Child Abuse and Neglect

Child Abuse and Neglect

Forensic Issues in Evidence, Impact, and Management

Edited By

India Bryce
University of Southern Queensland, Toowoomba, Queensland, Australia

Yolande Robinson
School of Criminology and Criminal Justice, Griffith University, Queensland, Australia

Wayne Petherick
Faculty of Society and Design, Bond University, Gold Coast, Queensland, Australia

Academic Press is an imprint of Elsevier
125 London Wall, London EC2Y 5AS, United Kingdom
525 B Street, Suite 1650, San Diego, CA 92101, United States
50 Hampshire Street, 5th Floor, Cambridge, MA 02139, United States
The Boulevard, Langford Lane, Kidlington, Oxford OX5 1GB, United Kingdom

Notices

Knowledge and best practice in this field are constantly changing. As new research and experience broaden our understanding, changes in research methods, professional practices, or medical treatment may become necessary.

Practitioners and researchers must always rely on their own experience and knowledge in evaluating and using any information, methods, compounds, or experiments described herein. In using such information or methods they should be mindful of their own safety and the safety of others, including parties for whom they have a professional responsibility.

To the fullest extent of the law, neither the Publisher nor the authors, contributors, or editors, assume any liability for any injury and/or damage to persons or property as a matter of products liability, negligence or otherwise, or from any use or operation of any methods, products, instructions, or ideas contained in the material herein.

Library of Congress Cataloging-in-Publication Data
A catalog record for this book is available from the Library of Congress

British Library Cataloguing-in-Publication Data
A catalogue record for this book is available from the British Library

ISBN 978-0-12-815344-4

For information on all Academic Press publications
visit our website at https://www.elsevier.com/books-and-journals

Publisher: Stacy Masucci
Acquisition Editor: Elizabeth Brown
Editorial Project Manager: Sam Young
Production Project Manager: Paul Prasad Chandramohan
Cover Designer: Christian J. Bilbow

Typeset by SPi Global, India

Contents

Part 3 Management: Responding to Child Abuse 261

Contributors

Karen Broadley RMIT University, Melbourne, VIC, Australia

India Bryce University Southern Queensland, Toowoomba, QLD, Australia

Jeffery Chin Home Team Behavioural Sciences Centre, Ministry of Home Affairs, Singapore, Singapore

Grace S. Chng Centre for Research on Rehabilitation and Protection, Ministry of Social and Family Development, Singapore, Singapore

Larissa S. Christensen School of Law, University of the Sunshine Coast, Sippy Downs, QLD, Australia

Chi Meng Chu Centre for Research on Rehabilitation and Protection, Ministry of Social and Family Development, Singapore, Singapore

Ella Cockbain Department of Security and Crime Science, University College London (UCL), London, United Kingdom

Lesley-Anne Ey University of South Australia, Adelaide, SA, Australia

David P. Farrington Institute of Criminology, Cambridge University, Cambridge, United Kingdom

Ruth Gan Home Team Behavioural Sciences Centre, Ministry of Home Affairs, Singapore, Singapore

Chris Goddard University of South Australia, Adelaide, SA, Australia

Daryl Higgins Institute of Child Protection Studies, Australian Catholic University, Melbourne, VIC, Australia

Vaishnavi Honnavalli Home Team Behavioural Sciences Centre, Ministry of Home Affairs, Singapore, Singapore

Katelyn Jansen School of Criminology and Criminal Justice, Griffith University, Southport, QLD, Australia

Jatinder Kaur JK Diversity Consultants, Accredited Mental Health Social Worker, M.SocWk, M.Soc.Admin, B.A. (Psy), Cleveland, QLD, Australia

Majeed Khader Home Team Behavioural Sciences Centre, Ministry of Home Affairs, Singapore, Singapore

Dongdong Li Centre for Research on Rehabilitation and Protection, Ministry of Social and Family Development, Singapore, Singapore

Andrew Lowe Queensland Police Service, Toowoomba, QLD, Australia

Catia G. Malvaso School of Psychology, University of Adelaide, Adelaide, SA, Australia

Victoria Marshall Monash University, Melbourne, VIC, Australia

Elena Martellozzo Middlesex University, London, United Kingdom
Nadine McKillop USC Law School, Faculty of Arts, Business and Law, USC Australia, Sippy Downs, QLD, Australia
Tim Moore Australian Centre for Child Protection, University of South Australia, Adelaide, SA, Australia
Loo Seng Neo Home Team Behavioural Sciences Centre, Ministry of Home Affairs, Singapore, Singapore
Kristen Olver Department of Security and Crime Science, University College London (UCL), London, United Kingdom
Amelie Pedneault Department of Criminal Justice and Criminology, Washington State University, Pullman, WA, United States
Wayne Petherick Faculty of Society and Design, Bond University, Gold Coast, QLD, Australia
Yolande Robinson Griffith Criminology Institute, Griffith University, Gold Coast, QLD, Australia
Bernadette J. Saunders Monash University, Caulfield East, VIC, Australia
Rosemary Sheehan Monash University, Melbourne, VIC, Australia
Grant C.B. Sinnamon Bela Menso Brain and Behaviour Centre, Gold Coast, QLD, Australia
Shi Hui Tee Home Team Behavioural Sciences Centre, Ministry of Home Affairs, Singapore, Singapore
Ming Hwa Ting Centre for Research on Rehabilitation and Protection, Ministry of Social and Family Development, Singapore, Singapore

Foreword

I am pleased to be able to provide the foreword for this book.

In my view, its topic—*Child Abuse and Neglect*—is one of the most significant issues within the broader Australian community in the present time. Other countries however face similar issues, and its contents are not confined to any one location.

Whilst many articles have been written and reports produced about child abuse and neglect, there is a lack of a publication where in a comprehensive way the wide range of associated issues and topics are brought together in one volume that reflects the most recent and contemporary knowledge and understanding.

The structure and holistic content are combined to provide a valuable reference for students, lectures, practitioners, and managers.

I would hope that this is the first of further editions as more evidence-based information becomes available.

There is a significant economic cost to our community as the result of *Child Abuse and Neglect*. That economic cost is far outweighed by the social cost when a child's future wellbeing and potential are stolen from them.

In any civilised society, there is a duty to protect children, our most vulnerable members. This book provides a valuable contribution to that important responsibility.

Bob Atkinson AO APM
Commissioner—Queensland Police Service 2000–12
Commissioner—Royal Commission into Institutional Responses to Child Sexual Abuse 2013–17
Special Advice to the Minister (Queensland) for Child Safety, Youth and Women—2018

Preface

We are delighted to offer this first edition of *Child Abuse and Neglect: Forensic Issues in Evidence, Impact, and Management*. Nationally and internationally, the growing complexity of child abuse and neglect continues to affect practitioners across a range of disciplines within welfare, legal, and forensic sectors. Additionally, the evolving diversity of individuals and families, social environments, and methods of communication further confounds and challenges efforts to effectively impact this global problem. These expanding and rapidly unfolding challenges stress the need for a more integrated and evidence-based forensic response to improving knowledge and developing frameworks of practice, research, advocacy, and collaboration to meet the human rights, social justice, and legal needs of victims, perpetrators, practitioners, students, and educators. As practitioners in forensic sectors encounter human rights violations, trauma and abuse, outmoded and outdated policies and procedures, systemic gaps, barriers, and cross-cultural legal disparity, the investigative and clinical landscape may be described as (to say the least) intimidating.

The forensic focus of this text acknowledges the nature of the professional roles currently engaging and intersecting in the child abuse area and the highly specialised skills that are demanded within law, mental and behavioural health, criminal and juvenile justice, and child protection. We specifically acknowledge the role of forensic social workers, forensic psychologists, forensic criminologists, forensic architects, and forensic medical practitioners. Consequently, this book is aimed at preservice and practicing professionals in education, psychology, criminology, criminal justice, child and family welfare, and law enforcement, highlighting the relevance of a multidisciplinary approach to the topic.

The terms *child abuse*, *child neglect*, and *child maltreatment* have often been used interchangeably. Indeed, the subject title of this work, *Child Abuse and Neglect*, reflects this divarication. From this point, this volume adopts *child abuse* as an umbrella term to cover all forms of abuse, including neglect, exploitation, and trafficking, thereby espousing the view that any offence against a child, any act of omission or commission, or any violation of a child's basic human rights constitutes abuse. This text, therefore, supports and reflects a broader view of child abuse than has thus far been published and supports a global definition supported by principle documents supplied by the United Nations Convention on the Rights of the Child (1989), The Universal Declaration of Human Rights (1948), The United Nations

Millennium Declaration (2000), Millennium Development Goals (2015), A World Fit for Children (2001), and State of the World's Children (2016).

Whilst it is difficult to ascertain the exact extent and frequency of child abuse, overwhelming evidence indicates that the magnitude of the problem is significant. Studies suggest that 25%–70% of children around the world experience physical abuse, 20% of female children and 5%–10% of male children suffer sexual abuse, and 24%–30% of children experience emotional abuse (ISPCAN International Congress on Child Abuse and Neglect, 2012). In Australia, from 2014 to 2015, over 320,100 child protection notifications were received—152,086 of which were investigated and 56,423 substantiated, resulting in 48,730 children on child protection orders and 43,399 of those children entering out-of-home care (Australian Institute of Family Studies, 2016). In recent years, there has been an influx of media attention, government inquiries into departmental responses to child abuse and neglect, and a host of research identifying an unacceptable prevalence of child abuse in our society.

When planning this volume, we reviewed the current offerings for a textbook for this topic. We were surprised to find very little in the way of scholarly work, and none published within Australia let alone an international scope, such as this one has. Most textbooks with a curriculum-based format predate 1990 and focus on limited aspects of child abuse, such as management. The more recent works dealing with a comprehensive array of issues surrounding child abuse (c.2006) do not reflect the myriad of significant advances in knowledge in areas such as disclosure, child trafficking, and online and virtual child abuse. This alone is call for new work in the area.

This work is distinguished from the wider literature in a variety of ways. First, types of child abuse not previously explored such as child trafficking, child abuse and extremism, the consequences of child abuse, physical discipline, and online predation are addressed. Second, impacts will be considered through the lenses of both victimology and offending, as well as chronicity, posttraumatic outcomes, and lifespan development. Third, the contributions included in this volume are recent, many of which report recent findings and evidence from exciting and controversial studies. Fourth, although empirical scholarship will inform much of the content, there will be applied material from experts and practitioners in the field—from policing to child safety to intelligence—which is a significant divergence from literature most commonly provided by textbooks and academic journals. Additionally, the text provides perspectives of the international experience, rather than those of one country or jurisdiction.

So, given the complexity and sheer number of profound issues and challenges surrounding child abuse, we deliberated (agonised even!) about the most appropriate content and layout of this work. One specific problem we faced was the amount of immensely valuable material submitted by esteemed authors dealing with child sexual abuse. Here, the burgeoning amount of media, political, and legal attention currently being given to sexual abuse against children is attracting similar empirical attention in direct response to the lights being shone deep into the underbellies of churches and other institutions that have, historically, enjoyed unrestricted, frequent, and unsupervised access to children. We knew we had only two options to deal with this issue: create a discrete section for this abuse type, which may create an imbalance in the overall work and detract from the profound impacts and challenges associated with other abuse types, or hold contributions over for a stand-alone work focussing on sexual abuse against children. We chose the latter.

In the opening chapter, Yolande introduces the reader to the common domains of child abuse—physical, sexual, and emotional/psychological—and neglect. The chapter broadens to scope of child abuse types, with the addition of foetal abuse and the associated subtypes that must be considered in the context of pregnancy, including maternal substance misuse and intimate partner violence (IPV).

The next chapter, written by Victoria Marshall, Dr Lesley-Anne Ey, and Professor Chris Goddard, examines IPV as a form of child abuse and explores the challenges and complexities relating to language, definitions, and data. The authors discuss patterns of abusive and violent behaviour, children's responses to this behaviour, and the subsequent impact on the child. The authors consider the various contexts in a child's life and the review of theoretical frameworks relevant to understanding child abuse and IPV. The authors explore the problem of violence experienced by children in the home and community responses to protecting children from it.

Chapter 3 draws on the research published by the Australia Royal Commission into Institutional Responses to Child Sexual Abuse and explores the nature and extent of child sexual abuse in institutions. In this chapter, authors Daryl Higgins and Tim Moore use a situational prevention approach to examine the organisational, contextual, and individual factors that enable institutional child sexual abuse to occur and flourish. With a focus on prevention initiatives, the chapter presents similarities and differences between institutional child sexual abuse and other forms of child abuse. The chapter concludes with an emphasis on the role of both individuals and organisational culture in promoting safety and preventing child sexual abuse.

In Chapter 4, Dr Elena Martellozzo draws on her extensive research experience in online child behaviour and abuse and her valuable partnership with the London Metropolitan Police's Paedophile and High Tech Crime Unit (2003–09). The aim of the chapter is to offer an overview of the nature of online child sexual abuse, a domain of abuse that has become increasingly prevalent with the influx of social media platforms and internet-based services. The chapter investigates the issues of sexual solicitation, online grooming, and the production and distribution of child abuse images. The chapter closes by highlighting the complexities associated with policing in the field of cybercrime as we struggle to accommodate these 'new manifestations of old modus operandi'.

In compiling our list of authors, we sought to engage both national and international experts, in a range of child welfare disciplines, not previously explored in a single text. We were delighted to include the work of Vaishnavi Honnavalli, Loo Seng Neo, Ruth Gan, Shi Hui Tee, Majeed Khader, and Jeffery Chin from the Home Team Behavioural Sciences Centre, Ministry of Home Affairs, and Singapore. Their chapter investigates child abuse in the context of violent extremism and proposes implications for practitioners and academics alike, drawing connections between nonterror-related child abuse and terror-related trauma in children.

In order to meet our goal of broadening the scope of what constitutes child abuse in our increasingly complex global society, it was apparent from the outset that child trafficking needed to be featured in our text. In their chapter, Dr Ella Cockbain and Kristen Olver provide a comprehensive introduction to this complex and far-reaching abuse type. Law, policy, and practice will be discussed, and the numerous forms of exploitation will be presented, moving beyond the well-publicised sex trade. Using the United Kingdom as an example, Ella and Kristen present cases of child trafficking for purposes of domestic servitude, organ harvesting, forced begging, and cannabis cultivation. The chapter finishes by highlighting important theoretical and practical challenges in future responses to child trafficking.

Whilst much has been achieved in our understanding of male perpetrators of child sexual abuse, there is a dearth of research examining the female perpetrator. This topic has been the subject of much conjecture and myth, and in Chapter 7, Dr Lara Christensen and her coauthor, Katelyn Jansen, synthesise the differences and similarities across males and females who sexually abuse children. Following a discussion on the prevalence and case characteristics of male and female perpetrators, the authors review typologies that have been used to explain gendered sexual abuse of children. The chapter clarifies our understanding of the public and professional perception of gendered sexual abuse of children and the perceived level of harm and severity it inflicts.

To begin Part 2 of this text, Chapter 8 by Dr Wayne Petherick discusses victimology, which is the study of victims of crime. Specifically, this chapter discusses forensic victimology, which is the study of victims to answer investigative and legal questions. In this chapter, the various components of a victimology are discussed, including medical, psychological, residential, and financial histories, which serve as the basis for a risk assessment of the victim of crime. As the child victim will be too young to have a lot of information of their own relating to each domain, a victimology conducted on a child will usually be based on information pertinent to the parents or caregivers. This will also be discussed.

Highlighting the body of research concluding that maltreatment is more likely to be experienced by children as multiple incidents rather than as an isolated incident, India Bryce explores the concept of multiplicity and chronicity as it pertains to an accumulation of maltreatment experiences and adversity in childhood. Chapter 9 examines the broad range of theoretical perspectives, including developmental victimology, polyvictimisation, and revictimisation, which construct our understanding of cumulative harm and its pervasive impact across the lifespan.

In Chapter 10, Dr Grant Sinnamon, clinical psychologist and academic, provides insights about the immediate and medium-term neurodevelopmental consequences of childhood exposure to chronic and acute stress, duress, trauma, and neglect. Grant clarifies our understanding of the potential consequences for adult survivors of early-life stress (ELS) and presents an overview of child maltreatment, in particular domestic and family violence, and the related sequelae of these experiences.

Chapter 11 addresses the intersection of two critical topics in child abuse research, intergenerational transmission of abuse and corporal punishment. In this chapter, Dr David Farrington and Dr Catia Malvaso present their original research with new analyses to investigate the intergenerational transmission of physical punishment and its relationship to offending.

Chapter 12 sees Dr Bernadette Saunders review the most recent existing research on corporal punishment and its association with child abuse. Chapter 12 draws attention to international law and the human rights context within which children's physical discipline continues to be tolerated in many countries, including Australia. The chapter argues that corporal punishment has no place in any child's life.

As highlighted earlier, sexual abuse is a widely researched and publicised topic, but the heterogeneity of perpetrator behaviour, abuse incidents, and responses can inhibit effective prevention. Dr Nadine McKillop of the University of the Sunshine Coast employs research examining the individual, situational, and social-ecological aspects of child sexual abuse that contribute to onset, progression, and desistance across the life course. The chapter proposes multitiered prevention strategies, evaluating their efficacy for reducing the extent and impact of abuse in the community.

We explore, in Part 3, responses to abuse and neglect, including approaches to policy- and decision-making, recidivism, media influence, and cultural considerations, commencing with Petherick's invaluable chapter on the issue of false reports in child abuse and neglect cases. The contentious nature of these false reports is discussed in Chapter 14, along with the relevance and importance of their recognition among those who investigate cases relating to child victims. The definitions of false reports are provided, along with the different types of false reports. This is followed by the incidence of false reports in general, especially among sexual crimes in adults, and a number of studies that have been conducted on false reports in child abuse and neglect cases. This chapter closes with the motivations for false reports, the effects of false reports, and a variety of ways that false reports can be assessed.

As the prevalence of child abuse increases and our professional obligations intensify, it has become increasingly necessary to address the complexities of mandatory reporting. In his chapter, Detective Sergeant Andrew Lowe draws on his 15 years in the Queensland Police Service, 13 of those spent in the Child Protection Investigation Unit. Drawn from observations of the dearth of resources available to helping professions in meeting their mandatory reporting obligations, Chapter 15 discusses issues of language, definition, and decision-making. Given the significance of information gathering in making a report of suspected abuse, Andrew discusses strategies for speaking with children around disclosures of child abuse and neglect, so as to provide child protection agencies with better information, both in quantity and quality.

The rise in notifications to child protection over recent years has resulted in increased workloads for child protection practitioners. This has increased the complexity and importance of first-level decision-making about whether the concerns meet the threshold for a statutory investigation and the priority. In Chapter 16, Karen Broadley provides an invaluable decision-making framework for the intake phase.

In a chapter that is both enlightening and encouraging, Karen Broadley takes a novel approach to understanding decision-making in child protection. Drawing on Aristotle's virtue ethics as an organising framework to describe professional judgement, Karen engagingly explains how professional judgement is learned and how modern child protection systems hinder its development. Karen concludes by recommending a way forward.

Dr Sinnamon contributes a second chapter, complimenting his earlier contribution in Chapter 10. Trauma experienced through domestic and family violence (DFV) is related to numerous deleterious outcomes across the biopsychosocial spectrum. Moreover, the prevailing consensus is that current treatments offer little efficacy in improving the psychosocial pathology that results. This chapter presents a brief overview of eight core principles that the author proposes should be used to inform both adult and paediatric clinical intervention practices where trauma is an aetiological factor.

Chapter 19 is provided by Dongdong Li, Chi Meng Chu, Grace S. Chng, and Ming Hwa Ting and adopts a Singaporean perspective to examine the prevalence, predictors, outcomes, and interventions of childhood maltreatment and reentry into the child protection system (CPS). The authors conduct a critical analysis of the risk factors for reentry into the CPS using a cumulative ecological-transactional framework with a view to facilitating informed decision-making and enhancing positive outcomes for families engaged in the child protection system.

Having been fortunate enough to attend a professional development seminar by Jatinder Kaur on culturally sensitive child protection practice, inviting Jatinder to contribute her expertise to our text was considered logical, if not imperative. Child maltreatment occurs across all cultures, and there is a growing need for the Australian Child Protection System to recognise and respond to migrant and refugee communities in a culturally responsive manner. Chapter 20 will provide an overview, using ethnic case studies, for understanding child maltreatment across migrant and refugee communities. The chapter provides a framework for practitioners to support ethnic minority families across the child protection continuum, from early intervention to supporting cultural identity of children and young people from diverse backgrounds in foster care placements.

In Chapter 21, Dr Rosemary Sheehan of Monash University argues that the adversarial paradigm that operates in the judicial context creates considerable tension between the child protection and legal systems and distracts from the child protection concerns and best interests of the child. Rosemary's chapter investigates the factors, which undermine collaborative service delivery and advocates to a legal process that minimises disputation, is agreement-focussed, is more child-centred, and works collaboratively with key child welfare professionals.

In the final chapter, Dr Amelie Pedneault of Washington State University delves into the nature of public perceptions of individuals who sexually abuse children and the ineffective and reactionary legislation that results. Amelie applies Cohen's theory of moral panic to abusers and presents reactionary pieces of legislation from the United States, the United Kingdom, Canada, and Australia along with empirical evidence questioning their effectiveness, introducing the concept of crime control theatre. Referring, as have many of our authors, to the need to clear and accurate terminology, Chapter 22 concludes by identifying ways to educate the public about sexual abuse of children and those who perpetrate it, to achieve effective prevention.

Rather than tackling the broad and diverse array of topics alone, we have called upon contacts, networks, friends, and colleagues to contribute to this text. They have provided a rich and fertile ground through which a diverse range of topics are uncovered, each within the unique perspective of the author tempered by the aggregate literature and research. Adopting this approach, we feel not only that the information represents the best practice in each respective authors' field and region but also that it represents a global and often unified approach to deal with issues of child abuse and neglect. We urge the reader to take what they can from each chapter, with the knowledge and understanding that things may be different in their jurisdiction than that of the chapters' author(s). More information is better, and a diverse array of viewpoints improve our understanding of the global issues that impact a vast and complex topic such as child abuse and neglect. We present this current volume with the complete understanding that certain issues will differ from one location to the next and remind the reader that concepts, terms, approaches, and legal recourse will be different from one place to the next.

We suspect that you, as professionals and practitioners interested in informing and impacting child abuse in our lifetime, have more than a scholarly and practical interest in this issue.

We suspect that you have the heart to protect children from those who both intentionally and unintentionally harm them. We suspect that your intention is to reach beyond the classroom, office, and the pages of this book to improve outcomes for children. We suspect that you want to extend your influence beyond your own children or the children of others you hold dear. We suspect that you recognise the right of all children to live in safe, nurturing, and healthy environments. We hope this book contributes to your journey.

Acknowledgements

Having 'done my time' in the field, education, counselling, and front-line child protection, I know intimately the value of collaboration, and this project was a true embodiment of collaborative practice, warts, and all. We have been blessed to engage a dynamic, passionate, and knowledgeable community of authors, whose dedication to our project has been the cornerstone of its success. Without our contributors, there would simply be no book, and their commitment and generosity have not gone unnoticed. So, my first statement of gratitude is to our authors, for their patience, tenacity, open communication, and the provision of their exceptional expertise. This book is an exciting achievement, and it's only made possible by the contributions of our authors.

Thank you to Wayne and Yolande, for inviting me into the project and providing me an opportunity to bring to life a longstanding dream to 'write the book' on child abuse, to fill the noticeable gap in the literature for my students, and to broaden the scope of what no constitutes 'child abuse'. I am extremely grateful for the invitation to join you in embarking on this journey and for the partnerships and friendships this process has helped to cement. Having enjoyed a friendship with Wayne and his beautiful family for a number of years, I've enjoyed the opportunity to add a layer to our friendship.

A huge thank you to Liz and Sam at Elsevier, for taking the chance on this book, for their support and assistance in making an idea a reality, and for their patience in answering my endless barrage of questions, as I felt my way through this new world of editing.

My sincerest thank you to my husband, Andrew, whose unwavering support, enduring willingness to listen, quiet patience, and unconditional love have meant the world to me, especially through this often trying editorial process. These achievements are only possible because of you and all you do for me, and celebrating these successes is made meaningful by sharing them with you.

To my Mum, Dad, and Nenna, without your support and willingness to step in when I am simply too busy to meet my other obligations, listen when I need to vent, and generally 'be in my corner', I would not be able to achieve goals, such as this book. I am me, because of you.

To those who will read this book, the practitioners, the students, the researchers, the people… thank you, for taking the time to read our humble contribution to the discipline and for fighting the good fight. I hope all that you read here serves to arm you as you walk into the 'field' and do good.

India Bryce

> *In order for a child to develop normally, a child needs progressively more complex joint activity with one or more adults who have an irrational emotional relationship with the child. Somebody's got to be crazy about the kid. That's number one. First, last, and always.*

Urie Bronfenbrenner

This book is dedicated to the inner children in all of us. My prayer is that they learn not to be the sum of their past, but that they know they can be safe to learn, to heal, and to love—and to laugh, a lot, with joy and hilarity. Thank you Pamella Pope.

Thank you Mum. You have always been 'crazy about that kid' and my greatest champion and advocate.

Thank you to my beautiful daughters, Alex and Christina—my moral compass and the greatest joys in my life. I am proud of the young women you have become, your sense of social justice, your constant regard for people who need encouragement, and your strength and wisdom beyond your years. If I could choose that of which I am most proud, it is that you speak these qualities into the lives of your own families.

To my dear friends Jilly and Capt'n Dave, who always intent on making the world a brighter and better place and who cause me to smile no matter what.

We are enormously grateful to Sam Young, Liz Brown, and the editorial team at Elsevier for your generosity, time, and direction (and flexibility!). Thank you to our amazing contributors, of whom all are working to prevent, treat, examine, detect, and prosecute within the child welfare arena—and who are aiming to improve the lives of children at risk of experiencing abuse and facing life-long outcomes of early-life trauma. Our gratitude extends also to Dr Kerryann Walsh and Dr Claire Fergusson for your reviews of and recommendations for our original proposal. All in all, this book is the product of an extraordinary team.

Finally, yes finally. To Len and Margaret Hilliard, for an unforeseen legacy, one to be long remembered and oft recalled. For that I am grateful.

Yolande

It is always a pleasure to work talented and passionate people. And this volume represents some of the most talented people you could have the pleasure to work with. Those who work within child abuse and child protection tend to be some of the most passionate professionals you can find, and this talent and passion oozes from every page of their work. To all those who volunteered their time, I would like to say a heartfelt thank you. Not only did your works exceed my expectation for this book, but also they exceeded it in every regard. I won't name you all individually, but you know who you are, and you should be both please with and proud of yourself for what you have done.

As always, a huge thank you to Tash, my partner in crime, for her continued support and advice. She is always ready to proofread my writing and to offer some guidance and theoretical advice on content and direction. Her motivation never ceases to amaze me, nor does her energy. I really feel like I couldn't do this without her, and do not think I would want to, and for that, I am thankful.

As I have said elsewhere, I often get asked why I don't publish a few works with another publisher. My response to this is always the same, 'why would I? I already work with the best there is'. A huge shout out to Liz and the team and especially thanks to Sam who has been a huge help along every step of the way. Always ready to help with support and guidance, the whole crew at Elsevier really go above and beyond each and every time.

Thanks to Yolande and India. Yolande approached me with this project some time ago, and I felt that it was a worthwhile project to be involved in, so I eagerly accepted and came on board. Thanks to India for your passion and motivation and for bringing it all together at the end. It has been a lot of fun working with you both, and I really can't wait to have my hands on the final product!

Thank you once again to all those involved. Another journey done and dusted. After I take a pause for the cause, I will start to put my thoughts together for the next project, so sit back and wait for an e-mail from me.

Wayne

About the Authors

Yolande Robinson

Yolande Robinson is a current PhD scholar whose research and teaching interests include abuse in childhood, school-based bullying (specifically focused on the bully), Internet predation of children, and life-course offending and victimisation prevention. Yolande has spoken at a number of conferences and seminars on issues particularly relating to Internet safety for children and crime prevention. Yolande has two children who have followed her own passion for social justice and relishes the crisp winters in beautiful Toowoomba, Queensland.

Victoria Marshall

Victoria Marshall is a PhD candidate at Monash University researching children who have experienced intimate partner violence and identity. She is an experienced social worker in the field of family violence, having worked with male perpetrators of family violence and women and children living with family violence.

Lesley-anne Ey

Lesley-anne Ey lectures in child development, educational psychology, and child protection in the bachelor and master of teaching program at University of South Australia. Before undertaking her PhD, she taught in preschools and primary schools across a variety of government and independent sectors. Her PhD research focused on young children's engagement with contemporary music media and their gender role and self-identity development. Her research revolves around the impacts of media on children's healthy development, bullying in early childhood, children's problematic sexual behaviours, and child protection issues with the aim to support teachers and inform curriculum. Lesley-anne is involved in international, national, and state research. She is interested in supporting the wellbeing of children and educators and is a great advocate for placing children's voice at the centre of her research.

Chris Goddard

Professor Goddard is visiting professor in social work at the University of Hertfordshire and adjunct research professor in education, arts, and social sciences at the University of South Australia. On moving to Australia, he was appointed as deputy chief social worker at the Royal Children's Hospital, Melbourne, where he established the first child protection team. In 1986, together with other professionals and concerned individuals, he assisted in founding what is now known as the Australian Childhood Foundation. In his early years at Monash University, he undertook research that attracted national attention, including an ABC TV Four Corners' investigation. In 1998, he was appointed head of social work, Monash University; from 2004, he was director of research teams specialising in child abuse and child protection at Monash University. A major focus of Professor Goddard's research has been the experiences of health and welfare workers in child protection practice. His work with Dr Janet Stanley on violence against child protection workers, *In the Firing Line: Violence and Power in Child Protection Work* (published by Wiley), is internationally recognised. In 2010, he published *Physical Punishment in Childhood: The Rights of the Child* (Wiley) with Dr Bernadette Saunders. In 2006, he was named one of Australia's Smart 100 Thinkers. Also in 2006, with Dr Neerosh Mudaly, he coauthored *The Truth is Longer than a Lie* (Jessica Kingsley), one of the first works to give children who had been abused a voice. This was recently adapted as a play of the same title by Keiran O'Carroll. In 2008, he and his colleagues Professor Linda Briskman and Dr Susie Latham were awarded an Australia Human Rights Award for their research, Human Rights Overboard (Scribe). Professor Goddard has published many journal articles and book chapters. He has also written more than 50 newspaper articles for major newspapers, including *The Age*, *The Australian*, and *The Sydney Morning Herald* including, in recent years, opinion pieces on child abuse and child protection failures in churches. He is currently completing a study of child abuse deaths with Victoria Police.

Daryl Higgins

Professor Daryl Higgins commenced as the director of the Australian Catholic University's Institute of Child Protection Studies in February 2017. His research focuses on public health approaches to protecting children and child-safe organisational strategies. A registered psychologist, Prof Higgins has been researching child abuse impacts and prevention, family violence, and family functioning for 25 years. Prior to joining ACU, Prof Higgins was the deputy director (research) at the Australian Institute of Family Studies, where he had responsibility for the research program, knowledge translation, and exchange functions focusing on issues affecting families in Australia. Prof Higgins has contributed to over 230 publications and more than 400 presentations and media engagements. He has extensive experience in managing and supervising research looking at child abuse and neglect, child protection, children in out-of-home care, child-safe organisations, family law and allegations of child abuse, disability and family care, welfare reform, family and interpersonal violence, jobless families, past adoption and forced family separation practices, and community development approaches to child and family welfare issues. He has considerable experience in qualitative and quantitative evaluation methodology and frameworks and a sound knowledge of state and territory policy and service delivery contexts across Australia.

Tim Moore

A/Prof Tim Moore is deputy director (Practice Solutions) at the Australian Centre for Child Protection at the University of South Australia. After a decade of working directly with children, young people, and families, he moved into academia in 2005 to better understand children's lives and the best ways to support them and their families during periods of adversity. Having first-hand experience of the challenges that families face and the difficulties that many encounter when attempting to navigate the service sector, his research has always been underpinned by a commitment to promoting the needs, views, and experiences of children and young people and supporting the development of practices, policies, and programs that respond to them. Over the past 13 years, he has worked directly with children and young people in participatory research projects focusing on issues such as homelessness, youth justice, child protection, residential care, young caring, and child sexual abuse prevention. His research continues to consider not only how children live their lives but also the best ways to account for their childhoods and to conduct work that focuses on the practice of ethical research and the development of appropriate and rigorous methodologies that explore the issues that they encounter.

Elena Martellozzo

Dr Elena Martellozzo is a criminologist and a senior lecturer at Middlesex University. Elena's research includes exploring children and young people's online behaviour, the analysis of sexual grooming, and police practice in the area of child sexual abuse. She works closely with the media and provides regular expert advice to a number of leading agencies and charities. Elena is the author of *Online Child Sexual Abuse* (2012) and coauthor of *Cybercrime and Its Victims* (2017), which have become seminal texts.

Vaishnavi Honnavalli

Vaishnavi Honnavalli is a behavioural sciences research analyst at the Home Team Behavioural Sciences Centre, Ministry of Home Affairs, Singapore. She has an undergraduate degree in psychology and a masters each in criminology and forensic psychology from the United Kingdom. As a postgraduate student, her core area of research included rehabilitative studies and perspective studies on criminal behaviour. She has been with the research and training outfit for 2 years, conducting research in the area of online radicalisation, leadership in violent extremist groups, and the psychology of violent extremism. She regularly conducts trainings and workshops for law enforcement officers and organisations in the private sector on these topics. She has published many research reports on the topic of violent extremism and contributed to books written on violent extremism and child abuse. She enjoys sharing her research findings with practitioners, policymakers, and experts at various platforms and is enthusiastic about the dynamic and evolving research on violent extremism. She has also coedited a four-volume compendium titled *A Behavioural Sciences Approach to Understanding Terrorism*. She is a member of the British Psychological Society (BPS). Her most recent area of work is in *Insider Threat*.

Loo Seng Neo

Loo Seng Neo is a principal behavioural sciences research analyst with the Home Team Behavioural Sciences Centre at the Ministry of Home Affairs, Singapore. For the past 12 years, Loo Seng has been specialising in the area of violent extremism, particularly in the fields of online radicalisation, online threat assessment, preattack warning signs, and psychology of violent extremism. He works with a team of research analysts undertaking behavioural sciences research on violent extremism, resilience, and intergroup conflict. He has presented at many international conferences, trained law enforcement officers, and published many government research reports and peer-reviewed journals and book chapters on the topic of violent extremism. He has also coedited two books titled *Combating Violent Extremism and Radicalisation in the Digital Era* in 2016 and *Learning from Violent Extremist Attacks: Behavioural Insights for Practitioners and Policymakers* in 2018 and a four-volume compendium titled *A Behavioural Sciences Approach to Understanding Terrorism* in 2017. Loo Seng is currently pursuing his PhD in psychology researching on the personality profile of violent extremists at Nanyang Technological University.

Ruth Gan

Ruth Gan is a behavioural sciences research analyst with the Home Team Behavioural Sciences Centre at the Ministry of Home Affairs, Singapore. Ruth specialises in violent extremism research and is currently working on a project to improve bystander reporting of suspicious behaviours by nonsecurity airport staff. She is part of the core team that conducts trainings for Home Team officers and other stakeholders. She is also mostly familiar with the Buddhist violent extremist landscape in South Asia, particularly in Sri Lanka. Prior to this, Ruth worked with the Police Psychological Services Department where she was part of a team that handled the selection and leadership training for police officers. She also looked into the topic of negotiation for lone-wolf terrorists during her time there. Ruth has a keen interest in dealing with forensic and police psychology and is hoping to continue pursuing a career in this field.

Shi Hui Tee

Shi Hui Tee is a behavioural sciences research analyst with the Home Team Behavioural Sciences Centre at the Ministry of Home Affairs, Singapore. Shi Hui specialises in research on violent extremism. Her research areas include the motivations and personality of lone-wolf violent extremists in both terrorist organisations and right-wing organisations. She also looks into the development of trust relationships between violent extremists in the online community. She has also held seminars and conducted trainings for officers and relevant stakeholders on the topic of violent extremism. She is a member of the Online Radicalisation Research Community of Practice (ORRCOP) that comprises Singaporean practitioners and subject-matter experts involved in research related to online radicalisation. Shi Hui has published several research reports on violent extremism and related topics.

Majeed Khader

Majeed Khader is the director of the Home Team Behavioural Sciences Centre under the Ministry of Home Affairs and deputy director of the Police Psychological Services Division. Dr Majeed is also the chief psychologist of the Ministry of Home Affairs and Singapore Police Force. He teaches criminal psychology part time as an assistant professor (adjunct) at the School of Humanities and Social Sciences at Nanyang Technology University, Singapore. For the past 23 years, Dr Majeed has overseen the development of psychological services in the areas of stress, resilience, employee selection, deception psychology, leadership, crisis negotiations, crime profiling, and crisis psychology. For his work on the psychology of terrorism, he was awarded the National Day Public Administration Award (Bronze) in 2006 by the president of Singapore and once again the Public Administration Award (Silver) in 2014. A forensic psychologist by training, Majeed holds a PhD in psychology (specialising in personality and crisis leadership) from the University of Aberdeen, Scotland. Dr Majeed has been the chairman of three major international conferences held in Singapore titled the 'Asian Conference of Criminal and Operations Psychology'. He is a registered psychologist with the Singapore Psychological Society and a member of the British and American Psychological Societies.

Jeffery Chin

Jeffery Chin is a senior psychologist at the Home Team Behavioural Sciences Centre. Key areas of his work at the centre include applied research in violent extremism, investigative interviewing, deception, and leadership during critical incidents. As a concurrent appointment, Jeffery also supports the operations of the Crisis Negotiation Unit, Singapore Police Force, as a psychologist. Jeffery holds a master's degree in investigative and forensic psychology from the University of Liverpool (the United Kingdom). His master's dissertation topic was on critical incident leadership.

Ella Cockbain

Dr Ella Cockbain is a lecturer in Security and Crime Science at University College London (UCL) and 'Future Research Leaders' fellow of the Economic and Social Research Council (ESRC). Her research focuses on serious and organised crime and its prevention, in particular human trafficking, sexual exploitation, and labour exploitation. She teaches and publishes widely on these topics, including numerous peer-reviewed journal articles and book chapters; several edited collections; and a recent monograph, *Offender and Victim Networks in Human Trafficking* (Routledge, 2018). She is on the editorial board of three scientific journals and reviews for many others, as well as providing expert reviews for the UK Home Office, the Centre of Expertise on Child Sexual Abuse, and others. Ella has collaborated extensively with organisations across the public, private, and third sectors, including the National Crime Agency, numerous police forces, and leading children's charity Barnardo's. She is regularly invited to contribute at national and international level to policy, strategy, training, and practical interventions to tackle trafficking and exploitation (modern slavery). In recognition of the impact of her research, Ella was recently named one of the Top 100 Modern Slavery Influencers in the United Kingdom.

Kristen Olver

Kristen Olver is currently working at the Global Initiative against Transnational Organized Crime on the ENACT project, which builds knowledge and skills to enhance Africa's response to transnational organised crime. She has also held roles with the Senate of Canada and United Nations Development Programme in Rwanda. Her research interests include gender-based violence, human trafficking, the crime-terror nexus, and the role of security forces in addressing these challenges. She is currently completing her MSc in countering organised crime and terrorism at the Department of Security and Crime Science, University College London (UCL). She holds a BA in political studies from Queen's University at Kingston.

Lara Christensen

Dr Lara Christensen's primary research interest is sexual violence. Her PhD (psychology) focused on the attrition of child sexual abuse cases from the criminal justice process. Her current field of interest also encompasses female child sexual offenders. Overall, Lara has a broad, yet strong, knowledge base pertaining to child sexual offending, including the grooming process, cognitive distortions, crime scripts, online child predators, and victimology. You will find her research published in a number of prominent international journals. Prior to being appointed at the University of the Sunshine Coast in 2018, Lara was a lecturer in the School of Criminology and Criminal Justice at Griffith University, Gold Coast. During this time, Lara was the recipient of multiple teaching awards, which recognise excellence in the provision of engaging learning for students, and was awarded a 2017 Vice Chancellor's Teaching Excellence Award. In addition to her research and teaching, she is currently working on a number of joint innovative projects with key stakeholders.

Katelyn Jansen

Katelyn Jansen recently completed her bachelor of criminology and criminal justice at Griffith University on the Gold Coast, where she was a member of the elite Criminology

Academic Excellence Society. Further, Katelyn received the Griffith Award for Academic Excellence across 2016 and 2017. Her fields of interest include child exploitation, victimology, cybercrime, and gender issues in criminology. She was selected to study women's issues at the University Institute of Lisbon (ISCTE), Portugal, which contributed to her understanding of domestic violence, human trafficking, and other issues affecting women worldwide. Katelyn was awarded a research internship, in which she has worked closely with Dr Lara Christensen, assisting with publishing a paper on the portrayal of female child sex offenders in the media. She is also currently contributing to a research project on public attitudes towards released offenders. Katelyn aims to pursue further research on child exploitation through postgraduate studies.

Wayne Petherick

Dr Wayne Petherick is a forensic criminologist and is currently associate professor of criminology at Bond University, Gold Coast, Queensland, Australia. In addition to teaching and research, Wayne works on cases from risk and threat to stalking, sexual assault, and homicide. These are for private clients, legal professionals, and various criminal justice agencies. Wayne has lectured in Australia and many states of the United States in the areas of criminal motivations, forensic victimology, criminal profiling, applied crime analysis, stalking, sexual assault, and homicide (including multiple homicide). Over the last 20 years in the tertiary education sector, Wayne has worked as the author or coauthor of over 60 book chapters and on textbooks and journal publications. Wayne has published in specialised texts in the United States, Portugal, Australia, the United Kingdom, and Georgia where his text *Forensic Criminology* was translated into Georgian. Over the course of his teaching, researching, and working on various cases, Wayne has developed a unique approach to crime analysis called *Applied Crime Analysis* to distinguish it from other types of analysis conducted. This provides a holistic approach to understanding all aspects of a case, from the basics of the physical evidence to considerations of the crime scene, victimology, criminal motivations, and investigative strategies that can still be undertaken. While this approach to analysis is generic in that it can be applied to any criminal or victim behaviour, whether civil or criminal, it is an extremely powerful tool that can disentangle the often complex interactions between criminals, victims, and the environment.

India Bryce

India Bryce began her career as early childhood teacher in independent schools in Queensland, Australia, before taking a position as a front-line child safety officer in the Investigation and Assessment Team, in the previously named Queensland Department of Communities, Child Safety and Disabilities. India first completed a bachelor of education (primary and middle School) through the University of Southern Queensland (USQ) and then a masters of guidance and counselling through James Cook University and has achieved a masters of social work (forensic studies) through Monash University. India is currently undertaking her PhD, which explores the lived experience of cumulative harm and its influence on career choice. India is now a lecturer of Human Development, Wellbeing and Counselling in the School of Linguistics, Adult and Specialist Education, at USQ. She is also specialist consultant in the field of child maltreatment, specialising in cumulative harm. She has worked closely with government and nongovernment agencies in the design and implementation of family intervention, prevention, and preservation programs and has delivered training in child maltreatment and cumulative harm to a broad range of helping professionals across the forensic sector. India has presented on topics related to cumulative harm and child maltreatment at workshops, conferences, and symposiums, nationally and internationally. India has published books, book chapters, and journal articles on the topic of child protection, maltreatment, and cumulative harm.

Grant Sinnamon

Dr Grant Sinnamon, BPsych (Hons), MCouns, MPsych (clinical) with distinction, and PhD (medicine: psychiatry and psychiatric neurosciences). Grant is married to Natalie, and together, they have four children. Grant is the creator of the REPAIR™ Model: a six-step intervention model for working with children and adults with complex needs, mental illness, and trauma. The model is an evidence-based intervention platform that emphasises the need to recognise, manage, and address the systemic neurofunctional, emotional, cognitive, and behavioural challenges associated with childhood maltreatment and trauma, mental illness, and neurodevelopmental disorders. Grant is the director of research and clinical services and the founder of the Bela Menso Brain and Behaviour Centre on the Gold Coast, in Australia. With a focus on the clinical application of regenerational and translational mental and neurophysiological health, psychogenetics, and the emerging field of clinical psychoneuroimmunology, Grant's work encompasses two great passions: the psychoneuroimmunology of childhood onset autoimmune diseases and their psychological and neurological complications and developmental neurobiology and the structural, systemic, and functional impact of early-life experiences on the growing brain and on later-life health and wellbeing. Grant has published a number scientific papers in leading peer-reviewed journals including *Science*, *Nature*, *Nature Genetics*, *Molecular Psychiatry*, and *JAMA Psychiatry*; is the coauthor of *The Psychology of Criminal and Antisocial Behavior* (also published by Elsevier); and has contributed both victim- and perpetrator-related psychological content chapters to other books in the areas of serial crime, criminal profiling, and applied crime analysis.

David Farrington

David P. Farrington is emeritus professor of Psychological Criminology at the Institute of Criminology, Cambridge University. He has been chosen to receive the John Paul Scott Award of the International Society for Research on Aggression in 2018, for significant lifetime contributions to aggression research, and the Herbert Bloch Award of the American Society of Criminology in 2018, for outstanding service contributions to criminology. He received the Stockholm Prize in Criminology in 2013. He has been president of the American Society of Criminology, president of the European Association of Psychology and Law, president of the British Society of Criminology, president of the Academy of Experimental Criminology, and chair of the Division of Developmental and Life-Course Criminology of the ASC. He received BA, MA, and PhD degrees in psychology from Cambridge University and an honorary degree of ScD from Trinity College Dublin. His major research is in developmental criminology, and he is director of the Cambridge Study in Delinquent Development, which is a prospective longitudinal survey of over 400 London males from age 8 to age 61. In addition to 749 published journal articles and book chapters on criminological and psychological topics, he has published 108 books, monographs, and government publications and 152 shorter publications (total = 1009).

Catia G. Malvaso

Catia G. Malvaso is a postdoctoral research fellow in the School of Psychology at the University of Adelaide. She recently completed her PhD and was awarded the Frank Dalziel Prize for the best psychology thesis in 2017. The focus of her thesis was on the association between child maltreatment and youth offending, and it involved linking administrative government data and survey information collected by child protection and youth justice agencies in South Australia. She has experience working with large datasets and longitudinal data and has managed a number of research projects on vulnerable youth. She recently had the opportunity to work as a research consultant for the Royal Commission into the Protection and Detention of Children in the Northern Territory, because of her expertise on the crossover of children between the child protection and youth justice systems.

Bernadette Saunders

Bernadette has professional qualifications in Social Work and Education. Her PhD research, in which she interviewed 40 adults (professionals who work with children, parents, and grandparents) and 31 children, focused upon the physical punishment of children and the intergenerational transmission of disciplinary violence. For 20 years, she has been advocating through academic writing, national and international conference presentations, and the Australian media, for law reform in Australia that recognises children's rights to freedom from all forms of assault and the removal of the defence to assault, available to parents, of reasonable physical chastisement or lawful correction. Her publications and research largely focus upon injustices, resulting from law, language, and culture, impacting disadvantaged groups, especially children. She is a senior lecturer, PhD supervisor, and master of social work course coordinator in the Department of Social Work, Monash University, where she coordinates and teaches postgraduate students in the units: 'Human rights, law and ethics' and 'The child in society: Promoting child well-being and responding to child maltreatment'. In 2010, Wiley published her coauthored book, stemming from her PhD research, *Physical Punishment in Childhood: The Rights of the Child.*

Nadine McKillop

Dr Nadine McKillop is a lecturer in Criminology and Justice at USC Australia. She is also a psychologist and worked with both offenders and victims within criminal justice settings prior to entering academia. Her applied research interests include understanding and preventing sexual violence and abuse, the assessment and treatment of youth and adult sexual offenders, and factors associated with the onset of youth and adult offending to reduce the extent and impacts of sexual violence and abuse in the community. Nadine is an adjunct research fellow with the Griffith Criminology Institute and honorary research fellow with the Centre for Advances in Behavioural Sciences, Coventry University. She also serves as associate editor for the Journal of Sexual Aggression: *An International, Interdisciplinary Forum for Research, Theory and Practice.*

Andrew Lowe

Andrew Lowe is a detective sergeant of police with the Queensland Police Service. Andrew has over 13 years' experience as an investigator, the majority of which has been involved in the investigation of child abuse matters and youth offending as well as a variety of other serious and complex matters including, but not limited to, homicides, child abuse, online child abuse, property crime, and drug offences. Andrew holds an advanced diploma of public safety (police investigations), a bachelor of arts (criminology), and masters of criminology and criminal justice (first class honours) during which he examined the relationship between prolific offending and repeatedly victimised locations. Andrew has commenced his doctorate of philosophy in criminology.

Karen Broadley

Karen Broadley, MSocSci, BA, has more than 20 years' experience working in child welfare. She has held a number of roles within the child protection system, including management and leadership positions. Karen has researched in various areas of child protection, including a critique of the public health model, intervening to protect children from cumulative harm, risk assessment, and child protection decision-making. Karen is currently completing a PhD at RMIT University.

Dongdong Li

Dongdong Li, PhD, is a principal research specialist at the Centre for Research on Rehabilitation and Protection, Ministry of Social and Family Development, Singapore. Her research involves the study of child protection issues and youth offender rehabilitation, such as the predictors and outcomes of involvement in child protection service, the effects of childhood maltreatment in offending, and the cycle of violence. She also studies media effects on child development, specifically the effects of the Internet and digital games on children and adolescents' educational and psychological outcomes. She is an adjunct research fellow at the Social Service Research Centre, National University of Singapore.

Chi Meng Chu

Chi Meng Chu, PhD, is a registered psychologist in Singapore and Australia, with specialist training and experience in clinical and forensic psychology. He currently heads the Centre for Research on Rehabilitation and Protection at the Ministry of Social and Family Development (MSF) as a deputy director and is also concurrently the senior principal clinical and forensic psychologist at the Clinical and Forensic Psychology Service at MSF. Dr Chu has research interests in child protection and welfare issues as well as offender assessment and rehabilitation topics. He is also an adjunct associate professor at the Department of Psychology, National University of Singapore.

Grace S. Chng

Grace S. Chng, PhD, is a senior research specialist at the Centre for Research on Rehabilitation and Protection, Ministry of Social and Family Development, Singapore. Her research interests lie in family and child development, resilience, and inequality. Her current work deals with child protection and youth rehabilitation issues, and she has published on family profiles in both child protection clients and youth offenders in Singapore. Previously in education, she examined parenting and family communication on children's informal reasoning and youths' online risky behaviours. She is an adjunct investigator at the Singapore Institute for Clinical Sciences, Agency for Science, Technology and Research.

Ming Hwa Ting

Ming Hwa Ting, PhD, is currently senior manager/senior research specialist in the Centre for Research on Rehabilitation and Protection/Clinical and Forensic Psychology Service in the Ministry of Social and Family Development. He is also an adjunct investigator at the Singapore Institute of Clinical Science, Agency for Science, Technology and Research. His current research focuses on the analysis of linked administrative data at the population level. Prior to his current stint at the Ministry of Social and Family Development, he was working in the Department of Education and Child Development and the Department of Further Education, Employment, Science and Technology in Adelaide, South Australia.

Jatinder Kaur

Ms Jatinder Kaur is the director of JK Diversity Consultants, is an accredited mental health social worker, and specialises in working with migrant and refugee communities. Her professional career spans 15 years and across various scopes of practice: research, child protection, family support, refugee settlement support, domestic violence counselling, policy roles, and teaching social work practice. She is recognised as 'multicultural child protection expert' and has published various research papers, reports, and numerous policy submissions to various child protection inquiries in Victoria, Qld, and the senate inquiry into out-of-home care. In 2017, she was summoned as expert witness for the Royal

Commission into Institutional Responses to Child Sexual Abuse and presented her research evidence. She has delivered cultural competency training workshops across Australia to build cultural capability for front-line practitioners to meet the needs of migrant and refugee children and young people who come to the attention of child protection system.

Rosemary Sheehan

Rosemary Sheehan is a professor in the Department of Social Work, Monash University, Australia, and held for 17 years the post of Dispute Resolution Convenor in the Family Division of the Children's Court of Victoria. Her published research has looked at child welfare and the law, mental health, and judicial and correction responses to offenders, with particular reference to women offenders. Her research led to the establishment of a specialist Victorian Children's Court judicial list for the hearing of child sexual abuse matters, a major Australian innovation. Currently, she is exploring the extent to which children before the court on offending matters are also clients of the child protection system and what factors propel them into this trajectory. Her 2013 national profile of Australia's Children's Courts, with Allan Borowski, is the first such study of how the justice system manages vulnerability, child harm, and child offending across the Australian community.

Amelie Pedneault

Amelie Pedneault is an assistant professor in the Department of Criminal Justice and Criminology at Washington State University. She earned her PhD in criminology from Simon Fraser University in 2015, after completing her doctoral research at the Centre for Research on Sexual Violence. Her research examines various aspects of sexual offending, including more recently a large-scale study of public opinions about offenders who commit sexual crimes in Washington State.

PART 1

Types of Child Abuse

CHAPTER 1

Child Abuse: Types and Emergent Issues

Yolande Robinson
Griffith Criminology Institute, Griffith University, Gold Coast, QLD, Australia

1 Introduction

> *Someday, maybe, there will exist a well-informed, well considered, and yet fervent public conviction that the most deadly of all possible sins is the mutilation of a child's spirit; for such mutilation undercuts the life principle of trust, without which every human act, may it feel ever so good, and seem ever so right, is prone to perversion by destructive forms of consciousness.*
>
> **Densen-Gerber & Hutchinson (1979, p. 61)**

The identification of child abuse as an individual, social, health, educational, and forensic concern is very 'present-orientated', having moved well beyond the first prosecuted child abuse case in the United States in 1874 and the 'discovery' by Kempe and associates of the battered-child syndrome (Corby, 2006, p. 8; Kempe, Silverman, Steele, Droegemueller, & Silver, 1962). Indeed, it was only in the early 1980s that sexual abuse of children was first formally identified in Britain, and until just a few decades ago, empirical, legal, welfare, and treatment concerns surrounding child abuse and neglect were narrowly focussed on intrafamilial abuse, specifically in the forms of physical and emotional abuse, sexual abuse, and neglect, with sexual abuse at that time being considered rare (Corby, 2006; Negriff, Schneiderman, Smith, Schreyer, & Trickett, 2014).

Since these early developments, the scope of child-protection-focussed research and practice continues to expand, with other forms of child abuse and their aetiologies, victim/offender typologies, and prevalence rates well documented (Negriff et al., 2014). From the 1990s, media- and research-driven enquiry into organised sexual abuse and commercial exploitation of children, particularly within institutional settings and via the Internet, has increased exponentially, casting a blazing light on the nature, extent, and consequences for victims of these abuse settings and modus operandi (Corby, 2006). Likewise, foetal abuse, as a form of child abuse, is another area attracting significant attention. Here, a variety of disciplines including sociology, neuropsychology, criminal justice, and law are examining appropriate responses to a plethora of reported negative outcomes over the life course for children exposed to domestic violence and substance misuse in utero (Kelly, 2014).

Child Abuse and Neglect. https://doi.org/10.1016/B978-0-12-815344-4.00001-5

There are, of course, overlaps in the types and impacts of child abuse, where a child might be neglected and physically and/or sexually abused or might be emotionally and sexually abused. Furthermore, one abuse type can include a variety of acts. For example, Shevlin and colleagues identified, modelled, and measured 18 different contact and noncontact child sexual abuse acts such as the following: questioned about own sexuality, kissed and fondled in a certain way, teased about sexual development, had to present own genitals to someone else, had to masturbate while someone was watching, and had genital intercourse. Indeed, inconsistencies in estimates of abuse across scholarship may well be the result of inconsistent definitions and restrictive measurements of child abuse across domains, jurisdictions, and scientific methods of enquiry (Shevlin, Murphy, Elklit, Murphy, & Hyland, 2018; Stoltenborgh, van IJzendoorn, Euser, & Bakermans-Kranenburg, 2011).

Although research attests to the importance of recognising the emotional impact of all forms of abuse of a child, identifying types of abuse in a systematic and exhaustive manner can assist practitioners and scholars to more closely examine and accurately identify outcomes and specific risk profiles (Shevlin et al., 2018). To illustrate this point, a wide literature reports psychological outcomes of child sexual abuse (as an overarching type of abuse) to include posttraumatic stress disorder, depression, suicide ideation, and difficulties in forming and maintaining positive social and intimate relationships into adulthood. However, as discrete characteristics within abuse types are expanded, evidence also suggests that psychological outcomes can vary according to the duration, severity, type of abuse, and the relationship of the perpetrator to the target (Briere & Elliott, 2003; Kendall-Tackett, 2012; Shevlin et al., 2018).

With a key goal of *Child Abuse and Neglect: Forensic Issues in Evidence, Impact, and Management* being to influence treatment perspectives and efficacy, the importance of a comprehensive approach to classifying discrete forms of child abuse cannot be overstated and is certainly a challenge for child abuse research. Careful consideration of characteristics, patterns, and cooccurrences of various types of child abuse offending may serve to strengthen the validity of empirical questions and hypotheses (that might include, for instance, risk profiles) and improve the reliability of measured outcomes (such as responses to treatment). Therefore, this chapter expands upon the most commonly reported and examined types of abuse, those being physical abuse, emotional abuse, neglect, and sexual abuse, and adds to this list violations of Internet predation, foetal abuse, and witnessing family violence. Although these might not be deemed subtypes within their own right, they bear inclusion within the types being discussed. For instance, Internet child sexual abuse is now included as a subcategory of sexual abuse along with rape and sexual assault. Likewise, witnessing family violence is included as a form of emotional abuse due to the effects of exposure to family violence and persistent discord on a child's perception of appropriate behavioural boundaries and overall cognitive and social development. These additions reflect both the burgeoning changes in communications relating to the Internet and the recognition of the deleterious effects of Internet predation, substance abuse, and family violence.

Overarching typologies are presented in alphabetical order so as not to suggest a more profound significance or measure of harm for one form of abuse over another, as child abuse in any form, duration, and level of severity has the potential for serious and life-long consequences for children and as such is, individually and collectively, a major public health concern.

2 Emotional Abuse

Much like neglect, research into the developmental outcomes for children who have experienced psychological/emotional abuse has lagged behind research on childhood physical and sexual abuse (Taillieu, Brownridge, Sareen, & Afifi, 2016; Trickett, Kim, & Prindle, 2011). Emotional abuse can be defined as 'a repeated pattern of caregiver behavior or extreme incident(s) that convey to children that they are flawed, unloved, unwanted, endangered, or of value only in meeting another's needs' (American Professional Society on the Abuse of Children (APSAC), 1995, p. 2). Whether this type of abuse should be termed *emotional* or *psychological* is open to debate (Glaser, 2002, p. 698), since cognition and emotion are necessarily dependent on each other, where 'cognitive appraisal of experiences contribute to the affective experience and vice versa'. Scholarship generally identifies two subtypes of emotional abuse: acts of commission (emotional abuse) and acts of omission (emotional neglect) (Coates & Messman-Moore, 2014; Ferguson & Dacey, 1997; Taillieu et al., 2016). The APSAC (1995) describes six indicators of emotional abuse: spurning (verbal and nonverbal hostile rejecting/degrading); terrorising (behaviour that threatens or is likely to physically harm the child or place the child or the child's loved objects in danger); exploiting/corrupting (encouraging the child to develop inappropriate behaviours); denying emotional responsiveness (ignoring child's needs to interact, failing to express positive affect to the child, and showing no emotion in interactions with the child); isolating (denying child opportunities for interacting/communicating with peers or adults); and mental, health, medical, and educational neglect (ignoring or failing to ensure provision for the child's needs) (APSAC, 1995, as cited in Glaser 2002, p. 702).

Across a wide literature, similar estimates of experiencing emotional abuse in childhood lie at around 15% (Finkelhor, Turner, Ormrod, & Hamby, 2009), with a study by Taillieu and colleagues (2013) finding that around 6% of respondents experienced emotional neglect only and 5% experienced emotional abuse only and that experiencing both emotional abuse and neglect is less common at around 3%. Although less is known about emotional abuse, it is widely asserted that it is an underlying feature of other forms of abuse and may lead to more serious developmental, social, and psychological harm (Chamberland, Fallon, Black, & Trocmé, 2011; Taillieu et al., 2016).

Childhood emotional abuse per se has been associated with a range of negative impacts on long-term mental health issues such as depression (Bruce et al., 2012; Ferguson & Dacey, 1997; Gibb, Chelminski, & Zimmerman, 2007), posttraumatic stress disorder (Gibb et al., 2007; Taillieu et al., 2016), anxiety disorders (Hamilton et al., 2013), and dissociative and psychotic disorders (Ackner, Skeate, Patterson, & Neal, 2013; Taillieu et al., 2016). Additionally, emotional abuse has been said to 'destroy a child's sense of self and personal security' (Kairy's et al., 2002, p. 2) and is considered particularly disruptive to the development of secure attachment to primary caregivers. Indeed, it is this insecure or ambivalent attachment that is believed to underpin a relationship between emotional abuse and mental disorders (Taillieu et al., 2016).

Black, Smith Slep, and Heyman (2001) identify a number of risk factors significantly associated with a child being emotionally abused and report them within three categories: characteristics of the child, characteristics of the parent/s, and marital relationships. Child risk factor characteristics include child aggression (e.g. physical fights with other children), child delinquency (e.g. vandalism), and child interpersonal problems (e.g. trouble socialising and making friends). Parent characteristics include depressive, anger or hostility, or neurotic symptoms; higher levels of social anxiety and neuroticism; and lower levels of self-esteem. Psychologically abusive parents were also more socially isolated and scored lower on measures of verbal reasoning (Black et al., 2001). Indeed, risk factors for emotional abuse (mainly consisting of problematic personality traits) can be interpreted to contrast, to an extent, with risk factors for physical abuse that, although still proximal, reflect issues such as intimate partner violence (IPV), the lack of social support, intimate partner difficulties, and stressful life situations.

3 Foetal Abuse

The intention of the current section is not to open or inflame contemporaneous debate surrounding issues of 'when a child becomes a child', but to address foetal abuse as a contributor to adverse outcomes suggested to extend beyond neonatal concerns, to impact developmental and social and behavioural outcomes later in childhood. In this regard, research indicates that prenatal exposure to traumatic conditions in utero can have negative effects across multiple physical and neurodevelopmental domains such as birth abnormalities (Kelly, 2014; Schroedel & Peretz, 1994); neurodevelopmental deficits (Zhou, Mason, & Open Access Publishing in European Networks, 2015); and deficits in language, reduction in fine and gross motor skills, attention and memory deficits, conduct disorders, and social problems (Zhou et al., 2015). Foetal abuse is additionally relevant to the issue of child abuse with research suggesting that, like child abuse, foetal abuse may be predictive of long-term biopsychosocial outcomes in adulthood and that an expanding scholarship proffers a potential relationship between foetal abuse and later child abuse (Condon, 1986).

Until the early 21st century, little attention was given to the welfare of a foetus subject to direct physical assault, neglect, or failure to protect the foetus from chemical assault by alcohol or drugs (Kent, Laidlaw, & Brockington, 1997). Moreover, early scholarship and debate focussed primarily on problems dealing with maternal substance abuse rather than trauma due to the partner (Newberger et al., 1992). Since that time, research has widely examined the impact of events caused by intimate partner violence and maternal behaviours such as drug and alcohol abuse on neonatal and child health. Indeed, paediatric providers are now encouraged to routinely screen for the occurrence and cooccurrence of these risk factors for poor neonatal outcomes (Alhusen, Lucea, Bullock, & Sharps, 2013). Although the effects of adverse prenatal conditions on neonatal and later outcomes have long been known, the significant social cost of caring for children who may develop into adults with very real challenges to their health and functioning is raising the policy salience of foetal health and holding the plethora of prenatal risks to heightened scrutiny (Kelly, 2014; Schroedel & Peretz, 1994).

3.1 Intimate Partner Violence

The World Health Organisation (WHO) presents intimate partner violence (IPV) as one of the most prevalent forms of abuse against women, which includes acts of physical, sexual, emotional, and financial abuse and violent behaviours (Garcia-Moreno, Gueses, & Knerr, 2012). Specifically, acts of violence include slapping, kicking, hitting, or beating; sexual violence includes rape and other forms of sexual coercion; emotional abuse refers to threats of harm, belittling, humiliation, destruction of property, and threats to abscond with children; and controlling behaviours include social isolating, monitoring of movements or financial affairs, and restrictions to necessary resources such as employment, education, or medical care (Centers for Disease Control and Prevention, 1999; World Health Organization, 1999).

Pregnancy presents a unique suite of circumstances for vulnerability to IPV at this time as women are prone to experience significant challenges to their physical health and needs, strength and responsivity, social supports, and financial situation (Alhusen et al., 2013). Moreover, IPV in pregnancy is a global public health issue that can profoundly impact maternal and foetal outcomes (Finnbogadóttir, Dykes, & Wann-Hansson, 2014; James, Brody, & Hamilton, 2013). Although estimates of exposure to IPV around the time of pregnancy vary widely, principally due to variations in types of IPV measured, differences in definitions, characteristics, study samples, and jurisdictions (Alhusen et al., 2013; James et al., 2013), one meta-analysis across 92 independent studies estimates the prevalence of emotional abuse at 28%, physical abuse at 14%, and sexual abuse around 8% of all pregnant women examined (James et al., 2013).

Although IPV in pregnancy occurs across settings and among all socioeconomic, cultural, and religious groups, a number of risk factors are consistently reported across a wide scholarship.

These are low socioeconomic status (Cokkinides & Coker, 1998; Goodwin, Gazmararian, Johnson, Gilbert, & Saltzman, 2000; James et al., 2013; Schumacher, Slep, & Heyman, 2001), lower educational attainment (Stith et al., 2000), living in an urban area (Alhusen et al., 2013), unintended pregnancy (Cokkinides, Coker, Sanderson, Addy, & Bethea, 1999; James et al., 2013, Jasinski, 2001), experiencing immediate stressful life events, long-term exposure to violence as a child or adult (Jasinski & Kaufman Kantor, 2001), low levels of social support or social isolation and maternal or paternal drug and alcohol abuse (James et al., 2013; Martin, English, Clark, Cilenti, & Kupper, 1996).

Physical or sexual victimisation against the mother may result in a number of postpartum risks for the born child. For instance, women experiencing IPV are at a heightened risk of postpartum depression and associated preeclampsia, preterm birth, and low birth weight (Kim et al., 2013; McCoy, Monica, Keen, and EBSCOhost, 2011); posttraumatic stress disorder and an associated risk of preterm birth (Yonkers et al., 2014); smoking and illicit substance use and dependency in pregnancy (Alhusen et al., 2013; Newberger et al., 1992); and premature rupture of membranes, antepartum haemorrhage, poor weight gain during pregnancy, low birth weight, and prematurity (Khaironisak, Zaridah, Hasanain, & Zaleha, 2017).

The current section does not allow for a comprehensive discussion of the full array of outcomes for children exposed to adversity in utero. However, even the most cursory examination and presentation of studies that have measured effects in pre-school-aged and early-primary-school-aged children reveals significant effects. For instance, neuropsychiatric outcomes suggest that maternal exposure to IPV and related maternal stress, anxiety, and depression is associated with thinning of selective cortical regions with commensurate cognitive and emotional deficits (Sandman et al., 2018), increased risk of psychopathology (Monk, Spicer, & Champagne, 2012), and neurodevelopmental disorders (Susser, Hoek, & Brown, 1998). Some potential underlying mechanisms for these neuropsychiatric outcomes have been examined, and it is preferred that mothers distressed by IPV might be less able to meet primary parenting demands of establishing both a secure attachment with their child and developing the child's emotion regulation. A secure parental attachment and emotional regulation are suggested to be primary protective factors for children, particularly for children being raised in adverse or disadvantaged circumstances. For instance, insecure attachment styles have been associated with exhibiting increased fear reactivity and negative cognition, affect, and behavioural affects and less positive responsivity, with these mood and stress-related reductions potentially serving as conduits for delayed or reduced psychological and physical development (Monk et al., 2012).

3.2 Maternal Substance Abuse

Maternal drug and alcohol abuse during pregnancy presents as a chronic social and public concern across national and international jurisdictions (NIDA, 2011) and a major contributor to the burden of disease (Davis, Rotheram-Borus, Weichle, Rezai, & Tomlinson, 2017). Drug and alcohol abuse during pregnancy is significant to the issue of child abuse for two reasons: first, for the negative effects on the physical and neuropsychological development of the foetus and subsequent born child and as a reliable risk factor for future child maltreatment, neglect, and exposure to the public welfare system (Fluke, Chabot, Fallon, MacLaurin, & Blackstock, 2010; Goodwin et al., 2000; Huang, Bory, Caron, Tebes, & Connell, 2014). In the United States, it is estimated that 6% of pregnant women use illicit drugs and 9% consumed alcohol (3% in a binge pattern) (U.S. Department of health and human services, 2012). Further studies in England found that 3% of pregnant women studied reported using illicit drugs (Smith et al., 2015) and a quarter of women studied reported drinking alcohol while knowing they were pregnant, 9% in a binge pattern (Smith, Savory, Couves, & Burns, 2014).

Despite the global prevalence of prenatal drug and alcohol abuse reported globally, studies have indicated that only a minority of pregnant women who abuse drugs (including prescription medication) or alcohol are identified within healthcare systems (Lehikoinen, Ordén, Heinonen, & Voutilainen, 2016; Pajulo, Savonlahti, Sourander, Helenius, & Piha, 2001; U.S. Department of health and human services, 2012) and therefore receive appropriate interventions. The most commonly identified substances found in pregnant women include alcohol, marijuana, opioids, and cocaine (Lehikoinen et al., 2016), with evidence; however, the trends for specific substances being used are changing. Alcohol and marijuana continue to be the most widely reported substances both detected in and reported by pregnant women (Chasnoff, Landress, & Barrett, 1990). However, cocaine rates appear decreasing over time, with apparent increases in the ingestion or administration of opioids (Azadi & Dildy, 2008; Lehikoinen et al., 2016).

Regarding alcohol, the negative effects of excessive consumption are well documented and include a range of foetal alcohol spectrum disorders (FASD) (Abel, 1998; Smith et al., 2014). FASD is the general term for a range of life-long adverse physical, neurocognitive, and behavioural problems associated with excessive alcohol consumption, of any type, in pregnancy. These manifestations range from mild to severe and include (but are not limited to) distinct facial (such as thin upper lip and smooth philtrum) and other physical characteristics (such as limitation to extension of fourth and fifth fingers, small head circumference, midface hyperplasia, and various birth defects) (del Campo & Jones, 2017; May et al., 2018). Accurate diagnoses of FASD must also include the presence of specific abnormalities in brain growth or structure and neurobehavioural impairment (May et al., 2018). Importantly, it is increasingly apparent that children diagnosed with FASD are identified and engaged with appropriate and best-practice interventions, as these are demonstrated to lead to significant improvements (see Nash et al., 2015, for valuable examples).

Drug misuse may also expose the foetus to maternally administered drugs and provides an interdisciplinary challenge for practitioners (from social, psychological, pharmacological, and obstetric specialists to addiction psychiatry/psychology disciplines) faced with the complexity of effects caused by a wide range of substances with the potential to harm both the foetus and born child (Havemann-Reinecke, 2008). This text cannot possibly address the plethora of effects of single-substance or multiple-substance abuse, whether opiates, cannabinoids, psychostimulants, benzodiazepines (as well as alcohol), or various combinations. However, scholarship accords overarching deleterious outcomes of both licit (prescribed or legally obtained) and illicit drug abuse. These include (but are not limited to) disruptions in angiogenesis, neurogenesis, replication, cellular development, tissue differentiation, and miscarriage, as well as delays in cognition and development, low birth weight, and birth defects in the born child (Hamplová, Sedláčková, & Veselý, 2015; Hennessy, 2018; Marangoni & Oliveira, 2015; Worley, 2014).

4 Neglect

Child neglect is suggested to be one of the most common types of child abuse globally (Mennen, Kim, Sang, & Trickett, 2010), with one meta-analytic review of specialised journals estimating global child neglect prevalence rates (among almost 60,000 participants) to be around 16% of children for physical neglect and just over 18% for emotional neglect. Despite this, child neglect is considered to have the least scholarly and public attention of all other forms of abuse, a situation having been coined by researchers as 'the neglect of neglect' (Mulder et al., 2018; Stoltenborgh, Bakermans-Kranenburg, & Van IJzendoorn, 2013). An overarching definition of child neglect could be the repeated failure to meet a child's physical or psychological needs that results in serious impairment of child health or development (Dubowitz, 2014). Of course, this broad definition is problematic for a number of reasons. First, it may not concur with definitions across jurisdictions leading to issues with translational validity and interpretation. Second, neglect most often infers the *omission* of care, rather than the *commission* of harm/s, which may muddy perceptions of severity, and third, societal norms across cultures, socioeconomic status and areas, and governmental jurisdictions are likely to affect expectations for what is 'good' parenting and what is not (Elliott & Urquiza, 2006; Mennen et al., 2010). Five subtypes of neglect have been proffered: care neglect, medical neglect, educational neglect, supervisory neglect, and environmental neglect (Mennen et al., 2010, p. 647) (Table 1).

Scholarship attests that neglect plays a significant role in a suite of problematic effects such as increased presentation of internalising and externalising behaviours (Stoltenborgh, Bakermans-Kranenburg, & Van IJzendoorn, 2013) and a lack of ego resilience (Manly, Kim, Rogosch, & Cicchetti, 2001). Reported long-term effects of child neglect include delays in cognitive and emotional development (Hildyard & Wolfe, 2002); poor school performance

Table 1: Child neglect types and examples

Subtype	Definition	Indicators
Care neglect	Failure to provide a child's basic needs for adequate food, clothing, and sanitation	A child reports to school without having breakfast, no lunch, without warm clothes in winter, a dirty and unkempt uniform, and chronically untreated head lice
Medical neglect	Failure to provide assessment or medical care for injury, illness, or disability	A child reports to school with untreated abrasions and swelling of the ankle, indicating significant trauma
Educational neglect	Failure to enrol a child for school or provide necessary educational tools	A child is absent for a significant time in the school term without reasonable explanation and, when present, does not have necessary books and stationary
Supervisory neglect	Failure to provide adequate supervision, whether in the immediate proximity of a child or not	Parent/carer is drunk or drug-affected and, although present, is unable to appropriately care for a child's needs
Environmental neglect	Failure to provide a clean, healthy environment for a child	A child is found to be living among rat-infested and filthy conditions and animal faeces

Adapted from Mennen et al. (2010).

(Thornberry, Ireland, & Smith, 2001); antisocial behaviour and association with deviant peers (Bolger & Patterson, 2001; Chapple & Vaske, 2010); insecure attachments (Bolger & Patterson, 2001; Bolger, Patterson, & Kupersmidt, 1998); difficulties with emotional regulation; and increased fear reactivity and negative cognition, affect, and behavioural effects (Chapple, Tyler, & Bersani, 2005; Chapple & Vaske, 2010; Ireland, Smith, & Thornberry, 2002). Moreover, studies support the overrepresentation of neglected children in welfare samples (Mennen et al., 2010).

As with all programs or interventions intended to ameliorate or mediate the impact of trauma, knowledge of the aetiology of child neglect and risk factors and their effects is vital. Given the prevalence and consequences of child neglect as a type of child abuse, empirical enquiry and the application of subsequent evidence-based protocols are essential. Overall, research has suggested that a convergence of ecologically based risk factors, rather than just one or two factors, is involved in the occurrence of child neglect (Bronfenbrenner, 2000; Mulder et al., 2018). Moreover, proximal, rather than distal risk, factors or social systems more reliably influence the onset and maintenance of child neglect (Mulder et al., 2018). More specifically, young, single, disadvantaged mothers are most likely to neglect their children (Coulton, Korbin, & Su, 1999), as well as those with current biopsychosocial problems or parents/carers with a history of their own child abuse and neglect, a large current family size, or families that display coercive, drug/alcohol-related, or otherwise problematic family behaviours (Mulder et al., 2018).

5 Physical Abuse

Child physical abuse is defined by the World Health Organisation (1999) as actions or inactions, which result in actual or potential physical harm, that are within the control of or preventable by the parent, carer, or authorised person (such as a school teacher). One global meta-analysis involving 111 studies and just under 10 million participants estimates the prevalence of child physical abuse to be upward of 22% and asserts that child physical abuse is a 'widespread global problem affecting the lives of millions of children all over the world [and is in] sharp contrast with the United Nation's Convention on the Rights of the Child' (Stoltenborgh, Bakermans-Kranenburg, IJzendoorn, & Alink, 2013; Stoltenborgh, Bakermans-Kranenburg, & Van IJzendoorn, 2013, p. 81).

Modern shifts in societal and intergenerational attitudes and experiences and even religious teachings have led to changes in the way corporal punishment of children is viewed or accepted as an effective form of discipline (Russa, Rodriguez, & Silvia, 2014). Indeed, corporal punishment has been, until quite recently, an accepted practice within families and schools, where belts, rulers, whips of various sorts, and other weapons have been fervently selected to most appropriately deal with a rebellious or otherwise difficult child. Indeed, the Christian Bible contains references to the worth of physical punishment as a form of discipline, including 'He that spareth the rod hateth his son; but he that loveth him chasteneth him betimes' (Proverbs, XIII, 24, King James Version) and 'Foolishness is bound in the heart of a child; but the rod of correction shall drive it from him' (Proverbs, XXII, 15, King James Version). However, parental use of physical discipline has been identified by a wide contemporary scholarship as generally deleterious to a child's healthy development, with negative effects being listed as increased risk-taking behaviours such as delinquency and sexual risk-taking and child aggression (Annerbäck, Sahlqvist, Svedin, Wingren, & Gustafsson, 2012), posttraumatic stress disorder (Rosner, König, Neuner, Schmidt, & Steil, 2014), negative health outcomes such as use of tobacco and drugs, and decreased understanding and acceptance of what constitutes reasonable and acceptable behaviour (Gershoff, 2002; Thornberry, Freeman-Gallant, Lizotte, Krohn, & Smith, 2003).

Child physical abuse includes physical acts against a child or the omission of acts that protect a child from physical abuse (here, problems with definitions of physical abuse and neglect can be methodologically unclear). These acts include hitting with a body part or weapon (such as a stick or belt), kicking, punching, shoving, throwing the child, dragging and dropping, shaking, choking, burning, and poisoning. Physical abuse tends to relate to actions at the hands of a parent/carer/authorised person, making it (by definition) a discrete type of abuse from, say, sexual abuse. Although sexual abuse can also be considered a form of physical abuse, particularly when trauma is involved, sexual abuse can be perpetrated by noncaregivers, such as acquaintances, distant family members, or strangers

(Jackson, Kissoon, & Greene, 2015). Of course, this discussion highlights problems faced by scientific enquiry but further underpins the importance of robust and consistent definitions of types of abuse and applications of variables.

A wide body of literature has examined and reported findings from studies evaluating risk factors for child physical abuse and not surprisingly most mirror risk factors for other abuse types. These include young parental age and low parental education, parental history of child abuse, psychiatric treatment, or violence history (Dakil, Cox, Lin, & Flores, 2012); family history of IPV (Taylor, Guterman, Lee, & Rathouz, 2009); and low socioeconomic status (Dakil et al., 2012; Sidebotham, Heron, and the ALSAC Team, 2006). Several cognitive risk factors are also presented, including parental empathy and emotional intelligence, parental locus of control, and levels of parental frustration and tolerance (McElroy & Rodriguez, 2008). Recent research indicates that child physical abuse rates may be reduced if environmental risk factors and early signs of physical abuse (such as atypical bruising or sentinel injuries) are identified and addressed (Pierce et al., 2017). Of particular interest is that an overrepresentation of negative cognitions in a caregiver can increase risk of physical harm to a child, whereby the caregiver interprets a child's action or behaviours as hostile or intentionally negative (Berlin, Dodge, & Reznick, 2013; Pierce et al., 2017).

6 Sexual Abuse

Expansion of (particularly prevalence) research into sexual abuse generally began around the time of Finkelhor's (1994) *The international epidemiology of child sexual abuse.* Since that time, the negative effects of child sex abuse (CSA) on short- and long-term biopsychosocial outcomes, regardless of gender, is without question (Chapman et al., 2004; Jumper, 1995; Spatz Widom, DuMont, & Czaja, 2007; Stoltenborgh et al., 2011). Prevalence rates around the world vary significantly regarding gender and geographical location, largely due to differences in social, religious, and cultural norms or beliefs (Kenny & McEachern, 2000; Pereda, Guilera, Forns, & Gomez-Benito, 2009; Stoltenborgh et al., 2011). However, one comprehensive meta-analysis reported in 2017 of specialist publications published between 1980 and 2008, with almost 2 million participants, reported that the overall prevalence was 13% in self-report studies and 4/1000 in informant studies. Self-reported CSA was more common among female (18%) than among male participants (8%). The lowest rates for both girls (12%) and boys (<1%) were found in Asia, and the highest rates were found for girls in Australia (20%) and for boys in Africa (19%). These rates, the authors note, confirm both the extent of the problem and methodological challenges, particularly in self-reported measurements (Stoltenborgh et al., 2011). Trends in CSA prevalence rates over time is a matter of controversy across scholarship, with some researchers reporting reductions from the 1990s to 2005 (Gilbert et al., 2009) and others finding little significant variation (Goldman & Padayachi, 2000).

Again, these differences may be explained by a range of methodological issues, such as differences in definition and issues of recollection bias in adult populations (Barth, Bermetz, Heim, Trelle, & Tonia, 2013).

The World Health Organisation (WHO) (1999) delineates a number of types of child sexual abuse including (a) rape, defined as oral, anal, or vaginal penetration by a perpetrator; (b) sexual assault, a broader term that refers to fondling and sexual nonpenetration behaviours; (c) incest, which refers to familial sexual contact (immediate family and/or up to fifth degree relations); and (d) sexual exploitation, defined as non-sexual contact in which the child is involved in pornography, witnesses sexual activity, sees adults exposing themselves to the child, or engages in other inappropriate behaviour for the sexual pleasure of the perpetrator. More recently, the term has been expanded to include Internet pornography and other Internet-enacted acts as listed above (Greydanus & Merrick, 2017). The WHO also outlines a number of necessary conditions for an accurate definition of child sexual abuse which are the following: (a) The child is deemed incapable of informed consent, (b) the abuser violates a county's set of laws or social taboos, (c) the abuse is perpetrated by an adult or an older child or adolescent in position to take sexual advantage, and (d) the sexual abuse of the victim is for the sexual gratification of the abuser (World Health Organization, 1999). Additionally, the World Health Organization (1999) asserts that even though the child may indicate consent, the child is most often involved in a sexual activity that he/she does not fully comprehend, that children can be unlawfully involved in prostitution or pornography as part of the spectrum of child sexual abuse types, and that perpetrators are most commonly trusted persons in a position of power over the vulnerable child.

The outcomes and consequences of child sexual abuse in childhood and through to adulthood are widely reported by a plethora of literature. The most widely examined and reported are posttraumatic stress disorder (Barrera, Calderón, & Bell, 2013), problematic cognition and externalising and internalising problems (Miragoli, Procaccia, & Di Blasio, 2014), disorganised or insecure attachments to primary caregivers translating to relationships in adulthood (Briere, Runtz, Eadie, Bigras, & Godbout, 2017), social isolation (Miner et al., 2016), and reports of more traumatic events in later life (Nacak, Morawa, Tuffner, & Erim, 2017). Notably, a growing literature suggests that CSA sexuality-related outcomes in adulthood are significant and wide ranging and include hypersexuality, sexual compulsivity, and risky sexual behaviours in adulthood (Miner et al., 2010; Vaillancourt-Morel et al., 2016), as well as sexual inhibition, sexual avoidance or aversion, low desire, and vaginal or pelvic pain (Vaillancourt-Morel et al., 2016).

The range and prevalence of risk factors for CSA are at least as wide ranging and varied as the consequences of CSA. Commonly, CSA is concurrent with other forms of child abuse, in particular, physical neglect and abuse and emotional neglect and abuse

(Laaksonen et al., 2011). Children are also more likely to experience CSA with parental substance abuse or not growing up with both parents (Laaksonen et al., 2011; Vaillancourt-Morel et al., 2016). Here, the association appears due to the lack of adequate and capable parental guardianship, if the parents are not the perpetrators of the abuse. Overall, the risk factors for CSA are too numerous to be synthesised within this text. However, a representation of the variables most commonly measured by scholarship when assessing prevalence rates is valuable for this discussion and includes exposure to bullying, sexual violence, witnessing family violence, social isolation, socioeconomic status, family structure, caregiver-child relationships, physical health, behaviour, and gender.

7 Conclusion

Since the earliest recognition, at least in a legislative sense, children have have the right to be treated fairly, to be safe, to have access to education, and to be immersed in an environment that supports their healthy physical and emotional development, scholarship has continued to cast light on those things that harm a child, those things we can do to both protect them, and those things that might serve to heal them when violations occur. This chapter has outlined a broad range of conditions or actions that whether deliberate or not, when experienced by a child, have the potential to impact their development on a range of biopsychosocial fronts. Those conditions or acts discussed were emotional abuse that include both acts of commission and omission, including witnessing family violence; foetal abuse that, whether the result of intimate partner violence or maternal substance abuse, has the potential to impact the born child well into adulthood; neglect, categorised into five areas—care, medical, educational, supervisory, and environmental; physical abuse that, despite historical endorsements, is now widely discouraged or sanctioned in a number of global jurisdictions; sexual abuse that includes acts of rape and sexual assault; and abuse via the Internet, which includes rape and sexual assault, as well as the sexual exploitation of children. Sexual assault, as with all types of abuse, can be exacted by family, acquaintances, and strangers but most commonly at the hands of immediate family.

This chapter has also outlined a number of important and contemporaneous issues faced by scholarship and those issues that impel research and drive continued empirical effort. There is conclusive evidence that CSA is a global issue of immense proportions and significance that has major and long-lasting effects on individuals, communities, and the burden of disease. It is with this in mind that *Child Abuse and Neglect: Forensic Issues in Evidence, Impact, and Management* presents an opportunity for esteemed scholars, those who are carrying the baton of CSA enquiry into the future, to present their findings, inform the most current science, and influence the work of practitioners and policymakers who have chosen to influence this profoundly important field.

Chapter Review Questions

(1) What are the two most commonly addressed issues in regard to foetal abuse?
(2) T/F: Child sexual abuse types generally overlap, where a child might be victim to multiple types. Explain.
(3) What is the difference between rape and sexual assault?
(4) List and give examples of five types of child neglect.
(5) List four risk factors for child physical abuse.
(6) A number of challenges are faced by scholars researching child abuse. List three and explain.
(7) Define emotional abuse and provide three examples.
(8) Risk factors for emotional abuse can be interpreted to contrast with risk factors for physical abuse. Explain.

References

Abel, E. (1998). Foetal alcohol syndrome: the 'American paradox'. *Alcohol, 33*, 195–201.

Ackner, S., Skeate, A., Patterson, P., & Neal, A. (2013). Emotional abuse and psychosis: a recent review of the literature. *Journal of Aggression, Maltreatment & Trauma, 22*(9), 1032–1049. https://doi.org/10.1080/10926771.2013.837132.

Alhusen, J. L., Lucea, M. B., Bullock, L., & Sharps, P. (2013). Intimate partner violence, substance use, and adverse neonatal outcomes among urban women. *Journal of Pediatrics, 163*(2), 471–476. https://doi.org/10.1016/j.jpeds.2013.01.036.

American Professional Society on the Abuse of Children. (1995). *Psychosocial evaluation of suspected psychological maltreatment in children and practice guidelines*. Chicago, IL: American Professional Society on the Abuse of Children.

Annerbäck, E., Sahlqvist, L., Svedin, C. G., Wingren, G., & Gustafsson, P. A. (2012). Child physical abuse and concurrence of other types of child abuse in Sweden—associations with health and risk behaviors. *Child Abuse & Neglect, 36*(7), 585–595. https://doi.org/10.1016/j.chiabu.2012.05.006.

Azadi, A., & Dildy, G. A. (2008). Universal testing for substance abuse at the time of parturition. *American Journal of Obstetrics and Gynaecology, 198*, 30–32.

Barrera, M., Calderón, L., & Bell, V. (2013). The cognitive impact of sexual abuse and PTSD in children: a neuropsychological study. *Journal of Child Sexual Abuse, 22*(6), 625–638. https://doi.org/10.1080/10538712.2013.811141.

Barth, J., Bermetz, L., Heim, E., Trelle, S., & Tonia, T. (2013). The current prevalence of child sexual abuse worldwide: a systematic review and meta-analysis. *International Journal of Public Health, 58*(3), 469–483. https://doi.org/10.1007/s00038-012-0426-1.

Berlin, L. J., Dodge, K. A., & Reznick, J. S. (2013). Examining pregnant women's hostile attributions about infants as a predictor of offspring maltreatment. *JAMA Pediatrics, 167*(6), 549–553.

Black, D. A., Smith Slep, A. M., & Heyman, R. E. (2001). Risk factors for child psychological abuse. *Aggression and Violent Behavior, 6*(2), 189–201. https://doi.org/10.1016/S1359-1789(00)00022-7.

Bolger, K. E., & Patterson, C. J. (2001). Developmental pathways from child maltreatment to peer rejection. *Child Development, 72*, 549–568.

Bolger, K. E., Patterson, C. J., & Kupersmidt, J. B. (1998). Peer relationships and self-esteem among children who have been maltreated. *Child Development, 69*, 1171–1197.

Briere, J., & Elliott, D. M. (2003). Prevalence and psychological sequelae of self-reported childhood physical and sexual abuse in a general population sample of men and women. *Child Abuse & Neglect, 27*, 1205–1222. https://doi.org/10.1016/j.chiabu.2003.09.008.

Briere, J., Runtz, M., Eadie, E., Bigras, N., & Godbout, N. (2017). Disengaged parenting: structural equation modeling with child abuse, insecure attachment, and adult symptomatology. *Child Abuse & Neglect, 67*, 260–270. https://doi.org/10.1016/j.chiabu.2017.02.036.

Bronfenbrenner, U. (2000). Ecological theory. In A. Kazdin (Ed.), *Encyclopedia of psychology*. Washington, DC: American Psychological Association and Oxford University Press.

Centers for Disease Control and Prevention. (1999). *PRAMS 1996 surveillance report*. Atlanta, GA: Division of Reproductive Health, National Center for Chronic Disease Prevention and Health Promotion, Centers for Disease Control and Prevention.

Chamberland, C., Fallon, B., Black, T., & Trocmé, N. (2011). Emotional maltreatment in Canada: prevalence, reporting and child welfare responses (CIS2). *Child Abuse & Neglect, 35*, 841–854. https://doi.org/10.1016/j.chiabu.2011.03.010.

Chapman, D. P., Whitfield, C. L., Felitti, V. J., Dube, S. R., Edwards, V. J., & Anda, R. F. (2004). Adverse childhood experiences and the risk of depressive disorders in adulthood. *Journal of Affective Disorders, 82*, 217–225. https://doi.org/10.1016/j.jad.2003.12.013.

Chapple, C. L., Tyler, K. A., & Bersani, B. E. (2005). Child neglect and adolescent violence: examining the effects of self-control and peer rejection. *Violence and Victims, 20*, 39–53.

Chapple, C. L., & Vaske, J. (2010). Child neglect, social context, and educational outcomes: examining the moderating effects of school and neighborhood context. *Violence and Victims, 25*(4), 470–485. https://doi.org/10.1891/0886-6708.25.4.470.

Chasnoff, I. J., Landress, H. J., & Barrett, M. E. (1990). The prevalence of illicit-drug or alcohol use during pregnancy and discrepancies in mandatory reporting. *Northern English Journal of Medicine, 322*, 1202–1206.

Coates, A. A., & Messman-Moore, T. L. (2014). A structural model of mechanisms predicting depressive symptoms in women following childhood psychological maltreatment. *Child Abuse & Neglect, 38*, 103–113. https://doi.org/10.1016/j.chiabu.2013.10.005.

Cokkinides, V. E., & Coker, A. L. (1998). Experiencing physical violence during pregnancy: prevalence and correlates. *Family and Community Health, 20*, 19–38.

Cokkinides, V. E., Coker, A., Sanderson, M., Addy, C., & Bethea, L. (1999). Physical violence during pregnancy: maternal complications and birth outcomes. *Obstetrics & Gynecology, 93*, 661–666.

Condon, J. T. (1986). The spectrum of foetal abuse in pregnant women. *Journal of Nervous and Mental Disease, 174*(9), 509–516.

Corby, B. (2006). *Child abuse: Towards a knowledge base* (3rd ed.). New York, NY; Maidenhead, England: Open University Press.

Coulton, C. J., Korbin, J. E., & Su, M. (1999). Neighborhoods and child maltreatment: a multi-level study. *Child Abuse and Neglect, 23*, 1019–1040.

Dakil, S. R., Cox, M., Lin, H., & Flores, G. (2012). Physical abuse in U.S. children: risk factors and deficiencies in referrals to support services. *Journal of Aggression, Maltreatment & Trauma, 21*(5), 555–569. https://doi.org/10.1080/10926771.2012.680007.

Davis, E. C., Rotheram-Borus, M. J., Weichle, T. W., Rezai, R., & Tomlinson, M. (2017). Patterns of alcohol abuse, depression, and intimate partner violence among township mothers in South Africa over 5 years. *AIDS and Behavior, 21*(S2), 174–182. https://doi.org/10.1007/s10461-017-1927-y.

del Campo, M., & Jones, K. L. (2017). A review of the physical features of the foetal alcohol spectrum disorders. *European Journal of Medical Genetics, 60*(1), 55–64. https://doi.org/10.1016/j.ejmg.

Densen-Gerber, J., & Hutchinson, S. F. (1979). Sexual and commercial exploitation of children: legislative responses and treatment challenges. *Child Abuse & Neglect, 3*(1), 61–66. https://doi.org/10.1016/0145-2134(79)90012-7.

Dubowitz, H. (2014). Child neglect. *Pediatric Annals, 43*(11), 444–445. https://doi.org/10.3928/00904481-20141022-07.

Elliott, K., & Urquiza, A. (2006). Ethnicity, culture, and child maltreatment. *Journal of Social Issues, 62*, 787–809.

Ferguson, K. S., & Dacey, C. M. (1997). Anxiety, depression, and dissociation in women health care providers reporting a history of childhood psychological abuse. *Child Abuse & Neglect, 21*(10), 941–952.

Finkelhor, D. (1994). The international epidemiology of child sexual abuse. *Child Abuse & Neglect, 18*(5), 409–417. https://doi.org/10.1016/0145-2134(94)90026-4.

Finkelhor, D., Turner, H., Ormrod, R., & Hamby, S. L. (2009). Violence, abuse, and crime exposure in a national sample of children and youth. *Pediatrics, 124*(5), 1411–1423. http://dx.doi.org/10.1542/peds.2009-0467.

Finnbogadóttir, H., Dykes, A., & Wann-Hansson, C. (2014). Prevalence of domestic violence during pregnancy and related risk factors: a cross-sectional study in Southern Sweden. *BMC Women's Health, 14*(1), 63. https://doi.org/10.1186/1472-6874-14-63.

Fluke, J. D., Chabot, M., Fallon, B., MacLaurin, B., & Blackstock, C. (2010). Placement decisions and disparities among aboriginal groups: an application of the decision making ecology through multi-level analysis. *Child Abuse & Neglect, 34*(1), 57–69. https://doi.org/10.1016/j.chiabu.2009.08.009.

Garcia-Moreno, C., Gueses, A., & Knerr, W. (2012). *Understanding and addressing violence against women.* World Health Organisation. http://apps.who.int/iris/bitstream/handle/10665/77432/WHO_RHR_12.36_eng.pdf?sequence=1.

Gershoff, E. T. (2002). Corporal punishment by parents and associated child behaviors and experiences: a meta-analytic and theoretical review. *Psychological Bulletin, 128*, 539–579.

Gibb, B. E., Chelminski, I., & Zimmerman, M. (2007). Childhood emotional, physical, and sexual abuse, and diagnoses of depressive and anxiety disorders in adult psychiatric outpatients. *Depression and Anxiety, 24*, 256–263. https://doi.org/10.1002/da.20238.

Gilbert, R., Widom, C., Browne, K., Fergusson, D., Webb, E., & Janson, S. (2009). Child maltreatment 1 burden and consequences of child maltreatment in high-income countries. *Lancet, 373*(9657), 68–81. https://doi.org/10.1016/S0140-6736(08)61706-7.

Glaser, D. (2002). Emotional abuse and neglect (psychological maltreatment): A conceptual framework. *Child Abuse & Neglect, 26*(6), 697–714. https://doi.org/10.1016/S0145-2134(02)00342-3.

Goldman, J. D. G., & Padayachi, U. K. (2000). Some methodological problems in estimating incidence and prevalence in child sexual abuse research. *The Journal of Sex Research, 37*, 305–314. https://doi.org/10.1080/00224490009552052.

Goodwin, M., Gazmararian, J. A., Johnson, C. H., Gilbert, B. C., & Saltzman, L. E. (2000). Pregnancy intendedness and physical abuse around the time of pregnancy: findings from the pregnancy risk assessment monitoring system, 1996-1997. *Maternal and Child Health Journal, 4*(2), 85–92.

Greydanus, D. E., & Merrick, J. (2017). A review of child sexual abuse. *International Journal of Child and Adolescent Health, 10*(3), 289–294.

Hamilton, J. L., Shapero, B. G., Stange, J. P., Hamlat, E. J., Abramson, L. Y., & Alloy, L. B. (2013). Emotional maltreatment, peer victimization, and depressive versus anxiety symptoms during adolescence: hopelessness as a mediator. *Journal of Clinical Child & Adolescent Psychology, 42*(3), 332–347. https://doi.org/10.1080/15374416.2013.777916.

Hamplová, L., Sedláčková, S., & Veselý, Z. (2015). Problems of addictive drug abuse in pregnancy. *Hygiena, 60*(3), 112–115. https://doi.org/10.21101/hygiena.a1402.

Havemann-Reinecke, U. (2008). Management of illicit drug misuse and maternal and child outcomes. *European Psychiatry, 23*, S57. https://doi.org/10.1016/j.eurpsy.2008.01.210.

Hennessy, G. (2018). Marijuana and pregnancy. *The American Journal on Addictions, 27*(1), 44–45. https://doi.org/10.1111/ajad.12671.

Hildyard, K. L., & Wolfe, D. A. (2002). Child neglect: developmental issues and outcomes. *Child Abuse and Neglect, 26*, 679–695. https://doi.org/10.1016/S0145-2134(02)00341-1.

Huang, C. Y., Bory, C. T., Caron, C., Tebes, J. K., & Connell, C. M. (2014). Relationship of risk assessment to placement characteristics in a statewide child welfare population. *Children and Youth Services Review, 46*, 85–90. https://doi.org/10.1016/j.childyouth.2014.07.012.

Ireland, T. O., Smith, C. A., & Thornberry, T. P. (2002). Developmental issues in the impact of child maltreatment on later delinquency and drug use. *Criminology, 40*, 359–399.

Jackson, A., Kissoon, N., & Greene, C. (2015). Aspects of abuse: recognizing and responding to child maltreatment. *Current Problems in Pediatric and Adolescent Health Care, 45*(3), 58–70. https://doi.org/10.1016/j.cppeds.2015.02.001.

James, L., Brody, D., & Hamilton, Z. (2013). Risk factors for domestic violence during pregnancy: a meta-analytic review. *Violence and Victims*, *28*(3), 359–380. https://doi.org/10.1891/0886-6708.VV-D-12-00034.

Jasinski, J. L. (2001). Pregnancy and violence against women: an analysis of longitudinal data. *Journal of Interpersonal Violence*, *16*, 713–734.

Jasinski, J. L., & Kaufman Kantor, G. (2001). Pregnancy, stress and wife assaults: ethnic differences in prevalence, severity and onset in a national sample. *Violence and Victims*, *16*, 1–14.

Jumper, S. A. (1995). A meta-analysis of the relationship of child sexual abuse to adult psychological adjustment. *Child Abuse & Neglect*, *19*, 715–728. https://doi.org/10.1016/0145-2134(95)00029-8.

Kairys, S. W., Johnson, C. F., & The Committee on Child Abuse and Neglect. (2002). The psychological maltreatment of children: technical report. *Pediatrics*, *109*(4), 1–3.

Kelly, M. (2014). Increasing victimization through fetal abuse redefinition. *William & Mary Journal of Women and the Law*, *20*(3), 685.

Kempe, C., Silverman, F., Steele, B., Droegemueller, W., & Silver, H. (1962). The battered child syndrome. *Journal of the American Medical Association*, *181*, 17–24.

Kendall-Tackett, K. (2012). The long-term health effects of child sexual abuse. In P. Goodyear-Brown (Ed.), *Handbook of child sexual abuse: Identification, assessment, and treatment* (pp. 49–67). Hoboken, NJ: Wiley.

Kenny, M., & McEachern, A. G. (2000). Prevalence and characteristics of childhood sexual abuse in multiethnic female college students. *Journal of Child Sexual Abuse*, *9*, 57–70. https://doi.org/10.1300/J070v09n02_04.

Kent, L., Laidlaw, J. D. D., & Brockington, I. F. (1997). Fetal abuse. *Child Abuse and Neglect*, *21*(2), 181–186.

Khaironisak, H., Zaridah, S., Hasanain, F. G., & Zaleha, M. I. (2017). Prevalence, risk factors, and complications of violence against pregnant women in a hospital in peninsular Malaysia. *Women & Health*, *57*(8), 919–923. https://doi.org/10.1080/03630242.2016.1222329.

Kim, D. R., Sockol, L. E., Sammel, M. D., Kelly, C., Moseley, M., & Epperson, C. N. (2013). Elevated risk of adverse obstetric outcomes in pregnant women with depression. *Archives of Women's Mental Health*, *16*(6), 475–482. https://doi.org/10.1007/s00737-013-0371-x.

Laaksonen, T., Sariola, H., Johansson, A., Jern, P., Varjonen, M., von der Pahlen, B., et al. (2011). Changes in the prevalence of child sexual abuse, its risk factors, and their associations as a function of age cohort in a Finnish population sample. *Child Abuse & Neglect*, *35*(7), 480–490. https://doi.org/10.1016/j.chiabu.2011.03.004.

Lehikoinen, A., Ordén, M., Heinonen, S., & Voutilainen, R. (2016). Maternal drug or alcohol abuse is associated with decreased head size from mid-pregnancy to childhood. *Acta Paediatrica*, *105*(7), 817–822. https://doi.org/10.1111/apa.13416.

Manly, T., Kim, J., Rogosch, J. E., & Cicchetti, D. (2001). Dimensions of child maltreatment and children's adjustment: contributions of developmental timing and subtype. *Development and Psychopathology*, *13*, 759–782.

Marangoni, S. R., & Oliveira, M. L. F. (2015). Women users of drugs of abuse during pregnancy: characterization of a series of cases. *Acta Scientiarum Health Sciences*, *37*(1), 53–61. https://doi.org/10.4025/actascihealthsci.v37i1.16754.

Martin, S. L., English, K. T., Clark, K. A., Cilenti, D., & Kupper, L. L. (1996). Violence and substance abuse among North Carolina pregnant women. *American Journal of Public Health*, *86*, 991–998.

May, P., Chambers, C., Kalberg, W., Zellner, J., Feldman, H., Buckley, D., et al. (2018). Prevalence of foetal alcohol spectrum disorders in 4 US communities. *JAMA-Journal of the American Medical Association*, *319*(5), 474–482. https://doi.org/10.1001/jama.2017.21896.

McCoy, Monica, L., Keen, S. M., & EBSCOhost. (2011). *Child abuse and neglect*. New York: Psychology Press.https://doi.org/10.4324/9781410616388.

McElroy, E. M., & Rodriguez, C. M. (2008). Mothers of children with externalizing behavior problems: Cognitive risk factors for abuse potential and discipline style and practices. *Child Abuse & Neglect*, *32*(8), 774–784. https://doi.org/10.1016/j.chiabu.2008.01.002.

Mennen, F. E., Kim, K., Sang, J., & Trickett, P. K. (2010). Child neglect: definition and identification of youth's experiences in official reports of maltreatment. *Child Abuse & Neglect*, *34*(9), 647–658. https://doi.org/10.1016/j.chiabu.2010.02.007.

Miner, M. H., Robinson, B. E., Knight, R. A., Berg, D., Swinburne Romine, R., & Netland, J. (2010). Understanding sexual perpetration against children: effects of attachment style, interpersonal involvement, and hypersexuality. *Sexual Abuse: A Journal of Research and Treatment*, *22*(1), 58–77. https://doi.org/10.1177/1079063209353183.

Miner, M. H., Swinburne Romine, R., Robinson, B. E., Berg, D., & Knight, R. A. (2016). Anxious attachment, social isolation, and indicators of sex drive and compulsivity: predictors of child sexual abuse perpetration in adolescent males? *Sexual Abuse: A Journal of Research and Treatment*, *28*(2), 132–153. https://doi.org/10.1177/1079063214547585.

Miragoli, S., Procaccia, R., & Di Blasio, P. (2014). Language use and PTSD symptoms: content analyses of allegations of child sexual abuse. *Journal of Forensic Psychology Practice*, *14*(5), 355–382. https://doi.org/10.1080/15228932.2014.970423.

Monk, C., Spicer, J., & Champagne, F. A. (2012). Linking prenatal maternal adversity to developmental outcomes in infants: the role of epigenetic pathways. *Development and Psychopathology*, *24*(4), 1361–1376. https://doi.org/10.1017/S0954579412000764.

Mulder, T. M., Kuiper, K. C., van der Put, C. E., Claudia, E., Stams, G. J. M., & Assink, M. (2018). Risk factors for child neglect: a meta-analytic review. *Child Abuse & Neglect*, *77*, 198–210. https://doi.org/10.1016/j.chiabu.2018.01.006.

Nacak, Y., Morawa, E., Tuffner, D., & Erim, Y. (2017). Insecure attachment style and cumulative traumatic life events in patients with somatoform pain disorder: a cross-sectional study. *Journal of Psychosomatic Research*, *103*, 77–82. https://doi.org/10.1016/j.jpsychores.2017.10.003.

Nash, K., Stevens, S., Greenbaum, R., Weiner, J., Koren, G., & Rovet, J. (2015). Improving executive functioning in children with fetal alcohol spectrum disorders. *Child Neuropsychology*, *21*(2), 191–209. https://doi.org/10.1080/09297049.2014.889110.

National Institute on Drug Abuse (NIDA). (2011). *Prenatal exposure to drugs of abuse*. NIDA Topics in Brief (http://www.drugabuse.gov/sites/default/files/prenatal.pdf.

Negriff, S., Schneiderman, J., Smith, C., Schreyer, J., & Trickett, P. (2014). Characterizing the sexual abuse experiences of young adolescents. *Child Abuse & Neglect*, *38*(2), 261–270. https://doi.org/10.1016/j.chiabu.2013.08.021.

Newberger, E. H., Barkan, S. E., Lieberman, E. S., McCormick, M. C., Yllo, K., Gary, L. T., et al. (1992). Abuse of pregnant women and adverse birth outcome: current knowledge and implications for practice. *JAMA*, *267*(17), 2370–2372. https://doi.org/10.1001/jama.1992.03480170096037.

Pajulo, M., Savonlahti, E., Sourander, A., Helenius, H., & Piha, J. (2001). Antenatal depression, substance dependency and social support. *Journal of Affective Disorders*, *65*, 9–17.

Pereda, N., Guilera, G., Forns, M., & Gomez-Benito, J. (2009). The international epidemiology of child sexual abuse: a continuation of Finkelhor (1994). *Child Abuse & Neglect*, *33*, 331–342. https://doi.org/10.1016/j.chiabu.2008.07.007.

Pierce, M. C., Kaczor, K., Acker, D., Webb, T., Brenzel, A., Lorenz, D. J., et al. (2017). History, injury, and psychosocial risk factor commonalities among cases of fatal and near-fatal physical child abuse. *Child Abuse & Neglect*, *69*, 263–277. https://doi.org/10.1016/j.chiabu.2017.04.033.

Rosner, R., König, H., Neuner, F., Schmidt, U., & Steil, R. (2014). Developmentally adapted cognitive processing therapy for adolescents and young adults with PTSD symptoms after physical and sexual abuse: Study protocol for a randomized controlled trial. *Trials*, *15*(1), 195. https://doi.org/10.1186/1745-6215-15-195.

Russa, M. B., Rodriguez, C. M., & Silvia, P. J. (2014). Frustration influences impact of history and disciplinary attitudes on physical discipline decision making. *Aggressive Behavior*, *40*(1), 1–11. https://doi.org/10.1002/ab.21500.

Sandman, C. A., Curran, M. M., Davis, E. P., Glynn, L. M., Head, K., & Baram, T. Z. (2018). Cortical thinning and neuropsychiatric outcomes in children exposed to prenatal adversity: a role for placental CRH? *American Journal of Psychiatry*, *175*(5), 471–479. https://doi.org/10.1176/appi.ajp.2017.16121433.

Schroedel, J. R., & Peretz, P. (1994). A gender analysis of policy formation: the case of fetal abuse. *Journal of Health Politics, Policy and Law*, *19*(2), 335–360. https://doi.org/10.1215/03616878-19-2-335.

Schumacher, J. A., Slep, A. M. S., & Heyman, R. E. (2001). Risk factors for male-to-female partner physical abuse. *Aggression and Violent Behavior*, *6*, 281–352.

Shevlin, M., Murphy, S. M., Elklit, A., Murphy, J., & Hyland, P. (2018). Typologies of child sexual abuse: an analysis of multiple abuse acts among a large sample of Danish treatment-seeking survivors of childhood sexual abuse. *Psychological Trauma: Theory, Research, Practice, and Policy*, *10*(3), 263–269. https://doi.org/10.1037/tra0000268.

Sidebotham, P., Heron, J., & the ALSAC Team. (2006). Child maltreatment in the "Children of the Nineties," a cohort study of risk factors. *Child Abuse & Neglect*, *30*, 497–522.

Smith, L. K., Draper, E. S., Evans, T. A., Field, D. J., Johnson, S. J., Manktelow, B. N., et al. (2015). Associations between late and moderately preterm birth and smoking, alcohol, drug use and diet: A population-based case-cohort study. *Evidence-Based Mental Health*, *100*(6), F486–F491. https://doi.org/10.1136/archdischild-2014-307265.

Smith, L., Savory, J., Couves, J., & Burns, E. (2014). Alcohol consumption during pregnancy: cross-sectional survey. *Midwifery*, *30*(12), 1173–1178. https://doi.org/10.1016/j.midw.2014.04.002.

Spatz Widom, C., DuMont, K., & Czaja, S. (2007). A prospective investigation of major depressive disorder and comorbidity in abused and neglected children grown up. *Archives of General Psychiatry*, *64*, 49–56. https://doi.org/10.1001/archpsyc.64.1.49.

Stith, S. M., Rosen, K. H., Middleton, K. A., Busch, A. L., Lundeberg, K., & Carlton, R. P. (2000). The intergenerational transmission of spouse abuse: a meta-analysis. *Journal of Marriage and the Family*, *62*, 640–654.

Stoltenborgh, M., Bakermans-Kranenburg, M. J., IJzendoorn, M. H., & Alink, L. R. A. (2013). Cultural–geographical differences in the occurrence of child physical abuse? A meta-analysis of global prevalence. *International Journal of Psychology*, *48*(2), 81–94. https://doi.org/10.1080/00207594.2012.697165.

Stoltenborgh, M., van IJzendoorn, M. H., Euser, E. M., & Bakermans-Kranenburg, M. J. (2011). A global perspective on child sexual abuse: meta-analysis of prevalence around the world. *Child Maltreatment*, *16*, 79–101. https://doi.org/10.1177/1077559511403920.

Susser, E., Hoek, H. W., & Brown, A. (1998). Neurodevelopmental disorders after prenatal famine: the story of the Dutch famine study. *American Journal of Epidemiology*, *147*, 213–216. https://doi.org/10.1093/oxfordjournals.aje.a0094399482494.

Taillieu, T. L., Brownridge, D. A., Sareen, J., & Afifi, T. O. (2016). Childhood emotional maltreatment and mental disorders: results from a nationally representative adult sample from the United States. *Child Abuse & Neglect*, *59*, 1–12. https://doi.org/10.1016/j.chiabu.2016.07.005.

Taylor, C. A., Guterman, N. B., Lee, S. J., & Rathouz, P. J. (2009). Intimate partner violence, maternal stress, nativity, and risk for maternal maltreatment of young children. *American Journal of Public Health*, *99*, 175–183.

Thornberry, T. P., Freeman-Gallant, A., Lizotte, A. J., Krohn, M. D., & Smith, C. A. (2003). Linked lives: the intergenerational transmission of antisocial behavior. *Journal of Abnormal Child Psychology*, *31*, 171–184.

Thornberry, T. P., Ireland, T. O., & Smith, C. A. (2001). The importance of timing: the varying impact of childhood and adolescent maltreatment on multiple problem outcomes. *Development and Psychopathology*, *13*, 957–979.

Trickett, P. K., Kim, K., & Prindle, J. (2011). Variations in emotional abuse experiences among multiply maltreated young adolescents and relations with developmental outcomes. *Child Abuse & Neglect*, *35*(10), 876–886. https://doi.org/10.1016/j.chiabu.2011.08.001.

U.S. Department of Health and Human Services. (2012). *Substance abuse and mental health services administration: Results from the 2011 national survey on drug use and health: Summary of national findings*. . Available from: URL: http://www.samhsa.gov/data/sites/default/files/NSDUHresults PDFWHTML2013/Web/NSDUHresults2013.pdf.

Vaillancourt-Morel, M., Godbout, N., Sabourin, S., Briere, J., Lussier, Y., & Runtz, M. (2016). Adult sexual outcomes of child sexual abuse vary according to relationship status. *Journal of Marital and Family Therapy*, *42*(2), 341–356. https://doi.org/10.1111/jmft.12154.

World Health Organization. (1999). *Report of the consultation on child abuse prevention, 29–31 March 1999*. Geneva, Switzerland: World Health Organization.

Worley, J. (2014). Identification and management of prescription drug abuse in pregnancy. *The Journal of Perinatal & Neonatal Nursing*, *28*(3), 196–203. https://doi.org/10.1097/JPN.0000000000000039.

Yonkers, K. A., Smith, M. V., Forray, A., Epperson, C. N., Costello, D., Lin, H., et al. (2014). Pregnant women with posttraumatic stress disorder and risk of preterm birth. *JAMA Psychiatry*, *71*(8), 897–904. https://doi.org/10.1001/jamapsychiatry.2014.558.

Zhou, F. C., Mason, S., & Open Access Publishing in European Networks. (2015). *Genetics and epigenetics of fetal alcohol spectrum disorders*. Lausanne, Switzerland: Frontiers Media SA.

CHAPTER 2

Intimate Partner Violence as a Form of Child Abuse

Victoria Marshall*, Lesley-Anne Ey†, Chris Goddard†
Monash University, Melbourne, VIC, Australia †University of South Australia, Adelaide, SA, Australia

1 Introduction

According to the UN Convention on the Rights of the Child (1989), children have the right to protection from all forms of violence (including nonphysical forms of violence). Intimate partner violence and child abuse are two terms that have been used to describe violence that children may experience in the home. These have often been considered as separate types of violence—the former targeting an intimate partner with the risk to children arising from 'exposure' to this violence and its effects and the latter targeting children directly. However, from the child's perspective, both types of violence in the home constitute a fundamental disruption of the child's secure base of home and family relationships. Both may therefore be considered forms of child abuse.

This chapter will examine intimate partner violence (IPV) as one form of abuse or victimisation with which many children are forced to live. Some of the challenges and complexities relating to language, definitions and data in this area of practice and research will be highlighted, and our current understanding of IPV will be discussed. Children's experiences of and responses to IPV will be explored. Finally, the question of children's voices is discussed and considered in relation to their rights to participation under the UN Convention.

2 Definition and Terminology

IPV is a behaviour by an intimate partner or ex-partner that causes physical, sexual, or psychological harm, including physical aggression, sexual coercion, psychological abuse, and controlling behaviours (WHO, 2017). IPV is one of a number of terms that may be used to describe violence and abuse in intimate relationships. Other terms frequently used include 'domestic violence', 'family violence', and 'batterer violence' (Laing, Humphreys, & Cavanagh, 2013). For the purposes of this chapter, we have chosen to use the term intimate

Child Abuse and Neglect. https://doi.org/10.1016/B978-0-12-815344-4.00002-7

partner violence (hereafter IPV). This term captures the particular relational aspect of the violence from one intimate partner to another.

Several different terms may be used to describe children's relationship to IPV. Language can position children as central or as outsiders to the dynamic of IPV. Terms such as 'witnessing' and 'exposed to' position the child outside the dynamic of IPV and imply that it is the child's seeing or hearing the IPV that is problematic (Goddard & Bedi, 2010). This is a reductive view of children's experiences of IPV that focuses more on children's relationship to particular acts of violence than on their experience of the overall dynamic of IPV within the family and their responses to this. The language of 'witnessing' may conceal certain aspects of children's experiences of IPV, such as how parent–child relationships may be different as a result of IPV. The term primarily used in this chapter will be 'children living with IPV' as this captures more fully the influence of IPV in the life of the family and that this will likely have meaning in children's lives beyond their experience of a particular act or acts of violence. However, it is noted that the language of 'witnessing' is often used in the field and this language will be used if necessary for the purposes of consistency when referring to specific studies that use this language.

Although the prevalence of IPV is difficult to accurately determine, it is estimated that in Australia, 17% of women and 6.1% of men have experienced physical and/or sexual violence by a current or previous cohabiting partner since the age of 15 and that 23% of women and 16% of men have experienced emotional abuse by a current or previous partner since the age of 15 (AIHW, 2018, p. 20). It has been estimated that approximately one in three of Australian parents experience IPV and children often witness the violence (Kaspiew et al., 2017a, 2017b), with between 59% (Richards, 2011) and 72% (Kaspiew et al., 2009) of parents reporting that their children had witnessed the violence. This is likely to be an underestimate in terms of the number of children who have been affected by IPV in the family as children do not have to see a particular act of violence to be affected by the violence and its effects in the family. Price-Robertson, Bromfield, and Vassalo (2010) reviewed studies of child maltreatment in Australia to arrive at prevalence estimates. Their review notes that 'witnessing family violence' is a form of child maltreatment and they estimate the prevalence of 'witnessing of family violence' by children in Australia at between 12% and 23% (Price-Robertson et al., 2010).

3 Understanding IPV

IPV has existed as a social problem for centuries (Laing et al., 2013). Social workers in the early 20th century were documenting the problem and attempting to intervene (Edleson, 1991). This early approach was individual- and family-centred (Edleson, 1991). The current understanding of the problem has its roots in recent history as it was only in the 1970s that the significant step was taken of naming this form of violence as violence against women or domestic violence (Laing et al., 2013). IPV was recognised as a social problem arising from society's unequal treatment of women and male power and privilege within society (Edleson, 1991), and a more organised social response to the problem was instigated (Laing et al., 2013). Action against IPV therefore became part of a broader social movement in support of women's rights and gender equality (Laing et al., 2013). IPV was linked to the dominance of men over women in marriage and in society (Dobash & Dobash, 1979). Beginning in the early 1970s, the first refuges offering safety and shelter to women and children escaping IPV were established, and there was advocacy for legal reform and a stronger criminal justice response from feminist organisations (Laing et al., 2013; Stark, 2007). Critiques later emerged about the second-wave feminist approach to IPV as grounded in white middle-class experience and failed to address specific concerns of women from marginalised groups, such as women from indigenous or culturally diverse communities experiencing multiple forms of oppression (Sokoloff & Pratt, 2005).

There remain ongoing controversies and debates in relation to the nature and causes of IPV (Dobash & Dobash, 2004). Research findings can be contradictory, with some evidence of men and women perpetrating IPV at similar rates (gender symmetry) and other evidence that IPV is overwhelmingly perpetrated by males against female partners (gender asymmetry) (Dobash & Dobash, 2004). Johnson (2011) has addressed these problems by arguing that different types of violence are being measured by surveys that find contradictory results and developing a typology of IPV. Johnson's typology sets out three major types of IPV: intimate terrorism, violent resistance, and situational couple violence (Johnson, 2011, p. 290). Intimate terrorism and violent resistance are related to patterns of coercive control, whereas situational couple violence occurs when couple conflicts escalate to aggression and then to violence (Johnson, 2011; Stark, 2007). The concept of coercive control (Stark, 2007) has been increasingly employed in relation to IPV to indicate a systematic pattern of abuse that may include physical violation, denial of respect and autonomy, social isolation, appropriation or denial of resources, and surveillance (Laing et al., 2013; Stark, 2007). Coercive control can lead to a loss of a sense of self and the denying of basic rights including to privacy, self-respect, autonomy and equality, and the effects are cumulative (Candela, 2016). While both men and women can be victims of any form of IPV, coercive control is highly gendered with the vast majority of victims being women (Myhill, 2015). Coercive control is one way in which men's dominance of women is perpetuated in intimate relationships (Candela, 2016).

Another typology that goes further in exploring the diversity of patterns of IPV in families has been developed by Emery (2011). This typology takes account of whether power in the relationship is shared or unequal, whether there are existing relationship norms, and the relationship of the violence to these norms and incorporates the following types:

1 Anarchic: a lack of normative order in the relationship and multiple problems such as substance abuse, poverty, or mental illness
2 Violent conflict: an ordered relationship where power is more or less shared and there is a stable pattern of IPV

3 Tolerant dictatorship: the only violent acts being perpetrated by a subordinate partner likely to be female towards a dominant partner who may be a man who holds patriarchal beliefs but does not use (physical) violence
4 Despotic dictatorship: violent acts of inconsistent control
5 Totalitarian dictatorship: rigid order and rules in the household set by the perpetrator-dictator and backed up by violence

(Emery, 2011, p. 532)

This typology engages with the complexity and diversity of IPV. There may be significant differences in family life between households where different patterns of IPV are used, including differences in the experiences of violence and what is considered possible in terms of response. Variability in IPV means that IPV in different families may influence children differently and different dynamics underlying the IPV may convey very different messages to children with different outcomes for adjustment difficulties, for example externalising and internalising problems (Jouriles & McDonald, 2015).

Emery's (2011) work implies considerable diversity of children's experiences of IPV. For example, life in a household where anarchic IPV prevailed would be quite different from that in a 'totalitarian dictatorship' (p. 532). Herman (1992) observed differences in how some children who had been abused spoke of the rules that ordered life in their family. While many emphasised rules that were 'unpredictable' and 'chaotic' in their enforcement, others described 'a highly organised pattern of punishment and coercion' that Herman likens to life in a political prison (Herman, 1992, p. 99). This resonates with aspects of Emery's typology given the themes of chaos/unpredictability and extreme order. It is important to recognise the heterogeneity of IPV in families and that different patterns of IPV may structure family life and shape children's experiences in very different ways.

4 Children's Rights

Article 19 of the UN Convention on the Rights of the Child (UN General Assembly, 1989), to which Australia is a signatory, states that children have the right to be protected from all forms of physical or psychological violence, injury, or abuse while in the care of parents or other caregivers. However, children remain one of the most highly victimised groups in society and as a group experience particular forms of victimisation in addition to those that adults experience, such as 'child abuse' (Finkelhor, 2008). Adult privileges in families have historically been a barrier to the recognition of children's experiences of trauma and neglect in the home, and acts that would be considered serious offences against adults have often been minimised when committed against children (Finkelhor, 2008; Lansdown, 2000). Children's experiences of trauma, violence, and abuse within the family therefore unfold within particular socio-political contexts that structure adult-child relations and inform the operations of adult power on children's lives at all levels.

5 Research With Children Living With IPV

The past few decades have seen considerable shifts in our understanding of children and their place in social and political life and increasing interest in how they can be involved in research so that their views and experiences can be better understood and inform more effective responses (Corsaro, 2015; Graham & Fitzgerald, 2010; Ramsden, 2013). The 1989 United Nations Convention on the Rights of the Child, to which Australia is a signatory, states that children have rights to participate in decisions that impact on their lives and to have their views and opinions heard on matters that affect them (Graham & Fitzgerald, 2010; Salveron, Finan, & Bromfield, 2013).

In academia, there has been a trend towards the notion of research *with* or research *for* children rather than research *on* children, with children increasingly viewed as subjects rather than objects of research and as citizens with the rights to have their views and perspectives heard (Corsaro, 2015). Murray (2005) notes the key influence of the 'new sociology of childhood' theories that emerged from the discipline of sociology and were then adopted by other disciplines. This approach considers children as social agents capable of influencing their environment rather than simply being on the receiving end of environmental influence (Murray, 2005). It also draws attention to the social construction of childhood and the relationships between childhood and other social categories such as gender or class (Corsaro, 2015). The implication of this approach is that in research with children, attention needs to be paid to children's actions and intentions and their social location from a structural perspective.

Interest in researching the experiences of children living with IPV increased in the 1990s (Stanley & Humphreys, 2015). Our understanding of the experiences of children living with IPV has changed over time from a view that positions children outside the IPV dynamic to increasing recognition that children are a part of the IPV dynamic within a family, that IPV affects every aspect of children's lives, and that children actively respond to and try to make sense of IPV and its effects (Holt, Buckley, & Whelan, 2008).

6 Data and Research Challenges

Despite increased interest in children's experiences of IPV and recognition of children's rights under the UN Convention on the Rights of the Child to have their views and opinions heard, there are few studies focusing on IPV from children's perspectives, and in studies where children are research participants, quantitative methods with predetermined questions and structured response alternatives are most often used (Georgsson, Almqvist, & Broberg, 2011; O'Brien, Cohen, Pooley, & Taylor, 2013). Children living with IPV have therefore had few opportunities to freely express their thoughts and opinions on their experiences living with IPV on their own terms (Georgsson et al., 2011). This forms part of a broader issue of a lack of Australian research that attempts to directly engage with children's perspectives and experiences (McNamara, 2013). Data collected on experiences of IPV involving children is limited, and data gaps exist in relation to children's experiences of family, domestic (IPV), and sexual violence in many areas including attitudes, prevalence, severity, frequency, impacts, and outcomes (AIHW, 2018). There are also data gaps in relation to children's IPV experiences in diverse family contexts (AIHW, 2018). Much of the literature on children and IPV is drawn from low-income, shelter, or community samples with predominantly Caucasian North American participants (Levendovsky, Bogat, & von Eye, 2007). Many studies draw participants from services such as those supporting families living with IPV; however, the experiences of children engaged in these services may not be the same as many other children living with IPV (Georgsson et al., 2011). There is little research following families over a longer time period that would provide opportunities for the evaluation of theories of IPV's effects on children (Levendovsky et al., 2007).

Research on children's experiences living with IPV is complicated by a number of factors. There may be other stressors in children's lives, and it is not possible to be sure what impact IPV might have in isolation (Holt et al., 2008). The forms of violence and the particular dynamics of power and control that underpin IPV within a family may vary widely (Emery, 2011; O'Brien et al., 2013). Definitions may be inconsistent across studies with some studies focusing only on children's experiences of physical violence or not differentiating between different forms of violence, and the ways in which questions are asked can also affect research outcomes (AIHW, 2018; Campo, 2015; O'Brien et al., 2013; Price-Robertson et al., 2010). In the Australian context, definitions can also vary across states and territories (AIHW, 2018). It is not easy to get an accurate picture of the extent of IPV in the general population due to this pattern of behaviour often taking place in the privacy of the family home, being concealed and possibly denied by the perpetrator and sometimes also by those living with the violence (AIHW, 2018).

7 IPV and Other Violence in Children's Lives

Stanley and Goddard (2002, p. 150) have noted the coexistence of different forms of violence in some families and urge us to consider the 'totality of violence' in the lives of children in order to fully understand children's experiences. Some children live with other forms of child abuse alongside IPV (Bedi & Goddard, 2007). Abuse targeted specifically towards children is perpetrated at significant levels in families where IPV is perpetrated, with estimates of 40%–55% for the coexistence of IPV and direct physical abuse of children and 40% for IPV and sexual abuse of children (Bedi & Goddard, 2007). Children living with IPV are at greater risk of physical, psychological, emotional, and sexual abuse (Briggs, 2012; Holmes, 2013; Holt et al., 2008; Hornor, 2005; Richards, 2011).

In addition to abuse specifically targeting children, there may be other forms of violence that coexist with IPV such as sibling violence or other adult-to-adult violence that is significant in the lives of children. Different forms of abusive behaviour against children are not necessarily discrete and may overlap (Finkelhor, 2008). For example, the perpetrator may physically assault a child with the intention of hurting the nonabusive parent. When considering children's experiences living with IPV, we need to consider all forms of violence that may be present in the child's life and how these forms of violence may connect and influence the life of the family. Goddard and Hiller (1993) write that the presence of IPV in families can be.

> *the most overt expression of domination or the unequal distribution of power; it is also indicative of an atmosphere of coercion within which abuse of children has taken place... children having witnessed the beating of their mothers need no further reminder of the possible consequences of their resistance to the wishes of their fathers (or, indeed, of older males in general)*
>
> ***Goddard and Hiller (1993, p. 27)***

IPV creates a particular context of unequal power relations that is fundamentally coercive and that structures the options available for children in terms of response to violence and abuse. How will a child respond to a request from the perpetrating parent knowing that parent's potential for harm towards their other parent and towards the child? This context of coercion may be easily exploited by perpetrators, for example in the sexual abuse of children (Goddard & Hiller, 1993).

It is important to hold the concept of the 'totality of violence' (Stanley & Goddard, 2002, p. 150) in mind when considering children's experiences of IPV and to consider that IPV may facilitate other kinds of violence towards children, such as sexualised abuse. As Goddard and Hiller (1993) point out, IPV expresses power relationships within the family, and we must consider what other forms of violence that may emerge from these same power relationships.

8 Trauma Theory

Understanding how children's brains respond to experiences that are frightening or stressful is a key part of understanding IPV as a form of child abuse. Children have particular vulnerabilities due to developmental processes continuing throughout childhood and adolescence that can be influenced and disrupted by experiences of trauma and abuse (Finkelhor, 2008).

According to Perry (2001, p. 4), the developing brain forms in response to 'the pattern, intensity and nature of sensory perceptual and affective experience of events during childhood'. This means that the brain becomes wired based on children's early experiences. The infant or young child's brain organises itself in response to experience, and it is during the early stage of life that the brain is most receptive to environmental input (Perry, Pollard, Blakley, Baker, & Vigilante, 1995). Perry et al. (1995, p. 290) note that traumatic experiences during infancy and childhood can influence the permanent organisation and future functional capabilities of the brain. Although infants and younger children are more vulnerable to developmental impacts of trauma, older children are not safeguarded from potential harm. The latest neurological research suggests that the brain continues to develop throughput the lifespan (Siegel, 2012) and thus continues to be shaped by experiences.

All human beings have a set of 'built-in' physiological responses (such as increased heart rate) to environmental stress from birth to facilitate survival under stressful conditions (Campbell & Thompson, 2015). The brain has two primary patterns of response when faced with a threat of significant harm. These are the hyperarousal continuum (fight or flight) and the dissociation continuum (freeze and surrender) (Perry et al., 1995, p. 291). These responses are intended to be short term to assist us to take action to survive such as running away from danger; however, in situations of ongoing stress such as where there is repeated violence in the home, these responses may be called on repeatedly leading to a prolonged physiological response (Campbell & Thompson, 2015).

Changes in neurobiological stress systems following their repeated activation in response to threats in a young child's environment can lead to the habitual overactivity of these systems in response to adversity (National Scientific Council on the Developing Child, 2008). Perry (2009) notes that trauma can influence the developing brain by interfering with.

> *....normal patterns of experience guided neurodevelopment by creating extreme and abnormal patterns of neural and neurohormonal activity....in any brain-mediated function examined – from speech to motor functioning to social, emotional, or behavioural regulation – developmental trauma and maltreatment increase risk of dysfunction*
>
> ***Perry (2009, p. 241)***

From the perspective of neurodevelopment, experiences of IPV may repeatedly activate the brain's stress response system, potentially altering the development and structure of the children's brains. This in turn influences children's functional and regulatory capacities such as self-regulation and impulsivity (Delima & Vimpani, 2011). Children who live in continuous fear or threat will be affected by neurophysiological adaptations, altering the development and structure of the brain and resulting in changes in their physiological composition and their social, emotional, behavioural, and cognitive functioning (Briggs, 2012; Kaspiew et al., 2017a, 2017b; Perry, 2001).

Children living with violence and abuse such as IPV may experience pervasive feelings of fear including fear of death and feelings of helplessness (Herman, 1992). Children respond to these environments by developing capacities for constant alertness to danger and indications of threat and to be attuned to the adult who uses violence (Herman, 1992). While the development of such capacities is adaptive and potentially life-saving for children, experiences of abuse and having to remain alert and hypervigilant to threats in the environment can impact on development (Finkelhor, 2008; Perry, 2009).

After experiencing a traumatic event or events, children may experience trauma symptoms that mirror their responses to these events (Perry et al., 1995). For example, a child who dissociates (freezes or shuts down) in response to a traumatic experience may present with dissociation as a trauma symptom (Perry et al., 1995). Some trauma symptoms may be more outwardly visible than others, and children who dissociate may mistakenly be thought not to have been affected by their experiences, whereas children who become hyperaroused may display more noticeable behaviours such as physical aggression (Perry et al., 1995).

Ongoing traumatic experiences such as IPV can have a critical relational impact on children. According to Siegel (2012), relationships play an important role in the developing mind. He argues that 'human connections shape the mind' and attachment figures play a key role (Siegel, 2012, p. 4). All human beings form attachments. Although attachment is primarily associated with infants and children and their parents/caregivers, attachments to significant others are continuously established throughout the lifespan (Bowlby, 1969). During times of stress, children and adults will seek close proximity to their attachment figure (Bowlby, 1969). Children living in an environment of violence and fear may suffer disrupted neural development that may impact on their ability to form secure attachments (Kaspiew et al., 2017a, 2017b).

While immensely helpful in understanding the effects of some forms of violence, trauma theory may have limitations in understanding the effects of others. Finkelhor (2008) argues that viewing child victimisation exclusively through the lens of the literature on trauma has highlighted some aspects of children's experiences of victimisation while obscuring others. He writes that.

> *experiences of victimization may be degrading, humiliating and stigmatising but not necessarily frightening or threatening to bodily integrity; experiences may not be time limited, may not be intense in the manner of a violent attack*
>
> ***Finkelhor (2008, p. 67)***

He draws attention to the 'long-term distortions of development and self-perception' that he describes as '*mis*-socialisation' (Finkelhor, 2008, p. 67) and suggests that this can be just as damaging as the emotional intensity of experiencing a traumatic event. This is particularly relevant in the IPV context given that not all instances of IPV would be considered traumatic events in themselves. For example, a child may be told that their mother has made negative statements about them as part of a pattern of IPV where the perpetrator aims to undermine the mother's relationship with the child. This may not be traumatic in the sense of creating extreme fears for safety; however, this behaviour would be harmful to a child and their relationship with their mother over time and can be considered a form of psychological abuse.

9 Role of Developmental Stage

Children's experiences of IPV may vary greatly both between children of the same age and between children of different ages. Clearly, an infant's experiences living with IPV will be very different from those of a teenager. Children's responses to IPV are dynamic and changing over time as children move through different stages of development and new options become available to them in terms of responses (Finkelhor, 2008). For example, a younger child crying and seeking proximity to their mother in response to IPV may grow into an older child confronting the perpetrator and trying to protect their mother, or a younger child who has witnessed sexual abuse from their father towards their mother may understand more about the nature of these behaviours and related social norms as they get older and experience different emotional responses to the event as time goes by. It should be highlighted that children are not passively affected by IPV but actively respond to what is happening and are part of the dynamic of IPV within the family rather than outside it. In one qualitative study with children who lived with IPV, when one boy recognised that his father was behaving threateningly towards his mother, he would ask his father to arm wrestle with him knowing that his father would win but that this opportunity for his father to demonstrate his dominance would reduce the threat to his mother (Øverlien, 2016).

The roles of children in the context of IPV can change within the family environment over time (O'Brien et al., 2013). Children's responses to IPV can be dynamic and shifting as children evaluate the strategies they use and consider their usefulness or otherwise. For example, O'Brien et al. write that some participants in their study attempted to physically intervene between their parents when they entered the teenage years, but there was also a common realisation in adolescence that there was not much they could do to stop the abuse, so participants' 'adolescent coping strategies' soon switched to removing themselves from the situation and actively seeking out a safe place to withdraw for longer and longer periods of time (O'Brien et al., 2013, p. 103).

Children may not think of IPV in terms of discrete incidents. In one study of adults recalling experiences of IPV as children, the participants could not recall at what age they had first become aware of the abuse, how frequent the abuse was, and over how many years it occurred and instead suggested that they had grown up with a general background awareness of it and found it more confronting as they matured (O'Brien et al., 2013). Some children may experience the loss of a 'normal' childhood as a result of taking on a protective role and a loss of trust in adults (Swanston, Bowyer, & Vetere, 2014).

Children's developmental stage is important not only in relation to their own experiences and responses but also in relation to the social responses they receive from family, friends, or other social connections. Children may receive different social responses as a result of their age; for example teenagers may be more likely to be doubted when disclosing their experiences (Finkelhor, 2008).

10 Differentiating Children's Experiences by Age and Developmental Stage

Preschool and school-aged children often develop behavioural and adjustment problems. They are more prone to aggressive behaviour, low self-esteem, and lower social competence, resulting in peer conflict and peer isolation (Briggs, 2012; Evans, Davis, & DiLillo, 2008; Holt et al., 2008; Richards, 2011). Psychologically, children may suffer posttraumatic stress, depression, anxiety, despondency, flashbacks, and emotional withdrawal (Holt et al., 2008; Richards, 2011). Psychosomatic problems include headaches, nightmares, insomnia, stomach aches, bedwetting, and sleepwalking (Evans et al., 2008). Children living with IPV are also at risk of school absenteeism, bullying, and poor academic performance (Campo, Kaspiew, Moore, & Tayton, 2014; Holt et al., 2008; Hornor, 2005; Kaspiew et al., 2017a, 2017b), impacting their potential to live a fulfilling life.

Adolescents are equally at risk of the same impacts described above and are more likely to participate in high-risk and rebellious behaviours such as alcohol and drug abuse, risky sexual behaviour, truancy, running away from home, and leaving school (Campo et al., 2014; Hornor, 2005). Responses of older children and teenagers to IPV may include concealing events at home for fear of being teased, losing confidence and self-esteem, feeling different and being reluctant to trust others, feeling wary of being close to peers, fearing rejection and having difficulties making and retaining friendships, establishing a safe place of retreat, and seeking a secure relationship to deal with their experiences (Buckely, Holt, & Whelan, 2007; O'Brien et al., 2013).

As adults, children who have been exposed to or affected by IPV are at greater risk of entering and remaining in a relationship in which IPV is perpetrated, as either a perpetrator or victim (Campo et al., 2014; Holt et al., 2008; Hornor, 2005) creating an intergenerational cycle of IPV (Holt et al., 2008). Children and adolescents raised in an IPV environment are generally challenged to navigate multiple stressors and impacts resulting in them suffering many adversities throughout their lifespan.

11 Children's Experiences and Responses

IPV is a pattern of behaviour that takes place within the context of a family system and has the potential to shape the system or bring about its reorganisation. The totality of a child's experience therefore goes beyond their relationship with particular events, for example being physically present when their mother is assaulted. Consideration needs to be given to the chains of influence of the patterns of violence in the child's life over time and to the responses to the violence at both the individual and systemic levels. This involves thinking about trauma and thinking beyond trauma, thus considering a child's neurobiological response to frightening situations and also how the pattern of perpetrator behaviours and responses of family members may have shaped or reshaped the family system and family life.

Bunston (2015) notes that, for infants living with IPV, 'exposure to relational violence also creates its own routines' (p. 152). She advises us to learn from infants about what their particular routines have been like and the ways that they may try to communicate their expectations of their world. For infants, when terrifying and traumatic experiences are repeated, the infant's responses and behaviours adapt to this reality, and the neural pathways in the brain organise themselves accordingly (Bunston, 2015). In the same way, the family system may adapt itself to the reality of an ongoing pattern of abuse and violence and develop particular routines in response.

IPV may impact on children's sense of safety and security. Children may experience a pervasive sense of threat and fear not confined to the experience of actual violence or the family home (O'Brien et al., 2013; Swanston et al., 2014). IPV follows children through time and space; indeed, it may be more accurate to speak of IPV living with children rather than children living with IPV. IPV and its effects may have a significant presence and impact in children's lives in the short, medium, and longer term (Briggs, 2012; Campo et al., 2014; Holt et al., 2008; Hungerford, Wait, Fritz, & Clements, 2012; Richards, 2011; Russell, Springer, & Greenfield, 2010). Children may worry about their own safety and the safety of other family members and employ strategies such as creating their own safe spaces, taking preventative action to protect themselves and others in the family, trying to intervene, retreating, or observing (Buckely et al., 2007; Georgsson et al., 2011). Children may have to contact emergency services, see a parent being arrested or taken to hospital in an ambulance, witness the parent's injuries or help the parent attend to these, attend to their own injuries or trauma, or flee the family home (Richards, 2011). Children may be used instrumentally by the perpetrator to attack the nonabusive parent, for example being forced to spy on the nonabusive parent and report back to the perpetrator.

Some children may be told to go to their room or be locked in their rooms during their father's use of IPV (Georgsson et al., 2011). While they may not directly see what is happening, their experience may still be one of overwhelming fear knowing that their mother is being hurt and being unable to help her. For some children, the perpetrator's demonstration of the capacity for violence in behaviour towards objects or animals may leave children wondering what he could do to them (Georgsson et al., 2011). How a child is affected by a particular act of violence may be due to the theme or message underlying the act as much and to the form the violence takes (Campbell & Thompson, 2015).

IPV and its effects can shape, organise, and change everyday life in fundamental ways for children. Brennan (2006) notes that social isolation is a major factor in families where IPV is being used. Children may experience repeated movement between homes and schools with implications for social and family relationships and may be physically isolated through having to remain indoors or away from adults who may intervene such as support agencies or medical professionals (Brennan, 2006). Family and domestic violence is a leading cause of homelessness for children and for women with children, with 34,000 children reporting that family and domestic violence caused or contributed to their homelessness (AIHW, 2018; Campo, 2015). For these children, homelessness can affect their schooling, social connectedness, and sense of safety and belonging (AIHW, 2018).

Women who have lived with IPV may experience homelessness or housing problems more generally (late paying of rent, skipping meals, and being threatened with eviction) post separation (Baker, Cook, & Norris, 2003). Housing issues that follow from women's efforts to move towards safety may be on a spectrum including homelessness, struggle to keep up mortgage repayments or rental payments, and relying on the practical support of family members (e.g. moving in with parents) (Baker et al., 2003). Given that many of these women will have children, the effects of IPV could impact on children's most basic needs including the need for shelter, warmth, and food and on the mother–child relationship when women are under financial stress.

Part of children's active response to and engagement with IPV and its effects is their process of making sense of what is happening. Even within the same family, there may be significant differences in the meaning that children attach to events and people (Dryden, Doherty, & Nicolson, 2010). For example, in Dryden et al.'s (2010) study of two boys from the same family, one brother fantasised about being able to physically defeat their father, while the other felt his father's and brother's aggressive masculinity was irrational and rejected it. Children may have thoughts, beliefs, and fantasies about ways they would have liked to respond to the IPV, for example revenge fantasies (Georgsson et al., 2011).

Children and young people may experience many losses as a result of separation due to IPV including the loss of the family as one unit, loss of the everyday presence of their father, and loss of extended family relationships (Holt, 2011). Children and young people may also experience a loss of trust, and this may not be easily rebuilt (Lamb, Humphreys, & Hegarty, 2018).

Children may also experience a wide range of social responses to the IPV with which they live. Any action taken after an incident is called a 'response' to IPV (AIHW, 2018). Responses can be informal (friends and family networks) or formal (police, community services, and legal services). People are most likely to seek support through informal networks (friends and family) after experiencing IPV; however, a large proportion of people do not seek any advice or support, and most people do not contact the police about the violence (AIHW, 2018). The role of the child's support network of relatives or friends is a key factor in relation to positive outcomes for the child (Finkelhor, 2008; O'Brien et al., 2013). Many perpetrators do not face consequences after police contact (AIHW, 2018), and it is important to consider what this lack of accountability may mean for children.

12 Nonabusive Caregiver and Their Relationship With the Child

IPV may undermine and attack the relationship between children and the nonabusive parent (often the mother) (Goddard & Bedi, 2010; Humphreys, 2007). Bunston, Franich-Ray, and Tatlow (2017) write that.

> *family violence creates relational trauma for all family members, as it disrupts and disturbs all relationships within the family, not just the relationship between warring parents/adults*
>
> **Bunston et al. (2017, p. 3)**

The disruption of a child's relationships caused by IPV is significantly harmful to children's development, particularly for younger children and infants who are fully dependent on these relationships for survival. Some fathers may deliberately set out to undermine the relationship between a child and their mother, for example through humiliating the mother in front of the children (Harne, 2011). Others may use children instrumentally in the abuse of their mother, for example threatening to harm children in order to control the mother's behaviour (Harne, 2011). IPV may raise concerns for children about their mother's vulnerability, and this may shape their interactions with her, for example not expressing feelings of anger towards her to avoid making her sad (Georgsson et al., 2011).

IPV can impact on the capacity of the parent being abused, often the mother, to be emotionally present and available to her children and to exert appropriate parental authority (Holt et al., 2008). In this way, IPV can be understood as an attack on the mother–child relationship (Humphreys, Thiara, & Sharp, 2015). Humphreys et al. (2015) argue that the mother–child relationship should be a key consideration in IPV policy and practice; however, they note that more progress needs to be made in this regard as attention to the mother–child relationship remains limited in both these domains.

IPV may cause physical or mental health issues for the abused caregiver that may impact on their ability to provide the necessary day-to-day physical and emotional care for their child, inhibiting secure attachment (Briggs, 2012; Campo et al., 2014; Holt et al., 2008; Kaspiew et al., 2017a, 2017b). Children and young people are living not only with IPV but also with the effects it has on the physical and mental health of their mother. Women living with IPV are at increased risk of experiencing anxiety, low self-esteem, depression, and posttraumatic stress disorder, which in turn may disrupt their ability to be emotionally available to their children and model typical emotional expression, impacting on children's emotional development and attachment (Holt et al., 2008). IPV therefore can create blocks to emotional connection and attachment between child and mother. The capacity of some mothers to connect emotionally with their children may be compromised by the efforts and energy required to keep themselves and their children safe while coming under physical and emotional attack from their partner. Some mothers experiencing IPV may also respond by using abusive behaviours towards their children (Campbell & Thompson, 2015; O'Brien et al., 2013). As Campbell and Thompson (2015) point out, caregivers may have the best intentions to provide care and nurturing relationships for their children, but these intentions may be frustrated by the emotional impact of their experiences of IPV.

Humphreys et al. (2015) argue that, while noting that women's relationships with their children in the context of IPV can be resilient, insufficient consideration is given to how the perpetrator's use of IPV can undermine women's capacity to be physically and emotionally available to their children. In their 'Talking To My Mum' project (Humphreys et al., 2015), women and children were able to identify some of the tactics used by perpetrators of IPV to actively undermine the mother–child relationship such as undermining the mother's parenting in front of the children or excluding mothers from their children.

A recent report into child deaths in families where there was IPV noted that the concept of the 'protective parent' is often employed in the child protection context; however, the presence of IPV may undermine the capacity of the abused parent to protect their children, and so, there needs to be a thorough risk assessment undertaken of the person perpetrating the violence (Commission for Children and Young People, 2016). The regulation and active undermining of the mother–child relationship by the perpetrator is a key part of the dynamic of IPV. Repeated actions taken that potentially compromise one parent's capacity to care for the child constitute the denial of a child's right under the UN Convention of the Rights of the Child (UN General Assembly, 1989) to be cared for by his or her parents. The support and strengthening of the mother–child relationship is therefore a means to restore the child's right to be cared for by his or her parent.

McIntosh (2002) writes that part of the role of a parent is to 'bring the world to the child in manageable doses… making experience manageable, tolerable, and thinkable' (McIntosh, 2002, p. 231). IPV is potentially harmful to children living with IPV on several levels. Firstly, there is the harm caused by the experience of the violence itself, and secondly, the IPV may compromise the parental function obstructing the parent's ability to help make experience manageable for the child. For example, the mother may herself be traumatised, making it difficult for her to acknowledge the child's experience of IPV, and the perpetrator may not acknowledge or take responsibility for their use of IPV. The violence and abuse may not be discussed within the family, and children may be left with few or no opportunities to find language for and to make sense of their experiences (Georgsson et al., 2011). Children are often reliant on adults to disclose violence and abuse; however, adults may choose not to disclose abuse for a variety of reasons (Finkelhor, 2008). There may be a 'dynamic of secrecy' in children's lives, and children may experience emotional isolation from others, possibly including their parents (Brennan, 2006). Children may interpret the concealment of IPV as indicating that mothers do not want to speak about it, resulting in further silence (Humphreys et al., 2015). The use of IPV not only harms the adult victim/mother and child but also can damage the capacity of the parental system to make experience manageable and tolerable for the child. When the child's experience remains unintegrated and intolerable, this may impact on their development (McIntosh, 2002).

13 Postseparation Violence and Fathering

IPV may continue after separation and may escalate in severity and lethality, in the extreme escalating to lethal risk for both women and children (Holt et al., 2008). The perpetrator may use tactics of direct abuse of the child with the knowledge and intent that this will harm the mother (Buckley et al., 2008). Children may experience many changes and losses as a result of separation but have minimal to no control over the decision to separate or postseparation custody and contact arrangements (Stanley & Humphreys, 2015). Children are often ordered to maintain contact with fathers who have been abusive, and the abusive behaviour may continue post separation (Stanley & Humphreys, 2015). Child contact provides an opportunity for the perpetrator to continue the abuse 'through' the child, for example interrogating children about their mother's actions.

Holt (2011) points out the difference between frequency of contact and relationship quality between fathers who have used IPV and children. Being physically present does not necessarily make for a secure and meaningful relationship. Holt (2011) notes a number of themes emerging in her literature review relating to patterns of behaviour of fathers who have used IPV, including either behavioural inconsistency or rigidity, the absence of reciprocity in the father-child relationship, and fatherhood seen in terms of rights to children rather than caring for them. Any potential benefits of an ongoing relationship with the abusive parent must be weighed against children's rights to physical and emotional safety; however, there may be differing views on the relative importance of this relationship for children, on the risks presented by continued contact, and on the rights of parents to contact with their children (Starsoneck & Ake, 2018).

14 Children's Voices

Children as a group are further disadvantaged relative to adults as they have no political voice and their voices are generally absent from public discussions around these issues of victimisation. There are significant limitations on their capacity to advocate for their own interests in this area due to factors including adult-child power relations, children's differing developmental capacities, and the impacts of trauma (Finkelhor, 2008; Starsoneck & Ake, 2018).

According to the UN Convention on the Rights of the Child (UN General Assembly, 1989), children have the right to express their opinions and participate in decisions that impact on their lives. However, there may be barriers to children expressing themselves arising out of their fear of violence or desire to protect family or community (Neither seen nor heard, 2016). A recent inquiry into issues of family violence in child deaths found that there was 'insufficient understanding of the barriers to children expressing themselves' amongst professionals involved in the cases reviewed (Neither seen nor heard, 2016, p. 50).

The authors point out that when such barriers are not addressed, children's experiences of violence, its impacts on them, and their needs may remain concealed (Neither seen nor heard, 2016, p. 50). This suggests that it may not be enough to simply offer children and young people the opportunity to speak. Consideration needs to be given to how to support children and young people to express their opinions and participate in decision-making processes in a meaningful way.

Children may not be fully informed about significant changes that will affect their lives including parental separation, divorce, or future plans (Holt, 2011). Children have a wide range of views on contact with fathers who have perpetrated IPV. However, there may be a question as to whether all views hold equal weight. In Holt's (2011) study with children who have lived with IPV, those who did not want contact with their fathers felt that their opinions were not valued or observed. McIntosh (2002) writes that the trauma of children who have lived with IPV can be perpetuated by unthinking and unreflective legal and support systems. A child who feels their views are not cared about within these systems may experience this as an extension of the silencing they may already have been living with around the IPV. It is important to note how this silencing takes place in the context of adult-child power relations where children do not have the level of access to resources for help seeking that adults do and do not have the same level of access to court processes that impact on their lives.

Holt's (2011) study questions whose needs and rights are prioritised when children are ordered to have contact with abusive fathers and notes how for some children contact will provide opportunities for further abuse. Lamb et al.'s (2018) study of children and young people who had lived with IPV found that a key aspect of reparation for these children and young people was that they should have some control of the process and be able to decide the level of involvement that fathers should have in their lives after IPV. The potential for unthinking and unreflective system responses that perpetuate trauma for children and young people has been noted above (McIntosh, 2002). System responses that allow children and young people increased control and influence over the contact process if they wish to have this can be considered responses that are thoughtful and reflective around children's and young people's experiences of IPV and that support children's rights to participation in matters that affect them.

15 Conclusion

This chapter has explored a number of ways in which IPV can impact every aspect of children's lives and highlighted how this is a question not only of trauma but also of the ways in which the effects of IPV ripple through family and relationships and can shape the life of the family. IPV can set children's lives on a different course to that that they might otherwise have followed, and given IPV and its effects have the potential to be both severe and life changing for children, IPV must be seen as a form of child abuse. IPV is incompatible with children's realisation of their rights under the UN Convention (1989) to freedom from all forms of physical and mental violence. The onus is therefore on signatory states such as Australia to work to reduce and eradicate IPV in order to uphold the rights of children. Given the power of research to influence both IPV policy and practice and the many gaps in knowledge around children's experiences of IPV as discussed above (AIHW, 2018; Georgsson et al., 2011), further research into children's experiences of IPV that engages with children's perspectives is of fundamental importance in this regard.

Chapter Review Questions

1. In what ways are children's rights under the UN Convention on the Rights of the Child violated in the context of IPV?
2. Why do we need to consider other forms of violence when thinking about children's experiences of IPV?
3. What makes infants and young children particularly vulnerable in the context of IPV?
4. How can repeated experiences of IPV impact on the children's brains?
5. Why is it important to consider children's developmental stage in the context of IPV?
6. How can IPV affect children's everyday lives?
7. How does IPV attack and undermine the relationship between a child's nonabusive caregiver (usually the mother) and the child?
8. What are some of the issues for children living with IPV in relation to their rights to have a say in matters affecting them under the UN Convention on the Rights of the Child?

References

Australian Institute of Health and Welfare. (2018). *Family, domestic and sexual violence. Cat. No. FDV 2.* Canberra: AIHW. retrieved from https://www.aihw.gov.au/getmedia/d1a8d479-a39a-48c1-bbe2-4b27c7a321e0/aihw-fdv-02.pdf.aspx?inline=true.

Baker, C., Cook, S., & Norris, F. (2003). Domestic violence and housing problems: a contextual analysis of women's help-seeking, received informal support and formal system response. *Violence Against Women*, *9*(7), 754–783.

Bedi, G., & Goddard, C. (2007). Intimate partner violence: what are the impacts on children? *Australian Psychologist*, *42*(1), 66–77.

Bowlby, J. (1969). *Attachment and loss.* London: Hogarth Press.

Brennan, S. (2006). Sibling incest within violent families: children under 12 seeking nurture. *Health Sociology Review*, *15*, 287–292.

Briggs, F. (2012). *Child protection: The essential guide for teachers and other professionals whose work involves children.* Docklands, VIC: Jo-Jo Publishing.

Buckely, H., Holt, S., & Whelan, S. (2007). 'Listen to me!' children's experiences of domestic violence. *Child Abuse Review*, *16*, 296–310.

Bunston, W. (2015). Infant-led practice: responding to infants and their mothers (and fathers) in the aftermath of domestic violence. In N. Stanley & C. Humphreys (Eds.), *Domestic violence and protecting children: New thinking and approaches.* London: Jessica Kingsley.

Bunston, W., Franich-Ray, C., & Tatlow, S. (2017). A diagnosis of denial: how mental health classifications systems have struggled to recognise family violence as a serious risk factor in the development of mental health issues for infants, children, adolescents and adults. *Brain Sciences*, *7*(10), E133.

Campbell, A., & Thompson, S. (2015). The emotional maltreatment of children in domestically violent homes: identifying gaps in education and addressing some common misconceptions. *Child Abuse and Neglect, 48*, 39–49.

Campo, M. (2015). Children's exposure to domestic and family violence: key issues and responses. *Journal of the Home Economics Institute of Australia, 22*(3), 33.

Campo, M., Kaspiew, R., Moore, S., & Tayton, S. (2014). *Children affected by domestic and family violence: A review of domestic and family violence prevention, early intervention and response services.* Retrieved from Melbourne, VIC:https://aifs.gov.au/publications/children-affected-domestic-and-family-violence.

Candela, K. (2016). Protecting the invisible victim: incorporating coercive control in domestic violence statutes. *Family Court Review, 54*(1), 112–125.

Commission for Children and Young People. (2016). *Neither seen nor heard—Inquiry into issues of family violence in child deaths.* Melbourne: Commission for Children and Young People.

Corsaro, W. (2015). *The sociology of childhood* (4th ed.). Sage: California.

Delima, J., & Vimpani, G. (2011). The neurobiological effects of child maltreatment. *Family Matters, No. 89.*

Dobash, R., & Dobash, R. (1979). *Violence against wives.* New York: The Free Press.

Dobash, R., & Dobash, R. (2004). Women's violence to men in intimate relationships. *British Journal of Criminology, 44*, 324–349.

Dryden, C., Doherty, K., & Nicolson, P. (2010). Accounting for the hero: a critical psycho-discursive approach to children's experience of domestic violence and the construction of masculinities. *British Journal of Social Psychology, 49*, 189–205.

Edleson, J. L. (1991). Social workers' intervention in woman abuse: 1907–1945. *Social Services Review, 65*(2), 304–313.

Emery, C. (2011). Disorder or deviant order? Re-theorising domestic violence in terms of order, power and legitimacy. *Aggression and Violent Behaviour, 16*, 525–540.

Evans, S. E., Davis, C., & DiLillo, D. (2008). Exposure to domestic violence: a meta-analysis of child and adolescent outcomes. *Aggression and Violent Behaviour, 13*(2), 131–140. https://doi.org/10.1016/j.avb.2008.02.005.

Finkelhor, D. (2008). *Childhood victimization: Violence, crime and abuse in the lives of young people.* New York: Oxford University Press.

Georgsson, A., Almqvist, K., & Broberg, A. (2011). Naming the unmentionable: how children exposed to intimate partner violence articulate their experiences. *Journal of Family Violence, 26*, 117–129.

Goddard, C., & Bedi, G. (2010). Intimate partner violence and child abuse: a child-centred perspective. *Child Abuse Review, 19*(1), 5–20.

Goddard, C., & Hiller, P. (1993). Child sexual abuse: assault in a violent context. *The Australian Journal of Social Issues, 28*(1), 20–33.

Graham, A., & Fitzgerald, R. (2010). Children's participation in research: some possibilities and constraints in the current Australian research environment. *Journal of Sociology, 46*(2), 133–147.

Harne, L. (2011). *Violent fathering and the risks to children.* UK: The Policy Press.

Herman, J. (1992). *Trauma and recovery.* New York: Basic Books.

Holmes, M. R. (2013). Aggressive behavior of children exposed to intimate partner violence: an examination of maternal mental health, maternal warmth and child maltreatment. *Child Abuse & Neglect, 37*(8), 520–530. https://doi.org/10.1016/j.chiabu.2012.12.006.

Holt, S. (2011). Domestic abuse & child contact: positioning children in the decision-making process. *Child Care in Practice, 17*(4), 327–346.

Holt, S., Buckley, H., & Whelan, S. (2008). The impact of exposure to domestic violence on children and young people: a review of the literature. *Child Abuse & Neglect, 32*(8), 797–810.

Hornor, G. (2005). Domestic violence and children. *Journal of Pediatric Health Care, 19*(4), 206–212. https://doi.org/10.1016/j.pedhc.2005.02.002.

Humphreys, C. (2007). Talking to my mum: strengthening relationships between mothers and children in the aftermath of family violence. *Developing Practice, 19*, 53–63.

Jones, J. (2015). Supporting the relationship between mothers and children in the aftermath of domestic violence. In C. Humphreys, R. Thiara, C. Sharp, N. Stanley, & C. Humphreys (Eds.), *Domestic violence and protecting children: New thinking and approaches.* London: Jessica Kingsley.

Hungerford, A., Wait, S. K., Fritz, A. M., & Clements, C. M. (2012). Exposure to intimate partner violence and children's psychological adjustment, cognitive functioning, and social competence: a review. *Aggression and Violent Behavior*, *17*(4), 373–382. https://doi.org/10.1016/j.avb.2012.04.002.

Johnson, M. (2011). Gender and types of intimate partner violence: a response to an anti-feminist literature review. *Aggression and Violent Behavior*, *16*, 289–296.

Jouriles, E., & McDonald, R. (2015). Intimate partner violence, coercive control and child adjustment problems. *Journal of Interpersonal Violence*, *30*(3), 459–474.

Kaspiew, R., Grey, M., Weston, R., Moloney, L., Hand, K., Qu, L., et al. (2009). *Evaluation of the 2006 family law reforms.* Retrieved from Melbourne:https://aifs.gov.au/sites/default/files/publication-documents/evaluationreport.pdf.

Kaspiew, R., Horsfall, B., Qu, L., Nicholson, J., Humphreys, C., Diemer, K., et al. (2017a). *Domestic and family violence and parenting: Mixed method insights into impact and support needs: Final report.* Retrieved from Sydney:https://d2c0ikyv46o3b1.cloudfront.net/anrows.org.au/Parenting_Horizons_FINAL.pdf.

Kaspiew, R., Horsfall, B., Qu, L., Nicholson, J., Humphreys, C., Diemer, K., et al. (2017b). *Domestic and family violence and parenting: Mixed methods insights into impact and support needs: Key findings and future directions: Final report.* Retrieved from Sydney:https://d2c0ikyv46o3b1.cloudfront.net/anrows.org.au/Parenting_Compass.pdf.

Laing, L., Humphreys, C., & Cavanagh, K. (2013). *Social work and domestic violence: Developing critical and reflective practice*. London: SAGE Publications.

Lamb, K., Humphreys, C., & Hegarty, K. (2018). "Your behaviour has consequences": children and young people's perspectives on reparation with their fathers after domestic violence. *Children and Youth Services Review*, *88*, 164.

Lansdown, G. (2000). Children's rights and domestic violence. *Child Abuse Review*, *9*, 416–426.

Levendovsky, A., Bogat, G., & von Eye, A. (2007). New directions for research on intimate partner violence and children. *European Psychologist*, *12*(1), 1–5.

McIntosh, J. (2002). Thought in the face of violence: a child's need. *Child Abuse and Neglect*, *26*, 229–241.

McNamara, P. (2013). Giving voice to children and young people in research: applying rights-based frameworks to meet ethical challenges. *Developing in Practice*, *37*, 55–66.

Murray, C. (2005). Children and young people's participation and non-participation in research. *Adoption and Fostering*, *29*(1), 57–66.

Myhill, A. (2015). Measuring coercive control: What can we learn from national population surveys? *Violence Against Women*, *21*(3), 355–375.

National Scientific Council on the Developing Child. (2008). *Establishing a level foundation for life: Mental health begins in early childhood: Working paper 6 updated edition* Retrieved fromwww.developingchild.harvard.edu.

O'Brien, K., Cohen, L., Pooley, J., & Taylor, M. (2013). Lifting the domestic violence cloak of silence: resilient Australian women's reflected memories of their childhood experiences of witnessing domestic violence. *Journal of Family Violence*, *28*, 95–108.

Øverlien, C. (2016). Do you want to do some arm wrestling?Children's strategies when experiencing domestic violence and the meaning of age. *Child and Family Social Work*, *22*(2), 680–688.

Perry, B. D. (2001). The neurodevelopmental impact of violence in childhood. In D. Schetky & E. P. Benedek (Eds.), *Textbook of child and adolescent forensic psychiatry* (pp. 221–238). Washington, DC: American Psychiatric Press, Inc.

Perry, B. (2009). Examining child maltreatment through a neurodevelopmental lens: clinical applications of the neurosequential model of therapeutics. *Journal of Loss and Trauma*, *14*(4), 240–255.

Perry, B. D., Pollard, R., Blakley, T., Baker, W., & Vigilante, D. (1995). Childhood trauma, the neurobiology of adaptation, and use dependent development of the brain: how states become traits. *Infant Mental Health Journal*, *16*(4), 271–291.

Price-Robertson, R., Bromfield, L., & Vassalo, S. (2010). Prevalence matters: estimating the extent of child maltreatment in Australia. *Developing Practice*, *26*(Spring 2010), 12–20.

Ramsden, K. (2013). Children's perspectives on their own wellbeing: 'I don't think they can hear us'. *Developing Practice*, *36*, 18–30.

Richards, K. (2011). Children's exposure to domestic violence in Australia. *Trends & Issues in Crime and Criminal Justice*, *1*(419), 1–7.

Russell, D., Springer, K. W., & Greenfield, E. A. (2010). Witnessing domestic abuse in childhood as an independent risk factor for depressive symptoms in young adulthood. *Child Abuse & Neglect*, *34*(6), 448–453. https://doi.org/10.1016/j.chiabu.2009.10.004.

Salveron, M., Finan, S., & Bromfield, L. (2013). Why wait? Engaging with children and young people in child protection research to inform practice. *Developing Practice*, *37*, 24–34.

Siegel, D. (2012). *The developing mind: How relationships and the brain interact to shape who we are* (2nd ed.). New York: The Guilford Press.

Sokoloff, N., & Pratt, C. (Eds.), (2005). *Domestic violence at the margins: Readings on race, class, gender and culture*. New Jersey: Rutgers University Press.

Stanley, J., & Goddard, C. (2002). *In the firing line: Violence and power in child protection work*. Chichester: John Wiley and Sons.

Stanley, N., & Humphreys, C. (Eds.), (2015). *Domestic violence and protecting children: New thinking and approaches*. London: Jessica Kingsley.

Stark, E. (2007). *Coercive control: How men entrap women in personal life*. New York: Oxford University Press.

Starsoneck, L., & Ake, G. (2018). Reconsidering our domestic violence system. *North Carolina Medical Journal*, *79*(2), 127–129.

Swanston, J., Bowyer, L., & Vetere, A. (2014). Towards a richer understanding of school-age children's experiences of domestic violence: the voices of children and their mothers. *Clinical Child Psychology*, *19*(2), 184–201.

UN General Assembly, Convention on the rights of the child, 20 November 1989, United Nations, Treaty Series, Vol. 1577, p. 3, Available at: http://www.refworld.org/docid/3ae6b38f0.html.

WHO website. (2017). http://www.who.int/mediacentre/factsheets/fs239/en/.

CHAPTER 3

Keeping Our Eye on Sex, Power, Relationships, and Institutional Contexts in Preventing Institutional Child Sexual Abuse

Daryl Higgins[*], **Tim Moore**[†]
[*]*Institute of Child Protection Studies, Australian Catholic University, Melbourne, VIC, Australia*
[†]*Australian Centre for Child Protection, University of South Australia, Adelaide, SA, Australia*

1 Nature and Extent of Child Sexual Abuse in Institutions

Between 2012 and 2017, the Australian Royal Commission into Institutional Responses to Child Sexual Abuse (the Royal Commission) uncovered the widespread sexual abuse of children and young people in youth-serving organisations, historically and in modern times (Royal Commission into Institutional Responses to Child Sexual Abuse, 2017b). Similar inquiries into the abuse of children by those who work with them have been conducted in Australian states and territories (Anthony et al., 2015), Ireland (Powell, Geoghegan, Scanlon, & Swirak, 2012), England, the United States (Higgins, Kaufman, & Erooga, 2016), Canada, Norway, and Sweden (Royal Commission into Institutional Responses to Child Sexual Abuse, 2017b) and have focused on out-of-home and residential care (Sköld, 2013), faith-based settings, and schools. Although these settings are considered higher risk, Gallagher (2000, p. 796) notes 'It is likely that sexual abuse has occurred in most, if not all, types of institutions for children'.

In December 2017, the Royal Commission released its much anticipated 17-volume final report. The 189 recommendations it contains are based on the Commission's analysis of information drawn from 8013 people in private sessions and over 1000 written accounts, 57 public hearings, 59 research reports, and 35 policy roundtables since it commenced its work in 2013 (Royal Commission into Institutional Responses to Child Sexual Abuse, 2017b).

Although the Royal Commission anticipated to find that sexual abuse had occurred within Australian organisations, they reported that the extent of abuse was far greater than they had ever imagined. For example, in reviewing complaints received by the Catholic Church, the Commission found that 7% of priests working in the period 1950–2010 were accused of child sexual abuse (Royal Commission into Institutional Responses to Child Sexual Abuse, 2017a).

Child Abuse and Neglect. https://doi.org/10.1016/B978-0-12-815344-4.00003-9

Since being released, the Royal Commission's findings have sparked increased interest in Australia about the nature, risks, and approaches to both identifying and responding to child sexual abuse within institutional contexts. Australian organisations, like those in other countries, have been compelled to adopt 'child-safe' policies and practices and to account for the ways that they are minimising child sexual abuse in their services, supports, and programs (Moore, 2017a, 2017b). We would argue that to be successful in creating truly child-safe organisations, leaders and staff need to understand, identify, and adequately respond to risks; to increase the effort for potential perpetrators to offend; and, most importantly, to create cultures and climates that facilitate the protection of children and young people from harm. This requires an understanding of how organisational conditions and cultures can promote attitudes, behaviours, and practices that either enable or minimise the likelihood of abuse occurring.

1.1 The Nature and Extent of Institutional Child Sexual Abuse

At its most basic, institutional child sexual abuse refers to abuse that is perpetrated by an adult within an institutional context. Gallagher (2000) defined it as;

> *The sexual abuse of a child (under 18 years of age) by an adult who works with him or her. The perpetrator may be employed in a paid or voluntary capacity; in the public, voluntary or private sector; in a residential or non-residential setting; and may work either directly with children or be in an ancillary role (p. 797).*

In more recent times, the definition has been broadened to also include youth-to-youth sexual assault either when this assault occurs on-site or when the two young people are both engaged in activities conducted by the institution. Reflecting the broad range of experiences reported by victims of who were harmed within institutional contexts, the Royal Commission into Institutional Responses to Child Sexual Abuse (2017c) adopted a broad definition of child sexual abuse describing it as;

> *Any act which exposes a child to, or involves a child in, sexual processes beyond his or her understanding or contrary to accepted community standards. Sexually abusive behaviours can include the fondling of genitals, masturbation, oral sex, vaginal or anal penetration by a penis, finger or any other object, fondling of breasts, voyeurism, exhibitionism, and exposing the child to or involving the child in pornography. It includes child grooming, which refers to actions deliberately undertaken with the aim of befriending and establishing an emotional connection with a child, to lower the child's inhibitions in preparation for sexual activity with the child (p. 30).*

Institutional child sexual abuse can be one-off or can include multiple encounters over a prolonged period. Most witnesses appearing before the Royal Commission reported that they had been abused on multiple occasions (83%): on average, for more than 2 years, with some for over 10 years (Royal Commission into Institutional Responses to Child Sexual Abuse, 2017c).

Institutional child sexual abuse can be perpetrated on-site or while children are engaged in activities off-site (such as on excursions, holiday camps, or sports trips). Similarly, institutional child sexual abuse can occur online, when an adult or other young person exposes a child to pornographic material or engages them in virtual sexual encounters.

Due to its often hidden and covert nature, the delays in which victims report, and the few studies focusing on its prevalence, it is difficult to adequately estimate how many children and young people experience institutional child sexual abuse (Gallagher, 2000). A conservative estimate, drawn from the analysis of data collected through the Australian Bureau of Statistics' Personal Safety Survey, proposes that there are at least 69,000 people in Australia who were sexually abused in an institutional setting before they were 15, most often by a teacher, doctor, or minister of religion. Police data analysed for the Royal Commission showed that approximately 5% of abuse cases reported was experienced in an institutional context (Bromfield, Hirte, Octoman, & Katz, 2017).

2 Organisational, Contextual, Individual Risk Factors: A Situational Crime Prevention Approach

For child sexual abuse to occur, there must be an adult or young person who has the potential to offend a child or young person who is vulnerable and an *environment* that enables abuse to occur and provides the opportunity for the adult (or young person) to offend. In this chapter, we focus on understanding these environments.

Historically, much of the public concern (and indeed, some of the scholarship) has focused on concern about sexual predators who are unknown to their victims: stranger danger. It prompted action—particularly in the 1980s and 1990s—focused on warnings for children (and their parents) and equipping children with skill to protect themselves and speak up should they encounter such a stranger. Since then, researchers and advocates have rightly turned their attention to the site or context where child sexual abuse has most frequently occurred: in the family. However, more recently, attention has turned to yet another environment: youth-serving organisations (Royal Commission into Institutional Responses to Child Sexual Abuse, 2017e).

Across the different settings and contexts, it is important to look at the factors that increase the risk or likelihood of a child or young person being exposed to child sexual abuse. The risk of child sexual abuse can be thought of at three levels: factors that affect the risk that someone will have the propensity/interest to sexually offend against a child/young person, whether some children/young people are more vulnerable to sexual abuse, and whether some settings or contexts affect the likelihood of abuse occurring. In this section, we explore the factors that enable abuse in institutional settings and can be the focus of prevention activities.

(a) *Factors affecting the propensity/interest to sexually offend against a child/young person*
Criminological research has focused on the risk factors for *perpetration* of child sexual abuse. Reviewing the evidence regarding risk factors for perpetration in familial, extrafamilial, and care settings, Quadara, Nagy, Higgins, and Siegel (2015) found not only were there similarities in the risk factors for perpetration of sexual abuse (biologically unrelated male, younger age, highly sexualised environment, childhood neglect, violent behaviour, poor family cohesion, and domestic violence in the family) but also there were similarities in the behaviours engaged in by perpetrators, namely, grooming behaviours, based on long-term planning; based on the trust, authority, and respect; and supported by secrecy, shame, and isolation of the victim.

As summarised in the final report of the Royal Commission into Institutional Responses to Child Sexual Abuse (2017c),

> *Risk factors associated with adult perpetrators identified in research include adverse experiences in childhood, such as physical, emotional, and sexual abuse and neglect; interpersonal relationship and emotional difficulties, including difficulty connecting with other adults, intimacy problems, poor social skills, and emotional affiliation with children; distorted beliefs and 'thinking errors' that may facilitate child sexual abuse; and indirect influences, such as contextual or 'trigger' factors (p. 14).*

While gender is an important factor (most abusers being male), it is clearly not a sufficient causal factor—as women *can* abuse and most males do not abuse (Stathopoulos, 2014). When thinking about those who sexually offend against children/young people, it is not only adults but also other young people who can engage in offending behaviour that we need to consider. As with adult offenders, most young people who engage in abusive behaviours are male. Research conducted for the Royal Commission confirmed that particularly for a setting like residential out-of-home care, young people are concerned about the behaviour and risk of harm (including sexual harm) from their peers (Moore, McArthur, Death, Roche, & Tilbury, 2016).

(b) *Factors affecting the vulnerability of children/young people to being sexual abused*
Just as there is considerable cooccurrence between types of violence to which young people may be exposed, there is also overlap between risk/protective factors for these forms of violence (Higgins & McCabe, 2000; Wilkins, Tsao, Hertz, Davis, & Klevens, 2014). Within the category of sexual violence, we see many of the same risk factors at the individual level that increase vulnerability to offending—by peers or adults. A common risk factor is exposure to past violence/abuse, and other risk factors include living in families or communities where children/young people experience disadvantage, inequity, disconnection, conflict, violence, mental health problems, and substance misuse (Wilkins et al., 2014).

Although anyone could be vulnerable to sexual abuse, the available research shows that some characteristics and prior experiences of children/young people increase the likelihood of exposure to sexual harm within an institutional context. Common risk factors for young people identified across the research and case studies from the Royal Commission into Institutional Responses to Child Sexual Abuse (2017c) include previous experiences of child maltreatment and living with disability (particularly that leads to reliance on others for personal care, movement, or communication). Other factors that can increase the risk of sexual abuse occurring within an institutional context include social isolation, poor level of understanding of sexual behaviour and personal safety, and low self-esteem. Ironically, high achievers can also be at risk. Sexual diversity also affects risk, where young people who do not identify as heterosexual or who question their sexuality or assigned gender are at greater risk (Royal Commission into Institutional Responses to Child Sexual Abuse, 2017c). While this can be framed as a characteristic of young people that places them at risk, it can also be seen as a characteristic of organisations or societies: when they are gender stereotyped, restrictive, or homophobic, it increases the risk of sexual abuse for young people.

Similarly, there are historical, social, and economic factors (such as colonisation, cultural dislocation, racism, and discrimination) that means young people who are Aboriginal or Torres Strait Islander or whose families are recent migrants/asylum seekers or from culturally and linguistically diverse communities can be at higher risk (Royal Commission into Institutional Responses to Child Sexual Abuse, 2017c). Despite the plethora of potential risk factors, the convergence in creating conditions within which child sexual abuse can occur, flourish, or be excused but different contexts can exacerbate—or create new—risks or 'opportunities' for offending.

(c) *Factors affecting the likelihood of abuse occurring in different settings*
Strategies used to sexually offend against children/young people vary by context. This highlights the contribution of situational factors that enable or excuse offending behaviour and therefore the importance of targeting situational factors when thinking about offending (Royal Commission into Institutional Responses to Child Sexual Abuse, 2017c).

Although abuse can occur in a wide range of contexts, some of the features of youth-serving organisations and contexts that the Royal Commission identified as being linked with reports of sexual harm were activities that were unsupervised or poorly supervised, where an adult has high levels of authority/trust/responsibility, and activities that involve care or physical/intimate contact. From a risk-management perspective, the logical question to ask is the following: Are these risks inherent, or are they modifiable? It is hard to predict ahead of time which adults or young people might be more likely to engage in abusive behaviour or which young people are the ones who are going to be abused. Although risk factors tell us about which groups of young people may have increased vulnerability, such characteristics of potential abusers and victims cannot necessarily be changed, and individuals who will be abused cannot reliably be predicted, so identifying such characteristics has only limited value for implementing prevention strategies. It just tells you where additional or modified prevention efforts might need to be targeted. The basic question is the following: where are the risks that you as an organisation can do something concrete to reduce the risk profile for all children/young people?

'Situational crime prevention' is a theoretical approach from the field of criminology that can be used to understand how and why sexual abuse occurs within specific locations or contexts. But more importantly, it provides a framework to develop whole-of-organisation prevention strategies that focus on the policies, practices, and strategies that can target these risks in order to reduce children and young people's vulnerability and empower all adults to play an active part in their protection.

In thinking about the typical or routine activities of the organisation, managers and workers need to think about whether there is anything in the day-to-day activities that could influence the risk of abuse to children, particularly where opportunities for supervision are reduced. This could include situations such as:

- high volumes of children using a facility requiring privacy, such as change of rooms;
- changes to the nature of activities (e.g. excursions to public venues), where a risk assessment should be conducted to understand how the change in the nature of the activities might pose new risks and require different mitigation strategies—such as considering the ratio of adults to children to increase capacity for supervision and clearly stipulating the supervisory roles of adults during that time, including paid and volunteer staff;
- regular activities that require children to have unsupervised time with adults (e.g. medical or other health procedures, music lessons, sports coaching, counselling, or allied health sessions).

Situational crime prevention focuses on the modifiable risk factors that enable child sexual abuse to occur in organisations rather than just 'weeding out' potential offenders. This is particularly important given that the research on offenders (reviewed above) shows that characteristics of offenders are very hard to distinguish from those who do not offend and that until someone has already offended (and been detected), screening processes are unlikely to help detect those with a demonstrated history of offending or concerning behaviour. The fact that children and young people can be at risk from peers also means that situational prevention approaches are more likely to assist with putting in place protective strategies, regardless of the source of the potential harm (i.e. adults or peers). It focuses on the crime event (i.e. child sexual abuse) and its precursors (i.e. grooming behaviour), rather than the offender and their characteristics or intentions. Focusing on the specific environment, location, victim(s), and offender (rather than the historical causes of crime, such as the behavioural history or psychopathology of the offender), the aim is to change the physical or organisational environment to reduce crime. In this sense, situational crime prevention is about creating safer environments to make crime more risky and difficult, less rewarding, and/or less appealing (see Box 1).

Box 1 Examples of situational crime prevention strategies for preventing risk of institutional child sexual abuse.

Increasing effort for offenders:

- Teaching children self-protection skills and assertive behaviours that make them a 'harder' target for a potential offender
- Controlling 'tools' that an offender could use to engage in grooming behaviour (e.g. the internet and social media—using filtering software and limiting or monitoring social media contact with children)
- Controlling access to facilities and who attends the institution by assessing their motivation and suitability to work with children (however, relying on pre-employment screening checks, such as 'working with children' checks, alone is not sufficient—policies to define acceptable behaviours supported by ongoing policy and procedures are needed)
- Risk assessments for organisation/location design and workplace practices and eliminating risk 'hot spots'
- In sporting clubs and schools, conducting more group activities and training to minimise one-on-one activities or create mitigation strategies. Such efforts need to be undertaken cautiously, to be balanced, and to be monitored, so children do not miss out on learning or mentoring opportunities that do require one-on-one adult/child interactions

Increasing risks for offenders:

- Minimise opportunities for staff to be alone with children and situational triggers (e.g. intimate activities with children)
- Redesign rooms to assist natural surveillance and eliminate blind spots (e.g. doors with viewing windows)
- Children and staff are given opportunities to raise concerns or suspicions about abuse or behaviour of an adult that worries them
- Improving processes for responding to allegations of child abuse (noting that many jurisdictions in Australia are now implementing reportable conduct schemes)
- Staff provided with processes to report suspected child sexual abuse
- Increasing capable guardianship by staff training
- Decreasing the vulnerabilities of potential victims
- Encouraging managers responsible for particular locations where adults and young people may interact (e.g. pool attendants, librarians, and gym attendants) to be vigilant of opportunities to engage in offending behaviour

Removing excuses/reducing permissibility of the organisation:

- Set clear codes of conduct, organisational rules, and policies reinforcing acceptable standards of staff conduct and consequences (e.g. limit physical contact or unsupervised children)
- Address the dehumanisation of children (e.g. in residential or detention centres) that may make it permissible to exploit power over them
- Increase staff awareness of codes of conduct, and improve regular communication (e.g. induction processes, posters to raise awareness, and directions for how to undertake processes in a way that is child-focused and child-safe)

Adapted from Higgins and Morley (2017).

In sum, situational crime prevention is focused on three broad lines of work: (a) increasing effort for offenders, (b) increasing risks for offenders, and (c) removing excuses or reducing permissibility of the organisation. For an overview of the strategies identified in Kaufman et al.'s (2010) comprehensive model for youth-serving organisations to assess their own setting for all of the broader risks for child sexual abuse and to develop strategies for preventing abuse, see https://safeguardingchildren.acu.edu.au/practice_tools/situational_crime_prevention.

Key factors that organisations should assess to determine their 'risk level' for child sexual abuse include characteristics of the children you serve, the physical environment and routine activities of the organisation, and its policies and overall culture. However, a critical success factor is to ensure staff, volunteers, and carers are adequately trained to deal with child sexual abuse issues. When implementing new strategies or policies, it is also important to bring key stakeholders along with the journey: parents/carers and, of course, the young people themselves. An important principle outlined by the Royal Commission is that children/young people need to be consulted and participate in decisions affecting them, including the development and implementation of child safeguarding policies.

The value of fostering 'protective participation' (Moore, 2017a, 2017b) efforts within organisations, where adults and children form alliances to empower children and young people, talk about risks of abuse and harm, identify potential threats, strengthen children's capacity to identify issues and seek help, and create informed responses to child sexual abuse and other maltreatment, was stressed in a series of studies conducted for the Royal Commission (Moore, McArthur, Death, et al., 2016; Moore, McArthur, Heerde, Roche, & O'Leary, 2016; Moore, McArthur, Noble-Carr, & Harcourt, 2015; Robinson, 2016). These types of efforts are sometimes referred to as 'target hardening' (Wortley & Smallbone, 2006) and require that adults and organisations support children through education, ongoing dialogue, and formal and informal mechanisms through which children can raise their concerns. Similarly, parents and primary caregivers need support in their duty to protect children, for example, through public education about the risks of child sexual abuse, why organisations are implementing policies and prevention strategies, and how they can work at home to support these activities.

3 Institutional Child Sexual Abuse: Similarities and Differences to Other Abuse Contexts and Types

Institutional child sexual abuse has not only many similarities but also some key differences to other forms of child abuse and neglect. In this section, we consider the intersections that institutional child sexual abuse has with other risk/prevention paradigms (including other forms of child maltreatment and peer victimisation, homophobia, bullying, dating, and relationship violence). We consider the incremental steps that are typically encountered and the typical responses (or the lack of responses) that feed the climate that, in turn, becomes a driver of future risk.

3.1 Home and Away: Are the Risks for Child Sexual Abuse Dependent on Location/Context?

In exploring risk factors and the focus of prevention activities, we need to focus on what is unique about institutional contexts compared with the more prevalent site of abuse (i.e. the family/home environment) and the implications for both connecting up with other prevention paradigms while not losing the opportunities to respond to its unique nature.

While abuse in the home or in other community contexts (e.g. online) has many of the same elements (facilitating access to the young person, engaging in grooming behaviours to desensitise the young person to the attention and the progressive sexual advances and to ensure their compliance and silence, and using 'tools' such as trust and secrecy), there are many situational factors about institutions that can help facilitate the early stages of abuse. The focus of a situational prevention approach is to remove these risks that can lead to abuse by changing the characteristics of the situation. Again, the distinction between situational characteristics of some locations (e.g. 'closed' vs open institutions; see Quadara et al. (2015)) is associated with higher risk of child sexual abuse occurring. Where institutions have high levels of authority and hierarchical power structures and limited interactions with the rest of the community, it is easier for norms to develop that support or excuse the violation of appropriate boundaries between children and young people and less likely for outside observation or opportunities for children/young people to recognise that their experiences are abusive and that they deserve help and are able to speak up and seek help.

Child maltreatment and interpersonal victimisation experienced by children and young people are not always discrete events—they can cooccur, which means that any form of abuse or harm is in itself a risk factor for other types of maltreatment (Higgins & McCabe, 2000). One of the clear messages coming from the Royal Commission report is that the risk of child sexual abuse within an institutional context is increased when children/young people experience other forms of vulnerability, particularly other forms of abuse/neglect (i.e. multitype maltreatment; Higgins & McCabe, 2000). This is consistent with the broader literature on risk factors for child sexual abuse, where it has been demonstrated that risks cooccur and where young people have already been neglected or subjected to other forms of child maltreatment or harm from peers such as bullying that they have an increased vulnerability to child sexual abuse within an organisation.

Sometimes, the context means that inherently, children and young people are at greater risk of child sexual abuse, due to their exposure to other forms of child maltreatment. This is clearly the case for institutions such as residential out-of-home care and also juvenile justice facilities, where young people have already been exposed to (and, in many cases, continue to be exposed to) significant harm in their lives (Attar-Schwartz, 2011, 2014).

This raises the following question: do organisations know enough about the risk profile of the young people they serve? (Have they already been subjected to child maltreatment in the home? Are they being bullied at school or online?) Not only do these other experiences increase the risk of sexual abuse, but also the cumulative experiences of prior harm can compound or interact with the experience of sexual abuse in terms of its impact and the therapeutic/support needs of the child/young person.

Youth-serving organisations now need to focus on the knowledge and capability that adults within their service need to prevent and respond to harm to children. For example, the key messages emerging from the Royal Commission into Institutional Responses to Child Sexual Abuse (2017a, 2017b, 2017c, 2017d, 2017e, 2017f, 2017g) research and case studies have been translated into the ACU Safeguarding Children and Young People Capability Framework. It contains six broad areas of knowledge or skills that adults need in order to effectively implement safeguarding strategies:

- Nature of abuse and risk factors
- Child-safe organisational cultures and governance
- Risk-management strategies
- Participation of children and young people ('protective participation')
- Prevention education (including sexual healthy/respectful relationship education)
- Responsive care and support (see https://safeguardingchildren.acu.edu.au/about_us/acu_safeguarding_children_capability_framework)

4 Creating Cultures that Foster Positive Attitudes Towards Sex, Sexuality and Healthy Relationships

In this section, we turn our attention to the attitudes, beliefs, and behaviours related to sex and sexuality that may act to compromise children's safety and efforts to prevent and appropriately respond to child sexual abuse. We begin by considering organisational culture and the ways that it either promotes or restricts child-safe practice.

4.1 The Influence of Organisational Cultures

Organisational cultures have been shown to either enable or restrict child sexual abuse. It is influenced by and influences the values, beliefs, attitudes, and behaviours of leaders, staff, children, young people, and others interacting with the organisation. Organisational culture can affect the way that child sexual abuse is perpetrated, detected, and responded to in institutional contexts (Palmer, Feldman, & McKibbin, 2016). In their report for the Royal Commission, Munro and Fish (2015) argued that organisational culture not only is created by both explicit strategies and messages communicated by senior management but also is the covert messaging that is transmitted throughout organisations, influencing individual and collective behaviour.

Child-safe organisational cultures are therefore the ones that foster a commitment in keeping children safe and in promoting attitudes and behaviours that restrict inappropriate behaviours and enable concerns to be raised and adequately dealt with throughout the organisation (Palmer et al., 2016). Although positive organisational cultures can be protective, organisations can also be imbued with cultures that promote values, attitudes, beliefs, and behaviours that dismiss; enable; or, in worst cases, facilitate the abuse of children and young people (Royal Commission into Institutional Responses to Child Sexual Abuse, 2017e). Institutional cultures that dehumanise children and young people, prioritise the institution's reputation over their safety, and dissuade adults from preventing and responding to abuse are all examples of enabling cultures as are those that repress healthy sexuality or downplay and excuse or encourage hypersexual environments and behaviour (Munro & Fish, 2015; Palmer et al., 2016; Royal Commission into Institutional Responses to Child Sexual Abuse, 2017e). In many of the case studies considered by the Royal Commission, dangerous cultures were dominant and acted to enable horrific child sexual abuse to occur.

4.2 Attitudes and Behaviours Regarding Sex and Sexuality That may Compromise Children's Safety

In reporting on findings from victim testimonials, research, and public sessions, the Royal Commission highlighted the fact that child sexual abuse often occurs within cultures that have taboos and negative attitudes to sex and sexuality and demonstrates institutional homophobia. Strongly held views of what it means to be a man and to be a woman shaped the way that victims experienced their abuse and influenced the ways that did (and often did not) seek help. This plays out in a number of ways.

Firstly, children and young people who have not been adequately educated about sex, appropriate and inappropriate relationships, and encounters, and those who hold negative attitudes towards sexuality may be at greater risk of child sexual abuse and exploitation. Victims who appeared before the Royal Commission often reported that as they were unaware that their abuser's behaviour was illegal and 'wrong', they took responsibility for their own abuse and experienced self-loathing and shame (Royal Commission into Institutional Responses to Child Sexual Abuse, 2017c). This was a particular issue for young people in a residential care research project who reported that as they had not been exposed to 'normal' relationships, they assumed that being coerced into sex, being manipulated, and experiencing an imbalance in interactions with peers and adults were to be expected (Moore, McArthur, Death, et al., 2016).

Historically, this was also the experience of children and young people in boarding schools, orphanages, and other 'closed' communities and organisations (Palmer et al., 2016). Sometimes, these cultures were underscored by assumptions about children's asexuality, their innocence, and the view that discussions about sex and sexuality could corrupt children and compromise their innocence. When sex and sexuality is seen as shameful or sinful, open dialogue is difficult for all (Robinson, 2013).

Secondly, studies have also shown that when young people are bullied about their sexuality and when they are sexually harassed or assaulted within an organisation, they are more vulnerable to further sexual abuse by adults and peers who take advantage of their vulnerability and social exclusion (Attar-Schwartz, 2011, 2014; Royal Commission into Institutional Responses to Child Sexual Abuse, 2017c). In these situations, perpetrators can target vulnerable young people and either groom them by demonstrating affection, which they take advantage of or engage in abusive behaviour feeling safe that the already victimised young person will not seek support (Royal Commission into Institutional Responses to Child Sexual Abuse, 2017c, 2017f). The Royal Commission heard examples of times when perpetrators targeted young people who were being harassed by their peers, took them under their protection, and positioned themselves to take advantage of this new relationship by sexually abusing them.

In many institutional contexts, sex and sexuality have been considered shameful; 'dirty'; and, in the case of religious organisations, sinful. Within these environments, adults may be reluctant to talk about concerns about sex and the sexual behaviour of other adults, and children may be reluctant to raise concerns or disclose their abuse. The Royal Commission found that in such settings, offenders took advantage of adults' reluctance to talk about sex and sexuality, children's naiveté, and the shame that surrounded abuse, sometimes grooming the child to feel complicit in or responsible for the abuse (Royal Commission into Institutional Responses to Child Sexual Abuse, 2017c, 2017d, 2017g). In many instances, victims were told that they were 'disgusting' and that adults and their peers would revile them if they were to disclose their abuse.

Similarly, within organisations and cultures where homosexuality is denigrated, children and young people may experience difficulties in seeking help or alerting trustworthy adults to their assaults. In particular, the Royal Commission heard that homophobic attitudes and rigid notions of masculinity prevented many young men from disclosing at the time of their abuse and for adult survivors to come forward to discuss their experiences (Royal Commission into Institutional Responses to Child Sexual Abuse, 2017d). Male victims reported that sexual abuse affected their sexual identities and their own masculinity (Why was I chosen? Could I be gay? Am I a real man?) and led them to believe that they would never have value as a person or as a man. These views were reinforced within many of the organisational cultures that surrounded them (Palmer et al., 2016). They reported that pervasive cultural norms around masculinity also led them to fear disclosing their abuse because it would require them to confront what they thought were strong nonmasculine or feminine emotions: emotions they had been socialised to avoid.

As cultural notions of sexuality and homophobia influence young men's vulnerability to sexual abuse and their disclosing and help seeking, research shows that beliefs about female sexuality, virginity, and purity influence young women. Female victims reported to the Royal Commission that they were often reluctant to raise concerns about the behaviours of men for fear about the ways that they might be perceived and to disclose, worrying that their reputations might be tainted when their abuse was revealed (Royal Commission into Institutional Responses to Child Sexual Abuse, 2017d). They questioned whether other men would ever find them attractive and want them to be their wives or to mother their children and whether their abuse might be misperceived (that they were somehow responsible for their abuse or that they were promiscuous).

4.3 Hypersexualized and Macho Cultures

In contrast to organisational cultures where sex and sexuality are considered taboo, some organisational cultures can be hypersexual and enable or are overly permissive of behaviours that can be abusive. Such cultures built up over time—and it is the incremental impact of small behaviour and expressions of attitudes that create a culture that can make abuse more likely and disclosure of concerning behaviour more difficult. In its deliberations, for example, the Royal Commission pointed to sporting activities that traditionally have a high tolerance of sexualised practices and conversations (i.e. within changing rooms) and where abusive behaviours are normalised as 'part of the game' (Royal Commission into Institutional Responses to Child Sexual Abuse, 2017c). They found that within these environments, grooming was more likely to occur, and victims were more reluctant to report concerns or disclose abuse.

Similarly, residential care units where young people with problematic sexual behaviours are sometimes placed together may also facilitate 'a sexualised culture, in which sex is 'constantly in the air' and in which behaviours that would not be considered acceptable in other environments are permitted' (Royal Commission into Institutional Responses to Child Sexual Abuse, 2017f). In research conducted for the Royal Commission, young people in residential care units often reported that peer sexual victimisation was commonplace and intrinsic to unhealthy peer interactions. This echoed other studies that showed that staff in residential care often turn a blind eye to these problematic behaviours, believing that they are 'par for the course' when working with groups of young people.

These hypersexual cultures may be instigated by young people, but they are too often enabled and in some cases encouraged by adults within institutions who hold 'boys will be boys'-like attitudes that normalise and mislabel abusive behaviours, particularly amongst peers (Green, 2005). In these machoistic cultures, young men (and some male staff) seek to be dominant and use sexual behaviour, bullying, and innuendo to disempower young women and their weaker male peers and to assert dominance, hierarchies, and 'pecking orders' (Green, 2005; Parkin & Green, 1997).

4.4 Organisational Cultures and Responses to Abuse

As well as enabling abuse to occur, organisational cultures can also influence the ways that adults and institutions respond when children are harmed. Some adults and institutions might not believe children and young people, particularly when the offender is a highly regarded member of the community and when they have already determined the nature of that individual's character. Often, staff are reticent to consider that a peer might have acted inappropriately or abused a child. Similarly, adults might be apprehensive about labelling problematic sexualised behaviour of clients and mislabelling behaviour as 'developmentally appropriate' or otherwise excusable.

Conversely, some adults may find discussions about children's sexuality and sexual abuse confronting and try to ignore, downplay, or dismiss events. This reluctance plays out in other arenas and, according to Robinson (2013), requires adults to overcome limiting ideas about children's sexual naiveté and their inability to cope with discussions about sexual matters (no matter how sensitively and appropriately done). Children and young people in the Safety Studies reported that it was more likely for adults to feel uncomfortable talking about sex and dealing with disclosures and would often actively dissuade children from discussing or sharing this information (Moore et al., 2015; Moore, McArthur, Death, et al., 2016). It is useful to note that these restrictive attitudes and behaviours are compounded within organisations whose cultures dehumanise children; restrict children and adults from raising concerns, making complaints, or challenging behaviours; and actively prioritise their reputations over children's wellbeing (Palmer et al., 2016).

4.5 Promoting Child-Safe Cultures

In its final report, the Royal Commission has flagged a number of ways that organisational cultures can improve collective responsibility for children's safety and for improving the organisation's preventative strategies and enable concerning behaviours to be identified, discussed, and managed and for children to play a part in their protection (Royal Commission into Institutional Responses to Child Sexual Abuse, 2017e). The task of promoting child-safe cultures has many positive intersections with other prevention paradigms—particularly strategies to prevent and respond to bullying and other forms of peer victimisation (including online), homophobia, dating, and relationship violence. For each of these, the prevention focus is on education and dispelling myths and stereotypes that create a culture that excuses or hides abuse behaviours and the conditions that lead to and facilitate it.

We would argue that in addition to the efforts outlined by the Royal Commission, organisations might also:

- identify whether the organisation and its members hold attitudes and beliefs that create conditions within which abuse might occur;
- reflect on where and how organisations can confront and challenge homophobic, limiting, or disempowering views about gender, sex, and sexuality held by staff, volunteers, and the children/young people they serve;
- improve the awareness of staff, children, young people, and other stakeholders about sex, sexuality, and sexual abuse (through training, supervision, and dialogue) and how attitudes and beliefs shape behaviours;
- develop policies and other documentation (such as codes of conduct) that articulate the organisation's commitment to creating environments where all staff, children, and young people are protected from sexual harassment, bullying, and misogynistic and homophobic behaviour with clear expectations about the behaviour of all;
- articulate the organisation's commitment to fostering protective attitudes and behaviours that promote diversity and positive notions of masculinity and femininity and celebrate efforts to enhance; and
- assess and reflect on progress made in fostering positive cultures and challenging behaviours and practices that enable them to continue.

5 Conclusions

In this chapter, we have provided an overview of the nature of institutional child sexual abuse and how it is similar and different to other forms of abuse and maltreatment. Drawing on our research and the broader literature, we emphasised the importance of not only recognising individual risk factors but also, more importantly, promoting conditions of safety. This entails enhancing organisational cultures that prevent institutional child sexual abuse and appropriately responding when grooming behaviours and abuse occur. We provided examples of both safe and unsafe cultures and argued that limiting views about sex and sexuality, homosexuality, and masculinity/femininity can influence children's safety and the ways that young men and women experience grooming and abuse and its impact on disclosure and responses.

In addition to promoting organisational cultures that empower all adults to take responsibility for children's safety and challenge beliefs, attitudes, and behaviours that may place children at risk, we have discussed the ways that situational crime prevention approaches can remove excuses for the harm of children, increase the level of difficulty for someone to offend, and reduce the appeal of the crime and the vulnerability of the child.

Chapter Review Questions

1. Why is it hard to estimate how many children and young people experience institutional child sexual abuse?
2. What are the three broad groups of risk factors that combine to facilitate the occurrence of child sexual abuse within an organisational context?
3. From a situational perspective—what are some of the activities that carry higher risk?
4. What are the three key strands of a situational crime prevention approach?
5. What does 'protective participation' refer to, and why is it a critical ingredient in preventing child sexual abuse in organisations?
6. What are the key areas of knowledge and capability that adults within a youth-serving organisation need to prevent and respond to harm to children?
7. How do particular types of 'organisational culture' enable abuse and/or child-centred responses to abuse if it occurs?
8. What are some strategies for implementing child-safe cultures?

References

Anthony, T., Caruana, C., Hollingworth, S., Maher, S., Michaux, A., Mildon, R., et al. (2015). *Report of the parenting research centre for the royal commission into institutional responses to child sexual abuse: Implementation of recommendations arising from previous inquiries of relevance to the royal commission into institutional responses to child sexual abuse (1925289117).* Sydney: Royal Commission into Institutional Responses to Child Sexual Abuse. Retrieved from https://www.childabuseroyalcommission.gov.au/research, under "ensuring a positive impact".

Attar-Schwartz, S. (2011). Maltreatment by staff in residential care facilities: The adolescents' perspectives. *Social Service Review*, *85*(4), 635–664.

Attar-Schwartz, S. (2014). Experiences of sexual victimization by peers among adolescents in residential care settings. *Social Service Review*, *88*(4), 594–629.

Bromfield, L., Hirte, C., Octoman, O., & Katz, I. (2017). *Child sexual abuse in australian institutional contexts 2008–13: Findings from administrative data.* Retrieved from http://apo.org.au/node/107907.

Gallagher, B. (2000). The extent and nature of known cases of institutional child sexual abuse. *British Journal of Social Work*, *30*(6), 795–817.

Green, L. (2005). Theorizing sexuality, sexual abuse and residential children's homes: Adding gender to the equation. *British Journal of Social Work*, *35*(4), 453–481.

Higgins, D. J., Kaufman, K., & Erooga, M. (2016). How can child welfare and youth-serving organisations keep children safe? *Developing Practice: The Child, Youth and Family Work Journal*, *44*, 48.

Higgins, D. J., & McCabe, M. P. (2000). Multi-type maltreatment and the long-term adjustment of adults. *Child Abuse Review*, *9*(1), 6–18.

Higgins, D., & Morley, S. (2017). *Understanding situational crime prevention for child sexaul abuse: What services need to know.* Melbourne: ACU Institute of Child Protection Studies. Available at https://safeguardingchildren.acu.edu.au/practice_tools.

Kaufman, K., Hayes, A., & Knox, L. A. (2010). The situational prevention model: Creating safer environments for children and adolescents. In K. L. Kaufman (Ed.), *The prevention of sexual violence: A practitioner's source book.* Holyoke, MA: NEARI Press.

Moore, T. (2017a). *Protection through participation: Involving children in child-safe organisations*. Melbourne: Australian Institute of Family Studies. https://safeguardingchildren.acu.edu.au/research_and_resources/practice_paper_protection_through_participation_involving_children_in_child-safe_organisations.

Moore, T. P. (2017b). Children and young people's views on institutional safety: It's not just because we're little. *Child Abuse & Neglect*, *74*, 73–85.

Moore, T., McArthur, M., Death, J., Roche, S., & Tilbury, C. (2016). *Safe and sound: Exploring the safety of young people in residential care (1925289990)*. Retrieved from https://safeguardingchildren.acu.edu.au/research_and_resources/institute_of_child_protection_studies_report_safe_and_sound.

Moore, T., McArthur, M., Heerde, J., Roche, S., & O'Leary, P. (2016). *Our safety counts: Children and young people's perceptions of safety and institutional responses to their safety concerns*. Melbourne: ACU. Retrieved from https://safeguardingchildren.acu.edu.au/research_and_resources/institute_of_child_protection_studies_report_our_safety_counts.

Moore, T., McArthur, M., Noble-Carr, D., & Harcourt, D. (2015). *Taking us seriously: Children and young people talk about safety and institutional responses to their safety concerns*. Melbourne: ACU. Retrieved from: https://safeguardingchildren.acu.edu.au/research_and_resources/institute_of_child_protection_studies_report_taking_us_seriously.

Munro, E., & Fish, S. (2015). *Hear no evil, see no evil: Understanding failure to identify and report child sexual abuse in institutional contexts*. Retrieved from https://www.childabuseroyalcommission.gov.au/research.

Palmer, D., Feldman, V., & McKibbin, G. (2016). *The role of organisational culture in child sexual abuse in institutional contexts: Royal commission into institutional responses to child sexual abuse*. https://trove.nla.gov.au/work/217052530?selectedversion=NBD58984227.

Parkin, W., & Green, L. (1997). Cultures of abuse within residential child care. *Early Child Development and Care*, *133*(1), 73–86.

Powell, F., Geoghegan, M., Scanlon, M., & Swirak, K. (2012). The Irish charity myth, child abuse and human rights: contextualising the Ryan report into care institutions. *British Journal of Social Work*, *43*(1), 7–23.

Quadara, A., Nagy, V., Higgins, D., & Siegel, N. (2015). *Conceptualising the prevention of child sexual abuse: Final report*. Retrieved from https://aifs.gov.au/publications/conceptualising-prevention-child-sexual-abuse.

Robinson, K. H. (2013). *Innocence, knowledge and the construction of childhood: The contradictory nature of sexuality and censorship in children's contemporary lives*. London, New York: Routledge. https://doi.org/10.1080/14681811.2013.819684.

Robinson, S. (2016). *Feeling safe, being safe: What is important to children and young people with disability and high support needs about safety in institutional settings?*. Retrieved from Sydney https://epubs.scu.edu.au/ccyp_pubs/178/.

Royal Commission into Institutional Responses to Child Sexual Abuse. (2017a). *Analysis of claims of child sexual abuse made with respect to Catholic Church institutions in Australia*. Retrieved from Sydney https://www.childabuseroyalcommission.gov.au/sites/default/files/research_report_-_analysis_of_claims_of_made_with_respect_to_catholic_church_institutions_-_institutions_of_interest_0.pdf.

Royal Commission into Institutional Responses to Child Sexual Abuse. (2017b). *Final Report: Volume 1—Our Inquiry*. Retrieved from Sydney https://www.childabuseroyalcommission.gov.au/sites/default/files/final_report_-_volume_1_our_inquiry.pdf.

Royal Commission into Institutional Responses to Child Sexual Abuse. (2017c). *Final report: Volume 2—Nature and causes*. Retrieved from Sydney https://www.childabuseroyalcommission.gov.au/sites/default/files/final_report_-_volume_2_nature_and_cause.pdf.

Royal Commission into Institutional Responses to Child Sexual Abuse. (2017d). *Final report: Volume 4—Identifying and disclosing*. Retrieved from Sydney https://www.childabuseroyalcommission.gov.au/sites/default/files/final_report_-_volume_4_identifying_and_disclosing_child_sexual_abuse.pdf.

Royal Commission into Institutional Responses to Child Sexual Abuse. (2017e). *Final report: Volume 6—Making institutions child safe*. Retrieved from Sydney https://www.childabuseroyalcommission.gov.au/sites/default/files/final_report_-_volume_6_making_institutions_child_safe.pdf.

Royal Commission into Institutional Responses to Child Sexual Abuse. (2017f). *Final report: Volume 12—Contemporary out-of-home care*. Retrieved from Sydney https://www.childabuseroyalcommission.gov.au/sites/default/files/final_report_-_volume_12_contemporary_out-of-home_care.pdf.

Royal Commission into Institutional Responses to Child Sexual Abuse. (2017g). *Final Report: Volume 16, Book 1—Religious institutions*. Retrieved from Sydney https://www.childabuseroyalcommission.gov.au/sites/default/files/final_report_-_volume_16_religious_institutions_book_1.pdf.

Sköld, J. (2013). Historical abuse—a contemporary issue: Compiling inquiries into abuse and neglect of children in out-of-home care worldwide. *Journal of Scandinavian Studies in Criminology and Crime Prevention, 14*(suppl. 1), 5–23.

Stathopoulos, M. (2014). *The exception that proves the rule: Female sexual offending and the gendered nature of sexual violence. ACSSA research summary*. Melbourne: Australian Centre for the Study of Sexual Assault, Australian Institute of Family Studies. Available at: https://aifs.gov.au/publications/exception-proves-rule.

Wilkins, N., Tsao, B., Hertz, M. F., Davis, R., & Klevens, J. (2014). *Connecting the dots: An overview of the links among multiple forms of violence*. Retrieved from Atlanta, GA. https://www.cdc.gov/violenceprevention/pub/connecting_dots.html.

Wortley, R., & Smallbone, S. (2006). Applying situational principles to sexual offenses against children. In R. Wortley & S. Smallbone (Eds.), Vol. 19. *Situational prevention of child sexual abuse [Crime Prevention Studies]* (pp. 7–36). New York: Criminal Justice Press.

CHAPTER 4

Online Child Sexual Abuse

Elena Martellozzo
Middlesex University, London, United Kingdom

Sexual abuse through social networking sites has become increasingly concerning in recent years, with the Internet offering opportunities for sex offenders to engage in online grooming behaviour. The aim of this chapter is to offer a critical overview of the nature of online sexual abuse: it explores some of the risks children face online, including sexual solicitation. This chapter also presents the types of online groomers that have been identified in the latest studies and the classification of child abuse images, considered part of the abuse process. It suggests that on the one hand, more needs to be done in ensuring that children are fully aware of the online risks; on the other hand, governments worldwide need to direct more resources to ensure that high-quality training and support is available to frontline police officers to help tackle child sex offences, especially online.

1 Introduction

1.1 Online Risks: The Broad Picture

Online crimes perpetrated against children are complex to identify, research, and evaluate, as these are constantly shaped by technological advancements (O'Connell, Price, & Barrow, 2004a). This chapter shows that the Internet can be used as a vehicle for sex offenders to exploit children in at least three ways: producing child abuse images, sharing child abuse images of children, and grooming and/or procuring child victims online. No matter how these crimes are perpetrated, the impact they have on children may be devastating, leaving them to feel humiliated, depressed, or even suicidal.

The risks for children of online behaviour have been extensively researched (Davidson & Martellozzo, 2008; O'Connell, Price, & Barrow, 2004b), with 10% of 8- to 11-year olds reporting that they had encountered something nasty or worrying in the last year, a figure that rose to 19% of 12- to 15-year olds (Livingstone et al., 2017). One alarming example of the dangers young people face in this new Wi-Fi-connected smartphone world is the rise of the annual rate of self-harming. UK girls (37.4/10,000) self-harmed at three times the rate of boys (12.3/10,000) in 2014, and the sharpest increase was a 68% rise amongst 13- to 16-year-old girls between 2011 and 2014. In one of his latest publications on Internet suicide and

Child Abuse and Neglect. https://doi.org/10.1016/B978-0-12-815344-4.00004-0

community affirmation, Niezen (2013) argues that social media platforms such as Facebook and Twitter allow for communities to form in order to share ideas and practices that would not be accepted in wider society. He claims that one evident feature present in those communities is what could be seen as a rejection of professional intervention aimed at serious issues such as anorexia, self-harm, and obsession with suicide (Niezen, 2013).

Although a causal link remains unproven, the first Apple iPhone was launched in 2007 and the cheaper Android alternative a year late. However, it took a couple of years for smartphones to begin their mass proliferation (Android Central, 2015). Many would endorse the following interpretation of the increasingly harmful impacts that smartphones have been having amongst teenage girls:

> *24-hour connectivity has made teen girls more sensitive, more self-absorbed, more extreme and yet also less active, less happy, less confident and less sociable than they were 15 years ago. Self-harm was a niche syndrome in the 20th century. In the 21st, it is a mode of expression for an entire generation of girls...In the era of constant visual bombardment, "body image" has taken on a whole new meaning.*
>
> **Foreman (2017, p. 1)**

Research by the Seattle Children's Research Institute discovered that teenagers use covert terms (in the forms of #s) in social media to discover further information about the process of self-harming. By using terms such as 'self-harmmm', Instagram's filters were shown to have only picked up six out of 18 search terms entered by users, which then brought up a site block and an advisory health warning box for the person searching. '#Self-harmmm' as an entered search term, grew in incidence from 1.7 million to 2.4 million between 2014 and 2015 (Handy Kader, 2015). In terms of sexting, research by Martellozzo et al. (2016) found that 7.8% of 948 UK 11- to 16-year olds had either shown or sent a naked or seminaked image of themselves to another person online and that 65% of the same cohort had seen online pornography. Revenge porn victims have been found to be 90% female (Cyber Civil Rights, 2017), whilst there exist an estimated 3000 websites worldwide dedicated to 'nonconsensual pornography' (Citron & Franks, 2014). Estimates of cyberbullying online vary wildly between 6% and 25% + according to the same research, and up to 10% of children have faced sexual solicitation from online groomers. This chapter focuses on the latter issue of online grooming, which is the process whereby a perpetrator engages in online contact with young people with the intention of commencing sexual contact, either exclusively online or with a view to committing an eventual contact offence.

2 Understanding and Defining Online Grooming

We do not know the extent of children being targeted online for sexual purposes, and we will never have a precise answer to this question, as children may not want to come forward out of fear or embarrassment or may not recognise that they have been victimised. A recent report published by the National Society for the Prevention of Cruelty to Children (NSPCC), a British leading charity, indicates that the number of offences recorded in 2016–17 increased by 15% from the previous year, with an offence recorded on average every 8 min, both online and offline, and included rape, sexual assault, and grooming. In almost 14,000 cases, the complainant was aged 10 or under, with 2788 of the alleged offences perpetrated against children aged 4 or under. In 10% of cases, there was an online element involved (Sky News, 2018). However, given that the emergence of technologies in our everyday lives may constitute a contributing factor to the increase of sexual victimisation of children, it would come as no surprise if this 10% will increase in the near future.

Whatever the extent of online sexual offences against children might be, we have evidence on children's online experience revealing that the issue of online grooming is serious and requires close attention. Research suggests that the perpetrator's initial contact is made through freely available legitimate Internet chat rooms (Babchishin, Karl Hanson, & Hermann, 2011; DeMarco, Sharrock, Crowther, & Barnard, 2017; Martellozzo, 2015). These provide a fertile arena in which those who wish to sexually exploit children may lurk, waiting for vulnerable individuals who are seeking friendship and support to appear online. Children may then be lured into private chat rooms, where potentially illegal conversations take place and personal details are exchanged. This is often considered to be the preliminary states of online sexual 'grooming'. Online sexual grooming is perceived as a type of online behaviour designed to 'seduce' or lure children into sexual behaviour or conversations with or without children's knowledge (Ost, 2009; Rimer, 2017; Whittle, Hamilton-Giachritsis, Beech, & Collings, 2013). However, a particular problem that occurs when we attempt to define the grooming process is that it is not possible to establish when it starts or stops (Gillespie, 2008) or the scale of it. Technology certainly has a strong role to play in facilitating the grooming process to take place. For example, growing alongside Internet chat rooms is the increasing use of video communication, through mobile phones or portable devices such as tablets or iPads, providing a means for those who wish to sexually exploit children to incite them into unlawful sexual behaviour; to watch that behaviour take place; and, in all likelihood, to record such behaviour for later use. The child may then be forced into further unlawful acts (either online or in person), blackmailed into sending money to avoid the threat of having his or her images or video footage sent to others or posted on social networking sites (Webster, 2012).

But why do offenders groom children for sexual abuse in the first place? In his latest pioneering work, Michael Seto (Eke, Seto, & Williams, 2010; Seto, 2013; Seto & Eke, 2017) explains that there are three main variables that contribute to the commission of sexual abuse against children. These are the following: an antisocial trait in the offender, a sexual interest in children, and situational factors such as access to children. He argues that the presence of antisocial behaviour and opportunity factors can be the distinguishing factors that may trigger contact abuse. His 'Motivation-Facilitation Model of Sexual Offending against Children' is supported by the findings from the most recent meta-analysis on Internet sex offenders (Babchishin et al., 2011), which recognises that the main predictors of recidivistic contact sex offending amongst offenders who use indecent images of children are being antisocial, having access to children, and the lack of barriers to acting on one's deviant impulses.

Grooming is a crucial part of the so-called cycle of abuse (Babchishin et al., 2011; Finkelhor & Hotaling, 1984), and it does not only take place online, although this is a recent and major concern. The grooming process consists of sex offenders socialising and grooming children over prolonged periods of time to gain their trust and preparing them for sexual abuse (Webster, 2012) and will ensure that abuse will take place without being disclosed (Martellozzo & Jane, 2017). Grooming can be differentiated in stages and usually begins with befriending a child (termed 'hands-off offending' by Calder (2004)) and moves on to relatively inappropriate touching by a familiar adult in whom the child trusts. Calder (2004) terms this 'hands-on' sexual offending. In this manner, the child does not become distressed and is unaware of the importance of what is happening. This behaviour gradually continues and becomes more and more sexual in nature, so the child becomes accustomed to what is happening.

Gallagher (2000) defines this behaviour as 'entrapment', that is, the process in which 'perpetrators draw children into abusive situations and make it difficult for them to disclose' (Gallagher, 2000, p. 810). He argues that this method consists of a number of techniques, but 'chief amongst these is the involvement of children in increasingly intimate physical contact, and the provision of a variety of inducements, whether these are material, illicit or emotional in nature' (Gallagher, 2000, p. 810). Recent studies on sex offenders' grooming behaviour supports the idea that the Internet does not create new stages in the cycle of abuse, but allows the cycle of abuse to be quickened (Gillespie, 2008; Martellozzo, 2010).

Generally speaking, when people set up their profiles on social networking sites, they do so through the requirements (name, sex, and age) of standardised electronic membership forms of social networking and similar websites and the verification processes of service providers (Martellozzo, 2015). The data they insert are checked electronically but not physically by a person. Therefore, offenders can make any desired claim about their identity, including the use of any profile picture. These profiles and the messages posted are designed to attract either children or like-minded people. In many cases, it seems to work. Research conducted with victims of online abuse has shown that in a small number of cases, young people thought they met someone special whom they could implicitly trust. However, in reality, they had been talking to an adult who had a sexual interest (O'Connell et al., 2004a, 2004b). These adults target young people with the ultimate objective to abuse them. They achieve their aims by gaining the child's trust and by making the child feel special, loved, and comfortable. Some of the techniques used are so well planned that children may not understand, at least initially, that they have been groomed (Berliner & Conte, 1990). The victims then realise that they have engaged willingly in the previous behaviour and feel that it is too late to stop it. Owing to the gradual nature of abuse, some children cannot define such behaviour as wrong until a later stage.

However, finding potential child victims may not happen quickly, as not all children are at risk of online abuse. As argued by Sonia Livingstone (2010, p. 3), 'the identification of online risk does not imply that harm will follow, nor that all users are equally effected; rather, it is a probabilistic judgement regarding an outcome that depends on the particular and contingent interaction between user and environment'. Online risks in some cases may lead to harm, but in others, they may facilitate resilience. However, it appears to be the case that offline vulnerability extends its consequences online, as risk migrates from traditional to new sites. Therefore, children who are 'vulnerable' offline are more likely to be susceptible to online abuse.

3 Understanding the Types of Online Offenders

Up until very recently, the figure of the online offender or even the concept of a child being sexually groomed and abused via the Internet was difficult to fathom. Technology has certainly shaped the way in which people live, work, interact, and offend. Therefore, understanding the types of online offenders and their motivations for offending is crucial, as it may be used to predict perpetrator pathways, including the potential for noncontact perpetrators to become contact perpetrators. Furthermore, this analysis may also be used to inform our understanding of children's vulnerability when online and provide ways to protect young people from further victimisation.

Since 2000, a number of empirical studies have been carried out to ascertain, through the development of typologies and classifications of Internet sex offenders, what characterises these individuals and how they groom children online (Lanning, 1998; O'Connell et al., 2004a, 2004b; Martellozzo, 2012; Elliott, 2017). Typologies are based on the perpetrators' *modus operandi*, their behaviour, and the effects (real or hypothetical) their actions may have on children. In their recent review of assessment behaviour and characteristics of online-facilitated child sexual abuse and exploitation, De Marco and his colleagues (DeMarco et al., 2017) argue that typologies are useful in informing preventative practices and Internet safety for children and young people, assisting law enforcement with ongoing investigations, and informing the treatment of perpetrators post offence. Depending on the study, typologies can differ; some may explain behaviour by motivations or sexual interests, whilst others may define perpetrators by offence type. Regardless of how typologies are developed, many may be linked thematically. First, there are perpetrators who primarily access CSA materials but do not seek contact. Second, there are perpetrators who view children as sexually attractive. Third, there are those who are primarily contact offenders and use information and communication technology as a tool in the perpetration of these offences. Lastly, there are organised criminals who see the abuse of children and the production of CSA materials as commodities leading to financial gain. These offence goals may not be mutually exclusive (DeMarco et al., 2017).

Some of the most pioneering studies on online sex offenders have been conducted by colleagues in the United States and the United Kingdom, and for the purpose of this chapter, the main and most recent typologies will be discussed.

In the United Kingdom, Beech and colleagues (Beech, Elliott, Birgden, & Findlater, 2008) developed four distinct typologies. The first consists of individuals who access child abuse material impulsively and/or out of curiosity. This group includes those who never exhibited sexual problems until they discovered the Internet (Delmonico & Griffin, 2008). The second is composed of individuals who access or trade child abuse material to fuel their sexual interest in children (Beech et al., 2008). For these individuals, the Internet facilitates an extension of an already existing pattern of sexual deviance (Delmonico & Griffin, 2008). The third consists of sexual offenders who use the Internet as part of a pattern of offline contact offending, including those who use it to acquire victims and/or disseminate images that they produce (Beech et al., 2008; Delmonico & Griffin, 2008). The fourth group consists of individuals who download child abuse images for nonsexual reasons (e.g. financial gain).

One of the most recent typologies was developed by Webster (2012) for the European Online Grooming Project. Through the interviews with convicted online perpetrators, they identified three types of offenders. The first is the intimacy-seeking type who do not have previous convictions for sexual offending or engage in networking with other sex offenders and are unlikely to have child abuse material. They are likely to engage in an intimate relationship with the younger person and believe the contact to be consensual. The second is the adaptable style typologies of offenders who tend to have previous convictions for sexual offending against children and view young people as mature and capable. These offenders adapt their approach according to the young person being engaged and their reactions. The last is the hypersexualised type who tends to have significant collections of indecent images and network extensively with other online sex offenders. These offenders use deception, and contact with young people is likely to progress rapidly and be of sexual nature. Progression to contact offences with the young person is less likely with this type than the other types because their primary motivation is immediate sexual gratification.

In an innovative and collaborative partnership between operational policing and academic research, Martellozzo (2015) examined three online undercover operations at the London Metropolitan Police High Technological Crime Unit and Paedophile Unit and analysed over 160 transcripts of perpetrators interacting with undercover officers, posing as either young boys or girls. Because of the nature of the undercover operations, she was able to observe online predators in their 'natural environment'. She found that whilst there is no such thing as a typical online groomer using a typical profile, it is possible to identify distinctive grooming behaviours. She placed her selected sample of groomers on a spectrum of openness, with hyperconfident groomers on the one side of the spectrum and hypercautious groomers on the other end. According to Martellozzo (2015), this spectrum should be interpreted as fluid, as a wide range of grooming behaviours exist at every stage in between. That said, despite the fluidity of grooming behaviours, it is possible to discern certain characteristics that are common to all groomers, regardless of the levels of confidence. Hyperconfident groomers are perpetrators who are open about their sexual interests, share nude pictures of themselves, and are comfortable exposing themselves to their victims online. She also found that these types of offenders are the most familiar with the Internet. From their behaviour, it is clear that they have experience in chatting with a lot of people; newer ones to the 'game' are more cautious and may explore the risk further. At the other end of the spectrum, hypercautious groomers could possibly be the most dangerous, as they are not easy to identify. They do not post any sexual messages or indecent photos and spend time establishing if they are interacting with genuine individuals. They enjoy playing a passive role and request to view the victim on webcam, hearing the victim's voice, and being sent photographs of the victim. Only when they are sure that their victims are real, they would arrange to meet with them.

DeHart et al. (2017) carried out a similar study in the United States, and from their analysis of transcripts of 200 perpetrators with victims, they developed four typologies.

The first typology was that of 'cybersex-only' perpetrators who either expose themselves to their victims whilst communicating or seek to receive sexually explicit images or content. These perpetrators are interested in physical features of their victims and provide instructions on how to behave or act sexually whilst communicating online. They tend to engage in sustained communication over several months but never discuss any concrete plan to have a real-world encounter. This group of perpetrators resembles the same characteristics of the hyperconfident groomer in Martellozzo's study.

The second typology is that of the 'schedulers' who are perpetrators that attempt to schedule a meeting (e.g. time and place) for sexual purposes but are unlikely to expose themselves online. Instead, they request sexual images of the victim more often. The period of communication between the victim and the perpetrators is much shorter than for cybersex-only perpetrators. This group of perpetrators resembles the same characteristics of the hypercautious groomer in Martellozzo's study.

Cybersex schedulers form the third typology of perpetrators who have both sustained communication with their victims, seek information about their physical features, and often masturbate in real time whilst online with the victims. They also plan (or attempt to plan) a meeting in the foreseeable future with the victim. Although these individuals share more similar features with the cybersex-only perpetrators, they are not actually likely to follow through with a meeting once planned with their victims. There is debate over whether imagining the encounter is part of their fantasy or if there is genuine insecurity and fear of being caught. Finally, the fourth typology defined the buyers, who are individuals that prioritise the schedule for meeting the victim and negotiate over the exact types of sexual actions they wish to perform. Amongst these individuals are those who are seeking classified advertisements on notice boards and respond.

Independent of these classifications, online groomers seem to form two distinct groups: those whose offences relate to fantasy and developing relationships online so they can meet their sexual needs and those whose primary intention is to meet young people offline to carry out the abuse in person (Briggs, Simon, & Simonsen, 2011). Online, individuals have the opportunity to explore the dark side of their sexuality by assuming desired identities and by disclosing as much or as little about themselves as they wish to others (Cooper, McLoughlin, & Campbell, 2000). Moreover, by hiding behind their fictitious avatar, they may explore any opportunities offered in cyberspace and the dark web, including that of predating children online (Martellozzo & Jane, 2017).

4 Policy and Legislation Context in Dealing With Online Child Sexual Abuse

Legislation across the world has struggled to keep up with the rapid developments in online technology (Martellozzo, 2013). Old laws have been tailored to fit online criminal behaviour, missing vital opportunities to stop online sexual abuse and protect vulnerable children. Although the United Kingdom's laws to protect children are robust and well known across the world, it is still vital to respond rapidly to technological changes and dramatic advancements in electronic communication technologies. There is a difficulty in policing this area of cybercrime as it can be seen as simply new manifestations of old modus operandi that may not fall under old-fashioned criminal liability laws (Martellozzo, 2015). The law is constantly trying to catch up with this ever-changing and developing phenomenon. For example, in the United Kingdom, the offence of 'sexual communication with a child' was introduced through an amendment to the Serious Crime Act 2015, but in reality did not come into force until 2017 (Pegg, 2017).

Online grooming has been a difficult offence to combat as recent legislations fail to address sexual groomers' modus operandi. For instance, the Malicious Communications Act (1988) makes it an offence to send a communication with the intention of causing distress or anxiety. However, groomers tend to befriend the child rather than cause harm through communication, so anxiety and distress can be difficult to prove (NSPCC, 2014). The Communications Act (2003) Section 127 makes it an offence to send an electronic message that is grossly offensive or of an indecent, obscene, or menacing character. Again, it is often difficult to charge online groomers under this act.

More recently, the Crown Prosecution Service (2017) published guidelines to aid the prosecuting of child sexual abuse cases. These guidelines were put in place in order to help prosecutors when dealing with child sexual abuse cases and include reference to online grooming in paragraph 11:

> *Online grooming and abuse can take place through chat rooms and social networking sites and gaming devices which have the ability to connect to the internet. Offenders may target hundreds of children at a time and once initial contact with a child is made this can escalate into threats and intimidation. The online abuse can be an end in itself without any contact offences taking place, but in other cases contact offences can occur.*
>
> ***CPS (2017, p. 1)***

In response to the gaps in the law, which made it difficult to charge online groomers, the National Society for the Prevention of Cruelty to Children (NSPCC) ran a campaign in 2014, which suggested that a new offence was needed to target paedophiles who communicate sexually with a child. In response to this, the Government introduced a new offence into Section 67 of the Serious Crime Act (2015). The new offence criminalises a person aged 18 years or over who communicates with a child under 16 (who the adult does not reasonably believe to be 16 or over) if the communication is sexual or if it is intended to elicit from the child a communication that is sexual. It is believed that this will help ensure that young people are fully protected by the law and allow the authorities to intervene earlier to prevent more serious offending against children (Ministry of Justice, 2015).

5 Child Sexual Abuse Images on the Internet

As previously argued (Martellozzo, 2013), the sexual abuse of children and the production of child abuse images existed long before the advent of the Internet. However, the Internet has certainly contributed to the radical increase of this abusive material and has aided its distribution across the globe easily and with ill intent. There is a vast amount of literature suggesting that the production and distribution of child sexual abuse images on the Internet has serious and long-term repercussions on children (Gillespie, 2002) and, as a result, it is taken very seriously.

In the United Kingdom, Section 160 of the Criminal Justice Act 1988, Protection of Children Act 1978 (Section 1), possession of indecent photograph of child/indecent photographs of children is illegal. This law also covers distribution and production. For these offences, a 'child' is defined as anyone below 18 years of age (UN Convention on the Rights of the Child [UNCRC], 1989; Akdeniz, 1997). Most European countries adhere to the same statutes that makes it illegal to possess, distribute, and make indecent images of children (IIOC), more commonly referred to as 'child pornography' outside the United Kingdom (Gillespie, 2008).

6 Classification of the Severity of the Image

To distinguish between abusive content and to facilitate the sentencing process, Combating Paedophile Information Networks in Europe's (COPINE) typologies have been adopted into English law (Quayle & Taylor, 2003; Quayle, Vaughan, & Taylor, 2006; Taylor & Quayle, 2003). These are based upon five categories of pictures that may be sexualised by an adult with a sexual interest in children. They range from level one, where children pose as nude or seminude; to level four, where penetrative sexual assault takes place; to level five, where acts of sadism and bestiality are exercised. Although this levelling may contribute to the sanitation of indecent images, it represents an extremely important step forward in recognising the seriousness of what images depict (Martellozzo & Taylor, 2009).

To minimise the challenges presented by the classification of images, the Council proposed that the levels of images can be simplified further so that Levels 1–5 became A, B, and C offence categories (Kloess, Woodhams, Whittle, Grant, & Hamilton-Giachritsis, 2017). The proposed levels are set out in Table 1.

Category A images tend to involve sadism or bestiality and would involve child penetrative sexual activity, whilst Category B images would usually depict nonpenetrative sexual activity. Category C would relate to indecent images not falling within categories A or B. The Sentencing Advisory Panel adopted by the Court of Appeal advised that all child abuse images should be allocated to one of three categories as of April 2014 (Sentencing Guidelines Council, 2012).

There are no exact figures about the number of abuse images and videos being spread online. Some estimates indicate that there could be up to 200 million items available on the Internet (IWF, 2016). The Internet is the main distribution channel for material (images, films, etc.) depicting sexual abuse of children with alarming data. Thirty four percent of the content reported to the hotline in the United Kingdom in 2015, which shows sexual activity between

Table 1: Classification system (Sentencing Guidelines Council, 2012)

	Possession	Distribution	Production
Category A (Previously levels 4 and 5)	Possession of images involving penetrative sexual activity Possession of images involving sexual activity with an animal or sadism	Sharing images involving penetrative sexual activity Sharing images involving sexual activity with an animal or sadism	Creating images involving penetrative sexual activity Creating images involving sexual activity with an animal or sadism
Category B (Previously levels 2 and 3)	Possession of images involving non-penetrative sexual activity	Sharing of images involving non-penetrative sexual activity	Creating images involving non-penetrative sexual activity
Category C (Previously level 1)	Possession of images of erotic posing	Sharing of images of erotic posing	Creating images of erotic posing

adults and children, are about rape or sexual torture of a child, and 69% of the victims are under the age of 10. Three percent of the victims are not even 2 years old (IWF, 2015). The dimension of these crimes is global by nature and requires international cooperation of players. To give an example of the complication of this crime and to highlight the importance of collaboration, a child can be sexually abused and filmed in country A, but the perpetrator may be a travelling offender coming from country B. The images may be uploaded from country C to Internet service providers' hosting services in countries D. They may be viewed by paedophiles all over the world. They may be reported by an Internet user stumbling over them to a hotline in country E. The hotline of country E may trace the hosting server back to country D and will contact the hotline in country D, which will cooperate with law enforcement and the ISP in the country to remove the content.

7 Addressing the Problem of Child Abuse Images in the United Kingdom and in Europe

In the United Kingdom, the IWF was established in 1996 to fulfil an independent role in receiving, assessing, and tracing public complaints about child sexual abuse content on the Internet and to support the development of website rating systems. Since then, they have been operating a hotline service for the public to report potentially criminal content, and we have been issuing 'takedown notices' to UK ISPs in partnership with the police so they can remove the content. Prior to the founding of the IWF, 18% of child sexual abuse material was found to be hosted within the United Kingdom. Findings in 2009 suggested that this percentage had been reduced to below 1% (Smith, 2014).

Information regarding the child abuse images hosted in the United Kingdom is communicated with the UK police. If the sites are in the United Kingdom, then the police may act upon them directly, whereas if they are hosted elsewhere in the world, then a report will be passed to the relevant authorities in that country or to the International Association of Internet Hotlines[1] (INHOPE) contact in that country. Within the United Kingdom, the IWF will also pass the report directly to the ISP and, in the case of illegal images circulating on Usenet, will pass a report to all UK ISPs so that they can remove or block the article from their servers (Harrison, 2006).

For the past 15 years, the European Commission has been addressing the evolving needs of Internet safety through a succession of safer Internet funding, including actions to fight against online child sexual abuse material. The main activity of the programmes is to cofund a European network of Safer Internet Centres currently present in 27 EU member states, Norway, and Iceland and to fund projects for enhancing law enforcement agencies' identification and analysis of child sexual abuse material (Hilton & Carr, 2010). The INHOPE

[1] The IWF is a member of INHOPE, and it will send a report to another INHOPE member if the material appears to be hosted in their country.

network of Internet hotlines allows citizens to anonymously report child sexual abuse material they come across whilst online. All EU member states run hotlines, but the network has also a global outreach over all continents. Hotlines analyse the content reported and take quick action by passing on the reports deemed as illegal to law enforcement. In the last years, dedicated police units have been created in the EU member states and also beyond. Hotlines, with the exception of the IWF, currently work in a reactive way, that is, they take action only when they have received a report by an Internet user, but they do not themselves search actively for child sexual abuse content on the Internet. More recently, the INHOPE foundation (2010) has been established to develop new hotlines worldwide, particularly in emerging countries where the legislation does not recognise online offending and there is a lack of funding.

8 Conclusion

This chapter highlighted the darkest and possibly the ugliest corners of the cybersphere, where people have the ability to behave in ways that can cause real suffering to others, particularly children. Research evidence shows that grooming children online for sexual purposes has a detrimental impact on a child's life and often goes unreported. The large percentage of unreported cases is a symptom of an uncomfortable silence around the topic. The number of cases that the police have been dealing with over the last 15 years is high, and there is no evidence to suggest the problem is a short-term one or one that will disappear quickly. However, it is important to explore these issues under a somewhat brighter light. Whilst the Internet has created new platforms for sex offenders to groom and abuse children, it has also allowed for police forces to unmask sex offenders that would have continued to abuse without being noticed. It has also allowed for empirical research to take place and to study and understand the modus operandi of perpetrators and the response of victims, as presented in this chapter.

Many countries across the world are working hard to ensure that cyberspace is a safer place for both adults and children. This chapter has cited organisations such as the Internet Watch Foundation in the United Kingdom and INHOPE with its member hotlines in Europe being established to report indecent images online, to train and support new hotlines, and to foster ongoing Internet safety awareness and education. It is vital that children feel able to come forward to disclose abuse and that they are given the appropriate and supportive platforms to enable them to do so. However, it is equally critical to invest on preventing the abuse. The NSPCC's Speak out Stay safe programme, for example, visits primary schools across the United Kingdom to help children learn the signs of abuse in an age-appropriate way and what to do if they have been victims of such abuse.

Undoubtedly, it is important to continue the work in understanding the nature of the risk, the source of the reporting of the offending, and the potential risks and harm to children, particularly in the ever-changing online world. To succeed, the support of governments is needed worldwide to direct more resources to ensure that high-quality training is available to frontline police officers to tackle online child sex offences, to ensure that robust safeguarding procedures are in place and to help raise awareness.

Chapter Review Questions

1. Since the advent of the Internet, what is new or different about child sexual abuse?
2. What are the main risks that children are exposed to online?
3. Who are the 'online sex offenders', and are they the 'usual suspects' of the criminal justice system?
4. What methods do online sex offenders use to abuse children online?
5. Why is the concept of 'entrapment' important for the understanding of the lack of disclosure of the abuse?
6. What might children and young people themselves do in order to reduce their risk of victimisation?
7. How are indecent images classified, and do you think it is important to have a classification in place?
8. How has the problem of child abuse images been addressed in the Europe? Do you think this is an efficient way to address the problem?
9. Can the popularity of indecent images of children online be regarded as a social problem? Why?

References

Akdeniz, Y. (1997). *Governance of pornography and child pornography on the global Internet: a multi-layered approach*. In *Law and the Internet: Regulating cyberspace* (pp. 223–241). cyber-rights.org.

Android Central. (2015). *Android history*. . -10-21T12:00:11-04:00, 2015-last update. Available: https://www.androidcentral.com/android-history [Apr 17, 2018].

Babchishin, K. M., Karl Hanson, R., & Hermann, C. A. (2011). The characteristics of online sex offenders: a meta-analysis. *Sexual Abuse: A Journal of Research and Treatment*, *23*(1), 92–123.

Beech, A. R., Elliott, I. A., Birgden, A., & Findlater, D. (2008). The Internet and child sexual offending: a criminological review. *Aggression and Violent Behavior*, *13*(3), 216–228.

Berliner, L., & Conte, J. R. (1990). The process of victimization: the victims' perspective. *Child Abuse & Neglect*, *14*(1), 29–40.

Briggs, P., Simon, W. T., & Simonsen, S. (2011). An exploratory study of Internet-initiated sexual offenses and the chat room sex offender: has the Internet enabled a new typology of sex offender? *Sexual Abuse*, *23*(1), 72–91.

Calder, M. C. (2004). *Child sexual abuse and the Internet: Tackling the new frontier*. Russell House Pub Ltd.

Citron, D. K., & Franks, M. A. (2014). Criminalizing revenge porn. *Wake Forest Law Review*, *49*, 345.

Cooper, A., Mcloughlin, I. P., & Campbell, K. M. (2000). Sexuality in cyberspace: update for the 21st century. *Cyberpsychology & Behavior*, *3*(4), 521–536.

CPS. (2017). *Child sexual abuse: Guidelines on prosecuting cases of child sexual abuse*. CPS. https://www.cps.gov.uk/legal-guidance/child-sexual-abuse-guidelines-prosecuting-cases-child-sexual-abuse.

Cyber Civil Rights. (2017). *End revenge porn archives*. https://www.cybercivilrights.org/category/end-revenge-porn/.

Davidson, J., & Martellozzo, E. (2008). Protecting children online: towards a safer Internet. In G. Wetherby, K. Williams, P. Birch, & M. Cain (Eds.), *Sex as crime?* (pp. 338–355). Willan.

DeHart, D., Dwyer, G., Seto, M. C., Moran, R., Letourneau, E., & Schwarz-Watts, D. (2017). Internet sexual solicitation of children: a proposed typology of offenders based on their chats, e-mails, and social network posts. *Journal of Sexual Aggression*, *23*(1), 77–89.

Delmonico, D. L., & Griffin, E. J. (2008). *Online sex offending*. In *Sexual deviance: Theory, assessment, and treatment* (pp. 459). New York, London: The Guilford Press.

DeMarco, J., Sharrock, S., Crowther, T., & Barnard, M. (2017). Behaviours and characteristics of perpetrators of online-facilitated child sexual abuse and exploitation. In *A rapid evidence assessment*. Independent Inquiry into Child Sexual Abuse (IICSA). NatCen.Prepared for.

Eke, A. W., Seto, M. C., & Williams, J. (2010). Examining the criminal history and future offending of child pornography offenders: an extended prospective follow-up study. *Law and Human Behavior*, *35*(6), 466–478.

Elliott, I. A. (2017). A self-regulation model of sexual grooming. *Trauma, Violence & Abuse*, *18*(1), 83–97.

Finkelhor, D., & Hotaling, G. T. (1984). Sexual abuse in the national incidence study of child abuse and neglect: an appraisal. *Child Abuse & Neglect*, *8*(1), 23–32.

Foreman, A. (2017). *The truth about teenage girls*. 2017-last update. The Australian. Available: https://www.theaustralian.com.au/life/modernity-didnt-invent-teenage-girls/news-story/208a7f50864090b25e20bc1414f3101e [Apr 17, 2018].

Gallagher, B. (2000). The extent and nature of known cases of institutional child sexual abuse. *British Journal of Social Work*, *30*(6), 795–817.

Gillespie, A. A. (2002). Child protection on the Internet challenges for criminal law. *Child and Family Law Quarterly*, *14*, 411–426.

Gillespie, A. (2008). *Child exploitation and communication technologies*. Russell House Publishing.

Harrison, C. (2006). Cyberspace and child abuse images: a feminist perspective. *Affilia*, *21*(4), 365–379.

Hilton, Z., & Carr, J. (2010). *Combating child abuse images on the Internet: international perspectives*. In *Internet child abuse: Current research and policy* (pp. 64–90): Routledge-Cavendish.

IWF. (2015). *IWF Annual Report*. IWF, 2015.

IWF. (2016). *IWF Annual Report 2016*. 2016-last update. Available: https://www.iwf.org.uk/sites/default/files/reports/2017-04/iwf_report_2016.pdf.

Kader, H. (2015). *Study: Teens use covert self-harm hashtags on Instagram that escape content advisory filters*. Seattle Children Hospital Research Foundation.

Kloess, J. A., Woodhams, J., Whittle, H., Grant, T., & Hamilton-Giachritsis, C. E. (2017). The challenges of identifying and classifying child sexual abuse material. *Sexual Abuse*, 1–24. https://doi.org/10.1177/1079063217724768.

Lanning, K. V. (1998). Cyber "pedophiles": a behavioral perspective. *The APSAC Advisor*, *11*(4), 12–18.

Livingstone, S. (2010). *E-youth: (future) policy implications: Reflections on online risk, harm and vulnerability*, LSE.

Livingstone, S., Davidson, J., Bryce, J., Batool, S., Haughton, C., & Nandi, A. (2017). *Children's online activities, risks and safety: A literature review by the UKCCIS evidence group*, LSE.

Martellozzo, E. (2010). Sex offenders' use of the Internet. In J. Davidson & P. Gottschalk (Eds.), *Internet child abuse: Current research and policy* (pp. 104–125). London: Routledge-Cavendish.

Martellozzo, E. (2012). *Online child sexual abuse: Grooming, policing and child protection in a multi-media world*. Routledge.

Martellozzo, E. (2013). *Online child sexual abuse: Grooming, policing and child protection in a multi-media world*. Routledge.

Martellozzo, E. (2015). Policing online child sexual abuse—the British experience. *European Journal of Policing Studies*, *3*(1), 32–52.

Martellozzo, E., & Jane, E. (2017). *Cybercrime and its victims*. Routledge.

Martellozzo, E., Monaghan, A., Adler, J. R., Davidson, J., Leyva, R., & Horvath, M. A. H. (2016). *"I wasn't sure it was normal to watch it". A quantitative and qualitative examination of the impact of online pornography on the values, attitudes, beliefs and behaviours of children and young people*. Middlesex University, NSPCC, OCC.

Martellozzo, E., & Taylor, H. (2009). Cycle of abuse. *Index on Censorship*, *38*(1), 117–122.

Ministry of Justice. (2015). *Serious Crime Act 2015 fact sheet: Offence of sexual communication with a child. Fact sheet, Ministry of Justice*. . 2015-last update. Available: https://www.gov.uk/government/uploads/system/uploads/attachment_data/file/416003/Fact_sheet_-_Offence_of_sexual_communication_with_a_child.pdf.

Niezen, R. (2013). Internet suicide: communities of affirmation and the lethality of communication. *Transcultural Psychiatry*, *50*(2), 303–322.

NSPCC. (2014). *Changing childhoods together: Annual reports and accounts 2013/2014. *, NSPCC, 2014-last update.

O'Connell, R., Price, J., & Barrow, C. (2004a). *Cyber stalking, abusive cyber sex and online grooming: A programme of education for teenagers*. UK: Cyberspace Research Unit, University of Central Lancashire.

O'Connell, R., Price, J., & Barrow, C. (2004b). *Emerging trends amongst primary school children's use of the Internet*. UK: Cyberspace Research Unit, University of Central Lancashire.

Ost, S. (2009). *Child pornography and sexual grooming: Legal and societal responses*. Cambridge University Press.

Pegg, S. (2017). *Online grooming and the law*. Law Gazette, 2017-last update. Available: https://www.lawgazette.co.uk/legal-updates/online-grooming-and-the-law/5060841.article [Apr 17, 2018].

Quayle, E., & Taylor, M. (2003). Model of problematic Internet use in people with a sexual interest in children. *Cyberpsychology & Behavior*, *6*(1), 93–106.

Quayle, E., Vaughan, M., & Taylor, M. (2006). Sex offenders, Internet child abuse images and emotional avoidance: the importance of values. *Aggression and Violent Behavior*, *11*(1), 1–11.

Rimer, J. R. (2017). Internet sexual offending from an anthropological perspective: analysing offender perceptions of online spaces. *Journal of Sexual Aggression*, *23*(1), 33–45.

Sentencing Guidelines Council. (2012). *Sexual offences guideline consultation*. 2012-last update. Available: https://consult.justice.gov.uk/sentencing-council/indecent-images-children/supporting....

Seto, M. C. (2013). *Internet sex offenders*. American Psychological Association.

Seto, M. C., & Eke, A. W. (2017). Correlates of admitted sexual interest in children among individuals convicted of child pornography offenses. *Law and Human Behavior*, *41*(3), 305–313.

Sky News. (2018). https://news.sky.com/story/alleged-child-sex-crime-cases-reach-record-high-including-rape-and-sexual-assault-11258549.

Smith, S. (2014). *Global strategies for tackling child sexual abuse material online*. IWF.

Taylor, M., & Quayle, E. (2003). *Child pornography: An Internet crime*. Psychology Press.

UN Convention on the Rights of the Child [UNCRC]. (1989). https://www.unicef.org.uk/what-we-do/un-convention-child-rights/.

Webster, S. E. A. (2012). *European online grooming project*. . 2012-last update. Available: http://natcen.ac.uk/our-research/research/european-online-grooming-project/ [Apr 18, 2018].

Whittle, H., Hamilton-Giachritsis, C., Beech, A., & Collings, G. (2013). A review of online grooming: characteristics and concerns. *Aggression and Violent Behavior*, *18*(1), 62–70.

CHAPTER 5

Understanding Violent Extremism and Child Abuse: A Psychological Analysis

Vaishnavi Honnavalli, Loo Seng Neo, Ruth Gan, Shi Hui Tee, Majeed Khader, Jeffery Chin
Home Team Behavioural Sciences Centre, Ministry of Home Affairs, Singapore, Singapore

In early January 2016, the Islamic State of Iraq and Syria (ISIS) released a 10 min-long propaganda video—in English—that featured amongst other things the execution of five British spies and threats directed at former UK Prime Minister David Cameron, over the country's involvement in the coalition against ISIS (Withnall, 2016). In particular, the video included a segment in which a 4-year-old boy, Isa Dare, was seen detonating a car bomb with four prisoners inside. Before carrying out the detonation, Dare addressed the camera in a British accent stating that "we will kill the kuffar [nonbelievers] over there" (Bolton, 2016). As the son of a female British Muslim convert who had travelled to Syria in 2013, Dare is just one of many examples of children who were born in or brought by their parents into ISIS territory (van der Heide & Geenen, 2017).

Whilst often assumed to be passive agents, children have long been and will continue to be involved in violent extremist groups (Gray & Matchin, 2008). Recent decades also witnessed the involvement of children in conflict zones around the globe. Prominent examples include the deployment of child soldiers by government and opposition forces in South Sudan (Wheeler, 2015), recruitment of children by Taliban to carry out suicide operations in Afghanistan (Betonman & Malik, 2016), militarisation of children in Northern Ireland (Brocklehurst, 1999), and sexual exploitation of female child soldiers in Colombia (Singer, 2006). The recent strategy by ISIS on nurturing the next generation of fighters such as Dare is a further confirmation of this dangerous phenomenon.

Whilst the role of children in violent extremism appears more newsworthy than their adult counterparts, there is still a deplorable lack of awareness in perceiving such involvement of children as a form of child abuse. A child is defined here as "every human being below the age of 18 years unless under the law applicable to the child, majority is attained earlier"

Child Abuse and Neglect. https://doi.org/10.1016/B978-0-12-815344-4.00005-2

(Office of the United Nations High Commissioner for Human Rights [OHCHR], 2005). Research on the psychological trauma faced by children living in conflict zones suggests that the trauma and harm faced by the children will have long-term psychological, moral, and physical health consequences (Ardino, 2011; Horgan, Taylor, Bloom, & Winter, 2016). Thus, children should first and foremost be viewed as victims of their circumstances; even in the event that the child "state that they want to join a violent extremist movement, their capacity to make this choice is specious" (Horgan et al., 2016, p. 651).

From a psychological perspective, children's involvement in violent extremism provides a unique window to further explore the concept of 'child abuse'. Firstly, violent extremist groups have recruited children to perform a litany of roles that provide a powerful case in support of the violent extremists and their approaches. For example, Singer (2006) highlights that children were recruited to abet in smuggling weapons through military checkpoints without arousing suspicion. Similarly, Blattman (2007) opines that the impressionable nature and staying power of children provided a convenient and low-cost option to ensure a constant supply of new recruits. Moreover, there is a likelihood that the children themselves may not recognise that they are the victims of exploitation by violent extremist groups. For example, Wheeler (2015, p. 3) observes that.

> *Despite all these hardships, some [child soldiers] said they felt grateful to their commanders for taking them in. In the midst of a grossly abusive conflict, they believed that being part of an armed group afforded them some protection, and also the opportunity to fight to protect their community or to fulfil their desire for revenge for attacks or abuses.*

Consequently, besides examining the physical exploitation of children, it is also useful to explore how violent extremist groups psychologically 'abused' children.

Secondly, violent extremist groups have utilised the Internet to disseminate propaganda targeting children ("Indonesia police find ISIS", 2017). Prominent cases of children from Western countries being indoctrinated and 'brainwashed' to join ISIS underscore the potential threat of grooming and exposure to violent extremism as a form of child abuse. In fact, many of these children who travelled to Syria to join ISIS have disregarded the potentiality of alienating their own family and community (Neo, Pang, & Chin, in press). Examples from the Israeli-Palestinian conflict (Ayer et al., 2015) and the Northern Ireland conflict (Toner, 1994) further depict how hatred from the older generation has been transferred historically and generationally to their children. Thus, the long-term exposure to radical propaganda materials may affect the way children perceived their world and their moral implications towards the use of violence.

Thirdly, violent extremists have been known to travel to conflict zones with their wives and children (van der Heide & Geenen, 2017). This has been observed in many cases of ISIS foreign fighters, who have 'uprooted' and 'migrated' with their loved ones to the Islamic caliphate. Whilst this 'migration' entails potential trauma and acculturation stressors that the wives and children may face whilst living in the conflict zones, it also represents the loss of proper infrastructure (e.g. schools and hospitals) and the subsequent detrimental impact on the physical and psychological well-being of the children—that is, a form of child abuse.

To enhance our understanding about violent extremism and child abuse, this chapter proposes the adoption of the World Health Organisation's (WHO) typology of child abuse. In the first section, WHO's five-category classification will be illustrated with instances of child abuse in the context of violent extremism. The following two sections will examine two indepth case studies (ISIS in Syria and the Liberation Tigers of Tamil Eelam [LTTE] in Sri Lanka) of interest. The last section will discuss implications that could potentially address this phenomenon.

1 World Health Organisation's Classification of Child Abuse

The WHO defines child abuse as (World Health Organisation [WHO], 1999, p. 15):

> *[A]ll forms of physical and/or emotional ill-treatment, sexual abuse, neglect or negligent treatment or commercial or other exploitation, resulting in actual or potential harm to the child's health, survival, development or dignity in the context of a relationship of responsibility, trust or power.*

Child abuse is viewed as a public health problem that results in long-term health consequences, where health is being understood as "a state of complete physical, mental, and social well-being, not merely the absence of disease" (WHO, 1999, p. 14). In its report on the 'Consultation on Child Abuse Prevention', WHO (1999) lays out a five-category classification of child abuse—that is, physical, emotional, neglect and negligent treatment, sexual, and exploitation. For the purpose of this chapter, the WHO's classification has been adopted to examine child abuse in the violent extremism context.

1.1 Physical Abuse

Physical abuse in the violent extremism context takes various forms, right from coercion into physical and military training as a child soldier to working as spies or carrying out high-risk endeavours on the orders of the adult soldiers and finally ending in injury, disability or illness, and death through the participation in battles or suicide bombings. These examples highlight instances where interaction with a person in a position of power has resulted in physical harm to a child, which is in line with the definition of physical abuse by the World Health Organisation [WHO] (1999, p. 15): "results in actual or potential physical harm from an interaction or lack of an interaction, which is reasonably within the control of a parent or person in a position of responsibility, power or trust."

As security forces are likely to view children with less suspicion, they serve as an ideal choice for the role of spies, couriers, and suicide bombers (Hurd, 2017). Indeed, Weiner (2001, para 8) observes that:

> *Knowing that the soldiers of the Israel Defense Forces (IDF) are ordered not to shoot live ammunition at children, Palestinian snipers hid among and behind groups of youngsters, on rooftops, in alleys or orchards, often using kids as shields when aiming at exposed IDF soldiers. On some occasions, Palestinian gunmen may have inadvertently shot these children from behind.*

Therefore, some children have been used as cannon fodder in battles. Al-Qaeda training videos have also shown young boys being taught how to manufacture bombs and set explosive traps, whilst Palestinian Islamic Jihad—a Palestinian radical group—is known to have recruited children as young as 13 as suicide bombers (Singer, 2006). These high-risk endeavours place the children at a disadvantage in terms of securing their own physical well-being.

In comparison with adults, children are less likely to escape training camps, easier to intimidate and do as they are told, and not knowledgeable enough to look out for themselves—for example, demand specific salaries (Perešin, 2014a). Children generally receive the same treatment as adult recruits and undergo brutal training-induction ceremonies, which may involve beatings and humiliation (Singer, 2006). For example, in Paraguay, government military trainers would beat children as young as 12 with sticks or rifle butts and burn them with cigarettes, with the intent of trying to turn them into soldiers. Those who resisted or who attempted to escape were further beaten or even killed (Wessells, 1997). Furthermore, children who were born and raised in a conflict zone could be normalised to the level of violence, and their understanding of safety could be highly skewed as they are unable to comprehend the consequences of their involvement (Radicalisation Awareness Network [RAN], 2016). Thus, their inability to decipher potentially dangerous situations might not help to distance themselves from harm's way.

1.2 Emotional Abuse

Security in a child's life is dependent on the development and maintenance of a good attachment relationship, which provides the child with a secure base and safe refuge to deal with a frightening world (Catherall, 2011). Damage to the secure attachment could lead the child to become sensitive to losing others, face difficulties when allowing himself/herself to form a secure attachment again, and increase a child's risk for a variety of problems (WHO, 1999). According to Bowlby (1973), factors that can interfere with attachment security of children and adolescents include poverty, domestic conflict, and violence.

In the context of violent extremism, child soldiers are indoctrinated at a young age where they are being exposed to violence and isolated from mainstream influences and values, in order for the violent extremist groups to create the 'perfect fighters' who are willing to engage in extreme violence and die for the groups' cause (Anderson, 2016), sometimes to the extent of killing their own family members so as to preclude the possibility of them escaping and returning home (Beber & Blattman, 2013). More importantly, prolonged exposure to violence desensitises the children towards violence, and they become conditioned to the use of violence to resolve problems (Lasser & Adams, 2007), which in the long run may be detrimental to their psychological and moral development (Singer, 2006). In fact, research suggests that youths who exhibited tolerant attitudes towards the use of violence are more vulnerable towards the use of future violence—for example, criminal behaviour (Zhang, Loeber, & Stouthamer-Loeber, 1997). Thus, the violence, ideology, and concepts that children learn from being part of violent extremist groups greatly influence their understanding of what is 'normal'. This has a detrimental impact not only on the child but also on the society that has to deal with a generation of children who believed in the use of violence as a solution. Moreover, the children may become emotionally crippled, unable to express their true emotions, because if they do, they are likely to be shamed and punished by the violent extremist group (Perešin, 2014b). These manifestations of emotional abuse are in line with the definition by the WHO (1990, p. 15): "Acts include restriction of movement, patterns of belittling, denigrating, scapegoating, threatening, scaring, discriminating, ridiculing or other nonphysical forms of hostile or rejecting treatment."

Besides the issue of indoctrination, another manifestation of emotional abuse revolves around the concept of psychological distress. Psychological distress was found to be a prominent factor amongst a sample of child soldiers of the Lord's Resistance Army (Vindevogel et al., 2013). Approximately 93%–97% of these children displayed symptoms of posttraumatic stress disorder (PTSD), which include depression, anxiety, experiencing nightmares, and general emotional and behavioural difficulties. These symptoms incapacitate the child and prevent them from being able to function normally in society even after the conflict has ended, and they are moved to a safe environment, as the trauma will continue to manifest and impact various aspects of their lives. Trauma might just be one aspect of postconflict psychosocial consequences. Other such fears include revenge attacks, rerecruitment, stigmatisation, familial violence, and chronic poverty (Wessells, 1997).

1.3 Neglect and Negligent Treatment

Trauma experienced due to neglect inflicted by a primary caregiver may disrupt the normal development of secure attachments and lead to the disorganisation of attachments (Lyons-Ruth & Jacobvitz, 1999; Solomon & George, 1999). In the context of violent extremism, participation in conflict means that the children lose their right to play, the right to education, the right to live with their parents, and the right to form healthy relationships with friends and siblings (de Silva, 2013). They are deprived of a normal education but are indoctrinated with the radical ideology of the violent extremism group instead (Omar & Smith, 2017), which is redundant outside the context of the conflict zone. In some instances, families as a whole migrated from their home country into conflict zones (i.e. foreign fighters bringing their families along to join ISIS), and the children are removed from school and normal family life, disrupting their emotional and developmental needs.

According to the United Nations Convention on the Rights of the Child, every child has the right to his or her identity 'as a child'. A child, apart from a name, has to have an identity as an independent individual with self-esteem and personalised entity (Convention on the Rights of the Child, 1989). This identity is often replaced by a new, less significant identity when the child becomes part of a violent extremist group.

Thus, the involvement in violent extremism and the associated exposure to violence have broad implications on the child's normal development. They are not afforded a safe environment to learn, socialise, and integrate into the community, which in turn may lead to a number of developmental problems including dissociative symptoms (Carlson & Kashani, 1988) and symptoms of depression, anxiety, and acting out (Lyons-Ruth, 1996). These failures to provide for the development of the child are in line with the definition of neglect by the WHO (1990, p. 15): "failure to provide for the development of the child in all spheres: health, education, emotional development, nutrition, shelter, and safe living conditions."

Furthermore, one often overlooked consequence of child soldiering is the economic drain on the society. Child soldiers frequently face injuries such as loss of sight, hearing, or limbs, and these disabilities reduce their employability due to the inability to perform common tasks. With their physical disabilities, they are likely to be marginalised from already disadvantaged families and communities, who might not be able to cope with the additional burden of taking care of them (Brett & Specht, 2004). This eventually leads to a generation of children who are unable to regain a 'normal life'.

1.4 Sexual Abuse

It has been a common practice in most conflict zones for young girls to be brought in to become the wives of combatants (Obaji, 2016). They have been abducted and kept hostage by violent extremist groups, to be married to members or raped by the men in the open as young boys watched. This is a method used by violent extremists to teach the young boys on how to subdue a struggling female victim during sexual assault. These boys are then enticed to participate in battle in exchange for an opportunity to take advantage of the females (Obaji, 2016). Similarly, young girls escaping from Boko Haram recount numerous stories of being raped at gunpoint by boys as young as 13 years old (Obaji, 2016). Their purpose was to serve the men in the violent extremist group, or their husbands, and produce children who would grow up to join Boko Haram. Young girls who became pregnant due to rape are left to fend for themselves, and some resort to throwing themselves downstairs to force a miscarriage (Craw, 2017). Rape is also a form of punishment for females who do not obey the orders of the violent extremist groups or their husbands.

There are reports that claimed sexual abuse in conflict zones is not limited only to female children. According to the Human Rights Watch, accounts of children who were detained in northern Syria told of boys who were 13 years and above, being sexually abused in detention, beaten, and brutally tortured in detention facilities (Leigh, 2014).

Thus, the abuse children faced in these conflict zones is in line with the definition of sexual abuse by the WHO (1990, p. 15): "involvement of a child in sexual activity that he or she does not fully comprehend, is unable to give informed consent to, or for which the child is not developmentally prepared and cannot give consent." Of concern, these young victims face stigmatisation and discrimination when they return to their communities, because of which some of them decide to return to the violent extremist groups rather than live in a society that targets and rejects them (Olsson, 2017).

1.5 Exploitation

The ongoing Syrian conflict has been the result of close to 5 million children being exposed to violence and slavery by all parties involved in the conflict (Montgomery, 2014). Apart from abusing them physically, sexually, and psychologically, these children are also exploited for domestic purposes. They are used as labour for cooking, cleaning, fetching water, or providing medical aid for the wounded (Montgomery, 2014).

For violent extremist groups, child soldiers make for good cannon fodder, an effective way of increasing numbers. The Lord's Resistance Army in Uganda, for example, only had about 200 core adult members but was able to project a strong military power because of the estimated 12,000 abducted children (Singer, 2006). The abducted children are exploited to carry out duties such as guarding strategic locations, arresting civilians, and beheading enemies (RAN, 2016), which are usually carried out by adults. They are also sent to the front lines to function as body shields for the more experienced fighters (Breitenbücher, 2015; Crimi, 2012). According to the United Nations, Boko Haram had kidnapped as many as 1500 children, and some as young as 8 were deployed on the front lines as human shields (Obaji, 2015). Thus, these observations are in line with the definition of exploitation by the WHO (1990, p. 16): "to use of the child in work or other activities for the benefit of others… are to the detriment of the child's physical or mental health, education, or spiritual, moral or social-emotional development."

2 Case Study Analysis of Violent Extremism and Child Abuse

In the previous section, the WHO's classification of child abuse provided a useful perspective to understand the various aspects of child abuse in the violent extremism context. This section will provide a more indepth analysis on two conflict zones (Syria and Sri Lanka) where violent extremist groups have abused children.

2.1 Syria: The Islamic State of Iraq and Syria (ISIS)

Since the breakout of civil war in Syria and the rise of the jihadist violent extremist groups in Iraq and Syria, horrifying images of death and torture have plagued the news. ISIS rose to power and called on followers to travel to the Syria and Iraq to join them and fight a war that would lead to the creation of a so-called Islamic State. As the group evolved, it adopted a new paradigm of recruitment by involving children. Children came to join ISIS through multiple ways: children of foreigners who joined ISIS, children of supportive locals, abandoned children found in ISIS-controlled orphanages, children coercively taken from their parents, and runaway children who volunteered to join ISIS (Horgan & Bloom, 2015).

ISIS introduced many strategies to attract and influence potential young recruits. ISIS organised public events where children were handed out candy and toys whilst given the opportunity to wave the ISIS flag. Ice-cream trucks would attempt to allure the older children by telling them what ISIS could do for them. ISIS also took control of schools in their territories and ensured that only ISIS-approved curriculum was provided to the children (Horgan & Bloom, 2015).

The abuse of the children who joined ISIS were carried out on gradually increasing scales as the children performed multiple roles in ISIS. They were spies, preachers, soldiers, executioners, suicide bombers, sex slaves, wives to fighters, and human shields (Betonman & Malik, 2016; van der Heide & Geenen, 2017). They were exploited as labour and were forced to face psychologically and physically challenging situations endlessly just to fulfil the objectives of the commanders in the group. For example, as spies, they were required to share information on family members, neighbours, or friends who did not comply with the rules and practices of ISIS (Horgan & Bloom, 2015). As soldiers, they were trained in military camps to fight in combat on the front line, handle weapons, and manufacture and detonate explosives (Betonman & Malik, 2016). New batches of children arrived at orphanages every few weeks, and the older boys were sent to different towns for intensive military training ("Cubs of the Caliphate", 2017).

Children endured physical abuse on the battle field and within the training camps. Within the camps, they were beaten brutally if they were unable to endure military training or if they attempted to escape (Rakela, 2008). They were mostly used as cannon fodder on the field and to protect the adult fighters (Crimi, 2012). A lot of children have been used to carry out suicide attacks, leaving them either dead or gravely injured (Bloom, Horgan, & Winter, 2016). Like the adult fighters, these child soldiers were hailed and celebrated as heroes (Bloom et al., 2016).

Psychologically, the children were desensitised to violence, blood, and death. Exposing children to executions and encouraging children to participate in public brutality numbed them to emotions like fear and empathy. In fact, children were commonly captured observing executions (e.g. stonings, crucifixions, and beheadings) in ISIS propaganda videos, showing that they were not affected by the brutality (Betonman & Malik, 2016). The children were psychologically manipulated to such an extent that children as young as 10 years old were carrying out beheadings and parading around in public with the decapitated head for the purpose of propaganda videos (Hall, 2015). Alternatively, 3-year-old children were given stuffed toys to decapitate, as practice (Hurd, 2017).

As ISIS expanded their hold on regions in Northern Iraq, families were torn apart with ISIS' indiscriminate killings and capturing of residents of these towns. According to an Iraqi official, Vian Dakhil, "an estimated 6,383 Yazidis – mostly women and children – were enslaved and transported to ISIS prisons, military training camps, and the homes of fighters across eastern Syria and western Iraq, where they were raped, beaten, sold, and locked away" (Otten, 2017, para. 13). The victims were often drugged and raped repeatedly by multiple men. To prevent themselves from being sold as sex slaves, the young girls would scratch and harm themselves in an effort to come across as unattractive to their buyers; others have committed suicide to avoid being raped (Otten, 2017). Women who have escaped the ordeal are still not able to return to leading a normal life. Medical officials who have treated hundreds of rape victims describe symptoms of severe PTSD, severe shock, and psychological distress (Callimachi, 2017).

Since the onset of the war in 2011, more than 11 million Syrians have been on the run, together with 5.4 million who have been displaced from their homes into neighbouring countries; within Syria itself, more than 6 million people have been displaced (Syria Emergency, n.d.). Displacement from their home countries requires children to cope with challenging situations, relocating to and integrating into a new country and society (i.e. negligent treatment). According to UNICEF, more than 2 million children's educations have been impacted by the war in Syria. Whilst some children have never been inside a classroom, some have lost out on more than 4 years of schooling ("Millions of children", 2015). Approximately 5000 schools across the country have been destroyed or converted into shelters to hold displaced families or army bases ("Millions of children", 2015). This also means that these children are forced to live in shelters with minimum sanitation facilities, and with the lack of nutritional food, they are susceptible to illness and diseases.

In sum, hundreds of children have been killed and thousands robbed of their childhood, forced out of their homes, and coerced to fight in the conflict ("At least one in four children", 2018), amounting to accounts of child abuse.

2.2 Sri Lanka: The Liberation Tigers of Tamil Eelam [LTTE]

The civil war in Sri Lanka between the Sinhalese majority and the LTTE (i.e. Tamil minority) lasted for 26 years from 1983 to 2009 (Imtiyaz & Mohamed-Saleem, 2015). During this time, the LTTE recruited children to fight for their cause (Gray & Matchin, 2008). There were at least 3500 children who were recruited by the LTTE from 2002 to 2004 ("Sri Lanka: Tamil Tigers", 2004). The Tamil children, aged 16 and under, composed a unit called the LTTE Bakuts (translated as 'Baby Brigade') and formed at least 40% of the entire fighting force (Singer, 2006).

These children were a crucial support to the LTTE's operations (Gray & Matchin, 2008) and were recruited after the LTTE was unable to employ sufficient adult fighters due to a backlash from the local community (Singer, 2006). Children joined either willingly mostly due to peer influence or by force after they had been abducted and tortured (de Silva, 2013). All of them were made to go through an induction programme designed to instil hate for the enemy (de Silva, 2013).

Young children who willingly joined the LTTE usually joined for naive reasons such as protecting the social status of the group, but as they grew up, they started to believe that the oppression they were facing from the majority Sinhalese government made it a movement worth fighting for (Somasundaram, 2002). Most of these children came from poor family backgrounds and were largely orphans or refugees, which meant that they could be easily poached and manipulated to become soldiers for the group (Gray & Matchin, 2008). The LTTE specifically targeted Tamil families in the lower socio-economic strata, where it was common for parents to encourage or allow their children to join the LTTE because they believed it would help their children gain social status (Gray & Matchin, 2008). The innovative methods employed by the LTTE to entice children worked well under harsh economic and social conditions, especially for children of lower socio-economic status who were easily enthralled by physically attractive items such as new uniforms, boots, and shiny medals (Gray & Matchin, 2008).

Notwithstanding, the LTTE also made children join them by force. The LTTE resorted to recruiting from stable Tamil homes whereby parents were informed that they had to provide a child for the movement against the Sinhalese majority ("Living in Fear", 2004). Parents who defied the LTTE and refused to give up their child would face constant threat and violent harassment and eventually have their child abducted in the middle of the night or whilst they were walking home from school ("Living in Fear", 2004).

There were almost an equal number of boys and girls recruited by LTTE, with more than 40% of children being girls ("Sri Lanka: Tamil Tigers", 2004). The rationale behind the recruitment of girls and women was to directly oppose the current traditionalist system and promote gender equality ("Coalition to Stop", 2001). Interestingly, unlike most other conflict scenarios where girls are involved, the LTTE prohibited the sexual exploitation of girl soldiers, and relationships are not permitted between the sexes ("Living in Fear", 2004).

Upon joining the movement, all children were made to undergo a vigorous 4-month training programme in the jungle in order to prepare for battle (de Silva, 2013; Gray & Matchin, 2008).

Part of the training included an indoctrination of the ideology and goals of the LTTE. Children were repeatedly exposed to propaganda material (Gray & Matchin, 2008), horrific videos of battles, and weapons that were strategically placed in places such as a playground (de Silva, 2013). Successful attackers were hailed as heroes, which led children to believe that killing soft targets, such as Sinhalese women or children, was a noble action that garnered the support of their fellow fighters (de Silva, 2013). The dead were glorified as martyrs or heroes, which reinforced their young minds to believe that it would be magnanimous to give up their lives for the cause. If there were any children who refused to obey or comply with the LTTE's protocol, they would be harshly dealt with and punished, with beatings, clean-up duty, imprisonment, or death threats (de Silva, 2013).

Thus, LTTE essentially created an army of children who support the use of violence. The arduous 4 months spent training in the jungle was meant to separate the child from reality and help them suppress any memories of home (Gray & Matchin, 2008). All these experiences in effect left a deep and long-lasting psychological scar on the child soldiers who survived the war (Gray & Matchin, 2008). Despite governmental attempts at rehabilitating and reintegrating the children back into society, a huge number of Sri Lankan child soldiers still have readjustment problems that affect their daily functioning and psychosocial development (Jayatunge, 2012).

3 Implications for Academics and Practitioners

In order to reduce the threat of violent extremism, there is a need to undermine the success of violent extremist groups attempting to recruit children into their ranks. There is the need to first identify the different manifestations of child abuse in the context of violent extremism and understand the underlying reasons why children got involved in the first place; otherwise, academics and practitioners will continue to face an uphill task in trying to manage the threat of violent extremism.

However, the involvement of children in violent extremism demands an approach that goes beyond the victim perspective. Recognising the need for tailored intervention based on the types of abuse the child faces is essential; it also hinges on changes to the environment in terms of reintegration efforts such as providing a safe platform for children to recover from their trauma. Thus, this section identifies three implications that might help academics and practitioners to better manage the problem of children being used as soldiers and violent extremists.

Firstly, there is an increased likelihood of law enforcement officers coming into contact with children who are recruited by violent extremist groups, in their line of work. It is therefore imperative for officers to realise that these children will try to harm them as they have been indoctrinated and trained by the violent extremist groups to do so

(Gray & Matchin, 2008; van der Heide & Geenen, 2017). Some important questions for consideration are as follows: What are the boundaries (e.g. when to stop shooting) to consider when officers engage children who are active members of violent extremist groups? How to prepare officers on dealing with their emotion (e.g. guilt) if they were to kill a child in their line of work?

Secondly, traditional model of disarmament, demobilisation, and reintegration (DDR; see Hanson, 2007) may not provide an adequate solution to address the ideological indoctrination that the children have been exposed to. Instead, authorities should introduce interventions that take into account (RAN, 2016, p. 2) the following:

> *The bio-psychosocial needs of child returnees by maximizing their and their families' wellness and reducing the long-term consequences of trauma such as ill health, unemployment, poor educational attainment and involvement with the criminal justice system is the most appropriate means of ensuring a positive outcome.*

In other words, there is a need to address psychosocial needs (e.g. critical thinking and value-based support in their spiritual, intellectual, ideological, social, and emotional growth) on top of just addressing their immediate physical health needs. For example, the Aarhus model, which has been implemented in Denmark, adopts a model of mentorship for individuals who are at risk for or radicalised, through collaboration with local communities, dialogues with mosques, cultural societies, and other major players in local communities (Agerschou, 2014). This model serves to create an appropriate environment for the vulnerable individual to recover from trauma and develop resilient coping strategies. Moreover, there is also the need to provide personalised treatment determined by rigorous assessment. Some important questions for consideration are as follows: How to assess the children's degree of agency as the abuse they faced differ from one individual to another? Where should the children be housed when they returned from the conflict zone (i.e. with their families who are not radicalised or in temporary facilitates)? Who should be included as part of the multidisciplinary team to assess and manage the successful and safe reintegration of children from conflict zones?

Lastly, the engagement of the children would not be sufficient if the stigmas associated with their involvement in violent extremism are prevailing within the community. This may lead to a 'climate of fear' where distrust towards the mainstream community further alienates these children, which in turn acts as an obstacle to the successful reintegration of them back to the community (RAN, 2016). Thus, there is a need to raise awareness amongst the community about these reintegration programmes and emphasise that these children are victims of their circumstances (Neo et al., in press) and not 'willing participants' to the conflict (Betonman & Malik, 2016). Some important questions for consideration are as follows: Who should be involved (e.g. religious leaders or political leaders) in raising awareness about the reintegration programmes? What are the prevailing stigmas the community has towards violent extremism?

In concluding this chapter, it appears that there are merits in using the WHO's classification of child abuse to understand the manifestation of child abuse in the context of violent extremism. Whilst the focus of this chapter resides within the domain of psychology, there is an essential need to be cognisant of other disciplines (e.g. legal issues such as lowering the age of criminal responsibility to prosecute child soldiers; see van der Heide & Geenen, 2017) that also play a role in reducing and managing the risk of children getting involved in violent extremism.

4 Chapter Review Questions

1. For years, children have been involved in violent extremist groups, and this number continues to increase with recent conflicts.
2. Children in a violent extremist context are physically abused by being coerced into military training, carrying out high-risk endeavours, and sometimes participating in suicide missions.
3. Psychological distress and diagnosis of posttraumatic stress disorder (PTSD) are the results of children participating in violent extremism.
4. Children in conflict zones are deprived of a normal education and normal family life, which disrupts their emotional and developmental needs.
5. Children, who experience sexual abuse whilst being a part of violent extremist groups, face discrimination and stigmatisation when they return to society, because of which some of them choose to return to the conflict zones.
6. Rehabilitation and reintegration programmes need to be tailored to the type of abuse experienced by the child, providing them with the appropriate environment to recover from any trauma.
7. In order to enable the child's successful reintegration into society, efforts need to be made to prevent the stigmatisation of children who have participated in violent extremism.
8. Practitioners and academics need to continue research in this niche area of understanding why children get involved in violent extremism.

Acknowledgement

The views expressed in this chapter are the authors' only and do not represent the official position or view of the Ministry of Home Affairs, Singapore.

References

Agerschou, T. (2014). Preventing radicalization and discrimination in Aarhus. *Journal for Deradicalization, 1*, 5–22.

Anderson, K. (2016). *'Cubs of the caliphate': The systematic recruitment, training, and use of children in the Islamic state*. International Institute for Counter-Terrorism. Retrieved from https://www.ict.org.il/UserFiles/ICT-Cubs-of-the-Caliphate-Anderson.pdf.

Ardino, V. (2011). *Post-traumatic stress in antisocial youth: a multifaceted reality*. In *Post-traumatic syndromes in childhood and adolescence: A handbook of research and practice* (pp. 211–230). New York, NY: Wiley.

At least one in four children in Iraq impacted by conflict and poverty. (2018, January 19). *UNICEF*. Retrieved from http://cain.ulst.ac.uk/issues/children/brocklehurst/brocklehurst99.htm.

Ayer, L., Venkatesh, B., Stewart, R., Mandel, D., Stein, B., & Schoenbaum, M. (2015). Psychological aspects of the Israeli–Palestinian conflict: a systematic review. *Trauma, Violence & Abuse*, *18*(3), 322–338.

Beber, B., & Blattman, C. (2013). The logic of child soldiering and coercion. *International Organization*, *67*(01), 65–104.

Betonman, N., & Malik, N. (2016). *The children of Islamic state*. Quilliam Foundation. Retrieved from https://f-origin.hypotheses.org/wp-content/blogs.dir/2725/files/2016/04/the-children-of-islamic-state.pdf.

Blattman, C. (2007). In *The causes of child soldiering: theory and evidence from Northern Uganda Paper presented at the annual convention of the International Studies Association, Chicago, IL*.

Bloom, M., Horgan, J., & Winter, C. (2016). Depictions of children and youth in the Islamic State's martyrdom propaganda. *CTC Sentinel*, *9*(2).

Bolton, D. (2016). Child in Isis video is 'son of female British fanatic' with links to Lee Rigby killers. *Independent*. Retrieved from https://www.independent.co.uk/news/uk/home-news/isa-dare-isis-video-grace-khadija-dare-lee-rigby-a6796376.html.

Bowlby, J. (1973). *Attachment and loss. Vol. II: Separation: Anxiety and anger*. New York, NY: Basic Books.

Breitenbücher, D. (2015, August 27). *Somalia: The fate of children in the conflict*. International Committee of the Red Cross. Retrieved from https://www.icrc.org/casebook/doc/case-study/somalia-the-fate-of-children-in-the-conflict.htm.

Brett, R., & Specht, I. (2004). *Young soldiers: Why they choose to fight*. Boulder, CO: Lynne Rienner Publishers Inc.

Brocklehurst, H. (1999). *The nationalisation and militarisation of children in Northern Ireland*. University of Wales. Retrieved from http://cain.ulst.ac.uk/issues/children/brocklehurst/brocklehurst99.htm.

Callimachi, R. (2017, July 27). Freed from ISIS, Yazidi women return in 'severe shock'. *The New York Times*. Retrieved from https://www.nytimes.com/2017/07/27/world/middleeast/isis-yazidi-women-rape-iraq-mosul-slavery.html.

Carlson, G. A., & Kashani, J. H. (1988). Manic symptoms in a non-referred adolescent population. *Journal of Affective Disorders*, *15*, 219–226.

Catherall, D. (2011). The impact of lower magnitude stressors on child and adolescent development: the family context. In V. Ardino (Ed.), *Post-traumatic syndromes in childhood and adolescence: A handbook of research and practice* (pp. 61–76). New York, NY: Wiley.

Coalition to stop the use of child soldiers. (2001). *Child soldiers global report 2001*. Retrieved from https://www.child-soldiers.org/Handlers/Download.ashx?IDMF=adc88bff-1916-4317-b184-d9079e7b0bb8.

Convention on the Rights of the Child. (1989, November 20). *United Nation Resolution 25, session 44*. Retrieved from:http://www.ohchr.org/EN/ProfessionalInterest/Pages/CRC.aspx.

Craw, V. (2017). Inside my life as an ISIS sex slave. *New York Post*. Retrieved from https://nypost.com/2017/10/11/inside-my-life-as-an-isis-sex-slave.

Crimi, F. (2012, November 22). Al-Qaeda's child soldiers. *Frontpage Mag*. Retrieved from https://www.frontpagemag.com/fpm/166038/al-qaedas-child-soldiers-frank-crimi.

Cubs of the caliphate: How Islamic State groomed child soldiers in a Mosul orphanage. (2017, February 18). *South China Morning Post*. Retrieved from http://www.scmp.com/news/world/middle-east/article/2071818/cubs-caliphate-how-islamic-state-groomed-child-soldiers-mosul.

de Silva, D. G. H. (2013). The use of child soldiers in war with special reference to Sri Lanka. *Paediatrics and International Child Health*, *33*(4), 273–280.

Gray, D. H., & Matchin, T. O. (2008). Children: the new face of terrorism. *International NGO Journal*, *3*(6), 108–114.

Hall, J. (2015, July 17). ISIS film a child carrying out a beheading for the first time: 'Cub of the caliphate' is the first seen executing a prisoner by decapitation as the terror group increasingly use boys to kill. *The Guardian*. Retrieved from http://www.dailymail.co.uk/news/article-3164999/ISIS-film-CHILD-carrying-beheading-time-Cub-Caliphate-seen-executing-prisoner-decapitation-terror-group-increasingly-use-boys-kill.html.

Hanson, S. (2007, February 15). *Disarmament, demobilization, and reintegration (DDR) in Africa*. Council on Foreign Relations. Retrieved from https://www.cfr.org/backgrounder/disarmament-demobilization-and-reintegration-ddr-africa.

Horgan, J., & Bloom, M. (2015, July 8). This is how the Islamic State manufactures child militants. *Vice News*. Retrieved from https://news.vice.com/article/this-is-how-the-islamic-state-manufactures-child-militants.

Horgan, J. G., Taylor, M., Bloom, M., & Winter, C. (2016). From cubs to lions: a six stage model of child socialization into the Islamic state. *Studies in Conflict & Violent Extremism*, *40*(7), 645–664.

Hurd, D. (2017, February 11). *"Growing threat": terrorists training children, even toddlers, to kill*. CBN News. Retrieved from https://www1.cbn.com/cbnnews/world/2017/november/growing-threat-terrorists-training-children-even-toddlers-to-kill.

Imtiyaz, M. A. R., & Mohamed-Saleem, A. (2015). Muslims in post-war Sri Lanka: understanding Sinhala-Buddhist mobilization against them. *Asian Ethnicity*, *16*(2), 186–202.

Indonesia police find ISIS propaganda targeting children. (2017, June 26). *The Straits Times*. Retrieved from https://www.straitstimes.com/asia/se-asia/indonesia-police-find-isis-propaganda-targeting-children.

Jayatunge, R. M. (2012, December 29). Psychosocial problems of the Sri Lankan child soldiers. *Colombo Telegraph*. Retrieved from https://www.colombotelegraph.com/index.php/psychosocial-problems-of-the-sri-lankan-child-soldiers/.

Lasser, J., & Adams, K. (2007). The effects of war on children: school psychologists role and function. *School Psychology International*, *28*, 5–10.

Leigh, K. (2014, February 10). How Syrian children are recruited into battle. *Syria Deeply*. Retrieved from https://www.newsdeeply.com/syria/articles/2014/02/10/how-syrian-children-are-recruited-into-battle.

Living in fear: Child soldiers and the Tamil Tigers in Sri Lanka. (2004, November 10). *Human Rights Watch*. Retrieved from https://www.hrw.org/report/2004/11/10/living-fear/child-soldiers-and-tamil-tigers-sri-lanka.

Lyons-Ruth, K. (1996). Attachment relationships among children with aggressive behavior problems: the role of disorganized early attachment patterns. *Journal of Consulting and Clinical Psychology*, *64*(1), 64–73.

Lyons-Ruth, K., & Jacobvitz, D. (1999). Attachment disorganization: unresolved loss, relational violence, and lapses in behavioral and attentional strategies. In J. Cassidy & P. R. Shaver (Eds.), *Handbook of attachment: Theory, research, and clinical applications* (pp. 520–554). New York, NY: Guilford Press.

Millions of children across conflict-hit Syria deprived of education. (2015, September 15). UNICEF. *News Note*. Retrieved from https://www.unicef.org/media/media_85516.html.

Montgomery, K. (2014, November 27). ISIS sets a 'new paradigm' for child soldiers: ideology, combat and forced marriage. *News Deeply*. Retrieved from https://www.newsdeeply.com/syria/articles/2014/11/27/isis-sets-a-new-paradigm-for-child-soldiers-ideology-combat-and-forced-marriage.

Neo, L. S., Pang, J. S., & Chin, J. (in press). Bystander intervention to prevent radicalisation. In M. Khader, L. S. Neo, J. Tan, D. D. Cheong, & J. Chin (Eds.), Learning from violent extremist attacks: Behavioural sciences insights for practitioners and policymakers. Singapore: World Scientific Press.

Obaji, P. (2015, October 16). US troops vs Boko Haram's child soldiers in Cameroon. *The Daily Beast*. Retrieved from http://www.thedailybeast.com/articles/2015/10/16/u-s-troops-vs-boko-haram-s-child-soldiers-in-cameroon.html.

Obaji, P. (2016, December 27). Boko Haram teaching child soldiers to rape. *The Daily Beast*. Retrieved from https://www.thedailybeast.com/boko-haram-teaching-child-soldiers-to-rape.

Office of the United Nations High Commissioner for Human Rights [OHCHR]. (2005). *Convention on the rights of the child*. Retrieved from https://www.unicef.org/protection/files/CRCGC6_EN.pdf.

Olsson, S. (2017, June 19). Hear the voices of Congo's girl child soldiers. *IRIN News*. Retrieved from https://www.irinnews.org/opinion/2017/06/19/hear-voices-congo%E2%80%99s-girl-child-soldiers.

Omar, A. C., & Smith, S. (2017, October 21). Generation ISIS: when children are taught to be terrorists. *NBC News*. Retrieved from https://www.nbcnews.com/storyline/isis-uncovered/generation-isis-when-children-are-taught-be-terrorists-n812201.

Otten, C. (2017, July 25). *Slaves of Isis: the long walk of the Yazidi women*. The Guardian. Retrieved from https://www.theguardian.com/world/2017/jul/25/slaves-of-isis-the-long-walk-of-the-yazidi-women.

Perešin, A. (2014a). Al-Qaeda online radicalization and the creation of children terrorists. *Medij Istraž, 20*(1), 85–100.

Perešin, A. (2014b). New trends in terrorism: a new wave of martyrdom education. In D. Čaleta & P. Shemella (Eds.), *Intelligence and combating terrorism—New paradigm and future challenges*. Ljubljana, Slovenia: Institute for Corporative Security Studies.

Radicalisation Awareness Network [RAN]. (2016, November). *Child returnees from conflict zones*. Retrieved from https://ec.europa.eu/home-affairs/sites/homeaffairs/files/what-we-do/networks/radicalisation_awareness_network/ran-papers/docs/issue_paper_child_returnees_from_conflict_zones_112016_en.pdf.

Rakela, M. (2008, November 16). Child warriors around the world—manipulation without end. *Radio Free Europe Radio Liberty*. Retrieved from https://www.rferl.org/a/Child_Warriors_Around_The_World__Manipulation_Without_End/1349622.html.

Singer, P. (2006). *Children at war*. Los Angeles: University of California Press.

Solomon, J., & George, C. (1999). The place of disorganization in attachment theory. In C. George (Ed.), *Attachment disorganization* (pp. 3–31). New York, NY: Guilford Press.

Somasundaram, D. (2002). Child soldiers: understanding the context. *Journal of British Medicine, 324*, 1268.

Sri Lanka: Tamil Tigers forcibly recruit child soldiers. (2004, November 11). *Human Rights Watch*. Retrieved from https://www.hrw.org/news/2004/11/11/sri-lanka-tamil-tigers-forcibly-recruit-child-soldiers.

Syria Emergency. (n.d.). UNHCR. Retrieved from http://www.unhcr.org/syria-emergency.html.

Toner, I. J. (1994). Children of 'the troubles' in Northern Ireland: perspectives and intervention. *International Journal of Behavioral Development, 17*(4), 629–648.

van der Heide, L., & Geenen, J. (2017). *Children of the caliphate*. International Centre for Counter-Terrorism–The Hague. Retrieved from https://icct.nl/wp-content/uploads/2017/08/ICCT-vanderHeide-Geenen-Children-of-the-Caliphate-2.pdf.

Vindevogel, S., Coppens, K., De Schryver, M., Loots, G., Broekaert, E., & Derluyn, I. (2013). Beyond child soldiering: the interference of daily living conditions in former child soldiers, longer term psychosocial well-being in northern Uganda. *Global Public Health, 8*(5), 485–503.

Weiner, J. R. (2001). Child abuse: the new Islamic cult of martyrdom. *South Asia Terrorism Portal*. Retrieved from http://www.satp.org/satporgtp/publication/faultlines/volume16/article3.htm.

Wessells, M. (1997). Child soldiers. *Bulletin of the Atomic Scientists, 53*(6) [November/December].

Wheeler, S. (2015, December 14). *We can die too: recruitment and use of child soldiers in South Sudan*. Human Rights Watch. Retrieved from https://www.hrw.org/report/2015/12/14/we-can-die-too/recruitment-and-use-child-soldiers-south-sudan.

Withnall, A. (2016, January 3). Isis releases video showing execution of five 'British spies' and warning to 'imbecile' David Cameron. *Independent*. Retrieved from https://www.independent.co.uk/news/uk/home-news/isis-releases-video-showing-execution-of-five-british-spies-and-warning-to-david-cameron-a6794551.html.

World Health Organisation [WHO]. (1999). *Report of the consultation on child abuse prevention*. Retrieved from http://apps.who.int/iris/handle/10665/65900.

Zhang, Q., Loeber, R., & Stouthamer-Loeber, M. (1997). Developmental trends of delinquent attitudes and behaviors: replications and synthesis across domains, time, and samples. *Journal of Quantitative Criminology, 13*, 181–215.

CHAPTER 6

Child Trafficking: Characteristics, Complexities, and Challenges

Ella Cockbain, Kristen Olver

Department of Security and Crime Science, University College London (UCL), London, United Kingdom

1 Introduction

Child trafficking is a complex and far-reaching problem that presents numerous challenges for analysis and intervention. In this chapter, we provide a broad, inclusive, and nuanced introduction to the topic. We begin with an overview of key laws, policies, and definitions. We then sketch out some key dimensions to child trafficking, including internal (domestic) versus international trafficking and the broad array of contexts in which trafficked children can be exploited. We critique the overall evidence-base on trafficking, highlighting some important shortcomings. We briefly examine the international picture of child trafficking; since individual countries and regions vary in their child trafficking problems and responses, we then focus in on the United Kingdom as a case study. We discuss some specific forms of child trafficking commonly encountered here, considering the associated challenges and complexities: trafficking for child sexual exploitation, drug cultivation, 'county lines' criminal exploitation, and domestic servitude. We finish by drawing out overall conclusions and implications for future research into and responses to child trafficking.

2 Definitions, Laws, and Policies

Most national laws and policies on child trafficking have their main roots in two international agreements: the United Nations 'Convention of the Rights of the Child' (UNCRC) (1989) and 'Protocol to Prevent, Suppress and Punish Trafficking in Persons, especially Women and Children' (2000) (commonly known as the 'Palermo Protocol'). The UNCRC is the most comprehensive and widely ratified statement on the rights of children (Reynaert, Bouverne-de-Bie, & Vandevelde, 2009). Although it mandated that states take measures to prevent child trafficking, it provided no definition of this crime. From the 1990s onwards, efforts to combat human trafficking accelerated (Goodey, 2008; Van Der Laan, Smit, Busschers, & Aarten, 2011). The lack of consensus around definitions has long remained an impediment

Child Abuse and Neglect. https://doi.org/10.1016/B978-0-12-815344-4.00006-4

to coordination, collaboration, and coherence (Aronowitz, 2001). The adoption of Palermo Protocol was an important step to improved coordination as it set out the first internationally agreed and legally binding definition of human trafficking:

> *'Trafficking in persons' shall mean the recruitment, transportation, transfer, harbouring, or receipt of persons, by means of the threat or use of force or other forms of coercion, of abduction, of fraud, of deception, of the abuse of power, or of a position of vulnerability, or of the giving or receiving of payments or benefits to achieve the consent of a person having control over another person, for the purpose of exploitation. Exploitation shall include, at a minimum, the exploitation of the prostitution of others or other forms of sexual exploitation, forced labour or services, slavery or practices similar to slavery, servitude, or the removal of organs (UN, 2000, p. 32).*

The Palermo Protocol proved highly influential in galvanising governmental support for counter-trafficking and shaping national legislation and policies. By 2016, 158 countries had laws criminalising "most forms of trafficking in persons in line with the [Palermo] definition," up from 33 in 2003 (United Nations Office on Drugs and Crime, 2016c, p. 12). In accordance with this definition, trafficking is best conceived not as a single event but a process. It is often said to have three constituent parts: an 'act' (e.g. recruitment), a 'means' (e.g. fraud), and a 'purpose' (e.g. sexual exploitation). Children are a special case in that the act and purpose are enough for them to be considered trafficked (UNICEF, 2003). The assumption was that no manipulation is needed since children cannot give informed consent, a position later made explicit: "when a child is concerned, no possible consent should ever be considered valid" (European Parliament, 2011). While widely used, some have criticised this framing of child trafficking for embodying an idealised construct of childhood that is Anglo-Euro-centric, for being divorced from cultural norms and socio-economic realities of other communities (especially in the Global South), and/or for being premised on a misleadingly binary opposition between childhood and adulthood (Fussey & Rawlinson, 2016; O'Connell Davidson, 2005; Skilbrei & Tveit, 2008). The fact that consent is deemed irrelevant in child trafficking means barriers with overlapping but ostensibly distinct phenomena (e.g. child smuggling, child labour, and child sexual exploitation) rapidly blur in practice.

Some researchers have criticised the protocol for being too vague and flexible, limiting the extent to which it can be clearly and consistently interpreted and operationalised (Anderson & O'Connell Davidson, 2004; O'Connell Davidson, 2005, 2015). Others have argued the opposite, saying it is too narrow in its reach, capturing only a small subset of people exploited worldwide and enabling governments to boast of progress while doing relatively little to combat structural inequalities (Bales, 2012; Hathaway, 2008). In certain affluent countries—most notably the United Kingdom (UK), the United States (US), and Australia—recent years have seen a shift from focusing on 'human trafficking' towards 'modern slavery' an umbrella construct that encompasses trafficking and exploitation. An obvious benefit to the modern slavery construct is that it does away with a seemingly arbitrary distinction between exploitation that does and does not involve movement. There are also some serious drawbacks. The boundaries of modern slavery are even more amorphous than those of human trafficking. The term modern slavery is loaded, evoking inaccurate parallels with the transatlantic slave trade and chattel slavery (O'Connell Davidson, 2015). Finally, there is no international definition and legal standard for modern slavery (Doezema, 2013; O'Connell Davidson, 2015; United Nations Office on Drugs and Crime, 2016b). For these and other reasons, child trafficking is the preferred focus of this chapter.

We endeavour to discuss the issue of child trafficking as accurately as possible while acknowledging the potential for inconsistency around the Palermo Protocol definition that we use. We recognise that the territory of trafficking is not 'discursively neutral terrain' but rather shaped by politics and ideology (Doezema, 2013, p. 5). Nevertheless, the phenomenon defined and documented as human trafficking has been associated with very real social, economic, psychological, and physical harms (see, e.g. Belser, 2005; Cockbain, 2018; Cockbain, Bowers, & Dimitrova, 2018; Cockbain & Brayley-Morris, 2017; Kelly, 2002; Oram et al., 2012; Oram, Stöckl, Busza, Howard, & Zimmerman, 2012; Turner-Moss, Zimmerman, Howard, & Oram, 2014; Zimmerman et al., 2006). From a pragmatic perspective, the growing prioritisation of counter-trafficking efforts nationally and internationally means it is important to engage with child trafficking and understand its characteristics and challenges. The United Nations (2015) recently set taking "immediate and effective measures to…end modern slavery and human trafficking" as a target for its 2030 Sustainable Development Goals.

3 Different Dimensions to Child Trafficking

Child trafficking is not a homogeneous phenomenon but rather a broad and varied issue that can be divided along various dimensions, of which we discuss some key ones here. First, trafficking can involve movements between countries (known as international or transnational trafficking), within the borders of a single country (known as internal or domestic trafficking), or both. Although the Palermo Protocol was deliberately designed to accommodate both international and internal trafficking (Gallagher, 2008), many countries have focused primarily on international trafficking (Aronowitz, Theuermann, & Tyurykanova, 2010; Laczko & Gozdziak, 2005; Winterdyk & Reichel, 2010). For example, one Europe-wide study found that just seven countries had enacted laws specifically criminalising domestic trafficking (European Union Agency for Fundamental Rights, 2009). Internationally, there is considerable variation in the proportion of detected trafficking victims who are domestically trafficked: in many Latin American countries, for example, the majority of victims are local nationals (United Nations Office on Drugs and Crime, 2016b). Second, nations themselves have traditionally been described as a 'source', 'transit', or 'destination' for trafficking. This crude typology is based on rudimentary information on trafficking flows—geographical data are notoriously scarce (Cockbain & Bowers, 2018; Kangaspunta, 2003). Its explanatory roots are in the frameworks of trafficking that focus on economic, social, and political factors that push people from one country (e.g. poverty and conflict) and pull them towards another (e.g. stability and employment prospects). Nowadays, it is increasingly recognised that countries cannot be neatly categorised as source, transit, or destination as the same country may be all three (Kragten-Heerdink, Dettmeijer-Vermeulen, & Korf, 2017). Third, trafficking of children (and adults) can happen for a wide range of purposes, including sex, domestic servitude (work in private homes), adoption, child soldiering, organ harvesting, begging, child marriage, drug cultivation, agriculture, fishing, theft, benefit fraud, and numerous other ends. Responses to trafficking in the aggregate risk obscuring key distinctions, missing opportunities for more targeted intervention, and promoting an unhelpful 'uniform prescription of policy measures' (Cockbain and Bowers, in preparation; Efrat, 2016, p. 36). Being sensitive to variety between types, however, should not mean working in silos or overlooking the intersections between them.

4 The State of the Evidence-Base on Human Trafficking

Despite marked increases in prioritisation and investment for tackling human trafficking (Gozdziak & Bump, 2008), there is remarkably little empirical evidence available to inform policy and practice (Cockbain et al., 2018; Zhang, 2009). This dearth of research is likely to be at least partially a function of difficulties accessing and generating research-relevant data on this sensitive problem that plays out in the margins of society (Cockbain, Bowers, & Vernon, n.d.; Tyldum, 2010). The empirical literature has numerous and well-documented problems and pitfalls. In outlining some of the most important criticisms, we draw here on the general research on trafficking as little has been written specifically about the state of the literature on child trafficking. Although there are plenty of excellent publications that contain valuable information and insights, we advise readers to be critical in how they consume the literature.

There are pronounced skews in terms of the thematic and geographical foci of trafficking studies (Andrees & van der Linden, 2005; Kleemans, 2011; Laczko, 2005; Parmentier, 2010). For example, far more is known about victims than about offenders, about sex trafficking than other trafficking types, and about trafficking in the Global North than in the Global South. In addition, most research has been largely or exclusively qualitative in design, and robust quantitative studies are particularly scarce (Cockbain et al., 2018; Laczko & Gozdziak, 2005). There are notably few evaluations of counter-trafficking interventions (Cockbain et al., 2018; Van Der Laan et al., 2011), leaving pronounced knowledge gaps around 'what works' in tackling trafficking and—just as importantly from a realistic perspective (Johnson, Tilley, & Bowers, 2015; Pawson & Tilley, 1997)—under what circumstances and by what mechanisms.

Perhaps the most fundamental criticism of the trafficking literature is that far too many publications (including peer-reviewed ones) fall short of basic scientific standards in the design, conduct, and reporting of research (Cockbain et al., 2018; Kelly, 2005). Problems include unclear or inappropriate methods, questionable assumptions, and ill-founded inferences. A linked issue is that dispassionate analysis and neutrality are sometimes sacrificed to further particular political, economic, moral, and/or religious agendas (O'Connell Davidson, 2015). Statistical data on trafficking are particularly problematic, not least because "[m]essy definitions result in slippery statistics ridden with methodological problems" (Gozdziak & Collett, 2005, p. 107). Many groups of interest in human trafficking (e.g. victims, perpetrators, and consumers/clients) constitute 'hidden populations': groups whose size, parameters, and characteristics are unclear (Tyldum & Brunovskis, 2005). Although there are likely to be sampling biases in most official data and research datasets, without knowing how they compare with the wider population, it is not possible to establish their representativeness. At one end of the spectrum, one common source of statistical data on trafficking is official records. While these are useful in many aspects, they are widely considered to underrepresent trafficking's true scale. There are many reasons why trafficking victims may be unwilling or unable to report abuse, including: mistrust of the authorities; fear of recriminations from traffickers; physical, social, and linguistic isolation; fears of deportation; or concerns about their own involvement in illegal or stigmatised activity (Aronowitz, 2009; Cockbain, 2018; Cockbain & Brayley-Morris, 2017; Farrell & Pfeffer, 2014; Helfferich, Kavemann, & Rabe, 2011; Hopper & Hidalgo, 2006; Laczko, 2005; Raymond & Hughes, 2001). Even when incidents are identified, they may not be recognised and recorded as trafficking offences. Official data are also notoriously sensitive to fluctuations in awareness, prioritisation, resourcing, capacity, etc. (Aronowitz, 2009; Dandurand, 2017; Farrell, Owens, & McDevitt, 2014). At the other end of the spectrum, there are numerous estimates of the scale of trafficking. Some are based on explicit, rigorous, and appropriately caveated methods, such as Silverman's (2014) estimate that there were around 10,000–13,000 trafficking victims in the United Kingdom in 2013, compared with just 2744 known to the authorities. Yet, many estimates are flagrantly lacking in rigour, transparency, and validity in their generation and interpretation (Feingold, 2010; Goodey, 2008). Sweeping claims about the scale and profitability of trafficking are often ill-substantiated but are widely cited within and beyond the research literature, becoming 'fact' by merit of repetition. The widespread use of flawed and unsubstantiated statistics is not only misleading but also risks undermining the credibility of the whole field (Fedina, 2015).

5 Child Trafficking: The International Picture

Countries and regions vary greatly in the extent and specific configurations of (child) trafficking that they encounter (United Nations Office on Drugs and Crime, 2016b). To illustrate, some obvious examples are how child trafficking for camel jockeying is generally associated with destinations in the Middle East (Calandruccio, 2005) and trafficking for child soldiering with war-torn countries, particularly in Sub-Saharan Africa and the Middle East (United Nations Office on Drugs and Crime, 2016b). Since 2001, the US Department of State has produced an annual 'Trafficking in Persons Report' (e.g. U.S. Department of State, 2018). It collects data and reports on other countries' trafficking problems and counter-trafficking responses, categorising their performance against the standards of US legislation and threatening sanctions for noncompliance (O'Brien & Wilson, 2015). These reports are influential and widely cited but are better seen as a political instrument than a rigorous analytical product: they are not the 'gold standard' they purport to be (Cockbain et al., 2018). The same goes for the 'Global Slavery Index', widely publicised reports that claim to offer a 'complete picture' (The Global Slavery Index, 2018) of modern slavery and robust estimates of its prevalence, among other things. Yet, scholars have exposed numerous and significant flaws that together fundamentally undermine the index's credibility and validity, including methods that are 'highly suspect or simply not revealed' (Gallagher, 2017; Guth, Anderson, Kinnard, & Tran, 2014; O'Connell Davidson, 2015; Weitzer, 2015, p. 231). When dubious data generated by unsound methods become the basis for policies and interventions, very real damage can be done.

From an international perspective, probably the most useful source on child trafficking is the United Nations' Global Reports on Trafficking in Persons, which are at least transparent about their limitations. Drawing on a combination of open-source publications (e.g. national police reports) and dedicated questionnaires to governments, the most recent such report identified a total of 19,929 victims of trafficking in 2014 across 81 countries (United Nations Office on Drugs and Crime, 2016a). Of them, 28% were children (20% girls and 8% boys). The increased proportion of child victims (up from 13% in 2004) was one of several changes described as reflecting an evolving understanding of human trafficking and greater recognition of its diversity: a shift from the dominant focus on "women trafficked from afar into an affluent country for sexual exploitation" (United Nations Office on Drugs and Crime, 2016b, p. 6). In certain regions of the world (Sub-Saharan Africa, Central America, and the Caribbean), most identified victims were children. There were clear regional variations in the gender distribution of trafficked children and types of exploitation they experienced, meaning that "[g]lobal averages mask regional differences" (United Nations Office on Drugs and Crime, 2016b, p. 24).

It seems likely that the particular configurations of child trafficking encountered in specific countries and regions are driven by a complex and interwoven set of factors. These factors might include legal, political, socio-economic, demographic, historical, geographical, situational, institutional, and definitional considerations that together combine to influence vulnerabilities, susceptibilities, and opportunities for child trafficking and the identification of cases. Although many things are presented as 'push and pull' factors for trafficking (see, e.g. Perry & McEwing, 2013), few empirical studies have attempted to test empirically whether they are genuine determinants of trafficking, and the few that have (e.g. Cho, 2015; Jac-Kucharski, 2012) are limited by the shortcomings of national datasets, their limited comparability, and the inherent diversity in trafficking since different trafficking types may have different drivers.

6 A National Overview of Child Trafficking: The UK as a Case Study

In this section, we focus in on the UK and use it as a national case study of child trafficking. The UK is an affluent country and an established destination for international trafficking. Recent years have also seen growing recognition that trafficking can happen within the borders of the UK too, for example, through the internal trafficking of vulnerable adults for labour exploitation (Cockbain & Brayley-Morris, 2017) or of children for sexual exploitation (Brayley & Cockbain, 2014; Cockbain, 2018). There has been a clear diversification in the types of trafficking identified: in 2006/2007, the UK authorities reported only victims of sex trafficking (United Nations Office on Drugs and Crime, 2009), whereas in 2012, they found for the first time more victims of labour trafficking than of sex trafficking (Cockbain & Bowers, in preparation). Although there may be some genuine changes in the actual trafficking happening, the influence on official data of shifts in awareness, legislation, understanding, funding, and prioritisation should not be underestimated.

Since its introduction in 2009, the single largest source of information on human trafficking in the UK is the National Referral Mechanism (NRM). The NRM covers all four of the United Kingdom's constituent nations and acts as a centralised system for identifying, processing, and supporting victims of trafficking and informing the national intelligence picture on this crime (National Crime Agency, n.d.). With the introduction of the Modern Slavery Act 2015, the system was expanded to cover suspected victims of exploitation (slavery, servitude, and forced or compulsory labour) that can but need not involve trafficking. Various accredited authorities can make referrals into the system: Adults must consent to referral, but children need not. Decision-makers from law enforcement or the immigration authorities (depending on a suspected victim's nationality/immigration status) process each referral on a case-by-case basis, considering the available evidence and gathering further information to decide whether someone should be accorded victim status (National Crime Agency, 2018). The NRM has been criticised for failing to meet victims' support needs and the conflict of interest inherent in the immigration authorities' involvement in decision-making (Harvey, Hornsby, & Sattar, 2015; HMICFRS, 2017; Home Office, 2014b; Stepnitz, 2012; The Anti-Trafficking Monitoring Group, 2010, 2012; The Slavery Working Group, 2013). Following a major review (Home Office, 2014b), the system is currently undergoing reform.

To date, child victims of trafficking identified through this centralised system have been exploited in contexts including commercial and noncommercial sex, domestic servitude, begging, cannabis cultivation, benefit fraud, and various other forms of labour, including at least one case of organ trafficking (Cockbain & Bowers, in preparation). The classification of 'labour trafficking' used in the NRM is notably broad, covering exploitation in various licit and illicit contexts, including benefit fraud, forced marriage, and shoplifting as well as classics like agriculture and factory work (Cockbain & Bowers, 2018).

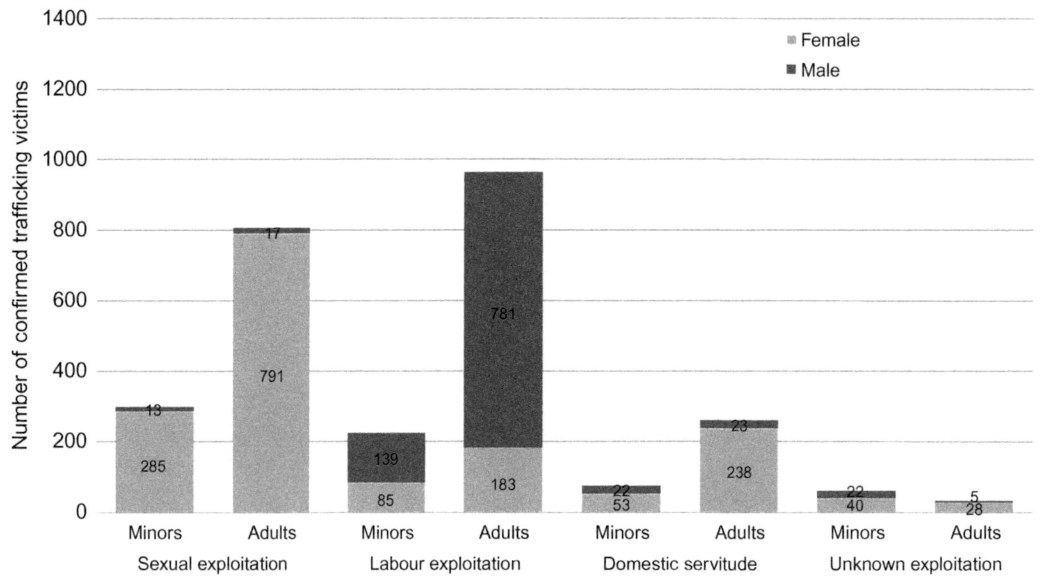

Fig. 1

Confirmed trafficking victims identified in the United Kingdom via the National Referral Mechanism April 2009–October 2014, excluding two organ trafficking cases. *Based on data used for Cockbain, E., & Bowers, K. (in preparation). What predicts the purpose for which people are trafficked? A nationwide comparison of human trafficking for sexual exploitation, domestic servitude and labour.*

Fig. 1 shows the breakdown of the 2727 confirmed trafficking victims identified by the UK authorities between April 2009 and October 2014,[1] split by age group, gender,[2] and exploitation type (Cockbain & Bowers, in preparation). At 24% ($n=660$), under 18-year-olds comprised a sizeable minority of the overall set of victims. Child victims were most commonly trafficked for sex (45%), followed by labour (34%) and then domestic servitude (11%). In contrast, adults were most commonly trafficked for labour (47%), then sex (39%), and then domestic servitude (13%). Clear gender distinctions are evident in the data: for example, girls made up the vast majority of child sex trafficking victims. Controlling for possible interactions between variables, certain characteristics of victims and their trafficking experiences (including gender, age, and region of origin) have been shown in the UK to be significant predictors of the purpose for which they are trafficked (Cockbain & Bowers, in preparation).

1 Numerous other suspected victims were referred into the system over the study period (from 1 April 2009 to 7 October 2014), but these figures are based only on those who had received positive conclusive ground decisions at the point of the data extraction, i.e. who had been assessed on the balance of probabilities to have been more likely to have been trafficked than not.

2 While we recognise that gender is broader than the male/female binary, all cases in our data fell into one of these two categories.

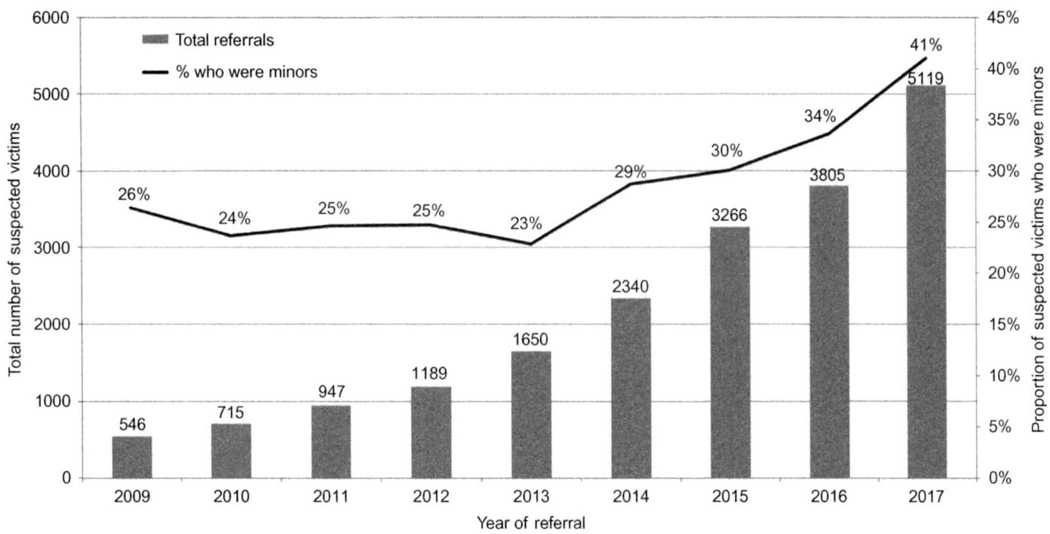

Fig. 2

Referrals into the United Kingdom's National Referral Mechanism 2009–17: total numbers of suspected victims and proportion that were minors. *Based on data from Cockbain, E., & Bowers, K. (in preparation). What predicts the purpose for which people are trafficked? A nationwide comparison of human trafficking for sexual exploitation, domestic servitude and labour; National Crime Agency. (2015). National referral mechanism statistics—End of year summary 2014. London: National Crime Agency; National Crime Agency. (2016). National referral mechanism statistics—End of year summary 2015. London: N. C Agency; National Crime Agency. (2017b). National referral mechanism statistics—End of year summary 2016. London: N. C. Agency; National Crime Agency. (2018). Modern slavery and human trafficking: National referral mechanism statistics annual report 2017. London: National Crime Agency.*

There has been a steady year-on-year increase in the number of referrals into the NRM, as shown in Fig. 2, and a particular growth in recent years. This development is almost certainly due to the introduction of the Modern Slavery Act 2015 and Modern Slavery Strategy (Home Office, 2014a), associated increases in publicity, awareness, prioritisation and funding for tackling this crime, and expansion of the NRM system also to cover all modern slavery. The increasing proportion of referrals involving children appears driven at least partially by the greater attention paid in recent years to child sexual exploitation and drug-related exploitation. Importantly, not all of these referrals will have resulted or will eventually result in the decision that the person in question was indeed a victim of trafficking/exploitation. While the outcome rates may have since changed, in the first 5 years of the system, approximately 45% of those referred were conclusively assessed to have been trafficking[3] (Cockbain & Bowers, in preparation). Disaggregated information on confirmed victims is not publically available for more recent years. The configurations may well have changed since those shown

[3] Proportion calculated based on decisions as of 7 October 2014 for referrals received into the system from 2009 to 2013 inclusive.

in Fig. 1, especially since by 2017, labour exploitation had become the prime reason (49% of cases) for which children were referred as suspected victims of modern slavery (data specifically for trafficking are no longer available) (National Crime Agency, 2018). The next most common category was sexual exploitation (27%), followed by unknown exploitation type (19%). There were comparatively few cases of suspected domestic servitude (6%).

The NRM data do not give a full picture of child trafficking in the UK: many cases will go undetected and unreported or might be identified but not recognised as involving trafficking. Problems with the availability and comparability of information on child trafficking (e.g. inaccessible or fragmented data or double counting across sources) make it difficult to build a clear and coherent picture of even the known parts of the problem. According to the National Society for the Prevention of Cruelty to Children (NSPCC, 2017, p. 70), which has run the national Child Trafficking Advice Centre since 2017, "currently available child protection data does not record information on whether or not a child has been trafficked." A recent inspection was highly critical of law enforcement responses to 'modern slavery', reporting that police lacked consistent training on human trafficking, confidence in identifying potential victims, and a good understanding of the indicators of human trafficking (HMICFRS, 2017). Since then, there has been a multimillion pound investment in improving police responses to modern slavery and legislative changes to how the crime is recorded. Recorded crime data on modern slavery are presented in the aggregate only, meaning it is unclear how many of the 3337 offences in England and Wales in the past year (Office for National Statistics, 2018) specifically involved child trafficking.

Unseen (a key nongovernmental organisation) has run a free round-the-clock 'Modern Slavery Helpline' since October 2016. In 2017, children represented a noticeably small proportion (just 6%, $n = 300$) of the 4886 potential victims of trafficking/exploitation indicated in calls or online contacts (Unseen UK, 2018)—especially when considering that 41% of NRM referrals that year were for children. Perhaps, children genuinely comprise a smaller proportion of the wider 'modern slavery' problem than previously thought. Equally, the patterns might be a result of pronounced publicity around certain issues involving adults (carwashes are a good example) or children/people concerned about children being less likely to contact the helpline and turning instead to other agencies (e.g. police, NSPCC, and children's services). We now move on to a detailed discussion of certain types of child trafficking encountered in the UK, selected to illustrate a range of complexities and challenges.

6.1 International Trafficking for Cannabis Cultivation

The trafficking of children into the UK to work in so-called cannabis factories/cannabis farms has attracted considerable concern since the mid-2000s (see, e.g. Beddoe, 2007;

Child Exploitation and Online Protection Centre, 2009, 2010, 2011; Silverstone & Savage, 2010). More so than most other forms of international child trafficking, this issue has been particularly associated with victims and offenders of a single nationality: Vietnamese. The growing prominence of this issue has been attributed to Vietnamese organised crime groups expanding into the cannabis cultivation industry in the UK (and elsewhere in the world) after first honing the necessary skills and technologies in Canada (Schoenmakers, Bremmers, & Kleemans, 2013; Silverstone & Savage, 2010). Traffickers and victims sharing a common ethnic background and language are not unique to this phenomenon but rather fairly typical of human trafficking (United Nations Office on Drugs and Crime, 2016b).

From the (very limited) available evidence, it seems that children coming to the UK to work in cannabis factories enter illegally but willingly in search of better opportunities (Child Exploitation and Online Protection Centre, 2011; Silverstone & Savage, 2010; The Anti-Trafficking Monitoring Group, 2010). Since consent is irrelevant in child trafficking, even those who are not deceived about the work in store may still be considered trafficked. In this sense, the dichotomy (Silverstone and Savage (2010, p. 26)) present between children who are "forcefully trafficked and those who migrate 'voluntarily'" is a false one. Debt bondage is central to trafficking for cannabis cultivation, with children coerced, compelled, or simply expected to repay the high costs of travel to the UK (Beddoe, 2007; Child Exploitation and Online Protection Centre, 2011; The Anti-Trafficking Monitoring Group, 2010). The dynamics of these cases highlight the complex interplay between trafficking, smuggling, and economic migration.

So-called gardeners are said to face serious occupational health hazards, including electrocution risks linked to dangerous wiring, burns from industrial lamps, fumes from the plants, and exposure to toxic fertilisers (see, e.g. Beddoe, 2007; The Guardian, 2018). Victims may be "isolated, locked in the property, and forced to sleep on the floor and in cupboards" (Anti-Slavery International, 2014, p. 15). Some children identified and rescued during police raids on cannabis factories subsequently went missing from care (Beddoe, 2007; ECPAT UK & Missing People, 2016). This issue is part of a broader problem of trafficked children going missing from residential care (ECPAT UK & Missing People, 2016), which highlights the dangers of focusing on 'rescue' without paying equivalent attention to safeguarding. Nongovernmental organisations have repeatedly criticised the authorities for prosecuting Vietnamese children for drug offences rather than recognising them as trafficking victims (Anti-Slavery International, 2014; Beddoe, 2007; The Anti Trafficking Monitoring Group, 2010, 2013). The criminalisation of trafficking victims violates the nonpunishment principle of trafficking, namely, "that people who commit offences in the course, or as a consequence, of being trafficked should not be held criminally accountable" (Piotrowicz & Sorrentino, 2016, p. 669).

6.2 Internal Trafficking for Child Sexual Exploitation

Although both local and foreign nationals can be internally trafficked, the movement of British children within the UK for the purposes of sexual exploitation has emerged as a particular concern in recent years (Brayley & Cockbain, 2014; Cockbain, 2018). A spate of high profile cases sparked claims that an epidemic of 'on-street grooming' involving 'Asian sex gangs' was sweeping the UK (Cockbain, 2013). Despite the obvious news appeal of such simplistic and sensationalist narratives, the scale of the problem remains largely unknown, and the racial dynamics have almost certainly been overstated (Cockbain, 2013, 2018). Although the focus thus far has been on female victims, the risk to boys and young men may be understated: a recent study into child sexual exploitation in the UK (a broad and varied category of which child sex trafficking is one subset) found that nearly a third of the 9042 affected children were male (Cockbain, Ashby, & Brayley, 2015).

A key factor distinguishing internal sex trafficking of British minors from many other forms of child trafficking—and indeed from most organised crime more generally—is that it is not necessarily profit-driven. Cockbain's (2018) research into six of the earliest and largest such investigations to date (including the now infamous Rochdale case) identified that only a minority of victims were commercially exploited. Another key distinction from standard international trafficking was that few victims were housed by offenders: instead, many described being trapped in a vicious cycle of being picked up, moved, sexually abused, and released. As one victim explained, "I could have walked away, but I never…It was like a lifestyle. Like get up, go out, and then do whatever—like you'd get up and go to work" (Cockbain, 2018, p. 93). The grooming process that facilitated abuse and reabuse was dynamic, varied, and multidirectional; there was evidence not only of offenders grooming victims but also of (some) offenders grooming other offenders, victims grooming other victims, and what was effectively 'self-grooming' on both their parts. Much of the abuse took place in social settings, and the vast majority of offenders committed offences collaboratively, unusual given that sexual offences in general have notoriously low co-offending rates (Andresen & Felson, 2012; Carrington, 2009; Van Mastrigt & Farrington, 2009). Although human trafficking and child sexual exploitation are both often characterised as involving highly organised and sophisticated criminal enterprises (e.g. Barnardo's, 2001, 2012; U.S. Department of State, 2018), close examination showed the offender networks to be structurally unsophisticated, disorganised, and often opportunistic.

The casual, everyday, and routinised nature of the abuse and offenders' unremarkable backgrounds and criminal histories should not detract from the severity of this form of trafficking; together, the 55 offenders across the six investigations subjected their 43 core victims to over 400 distinct offences, mostly serious and sexual in nature. Indicative of the sprawling nature of the crime, additional suspected victims and offenders mentioned in the investigative case files outnumbered the core victims and offenders by 3:1 and 4:1 respectively. Investigators and prosecutors interviewed for the research described the cases as unusually complex and challenging. Many of the victims were very vulnerable (with histories including youth offending, prior abuse, and social service involvement), and professionals were concerned they would not be seen as credible witnesses. Yet, eventual conviction rates across the six cases were in line with or above comparable national averages for sexual offences, showing that successful enforcement *is* possible.

Cockbain (2018, p. 164) concluded that complexity and social connectivity were among the defining characteristics of this crime and that it seemed to be socially contagious: "the structures, processes, and dynamics of offender and victim networks appear to promote, provoke, facilitate, spread and sustain trafficking activity and to impede and complicate criminal justice responses". While unusual for the trafficking field, the study clearly demonstrates how a bottom-up, multimethod, and case-study-based approach to researching child trafficking can help unravel the complexities of specific issues, debunk myths and stereotypes, and inform more nuanced and targeted interventions.

6.3 Internal Trafficking for 'County Lines' Activity

'County lines' is a popular but peculiarly British term to describe the exploitation of young and/or vulnerable persons, who are tricked, coerced, forced, or otherwise manipulated to transport, store, and sell drugs (especially heroine or crack cocaine) from 'urban hubs to provincial towns and cities'[4] (Coomber & Moyle, 2017, p. 2; HM Government, 2018; National Crime Agency, 2017a). According to a recent law enforcement assessment, victims are predominantly 15–17-year-old boys groomed to sell drugs on behalf of gangs and vulnerable adults (often drug addicts) forced or coerced into providing their homes to store drugs (a practice known as 'cuckooing') (NCA, 2017). In 2018, the first convictions under trafficking legislation in relation to county lines activity were secured: the victim in question was a teenage girl (The Independent, 2018).

County-lines-related referrals are a key driver behind recent increases in referrals of children into the NRM (National Crime Agency, 2018). This development suggests that children previously criminalised as gang-involved youth offenders are increasingly being treated as victims of (internal) trafficking and exploitation. This reframing of drug-related exploitation echoes the shift to recognising sexually exploited children as such rather than dismissing them as 'streetwise' or 'promiscuous' or consenting 'child prostitutes' (Barrett & Melrose, 2003; Chase & Statham, 2005). Unsurprisingly given its relative novelty (conceptually if not actually), there is virtually no academic research on trafficking specifically related to county lines.

[4] British subregional districts are known as 'counties'.

At a recent count, 88% of police forces reported local evidence of county lines activity, and there was an estimated minimum of 720 lines UK-wide (39% stemming from London)—although the exact parameters of 'a line' were unclear.[5] Highlighting how specific forms of child trafficking can intersect with other vulnerabilities and risky and/or criminal behaviour, victims of county-lines-related exploitation may also go missing repeatedly, have prior histories of abuse or neglect, and be involved in weapon crimes, serious violence, and gang-related sexual exploitation (Crown Prosecution Service, 2017; HM Government, 2018; National Crime Agency, 2017a; The Children's Society, Victim Support, and The National Police Chief's Council, 2018). Victims may also recruit, groom, or exploit others, either while at the bottom of the ladder or as they ascend the gang hierarchy. Previously documented for other forms of child trafficking and exploitation (Cockbain, 2018; Firmin, 2013),[6] this overlap between victim and offender roles presents serious ethical and logistical challenges for safeguarding, crime prevention, and criminal justice.

Another challenge common to other forms of child trafficking is that children involved in county-lines-related exploitation may neither self-identify as victims nor want to engage with services (The Children's Society et al., 2018). Although involvement in county lines carries obvious social, economic, and health risks, it can also offer marginalised young people both perceived and genuine benefits (e.g. unparalleled earning potential). In many ways, county-lines-related trafficking is the perfect storm of tensions around capacity, consent, constrained choice, and criminal responsibility, the age for which is just 10 years in England, Wales, and Northern Ireland and only 8 in Scotland. To encourage victims of trafficking/exploitation to "come forward and give evidence without the fear of being convicted" (House of Commons, 2014, p. no page), the Modern Slavery Act 2015 introduced a new statutory defence (Section 45) for those who commit certain offences under compulsion (if 18 years or over at the time) or as a 'direct result' of being trafficked (if under 18 years at the time)[7] (Crown Prosecution Service, 2018). New research shows some professionals see the use (and sometimes the misuse) of this defence as a key reason why young people involved in this form of criminal exploitation are increasingly referred to the authorities as potential victims of child trafficking (Olver, 2018).

---

[5] The 'line' in county lines is used variously and often interchangeably to refer to the phone number used to sell the drugs and the supply route. The National Crime Agency explains the general activity it considers to be county lines (as distinct from traditional drug supply lines) but is not specific about whether these 720 lines refer to phone lines or supply routes (one of which might feasibly involve multiple phone lines).

[6] The issue of victim-offender hybrids has also been documented in the context of trafficking of adults for labour exploitation (Cockbain & Brayley-Morris, 2017) and sexual exploitation (Mancuso, 2014; Monzini, 2005).

[7] The defence also holds for victims of 'slavery'. While it applies to drug trafficking and money laundering offences, the defence does not apply to certain offences, including serious, violent, and sexual offences. The burden of proof is reversed: 'it is for the defendant to prove on the balance of probabilities'. The distinction between requirements for adults and children likely links back to the position that children cannot consent to their own trafficking.

6.4 International Trafficking for Domestic Servitude

The trafficking of children into the UK for domestic servitude is a particularly hidden, underresearched, and poorly understood form of child trafficking. Responding to child trafficking is challenging in general, but this issue presents some very specific difficulties. By nature, domestic servitude occurs behind closed doors in private household settings, although victims may leave the home for errands etc., which could open up avenues for identification, intervention, and escape. Although children trafficked for domestic servitude have come from many different places, it is an issue particularly associated with victims from countries in Africa (especially Nigeria) and Asia (Beddoe, 2007; Bokhari, 2008; Child Exploitation and Online Protection Centre, 2010; National Crime Agency, 2018). Without the support of local diaspora communities in which the trafficking victims are hidden, it is said to be difficult to respond (Bokhari, 2008). Cultural and attitudinal differences can create additional barriers to intervention: sending a child with otherwise limited prospects away to do domestic work "is not always seen as an abuse of human rights but rather an opportunity for a better future abroad" (Bokhari, 2008, p. 205; see also Anti-Slavery International, 2005; Blagbrough, 2008). Private fostering arrangements reportedly facilitate this form of child trafficking, with victims entering the UK with adults purporting to be their guardians or carers (Beddoe, 2007; Pearce, Hynes, & Bovarnick, 2009). Insufficient oversight of private fostering can leave children vulnerable to this and other forms of abuse (The Children's Society, 2009).

Further complicating the situation, members of the diplomatic community have been implicated in trafficking (of both adults and children) for domestic servitude (Organisation for Security and Co-operation in Europe, 2014), including in the UK (BBC, 2016). Quite aside from the obvious power imbalance between victims and their diplomatic agent 'employers', diplomatic immunities and privileges can severely limit the recourse and assistance available (Organisation for Security and Co-operation in Europe, 2014). For example, the fact that diplomatic cars and residences are 'inviolable and cannot be entered and searched' poses serious barriers for identifying and supporting victims (Organisation for Security and Co-operation in Europe, 2014, p. 14).

Children trafficked for domestic servitude may have to work very long hours under poor conditions and may be particularly vulnerable to other forms of verbal, physical, and sexual abuse and neglect (Bokhari, 2008; Dowling, Moreton, & Wright, 2007; Pearce, 2011). There are also documented links between trafficking for domestic servitude and for benefit fraud (Beddoe, 2007; The Children's Society, 2009). As well as potentially heightening victims' vulnerabilities and support needs, such intersections of issues demonstrate once again how the boundaries between trafficking types can blur in practice. Overall, children trafficked for domestic servitude are thought to be extremely isolated socially, physically, and economically. Writing from an international perspective on child domestic labour more generally, Blagbrough (2008, p. 186) argues that victims' extreme dependency on their exploiters renders them more likely to accept violence 'as an occupational hazard' and less likely to report abuses.

Among the control mechanisms documented in cases of child trafficking to the UK for domestic servitude are the use of threats against victims and their families, confiscation of identity documents, fear and threats of deportation and other recriminations, violence, and intimidation (Child Exploitation and Online Protection Centre, 2010; The Children's Society, 2009). These manipulations are not specific to this particular issue but rather commonly associated with trafficking in adults and children in general (see e.g. Aronowitz, 2009; International Labour Office, 2009). An additional control mechanism that may be relevant as it is linked specifically to Nigerian trafficking victims—a key nationality in this context—is the use of 'juju'. Accordingly, victims may be ceremonially bound to their traffickers, and their fears of 'spiritual retribution' can deter subsequent escape and disclosure (Dunkerley, 2018, p. 83; van der Watt & Kruger, 2017).

7 Conclusions and Implications

In this chapter, we demonstrated that child trafficking is a far-reaching, complex, and challenging phenomenon that does not lend itself readily to easy quantification, simple explanation, and one-size-fits-all interventions. Recognising the difficulties and tensions inherent in conceptualising, identifying, and responding to child trafficking is a vital first step towards designing and delivering research and responses that are better grounded in the messy realities of this serious social problem. Using the UK as a case study, we identified numerous, intersecting, and sometimes competing challenges and considerations for counter-trafficking efforts, including: unresolved tensions between child protection, criminal justice, and immigration control; the impact of external factors on the evolving child trafficking landscape; thorny issues around children's agency, criminal responsibility, and consent; victims' complex needs and vulnerabilities; and the impacts of grooming and other control mechanisms. Beyond all that, we barely scratched the surface on the underlying systems of disadvantage that may make children susceptible to trafficking in the first place.

We highlighted the considerable weaknesses of the trafficking research literature. Robust, transparent, and rigorous research is much needed if we are to build a strong foundation for policy and practice in this field. It is time to move away from simplistic appeal of emotive rhetoric and sweeping claims, challenge received wisdom, and delve further into the empirical realities of child trafficking. As well as research on child trafficking in its various forms, evaluations of counter-trafficking interventions are needed to tease out what constitutes good practice, how it delivers the intended benefits, and under what circumstances it is effective (or not). Otherwise, there is a danger that resources will be wasted on counter-measures that are ineffective or even actively detrimental.

While child trafficking will likely never be fully eradicated, there is clearly much more that could be done to intervene in systems and situations that further this form of abuse and impede effective responses. Formulating good laws, policy, and strategy is important but so too is closing the implementation gap: doing so requires real commitment and adequate resources. As this chapter has shown, child trafficking is a far broader phenomenon than a crime problem alone, and it is misguided to think that criminal justice agencies can tackle it alone. Although multi-agency working is a bit of a buzzword, there are real gains to be had through better communication, collaboration, and contributions involving diverse groups, including health, social care, education, not-for-profits, private sector companies, and the general publics. Trafficking convictions are all too often implicitly treated as the ultimate metric of success in counter-trafficking. Yet, if the overall goal is harm reduction—and surely it should be—then it is vital to increase the focus on preventing child trafficking in the first place, improving early intervention and mitigating its impacts.

Acknowledgements

This chapter was written under Dr Ella Cockbain's 'Future Research Leaders' fellowship, funded by the Economic and Social Research Council of the United Kingdom (grant reference: ES/K008463/1). A big thank you goes to the National Crime Agency for their invaluable facilitation and support of the research conducted under that fellowship, some of which is drawn on in this chapter.

References

Anderson, B., & O'Connell Davidson, J. (2004). *Trafficking—A demand led problem? Part 1: Review of evidence and debates*. Stockholm: S. t. C. Sweden.

Andrees, B., & van der Linden, M. N. J. (2005). Designing trafficking research from a labour market perspective: the ILO experience1. *International Migration*, *43*(1–2), 55–73.

Andresen, M. A., & Felson, M. (2012). Co-offending and the diversification of crime types. *International Journal of Offender Therapy and Comparative Criminology*, *56*(5), 811–829.

Anti-Slavery International. (2005). *Child domestic workers: A handbook on good practice in programme interventions*. London: A.-S. International.

Anti-Slavery International. (2014). *Trafficking for forced criminal activities and begging in Europe: Exploratory study and good practice examples*. London: Anti-Slavery International.

Aronowitz, A. A. (2001). Smuggling and trafficking in human beings: the phenomenon, the markets that drive it and the organisations that promote it. *European Journal on Criminal Policy and Research*, *9*(2), 163–195.

Aronowitz, A. A. (2009). *Human trafficking, human misery: The global trade in human beings*. Plymouth: The Scarecrow Press.

Aronowitz, A. A., Theuermann, G., & Tyurykanova, E. (2010). *Analysing the business model of trafficking in human beings to better prevent the crime*. Vienna: Organization for Security and Co-operation in Europe.

Bales, K. (2012). *Disposable people: New slavery in the global economy, updated with a new preface*. University of California Press.

Barnardo's. (2001). *No son of mine! Children abused through prostitution*. Barkingside: Barnardo's.

Barnardo's. (2012). *Reducing the risk, cutting the cost: An assessment of the potential savings on Barnardo's interventions for young people who have been sexually exploited*. Barkingside: Barnardo's.

Barrett, D., & Melrose, M. (2003). Courting controversy—Children sexually abused through prostitution—Are they everybody's distant relatives but nobody's children? *Child and Family Law Quarterly*, *15*(4), 371–382.

BBC. (2016). *Foreign embassy staff accused of human trafficking and child sex offences*. BBC. (21/07/16). Retrieved from https://www.bbc.co.uk/news/uk-politics-36856918.

Beddoe, C. (2007). *Missing out: A study of child trafficking in the north-west, north-east and west midlands*. London: E. UK.

Belser, P. (2005). *Forced labour and human trafficking: Estimating the profits*. Geneva: International Labour Organization.

Blagbrough, J. (2008). Child domestic labour: A modern form of slavery. *Children & Society*, *22*(3), 179–190.

Bokhari, F. (2008). Falling through the gaps: safeguarding children trafficked into the UK. *Children & Society*, *22*(3), 201–211.

Brayley, H., & Cockbain, E. (2014). British children can be trafficked too: towards an inclusive definition of internal child sex trafficking. *Child Abuse Review*, *23*(3), 171–184. https://doi.org/10.1002/car.2307.

Calandruccio, G. (2005). A review of recent research on human trafficking in the middle east1. *International Migration*, *43*(1–2), 267–299.

Carrington, P. J. (2009). Co-offending and the development of the delinquent career. *Criminology*, *47*(4), 1295–1329.

Chase, E., & Statham, J. (2005). Commercial and sexual exploitation of children and young people in the UK—A review. *Child Abuse Review*, *14*(1), 4–25. https://doi.org/10.1002/car.881.

Child Exploitation and Online Protection Centre. (2009). *Strategic threat assessment: Child trafficking in the UK*. London: Child Exploitation and Online Protection Centre.

Child Exploitation and Online Protection Centre. (2010). *Strategic threat assessment: Child trafficking in the UK*. London: Child Exploitation and Online Protection Centre.

Child Exploitation and Online Protection Centre. (2011). *The trafficking of women and children from Vietnam*. Child Exploitation and Online Protection Centre: London.

Cho, S.-Y. (2015). Modelling for determinants of human trafficking (July 15, 2015). *Social Inclusion 3 (Special Issue "Perspectives on human trafficking and modern forms of slavery"): 2-21, 2015*. Retrieved from SSRN: https://ssrn.com/abstract=2117838 or http://dx.doi.org/10.2139/ssrn.2117838.

Cockbain, E. (2013). Grooming and the 'Asian sex gang predator': the construction of a racial crime threat. *Race & Class*, *54*(4), 22–32. https://doi.org/10.1177/0306396813475983.

Cockbain, E. (2018). *Offender and victim networks in human trafficking*. Abingdon: Routledge.

Cockbain, E., Ashby, M., & Brayley, H. (2015). Immaterial boys? A large-scale exploration of gender-based differences in child sexual exploitation service users. *Sexual Abuse: A Journal of Research and Treatment*, *29*(7), 658–684.

Cockbain, E., & Bowers, K. (2018). In *Applying data science techniques to human trafficking research. Paper presented at the United Nations on Drugs and Crime (UNODC) 4th international conference on governance, crime and justice statistics, Lima, Peru*. [04/06/18].

Cockbain, E., & Bowers, K. (in preparation). What predicts the purpose for which people are trafficked? A nationwide comparison of human trafficking for sexual exploitation, domestic servitude and labour.

Cockbain, E., Bowers, K., & Dimitrova, G. (2018). Human trafficking for labour exploitation: the results of a two-phase systematic review mapping the European evidence base and synthesising key scientific research evidence. *Journal of Experimental Criminology*, *14*(3), 319–360.

Cockbain, E., Bowers, K., & Vernon, L. (n.d.). Using law enforcement data in trafficking research. In J. Winterdyk & J. Jones (Eds.), The Palgrave international handbook of human trafficking. Basingstoke: Palgrave Macmillan.

Cockbain, E., & Brayley-Morris, H. (2017). Human trafficking and labour exploitation in the casual construction industry: an analysis of three major investigations in the United Kingdom involving Irish traveller offending groups. *Policing: A Journal of Policy and Practice*, *12*(2), 129–149.

Coomber, R., & Moyle, L. (2017). The changing shape of street-level heroin and crack supply in England: commuting, holidaying and cuckooing drug dealers across 'County lines'. *The British Journal of Criminology*.

Crown Prosecution Service. (2017). *'County lines': Typology*. London: C. P. Service.

Crown Prosecution Service. (2018). *Legal guidance on 'human trafficking, smuggling and slavery' (28/06/2018: Suspects who might be victims of trafficking or slavery)*. London: C. P. Service.

Dandurand, Y. (2017). Human trafficking and police governance. *Police Practice and Research, 18*(3), 322–336.

Doezema, J. (2013). *Sex slaves and discourse masters: The construction of trafficking*. London: Zed Books Ltd.

Dowling, S., Moreton, K., & Wright, L. (2007). *Trafficking for the purposes of labour exploitation: A literature review*. London: The Home Office.

Dunkerley, A. W. (2018). Exploring the use of juju in Nigerian human trafficking networks: considerations for criminal investigators. *Police Practice and Research, 19*(1), 83–100.

ECPAT UK & Missing People. (2016). *Heading back to harm: A study on trafficked and unaccompanied children going missing from care in the UK*. London: E. UK.

Efrat, A. (2016). Global efforts against human trafficking: the misguided conflation of sex, labor, and organ trafficking. *International Studies Perspectives, 17*(1), 34–54.

European Parliament. (2011). *Directive 2011/36/EU of the European Parliament and of the council on preventing and combatting trafficking in human beings and protecting its victims.* . Strasbourg.

European Union Agency for Fundamental Rights. (2009). *Child trafficking in the European Union: Challenges, perspectives and good practices*. Luxembourg: European Union Agency for Fundamental Rights.

Farrell, A., Owens, C., & McDevitt, J. (2014). New laws but few cases: understanding the challenges to the investigation and prosecution of human trafficking cases. *Crime, Law and Social Change, 61*(2), 139–168.

Farrell, A., & Pfeffer, R. (2014). Policing human trafficking: cultural blinders and organizational barriers. *The Annals of the American Academy of Political and Social Science, 653*(1), 46–64.

Fedina, L. (2015). Use and misuse of research in books on sex trafficking: implications for interdisciplinary researchers, practitioners, and advocates. *Trauma, Violence & Abuse, 16*(2), 188–198.

Feingold, D. (2010). Trafficking in numbers: the social construction of human trafficking data. In P. Andreas & K. Greenhill (Eds.), *Sex, drugs and body counts: The politics of numbers in global crime and conflict* (pp. 46–74). New York: Cornell University Press.

Firmin, C. (2013). Busting the 'gang-rape' myth: girls' victimisation and agency in gang-associated sexual violence. In M. A. Horvath & J. Woodhams (Eds.), *Handbook on the study of multiple perpetrator rape* (pp. 97–115). Abingdon: Routledge.

Fussey, P., & Rawlinson, P. (2016). *Child trafficking in the EU: Policing and protecting Europe's most vulnerable*. Abingdon: Routledge.

Gallagher, A. T. (2008). Human rights and human trafficking: quagmire or firm ground—a response to James Hathaway. *Virginia Journal of International Law, 49*, 789.

Gallagher, A. T. (2017). What's wrong with the global slavery index? *Anti-Trafficking Review, 8*.

Goodey, J. (2008). Human trafficking sketchy data and policy responses. *Criminology and Criminal Justice, 8*(4), 421–442.

Gozdziak, E., & Bump, M. (2008). *Data and research on human trafficking: Bibliography of research-based literature*. Washington, DC: Georgetown University.

Gozdziak, E., & Collett, E. (2005). Research on human trafficking in North America: a review of literature. *International Migration, 43*(1/2), 99–128.

Guth, A., Anderson, R., Kinnard, K., & Tran, H. (2014). Proper methodology and methods of collecting and analyzing slavery data: An examination of the global slavery index. *Social Inclusion, 2*(4), 14–22.

Harvey, J. H., Hornsby, R. A., & Sattar, Z. (2015). Disjointed service: an English case study of multi-agency provision in tackling child trafficking. *British Journal of Criminology, 55*(3), 494–513. https://doi.org/10.1093/bjc/azu115.

Hathaway, J. C. (2008). The human rights quagmire of human trafficking. *Virginia Journal of International Law, 49*, 1.

Helfferich, C., Kavemann, B., & Rabe, H. (2011). Determinants of the willingness to make a statement of victims of human trafficking for the purpose of sexual exploitation in the triangle offender–police–victim. *Trends in Organized Crime, 14*(2–3), 125.

HM Government. (2018). *Serious violence strategy*. London: H. Government.

HMICFRS. (2017). *Stolen freedom: The policing response to modern slavery and human trafficking*. London: HMICFRS.

Home Office. (2014a). *Modern slavery strategy*. London: T. S. Office.

Home Office. (2014b). *Review of the national referral mechanism for victims of human trafficking*. London: H. Office.

Hopper, E., & Hidalgo, J. (2006). Invisible chains: psychological coercion of human trafficking victims. *Intercultural Human Rights Law Review*, *1*, 185.

House of Commons. (2014). Modern slavery bill: explanatory notes. In *These notes refer to the modern slavery bill as introduced in the house of commons on 10 June 2014 [bill 8]*. London: H. o. Commons.

International Labour Office. (2009). *Operational indicators of trafficking in human beings*. Geneva: International Labour Office.

Jac-Kucharski, A. (2012). The determinants of human trafficking: a US case study. *International Migration*, *50*(6), 150–165.

Johnson, S. D., Tilley, N., & Bowers, K. J. (2015). Introducing EMMIE: an evidence rating scale to encourage mixed-method crime prevention synthesis reviews. *Journal of Experimental Criminology*, *11*(3), 459–473. https://doi.org/10.1007/s11292-015-9238-7.

Kangaspunta, K. (2003). Mapping the inhuman trade: Preliminary findings of the human trafficking database. *Forum on Crime and Society*, *3*(1 and 2), 81–101.

Kelly, L. (2002). *Journeys of jeopardy: A review of research on trafficking in women and children in Europe*. Geneva: International Organization for Migration.

Kelly, L. (2005). "You can find anything you want": a critical reflection on research on trafficking in persons within and into Europe. *International Migration*, *43*(1–2), 235–265.

Kleemans, E. R. (2011). Expanding the domain of human trafficking research: introduction to the special issue on human trafficking. *Trends in Organized Crime*, *14*(2–3), 95–99.

Kragten-Heerdink, S. L., Dettmeijer-Vermeulen, C. E., & Korf, D. J. (2017). More than just "pushing and pulling": conceptualizing identified human trafficking in the Netherlands. *Crime & Delinquency*, . 0011128717728503.

Laczko, F. (2005). Data and research on human trafficking. *International Migration*, *43*(1–2), 5–16.

Laczko, F., & Gozdziak, E. (2005). *Data and research on human trafficking: A global survey*. Geneva: International Organization for Migration.

Mancuso, M. (2014). Not all madams have a central role: analysis of a Nigerian sex trafficking network. *Trends in Organized Crime*, *17*(1–2), 66–88.

Monzini, P. (2005). *Sex traffic: Prostitution, crime and exploitation*. London: Zed Books.

National Crime Agency. (2015). *National referral mechanism statistics—End of year summary 2014*. London: National Crime Agency.

National Crime Agency. (2016). *National referral mechanism statistics—End of year summary 2015*. London: N. C. Agency.

National Crime Agency. (2017a). *County lines violence, exploitation & drug supply*. London: N. C. Agency.

National Crime Agency. (2017b). *National referral mechanism statistics—End of year summary 2016*. London: N. C. Agency.

National Crime Agency. (2018). *Modern slavery and human trafficking: National referral mechanism statistics annual report 2017*. London: National Crime Agency.

National Crime Agency. (n.d.). National referral mechanism. Retrieved from http://www.nationalcrimeagency.gov.uk/about-us/what-we-do/specialist-capabilities/uk-human-trafficking-centre/national-referral-mechanism

NCA. (2017). *County lines violence, exploitation & drug supply 2017*. Retrieved from http://www.nationalcrimeagency.gov.uk/publications/832-county-lines-violence-exploitation-and-drug-supply-2017/file.

NSPCC. (2017). *How safe are our children? The most comprehensive overview of child protection in the UK*. NSPCC.

O'Brien, E., & Wilson, M. (2015). *Clinton, Bush, and Obama: Changing policy and rhetoric in the United States annual trafficking in persons report*. In *Global human trafficking: Critical issues and contexts*. Taylor & Francis Group.(pp. 123–139).

O'Connell Davidson, J. (2005). *Children in the global sex trade*. Cambridge: Polity Press.

O'Connell Davidson, J. (2015). *Modern slavery: The margins of freedom*. Basingstoke: Palgrave Macmillan.

Office for National Statistics. (2018). *Crime in England and Wales: Year ending March 2018*. Newport: Office for National Statistics.

Olver, K. (2018). *'County lines' criminal exploitation in the West Midlands, UK: professionals' perspectives on the Modern Slavery Act in practice, organisational challenges, and strengthening the collective response*. [MSc in countering organised crime and terrorism MSc dissertation]London: University College London.

Oram, S., Ostrovschi, N. V., Gorceag, V. I., Hotineanu, M. A., Gorceag, L., Trigub, C., et al. (2012). Physical health symptoms reported by trafficked women receiving post-trafficking support in Moldova: prevalence, severity and associated factors. *BMC Women's Health*, *12*(1), 1–9.

Oram, S., Stöckl, H., Busza, J., Howard, L. M., & Zimmerman, C. (2012). Prevalence and risk of violence and the physical, mental, and sexual health problems associated with human trafficking: systematic review. *PLoS Medicine*, *9*(5), e1001224.

Organization for Security and Co-operation in Europe. (2014). *How to prevent human trafficking for domestic servitude in diplomatic households and protect private domestic workers*. Vienna: OSCE Special Representative and Co-ordinator for Combating Trafficking in Human Beings.

Parmentier, S. (2010). Epilogue: human trafficking seen from the future. *European Journal of Criminology*, *7*(1), 95–100.

Pawson, R., & Tilley, N. (1997). *Realistic evaluation*. London: Sage.

Pearce, J. (2011). Working with trafficked children and young people: complexities in practice. *British Journal of Social Work*, *41*(8), 1424–1441. https://doi.org/10.1093/bjsw/bcr029.

Pearce, J., Hynes, H. P., & Bovarnick, S. (2009). *Breaking the wall of silence: Practitioners' responses to trafficked children and young people*. London: NSPCC.

Perry, K. M., & McEwing, L. (2013). How do social determinants affect human trafficking in Southeast Asia, and what can we do about it? A systematic review. *Health and Human Rights*, *15*(2), 138–159.

Piotrowicz, R. W., & Sorrentino, L. (2016). Human trafficking and the emergence of the non-punishment principle. *Human Rights Law Review*, *16*(4), 669–699.

Raymond, J., & Hughes, D. M. (2001). Sex trafficking of women in the United States: International and domestic trends. *Research Report submitted to the US Department of Justice by the Coalition Against Trafficking in Women*. Retrieved from: https://www.ncjrs.gov/pdffiles1/nij/grants/187774.pdf.

Reynaert, D., Bouverne-de-Bie, M., & Vandevelde, S. (2009). A review of children's rights literature since the adoption of the United Nations convention on the rights of the child. *Childhood*, *16*(4), 518–534.

Schoenmakers, Y. M., Bremmers, B., & Kleemans, E. R. (2013). Strategic versus emergent crime groups: the case of Vietnamese cannabis cultivation in the Netherlands. *Global Crime*, *14*(4), 321–340.

Silverman, B. (2014). *Modern slavery: An application of multiple systems estimation*. London: Home Office.

Silverstone, D., & Savage, S. (2010). Farmers, factories and funds: organised crime and illicit drugs cultivation within the British Vietnamese community. *Global Crime*, *11*(1), 16–33.

Skilbrei, M.-L., & Tveit, M. (2008). Defining trafficking through empirical work: blurred boundaries and their consequences. *Gender, Technology and Development*, *12*(1), 9–30.

Stepnitz, A. (2012). A lie more disastrous than the truth: asylum and the identification of trafficked women in the UK. *Anti-Trafficking Review*, *1*, 104.

The Anti Trafficking Monitoring Group. (2013). *In the dock: Examining the UK's criminal justice response to trafficking*. London: A.-S. International.

The Anti-Trafficking Monitoring Group. (2010). *Wrong kind of victim? One year on: An analysis of UK measures to protect trafficked persons*. London: A.-S. International.

The Anti-Trafficking Monitoring Group. (2012). *All change: Preventing trafficking in the UK*. London: A.-S. International.

The Children's Society. (2009). *Hidden children—Separated children at risk*. London: T. C. s. Society.

The Children's Society, Victim Support and The National Police Chief's Council. (2018). *Children and young people trafficked for the purpose of criminal exploitation in relation to county lines: A toolkit for professionals*. London: T. C. s. Society.

The Global Slavery Index. (2018). *The global slavery index 2018*. Nedlands, Australia: W. F. Foundation.

The Guardian. (2018). Trafficked, beaten, enslaved: the life of a Vietnamese cannabis farmer. *The Guardian*, . (31/01/18). Retrieved from https://www.theguardian.com/world/2018/jan/31/trafficked-beaten-ensaved-life-of-cannabis-farmer-vietnam.

The Independent. (2018). Gang leaders who imprisoned teenager, beat her and forced her to conceal drugs inside her jailed. *The Independent*. (13/4/18). Retrieved from https://www.independent.co.uk/news/uk/crime/modern-slavery-drugs-london-county-lines-gangs-swansea-girl-teenage-jailed-a8303691.html.

The Slavery Working Group. (2013). *It happens here: Equipping the United Kingdom to fight modern slavery*. London: T. C. f. S. Justice.

Turner-Moss, E., Zimmerman, C., Howard, L. M., & Oram, S. (2014). Labour exploitation and health: a case series of men and women seeking post-trafficking services. *Journal of Immigrant and Minority Health*, *16*(3), 473–480.

Tyldum, G. (2010). Limitations in research on human trafficking. *International Migration*, *48*(5), 1–13.

Tyldum, G., & Brunovskis, A. (2005). Describing the unobserved: methodological challenges in empirical studies on human trafficking. *International Migration*, *43*(1–2), 17–34.

U.S. Department of State. (2018). *Trafficking in persons report June 2011*. Washington, DC: U.S. Department of State.

UN. (2000). *United Nations convention against transnational organized crime*. Retrieved from http://www.refworld.org/docid/3b00f55b0.html.

UNICEF. (2003). *End child exploitation: Stop the traffic!*. London: UNICEF UK.

United Nations. (1989). *United Nations convention on the rights of the child*. New York: United Nations.

United Nations. (2000). *Protocol to prevent, suppress and punish trafficking in persons especially women and children*. Vienna: United Nations.

United Nations. (2015). *Sustainable development goals: 17 goals to transform our world*. New York: United Nations.

United Nations Office on Drugs and Crime. (2009). *Trafficking in persons: A global report*. Vienna: United Nations Office on Drugs and Crime.

United Nations Office on Drugs and Crime. (2016a). *Annex to the global report on trafficking in persons. Annex I: Methodology and coverage*. Annex to the Vienna: United Nations Office on Drugs and Crime (UNODC).

United Nations Office on Drugs and Crime. (2016b). *Global report on trafficking in persons 2016*. Vienna: United Nations Office on Drugs and Crime (UNODC).

United Nations Office on Drugs and Crime. (2016c). *Global report on trafficking in persons*. Vienna: United Nations Office on Drugs and Crime (UNODC).

Unseen UK. (2018). *Annual assessment 2017*. Bristol: Unseen.

Van Der Laan, P., Smit, M., Busschers, I., & Aarten, P. (2011). Cross-border trafficking in human beings: prevention and intervention strategies for reducing sexual exploitation: a systematic review. *Campbell Systematic Reviews*, *7*(9), 1–51.

van der Watt, M., & Kruger, B. (2017). Exploring 'juju' and human trafficking: towards a demystified perspective and response. *South African Review of Sociology*, *48*(2), 70–86.

Van Mastrigt, S. B., & Farrington, D. P. (2009). Co-offending, age, gender and crime type: implications for criminal justice policy. *British Journal of Criminology*, *49*, 552–573.

Weitzer, R. (2015). Human trafficking and contemporary slavery. *Annual Review of Sociology*, *41*, 223–242.

Winterdyk, J., & Reichel, P. (2010). Introduction to special issue: human trafficking issues and perspectives. *European Journal of Criminology*, *7*(1), 5–10.

Zhang, S. X. (2009). Beyond the 'Natasha' story—a review and critique of current research on sex trafficking. *Global Crime*, *10*(3), 178–195.

Zimmerman, C., Hossain, M., Yun, K., Roche, B., Morison, L., & Watts, C. (2006). *Stolen smiles: A summary report on the physical and psychological health consequences of women and adolescents trafficked in Europe*. London: The London School of Hygiene & Tropical Medicine.

CHAPTER 7

Gender Comparisons of Offenders: Males and Females Who Sexually Offend Against Children

Larissa S. Christensen*, **Katelyn Jansen**†
*School of Law, University of the Sunshine Coast, Sippy Downs, QLD, Australia †School of Criminology and Criminal Justice, Griffith University, Southport, QLD, Australia

1 Introduction

The current chapter provides a discussion of differences and similarities across males and females who sexually offend against children and comprises five sections. The first commences with a discussion of differences in prevalence rates across male- and female-perpetrated child sexual abuse (CSA) and follows with comparisons of case characteristics of male and female perpetrators in terms of offender age, relationship to victim, preference in victim gender and victim age, and type of sexual abuse perpetrated. Next, offender typologies and models that have been formulated to explain offending across these two groups are discussed. The impacts of male- and female-perpetrated sexual abuse on victims are then explored, along with barriers to disclosure faced by victims of CSA. The chapter concludes with a discussion on public and professional perceptions between male- and female-perpetrated sexual abuse in terms of the perceived level of harm and severity inflicted.

2 Scope of Issue

CSA is a significant global problem (Stoltenborgh, van IJzendoorn, Euser, & Bakermans-Kranenburg, 2011). In their meta-analysis of 217 publications on CSA involving 9,911,748 participants, Stoltenborgh et al. (2011) calculated the global prevalence of CSA to be around 12%—a figure consistent with Pérez-Fuentes et al. (2013) who calculated the prevalence of CSA from a large national study in the United States involving >34,000 adults aged 18 years and older. Here, Pérez-Fuentes et al. (2013) concluded that approximately 1 in 10 individuals

Child Abuse and Neglect. https://doi.org/10.1016/B978-0-12-815344-4.00007-6

have experienced sexual abuse in the first 17 years of their lives. Whilst it is widely accepted that most perpetrators of CSA are male, several scholars have sought to determine the prevalence of sexual abuse perpetrated by females.

Early studies have estimated that females offend in up to 5% of all CSA cases (Graystona & De Luca, 1999; Hislop, 2001). However, more recent studies argue this figure is much higher (e.g. Cortoni, Babchishin, & Rat, 2017; Hayes & Carpenter, 2013; McLeod, 2015; Peter, 2009). For instance, Peter (2009) examined official records from Canadian child welfare records and found that females perpetrated around 11% of CSA cases. A recent meta-analysis conducted by Cortoni et al. (2017) reported that, although only about 2% of sexual offences reported to the police were said to be committed by females, victimisation surveys showed the figure to be around 12%. The higher prevalence rate reported in victimisation surveys is thought to be due to CSA perpetration being hidden within women's routine child care duties (e.g. bathing and dressing) and the additional social barriers to disclosure faced by victims of female-perpetrated abuse. Controlling for this, Hayes and Carpenter (2013) suggest that the true prevalence rate of female-perpetrated CSA could comprise up to 20% of cases. In support of this, in a sample of 66,765 substantiated cases of CSA reported to child protection services in the United States in 2010, McLeod (2015) found that females were the primary perpetrator in about 21% of CSA cases. Despite some discrepancies in the literature surrounding prevalence rates, female-perpetrated sexual abuse appears to be much more common than previously thought (Cortoni et al., 2017).

3 Characteristics Across Male- and Female-Perpetrated Sexual Abuse

There are several stable dissimilarities between males and females who perpetrate sexual abuse, including the offender age, relationship to victim, preference in victim gender and victim age, and type of sexual abuse perpetrated (see Table 1).

Offender age. Female perpetrators of sexual abuse tend to be younger than their male counterparts (Faller, 1995; Johansson-Love & Fremouw, 2006; Peter, 2009; Vandiver & Kercher, 2004). Faller (1995) found the average age of female perpetrators was 28 years, whilst male perpetrators had an average age of 33 years. In Vandiver and Kercher's (2004) study of 471 incarcerated female sexual offenders, most had an average age of 30 years,

Table 1: Summary of case characteristics

	Male Offender	Female Offender
Average offender age	Early to mid-thirties	Late twenties to early thirties
Relationship to victim	'Other' relatives	Child's mother
Victim gender	Female	Less discriminatory
Average victim age	11 years	10 years
Type of sexual abuse	Touching/fondling	Higher rate of touching/fondling

whereas Wortley and Smallbone (2000) found males to have a late onset of offending behaviour, with an average age of 32.4 years at the time of their first contact sexual offence. Conversely, McLeod (2015) found a higher average age for female perpetrators (33.7 years) than male perpetrators (33.2 years); however, the results of this study suggested that male perpetrators have a larger window of offending across their lifespan as they manifest offending behaviour at an earlier age and continue offending late into adulthood.

Relationship to victim. Whilst CSA is most often committed by someone known to the child (Wortley & Smallbone, 2000), there appears to be stable dissimilarities in terms of the victim-offender relationship between male and female perpetrators, with females more likely to be listed as the parent of the victim (78%) than male perpetrators (31%) (McLeod, 2015).[1] Indeed, in comparison with female perpetrators, male perpetrators were more likely to be listed as other relatives (28%), de facto partners to the victim's parent (9%), or friends or neighbours to the victim's family (3%). In Australia, the Australian Personal Safety Survey found that male perpetrators of sexual abuse were most likely to be cousin or uncle (30%), a family friend (16%), an acquaintance or neighbour (16%), another known person (15%), a father or stepfather to the victim (14%), or a stranger (11%) (Australian Bureau of Statistics, 2005). Similar to McLeod's findings (2015), Faller's earlier (1995) work identified that most female perpetrators (40/72 cases) had offended against at least one of their own children. Other relationships included the role of a professional caretaker (21 cases), the victim's grandmother (4 cases), the victim's stepmother/father's partner (3 cases), neighbour/family friend (2 cases), and other female relative (2 cases) (Faller, 1995). This finding is consistent with Nathan and Ward's (2002) and Lewis and Stanley's (2000) studies that suggested over 50% of female-perpetrated sexual abuse victims are sexually abused by their mothers.

Interestingly, a study by Bader, Scalora, Casady, and Black (2008) presented a significant contrast between the percentages of female-perpetrated intrafamilial abuse in a child protection sample and criminal justice sample, with 98% of the victims reported as intrafamilial in the child protection sample, compared with 30% in the criminal justice sample (Bader et al., 2008). This finding suggests that child protective agencies almost exclusively manage female-perpetrated intrafamilial sexual abuse cases to the exclusion of criminal justice agencies.

Victim gender. Regarding victim gender, female perpetrators appear to be less discriminatory in victim preference compared with male perpetrators. According to McLeod (2015), male perpetrators tend to target female victims (81%) over male victims (19%) and, whilst female perpetrators also target female victims over male victims, they did so at a lower rate (68% and 32%, respectively). Indeed, a number of studies have found females to have a slight preference for male victims (Bourke, Doherty, McBride, Morgan, & McGee, 2014; Cortoni et al., 2017; Lewis & Stanley, 2000). For example, in one victimisation survey,

[1] These percentages have been rounded to the nearest whole number.

Cortoni et al. (2017) found female-perpetrated sexual abuse was more prevalent amongst male victims (40%) than female victims (4%).

Victim age. Female perpetrators of sexual abuse also appear to be less discriminatory in their preferences for victim age than male perpetrators, abusing across a range of age groups. For example, in their sample of female perpetrators, Lewis and Stanley (2000) found the ages of the victims ranged between 3 and 17 years old, with an average age of 10 years old. In McLeod's (2015) study, victims of male-perpetrated sexual abuse had a mean age of 11 years old, and victims of female-perpetrated sexual abuse had a mean age of 10 years old. Although there was a similar upper victim age range across male and female perpetrators in McLeod's (2015) study, female perpetrators targeted children, on average, 2 years younger (5-year-old victims) than male perpetrators (7-year-old victims).

Types of sexual abuse. There are also stable dissimilarities in the types of sexual abuse perpetrated across male and female perpetrators. In particular, whilst male and female perpetrators most commonly take part in touching/fondling of the genitals, females take part in touching/fondling at a proportionally higher rate than males. For example, Peter (2009) found 51% of female perpetrators had engaged in touching/fondling of genitals compared with 49% of male perpetrators; further, only 19% of female perpetrators had engaged in attempted or completed penetration in comparison with 48% of male perpetrators. However, Bourke et al. (2014) found no significant differences across male- and female-perpetrated sexual abuse: contact sexual abuse (66% and 58%, respectively), penetrative acts (21% and 17%, respectively), and noncontact abuse (13% and 25%, respectively).

4 Typologies/Pathways to Offending

A number of typologies and models have been developed in order to explain motivations for CSA, a key element in the design of treatment and prevention programs. These typologies and models appear to differ across male and female perpetrators of sexual abuse. Regarding male perpetrators, Finkelhor (1984) identified the precondition model to explain the underlying reasons behind child sexual offending. This model considers contextual and situational variables and is composed of factors including emotional congruence, sexual arousal, blockage, and disinhibition (Finkelhor, 1984). According to the precondition model, an individual may develop sexual interests in children due to emotional congruence, finding sexual activity with children to be emotionally satisfying, and gratifying the perpetrator's need for safety and closeness. Sexual arousal refers to the perpetrator finding sexual activity with children as sexually arousing. Blockage denotes the individual being unable to meet their sexual needs in socially appropriate ways (e.g. sexual activity with adults). Finally, disinhibition refers to the individual becoming disinhibited and behaving in deviant ways; for example, the perpetrator may be under the influence of drugs or alcohol, unlocking their self-regulatory mechanisms. Similarly, the pathways model, developed by

Ward and Siegert (2002), is a multifactorial model that identifies the pathways that create a predisposition for sexual offending. Essentially, Ward and Siegert (2002) suggested that sexual offending is the result of interacting psychological mechanisms, along with the effects of cultural and biological factors and learning events. Different psychological profiles reflect different etiologies and are associated with different offending pathways.

More recently, Heffernan and Ward (2015) proposed the agency model of risk, suggesting four major risk factors in the perpetration of CSA, including intimacy deficits, cognitive distortions, self-regulation problems, and sexual deviance. Intimacy deficits as a risk factor indicate a lack of appropriate intimacy and interpersonal relationships, leading to subsequent emotional identification with children. Attachment issues and interpersonal problems have a significant influence on emotional states and can act as offence triggers (Heffernan & Ward, 2015). Cognitive distortions are also widely accepted as a central cause for sexual offending. Norm-violating attitudes, biased interpretations, excuses, minimisations, and rationalisations are examples of cognitive distortions, which lead to deviant behaviour due to an individual's distorted belief system (Heffernan & Ward, 2015). Self-regulation consists of the internal and external processes that allow an individual to engage in behaviours over time and across different contexts; a lack of self-regulation can lead to high-risk and impulsive sexually abusive behaviours (Heffernan & Ward, 2015). Finally, sexual deviancy is an influence that drives harmful sexual behaviour alongside other factors including maladaptive core beliefs, interpersonal issues, and poor self-regulation. Whilst sexual arousal must be present to some degree in sexual offending, its causal role will vary depending on situational and psychological factors (Heffernan & Ward, 2015).

In contrast with the development of the models of offending, several scholars have identified typologies of females who perpetrate sexual abuse. Such typologies focus on the background factors and possible motivations for offending. Fundamental research by Mathews, Matthews, and Speltz (1989; cited in Matthews, Mathews, & Speltz, 1991) identified some of the most long-standing typologies of female sexual offenders: the teacher/lover, the intergenerationally predisposed, and the male-coerced. The teacher/lover offender is one who seeks a loving sexual relationship and most often offends against an adolescent male. Female educators who abuse adolescent children often believe that they are in a consensual relationship and do not regard their behaviour as being abusive (West, Hatters-Friedman, & Knoll IV, 2010). The abuse is unlikely to be premeditated and is usually the result of poor judgement or immaturity. In contrast, women who offend against elementary school-aged children do so differently to those who offend against adolescent students. Females who abuse elementary school-aged children are often high achievers who use their positive standing to gain the trust of their students and their families (West et al., 2010). These women are more likely to be serial offenders, and allegations of abuse are often dismissed due to the reputation of the offender. Sullivan and Beech (2002) would argue that this category is part of a broader typology of 'professional perpetrators', a group of offenders who use their work with children to facilitate sexually abusive behaviours.

The second typology identified by Mathews et al. (1989; cited in Matthews et al., 1991) is the intergenerationally predisposed offender. These women have strong histories of being victimised and offend alone, usually against young victims. The prevalence of prior traumatic experiences amongst female perpetrators of sexual abuse has been further highlighted in more recent studies. For example, research conducted by Levenson, Willis, and Prescott (2015) explored the prevalence of childhood traumatic experiences amongst a sample of 47 female perpetrators. Compared with females in the general population, this sample demonstrated a significantly higher prevalence of CSA, verbal abuse, and emotional neglect; only 20% of female perpetrators reported zero adverse childhood experiences compared with 35% of the general female population. In addition, 41% of the female perpetrators reported four or more adverse childhood experiences, compared with 15% of the general female population (Levenson et al., 2015). The study also found that higher scores on the adverse childhood experiences scale (measuring neglect, abuse, and household dysfunction) were associated with offending against younger victims. The findings from this study indicate that female perpetrators who abuse young children are much more likely to have experienced childhood trauma than the general female population. In a different study, Lewis and Stanley (2000) found that 80% of their sample of females who had perpetrated sexual abuse reported histories of being victim of sexual abuse. Such findings support the typology developed by Mathews et al. (1989; cited in Matthews et al., 1991) of females who are predisposed to offending against children as a result of their own childhood victimisation.

Mathews et al. (1989; cited in Matthews et al., 1991) identified the final typology, the male-coerced, as females who are involved in the abuse with male cooffenders. These perpetrators display varying levels of passivity, from being a bystander to actively initiating the abuse. The male-coerced offender is suggested to be compelled by a male coperpetrator to participate in abuse and is often motivated by fear or emotional dependency. These women appear to play a passive role, for example, mothers who act as bystanders or who provide opportunities for the abuse to occur (Wijkman, Bijleveld, & Hendriks, 2010). Gannon and Rose (2008) argue that, due to their own histories of victimisation, female perpetrators tend to display emotional dependency, passivity, and low self-esteem. These women are also likely to experience domestic violence and be socially isolated and are vulnerable to coercion by a male (Gannon & Rose, 2008). Often in discussions of female-coperpetrated CSA, there is an assumption that female offenders participate in abuse under the influence of male cooffenders. However, this typology also includes the male-accompanied offender, who plays a more active role in the abuse (Mathews et al., 1989; cited in Matthews et al., 1991). In fact, Nathan and Ward (2002) proposed a new category within the male-accompanied typology: the rejected/revengeful. They found that only a minority of women with male cooffenders were coerced into offending against children. Instead, rejection, jealousy, and revenge were identified as motivating factors for females who abused children, with these women generally playing an active role in the abuse (Nathan & Ward, 2002).

Within the male-coerced offender category, Mathews et al. (1989; cited in Matthews et al., 1991) identified a subcategory of psychologically disturbed offenders. These offenders usually have dependency and self-esteem issues, which lead to significant psychopathology (Mathews et al., 1989; cited in Matthews et al., 1991). However, the effect of psychological disorders and mental illness on female perpetrators of sexual abuse is a contentious topic in the literature. In one study that involved a sample of 111 female perpetrators, Wijkman et al. (2010) found that mental disorders were prominent amongst 59% of the sample; psychiatric syndromes such as depression, paraphilia, anxiety disorders, and personality disorders were apparent. Lewis and Stanley (2000) also found that a majority (67%) of female perpetrators in their sample had been seen in outpatient psychiatric clinics. Contrary to these figures, Strickland (2008) found no significant differences in the prevalence of personality disorders or cognitive distortions between female perpetrators and nonsexual perpetrators. Not all scholars agree that poor mental functioning is a significant risk factor for female perpetrators of sexual abuse (for an overview, see Gannon & Rose, 2008).

5 Impact of Sexual Abuse on Victims

The short- and long-term impacts of CSA on victims can range in severity, from no apparent effects to very severe effects (Shakespeare-Finch & de Dassel, 2009). Childhood sexual abuse can have enduring effects on brain development, social functioning, mental health, personality, sleep, substance abuse, and self-harm (Australian Psychological Society [APS], 2013; Perry, Pollard, Blakley, Baker, & Vigilante, 1995). It is well established that CSA is a significant determinant of psychological disorders later in life (APS, 2013; Perry et al., 1995). Psychological disorders commonly experienced by CSA survivors include anxiety, depression, somatoform conditions, eating disorders, posttraumatic stress disorder (PTSD), and sexual dysfunction (APS, 2013). PTSD and depression appear to be two of the most prevalent outcomes for victims of CSA. For example, in one Australian study, 95% of the sample of adults who had experienced childhood sexual abuse were experiencing significant PTSD symptoms (Shakespeare-Finch & de Dassel, 2009). Regarding depression, a nationally representative study conducted in the United States found 52% of CSA survivors had suffered depression, compared with 27% of nonvictims (Saunders, Kilpatrick, Hanson, Resnick, & Walker, 1999). Further, PTSD and depression have been linked to smaller hippocampal volumes in female CSA survivors (Vythilingam et al., 2002).

Importantly, of the limited studies that have explored the impacts on victims between male- and female-perpetrated sexual abuse, female-perpetrated sexual abuse appears to be equally, if not more, damaging to the victim compared with male-perpetrated abuse. In one study, Denov (2004) found that of the victims who had disclosed sexual abuse by both men and women, all victims reported that the female-perpetrated abuse was more traumatic than the male-perpetrated abuse. The effects of sexual abuse perpetrated by women in Denov's (2004) study included substance abuse, self-injury, suicidal ideation, depression, problematic relationships with women, and difficulties with sexuality. Another effect related to female-perpetrated sexual abuse was the victim's fear of going on to sexually abuse children themselves; this fear was present for 86% of the sample. Interestingly, this effect has been found in studies that have explored the link between female-perpetrated abuse and later sexual offending in victims. In one of these studies, Salter et al. (2003) conducted longitudinal research with a sample of 224 male victims of sexual abuse and found that 38% of victim-abusers (victims who had become sexual abusers) had been victimised by a female, compared with only 17% of nonabusers (victims who had not become sexual abusers). This study identified female-perpetrated sexual abuse as a significant childhood risk factor for sexual offending later in life. In a different study, Glasser et al. (2001) reported similar findings using a retrospective clinical case note review. In a sample of 24 males who had been sexually abused by a female, 79% went on to become perpetrators of sexual abuse, compared with 54% in a sample of 111 males who had been sexually abused by a male. Male victims who were abused by a mother or sister were associated with the highest likelihood of becoming perpetrators (Glasser et al., 2001).

6 Barriers to Disclosure

The most common way CSA is discovered is through a child's disclosure of sexual abuse (Goodman-Brown, Edelstein, Goodman, Jones, & Gordon, 2003). However, many children do not disclose the sexual abuse, even as adults (Smith et al., 2000; Sorenson & Snow, 1991). Barriers to disclosure surround the perpetrator's grooming ability and motivational factors relating to the child, the family, and the perpetrator (Paine & Hansen, 2002). For example, regarding motivational factors concerning the perpetrator, a child who is abused by a person close to them (e.g. a mother or stepfather) might be concerned for the perpetrator's wellbeing if they were to disclose the sexual abuse. Several case characteristics have also been associated with a child's likelihood of disclosure, such as victim gender and abuse severity. Regarding victim gender, in their study of all CSA incidents that were reported to police in 2011 in one jurisdiction of Australia, Christensen, Sharman, and Powell (2016) found male victims were less likely to disclose the sexual abuse in comparison with female victims. Further, children were more likely to disclose when the sexual abuse was more severe (Christensen et al., 2016). It may be that as abuse severity increases, the child's perceived negative consequences of the sexual abuse override their anticipated negative consequences of disclosing the sexual abuse (Lam, 2014).

Importantly, female-perpetrated sexual abuse adds an additional layer to the complexities of victims disclosing the abuse (Denov, 2003). In Denov's (2003) study with victims who had disclosed female-perpetrated sexual abuse, all victims reported that they were fearful of disclosing the abuse due to the taboo nature of female-perpetrated sexual abuse (Denov, 2003). It is therefore important to consider public reactions to CSA as a significant barrier to victim disclosure (Arata, 1998). Upon disclosure of CSA, victims can potentially experience negative reactions from others. Negative reactions to disclosure include the victim not being believed and being blamed, judged, and/or punished. Negative and unsupportive reactions may compound the impact of the abuse on the victim, leading to secondary victimisation and poor psychological outcomes (APS, 2013; Ullman, 2007).

7 Public and Professional Perceptions Across Male and Female Perpetrators

Due to the assumption that sexual abuse was exclusively a male-perpetrated problem, women's sexual behaviour against children has traditionally been viewed as something other than abusive. Traditional sex scripts dictated that females, particularly mothers, are incapable of sexually abusing children, resulting in the minimisation or denial of abuse (Hetherton, 1999). Due to women being perceived as the caretakers and nurturers, female-perpetrated abuse was viewed as loving expressions of intimacy and caring (Hetherton, 1999). Alongside this perception was the belief that females were incapable of committing sexually abusive acts due to their physical construction (Hetherton, 1999). Sexual socialisation might play a role in reinforcing this myth, as women learn to be sexually vulnerable whilst men are framed as sexual aggressors (Burt & Estep, 1981, cited in Hayes & Baker, 2014). It has been argued that recognition of female-perpetrated CSA was obstructed by these cultural myths about women (Allen, 1990). Such beliefs are contrary to the reality that females perpetrate acts along the entire spectrum of sexual abuse, from fondling of the child to the penetration of objects and forced sexual intercourse with them or even with animals (Cain & Anderson, 2013).

Whilst the topic of females who perpetrate sexual abuse is slowly becoming more recognised in the public domain, gendered assumptions still surround this offending group. In particular, there is reframing of female-perpetrated sexual abuse to return female offenders to a socially acceptable form of femininity (Hayes & Carpenter, 2013). This means that in many cases where sexual abuse by women is recognised, it is often understood to be an outcome of male coercion. On the other hand, when women offend alone, their own histories of victimisation are used to minimise their behaviour and return them to a more acceptable form of femininity (Hayes & Carpenter, 2013). Further, it is argued that factors such as mental illness and substance abuse are considered in order to keep the concepts of 'abuse' and 'femininity' separate from one another (Hetherton, 1999). Thus, cognitive dissonance is theorised to contribute to public perceptions of female-perpetrated abuse that is characterised by denial and minimisation (Hetherton, 1999). When the behaviour of female perpetrators is no longer subject to these objections, these women tend to be characterised as evil and unnatural

(Hayes & Carpenter, 2013). Due to traditional views of femininity, female perpetrators incite a sense of fear and betrayal, which is less apparent in discussions of male-perpetrated sexual abuse (Hayes & Carpenter, 2013). Female perpetrators of sexual abuse are therefore repositioned to remove notions of femininity from their behaviour.

Several studies that have explored public perceptions across male and female perpetrators of sexual abuse have documented a gender bias toward female perpetrators (e.g. Geddes, Tyson, & McGreal, 2013; Hayes & Carpenter, 2013; Zack, Lang, & Dirks, 2016). In one study, Geddes et al. (2013) sought to examine the apparent gender double standard in perceptions of teacher-student sexual relationships. This study involved randomly selected participants who responded to two hypothetical vignettes: one being a male teacher-female student sexual relationship and the other being a female teacher-male student sexual relationship. They found that participants expressed significantly greater anger toward the male teacher than the female teacher in these scenarios, despite there being no difference in perceived responsibility for the incident between male and female teachers. In a different study, Zack et al. (2016) analysed over 900 online comments on five Huffington Post news articles about female teachers who perpetrated sexual abuse. They found that a substantial number of comments (35%) adhered to traditional sex scripts and neutralised the offenders' behaviour. This reinforcement of traditional sex scripts, contributing to the denial of women as perpetrators, has become institutionalised within the criminal justice system, the media, the public, and the victims themselves (Hayes & Baker, 2014).

Media representations have a major influence on public perceptions of perpetrators of sexual offending. Five studies to date have analysed the textual representation of female perpetrators in the media (Chiotti, 2009; Christensen, 2018a; Hayes & Baker, 2014; Landor, 2009; Landor & Eisenchlas, 2012). In most of these studies, there was a clear distinction in the overall tone of cases: Males were portrayed as evil, and females were portrayed as mentally ill or having an emotional connection to the victim. For example, Hayes and Baker (2014) examined 487 media reports from Australia and the United Kingdom to analyse the ways in which media reports of female perpetrators reinforce gender stereotypes. The study found that most women who offended against prepubescent victims were associated with male offenders as an accomplice. This suggests that women's behaviour is excused on some level or, at the very least, made coherent in terms of traditional sex scripts. However, the researchers also found that female perpetrators were seen as 'horrific' and their behaviour was described as the 'ultimate female betrayal', painting them as either vulnerable victims or unnatural women (Hayes & Baker, 2014). More recently, Christensen (2018a) identified a potential advancement in the reporting of female perpetrators of sexual abuse through a qualitative content analysis of the print media at an international level. Christensen (2018a) found female perpetrators were depicted as dangerous and accountable for their actions. Even in cases reporting coperpetrators, the females were depicted as willing or even playing a central role in the abuse. Such developments in the portrayal of female perpetrators of sexual abuse in the media may, over time, assist victim disclosure and responses to victims by the public and professionals.

Similar to public perceptions of perpetrators of sexual abuse, research on professionals' perceptions of male and female perpetrators has identified dismissive responses and attitudes in relation to female perpetrators (e.g. Denov, 2001; Finkelhor, Williams, Burns, & Kalinowski, 1988; Hetherton & Beardsall, 1998). In one study, Hetherton and Beardsall (1998) explored police officers' and social workers' attitudes. They found these professionals did not perceive female-perpetrated sexual abuse cases as being of the same severity as male-perpetrated sexual abuse cases. Professionals' responses to questionnaires indicated that they considered the case registration and imprisonment as more appropriate in incidents involving male perpetrators in comparison with female perpetrators. Hetherton and Beardsall (1998) highlighted a significant implication of such attitudes: victims of female-perpetrated abuse are less likely to be afforded protection than victims of male-perpetrated abuse, due to the abuse being considered as less harmful by professionals.

Denov (2001) conducted semistructured interviews with psychiatrists and police officers. The researcher found that these professionals minimised the seriousness of female-perpetrated sexual abuse, with female suspects being perceived as less harmful in comparison with male suspects. Denov (2001) coined the term 'culture of denial' (p. 303) to explain the minimisation of female-perpetrated sexual abuse amongst professionals. Such responses are problematic, particularly when professional responses are vital to the wellbeing of victims (Denov, 2003). In a different study, Denov (2003) conducted semistructured interviews with victims of female-perpetrated sexual abuse. During the interviews, victims discussed their experiences disclosing the abuse to a professional and the influence of professional responses. Denov (2003) found positive professional responses (i.e. validation and acknowledgement of the sexual abuse experienced by victims) mitigated negative impacts of the sexual abuse. In contrast, negative professional responses (i.e. disbelief and minimisation of the sexual abuse experienced by victims) exacerbated the negative impacts of the sexual abuse, essentially leading to secondary victimisation for some of the victims (Denov, 2003). Denov (2003) concluded that professional responses to victim disclosures of female-perpetrated sexual abuse play a vital role in the victim's wellbeing, regardless of the response being positive or negative.

Due to the changes in gender roles in Western society over the last 20 years, toward more egalitarian roles, Christensen (2018b) set out to explore whether professionals in the justice and community response sectors still appear to hold dismissive attitudes and responses toward female perpetrators of sexual abuse in comparison with male perpetrators of sexual abuse. Similar to Denov (2001), Christensen (2018b) conducted semistructured interviews. The sample involved a heterogeneous group of professionals in the sector, including social workers, police officers, counsellors, child and family support workers, case managers, and legal professional. Professionals acknowledged the pervasive negative impacts on victims inflicted by female-perpetrated sexual abuse—both physical and psychological—and suggested that the gender of the perpetrator was insignificant in their individual professional dealings of such cases. However, some professionals acknowledged that they had experienced some difficulty when conversing with other professions, even amongst some colleagues, in cases involving female perpetrators. Further, professionals highlighted the need for a more open discussion in society concerning female-perpetrated sexual abuse to assist victims disclosing and reporting the sexual abuse.

8 Conclusion

The current chapter provided a discussion on the differences between males and females who perpetrate CSA. Whilst male-perpetrated sexual abuse is most prevalent, female-perpetrated sexual abuse is much more common than it was once thought to be. There appears to be distinct characteristics between male and female perpetrators of CSA including offender age, relationship to victim, preference in victim gender and victim age, and type of sexual abuse perpetrated. The impacts of sexual abuse on the victims and the barriers to disclosure that victims face were discussed. It is clear that female-perpetrated sexual abuse can be equally, if not more, damaging than male-perpetrated sexual abuse and that the disclosure of female-perpetrated sexual abuse adds an additional layer due to the taboo nature of the topic. Finally, the literature on public and professional perceptions across male and female perpetrators was explored. Whilst it is evident that public and professional perceptions of female perpetrators of sexual abuse are moving away from dismissive attitudes and responses, perhaps attributable to a change in media reporting of female perpetrators, it is evident that a greater discussion on the topic amongst the public is required.

9 Chapter Review Questions

1. Historically, why has child sexual abuse exclusively been perceived as a male-perpetrated problem?
2. Name and explain Mathews, Matthews, and Speltz's (1989) typologies of females who perpetrate sexual abuse.
3. Compare the characteristics across male- and female-perpetrated sexual abuse in terms of offender age, relationship to victim, preference in victim gender and victim age, and type of sexual abuse perpetrated.
4. How does cognitive dissonance relate to public perceptions of female-perpetrated sexual abuse?
5. Why does female-perpetrated sexual abuse appear to be much more common than previously thought?
6. Highlight some of the short- and long-term psychological impacts of child sexual abuse

7. Why might a child not disclose child sexual abuse and, in particular, female-perpetrated sexual abuse?
8. Why is research on professional perceptions of child sexual offenders important, and how have professional perceptions of female child sexual offenders changed over time?

References

Allen, C. M. (1990). Women as perpetrators of child sexual abuse: recognition barriers. In A. L. Horton, B. L. Johnson, L. M. Roundy, & D. Williams (Eds.), *The incest perpetrator: A family member no one wants to treat* (pp. 108–125). Newbury Park, CA: Sage Publications.

Arata, C. M. (1998). To tell or not to tell: current functioning of child sexual abuse survivors who disclosed their victimization. *Child Maltreatment*, *3*(1), 63–71. https://doi.org/10.1177/1077559598003001006.

Australian Bureau of Statistics. (2005). *Personal safety survey Australia* (Report No. 4906.0). Retrieved from http://www.abs.gov.au/AUSSTATS/abs@.nsf/Lookup/4906.0Main+Features12012?OpenDocument.

Australian Psychological Society. (2013). *Child sexual abuse in the general community and clergy-perpetrated child sexual abuse*. Melbourne, VIC: Australian Psychological Society.

Bader, S. M., Scalora, M. J., Casady, T. K., & Black, S. (2008). Female sexual abuse and criminal justice intervention: a comparison of child protective service and criminal justice samples. *Child Abuse & Neglect*, *32*(1), 111–119. https://doi.org/10.1016/j.chiabu.2007.04.014.

Bourke, A., Doherty, S., McBride, O., Morgan, K., & McGee, H. (2014). Female perpetrators of child sexual abuse: characteristics of the offender and victim. *Psychology Crime and Law*, *20*(8), 769–780. https://doi.org/10.1080/1068316X.2013.860456.

Cain, C. M., & Anderson, A. L. (2013). *Female sex offenders: Public awareness and attributions*. University of Nebraska at Omaha, Springer Publishing Company.

Chiotti, J. M. (2009). *The "illusive" female sex offender: A quantitative content analysis of media exposure* [Doctoral dissertation]Washington State University.

Christensen, L. S. 2018a. The new portrayal of female child sexual offenders in the print media: a qualitative content analysis. *Sexuality and Culture*, *22*(1), 176–189.

Christensen, L. S. 2018b. Professionals' perceptions of female child sexual offenders. Journal of Interpersonal Violence (advance online publication).

Christensen, L. S., Sharman, S., & Powell, M. (2016). Identifying the characteristics of child sexual abuse cases that exit the criminal justice system before the forensic interview. *An International Journal of Police Strategies & Management*, *18*(2), 104–111. https://doi.org/10.1177/1461355716641973.

Cortoni, F., Babchishin, K. M., & Rat, C. (2017). The proportion of sexual offenders who are female is higher than thought. *Criminal Justice and Behavior*, *44*(2), 145–162.

Denov, M. S. (2001). A culture of denial: exploring professional perspectives on female sex offending. *Canadian Journal of Criminology*, *43*, 303–329.

Denov, M. (2003). To a safer place? Victims of sexual abuse by females and their disclosures to professionals. *Child Abuse & Neglect*, *27*(1), 47–61. https://doi.org/10.1016/S0145-2134(02)00509-4.

Denov, M. (2004). The long-term effects of child sexual abuse by female perpetrators: a qualitative study of male and female victims. *Journal of Interpersonal Violence*, *19*(10), 1137–1156. https://doi.org/10.1177/0886260504269093.

Faller, K. C. (1995). A clinical sample of women who have sexually abused children. *Journal of Child Sexual Abuse*, *4*(3), 13–30. https://doi.org/10.1300/J070v04n03_02.

Finkelhor, D. (1984). *Child sexual abuse*. New York, NY: Free Press.

Finkelhor, D., Williams, L. M., Burns, N., & Kalinowski, M. (1988). *Sexual abuse in day care: A national study*. Final report Durham, NH: University of New Hampshire.

Gannon, T. A., & Rose, M. R. (2008). Female child sexual offenders: towards integrating theory and practice. *Aggression and Violent Behavior*, *13*(6), 442–461. https://doi.org/10.1016/j.avb.2008.07.002.

Geddes, R. A., Tyson, G. A., & McGreal, S. (2013). Gender bias in the education system: perceptions of teacher-student sexual relationships. *Psychiatry, Psychology and Law*, *20*(4), 608–618. https://doi.org/10.1080/13218719.2012.728428.

Glasser, M., Kolvin, I., Campbell, D., Glasser, A., Leitch, I., & Farrelly, S. (2001). Cycle of child sexual abuse: links between being a victim and becoming a perpetrator. *The British Journal of Psychiatry*, *179*(6), 482–494. https://doi.org/10.1192/bjp.179.6.482.

Goodman-Brown, T. B., Edelstein, R. S., Goodman, G. S., Jones, D. P., & Gordon, D. S. (2003). Why children tell: a model of children's disclosure of sexual abuse. *Child Abuse & Neglect*, *27*(5), 525–540. https://doi.org/10.1016/S0145-2134(03)00037-1.

Graystona, A. D., & De Luca, R. V. (1999). Female perpetrators of child sexual abuse: a review of the clinical and empirical literature. *Aggression and Violent Behavior*, *4*(1), 93–106. https://doi.org/10.1016/S1359-1789(98)00014-7.

Hayes, S., & Baker, B. (2014). Female sex offenders and pariah femininities: rewriting the sexual scripts. *Journal of Criminology*, *2014*, 1–8. https://doi.org/10.1155/2014/414525.

Hayes, S., & Carpenter, B. (2013). Social moralities and discursive constructions of female sex offenders. *Sexualities*, *16*(1–2), 159–179. https://doi.org/10.1177/1363460712471112.

Heffernan, R., & Ward, T. (2015). The conceptualization of dynamic risk factors in child sex offenders: an agency model. *Aggression and Violent Behavior*, *24*, 250–260. https://doi.org/10.1016/j.avb.2015.07.001.

Hetherton, J. (1999). The idealization of women: its role in the minimization of child sexual abuse by females. *Child Abuse & Neglect*, *23*(2), 161–174. https://doi.org/10.1016/S0145-2134(98)00119-7.

Hetherton, J., & Beardsall, L. (1998). Decisions and attitudes concerning child sexual abuse: does the gender of the perpetrator make a difference to child protection professionals? *Child Abuse & Neglect*, *22*(12), 1265–1283. https://doi.org/10.1016/S0145-2134(98)00101-X.

Hislop, J. (2001). *Female sex offenders: what therapists, law enforcement and child protective services need to know*. Ravensdale, WA: Issues Press.

Johansson-Love, J., & Fremouw, W. (2006). A critique of the female sexual perpetrator research. *Aggression and Violent Behavior*, *11*(1), 12–26. https://doi.org/10.1016/j.avb.2005.05.001.

Lam, K. (2014). Factors associated with adolescents' disclosure of sexual abuse experiences in Hong Kong. *Journal of Child Sexual Abuse*, *23*(7), 768–791. https://doi.org/10.1080/10538712.2014.950398.

Landor, R. V. (2009). Double standards? Representation of male vs. female sex offenders in the Australian media. *Griffith Working Papers in Pragmatics and Intercultural Communication*, *2*(2), 84–93.

Landor, R. V., & Eisenchlas, S. A. (2012). "Coming clean" on duty of care: Australian print media's representation of male versus female sex offenders in institutional contexts. *Sexuality and Culture*, *16*(4), 486–502. https://doi.org/10.1007/s12119-012-9134-5.

Levenson, J. S., Willis, G. M., & Prescott, D. S. (2015). Adverse childhood experiences in the lives of female sex offenders. *Sexual Abuse: A Journal of Research and Treatment*, *27*(3), 258–283. https://doi.org/10.1177/1079063214544332.

Lewis, C. F., & Stanley, C. R. (2000). Women accused of sexual offenses. *Behavioral Sciences & the Law*, *18*(1), 73–81. https://doi.org/10.1002/(SICI)1099-0798(200001/02)18:1<73::AID-BSL378>3.0.CO;2-#.

Matthews, J. K., Mathews, R., & Speltz, K. (1991). Female sexual offenders: a typology. In M. Patton (Ed.), *Family sexual abuse: Frontline research and evaluation* (pp. 199–219). Newbury Park, CA: Sage Publications.

McLeod, D. A. (2015). Female offenders in child sexual abuse cases: a national picture. *Journal of Child Sexual Abuse*, *24*(1), 97–114. https://doi.org/10.1080/10538712.2015.978925.

Nathan, P., & Ward, T. (2002). Female sex offenders: clinical and demographic features. *Journal of Sexual Aggression*, *8*(1), 5–21. https://doi.org/10.1080/13552600208413329.

Paine, M. L., & Hansen, D. J. (2002). Factors influencing children to self-disclose sexual abuse. *Clinical Psychology Review*, *22*(2), 271–295. https://doi.org/10.1016/S0272-7358(01)00091-5.

Pérez-Fuentes, G., Olfson, M., Villegas, L., Morcillo, C., Wang, S., & Blanco, C. (2013). Prevalence and correlates of child sexual abuse: a national study. *Comprehensive Psychiatry*, *54*(1), 16–27. https://doi.org/10.1016/j.comppsych.2012.05.010.

Perry, B., Pollard, R., Blakley, T., Baker, W., & Vigilante, D. (1995). Childhood trauma, the neurobiology of adaptation, and "use-dependent" development of the brain: how "states" become "traits". *Infant Mental Health Journal*, *16*(4), 271–291. https://doi.org/10.1002/1097-0355(199524)16:4<271::AID-IMHJ2280160404>3.0.CO;2-B.

Peter, T. (2009). Exploring taboos: comparing male- and female-perpetrated child sexual abuse. *Journal of Interpersonal Violence*, *24*(7), 1111–1128. https://doi.org/10.1177/0886260508322194.

Salter, D., McMillan, D., Richards, M., Talbot, T., Hodges, J., Bentovim, A., et al. (2003). Development of sexually abusive behaviour in sexually victimised males: a longitudinal study. *The Lancet*, *361*(9356), 471–476. https://doi.org/10.1016/S0140-6736(03)12466-X.

Saunders, B. E., Kilpatrick, D. G., Hanson, R. F., Resnick, H. S., & Walker, M. E. (1999). Prevalence, case characteristics, and long-term psychological correlates of child rape among women: a national survey. *Child Maltreatment*, *4*(3), 187–200. https://doi.org/10.1177/1077559599004003001.

Shakespeare-Finch, J., & de Dassel, T. (2009). Exploring posttraumatic outcomes as a function of childhood sexual abuse. *Journal of Child Sexual Abuse*, *18*(6), 623–640. https://doi.org/10.1080/10538710903317224.

Smith, D., Letourneau, E., Saunders, B., Kilpatrick, D., Resnick, H., & Best, C. (2000). Delay in disclosure of childhood rape: results from a national survey. *Child Abuse & Neglect*, *24*(2), 273–287. https://doi.org/10.1016/s0145-2134(99)00130-1.

Sorenson, T., & Snow, B. (1991). How children tell: the process of disclosure in child sexual abuse. *Child Welfare League of America*, *70*(1), 3–15. Retrieved from http://web.a.ebscohost.com.ezproxyb.deakin.edu.au/ehost/detail/detail?sid=a052c195-4108-40ae-b4fcd3beb4324bf1%40sessionmgr4002&vid=0&hid=4104&bdata=JnNpdGU9ZWhvc3Qt bGl2ZSZzY29wZT1zaXRl#db=mdc&AN=1997290.

Stoltenborgh, M., van IJzendoorn, M. H., Euser, E. M., & Bakermans-Kranenburg, M. J. (2011). A global perspective on child sexual abuse: meta-analysis of prevalence around the world. *Child Maltreatment*, *16*(2), 79–101. https://doi.org/10.1177/1077559511403920.

Strickland, S. M. (2008). Female sex offenders: exploring issues of personality, trauma, and cognitive distortions. *Journal of Interpersonal Violence*, *23*(4), 474–489. https://doi.org/10.1177/0886260507312944.

Sullivan, J., & Beech, A. (2002). Professional perpetrators: sex offenders who use their employment to target and sexually abuse the children with whom they work. *Child Abuse Review*, *11*(3), 153–167. https://doi.org/10.1002/car.737.

Ullman, S. E. (2007). Relationship to perpetrator, disclosure, social reactions, and PTSD symptoms in child sexual abuse survivors. *Journal of Child Sexual Abuse*, *16*(1), 19–36. https://doi.org/10.1300/J070v16n01_02.

Vandiver, D. M., & Kercher, G. (2004). Offender and victim characteristics of registered female sexual offenders in Texas: a proposed typology of female sexual offenders. *Sexual Abuse: A Journal of Research and Treatment*, *16*(2), 121–137. https://doi.org/10.1177/2F107906320401600203.

Vythilingam, M., Heim, C., Newport, J., Miller, A. H., Anderson, E., Bronen, R., et al. (2002). Childhood trauma associated with smaller hippocampal volume in women with major depression. *American Journal of Psychiatry*, *159*(12), 2072–2080. https://doi.org/10.1176/appi.ajp.159.12.2072.

Ward, T., & Siegert, R. (2002). Toward a comprehensive theory of child sexual abuse: a theory knitting perspective. *Psychology, Crime & Law*, *8*(4), 319–351. https://doi.org/10.1080/10683160208401823.

West, S. G., Hatters-Friedman, S., & Knoll, J. L., IV. (2010). Lessons to learn: female educators who sexually abuse their students. *Psychiatric Times*, *27*(8), 9–10.

Wijkman, M., Bijleveld, C., & Hendriks, J. (2010). Women don't do such things! Characteristics of female sex offenders and offender types. *Sexual Abuse*, *22*(2), 135–156.

Wortley, R., & Smallbone, S. (2000). *Child sexual abuse in Queensland: offender characteristics and modus operandi*. Brisbane: Queensland Crime Commission and Queensland Police Service.

Zack, E., Lang, J. T., & Dirks, D. (2016). "It must be great being a female pedophile!": the nature of public perceptions about female teacher sex offenders. *Crime, Media, Culture: An International Journal*, *14*(1), 1–19. https://doi.org/10.1177/1741659016674044.

PART 2

Impact and Outcomes of Child Abuse

CHAPTER 8

Forensic Victimology Assessments in Child Abuse and Neglect Cases

Wayne Petherick
Faculty of Society and Design, Bond University, Gold Coast, QLD, Australia

1 Introduction

In general terms, victimology is the study of victims. This broad definition does little to aid in our understanding of victims of different types, who have fallen prey to natural disaster or who have suffered at the hands of others as victims of criminal acts. The associated field of study of victims of a variety of events is called *general victimology* and concerns itself as much with victims of war and natural disaster as it does victims of crime (van Dijk, 1999). For the purpose of this chapter, we are concerned only with the subfield of victimology known as *forensic victimology*, which focuses on victims of interpersonal crime and violence in an attempt to answer investigative and legal questions (Ferguson, Petherick, & Turvey, 2010). This is more akin to interactionist or penal victimology (van Dijk, 1999), which is the study of the interactions between offenders and victims (Ferguson et al., 2010).

The study of victimology as a formal discipline has been around for less than one century. The first person to formally use the term victimology was Benjamin Mendelsohn while presenting in Bucharest for the Romanian Psychiatric Association (Wilson, 2009). Mendelsohn interviewed victims and found that many of them had a personal relationship with the offender. He continued his work that lead to the development of a typology focusing on the degree of culpability of the victim (Wilson, 2009).

One of the first uses of the term victimology is by Fredric Wertham (1949) who wrote *The Show of Violence*. Wertham was a psychiatrist in New York, and he was to later go on to author *Seduction of the Innocents*, a book about the dangers of comics and the role they played in juvenile delinquency. In *The Show of Violence*, Wertham notes that the focus at the time was on offenders, such as their developmental history and

Child Abuse and Neglect. https://doi.org/10.1016/B978-0-12-815344-4.00008-8

rationalisations for the act. Emphasising the importance of the victim, he goes on to argue that (p. 259)

> *The murder victim is the forgotten man. What with sensational discussions on the abnormal psychology of the murderer, we have failed to emphasize the unprotectedness of the victim and the complacency of the authorities. One cannot understand the psychology of the murderer if one does not understand the sociology of his victim. What we need is a science of victimology.*

Many later victimologists were lawyers who used the study of victims to determine the degree of legal culpability of their clients. Hans von Hentig was a German lawyer who wrote *The Criminal and His Victim*, Steven Schafer was a Hungarian-born American lawyer who wrote *The Victim and His Criminal* (presumably in homage to von Hentig), and Benjamin Mendelsohn was a Romanian lawyer. Their typologies outlined features or characteristics of victims that contribute towards an active or passive precipitation (these will be discussed in the next section). For example, von Hentig (1948) includes the acquisitive who is greedy and looking for personal gain. Schafer (1977) includes provocative victims where the offender is reacting to something the victim has done and the precipitative type where the victim puts themselves in harm's way by virtue of how they dress, speak, act, and so forth.

2 Victim Precipitation

The attribution of responsibility will depend on a number of factors, not limited to the sex of the victim, drug and alcohol use, manner of dress, and their behaviour at the time of the offence. Blame is often placed upon the victim when they have done something that some find personally or morally offensive such as 'she shouldn't have worn a skirt so short!' or 'he shouldn't have been so drunk!' There may also be a tendency to absolve a victim of blame when they possess characteristics that are socially desirable or faultless such as 'she was just a little child!' Such attributions serve a psychological or emotional purpose: if we can identify something in another that we do not do personally possess or believe to be peculiar to the victim, this reassures us that a similar fate cannot or will not befall us.

Of course, such thinking is perhaps more of a common or popular attempt to understand crime by identifying very simple cause and effect relationships, and while they may make us feel better, they do little to aid in the professional or structured understanding of a criminal event. This is to say nothing of the very complex relationship between victim and criminal. Therefore, any attempt to understand crime and victimisation must include an attempt to understand the context and circumstances of the criminal event. This includes what the victim was doing, who they are, how they were behaving, and what they were doing at the crime scene. But our attempt to understand doesn't end there, and while we must consider these factors as related to the victim, we must also incorporate the same attempt in our understanding of the offender.

Victim precipitation is a contentious area within the study of victims of crime, as it is often equated with victim blaming. Indeed, Moriarty's (2008) *Controversies in Victimology* has in it a chapter covering victim precipitation by Eigenberg and Garland (2008), which is titled Victim Blaming. In it, the authors state (p. 22)

> *Ironically, one of the ways that victims re-emerged in the study of crime related to the ways that they contributed to their victimization. Victim blaming, victim facilitation, and victim precipitation are some of the many labels used to examine the concept of shared responsibility for criminal acts. Generally speaking, victim precipitative behaviours are those which cause victims to bring about their own victimization... As one might image [sic], this type of approach has caused a great deal of controversy.*

This somewhat simple link between precipitation and blame dichotomises the relationship between the victim and the offender as one in which the offender is entirely at fault and the victim is not at all. This ignores the complex interplay of factors between the victim and offender, victim and the crime scene, and offender and the crime scene, along with any other variables that occur within any given criminal event. This also reduces the argument to one where we are attempting to find fault, resulting in a value judgement being placed upon a variety of behaviours and interactions. This typically takes the form of 'if you weren't doing X, Y wouldn't have happened to you'.

Not only is this unhelpful, but also it is usually the responsibility of the legal professional to introduce fault at trial within the scope of the criminal law (such as may occur with provocation defences as but one example). It is generally not within the purview of the social and behavioural scientist to try to ascribe blame, only to examine and outline the case in such a way that they can assist others in their understanding of the case. To put it another way, it is the expert's job to provide content and connection, and this can only be done through a detailed and thorough understanding of the roles played by all of the parties concerned. Much of what is seen in a crime is a reaction to an action that may in itself produce a reaction and on and on until one party is hurt or killed by another. The skill is in disentangling the complexities of these interactions and explaining them in such a way that each respective action and reaction can be understood. It is in this understanding that the author suggests an examination of precipitation can be useful. This will allow for a more holistic understanding of the case, and it may inform decision makers about complex issues that may be outside of their education, training, and experience to understand.

A critical point to consider with regard to victim precipitation and one that would render any accusation of precipitation equating to blame redundant is that of perception. Within any given crime, there are a variety of viewpoints, even amongst those directly involved. There is how the victims see themselves, how other people see them, and how they see the offender/s. There is how the offenders see themselves, how other people see them, and how they see the victim/s. What this means is that precipitation is as much about perception as it is reality, and blaming a victim for another person's perception is like blaming the neighbour's dog for what your dog left by the back door.

3 Victimology in Child Abuse and Neglect Cases

Victimological assessments in child abuse and neglect cases are not fundamentally different to those conducted on adults or teenagers. That is, they contain the same information from much the same sources as other assessments. One key difference though is that a child victim will not have the same degree of autonomy or independence as an adult and therefore will often not have their own information to report on in the sections discussed below. For example, a child, depending on their age, won't usually have an employment history or a drug and alcohol history. Because of this, we cannot just ignore that information especially seeing as so much violence may indeed be predicated upon it: a parent's drug and alcohol history will certainly impact upon the child's risk of becoming a victim of crime, as will their employment and financial history. Speaking specifically to this point on infanticide, Piers (1978, p. 13) just as relevant now as it was when it was written, states that

> *The total helplessness of the human child at birth and the near endless years of subsequent dependence on adults make him a ready target for their destructive impulses. Children die because adults neglect or abuse them or kill them at birth.*

The role of the parents in the victimisation of the child is also echoed in the factors that relate to filicide, as stated by Almeida and Vieira (2017, p. 168):

> *Several studies have suggested, among other causes, child maltreatment (which turns out to be fatal), altruistic reasons, psychotic symptoms, spouse revenge, social factors (e.g. socioeconomic conditions), or the existence of diseases or malformations in children as causal of crime.*

All of this to say that, the younger the child and more heavily dependent they are on their caregivers, the greater the influence of the parent's behaviour on their risk of victimisation.

3.1 Positive and Negative Documentation

There are two general styles of documentation that can be done in a victimology. The first is called *positive documentation* where evidence exists regarding a particular facet, and this information is provided in the correct history section. Positive documentation effectively says, 'we have evidence for this, and here it is'. The second type is called *negative documentation* and is used when there is no evidence for a particular section or facet of the victimology or where no evidence was provided to the examiner (though it may exist elsewhere). This tells the reader of the report that this information was considered but wasn't available, preventing them from questioning whether it was even considered in the first instance. The format for this style of documentation usually follows along the lines of 'no information about psychological history was provided to this analyst'.

3.2 Administrative Inclusions

This section is usually amongst the first and contains the basic contact and administrative information for the report such as who wrote it, when, who it was written for, and contact information. This is a very important part of the report as it details not only who wrote the report and under what circumstances but also who requested the report and under what circumstances this was done. Contact information is important for obvious reasons. The author usually advises that three types of contact information be provided because affiliations and employment status can change over time, subsequently changing e-mail and mobile and telephone numbers, but there is less chance that all three will change at once. This will allow someone to contact you after the fact should they not be amongst the original people who contracted the report. Perhaps, a new lawyer has taken on the case, or the report is wanted to be able to argue a different aspect of the same case through another agency. The author was involved in a case in 2000 in an appellate matter and then contacted again in 2010 or so for a copy of the report to be used in an extradition matter. It was only because one type of contact information provided had stayed the same that the client was able to establish contact after so many years.

This section includes any caveats or disclaimers such as whether you were able to visit the crime scene, whether you discuss the matter with relevant parties, or where there may be conflicts of interest that need to be disclosed. This author also includes a discovery chain where a description or explanation is provided explaining the specific approach the client made for the examination, how many discussions were held over time and when, and whether any other persons were spoken to or interviewed in relation to the case or report.

3.3 Demographics

The demographic section of the report contains basic information about the victim or victims such as height, weight, age, sex, religion, aliases, tattoos or identifying marks, eye colour, hair colour, and anything else about their physical appearance. This information should be obtained through primary sources where possible such as official or government identification, recent photographs, or social media posts. Where the information is vague, equivocal, or cannot be established as fact, then this should be clearly stated so that the reader of the report knows the appropriate degree of caution they need to attach to the information.

Recording this information is more than an academic exercise of cataloguing. A frequent change of appearance may signal an attempt to conceal or disguise identity, a gross fluctuation in weight may signal a period of emotional turmoil, and tattoos can provide connections and relationships. Of course, such information may not be proof of any of this, but unless it is documented and investigated properly, the victimologist cannot know what weight, if any, to attach to it.

3.4 Medical History

It may be difficult to acquire information related to certain sections of the victimology owing to the confidential nature of that information. The medical history is one such section. Ideally, medical records would be the best place to acquire this information unless this is provided by the victim, a family member, or a legal representative. Sometimes, a living victim will be entirely forthcoming with this information and sometimes not. Sometimes, a proxy measure of medical history could be used such as medications prescribed (type of medicine, dosage, recency of prescriptions, how much of the prescription has been taken, and anything else relevant to the medical domain).

This section should include not only those medical issues that have been subject to formal diagnosis but also any conditions that the victim claims to have. For formal diagnoses, the exact date, identity, and qualifications of the person making the diagnosis should be provided if available. The nature and degree of any impact this had on the victim's functioning should also be included here.

If there is scant medical information available or where this information overlaps significantly with other information, it may not be appropriate to combine this section with others. For example, if there is a lot of medical history and a lot of psychological history, it would make more sense to keep these as discrete sections in the report. However, if the only information is that the victim had depression, was prescribed an antidepressant, and was receiving ongoing counselling, then this could be combined into a medical and psychological history section.

There will be circumstances in which it is not clear where a specific piece of history should be placed. The author always advises that this should be done where this information makes most sense within the context of the case. If the examiner feels that a certain thing is better suited to medical history, then that is where it should be placed. If related more to psychological history, then this would be the best home for it.

3.5 Psychological History

Like medical history, psychological history may be difficult to establish owing to the confidential nature of any psychological or psychiatric examination. As above, some victims may keep extensive documentation, and others may keep nothing at all. The highly paranoid individual may obsessively keep records of everything they go through, thinking it is all part of some conspiracy or action against them. The complacent victim may dispose of or lose any of this information.

Many children will be too young to be diagnosed with certain disorders, perhaps especially true of personality disorders and other disorders of functioning because symptoms may be a normal part of the developmental process (attachment issues as but one example). It is equally true that they are often simply not old enough to be symptomatic or to have experienced sufficient emotional development for a disorder to surface. Despite this, there may still be some evidence of psychological dysfunction in the child, and this may be particularly relevant when there is associated reactivity or complementarity in the behaviour of the adult. For example, a child with strong attachment needs coupled with an emotionally ambivalent mother may act out in various ways.

Because of this, it is vital to include any and all information regarding the psychological functioning of the parents when this is available. This would include not only any evidence of thought disorders, but also and perhaps more importantly evidence of relationship and emotional functioning or disorder. When a parent has characteristics or evidence of borderline personality disorder (BPD) and the child is displaying significant attachment problems with this parent, risks of harm to the child may be heightened (see de Barros & de Pádua Serafim, 2008 and others).

If the parent or parents have multiple children, the psychological functioning with each of the children and also amongst the children will be important to examine. This may highlight which, if any, of the specific relationships were problematic and the nature and degree of any dysfunction between people.

3.6 Justice System History

It is unlikely that a child will have had contact with the prison system, but this section of the victimology is for contact with all branches of the justice system, not just its penal arm. Children may have had contact with the family court system in a custodial dispute; they may have been through various degrees of contact with child safety or the foster care system, juvenile justice (if old enough), and any other branches that exist within the myriad criminal justice and social systems around the world. A child may also have had formal assessments conducted that could be available to the analyst, and these may inform on family functioning, psychological functioning, emotional adjustment, or anything else of victimological concern.

Evidence of the criminal justice history of the parents or caregivers would also be included here if present and available. Not only does this provide an understanding of their contact with various branches of the justice system, but also it will provide insight into the kinds of behaviours they have engaged in previously. It may also provide information about an ongoing contact with the system or provide information about potential criminal contacts.

3.7 Drugs and Alcohol History

Certain drugs have a heightened relationship to violence and can play a role in victimisation and offending (methamphetamine users are involved in about one-quarter of violent and property offences; see Goldsmid & Willis, 2016), and even drug dealing has been shown to be associated with an increased risk of violence (Seffrin & Domahidi, 2014). Being under the influence of drugs or alcohol can alter an individual's perception, their ability to identify risks in their environment, and their ability to make rational choices or decisions. Living in a home in which there is drug use or drug dealing can increase a child victim's risk.

The nature of the particular drugs must be identified and documented, and this should include any illegal drugs and legal drugs that they may be taking outside of medical care. Any contraindications for each particular medicine must be included along with the frequency, recency, and duration of the medication. The frequency relates to how often it is taken, recency relates to the last taken dosage, and duration is how long they have been taking the medication in total. If the victim is taking drugs prescribed by a doctor, this information would be better suited in the medical history section.

Anything being taken by the parents should be included here. This would include the specific drug and how this is sourced (does the parent go to a well-known drug location? Does the dealer visit or deliver to the house? Do the parents or caregivers produce or grow their own?). If known, the effect of the drug on each individual user should be included. This may show, for example that when consuming alcohol, they may become sullen and moody, happy, or aggressive and violent. Drugs affect each person differently, and thus, the effects should be factored into any assessment. The alcohol and drug history should be compared with any toxicological results that are available. This not only will help validate the historical discovery but also may identify other substances not previously known about.

3.8 Relationship History

Criminal and victim behaviours do not occur in a vacuum, and there are potentially a large number of people who have information regarding a victim's history (Petherick & Ferguson, 2015). How someone functions in a relationship can be instructive in understanding why and how they were targeted by an offender. A victim who is willing to take a lot of abuse from their partners may open themselves up for domestic abuse and those with reassurance-oriented needs (see Petherick & Sinnamon, 2014; Petherick, 2014a). A victim's motivation for behaving in a particular way has been shown to be predictive for the type of offence they will fall victim to (Brotto, Sinnamon, & Petherick, 2017).

The relationship history should be detailed chronologically including the nature of the relationship, duration, level of functioning, and how and why it ended if at all. Consideration should be given to any differences in relationship style or functioning such as whether this was worse with one person than another. For a child, whether they bonded better with one parent or whether they had more conflict with one parent might be important in understanding the context of victimisation.

3.9 Residential History

A residential history should be compiled to determine the physical locations where the victim has lived and the amount of time they spent living there and the status of the occupancy. If the child lives across multiple dwellings, these should be identified and documented, including the amount of time they spent at each address. Because exposure to harm or loss can be based on the physical proximity to crime or criminals, the crime rate of the location should be investigated. This is done to identify whether the danger was coming from inside the house or from the environment in which the house was located.

3.10 Employment History

As a child won't typically have an employment history, this would be based entirely on the parent's employment status. The type of employment will provide information about the amount of time guardians are out of the house, where they are when out of the house, hours kept, and who they have contact with. Any formal employment should be recorded along with informal or 'off the books' employment. Any volunteer work undertaken could be included here. As with other sections of the victimology (e.g. relationship and technological), the idea here is to document the number of people the victim may have had contact with over time and the context under which these contacts occurred.

3.11 Financial History

Financial history will usually be inextricably linked to employment history, but not in every instance. For example, someone might not only have a job but also be independently wealthy based on family money or an inheritance. Income sources from both legitimate and illegitimate streams should be documented where available, such as when a victim or family member has both a paid job and supplementary income from dealing drugs. Bank and credit card statements may be available and should be consulted. If the victim was living beyond their means but still managing to meet their financial commitments, the way this is done should be established. It may well be that there are previously undiscovered income streams or someone else may be helping out financially.

3.12 Technological History

The technological history relates to the various ways in which the victim or those around them connect to the world. This would include the specific type of connections available (home-based broadband service or mobile data) and the number and nature of devices used. The more connected a child is the greater their exposure is to those outside of the house who may do them harm. It is therefore important to establish the variety of different ways a child may come into contact with any other persons through technology. However, while intuitively correct, some evidence suggests that an increase in time spent online does not necessarily result in an increased exposure to victimisation (see Livingstone & Smith, 2014).

The number of connections should be chronicled, as should the number of devices. Laptop computers, tablets, mobile phones, e-readers, games consoles, and any other connected technology should be included here. The amount of time spent online and the number of different accounts reflecting an online presence should be established. Nicknames or 'gamer tags' should be established, as well as online searches made of these. The idea is to determine whether the harm or loss came to the victim through a device or connected account by virtue of who they were in contact with. Similarly, posts made to social media, blogs, bulletin boards, or text and messaging clients may help establish what has happened, how long it has been going on, and who else is involved. For example, they may have discussed their victimisation with someone online, and this could be used in conjunction with information already known, or it may provide new information that the analyst was not aware of.

3.13 Media History

Of all sections of the victimology, the media history may be the least predictive or valid and the most speculative in terms of the meaning that can be derived from it. The idea in establishing a victim's media history is to determine whether there are any themes running throughout the media they use. This would include the books and magazines they read, the types of television shows or movies they watch, or the type of music they listen to. This would also include their internet searches and websites visited. If a victim is doing a lot of searches relating to 'child abuse' or 'bad touching', this may provide a window into what is happening to them. Musical genres depicting despair, hopelessness, or helplessness may be similarly instructive.

It is also important to understand that this may amount to nothing meaningful at all. Even a cursory perusal of the author's media would show nothing more than a musical taste from the 1960 through top 40, movies from a variety of genres including romcoms and action, and books ranging from fiction to military history and political intrigue. However, as with all information, inquiries must be made in case something meaningful can be found. The victimologist would not want to find themselves in the unenviable position of having something of merit available to them but not knowing about it because they didn't look.

3.14 Past Victimisation

According to Tseloni and Pease (2003, p. 196) 'victimisation is a good, arguably the best readily available, predictor of future victimisation'. Some individuals will suffer repeatedly as the hands of others, either for the same type of crime or for different types of crime with different people. A repeated or regular exposure to the same type of offending may indicate a lack of insight or introspection on the part of the victim, or it could communicate a lack of self-worth. In children, there will be conflict between what is happening ('mummy/daddy hurts me') and how, in their limited understanding, they should feel ('I love my mummy/daddy'). The younger the victim the less able they may be to extricate themselves from the situation or even to understand what is happening to them. As they won't have a knowledge of the law, they will not and cannot appreciate that what is happening to them is wrong. We also cannot expect child victims to have the executive functioning to know that they need to extract themselves from a dangerous situation or to even understand what a dangerous situation looks like. For those who grow up in abusive environments, the abuse may indeed be their normal.

3.15 Wounds

Wounds should be differentiated from injuries. An injury is something like a cut, bruise, scrape, or other trauma relating to some environmental event or accident between people and people or the environment. Injuries, such as a graze from falling down while learning to ride a bicycle, would be considered under medical history. This section of the victimology is entirely reserved for those defects or traumas imparted to the victim as a result of deliberate action by another person or persons. An injury results when two people while playing accidentally bump heads. A wound happens when one person has his/her head banged against an object deliberately by another as punishment or whim. The goal here is therefore to distinguish between those defects caused by accident and those caused deliberately. For obvious reasons, when considering victimology, we only want to incorporate those aspects that are the result of criminal or negligent events as these will be related to the criminal event under consideration.

3.16 Risk Assessment

The risk assessment could be considered the capstone of the victimology. Information from all other histories is used to determine where the danger was coming from in the victim's life. This includes not only whether there was a danger but also the nature and degree of the danger.

Victim risk is different to the more commonly understood violence risk assessment. It is necessary to understand these types of risk and the difference between them so as to ensure that the proper and appropriate risk assessment is conducted in a given case and also that the right questions are being asked and answered. Generally speaking, the difference between the two is in the timeframe of the assessment and whether it is retrospective (victim risk assessment) or predictive (violence risk assessment).

A victim risk assessment seeks to determine the victim's risk of suffering what actually happened to them. So in a homicide case, we are trying to answer the question *what was this person's risk of being a victim of homicide?* In this context, we are not necessarily interested in what might happen to them in the future, only in establishing whether what happened to them could have been expected, and to what degree (classed as low, medium, or high). For a victim risk assessment to be required, an event has occurred (a victimisation of some type), and a request has been made to determine this victim's risk of that event. We are thus starting at a point in time (the criminal event) and looking back at the victim's overall lifestyle and situational factors to determine the victim's exposure to this specific type of event.

A violence risk assessment is a predictive assessment involving a prediction of violence towards a specific person or group of people at some point in time in the future. This could be a fixed point such as within a month or year, or it could be a vague or nonspecific timeframe such as 'at some point in the future'.

4 Determine Patterns, Themes, and Associations

The general rule with information in any analysis conducted from a social scientific approach is that all information is relevant until proven otherwise. This is the philosophy of Applied Crime Analysis (see Petherick, 2014b), which is a holistic attempt to understand an individual case in depth. When done properly, the analyst should come to learn more about the current case than any other person, though usually with a few exceptions (parents, partners, family members, original investigators, and the legal team may be just as well or better versed on the particulars of the case).

Once all of the information is assembled and has been examined, the goal is to develop hypotheses that potentially explain the behaviours and interactions. Once these hypotheses have been developed, the next step is to test these against the evidence in the case. Weaker theories that don't stand up to scrutiny will be excluded relatively easily, from which we can move on to more robust theories of the case. When we have systematically excluded all theories on the case but one, this becomes the working theory of the case and can be used to explain the event in specific light of questions the analyst has been asked to address.

The reader familiar with this process will know it as the scientific method, which is a systematic process for obtaining knowledge through testing and falsification. In an ideal world, there will be enough information to be able to test and exclude every hypothesis but one, though in reality there will be missing or incomplete information or information about the case that is still equivocal, that is, subject to more than one interpretation. In situations such as this, we may be left with what is known as reasoning to the best explanation, or adduction, where the strongest argument is put forward based on the evidence. Where a number of competing hypotheses remain, then each of the surviving hypotheses should be put forward along with the relative merits of each argument. If sufficient evidence exists, then the analyst may even go so far as to rank order the hypotheses according to the amount of data that supports or refutes each one.

In situations where the analyst is left with a number of possibilities, the Applied Crime Analysis (ACA) or analysis of competing hypotheses model is of use. This is presented by Heuer (1999) in a publication for the United States Central Agency. In it, Heuers proposes that a matrix be produced with the competing hypotheses on one axis, along with the evidence supporting or refuting each hypothesis along another axis. The evidence in support of a given hypothesis can then be tallied, and this may be a useful indicator of the merits of each alternative scenario.

The key to determining what actually happened or which of the scenarios best accounts for the available data is to look for patterns, themes, and associations between the various components of the victimology. An assertion about how someone functions in the company of other people that is drawn from multiple domains of the victimology will be a stronger and easier case to make than if information from only one domain supports it. For example, in an analysis, evidence of interpersonal conflict where there is considerable information in the psychological history, relationship history, and employment history will strengthen the case compared with conflict between just the victim and one other person drawn from the relationship information.

All of the information in the victimology and the conclusions that arise from this should be presented in accordance to the validity, reliability, and sufficiency of that information (Petherick & Rowan, 2015). The use of these terms within the context of ACA and victimology differ a little to their traditional use in research, so they will be discussed briefly herein.

In a research context, validity refers to whether something measures what it is supposed to measure. A depression instrument that measures depression is valid. A research project that produces genuine findings is valid. In ACA, something is valid when it is an accurate representation of what it actually is. A stain on a carpet that has been presumptively tested for blood and then sent to the crime laboratory for testing that verifies it is human blood means that this stain in a crime scene can be validly accepted as human biological fluid. A brown stain on a carpet that has not been further tested could be a chocolate milkshake, red wine, or any other variant of contaminant. Validity relates to trust, that is, can we trust the information? Validity and accuracy are functional equivalents.

Reliability typically refers to whether a test or procedure can yield the same findings. If a measure for depression measures this accurately across groups or across repeated testing with the same person, then it could be said to be reliable. In ACA, reliability refers to whether we can trust the information itself or the source of the information. Information given to us by someone who is a suspect or who has questionable motives may not be reliable, while information from a third party who has no vested interest in an outcome may be more trustworthy. Reliability and trust are functional equivalents.

The final aspect of information that is necessary to establish is called sufficiency. This refers to the quantity of the information available. Obviously, more information is better, and more limited information will likely result in more limited conclusions that can be formed. At the least, any conclusions must be identified as circumspect or speculative when information is not of considerable volume.

Each piece of information must be assessed according to its accuracy (validity), trust (reliability), and quantity (sufficiency). Where the rating of this information is low across all three, this must be communicated appropriately in the language used within the report. It wouldn't typically be acceptable to state something as fact when we only have an allegation, so the language must reflect the evidence we have for any given conclusion or domain. For example, if John claims he last spoke to the victim at 8:00 pm and this is the only evidence supporting this, then the language 'John states he spoke to the victim at 8:00 pm' would be appropriate. If this were a matter of verifiable fact, such as established through phone records, 'John spoke to the victim at 8:00 pm' would be acceptable.

5 Conclusion

Establishing the nature and context of any victimisation is paramount. This will dictate the direction of the investigation and any subsequent inquiries that arise from it, such as civil litigation or further criminal charges against those liable for victimisation. While this can be a statistical picture established through research and literature, it is the author's contention that this be properly established through an idiographic analysis of the case. This is accomplished through an examination of the number of histories of the victim including the medical and psychological history, residential, technological, and media history. This information then informs an overall risk assessment to determine where in the victim's like the harms or potential harms were coming from. As the child will be too young to have established much autonomy from parents and caregivers, the child's victimology will include any information about them that has been established up until the index event but will likely be substantively based on information about the parents. The higher the degree of reliance on the parents, the higher the impact of their functioning and environment on the child's risk of harm.

Chapter Review Questions

1. Name five different histories included in a victimology.
2. The media history includes information about whether the victim has ever been interviewed on the radio or on television. True or False?
3. Identify two of the histories that may overlap with other histories.
4. A victimology done on a child victim should only include information about the child and never about other persons such as caregivers or parents. True or false?
5. Briefly define victim precipitation and why it is not necessarily about blaming the victim.

6. The two different types of victim precipitation are
   a. Active and overt
   b. Overt and Covert
   c. Overt and Passive
   d. Active and Passive
   e. None of the above

References

Almeida, F., & Vieira, D. N. (2017). Profiling in violent crimes: the perpetrator and the victim in cases of filicide. In W. A. Petherick & G. C. B. Sinnamon (Eds.), *The psychology of criminal and antisocial behaviour: Victim and offender perspectives*. San Diego: Elsevier Science.

Brotto, G. L. M., Sinnamon, G. C. B., & Petherick, W. A. (2017). Victimology and predicting victims of personal violence. In W. A. Petherick & G. C. B. Sinnamon (Eds.), *The psychology of criminal and antisocial behaviour: Victim and offender perspectives*. San Diego: Elsevier Science.

de Barros, D. M., & de Pádua Serafim, A. (2008). Association between personality disorder and violent behavior pattern. *Forensic Science International*, *179*(1), 19–22. https://doi.org/10.1016/j.forsciint.2008.04.013.

Eigenberg, H., & Garland, T. (2008). Victim blaming. In L. J. Moriarty (Ed.), *Controversies in victimology*. (2nd ed.). Newark: Anderson Publishing.

Ferguson, C. E., Petherick, W. A., & Turvey, B. E. (2010). Forensic victimology. In W. A. Petherick, C. E. Ferguson, & B. E. Turvey (Eds.), *Forensic criminology*. San Diego: Academic Press.

Goldsmid, S., & Willis, M. (2016). Methamphetamine use and acquisitive crime: evidence of a relationship. In Vol. 516. *Trends and issues in crime and justice*. Canberra: Australian Institute of Criminology.

Heuer, R. J. (1999). *The psychology of intelligence analysis. Centre for the study of intelligence*. Washington: Central Intelligence Agency.

Livingstone, S., & Smith, P. K. (2014). Annual research review: harms experienced by child users of online and mobile technologies: the nature, prevalence and management of sexual and aggressive risks in the digital age. *Journal of Child Psychology and Psychiatry*, *55*(6), 635–654. https://doi.org/10.1111/jcpp.12197.

Petherick, W. A. (2014a). Motivations. In W. A. Petherick (Ed.), *Applied crime analysis: A social science approach to understanding crime, criminals and victims*. Sand Diego: Elsevier Science.

Petherick, W. A. (Ed.), (2014b). *Applied crime analysis: A social science approach to understanding crime, criminals and victims*. Sand Diego: Elsevier Science.

Petherick, W. A., & Ferguson, C. E. (2015). Forensic victimology. In W. A. Petherick (Ed.), *Applied crime analysis: A social science approach to understanding crime, criminals and victims*. Sand Diego: Elsevier Science.

Petherick, W. A., & Rowan, A. (2015). Physical evidence and the crime scene. In W. A. Petherick (Ed.), *Applied crime analysis: A social science approach to understanding crime, criminals, and victims*. San Diego: Elsevier Science.

Petherick, W. A., & Sinnamon, G. C. B. (2014). Motivations: offender and victim perspectives. In W. A. Petherick (Ed.), *Profiling and serial crime: Theoretical and practical issues*. San Diego: Academic Press.

Piers, M. W. (1978). *Infanticide: Past and present*. New York: W. W. Norton and Company Inc.

Schafer, S. (1977). *Victimology: The victim and his criminal*. Virginia: Reston Publishing Company.

Seffrin, P. M., & Domahidi, B. I. (2014). The drugs-violence nexus: a systematic comparison of adolescent drug dealers and drug users. *Journal of Drug Issues*, *44*(4), 394–413. https://doi.org/10.1177/0022042614526994.

Tseloni, A., & Pease, K. (2003). Repeat personal victimisation. *British Journal of Criminology*, *43*, 196–212.

van Dijk, J. J. M. (1999). Introducing victimology. In J. J. M. van Dijk, R. G. H. van Kaam, & J. Wemmers (Eds.), *Caring for crime victims: Selected proceedings of the ninth international symposium on victimology, Amsterdam, August 25–29, 1997* (pp. 1–12). Monsey, NY: Criminal Justice Press.

Von Hentig, H. (1948). *The criminal and his victim*. New Haven: Yale University Press.

Wertham, F. (1949). *The show of violence*. New York: Doubleday and Company, Inc.

Wilson, J. K. (2009). *The Praeger handbook of victimology*. Santa Barbara: ABC-CLIO LLC.

CHAPTER 9

Cumulative Harm: Chronicity, Revictimisation, and Developmental Victimology

India Bryce

University Southern Queensland, Toowoomba, QLD, Australia

1 Introduction

The impact of adverse childhood conditions and the associated complex trauma that often results is a pervasive social concern, both nationally and internationally. Trauma that is experienced early in life has the potential for lifelong negative outcomes across the major domains of personal and social functioning. Evidence for this is growing, and the implications for individuals, families, and support services, as well as social policy for prevention, protection, and intervention, are continually being clarified. The Australian Royal Commission into Institutional Responses to Child Sexual Abuse identified that 80% of the 5000 participants they have interviewed to date had experienced multiple incidents of abuse, by multiple perpetrators, with the average length of abuse being 2.5 years (Fitzgerald, 2016). Commissioner Robert Fitzgerald argued that "the lack of trauma-informed practice and inadequate understanding of the long-term impacts of trauma are the reasons for the large population of dysfunctional and struggling traumatised individuals in Australia" (Fitzgerald, 2016). In an Australian study, Kezelman, Hossack, Stavropoulos, and Burley (2015) calculated that the annual cost of childhood trauma to the government is $16 billion. The report further stated that, "a minimum of $9.1 billion could be gained from addressing the problem of childhood trauma more generally in the 5 million Australian adults affected by it" (Kezelman et al., 2015, p. 43). In addition to this, Australian research has reflected international studies that, "the majority of children who experience child maltreatment will have multiple incidents of maltreatment over a prolonged period of time" (Bromfield & Higgins, 2005, p. 38). The impact of the accumulation of adverse childhood experiences (ACEs) has been labelled 'cumulative harm' (Bromfield, Gillingham, & Higgins, 2007).

This chapter will explore the broad range of theoretical perspectives that construct our current understanding of cumulative harm and will investigate concepts of chronicity, developmental

Child Abuse and Neglect. https://doi.org/10.1016/B978-0-12-815344-4.00009-X

victimology, polyvictimisation, and revictimisation. The chapter will highlight the pervasive impact on the individual, behaviourally, physically, and psychologically, across the lifespan and emphasise additional considerations such as resilience. Finally, prevention and intervention approaches specific to cumulative harm will be discussed.

2 Cumulative Harm

2.1 The Adverse Childhood Experiences Study

In the 1990s, researchers discovered a phenomenon that had profound impact on individuals across the lifespan, lowering life expectancy, increasing risk of chronic illness and disease, impairing functioning, and diminishing capacity—this phenomenon was exposure to childhood trauma (Felitti et al., 1998). The adverse childhood experience (ACE) study was a ground breaking, large-scale investigation of negative childhood experiences and poor adult outcomes. Between 1995 and 1997, 17,000 participants completed surveys providing information regarding their childhood experiences, health status, and behaviour. These results, combined with physical exams, formed the study's findings. The study provided the evidential weight to an instinctive belief, long held by practitioners in the field, that childhood trauma has pervasive and far-reaching implications, often unseen until later life and long after the adversity is resolved. The original study found more than half the respondents (52%) had experienced one or more ACEs, more than one in five reported three or more ACEs, and approximately 6% indicated more than four ACEs (Felitti et al., 1998). The study further highlighted that, for persons experiencing at least one ACE, the probability of exposure to additional categories of ACEs ranged from 62% to 93%, and experiencing more than two additional categories ranged from 40% to 74% (Felitti et al., 1998). Noting the commonality of multiple ACEs, further research was conducted into the relationship between multiple ACEs and long-term outcomes. Edwards, Holden, Felitti, and Anda (2003) found that, in his study of multicategory maltreatment, of the 43% of individuals who identified experiences of some form of childhood abuse, around one-third experienced at least two types of maltreatment and that the higher the number of ACEs experienced, the poorer the physical, mental, and behavioural outcomes in adulthood. According to Gillespie and Folger (2017), the ACE study was transformative to our understanding of the role cumulative ACEs play in lifespan health and wellbeing outcomes. Felitti (2017) muses that:

> *The prevalence of ACEs was found to be so common, and their powerful dose-related relationship so strong, that one can only wonder why the relationship of life experiences in the developmental years to adult functionality, disease and lifespan was not recognised long ago (p. 205).*

2.2 Cumulative Harm: Theoretical Perspectives

Research to date has shifted from a conceptualisation of isolated events of maltreatment to an understanding of the chronicity of abuse and neglect and the lifespan implications of prolonged and repetitive trauma (Bromfield et al., 2007; Dong et al., 2004; Edwards et al., 2003; Frederico, Jackson, & Black, 2008; Higgins, 2004). Bromfield et al. (2007) coined the term 'cumulative harm' as an overarching label to describe the impact of chronic maltreatment that applied to the "impact of patterns of circumstances and events in a child's life, which diminish a child's sense of safety, stability, and wellbeing" (Miller, 2007, p. 1). Gilmore (2010) likened cumulative harm to global warming, in that it is a seemingly intractable problem, involving a culmination of human and environmental factors. Miller (2007) argues for an all-encompassing definition of cumulative harm as it is:

> *...experienced by a child as a result of a series or pattern of harmful events and experiences that may be historical, or ongoing, with the strong possibility of the risk factors being multiple, interrelated and coexisting over critical developmental periods (p. 1).*

Howard Bath (2014), Children's Commissioner for the Northern Territory, highlighted that although discussions regarding cumulative harm in child protection literature have been present for some time, there has been a dearth of specific research relating to the impact of multitype abuse or the prevalence of chronic maltreatment leading to cumulative harm. Bath (2014) drew on the Australian Early Development Index (AEDI) that provides a census of population-based wellbeing indicators, undertaken by educators in a child first year of school. He argued that "the problematic AEDI scores for Indigenous children across Australia, and especially in the Northern Territory, provide a clear illustration of the impact of adverse experiences in early childhood and, by proxy, the phenomenon of cumulative harm" (Bath, 2014, p. 6). Bath (2014) emphasised that despite the lack of studies specifically exploring cumulative harm, there was no lack of evidence for the phenomenon, drawing on statutory legislation as an indicative example. He purported that, by definition, child protection legislation recognises cumulative harm in that it emphasises the need for neglect to be persistent and a child's basic needs repeatedly unmet (Bath, 2014). Further to this, Bath (2014) highlighted the presence of cumulative harm as an operational definition of maltreatment, present in child protection legislation within Australia.

Cumulative harm is largely an Australian term, with international research using the more global terminology of complex trauma, to encapsulate the lifespan implications of the accumulation of childhood adversity. However, the term cumulative harm, cumulative abuse, cumulative trauma, or cumulative risk has been utilised in research in the United States. In a study conducted in the mid-1990s, Follette, Polusny, Bechtle, and Naugle (1996) referred to cumulative trauma in their exploration of trauma symptomology and childhood and adult sexual and physical abuse. Follette et al. (1996) sought to address the gap in literature regarding cumulative impacts of sexual and physical trauma, in both childhood and adulthood. They hypothesised that "multiple trauma experiences would lead to increased trauma symptoms, and that as the number of different types of traumatic experiences increased, subjects would demonstrate a cumulative impact of trauma" (Follette et al., 1996, p. 27). Follette et al. (1996) concluded exposure to multiple interpersonal traumas is cumulative in their impact on an individual. Comparatively, Mcnutt, Carlson, Persaud, and Postmus (2002) investigated the relationship between cumulative abuse experiences, physical health, and health behaviour, concluding that both repeat victimisation in childhood and revictimisation in adulthood influenced health in adulthood. Further to this, the US Department of Health and Human Services published a paper in 2013 highlighting the cumulative impact of chronic child neglect, drawing specifically from the research of Kaplan, Schene, DePanfilis, and Gilmore (2009) to emphasise that chronically neglected children experience cumulative harm because of an ongoing pattern of deprivation of basic physical, psychological, and developmental needs.

Whilst the publication of specific cumulative harm research has stagnated in recent years, the literature and dialogue surrounding the issue clearly indicate a consensus on the value of prioritising cumulative harm. Practitioners and researchers vehemently agree that it is vitally important that research findings and clinical knowledge about chronic maltreatment and its legacy of cumulative harm find a central place in our legislative frameworks, our practice guidelines, our data collection processes, and our intervention models (Bromfield et al., 2007; Broadley, 2014; Bath, 2014; Bryce, 2018.)

2.3 Chronic Child Maltreatment

Chronicity is not a new concept in child abuse research. Since its public recognition in 1962 (Kempe, Silverman, Steele, Droegemueller, & Silver, 2013), child maltreatment has been acknowledged in research and in practice as occurring in either isolated or repeated incidents. From this, however, research into child maltreatment has historically been located in two dominant areas: factors increasing vulnerability to maltreatment and the impact of maltreatment on individuals (Anderson, 2010; Bromfield & Higgins, 2005; Higgins, 2004). Researchers have typically explored maltreatment in terms of specific subtypes: physical, psychological, sexual abuse, and witnessing family violence (Herrenkohl & Herrenkohl, 2009; Higgins, 2004; James, 2000; Miller-Perrin & Perrin, 2007). Bromfield and Higgins argued that this perspective on maltreatment fails to adequately acknowledge that "some children's development is characterised by maltreatment over prolonged periods of time and fails to address the cumulative impact" (Bromfield & Higgins, 2005, p. 38). Higgins (2004) argued that an abuse type may not be considered detrimental in isolation but may in fact be detrimental over those prolonged periods. Although contributing to the discipline, attempts to identify the risk factors and outcomes for individual abuse types have been largely unsuccessful due to the prevalence of individuals experiencing multiple forms of maltreatment in combination and over extended episodes (Higgins, 2004). Dong et al. (2004) argued that "adults who reported any single form of adverse childhood experience were likely to have suffered multiple other adverse experiences during childhood" (p. 781). Bromfield and Higgins indicate "the majority of children who experience child maltreatment will have multiple incidents of maltreatment over a prolonged period of time" (Bromfield & Higgins, 2005).

Early typologies of chronic maltreatment emerged in the 1990s and proposed theoretical frameworks for understanding repeat victimisation of children (Hamilton & Browne, 1998; Higgins & McCabe, 2000; Robbie Rossman & Rosenberg, 1998). These typologies contributed to a reconceptualisation of child maltreatment as an issue of chronicity rather than episodic, isolated events (Bromfield & Higgins, 2005). The following dimensions were proposed as valuable in conceptualising the experience of repeat victimisation: number of incidents (Hamilton & Browne, 1998; Higgins & McCabe, 2000; Robbie Rossman & Rosenberg, 1998); number of maltreatment subtypes (Higgins & McCabe, 2000; Robbie Rossman & Rosenberg, 1998); number of perpetrators (Hamilton & Browne, 1998; Higgins & McCabe, 2000); duration of time over which maltreatment took place (Robbie Rossman & Rosenberg, 1998); the child's familial network and embeddedness, ecological factors of community, and cultural environment (Robbie Rossman & Rosenberg, 1998); victimological factors (Hamilton & Browne, 1998); and the child's developmental stage (Hamilton & Browne, 1998). Although maltreatment severity and the relationship of the perpetrator to the child (intra- or extrafamilial) had been discussed in the literature, these elements had been absent from any of the typologies for multiple victimisation prior to the chronic maltreatment study conducted by Bromfield and Higgins (2005).

To give due weight to the phenomena of chronicity, the term *chronic child maltreatment* has been adopted and applied to the definition of "recurrent incidents of maltreatment over a prolonged period of time" (Bromfield et al., 2007). In their chronic maltreatment study, Bromfield and Higgins (2005) identified that 65% of participants, gathered from a child protection sample, had experienced chronic maltreatment, with multiple, interrelated issues. Their *chronic child maltreatment typology* (Bromfield & Higgins, 2005) included the following five dimensions: *frequency*, number of incidents; *subtype*, number of subtypes and categorical classification of the different subtypes (physical abuse, neglect, sexual abuse, emotional abuse, and witnessing family violence); *severity*, severity of the adult behaviour and severity of harm to the child; *perpetrators*, number of perpetrators and relationship of perpetrator to child (intra- or extrafamilial); and *duration*, period of time over which maltreatment occurred. Prolonged and persistent experiences of child abuse and neglect, occurring over various developmental periods, can cause cumulative harm and have a profound and exponential impact on a child's life (Bromfield et al., 2007; Frederico et al., 2008; Miller, 2007).

2.4 Cumulative Harm: Multitype Maltreatment, Polyvictimisation and Revictimisation

Cumulative harm is the accumulation of maltreatment experiences in childhood, which have profound and pervasive impact on the lifespan of an individual. When considering the literature around cumulative harm, Miller (2007) states that "it has been relevant to study theory and research that documents multiple-victimisation, multiple harmful experiences that are interrelated, and maltreatment that is recurrent over prolonged periods" (p. 7).

This accumulation of child abuse, neglect, and adversity can take many forms, which are accounted for in the research as multitype maltreatment, polyvictimisation, and more broadly revictimisation. *Multitype maltreatment* has been proposed as a theoretical framework for understanding the interrelatedness of the five abuse types; however, polyvictimisation is a model that focuses on traumatisation in the broader sense, taking into account other forms of victimisation, including, but not limited to, bullying, neighbourhood conflict, and crime that might cooccur in childhood (Price-Robertson, Rush, Wall, & Higgins, 2013). *Revictimisation* is also a broader model, exploring the same adversities as polyvictimisation, although from a 'whole of lifespan' perspective.

In order to adequately communicate the interconnectedness of maltreatment experiences in childhood, Australian researchers, Higgins and McCabe (1998, 2000b), introduced the term *multitype maltreatment*. Although *single-type maltreatment* refers to experience of only one type of abuse (sexual, physical, emotional, neglect, or witnessing domestic violence), *multitype maltreatment* takes into account the coexistence of multiple abuse types (e.g. emotional abuse and physical abuse). Higgins and McCabe (2001) conducted a systematic review of existing studies that explored more than one type of child abuse or neglect and discovered two key findings: (1) A large percentage of adults who had experienced childhood maltreatment were subject to more than one type, and (2) those who reported multiple abuse subtypes had significantly poorer outcomes than those experiencing one or no abuse types. Comparatively, the findings of research conducted by Frederico et al. (2008) through the 'Take Two' program in Victoria, Australia, between 2004 and 2007, identified that of 1063 referrals, 96% of the referred clients had experienced multiple forms of abuse, with 25% experiencing all five domains of abuse.

There is a growing body of evidence to suggest that broader experiences of victimisation tend to accumulate for certain individuals or in certain environments (Fluke, Shusterman, Hollinshead, & Yuan, 2008; Hamilton & Browne, 1998; Price-Robertson et al., 2013). The dominant research tool used to measure polyvictimisation is the Juvenile Victimisation Questionnaire (JVQ) (Finkelhor, Ormrod, Turner, & Hamby, 2005). The JVQ measures the five general categories: conventional crime, child maltreatment, peer and sibling victimisation, sexual victimisation (peer or adult perpetrator), and witnessing and indirect victimisation. Polyvictimisation is indicated when an individual identifies experiencing an accumulation of four or more of these forms of victimisation over a 12 month period (Price-Robertson et al., 2013). The largest polyvictimisation studies found that almost a quarter of children in the United States experienced polyvictimisation in a 12 month period (Finkelhor et al., 2005; Finkelhor, Ormrod, & Turner, 2007a).

Finkelhor et al. (2007a) explored this cohort more closely and concluded that those children who had experienced four or more victimisations in 1 year were at high risk of revictimisation. Those who experience childhood maltreatment in the familial unit may be more susceptible than others to peer violence and exposure to crime; or childhood sexual abuse victims may be more vulnerable to further sexual victimisation as adults (Finkelhor, Ormrod, & Turner, 2007b; Tseloni & Pease, 2004). Finkelhor, Ormond, and Turner proposed that for many children, "victimisation is more of a *condition* than an *event*" (Finkelhor et al., 2007a, p. 9). They argue that:

> *...persistence is a pathway in which child maltreatment, domestic violence, family conflict, and disruption propel children into an intensively and generalized victimized condition that in turn generates general anger/aggression, which, by fuelling and sustaining defiant, challenging, rule-violating behaviour, tends to lock them into an even more persistent victimized condition (Finkelhor et al., 2007b, p. 493).*

Revictimisation occurs when a person or place is subject to an offence on more than one occasion (Farrell, 1992). Revictimisation has long been applied in the field of crime prevention; however, its application to child abuse has been limited (Hamilton & Browne, 1998). Revictimisation research has been framed around identified 'risks' in a person, object, or place and is aligned with rational choice theory, in which three elements must converge to result in a crime occurring: (1) a motivated offender, (2) a suitable victim, and (3) the absence of a capable guardian (Farrell, Phillips, & Pease, 1995). This theory is appropriately applied to the polyvictimisation of children and thus revictimisation across the lifespan, as it highlights vital factors that increase vulnerability. In the case of abuse by the same perpetrator, the motivated offender possesses knowledge of the victim's suitability and the lack of capable guardians. In abuse by multiple perpetrators, the 'rational' decisions to target a specific victim are those that prompted previous offenders to target this same victim (Farrell et al., 1995). The concepts of both polyvictimisation and revictimisation place focus on issues of vulnerability and the role of the environment in the accumulation of victimisations.

Multitype maltreatment, polyvictimisation, and revictimisation can, but does not always, result in cumulative harm, and we do not as yet have a clear understanding of the factors that may mitigate its impact. Although it appears risk factors for chronic maltreatment and revictimisation and the consequences of trauma are closely aligned, it is unclear what factors lead some individuals to experience revictimisation and trauma whilst others do not (Price-Robertson et al., 2013). Research has identified polyvictimisation to be a strong predictor of trauma symptoms, and polyvictims were more symptomatic than their peers who had experienced repeated episodes of the same kind of victimisation (Finkelhor et al., 2005, 2007a). Papalia et al. (2017) identified that abuse and neglect occurring in adolescence may significantly increase an individual's exposure to revictimisation and factors such as mental health problems, substance misuse, and criminal histories were uniquely predictive of persistent revictimisation. These conclusions compliment the findings of the ACE study that links childhood adversity and victimisation to later-life substance abuse, mental illness, and criminality (Felitti et al., 1998).

This body of research characterises the pattern of cumulative harm. Child abuse and neglect, occurring in the early years, with the vulnerabilities of childhood itself as a risk factor, is exacerbated by the environment and ecological systems interacting in a child's life. This results in further victimisation (polyvictimisation) through familial dysfunction and disadvantage, thus predisposing an individual to behavioural, physical, and psychological issues, which further exposes them to revictimisation across their lifespan. Cumulative harm is a condition of lifespan victimisation.

3 Impact of Cumulative Harm

3.1 Developmental Victimology

When considering cumulative harm and the accumulation of maltreatment experiences across the lifespan, as explored earlier in this chapter, it is valuable to consider victimisation and revictimisation from a developmental perspective. Research has identified that development plays a significant role in both risk and impact of child abuse and neglect, and a field of study has evolved from the building momentum. Developmental victimology has been proposed as a "study of the diverse victimisations of children, including crime, child abuse, and other violences, across the various stages of development" (Finkelhor & Kendall-Tackett, 1997, p. 1). This field of study has two dominant aspects, the role of development in risk and impact across childhood. Analysis of developmental patterns has identified developmental stages and the associated milestones as being relevant to the risk of experiencing child abuse and neglect. Factors such as personal traits and characteristics, mastery of developmental tasks, capacity to self-protect, communication abilities, the activities they engage in at various stages, and behaviour and discipline can increase or decrease vulnerability to victimisation and polyvictimisation (Finkelhor et al., 2007a; Finkelhor & Kendall-Tackett, 1997). Age and developmental stage have been associated with vulnerability to perpetrators, with younger victims suffering higher rates of intrafamilial abuse and older child victims experiencing higher extrafamilial abuse (Finkelhor, 2007; Finkelhor & Dziuba-Leatherman, 1994; Finkelhor & Kendall-Tackett, 1997). Child homicide rates have demonstrated an interesting age-occurrence relationship, with rates elevated for children younger than 4 years and older than 15 years, likely due to physical frailty and dependence in the early years and involvement in risk-taking behaviours in adolescence (Finkelhor & Kendall-Tackett, 1997). In fact, the research conclusively articulates that some of the dependency-related victimisations are most concentrated in the under-12 age group and parental abduction is reported to be heavily concentrated among younger children (Finkelhor, 2007). In contrast, as children age and spend more time autonomously exploring their external environment, their exposure to extrafamilial offenders and victimisations increases, such as property crime, theft, and extrafamilial sexual abuse (DeCamp & Zaykowski, 2015; Finkelhor, 2007). Interestingly, according to Finkelhor (2007), only a few crimes, including kidnapping, forcible sodomy, and incest, appear somewhat evenly distributed across developmental stages.

The second aspect of developmental victimology explores development in the context of impact on an individual and how the effects of child maltreatment might differ across the lifespan. We understand from the body of literature that has emerged on human development that children must master various tasks and activities to successfully achieve a developmental stage and move onto the next. We can also infer at this point that disruptions to such mastery would interrupt healthy development, thus having significant implication for the growth and functioning of an individual. Many observations have been made in research regarding developmental impacts of child abuse and neglect, and debate has arisen from the relationship between the age of onset of sexual abuse and impact and whether comprehension and cognitive understanding might act as a protective mechanism in processing an abusive event (Finkelhor, 1997; Finkelhor & Baron, 1986). However, some studies suggest the earlier the sexual or physical abuse, the more likely the occurrence of chronic disassociation as a coping mechanism. Finkelhor (1997, 2007) proposed a model for conceptualising developmental victimology—the developmental dimensions model of victimisation impact. This model argues that developmental differences can affect four distinct dimensions of victimisation impact: understanding of the victimisation and its implications, disruptions to achieving developmental tasks, coping strategies, and environmental buffers located in their social and familial networks (Finkelhor, 1997, 2007).

3.2 Impact of Cumulative Harm on the Developing Child

The successful and healthy development of a child relies predominantly on the provision of basic needs, in an orderly and sequential manner (Miller, 2007). Failure to do so may and often does compromise the socioemotional, cognitive, and physical development of the child and impair their life potential (Felitti et al., 1998; Miller, 2007). Development is an enduring and dynamic process and is greatly influenced by the experiences that take place throughout our lifespan, the impact of which can be empowering and propelling or pervasive and debilitating. Just as trauma is cumulative, so too is development, as we build our capacity to achieve each milestone towards adulthood.

A large body of research on child welfare and development conclusively demonstrates that chronic child maltreatment in the early years can have a profoundly detrimental impact on children's overall long-term wellbeing, the effects of which are costly to the individual, their community, and the economy (Thomas, 2017). When cumulative harm occurs during critical periods of brain development in the first 5 years of life, it interrupts healthy development and can lead to potentially lifelong, permanent, and irreversible impairments in learning, behaviour, and physical and mental health. Disruptions to normal brain development in early life may also alter later development of other areas of the brain. According to Phillips and Shonkoff (2000), researchers investigating brain development have used the term 'toxic stress' to describe prolonged activation of stress management systems in the absence of support. If prolonged, such as when a child experiences multiple adverse circumstances or events, stress can disrupt the brain's architecture and stress management systems, leading to hypersensitivity and overactivity (Phillips & Shonkoff, 2000).

In the preverbal child, cumulatively harmful and traumatic experiences, such as witnessing domestic violence or neglect and inconsistent attachments, are stored in a child's preverbal memory (Miller, 2007). These memories are intense, perceptual experiences and often intrude on awareness later in life, in the form of hypervigilance, nightmares, and hyperarousal. Behaviour and feeling are directed by physiological processes; thus, in hypervigilant children, these impacts may manifest themselves in behaviour such as oversensitivity or misinterpreting nonverbal cues, perceiving eye contact as a threat, and interpreting any touch as an antecedent to abuse or seduction (Perry, 2006). The cumulative effect of childhood maltreatment, particularly in the first 5 years, of the anticipatory stress and fear of those events reoccurring can be, at the least, distracting and, at the most, debilitating. Osborn and Delfabbro's (2006) exploration of the characteristics of children and young people with 'high support' needs in out-of-home care found that 91.7% of the Victorian sample required psychological assistance in the past 6 months due to early childhood traumatic experiences of reoccurring, multiple forms of abuse (Miller, 2007).

Cumulative harm negatively affects the attachment process between parent and child. Trauma is particularly devastating when experienced at the hands of an attachment figure as it forms a 'dual liability' by creating extreme distress and undermining the development of the biological, emotional, and behavioural capacities that regulate that distress (Allen, 2002). The most devastating impacts exist in worryingly frequent cases, whereby a child experiences both neglect and abuse (Nader, 2008). In such cases, the interpersonal trauma, inflicted by someone with attachment to the child, may indeed override any genetic, constitutional, social, or psychological resilience (De Bellis et al., 1999). Children who are denied relationships with an attentive and nurturing primary caregiver are likely to have abnormal developmental processes and altered brain function, severely impairing the child's socioemotional development, including self-perception, emotional regulation, and social problem-solving (Thomas, 2017).

Ethier, Lemelin, and Lacharité (2004) and Frederico et al. (2008) have found that the earlier the abuse and neglect, the more probable behavioural problems will develop in adolescents. Behavioural manifestations include internalising such as withdrawal, sadness, isolation, and depression (Ethier et al., 2004) and externalising by way of aggression and hyperactivity (Frederico et al., 2008). Mental health problems including depressive and anxiety disorders have constantly been linked with abuse and neglect, particularly in adolescence, and major depression is shown to be approximately four times higher in adolescence than in younger children (Lamont, 2010), as well as an increase in substance abuse and criminal offending (Papalia et al., 2017). Another profound consequence of cumulative harm is the development of posttraumatic stress disorder (PTSD). Between one-third and one-half of all abused children meet the criteria for PTSD (Ackerman, Newton, McPherson, Jones, & Dykman, 1998). A significant impact cumulative harm can have on the developing adolescent self is the transition into adulthood, such as early pregnancy, marriage, educational disengagement, or abandoning cohort for an older set of friends, which can lead to risk-taking or unsafe behaviours (Lamont, 2010).

3.3 Later Life Implications of Cumulative Harm

Felitti (2002) emphasised the findings of the ACEs study as a means of illustrating that for some, time does not heal all wounds. Poor lifespan outcomes associated with past histories of child maltreatment often share an interrelatedness. Experiencing chronic and multitype maltreatment or polyvictimisation can increase the risk of more severe and damaging adverse consequences in adulthood. These adverse outcomes are often exacerbated by the impact of revictimisation across the life course. The ACE study assessed cumulative childhood stress and later-life adjustment, and the findings revealed powerful relationships between childhood adversities and poor adult health and wellbeing. This provided considerable insight into the trajectory we take to become who we are in adulthood. The ACE study and subsequent research found that as the number of ACEs increased, so too does the risk of a vast number of health and behavioural outcomes including chronic disease, health risk behaviours, mental health, sexual behaviours, revictimisation and perpetration, and other social issues (Anda et al., 2008, 2007, 2002; Anda, Tietjen, Schulman, Felitti, & Croft, 2010; Barile, Edwards, Dhingra, & Thompson, 2015; Brown et al., 2007, 2010; Chapman et al., 2004; Dietz et al., 1999; Dong et al., 2004; Dube et al., 2003, 2009; Edwards, Anda, Gu, Dube, & Felitti, 2007; Felitti et al., 1998; Hillis, Anda, Felitti, & Marchbanks, 2001; Ports, Ford, & Merrick, 2016; Remigio-Baker, Hayes, & Reyes-Salvail, 2014; Strine et al., 2012).

Whilst it is not a forgone conclusion that children who experience abuse perpetuate that abuse against their own offspring, there is a body of evidence that suggests those who are maltreated as children are at an increased risk of intergenerational abuse than their nonmaltreated peers (Ertem, Leventhal, & Dobbs, 2000; Kwong, Bartholomew, Henderson, & Trinke, 2003; Mouzos & Makkai, 2004; Pears & Capaldi, 2001). Research suggests that parenting styles are often passed from one generation to the next (Neppl, Conger, Scaramella, & Ontai, 2009), and retrospective studies have indicated that the children of parents with high ACE scores have higher rates of adversity (Randell, O'Malley, & Dowd, 2015). According to Pears and Capaldi (2001), parents who had experienced physical abuse in childhood were significantly more likely to engage in abusive behaviours towards their own children. This concept of modelling and transmission of abuse behaviours from parent to child to parent is reflected in the review by Oliver (1993) who concluded that one-third of abused and neglected children repeat these abusive patterns in their own parenting. Gillespie and Folger (2017) argue that this association is logical; a person who has experienced ACEs has a higher risk of substance dependence, mental illness, and incarceration—these conditions become the ACEs for the next generation. Moreover, parents who have experienced chronic child maltreatment in their own lives are likely to need additional support in understanding and implementing such concepts as positive parenting, appropriate discipline, good self-care, modelling conflict resolution, healthy coping skills, and developmental promotion and stimulation (Gillespie & Folger, 2017).

McCormack and Thomson (2017) stated that "unsurprisingly then, for these participants whose self has developed within environments of fear, psychopathology was an outcome in adulthood" (p. 162). Poor mental health outcomes are considered common consequences of childhood maltreatment. Mental health problems found to be resultant from child abuse and neglect include personality disorders, anxiety disorders, dissociative disorders, PTSD, depression, and psychosis (Afifi, Boman, Fleisher, & Sareen, 2009; Cannon, Bonomi, Anderson, Rivara, & Thompson, 2010; Chapman et al., 2004; Clark, Caldwell, Power, & Stansfeld, 2010; Maniglio, 2012; McQueen, Itzin, Kennedy, Sinason, & Maxted, 2009; Norman et al., 2012; Springer, Sheridan, Kuo, & Carnes, 2007). Widom, DuMont, and Czaja (2007) found children who experienced multitype abuse were at increased risk of major depressive disorder in adulthood. The research draws convincing conclusions regarding the relationship between maltreatment experiences in childhood and poor mental health in adulthood, with particular emphasis on the impact of an accumulation of these experiences on an individual. Finkelhor, Turner, and Ormrod (2006) argued that "cumulative exposure to multiple forms of victimization over a child's life-course represents a substantial source of mental health risk" (p. 13).

Adults who experienced child abuse and neglect are at increased risk of physical health problems such as chronic disease, diabetes, gastrointestinal problems, arthritis, headaches, gynaecological problems, stroke, lung cancer, hepatitis, and heart disease (Anda et al., 2008, 2010; Barile et al., 2015; Brown et al., 2010; Dong et al., 2004; Dube et al., 2009; Felitti et al., 1998; Sachs-Ericsson, Cromer, Hernandez, & Kendall-Tackett, 2009; Springer et al., 2007). In a comprehensive literature review, Sachs-Ericsson et al. (2009) found a majority of studies concluded that adults who had experienced child abuse had more medical issues than their nonabused peers. Further review of existing research by Wegman and Stetler (2009) uncovered the relationship between child maltreatment and an increased risk of neurological, musculoskeletal, respiratory, cardiovascular, and gastrointestinal problems but, contrary to other studies, not gynaecological problems. The ACE study (Felitti et al., 1998) highlighted the relationship between childhood maltreatment and poor health in adulthood, with subsequent ACE-related research by Corso, Edwards, Fang, and Mercy (2008) arguing that individuals who experienced childhood abuse and neglect had significant and sustained losses in health-related quality of life in adulthood, as compared with their nonabused peers.

There is a body of evidence, drawing the link between childhood maltreatment and substance misuse in adulthood (Anda et al., 2002; Dube et al., 2003; Gilbert et al., 2009; Simpson & Miller, 2002; Strine et al., 2012; Widom, White, Czaja, & Marmorstein, 2007). The ACE study provides support for these findings, reporting adults with four or more ACEs were seven times more likely to identify as an alcoholic, five times more likely to have used illicit drugs, and 10 times more likely to have used intravenous drugs, compared with adults with no adverse experiences (Felitti et al., 1998). Violence and criminal behaviour is also frequently identified as a potential long-term consequence of child maltreatment especially for those who have experienced physical abuse or witnessed domestic violence (Gilbert et al., 2009; Kwong et al., 2003; Miller-Perrin & Perrin, 2007). Hamilton, Falshaw, and Browne (2002) found that young people who have experienced revictimisation were more likely to engage in criminal or sexual offences than their nonabused peers. Further to this, they also discovered that those who experienced extrafamilial polyvictimisation or revictimisation or a combination of revictimisation inside and outside the family were the most likely of all to engage in criminal activity (Hamilton et al., 2002).

3.4 Cumulative Harm and Complex Trauma

Complex trauma is a concept that both parallels and shares a reciprocal connectedness to cumulative harm. Both cumulative harm and complex trauma are acknowledged as two popular models that account for the complexity of traumatic experience. Whereas cumulative harm focuses on the ongoing trauma and negative outcomes experienced by children and individuals who have endured childhood maltreatment, *complex trauma* is the model used to conceptualise the complexity of traumatic outcomes for survivors of victimisation across the whole lifespan. Complex trauma can occur at any point across an individual's lifetime and can be experienced as a result of not only childhood maltreatment but also war, oppression, conflict, civil unrest, accident, or loss (Price-Robertson et al., 2013). Complex trauma may be resultant of cumulative harm experiences due to the increased risk of revictimisation (Price-Robertson et al., 2013). Examining the relationship between complex trauma and cumulative harm and acknowledging broader impacts of childhood trauma and revictimisation through the lens of complex trauma are vital in understanding the pervasiveness of an accumulation of maltreatment experiences, as it manifests in adulthood. McCormack and Thomson (2017) concluded

> *In the aftermath of childhood trauma, these participants characteristically struggled to form a coherent sense of self, which left them vulnerable to difficulties forming and maintaining healthy relationships, in managing emotions, and in identifying and enacting values. Their representations of self, others, and the world were seriously impacted....living a satisfying life seemed out of their reach (p. 162).*

Complex trauma appears to manifest in individuals as an adaptive reaction to the experience of maltreatment but evolves into problematic and maladaptive behaviours (Cook et al., 2017).

Revictimisation appears to be common for individuals experiencing complex trauma due to the increased risk posed by multiple abuse types and in correlation with many of the key features of complex trauma such as psychiatric disorders, substance misuse, and powerlessness (Classen, Palesh, & Aggarwal, 2005). According to Cook et al., "children exposed to complex trauma often experience lifelong problems that place them at risk for additional trauma exposure and cumulative impairment, including psychiatric and addictive disorders; chronic medical illness; and legal, vocational, and family problems" (Cook et al., 2017, p. 390).

3.5 Cumulative Harm and Resilience

Resilience is the quality or set of qualities that allow an individual to bounce back in the face of adversity. According to research, resilience refers to one's capacity to positively adapt to change and stressful events in healthy and productive ways (Catalano, Berglund, Ryan, Lonczak, & Hawkins, 2002; Garmezy, 1991). For some adults, the effects of child abuse and neglect are chronic and debilitating, whilst others have more positive outcomes as adults, despite their abuse and neglect histories (Miller-Perrin & Perrin, 2007). Mental health outcomes are difficult to predict, and the concept of 'resilience' helps to explain in part why some individuals who exhibit serious risk factors and who could be expected to do poorly in this aspect of life, in fact, thrive and are very well adjusted. Resilience has been conceptualised as a dynamic process involving an interaction between both risk and protective processes that act to modify the effects of an adverse life event (Oliver, Collin, Burns, & Nicholas, 2006; Rutter, 1985, 1999). Resilience does imply not only invulnerability to stress but also a capacity to recover from traumatic experiences (Garmezy, 1991).

Resilience is not necessarily an innate attribute; rather, it may be best described as an adaptive process, involving interactions between risk and protective factors, across multiple levels of an individual's lived experience (Olsson, Bond, Burns, Vella-Brodrick, & Sawyer, 2003). Resilient individuals utilise a set of coping skills and resources that allow them to deal effectively with stress, and the development of resilience occurs when there is an interaction between an individual and stress (Blum, 1998). Researchers typically categorise resilient attributes into dispositional or personal characteristics (e.g. a sense of spirituality, positive social skills, and personal efficacy), family or social characteristics (e.g. connectedness to a parent or caregiver), and environmental characteristics (such as involvement in one's community, access to health services, and the presence of caring adults) (Blum, 1998; Garmezy, 1985). Resilient outcomes refer to particular patterns of functional behaviour despite risk (Olsson et al., 2003). Good mental health, social competence, and functional capacity are examples of resilient outcomes (Garmezy, 1991).

It has been proposed that experiencing some adversity in life can provide opportunity for growth and wellbeing (Seery, 2011; Tedeschi, 2004). When considering the amount of adversity experienced versus resilience, Seery (2011) argues for a 'U-shaped' relationship, one that acknowledges that experiencing *some* lifetime adversity may have its benefits and predict better outcomes than both a history of *high* adversity and a history of *no* adversity. Relative to a history of either no or high cumulative lifetime adversity, a history of *some* adversity may contribute to the development of subsequent propensity for resilience in the face of stress and distress, resulting in better mental health and wellbeing and less distress and disruption (Seery, 2011). A range of internal characteristics can emerge from adversity, including generating individual toughness, a sense of mastery over past adversity, fostering perceived control and confidence in coping ability, acquisition of coping skills, establishing social-support networks, and promoting cell growth in brain areas relevant for coping (e.g. Dienstbier, 1989; Lyons, Parker, & Schatzberg, 2010; Wortman & Silver, 1990). Scholarship suggests that, without any exposure to adversity, these internal resources may have little opportunity to develop; comparably, higher levels of adversity could prove overwhelming and disrupt these capacities (e.g. fostering perceived helplessness and the lack of toughness) (Seery, 2011).

Whilst resilience has been hailed as a protective factor valuable in mitigating the impact of maltreatment in childhood, even the most resilient child can be overcome by the pervasiveness of cumulative harm. As cumulative harm relates to adverse experiences that are multiple and prolonged in nature, the power of resilience in mitigating the effects of abuse and neglect is often diminished or worn down. An individual's lived experience and their response to the external factors impacting on it, such as trauma and adverse events, can increase or decrease their vulnerability or resilience. Bromfield and Miller emphasise that "an individual's level of resilience is not static, rather it is dynamic and evolves and changes over time in relation to the individual's life experiences" (Bromfield & Miller, 2012, p. 9).

Families in which cumulative harm exists often have a significant lack of adequate protective factors, and there is a common pattern of multiple abuse types impacting on the individual. These complexities of cumulative harm can diminish a child's resilience or can cause a child to develop maladaptive behaviours that have been necessary for survival. It is cautiously noted that characteristics developed for survival may become maladaptive if overused and/or not given up when the stressor no longer exists. Entrenched problems are most likely to develop when a child's life circumstances fail to change and the environment never becomes secure. This is especially relevant when there has been minimal genuine engagement with meaningful intervention for an extended period of time. Bromfield and Miller advise that "we must be cautious not to focus on resilience to the extent that we ignore the risks for the child. Children who appear to be coping well, but who in fact have internalising symptoms (such as depression, lack of self-worth), are vulnerable to being overlooked" (Bromfield & Miller, 2012, p. 9).

4 Prevention and Intervention

Literature widely asserts that prevention and intervention is the most effective response to child maltreatment (Bryce, 2018; Doyle, 2012; Doyle & Timms, 2014; Tilbury et al., 2007). Therefore, in response to cumulative harm and chronic maltreatment, it has been argued strongly that identifying indicators of potential cumulative risk and responding to prevent the onset of cumulative harm whilst intervening in the observable current harm are the best ways forward (Broadley, 2014; Bromfield et al., 2007; Bromfield & Higgins, 2005; Bromfield, Lamont, Antcliff, & Parker, 2011; Bromfield & Miller, 2012). Bryce (2018) conducted a comprehensive review of international child protection approaches to cumulative harm and concluded that, whilst a more holistic understanding of harm and the impacts of long-term maltreatment has emerged, "a collaborative level of consistent practice, which places cumulative harm and reoccurring maltreatment on an equal footing with episodic maltreatment, particularly in relation to notification and reporting, has not yet been achieved" (p. 7). Bryce (2018) argued that the pervasiveness of cumulative harm must be acknowledged in policy and procedure and that prevention and intervention should be implemented, regardless of whether the indicators of harm are observable at the time the maltreatment is identified.

Prevention of cumulative harm, based on the assessment of parental action and research, which supports the probable, evidence-based, lifespan outcomes, is a more appropriate response to this issue (Broadley, 2014). The need for assessment and prevention based on documented and research-based *potential* outcomes for a child, as they correlate with parental actions and inactions, is necessary to adequately mitigate the onset and impact of cumulative harm. As highlighted in literature regarding polyvictimisation and revictimisation, early detection of risk factors is needed to interrupt the likelihood of future victimisations occurring (Finkelhor, 2007; Dudfield, Angel, Sherman, & Torrence, 2017). The identification of indicators of cumulative harm and risk gathered at the referral stages of family support programs can inform prevention strategies, which can be combined effectively with intervention plans for a family. Purposeful referrals for families must be targeted at the vulnerabilities identified in assessment and based on understanding what has worked or not worked in the past (Frederico, Jackson, & Jones, 2006).

From a therapeutic perspective, repetition, logically, forms the cornerstone of intervention practices. Understanding parents' experience of trauma and deprivation informs us as to what types of intervention are most effective. Parents, who have experienced cumulative harm in their own lifetime, need repetitive positive experiences in order to provide these for their children (Frederico et al., 2008). According to Perry (2006), adequate repetition of positive, developmentally appropriate experiences can heal those parts of the brain formerly altered by trauma. "Effective therapeutic and enrichment interventions must recruit other adults in a child's life – caregivers, teachers, parents – to be involved in learning and delivering elements of these interventions, in addition to the specific therapy hours dedicated to them during the week." (Perry, 2006, p. 38). In other words, the various ecological systems interacting in that child's life must be employed to mitigate and repair cumulative harm.

5 Conclusion

Child abuse and neglect is acknowledged as a critical issue medically and socially, worldwide. Rarely occurring in isolation, many children may experience chronic and multiple types of abuse and neglect (Higgins & McCabe, 2000; Price-Robertson et al., 2013). Given the acknowledged multiplicity of child maltreatment experiences and adversities, we must grasp clearly the way in which these multiple experiences accumulate, through chronic singular and multitype maltreatment, polyvictimisation, and revictimisation.

Armed with a cognisance of the commonality of repeat victimisations and its manifestations, we begin to comprehend how an individual is affected by, made vulnerable by, and ultimately shaped by the condition of cumulative harm. We come to recognise the specific implications cumulative harm has on the developing child, from conception to adolescence, acknowledging the way in which childhood itself exacerbates risk, through dependency and autonomy alike.

This developmental victimology informs our understanding of both risk and impact, helping us to recognise the way in which we are made vulnerable to and exposed to victimisation and revictimisation. We see the ramifications for adulthood, the intergenerational, cyclical transition of abuse, neglect, and dysfunction. Cumulative harm must be a priority, for our practice, our policy, and our professional development. Once we are fully aware of these recurrent victimisation trajectories, we are convicted to act. Experiencing cumulative harm undermines even the most resilient individual and, through repetition, overrides our capacity to overcome. Our early victimhood predisposes us to a 'career' of victimisation; thus, without doubt, prevention and early intervention, informed by accurate and holistic risk assessment, is the way forward. We must use what we know: that an accumulation of ACEs paves a path to poorer outcomes, to get in front, to interrupt the cycle, to mitigate cumulative harm, and to promote healing.

6 Chapter Review Questions

1. ACEs study was a landmark study; explain its significance and contribution to our understanding of child maltreatment.
2. Define cumulative harm.
3. There has been a shift in the way we understand maltreatment, in terms of chronicity; explain this shift and the potential implications for your professional context.
4. Explain the difference between multitype maltreatment, polyvictimisation, and revictimisation and the relationship between these concepts.

5. How does development influence the way a child might experience cumulative harm?
6. How does cumulative harm differ from complex trauma?
7. Explain why being resilient does not mean less deserving of protection.
8. What is the most effective approach to preventing and intervening in cases that indicate cumulate harm or risk of cumulative harm?

References

Ackerman, P. T., Newton, J. E., McPherson, W. B., Jones, J. G., & Dykman, R. A. (1998). Prevalence of post traumatic stress disorder and other psychiatric diagnoses in three groups of abused children (sexual, physical, and both). *Child Abuse & Neglect, 22*(8), 759–774.

Afifi, T., Boman, J., Fleisher, W., & Sareen, J. (2009). The relationship between child abuse, parental divorce, and lifetime mental disorders and suicidality in a nationally representative adult sample. *Child Abuse & Neglect, 33*, 139–147.

Allen, J. (2002). *Traumatic relationships and serious mental disorders*. Chichester: Wiley.

Anda, R. F., Brown, D. W., Dube, S. R., Bremner, J. D., Felitti, V. J., & Giles, W. H. (2008). Adverse childhood experiences and chronic obstructive pulmonary disease in adults. *American Journal of Preventive Medicine, 34*(5), 396–403.

Anda, R. F., Brown, D. W., Felitti, V. J., Bremner, J. D., Dube, S. R., & Giles, W. H. (2007). Adverse childhood experiences and prescribed psychotropic medications in adults. *American Journal of Preventive Medicine, 32*(5), 389–394.

Anda, R., Tietjen, G., Schulman, E., Felitti, V., & Croft, J. (2010). Adverse childhood experiences and frequent headaches in adults. *Headache: The Journal of Head and Face Pain, 50*(9), 1473–1481.

Anda, R. F., Whitfield, C. L., Felitti, V. J., Chapman, D., Edwards, V. J., Dube, S. R., et al. (2002). Adverse childhood experiences, alcoholic parents, and later risk of alcoholism and depression. *Psychiatric Services, 53*(8), 1001–1009.

Anderson, K. L. (2010). Conflict, power, and violence in families. *Journal of Marriage and Family, 72*(3), 726–742.

Barile, J. P., Edwards, V. J., Dhingra, S. S., & Thompson, W. W. (2015). Associations among county-level social determinants of health, child maltreatment, and emotional support on health-related quality of life in adulthood. *Psychology of Violence, 5*(2), 183.

Bath, H. (2014). The accumulating evidence for cumulative harm. *Developing Practice: The Child, Youth and Family Work Journal, 38*, 6.

Blum, R. W. (1998). Healthy youth development as a model for youth health promotion: a review. *Journal of Adolescent Health, 22*(5), 368–375.

Broadley, K. (2014). Equipping child protection practitioners to intervene to protect children from cumulative harm: legislation and policy in Victoria, Australia. *Australian Journal of Social Issues, 49*(3), 265–284.

Bromfield, L. M., Gillingham, P., & Higgins, D. J. (2007). Cumulative harm and chronic child maltreatment. *Developing Practice: The Child Youth and Family Work Journal, 19*, 34–42.

Bromfield, L. M., & Higgins, D. J. (2005). Chronic and isolated maltreatment in a child protection sample. *Family Matters, 70*, 38.

Bromfield, L., Lamont, A., Antcliff, G., & Parker, R. (2011). *Practice guide: Cumulative harm*. Sydney, NSW: The Benevolent Society.

Bromfield, L., & Miller, D. (2012). *Cumulative harm: Best interests case practice model-specialist practice resource*. Melbourne: Victorian Government Department of Human Services.

Brown, D. W., Anda, R. F., Edwards, V. J., Felitti, V. J., Dube, S. R., & Giles, W. H. (2007). Adverse childhood experiences and childhood autobiographical memory disturbance. *Child Abuse & Neglect, 31*(9), 961–969.

Brown, D. W., Anda, R. F., Felitti, V. J., Edwards, V. J., Malarcher, A. M., Croft, J. B., et al. (2010). Adverse childhood experiences are associated with the risk of lung cancer: a prospective cohort study. *BMC Public Health, 10*(1), 20.

Bryce, I. R. (2018). A review of cumulative harm: a comparison of international child protection practices. *Children Australia*, *43*(1), 23–31.

Cannon, E. A., Bonomi, A. E., Anderson, M. L., Rivara, F. P., & Thompson, R. S. (2010). Adult health and relationship outcomes among women with abuse experiences during childhood. *Violence and Victims*, *25*(3), 291–305.

Catalano, R. F., Berglund, M. L., Ryan, J. A., Lonczak, H. S., & Hawkins, J. D. (2002). Positive youth development in the United States: research findings on evaluations of positive youth development programs. *Prevention & Treatment*, *5*(1), 15a.

Chapman, D., Whitfield, C., Felitti, V., Dube, S., Edwards, V., & Anda, R. (2004). Adverse childhood experiences and the risk of depressive disorders in adulthood. *Journal of Affective Disorders*, *82*, 217–225.

Clark, C., Caldwell, T., Power, C., & Stansfeld, S. A. (2010). Does the influence of childhood adversity on psychopathology persist across the lifecourse? A 45-year prospective epidemiologic study. *Annals of Epidemiology*, *20*(5), 385–394.

Classen, C. C., Palesh, O. G., & Aggarwal, R. (2005). Sexual revictimization: a review of the empirical literature. *Trauma, Violence & Abuse*, *6*(2), 103–129.

Cook, A., Spinazzola, J., Ford, J., Lanktree, C., Blaustein, M., Cloitre, M., et al. (2017). Complex trauma in children and adolescents. *Psychiatric Annals*, *35*(5), 390–398.

Corso, P. S., Edwards, V. J., Fang, X., & Mercy, J. A. (2008). Health-related quality of life among adults who experienced maltreatment during childhood. *American Journal of Public Health*, *98*(6), 1094–1100.

De Bellis, M. D., Keshavan, M. S., Clark, D. B., Casey, B. J., Giedd, J. N., Boring, A. M., et al. (1999). Developmental traumatology part II: brain development. *Biological Psychiatry*, *45*(10), 1271–1284.

DeCamp, W., & Zaykowski, H. (2015). Developmental victimology: estimating group victimization trajectories in the age–victimization curve. *International Review of Victimology*, *21*(3), 255–272.

Dienstbier, R. A. (1989). Arousal and physiological toughness: implications for mental and physical health. *Psychological Review*, *96*(1), 84.

Dietz, P. M., Spitz, A. M., Anda, R. F., Williamson, D. F., McMahon, P. M., Santelli, J. S., et al. (1999). Unintended pregnancy among adult women exposed to abuse or household dysfunction during their childhood. *Journal of the American Medical Association*, *282*(14), 1359–1364.

Dong, M., Anda, R. F., Felitti, V. J., Dube, S. R., Williamson, D. F., Thompson, T. J., et al. (2004). The interrelatedness of multiple forms of childhood abuse, neglect, and household dysfunction. *Child Abuse & Neglect*, *28*(7), 771–784.

Doyle, C. (2012). *Working with abused children: Focus on the child*. Hampshire: Palgrave Macmillan.

Doyle, C., & Timms, C. (2014). *Child neglect and emotional abuse*. London: Sage Publications Ltd.

Dube, S. R., Fairweather, D., Pearson, W. S., Felitti, V. J., Anda, R. F., & Croft, J. B. (2009). Cumulative childhood stress and autoimmune diseases in adults. *Psychosomatic Medicine*, *71*(2), 243.

Dube, S. R., Felitti, V. J., Dong, M., Chapman, D. P., Giles, W. H., & Anda, R. F. (2003). Childhood abuse, neglect, and household dysfunction and the risk of illicit drug use: the adverse childhood experiences study. *Pediatrics*, *111*(3), 564–572.

Dudfield, G., Angel, C., Sherman, L. W., & Torrence, S. (2017). The "power curve" of victim harm: targeting the distribution of crime harm index values across all victims and repeat victims over 1 year. *Cambridge Journal of Evidence-Based Policing*, *1*(1), 38–58.

Edwards, V. J., Anda, R. F., Gu, D., Dube, S. R., & Felitti, V. J. (2007). Adverse childhood experiences and smoking persistence in adults with smoking-related symptoms and illness. *The Permanente Journal*, *11*(2), 5–13.

Edwards, V. J., Holden, G. W., Felitti, V. J., & Anda, R. F. (2003). Relationship between multiple forms of childhood maltreatment and adult mental health in community respondents: results from the adverse childhood experiences study. *American Journal of Psychiatry*, *160*(8), 1453–1460.

Ertem, I. O., Leventhal, J. M., & Dobbs, S. (2000). Intergenerational continuity of child physical abuse: how good is the evidence? *The Lancet*, *356*(9232), 814–819.

Ethier, L. S., Lemelin, J. P., & Lacharité, C. (2004). A longitudinal study of the effects of chronic maltreatment on children's behavioral and emotional problems. *Child Abuse & Neglect*, *28*(12), 1265–1278.

Farrell, G. (1992). Multiple victimisation: its extent and significance. *International Review of Victimology*, *2*, 85–102.

Farrell, G., Phillips, C., & Pease, K. (1995). Like taking candy: why does repeat victimization occur? *The British Journal of Criminology*, 384–399.

Felitti, V. J. (2002). The relation between adverse childhood experiences and adult health: turning gold into lead. *The Permanente Journal*, *6*(1), 44–47.

Felitti, V. J. (2017). Future applications of the adverse childhood experiences research. *Journal of Child & Adolescent Trauma*, *10*(3), 205–206.

Felitti, V. J., Anda, R. F., Nordenberg, D., Williamson, D. F., Spitz, A. M., Edwards, V., et al. (1998). Relationship of childhood abuse and household dysfunction to many of the leading causes of death in adults: the adverse childhood experiences (ACE) study. *American Journal of Preventive Medicine*, *14*(4), 245–258.

Finkelhor, D. (1997). 5 The victimization of children and youth. *Victims of Crime*, *86*.

Finkelhor, D. (2007). Developmental victimology. *Victims of Crime*, 9–34.

Finkelhor, D., & Baron, L. (1986). *High-risk children*. In *A sourcebook on child sexual abuse*. Sage. (pp. 60–88).

Finkelhor, D., & Dziuba-Leatherman, J. (1994). Children as victims of violence: a national survey. *Pediatrics*, *94*(4), 413–420.

Finkelhor, D., & Kendall-Tackett, K. (1997). A developmental perspective on the childhood impact of crime, abuse, and violent victimization. In D. Cicchetti & S. L. Toth (Eds.), *Rochester symposium on developmental psychology, Vol. 8. Developmental perspectives on trauma: Theory, research, and intervention* (pp. 1–32). Rochester, NY: University of Rochester Press.

Finkelhor, D., Ormrod, R. K., & Turner, H. A. (2007a). Poly-victimization: a neglected component in child victimization. *Child Abuse & Neglect*, *31*(1), 7–26.

Finkelhor, D., Ormrod, R. K., & Turner, H. A. (2007b). Re-victimization patterns in a national longitudinal sample of children and youth. *Child Abuse & Neglect*, *31*(5), 479–502.

Finkelhor, D., Ormrod, R. K., Turner, H. A., & Hamby, S. L. (2005). Measuring poly-victimization using the juvenile victimization questionnaire. *Child Abuse & Neglect*, *29*(11), 1297–1312.

Finkelhor, D., Turner, H., & Ormrod, R. (2006). The effect of lifetime victimization on the mental health of children and adolescents. *Social Science & Medicine*, *62*(1), 13–27.

Fitzgerald, R. (2016, September 14). In *Evolution or revolution—emerging challenges from the royal commission. Address presented at Leneen Forde Address in Brisbane Supreme Court, Brisbane*.

Fluke, J. D., Shusterman, G. R., Hollinshead, D. M., & Yuan, Y. Y. T. (2008). Longitudinal analysis of repeated child abuse reporting and victimization: multistate analysis of associated factors. *Child Maltreatment*, *13*(1), 76–88.

Follette, V. M., Polusny, M. A., Bechtle, A. E., & Naugle, A. E. (1996). Cumulative trauma: the impact of child sexual abuse, adult sexual assault, and spouse abuse. *Journal of Traumatic Stress*, *9*(1), 25–35.

Frederico, M. M., Jackson, A. L., & Black, C. M. (2008). Understanding the impact of abuse and neglect on children and young people referred to a therapeutic program. *Journal of Family Studies*, *14*(2–3), 342–362.

Frederico, M., Jackson, A., & Jones, S. (2006). *Child death group analysis: Effective responses to chronic neglect*. Melbourne: Office of the Child Safety Commissioner, Victorian Child Death Review Committee.

Garmezy, N. (1985). Stress-resistant children: the search for protective factors. Recent research in developmental psychopathology. *Recent Research in Developmental Psychopathology*, *4*, 213–233.

Garmezy, N. (1991). Resilience in children's adaptation to negative life events and stressed environments. *Pediatric Annals*, *20*(9), 459–466.

Gilbert, R., Spatz Widom, C., Browne, K., Fergusson, D., Webb, E., & Janson, J. (2009). Burden and consequences of child maltreatment in high-income countries. *Lancet*, *373*, 68–81.

Gillespie, R. J., & Folger, A. T. (2017). Feasibility of assessing parental ACEs in pediatric primary care: implications for practice-based implementation. *Journal of Child & Adolescent Trauma*, *10*(3), 249–256.

Gilmore, D. (2010). Chronic child neglect: building knowledge, fostering hope. *Policy & Practice*, *68*(3), 12–13.

Hamilton, C. E., & Browne, K. D. (1998). The repeat victimization of children: should the concept be revised? *Aggression and Violent Behavior*, *3*(1), 47–60.

Hamilton, C. E., Falshaw, L., & Browne, K. D. (2002). The link between recurrent maltreatment and offending behaviour. *International Journal of Offender Therapy and Comparative Criminology*, *46*(1), 75–94.

Herrenkohl, R. C., & Herrenkohl, T. I. (2009). Assessing a child's experience of multiple maltreatment types: some unfinished business. *Journal of Family Violence*, *24*(7), 485–496.

Higgins, D. J. (2004). Differentiating between child maltreatment experiences. *Family Matters*, *69*, 50.

Higgins, D. J., & McCabe, M. P. (1998). Parent perceptions of maltreatment and adjustment in children. *Journal of Family Studies*, *4*(1), 53–76.

Higgins, D. J., & McCabe, M. P. (2000). Relationships between different types of maltreatment during childhood and adjustment in adulthood. *Child Maltreatment*, *5*(3), 261–272.

Higgins, D. J., & McCabe, M. P. (2000b). Multi-type maltreatment and the long-term adjustment of adults. *Child Abuse Review*, *9*(1), 6–18.

Higgins, D. J., & McCabe, M. P. (2001). Multiple forms of child abuse and neglect: adult retrospective reports. *Aggression and Violent Behavior*, *6*(6), 547–578.

Hillis, S. D., Anda, R. F., Felitti, V. J., & Marchbanks, P. A. (2001). Adverse childhood experiences and sexual risk behaviors in women: a retrospective cohort study. *Family Planning Perspectives*, 206–211.

James, M. (2000). Child abuse and neglect (Series of two parts) Part 1: redefining the issues. *Trends and Issues in Crime and Criminal Justice/Australian Institute of Criminology*, *146*, 1.

Kaplan, C., Schene, P., DePanfilis, D., & Gilmore, D. (2009). Introduction: shining light on chronic neglect. *Protecting Children*, *24*(1), 1–8.

Kempe, C. H., Silverman, F. N., Steele, B. F., Droegemueller, W., & Silver, H. K. (2013). The battered-child syndrome. In C. Henry Kempe (Ed.), *A 50 Year legacy to the field of child abuse and neglect* (pp. 23–38). Netherlands: Springer.

Kezelman, C., Hossack, N., Stavropoulos, P., & Burley, P. (2015). *The cost of unresolved childhood trauma and abuse in adults in Australia*. Sydney: Adults Surviving Child Abuse.

Kwong, M. J., Bartholomew, K., Henderson, A. J., & Trinke, S. J. (2003). The intergenerational transmission of relationship violence. *Journal of Family Psychology*, *17*(3), 288.

Lamont, A. (2010). *Effects of child abuse and neglect for children and adolescents*. Australian Institute of Family Studies.

Lyons, D. M., Parker, K. J., & Schatzberg, A. F. (2010). Animal models of early life stress: implications for understanding resilience. *Developmental Psychobiology*, *52*(7), 616–624.

Maniglio, R. (2012). Child sexual abuse in the etiology of anxiety disorders: a systematic review of reviews. *Trauma, Violence & Abuse*, *14*(2), 96–112.

McCormack, L., & Thomson, S. (2017). Complex trauma in childhood, a psychiatric diagnosis in adulthood: making meaning of a double-edged phenomenon. *Psychological Trauma: Theory, Research, Practice, and Policy*, *9*(2), 156.

Mcnutt, L. A., Carlson, B. E., Persaud, M., & Postmus, J. (2002). Cumulative abuse experiences, physical health and health behaviors. *Annals of Epidemiology*, *12*(2), 123–130.

McQueen, D., Itzin, C., Kennedy, R., Sinason, V., & Maxted, F. (2009). *Psychoanalytic psychotherapy after child abuse. The treatment of adults and children who have experienced sexual abuse, violence, and neglect in childhood*. London: Karnac Books Ltd.

Miller, R. (2007). *Cumulative harm: A conceptual overview*. Melbourne, Victoria: Victorian Government.

Miller-Perrin, C., & Perrin, R. (2007). *Child maltreatment: An introduction*. Thousand Oaks, CA: Sage Publications.

Mouzos, J., & Makkai, T. (2004). *Women's experiences of male violence: Findings from the Australian component of the international violence against women survey (IVAWS)*. (Vol. 56). Canberra: Australian Institute of Criminology.

Nader, K. (2008). *Understanding and assessing trauma in children and adolescents*. New York, NY: Routledge.

Neppl, T. K., Conger, R. D., Scaramella, L. V., & Ontai, L. L. (2009). Intergenerational continuity in parenting behavior: mediating pathways and child effects. *Developmental Psychology*, *45*(5), 1241.

Norman, R. E., Byambaa, M., De, R., Butchart, A., Scott, J., & Vos, T. (2012). The long-term health consequences of child physical abuse, emotional abuse and neglect: a systematic review and meta-analysis. *Public Library of Science Medicine*, *9*(11), 1–31.

Oliver, J. E. (1993). Intergenerational transmission of child abuse: rates, research, and clinical implications. *The American Journal of Psychiatry*, *150*(9), 1315.

Oliver, K. G., Collin, P., Burns, J., & Nicholas, J. (2006). Building resilience in young people through meaningful participation. *Australian e-Journal for the Advancement of Mental Health*, *5*(1), 34–40.

Olsson, C. A., Bond, L., Burns, J. M., Vella-Brodrick, D. A., & Sawyer, S. M. (2003). Adolescent resilience: a concept analysis. *Journal of Adolescence*, *26*(1), 1–11.

Osborn, A., & Delfabbro, P. H. (2006). *National comparative study of children and young people with high support needs in Australian out-of-home care*. Adelaide: University of Adelaide.

Papalia, N. L., Luebbers, S., Ogloff, J. R., Cutajar, M., Mullen, P. E., & Mann, E. (2017). Further victimization of child sexual abuse victims: a latent class typology of re-victimization trajectories. *Child Abuse & Neglect*, *66*, 112–129.

Pears, K., & Capaldi, D. (2001). Intergenerational transmission of abuse: a two-generational prospective study of an at-risk sample. *Child Abuse & Neglect*, *25*, 1439–1461.

Perry, B. (2006). Applying principles of neurodevelopment to clinical work with maltreated and traumatized children. In B. Wedd (Ed.), *Working with traumatized youth* (pp. 27–52). New York: Guildford Press.

Phillips, D. A., & Shonkoff, J. P. (Eds.), (2000). *From neurons to neighborhoods: The science of early childhood development*. National Academies Press.

Ports, K. A., Ford, D. C., & Merrick, M. T. (2016). Adverse childhood experiences and sexual victimization in adulthood. *Child Abuse & Neglect*, *51*, 313–322.

Price-Robertson, R., Rush, P., Wall, L., & Higgins, D. (2013). *Rarely an isolated incident: Acknowledging the interrelatedness of child maltreatment, victimisation and trauma*. Melbourne: AIFS, Child Family Community Information Exchange.

Randell, K. A., O'Malley, D., & Dowd, M. D. (2015). Association of parental adverse childhood experiences and current child adversity. *JAMA Pediatrics*, *169*(8), 786–787.

Remigio-Baker, R. A., Hayes, D. K., & Reyes-Salvail, F. (2014). Adverse childhood events and current depressive symptoms among women in Hawaii: 2010 BRFSS, Hawaii. *Maternal and Child Health Journal*, *18*(10), 2300–2308.

Robbie Rossman, B. B., & Rosenberg, M. S. (1998). The multiple victimization of children: incidence and conceptual issues. *Journal of Aggression, Maltreatment & Trauma*, *2*(1), 1–5.

Rutter, M. (1985). Resilience in the face of adversity: protective factors and resistance to psychiatric disorder. *The British Journal of Psychiatry*, *147*, 598–611.

Rutter, M. (1999). Resilience concepts and findings: implications for family therapy. *Journal of Family Therapy*, *21*(2), 119–144.

Sachs-Ericsson, N., Cromer, K., Hernandez, A., & Kendall-Tackett, K. (2009). A review of childhood abuse, health, and pain-related problems: the role of psychiatric-disorders and current life stress. *Journal of Trauma & Dissociation*, *10*(2), 170–188.

Seery, M. D. (2011). Resilience: a silver lining to experiencing adverse life events? *Current Directions in Psychological Science*, *20*(6), 390–394.

Simpson, T., & Miller, W. (2002). Concomitance between childhood sexual and physical abuse and substance use problems. A review. *Clinical Psychology Review*, *22*, 27–77.

Springer, K., Sheridan, J., Kuo, D., & Carnes, M. (2007). Long-term physical and mental health consequences of childhood physical abuse: results from a large population-based sample of men and women. *Child Abuse & Neglect*, *31*, 517–530.

Strine, T. W., Dube, S. R., Edwards, V. J., Prehn, A. W., Rasmussen, S., Wagenfeld, M., et al. (2012). Associations between adverse childhood experiences, psychological distress, and adult alcohol problems. *American Journal of Health Behavior*, *36*(3), 408–423.

Tedeschi, R. G. (2004). Posttraumatic growth: a new perspective on psychotraumatology. *Psychiatric Times*, *4*, 58.

Thomas, K. (2017). The lost children: why the United Nations is wrong about Australian child protection. *Policy: A Journal of Public Policy and Ideas*, *33*(1), 16.

Tilbury, C., Osmond, J., Wilson, S., & Clark, J. (2007). *Good practice in child protection*. Pearson Education Australia: New South Wales.

Tseloni, A., & Pease, K. (2004). Repeat personal victimization: random effects, event dependence and unexplained heterogeneity. *British Journal of Criminology*, *44*(6), 931–945.

Wegman, H. L., & Stetler, C. (2009). A meta-analytic review of the effects of childhood abuse on medical outcomes in adulthood. *Psychosomatic Medicine*, *71*, 805–812.

Widom, C., DuMont, K., & Czaja, S. (2007). A prospective investigation of major depressive disorder and comorbidity in abused and neglected children grown up. *Archives of General Psychiatry*, *64*, 49–56.

Widom, C. S., White, H. R., Czaja, S. J., & Marmorstein, N. R. (2007). Long-term effects of child abuse and neglect on alcohol use and excessive drinking in middle adulthood. *Journal of Studies on Alcohol and Drugs*, *68*(3), 317–326.

Wortman, C. B., & Silver, R. C. (1990). *Successful mastery of bereavement and widowhood: a life-course perspective*. In *Successful aging: Perspectives from the behavioral sciences* (pp. 225–264).

CHAPTER 10

The Pathological Consequences of Exposure to Domestic and Family Violence in Childhood

Grant C.B. Sinnamon

Bela Menso Brain and Behaviour Centre, Gold Coast, QLD, Australia

1 Introduction

Only relatively recently have longitudinal studies of brain development progressed to incorporate results that include the brain at full maturity. These studies have greatly improved our understanding of the developmental trajectory of the healthy brain over the first 30 years of life and the developmental impact of child maltreatment (Pechtel & Pizzagalli, 2011). The data illustrates a clear relationship between early childhood experience and brain development. A simplistic summation of the data is that positive experiences result in a positive impact on the development of the CNS, while negative experiences, defined by variations to the themes of stress, trauma, and neglect, including these experiences through the medium of DFV, result in neurodevelopmental deficits that produce clearly identifiable impairment right across the biopsychosocial spectrum (Coates, 2010; Diseth, 2005; Hedges & Woon, 2011; Shonkoff & Garner, 2012; Teicher, Anderson, & Polcari, 2012). This summation is perhaps an oversimplification as individual differences play a major role on the outcomes of our experiences (Howell & Sanchez, 2011; Rudolph, Troop-Gordon, & Granger, 2011). Nevertheless, the data demonstrates that the developmental trajectory of the brain has several definable characteristics. Further, the impact of early-life maltreatment on the developing brain and both the psychological and somatic sequelae can, increasingly, be quantified.

In the last three decades, paediatric health services have been increasingly informed by the advances in knowledge of developmental neurobiology. These advances have occurred largely as a result of two things: (1) the evolution in imaging technologies that have allowed us to observe the workings of the central nervous system (CNS) in ever-increasing detail and (2) the realisation (if not yet complete understanding) that the relationships between structures, systems, and functional outputs of the CNS are far more complex than the traditional mechanistic view has credited.

Child Abuse and Neglect. https://doi.org/10.1016/B978-0-12-815344-4.00010-6

2 An Overview of the Impact of Childhood Maltreatment Through DFV

Early-life stress (ELS) refers to any event that exposes a child to physical and/or psychological stimuli that exceeds their capacity to successfully cope (Gunnar & Quevedo, 2007). The most commonly cited stressors are those relating to variations to the themes of abuse, neglect, and traumatic experience (DFV, assault, accident, natural disaster, death, illness, and war). The stressor may involve a single-event exposure or a succession of exposures. It is the response to the stimuli that dictates the extent of the outcome rather than the event itself. One exposure to a significant emotional or physical event may be enough to trigger a series of recurrent memory-based reexposures. These memory-based reexposures can produce near identical psychological and physiological responses to the original physical event, thus reinforcing the trauma as if the child is being physically reexposed to the stimuli itself. The impact of repeated exposure (whether physical or memory-based) is more severe in children than it is in adults. The ability to modulate experience through rationalisation is largely a function of the prefrontal cortex (PFC), and while the PFC remains undeveloped, it is the lower-order sensorimotor brain systems that provide direct stimulus-affect interactions without the benefit of higher-order cognitive modulation. In this way, emotional responses to events will be more salient, thus potentially evoking stronger memories and (mal)adaptive functional and behavioural outcomes. Child maltreatment through DFV is a particularly insidious experience for children as parents or primary careers are supposed to be a child's go-to place of safety, security, and stability. When a child's innate need for secure attachment is unmet and their basic needs for security and stability are betrayed, the impact can be serious and pervasive.

Just how many children experience DFV is difficult to determine. Across jurisdictions, there are substantial variations in (1) the collection of DFV data, (2) the definitions of what constitutes DFV, (3) the rates of arrest, charge, and conviction of perpetrators, and (4) the attitudes of authorities and the wider community around DFV behaviours and the moral obligations, responsibilities, and rights of all involved. The wide variety of events that are studied as DFV and, indeed, maltreatment and ELS in general and the variation in the severity of these events make it very difficult to determine precisely how many children experience traumatic reactions to such adversities. Any attempt to discern accurate figures is often further exacerbated by the low levels of disclosure and under reporting by various stakeholders (Pereda, Guilera, Forns, & Gomez-Benito, 2009).

In Australia, figures show that in 2010, 187,314 Australian children (approximately 3.7%) were subject to child protection notifications for suspected maltreatment (AIHW, 2011b; Lamont, 2012). During this same period, 1:135 Australian children (37,730 or 0.74%) were subject to out-of-home care or child protection orders. Figures from the United States show that in 2010, 5.9 million American children (approximately 8%) were referred to child welfare services for suspected maltreatment (Child Maltreatment 2010, 2011). During this same period, it is estimated that 1560 children died as a result of child abuse (2.07 deaths per 100,000 American children). Of these fatalities, 80% were younger than 4 years of age, 33% were attributable exclusively to neglect, and 41% were the result of multiple maltreatment modalities. Figures from other Western nations suggest comparable statistics.

These numbers represent a specific group of children subjected to early-life maltreatment through DFV and do not include the multiple other modalities through which maltreatment may be experienced. For example, in Australia, it is estimated that 1:6 children will experience severe bullying by their peers (Rigby, 2003). This is important given that research indicates children exposed to DFV are at higher risk for other forms of violence and abuse such as bullying. Neither does it take into account the low reporting and substantiation difficulties that are involved in investigations that pit child testimony against that of adults (NAPCAN, 2007). According to the National Association for the Prevention of Child Abuse and Neglect (NAPCAN, 2007), conservative estimates place child abuse and neglect rates in Australia upwards of 10%–20% of children each year.

Despite the difficulty in accurately quantifying the prevalence of child adversity, it is clear that maltreatment through DFV is an extensive problem in many countries around the world. Furthermore, its impact is pervasive and, if not addressed, results in long-term, even life-long biopsychosocial deficits (Anda et al., 2008, 2009; Brown et al., 2009, 2010; Clark, Caldwell, Power, & Stansfeld, 2010; Corcoran, Gallagher, Keeley, Arensman, & Perry, 2006; Dube, Felitti, Dong, Giles, & Anda, 2003; Glaser, van Os, Portegijs, & Myin-Germeys, 2006; Green et al., 2010; Strine et al., 2012).

The stress response is designed as a means to deal with any situation that either has (or threatens to) knock the body out of homeostatic balance. It is a biological imperative if we wish to survive, as it is the means by which our bodies are able to effectively distribute resources in order to survive an immediate threat. During a stress response, resource distribution is prioritised to provide optimal physical efficiency and the energy requirements to fuel the physical needs of the 'fight or flight' mechanisms. These responses are very costly both physically and psychologically as the energy requirements and physical response efficiency come as a result of shutting down a number of other functions and redirecting the resources for immediate survival needs (Bruner & Woll, 2011; Charmandari, Kino, Souvatzoglou, & Chrousos, 2003; Charmandari, Tsigos, & Chrousos, 2005; Chrousos, 2000).

In the CNS, this means shutting down many of the higher cognitive functions in order to allow the reflexive survival mechanisms of the nervous system to respond to the threat. While an important survival function, if the stress response is triggered chronically, then some of the associated chemistry becomes neurotoxic, and the process will hinder normal brain function and development (Charmandari et al., 2003). Moreover, if this occurs in childhood, a period of hyperactivated brain and physiological development, then the impact risk is far more serious.

Children are, in essence, one large-scale building project. When children are subjected to continued stress, they are effectively operating in an environment designed to shut down their long-term building project in preference for immediate survival needs. Repeated exposure to threat results in the chronic activation of the sympathetic nervous system and the hypothalamic-pituitary-adrenal axis (HPA axis) (Bevans, Cerbone, & Overstreet, 2008; Heim & Nemeroff, 2001; Heim, Newport, Mletzko, Miller, & Nemeroff, 2008; Nemeroff, 2004; Yehuda et al., 2010). As the acute response to stress is a vital mechanism for survival, it is highly adaptive to environmental requirements. When chronically triggered, this sensitivity to adaptive processes, particularly in children who are in a state of constant development and adaptation to experience, can result in upregulated HPA axis and autonomic reactivity. Ultimately, pervasive brain adaptations occur including hyperresponsive neuroendocrine processes, alterations to the regulation of neuroimmune and monoamine function, and structural adaptation to stress-induced stimulation of specific brain structures and neural pathways (Charmandari et al., 2003; Glaser et al., 2006; Gunnar & Quevedo, 2007; Otte et al., 2005).

3 Characteristics of Normal Brain Development

Brain development can be described using five core characteristics. These characteristics form a useful framework through which the trauma of DFV can be seen to exert its influence on children.

Characteristic 1. Brain development is largely nonlinear (Shaw et al., 2008). Increased age in childhood does not necessarily reflect a uniform advancement in functional capacity. In this way, the consequences of DFV may differ dependent upon the stage of the development of the brain. Early childhood is a time of rapid growth and critical organisation of the brain, and therefore, any interference in the first several years may manifest more significant consequences than at other periods (Pechtel & Pizzagalli, 2011; Perry, 2009).

Characteristic 2. The brain develops from the bottom up and the inside out (Perry, 2009; Perry, Pollard, Blakley, & Vigilante, 1995). This means that lower-order sensorimotor regions develop structurally and functionally before the higher-order association cortices (Gogtay et al., 2004; Gogtay & Thompson, 2010; Pechtel & Pizzagalli, 2011; Shaw et al., 2008). It is believed that the protracted developmental trajectory and the necessary reliance on the success of lower-order brain development make the higher-order structures and functions of the brain (cortical and limbic) highly susceptible to early-life insult and the impacts of chronic stress through exposure to DFV (Pechtel & Pizzagalli, 2011).

Characteristic 3. Ontogeny recapitulates phylogeny (Lenroot et al., 2009; Pechtel & Pizzagalli, 2011). Put simply, brain development is sequenced to reflect evolutionary processes with the structures involved in the highest-order executive processes being among the last brain structures to reach maturity.

Characteristic 4. Brain development is modulated by a combination of genetic and environmental factors (Lenroot et al., 2009; Pechtel & Pizzagalli, 2011; Peper et al., 2009). While basic development and function is guided by genetics, the intricacies of brain function are sculpted by environmental experiences through the principles of neuroplasticity and use-dependent development (Perry, 2009; Perry et al., 1995). While there is little doubt that experience is a major driver of neurodevelopmental outcomes, genetics are also found to have a significant role. For example, 60% of cortical thickness is accounted for through genetic variance (Schmitt et al., 2008). Moreover, the relationship between heritability and region-specific brain development reflects developmental trajectory. In this way, earlier-developing brain regions have stronger genetic correlations earlier in life, and later-maturing regions have stronger genetic correlations later in life (Lenroot et al., 2009; Pechtel & Pizzagalli, 2011). Thus, it could be hypothesised that the fundamental structure of the brain is genetically programmed, while neural functionality is a product of both the needs and the influences of the developmental environment.

Characteristic 5. The neurodevelopmental trajectories of males and females differ. These differences appear to be primarily in areas that are most associated with sex hormones such as the hypothalamus and amygdala, which either contain high concentrations of sex hormone receptors (e.g. the hypothalamus) or are strongly connected to the areas that do (e.g. the amygdala) (Hines, 2011; Lenroot & Giedd, 2010). Male and female children who experience DFV at the same age may therefore experience different sex-specific outcomes.

4 Characteristics of Maltreatment-Induced Neurodevelopmental Impairment

4.1 Maltreatment and Gene Expression

ELS and particularly that experienced through maltreatment via DFV have been shown to alter gene expression through its impact on a number of physiological systems at the molecular level (de Nadal, Ammerer, & Posas, 2011; Park et al., 2012; Takahashi, Sakamoto, & Kimura, 2012). Stress-induced changes to gene expression have been shown in processes directly impacting brain function and myriad other physiological processes. In rat models of maltreatment-related and general stress-induced PTSD, serotonin receptor expression increases in response to stress resulting in increased anxiety and mood dysregulation (Luo, Han, & Shi, 2011). Similarly, in rat models of chronic social stress and abuse, serotonin mRNA was shown to be significantly altered in brain regions involved in reward and motivation (Furay, McDevitt, Miczek, & Neumaier, 2011). Further, Komatsu et al. (2011) found that social stress in mice resulted in alterations to the mu-opioid receptor that is involved in the behavioural responses to psychosocial stressors and in the regulation of brain-derived neurotrophic factor (BDNF) expression in the hippocampus. Hippocampal BDNF mediates a number of aspects of hippocampal-dependent learning processes and neuroplasticity (Vaynman, Ying, & Gomez-Pinilla, 2004). It is speculated that the mu-opioid receptor also plays an important role in the pathogenesis of a variety of psychopathologies in which stress predisposes, mediates, or precipitates the progression of the disorder such as depression, PTSD, and social anxiety disorder (Culverhouse et al., 2018; Direk et al., 2017; Komatsu et al., 2011; Witt et al., 2017; Wray et al., 2018).

4.2 Neuropsychological Impacts

Impaired higher cortical function is also associated with childhood maltreatment (Anderson & Ylvisaker, 2009; Hedges & Woon, 2011; Oomen et al., 2011; Shonkoff & Garner, 2012). A number of studies have identified poorer performance in global measures of cognitive function such as school performance (including higher inclusion rates in special education programs, lower school completion, and lower rates of progression into tertiary education) and general measures of intelligence (IQ) (Blair & Raver, 2012; Loman, Wiik, Frenn, Pollak, & Gunnar, 2009; Pechtel & Pizzagalli, 2011). These performance deficits have been linked to a number of neurobiological correlates including smaller intracranial volume, reduced hemispheric integration, and a smaller corpus callosum (Noble, Tottenham, & Casey, 2005; Pechtel & Pizzagalli, 2011). In domain specific assessments of cognitive function, individuals with histories of maltreatment and particularly from exposure to DFV-related stressors perform significantly poorer than their peers with no history of maltreatment in a range of areas including executive function (Butts, Weinberg, Young, & Phillips, 2011; DePrince, Weinzierl, & Combs, 2009; Polak, Witteveen, Reitsma, & Olff, 2012), memory and learning (Meiser-Stedman, Dalgleish, Smith, Yule, & Glucksman, 2007; Quesada, Wiemers, Schoofs, & Wolf, 2012; Yasik, Saigh, Oberfield, & Halamandaris, 2007), and emotional and social function (Pechtel & Pizzagalli, 2011; Perry, 2009).

4.2.1 Executive function

Deficits in executive function are consistently reported in maltreatment cohorts (Bos, Fox, Zeanah, & Nelson Iii, 2009; Colvert et al., 2008; Gould et al., 2012; Polak et al., 2012; Stevens et al., 2008) and are thought to be associated with the increased susceptibility to chronic stress resulting from the long developmental trajectory of the frontal lobe structures and circuitry and the density of glucocorticoid receptors and dopaminergic projections (Gogtay & Thompson, 2010).

Specific neurobiological correlates of executive impairments in maltreatment cohorts have been found in the PFC (e.g. increased activation in the inferior PFC and striatum associated with impaired inhibitory control and reduced PFC grey matter (GM)) (Frodl, Reinhold, Koutsouleris, Donohoe, et al., 2010; Mueller et al., 2010; Navalta, Polcari, Webster, Boghossian, & Teicher, 2006) and cerebellum (e.g. reduced volume in the right cerebellar lobe associated with impaired planning) (Bauer, Hanson, Pierson, Davidson, & Pollak, 2009). According to Bauer et al. (2009), the cerebellum, like the frontal cortex, has a long developmental trajectory and may therefore be similarly susceptible to the impact of chronic stress. The cerebellum, like the frontal cortex, is intimately involved in higher-order cortical processing including affect regulation, language, visual spatial learning, and working memory (O'Halloran, Kinsella, & Storey, 2012; Schmahmann & Caplan, 2006; Tiemeier et al., 2010).

4.2.2 Memory

Impairments in both verbal and nonverbal memory are associated with DFV-mediated maltreatment and ELS in general (Bos et al., 2009; Bremner et al., 2003a, 2003b; Gould et al., 2012; Hedges & Woon, 2011; Navalta et al., 2006). Human and animal studies consistently show a reduction in hippocampal volume (Frodl, Reinhold, Koutsouleris, Donohoe, et al., 2010; Jackowski et al., 2011; Teicher et al., 2012; Woon & Hedges, 2008; Woon, Sood, & Hedges, 2010), which are, in turn, associated with long-term learning and memory deficits (Karten, Olariu, & Cameron, 2005). One possible explanation is that the high density of glucocorticoid receptors in the hippocampus render it more susceptible to stress (Herman, Ostrander, Mueller, & Figueiredo, 2005). Sapolsky (1996) suggests that glucocorticoids bind to the glucocorticoid receptors in the hippocampus and hinder neurogenesis ultimately causing cell reductions. Carrion, Weems, and Reiss (2007) support this argument and posit that the cell reductions are long-term sequelae of glucocorticoid hypersecretion taking years to manifest. This may explain why both reductions in hippocampal volume and the associated learning and memory deficits are only consistently found in adult survivors of childhood maltreatment and not in child and adolescent cohorts (De Bellis, Hooper, Woolley, & Shenk, 2010; Karl et al., 2006; Teicher et al., 2003, 2012; Woon et al., 2010; Woon & Hedges, 2008).

Finally, in children with a history of physical maltreatment, memory performance was also associated with functional changes in areas of the cortex that were sensitive to dopaminergic projection (Sheu, Polcari, Anderson, & Teicher, 2010).

4.2.3 Affective function

Childhood exposure to DFV is associated with significant impairment to affect regulation and perception and reward processing. Impaired affective functioning is, in turn, thought to increase the risk for psychopathology (Baune, Czira, Smith, Mitchell, & Sinnamon, 2012; Beblo, Sinnamon, & Baune, 2011; Pechtel & Pizzagalli, 2011). Survivors of exposure to childhood DFV are subject to significant affective dysregulation that persists long after the termination of the maltreatment (Beblo et al., 2011; Pechtel & Pizzagalli, 2011). Dysregulated affect is associated with PFC-anterior cingulate cortex (ACC) and fronto-limbic circuitry (Beblo et al., 2011; Berthoz et al., 2002; Bryant et al., 2008; Cohen et al., 2006) and with increased amygdala reactivity (Beblo et al., 2011; Grant, Cannistraci, Hollon, Gore, & Shelton, 2011; Ochsner & Gross, 2005).

Emotional perception abnormalities are associated with reduced recognition and response to emotions in self and others in a context appropriate manner (Onozawa, Yagasaki, Izawa,

Abe, & Kawakami, 2011; Oomen et al., 2011; Pechtel & Pizzagalli, 2011; Perry, 2009). This includes a propensity towards increased negativity bias (West, Choi, & Travers, 2010) in which attentional focus characteristically 'locks on' to negative environmental elements and subsequent experiences are then interpreted and perceived negatively. In maltreatment cohorts, this has been observed to coincide with activation of the left rostromedial area of the PFC. This area is implicated in the retrieval of emotional knowledge and suggests the process is underpinned by emotive learning from past (adverse) experience (Ochsner et al., 2004; Ochsner & Gross, 2005). Negatively valenced affective apperception and its associated attentional bias are associated with a decreased capacity to actively control behaviours and cognitions and an increase in reactive cognitive function (West et al., 2010). This has a significant impact on the ability to interpret surrounding events, assess risk, and take appropriate and deliberate action in response. Instead, individuals rely on impulsive and often poorly constructed and deliberated reactions to experiences (Forbes, Cox, Schmader, & Ryan, 2011; Melcher, Born, & Gruber, 2011; West et al., 2010).

The processing of risk and reward also appears among the list of deficit functions resulting from childhood maltreatment. The mesolimbic dopaminergic pathways also appear to play an important role in reward motivation (incentive-salience) (Berridge, 2007; Pechtel & Pizzagalli, 2011; Waldinger, Schulz, Barsky, & Ahern, 2006). This is supported by the literature showing reduced mesolimbic dopamine expression in the presence of biopsychological symptomology such as anhedonia, the loss of libido, lassitude, and fatigue (Dillon et al., 2009; Dunlop & Nemeroff, 2007; Hasler et al., 2008; Pizzagalli et al., 2009).

Children who are removed from abusive, traumatic, or neglectful environments and placed in positive and stable placements show some performance gains (known as 'catch-up') over time but, even after spending significant time in quality care, still underperform compared with their peers (Bakermans-Kranenburg et al., 2011; Beckett et al., 2006; Johnson et al., 2010; Judge, 2003; Rutter et al., 1998). This suggests that cognitive function is strongly related to both the consistency of early-life experience and the neurobiological impairments observed. This is supported by the literature that shows a number of neural correlates to cognitive function in children and adult survivors of childhood maltreatment. For example, intelligence and GM volume are consistently correlated in studies of childhood maltreatment and exposure to DFV, with reductions in global measures of IQ being associated with reductions in GM in areas including the hippocampus, insula, orbitofrontal cortex, anterior cingulate gyrus, and caudate nuclei. This relationship increases in strength the earlier the age of initial exposure/experience and the longer the duration of the experience (De Bellis et al., 2002; Noble et al., 2005).

4.3 Neurobiological Impacts

Reductions in GM volume (Dannlowski et al., 2012; Frodl et al., 2012; Tomoda et al., 2009; Treadway et al., 2009), increased white matter (WM) volume and changes in WM tracts (Frodl et al., 2012; Frodl, Reinhold, Koutsouleris, Reiser, & Meisenzahl, 2010), reduced global intracranial volumes (De Bellis et al., 1999, 2010; Woodward et al., 2007), smaller corpus callosum (De Bellis et al., 1999) and hippocampus (Dannlowski et al., 2012; Jackowski et al., 2011; Oomen et al., 2011), increased amygdala volume and reactivity (Grant et al., 2011; Malykhin, Carter, Hegadoren, Seres, & Coupland, 2012), HPA axis dysregulation (Carpenter, Shattuck, Tyrka, Geracioti, & Price, 2011; Shea, Walsh, MacMillan, & Steiner, 2005; Tofoli, Baes, Martins, & Juruena, 2011), impaired autonomic function (Calkins, Graziano, Berdan, Keane, & Degnan, 2008; Gump et al., 2011; Miskovic, Schmidt, Georgiades, Boyle, & MacMillan, 2009; Scheeringa, Zeanah, Myers, & Putnam, 2004; Wright, 2010), and myriad additional neurobiological alterations are observed in child and adult survivors of childhood maltreatment. The present general consensus for the associated structural and functional brain alterations is that stressful early-life experiences impede normal developmental neuroplasticity via interruptions to critical periods of neurogenesis and the processes of synaptic connectivity and synaptic pruning (Frodl, Reinhold, Koutsouleris, Donohoe, et al., 2010; Huether, 1998; Pechtel & Pizzagalli, 2011; Teicher, Samson, Polcari, & McGreenery, 2006; Teicher, Tomoda, & Andersen, 2006).

A number of mechanisms are potentially involved in this impediment. For example, threat response involves the release of arginine vasopressin (AVP) and corticotrophin-releasing factor (CRF) into the anterior pituitary where they stimulate the secretion of adrenocorticotropic hormone (ACTH) (Bradley et al., 2008). In turn, ACTH travels to the adrenal glands and stimulates the release of glucocorticoids into both the body and the brain. In high or chronic stress load scenarios, glucocorticoids (through interaction with glucocorticoid receptors in the brain) are known to impede neuroplasticity. Brain regions with the highest concentrations of glucocorticoid receptors (e.g. the hippocampus and PFC) are also found to be the most susceptible to stress (Shonkoff & Garner, 2012). Exposure to DFV appears to increase the reactivity of this neuroendocrine stress response via alterations to the HPA axis, in turn altering the glucocorticoid receptors and creating long-lasting alterations to physiological functioning (McGowan et al., 2009; Shonkoff & Garner, 2012). Other factors such as impediments to the development and function of monoamine systems, oxidative stress mechanisms, and neuroinflammatory processes are also implicated. A detailed review of these mechanisms are outside the scope of this chapter; however, several good reviews have been published (see Hunter, Minnis, & Wilson, 2011; Karl et al., 2006; O'Halloran et al., 2012; Pereda & Gallardo-Pujol, 2011; Shaw et al., 2008; Tofoli et al., 2011; Twardosz & Lutzker, 2010).

4.3.1 Corporal punishment

In children exposed to physical maltreatment in the home, a number of these mechanisms have been shown to be associated with significant changes in the frontal cortices and other core areas of the brain associated with cognitive function and emotional regulation

(Sheu et al., 2010; Tomoda et al., 2009). Tomoda et al. (2009) and numerous other studies have concluded that exposing children to physical maltreatment can have significantly detrimental effects on the trajectory of the developing brain. These changes involve both structural and chemical alterations (Amodio & Frith, 2006; Anderson, Bechara, Damasio, Tranel, & Damasio, 1999; Glaser, 2000; Hart & Rubia, 2012; Heim, Shugart, Craighead, & Nemeroff, 2010). Reductions in GM volume in the frontal cortex have been shown to be a particularly robust finding (Sheu et al., 2010; Tomoda et al., 2009). Other consistent findings include functional changes associated with cognition and emotional regulation in several areas including the caudate, putamen, substantia nigra, thalamus, and accumbens (Sheu et al., 2010). In addition, physical maltreatment is associated with neurofunctional changes in dopaminergic projections that have been associated with substantial reductions in memory performance and a substantially increased risk for drug and alcohol abuse (Sheu et al., 2010).

4.3.2 Verbally aggressive parenting

It is not only physical maltreatment that creates high risk in children living in DFV. There is evidence that children exposed to verbally aggressive parenting are also at risk of substantial neurofunctional challenges (Choi, Jeong, Rohan, Polcari, & Teicher, 2009). Studies have shown that three WM tract regions appear to have significantly reduced functional performance that is related to exposure to parental verbal abuse. These are the arcuate fasciculus in the left superior temporal gyrus, the cingulum bundle at the posterior tail of the left hippocampus, and the left body of the fornix. In children exposed to verbally aggressive parenting, reduced functional performance in the arcuate fasciculus is correlated with reduced verbal IQ and reduced verbal comprehension. Reduced functional performance in the cingulum bundle is associated with higher rates of depression, dissociation, and emotional dysregulation. Finally, reduced functionality in the left fornix is associated with increased anxiety and somatisation (Choi et al., 2009).

4.4 Increased Risk of Psychiatric Disorder

In the United States, the National Comorbidity Survey found that 32% of all psychiatric illness can be explained by exposure to experiences of childhood maltreatment (Green et al., 2010). This figure rose to 44% when explaining psychiatric disorders with a childhood onset. This relationship has been illustrated in a number of studies, and the relative significance of the issue is robust (Thabrew, de Sylva, & Romans, 2012) and does not appear to attenuate with age (Clark et al., 2010).

This risk association extends through the spectrum of psychiatric conditions including personality disorders (PD). In the case of PD, there are several variants that are significantly associated with childhood trauma. Of particular note is borderline PD (BPD). The research shows a clear relationship between child maltreatment and BPD (Bornovalova, Gratz, Delany-Brumsey, Paulson, & Lejuez, 2006).

Those with BPD consistently report higher rates of childhood maltreatment across the areas of sexual, emotional, and physical abuse and emotional and physical neglect (Bornovalova et al., 2006; Kuo, Khoury, Metcalfe, Fitzpatrick, & Goodwill, 2015). Research shows that 40%–76% of those with BPD report that they were sexually abused as children, while 25%–73% report that they were physically abused (Bornovalova et al., 2006; Frias, Palma, Farriols, Gonzalez, & Horta, 2016; Kuo et al., 2015; Soloff, White, Omari, Ramaseshan, & Diwadkar, 2015; Westbrook & Berenbaum, 2017). The research indicates that it is emotional maltreatment that appears to be the primary driver of BPD formation with factors such as emotional abuse, emotional neglect, preoccupied attachment in career adults, and emotional invalidation, all associated with BPD formation (Chanen & Kaess, 2012; Fonagy, Luyten, & Strathearn, 2011; Frayn, Paris, & Zweig-Frank, 1991; Frias et al., 2016; Kuo et al., 2015; Soloff et al., 2015; Westbrook & Berenbaum, 2017). In those with BPD, childhood sexual abuse has been identified as being linked to an increased risk of suicidal behaviour (Soloff, Feske, & Fabio, 2008).

4.5 Increased Risk of Drug Addiction

Alterations to stress and reward physiology as a result of ELS are significantly linked to risk of drug abuse and increased risk for relapse after rehabilitation (Dube et al., 2003; Koob & Kreek, 2007; Koob & Le Moal, 2001; Kreek & Koob, 1998; Strine et al., 2012). Significant numbers of people presenting with drug related conditions have a history of childhood maltreatment and exposure to DFV specifically (Enoch, 2011; Navailles, Hof, & Schmauss, 2008; Reed, Anthony, & Breslau, 2007). A primary link to childhood maltreatment and ELS and increased risk for drug use appears to be derived through alterations to the release and reception of CRF and function in the HPA axis resulting in hyperresponsivity and elevated baseline levels of stress hormones (Heim, Newport, Bonsall, Miller, & Nemeroff, 2001; Kendler et al., 2000; Ladd et al., 2000; Pastor et al., 2008).

Two key findings are relevant to the foundations of this increased risk. Firstly, increased levels of hypothalamic CRF appears to increase the reinforcing effects of a number of drugs of abuse (Back et al., 2008; Bonci & Borgland, 2009; Sarnyai, Shaham, & Heinrichs, 2001; Shalev, Erb, & Shaham, 2010). Secondly, a number of illicit drugs (e.g. cannabis and opiates), while stimulating the HPA axis leading to increased reinforcement, also reduce the volume of hypothalamic CRF, thereby possibly serving to counter the increased anxiety and depression associated with elevated stress (Arzt & Holsboer, 2006; Bonci & Borgland, 2009). In this way, the self-medicating characteristics of drug use in individuals with elevated baseline CRF or hypersensitive CRF response patterns appear to be an important factor. Research supports this with results of clinical trials showing that some drugs of abuse such as ±3,4-methylenedioxymethamphetamine (MDMA) are effective in treating psychopathologies characterised by upregulated CRF and heightened anxiety responses such as PTSD (Mithoefer, Wagner, Mithoefer, Jerome, & Doblin, 2011).

Finally, physical maltreatment in children has been associated with altered activation in regions most impacted by dopaminergic projections, and this, in turn, is associated with increased risk for drug and alcohol abuse (Sheu et al., 2010).

4.6 Increased Suicide Risk

Consistent findings over time have shown that about two-thirds (~67%) of population-wide suicide risk can be attributed to factors associated with childhood maltreatment (Afifi et al., 2008; Corcoran et al., 2006; Dube et al., 2001; Dube, Felitti, Dong, Giles, & Anda, 2003). Imaging studies of children with backgrounds of maltreatment experience show substantially greater levels of both self-harming and suicidal behaviours. Further, these individuals show a range of structural brain differences compared with individuals who display neither characteristic, regardless of other pathology factors such as depression, bipolar disorder, or schizophrenia (Johnston et al., 2017; Tanti et al., 2017; Witt et al., 2018). This has also been reported in offender populations. In offender groups, suicide behaviours are significantly more likely in those with a history of abuse, whether or not the abuse was at the hands of a family member (Gunter, Chibnall, Antoniak, Philibert, & Black, 2013). However, this remains highly relevant to the issue of DFV, as the statistics across the vast majority of countries and jurisdictions where they have been made available show that all forms of abuse and maltreatment in children are far more commonly perpetrated by a close family member or career than by a stranger. These findings are consistent across numerous studies and in methodologically sound meta-analyses where results across studies have been assessed collectively (Dube, Felitti, Dong, Giles, & Anda, 2003; Jonson-Reid, Kohl, & Drake, 2012; Witt et al., 2018).

4.7 Increased Risk of Somatic Illness

The link between early-life maltreatment and poor physical health has shown to be robust in child, adolescent, and adult cohorts (Clark et al., 2010; Flaherty et al., 2006; Graham-Bermann & Seng, 2005; Thabrew et al., 2012). General poorer physical health is consistently reported, and increasingly, the literature is reporting a link with several specific illnesses, many of which are closely associated with increased mortality. Some examples include chronic headache and migraine (Anda, Tietjen, Schulman, Felitti, & Croft, 2010), heart disease (Dong et al., 2004; O'Rand & Hamil-Luker, 2005), pulmonary diseases (Anda, Brown, Dube, et al., 2008), some cancers (Brown, Young, Anda, Felitti, & Giles, 2006), autoimmune dysfunction related to diseases such as type 1 diabetes (Sepa, Frodi, & Ludvigsson, 2005; Sepa, Wahlberg, Vaarala, Frodi, & Ludvigsson, 2005), and a general increase in biomarkers of aging such as telomere length (Surtees et al., 2011). In the case of type 1 diabetes, experience of DFV in childhood is associated with an increased risk for the disease of 2.8 times that of children without a history of DFV (Sepa, Frodi, & Ludvigsson, 2005; Sepa, Wahlberg, et al., 2005).

4.8 Increased Risk of Early Mortality

Individuals who experience multiple episodes of early-life adversity are at significantly increased risk for early mortality (Anda et al., 2009; Brown et al., 2009; Dube, Felitti, Dong, Giles, & Anda, 2003; Felitti et al., 1998). Specifically, Brown et al. (2009) found that individuals with six or more early-life experiences of maltreatment are likely to die up to 20 years earlier than those without early-life maltreatment. Cohorts dating back as far as 1900 have shown increased early mortality associated with childhood maltreatment and a range of both mental and physical illnesses (Dube, Felitti, Dong, Giles, & Anda, 2003). Many long-term health outcomes linked to childhood maltreatment are additionally influenced by the presence of increased behaviours and somatic factors that are associated with poor health outcomes such as smoking (Edwards, Anda, Gu, Dube, & Felitti, 2007), alcoholism (Dube, Anda, Felitti, Edwards, & Croft, 2002; Strine et al., 2012), drug misuse (Anda, Brown, Felitti, Dube, & Giles, 2008; Dube, Felitti, Dong, Chapman, et al., 2003), poor mental health (Lu, Mueser, Rosenberg, & Jankowski, 2008; Oladeji, Makanjuola, & Gureje, 2010; Schilling, Aseltine, & Gore, 2007; Tonmyr, Jamieson, Mery, & MacMillan, 2005), obesity and type 2 diabetes (Thomas, Hypponen, & Power, 2008), and HIV contraction risk (Brown & Anda, 2009).

4.9 Additional Risks From Childhood Maltreatment

Consistent findings from Australia (AIHW, 2009, 2011a; Bromfield, Lamont, Parker, & Horsfall, 2010), the United States (Goldman, Salus, Wolcott, & Kennedy, 2003), and the United Kingdom (UKDH, 2010) suggest that childhood adversity has been further linked to a number of factors relating to social, educational, and economic characteristics. In brief summary, survivors of childhood exposure to DFV are at significantly increased risk to the following:

- Be in special education programs
- Not to finish high school (those who do are 30% less likely to go to higher education)
- Never hold a steady job
- Spend their whole lives in poverty
- Be arrested for a violent crime
- Become a teen parent
- Become a single parent
- Have children to multiple partners outside committed relationship (regardless of whether the survivor of childhood maltreatment is male or female)
- Be involved in adult domestic violence as either a victim or perpetrator
- Be involved with child protection intervention in some form (victim or perpetrator)

5 Summary and Conclusion

It is clear that there are significant links between childhood exposure to DFV, neurological deficits, a plethora of deleterious biopsychosocial sequelae, and ultimately increased mortality risk. Early-life experiences of maltreatment provide powerful influences over neurobiological development, and together, these factors collude to impede the psychobiological function, behaviour, and pathology of survivors. This interplay of influence is underpinned by genetic variants that may, in themselves, become subject to manipulation through the effects of DFV and its physiological correlates. The complexity of the human brain means that it is necessarily subject to a prolonged developmental trajectory in which the most complex of systems are the last to reach maturity, taking as long as 30 years to fully develop. Early-life is a period characterised by rapid and complex growth and organisation of neurophysiology. During this period, children are both highly dependent upon others for their welfare, while simultaneously lacking the physiological and cognitive capacity to self-protect from adverse experiences. Ultimately, this renders them at great risk of psychobiological insult and the consequent deleterious impact on neurodevelopmental progress.

6 Chapter Summary

- Only relatively recently have longitudinal studies of brain development progressed to incorporate results that include the brain at full maturity. These studies have greatly improved our understanding of the developmental trajectory of the healthy brain over the first 30 years of life and the developmental impact of child maltreatment.
- Positive experiences result in a positive impact on the development of the CNS, while negative experiences, defined by variations to the themes of stress, trauma, and neglect, including these experiences through the medium of DFV, result in neurodevelopmental deficits that produce clearly identifiable impairment right across the biopsychosocial spectrum.
- In the last three decades, paediatric health services have been increasingly informed by the advances in knowledge of developmental neurobiology. These advances have occurred largely as a result of two things: (1) the evolution in imaging technologies that have allowed us to observe the workings of the CNS in ever-increasing detail and (2) the realisation (if not yet complete understanding) that the relationships between structures, systems, and functional outputs of the CNS are far more complex than the traditional mechanistic view has credited.
- ELS refers to any event that exposes a child to physical and/or psychological stimuli that exceeds their capacity to successfully cope.
- The most commonly cited stressors are those relating to variations to the themes of abuse, neglect, and traumatic experience.
- A stressor may involve a single-event exposure or a succession of exposures. It is the response to the stimuli that dictates the extent of the outcome rather than the event itself.

- In the CNS, a stress response shuts down many of the higher cognitive functions in order to allow the reflexive survival mechanisms of the nervous system to respond to the threat. If the stress response is triggered chronically, then some of the associated chemistry becomes neurotoxic, and the process will hinder normal brain function and development. When this occurs in childhood, a period of hyperactivated brain and physiological development, then, the impact risk is far more serious.
- Brain development can be described using five core characteristics. These characteristics form a useful framework through which the trauma of DFV can be seen to exert its influence on children:
  1. Brain development is largely nonlinear.
  2. The brain develops from the bottom up and the inside out.
  3. Ontogeny parallels phylogeny.
  4. Brain development is modulated by a combination of genetic and environmental factors.
  5. The neurodevelopmental trajectories of males and females differ.
- Childhood maltreatment has been shown to alter gene expression through its impact on a number of physiological systems at the molecular level.
- Impaired higher cortical function is also associated with childhood maltreatment.
- Deficits in executive function are consistently reported in maltreatment cohorts and are thought to be associated with the increased susceptibility to chronic stress resulting from the long developmental trajectory of the frontal lobe structures and circuitry and the density of glucocorticoid receptors and dopaminergic projections.
- Impairments in both verbal and nonverbal memory are associated with DFV-mediated maltreatment and ELS in general.
- Childhood exposure to DFV is associated with significant impairment to affect regulation and perception and reward processing. Impaired affective functioning is, in turn, thought to increase the risk for psychopathology.
- Neuroanatomy is impacted in numerous ways including reductions in GM volume, increased WM volume and changes in WM tracts, reduced global intracranial volumes, smaller corpus callosum and hippocampus, increased amygdala volume and reactivity, HPA axis dysregulation, and impaired autonomic function.
- The present general consensus for the associated structural and functional brain alterations is that stressful early-life experiences impede normal developmental neuroplasticity via interruptions to critical periods of neurogenesis and the processes of synaptic connectivity and synaptic pruning. A number of these mechanisms have been shown to be associated with significant changes in the frontal cortices and other core areas of the brain associated with cognitive function and emotional regulation and significantly detrimental effects on the trajectory of the developing brain. These changes involve both structural and chemical alterations.

- Exposure to verbally aggressive parenting increases the risk of substantial neurofunctional challenges with studies showing that three WM tract regions appear to have significantly reduced functional performance: the arcuate fasciculus in the left superior temporal gyrus, the cingulum bundle at the posterior tail of the left hippocampus, and the left body of the fornix.
- Studies have suggested that about 1/3 of all psychiatric illness can be explained by exposure to experiences of childhood maltreatment. This figure rises to almost ½ when explaining psychiatric disorders with a childhood onset.
- Alterations to stress and reward physiology as a result of ELS are significantly linked to risk of drug abuse and increased risk for relapse after rehabilitation.
- Consistent findings over time have shown that about two-thirds (~67%) of population-wide suicide risk can be attributed to factors associated with childhood maltreatment.
- The link between early-life maltreatment and poor physical health has shown to be robust in child, adolescent, and adult cohorts.
- Individuals who experience multiple episodes of early-life adversity are at significantly increased risk for early mortality.

7 Chapter Review Questions

1. Describe the five characteristics of normal brain development.
2. Describe how gene expression is thought to be impacted by childhood maltreatment.
3. What are the three functional impacts on cognitive performance that can result from childhood maltreatment?
4. What are the five neuroanatomical impacts of childhood maltreatment?
5. How does corporal punishment impact the developing brain?
6. What the three areas of WM have been shown to be impacted by verbally aggressive parenting?
7. Name and describe the three psychiatric conditions associated with childhood maltreatment.
8. What percentage of psychiatric conditions in the population is thought to be associated with childhood maltreatment?
9. How is childhood maltreatment thought to influence the risk of drug abuse?
10. Describe the relationship between suicide risk and childhood maltreatment.
11. Numerous somatic illnesses have been linked to childhood maltreatment; describe three and the proposed mechanisms by which they are thought to be associated.
12. Childhood maltreatment is strongly linked to early mortality. What is the specific finding that was identified in this regard?
13. What are the five additional risks associated with childhood maltreatment?

References

Afifi, T. O., Enns, M. W., Cox, B. J., Asmundson, G. J., Stein, M. B., & Sareen, J. (2008). Population attributable fractions of psychiatric disorders and suicide ideation and attempts associated with adverse childhood experiences. *American Journal of Public Health*, *98*(5), 946–952. AJPH.2007.120253 [pii] https://doi.org/10.2105/AJPH.2007.120253.

AIHW. (2009). *Australian Institute of Health and Welfare 2009. A picture of Australia's children 2009. Cat. no. PHE 112*. Canberra: Australian Institute of Health and Welfare.

AIHW. (2011a). *Australian Institute of Health and Welfare 2011. Headline Indicators for children's health, development and wellbeing 2011. Cat. no. PHE 144*. Canberra: Australian Institute of Health and Welfare.

AIHW. (2011b). *Child Protection Australia 2009-10. Child Welfare Series no. 51. Cat. no. CWS 39*. Canberra: Australian Institute of Health and Welfare.

Amodio, D. M., & Frith, C. D. (2006). Meeting of minds: the medial frontal cortex and social cognition. *Nature Reviews Neuroscience*, *7*(4), 268.

Anda, R. F., Brown, D. W., Dube, S. R., Bremner, J. D., Felitti, V. J., & Giles, W. H. (2008). Adverse childhood experiences and chronic obstructive pulmonary disease in adults. *American Journal of Preventive Medicine*, *34*(5), 396–403. S0749-3797(08)00151-7 [pii] https://doi.org/10.1016/j.amepre.2008.02.002.

Anda, R. F., Brown, D. W., Felitti, V. J., Dube, S. R., & Giles, W. H. (2008). Adverse childhood experiences and prescription drug use in a cohort study of adult HMO patients. *BMC Public Health*, *8*, 198. 1471-2458-8-198 [pii] https://doi.org/10.1186/1471-2458-8-198.

Anda, R. F., Dong, M., Brown, D. W., Felitti, V. J., Giles, W. H., Perry, G. S., et al. (2009). The relationship of adverse childhood experiences to a history of premature death of family members. *BMC Public Health*, *9*, 106. 1471-2458-9-106 [pii] https://doi.org/10.1186/1471-2458-9-106.

Anda, R., Tietjen, G., Schulman, E., Felitti, V., & Croft, J. (2010). Adverse childhood experiences and frequent headaches in adults. *Headache*, *50*(9), 1473–1481. https://doi.org/10.1111/j.1526-4610.2010.01756.x.

Anderson, S. W., Bechara, A., Damasio, H., Tranel, D., & Damasio, A. R. (1999). Impairment of social and moral behavior related to early damage in human prefrontal cortex. *Nature Neuroscience*, *2*(11), 1032.

Anderson, V., & Ylvisaker, M. (2009). Executive function and the frontal lobes: themes for child development, brain insult and rehabilitation. *Developmental Neurorehabilitation*, *12*(5), 253–254. https://doi.org/10.3109/17518420903086899.

Arzt, E., & Holsboer, F. (2006). CRF signaling: molecular specificity for drug targeting in the CNS. *Trends in Pharmacological Sciences*, *27*(10), 531–538. S0165-6147(06)00203-3 [pii] https://doi.org/10.1016/j.tips.2006.08.007.

Back, S. E., Brady, K. T., Waldrop, A. E., Yeatts, S. D., McRae, A. L., & Spratt, E. (2008). Early life trauma and sensitivity to current life stressors in individuals with and without cocaine dependence. *The American Journal of Drug and Alcohol Abuse*, *34*(4), 389–396. 793247664 [pii] https://doi.org/10.1080/00952990802122614.

Bakermans-Kranenburg, M. J., Steele, H., Zeanah, C. H., Muhamedrahimov, R. J., Vorria, P., Dobrova-Krol, N. A., et al. (2011). Attachment and emotional development in institutional care: characteristics and catch up. *Monographs of the Society for Research in Child Development*, *76*(4), 62–91.

Bauer, P. M., Hanson, J. L., Pierson, R. K., Davidson, R. J., & Pollak, S. D. (2009). Cerebellar volume and cognitive functioning in children who experienced early deprivation. *Biological Psychiatry*, *66*(12), 1100–1106. S0006-3223(09)00769-0 [pii] https://doi.org/10.1016/j.biopsych.2009.06.014.

Baune, B. T., Czira, M. E., Smith, A. L., Mitchell, D., & Sinnamon, G. (2012). Neuropsychological performance in a sample of 13-25 year olds with a history of non-psychotic major depressive disorder. *Journal of Affective Disorders*, *141*(2–3), 441–448. https://doi.org/10.1016/j.jad.2012.02.041.

Beblo, T., Sinnamon, G., & Baune, B. T. (2011). Specifying the neuropsychology of affective disorders: clinical, demographic and neurobiological factors. *Neuropsychology Review*, *21*(4), 337–359. https://doi.org/10.1007/s11065-011-9171-0.

Beckett, C., Maughan, B., Rutter, M., Castle, J., Colvert, E., Groothues, C., et al. (2006). Do the effects of early severe deprivation on cognition persist into early adolescence? Findings from the English and Romanian adoptees study. *Child Development*, *77*(3), 696–711.

Berridge, K. C. (2007). The debate over dopamine's role in reward: the case for incentive salience. *Psychopharmacology*, *191*(3), 391–431. https://doi.org/10.1007/s00213-006-0578-x.

Berthoz, S., Artiges, E., Van De Moortele, P. F., Poline, J. B., Rouquette, S., Consoli, S. M., et al. (2002). Effect of impaired recognition and expression of emotions on frontocingulate cortices: an fMRI study of men with alexithymia. *The American Journal of Psychiatry*, *159*(6), 961–967.

Bevans, K., Cerbone, A., & Overstreet, S. (2008). Relations between recurrent trauma exposure and recent life stress and salivary cortisol among children. *Development and Psychopathology*, *20*(1), 257–272. S0954579408000126 [pii] https://doi.org/10.1017/S0954579408000126.

Blair, C., & Raver, C. C. (2012). Child development in the context of adversity: experiential canalization of brain and behavior. *The American Psychologist*, https://doi.org/10.1037/a0027493. Advance online publication. 2012-05396-001 [pii].

Bonci, A., & Borgland, S. (2009). Role of orexin/hypocretin and CRF in the formation of drug-dependent synaptic plasticity in the mesolimbic system. *Neuropharmacology*, *56*(Suppl 1), 107–111. S0028-3908(08)00298-0 [pii] https://doi.org/10.1016/j.neuropharm.2008.07.024.

Bornovalova, M. A., Gratz, K. L., Delany-Brumsey, A., Paulson, A., & Lejuez, C. (2006). Temperamental and environmental risk factors for borderline personality disorder among inner-city substance users in residential treatment. *Journal of Personality Disorders*, *20*(3), 218–231.

Bos, K. J., Fox, N., Zeanah, C. H., & Nelson Iii, C. A. (2009). Effects of early psychosocial deprivation on the development of memory and executive function. *Frontiers in Behavioral Neuroscience*, *3*, 16. https://doi.org/10.3389/neuro.08.016.2009.

Bradley, R. G., Binder, E. B., Epstein, M. P., Tang, Y., Nair, H. P., Liu, W., et al. (2008). Influence of child abuse on adult depression: moderation by the corticotropin-releasing hormone receptor gene. *Archives of General Psychiatry*, *65*(2), 190–200.

Bremner, J. D., Vythilingam, M., Vermetten, E., Southwick, S. M., McGlashan, T., Nazeer, A., et al. (2003a). MRI and PET study of deficits in hippocampal structure and function in women with childhood sexual abuse and posttraumatic stress disorder. *The American Journal of Psychiatry*, *160*(5), 924–932.

Bremner, J. D., Vythilingam, M., Vermetten, E., Southwick, S. M., McGlashan, T., Staib, L. H., et al. (2003b). Neural correlates of declarative memory for emotionally valenced words in women with posttraumatic stress disorder related to early childhood sexual abuse. *Biological Psychiatry*, *53*(10), 879–889. S0006322302018917 [pii].

Bromfield, L., Lamont, A., Parker, R., & Horsfall, B. (2010). *Issues for the safety and wellbeing of children in families with multiple and complex problems: The co-occurrence of domestic violence, parental substance misuse, and mental health problems*. Canberra: Australian Institute of Family Studies.

Brown, D. W., & Anda, R. F. (2009). Adverse childhood experiences: origins of behaviors that sustain the HIV epidemic. *AIDS*, *23*(16), 2231–2233. https://doi.org/10.1097/QAD.0b013e3283314769. 00002030-200910230-00024 [pii].

Brown, D. W., Anda, R. F., Felitti, V. J., Edwards, V. J., Malarcher, A. M., Croft, J. B., et al. (2010). Adverse childhood experiences are associated with the risk of lung cancer: a prospective cohort study. *BMC Public Health*, *10*, 20. 1471-2458-10-20 [pii] https://doi.org/10.1186/1471-2458-10-20.

Brown, D. W., Anda, R. F., Tiemeier, H., Felitti, V. J., Edwards, V. J., Croft, J. B., et al. (2009). Adverse childhood experiences and the risk of premature mortality. *American Journal of Preventive Medicine*, *37*(5), 389–396. S0749-3797(09)00506-6 [pii] https://doi.org/10.1016/j.amepre.2009.06.021.

Brown, D. W., Young, K. E., Anda, R. F., Felitti, V. J., & Giles, W. H. (2006). Re: asthma and the risk of lung cancer. Findings from the Adverse Childhood Experiences (ACE). *Cancer Causes & Control*, *17*(3), 349–350. https://doi.org/10.1007/s10552-005-0420-5.

Bruner, V. E., & Woll, P. (2011). The battle within: understanding the physiology of war-zone stress exposure. *Social Work in Health Care*, *50*(1), 19–33. 932374282 [pii] https://doi.org/10.1080/00981389.2010.513915.

Bryant, R. A., Kemp, A. H., Felmingham, K. L., Liddell, B., Olivieri, G., Peduto, A., et al. (2008). Enhanced amygdala and medial prefrontal activation during nonconscious processing of fear in posttraumatic stress disorder: an fMRI study. *Human Brain Mapping*, *29*(5), 517–523. https://doi.org/10.1002/hbm.20415.

Butts, K. A., Weinberg, J., Young, A. H., & Phillips, A. G. (2011). Glucocorticoid receptors in the prefrontal cortex regulate stress-evoked dopamine efflux and aspects of executive function. *Proceedings of the National Academy of Sciences of the United States of America*, *108*(45), 18459–18464. 1111746108 [pii] https://doi.org/10.1073/pnas.1111746108.

Calkins, S. D., Graziano, P. A., Berdan, L. E., Keane, S. P., & Degnan, K. A. (2008). Predicting cardiac vagal regulation in early childhood from maternal-child relationship quality during toddlerhood. *Developmental Psychobiology*, *50*(8), 751–766. https://doi.org/10.1002/dev.20344.

Carpenter, L. L., Shattuck, T. T., Tyrka, A. R., Geracioti, T. D., & Price, L. H. (2011). Effect of childhood physical abuse on cortisol stress response. *Psychopharmacology*, *214*(1), 367–375. https://doi.org/10.1007/s00213-010-2007-4.

Carrion, V. G., Weems, C. F., & Reiss, A. L. (2007). Stress predicts brain changes in children: a pilot longitudinal study on youth stress, posttraumatic stress disorder, and the hippocampus. *Pediatrics*, *119*(3), 509–516. 119/3/509 [pii] https://doi.org/10.1542/peds.2006-2028.

Chanen, A. M., & Kaess, M. (2012). Developmental pathways to borderline personality disorder. *Current Psychiatry Reports*, *14*(1), 45–53.

Charmandari, E., Kino, T., Souvatzoglou, E., & Chrousos, G. P. (2003). Pediatric stress: hormonal mediators and human development. *Hormone Research*, *59*(4), 161–179. https://doi.org/10.1159/000069325. 69325 [pii].

Charmandari, E., Tsigos, C., & Chrousos, G. (2005). Endocrinology of the stress response. *Annual Review of Physiology*, *67*, 259–284. https://doi.org/10.1146/annurev.physiol.67.040403.120816.

Child Maltreatment 2010. (2011). *Washington, DC: Administration for Children and Families, Administration on Children, Youth and Families, Children's Bureau.* Available fromhttp://www.acf.hhs.gov/programs/cb/stats_research/index.htm#can.

Choi, J., Jeong, B., Rohan, M. L., Polcari, A. M., & Teicher, M. H. (2009). Preliminary evidence for white matter tract abnormalities in young adults exposed to parental verbal abuse. *Biological Psychiatry*, *65*(3), 227–234.

Chrousos, G. P. (2000). The role of stress and the hypothalamic-pituitary-adrenal axis in the pathogenesis of the metabolic syndrome: neuro-endocrine and target tissue-related causes. *International Journal of Obesity and Related Metabolic Disorders*, *24*(Suppl 2), S50–S55.

Clark, C., Caldwell, T., Power, C., & Stansfeld, S. A. (2010). Does the influence of childhood adversity on psychopathology persist across the life course? A 45-year prospective epidemiologic study. *Annals of Epidemiology*, *20*(5), 385–394. S1047-2797(10)00031-1 [pii] https://doi.org/10.1016/j.annepidem.2010.02.008.

Coates, D. (2010). Impact of childhood abuse: biopsychosocial pathways through which adult mental health is compromised. *Australian Social Work*, *63*(4), 391–403.

Cohen, R. A., Grieve, S., Hoth, K. F., Paul, R. H., Sweet, L., Tate, D., et al. (2006). Early life stress and morphometry of the adult anterior cingulate cortex and caudate nuclei. *Biological Psychiatry*, *59*(10), 975–982. S0006-3223(06)00140-5 [pii] https://doi.org/10.1016/j.biopsych.2005.12.016.

Colvert, E., Rutter, M., Kreppner, J., Beckett, C., Castle, J., Groothues, C., et al. (2008). Do theory of mind and executive function deficits underlie the adverse outcomes associated with profound early deprivation?: findings from the English and Romanian adoptees study. *Journal of Abnormal Child Psychology*, *36*(7), 1057–1068. https://doi.org/10.1007/s10802-008-9232-x.

Corcoran, P., Gallagher, J., Keeley, H. S., Arensman, E., & Perry, I. J. (2006). Adverse childhood experiences and lifetime suicide ideation: a cross-sectional study in a non-psychiatric hospital setting. *Irish Medical Journal*, *99*(2), 42–45.

Culverhouse, R. C., Saccone, N. L., Horton, A. C., Ma, Y., Anstey, K. J., Banaschewski, T., et al. (2018). Collaborative meta-analysis finds no evidence of a strong interaction between stress and 5-HTTLPR genotype contributing to the development of depression. *Molecular Psychiatry*, *23*(1), 133–142. https://doi.org/10.1038/mp.2017.44.

Dannlowski, U., Stuhrmann, A., Beutelmann, V., Zwanzger, P., Lenzen, T., Grotegerd, D., et al. (2012). Limbic scars: long-term consequences of childhood maltreatment revealed by functional and structural magnetic resonance imaging. *Biological Psychiatry*, *71*(4), 286–293.

De Bellis, M. D., Hooper, S. R., Woolley, D. P., & Shenk, C. E. (2010). Demographic, maltreatment, and neurobiological correlates of PTSD symptoms in children and adolescents. *Journal of Pediatric Psychology*, *35*(5), 570–577.

De Bellis, M. D., Keshavan, M. S., Clark, D. B., Casey, B. J., Giedd, J. N., Boring, A. M., et al. (1999). Developmental traumatology part II: brain development. *Biological Psychiatry*, *45*(10), 1271–1284.

De Bellis, M. D., Keshavan, M. S., Shifflett, H., Iyengar, S., Beers, S. R., Hall, J., et al. (2002). Brain structures in pediatric maltreatment-related posttraumatic stress disorder: a sociodemographically matched study. *Biological Psychiatry*, *52*(11), 1066–1078.

de Nadal, E., Ammerer, G., & Posas, F. (2011). Controlling gene expression in response to stress. *Nature Reviews. Genetics*, *12*(12), 833–845. nrg3055 [pii] https://doi.org/10.1038/nrg3055.

DePrince, A. P., Weinzierl, K. M., & Combs, M. D. (2009). Executive function performance and trauma exposure in a community sample of children. *Child Abuse & Neglect*, *33*(6), 353–361. S0145-2134(09)00096-9 [pii] https://doi.org/10.1016/j.chiabu.2008.08.002.

Dillon, D. G., Holmes, A. J., Birk, J. L., Brooks, N., Lyons-Ruth, K., & Pizzagalli, D. A. (2009). Childhood adversity is associated with left basal ganglia dysfunction during reward anticipation in adulthood. *Biological Psychiatry*, *66*(3), 206–213. S0006-3223(09)00232-7 [pii] https://doi.org/10.1016/j.biopsych.2009.02.019.

Direk, N., Williams, S., Smith, J. A., Ripke, S., Air, T., Amare, A. T., et al. (2017). An analysis of two genome-wide association meta-analyses identifies a new locus for broad depression phenotype. *Biological Psychiatry*, *82*(5), 322–329. https://doi.org/10.1016/j.biopsych.2016.11.013.

Diseth, T. H. (2005). Dissociation in children and adolescents as reaction to trauma—an overview of conceptual issues and neurobiological factors. *Nordic Journal of Psychiatry*, *59*(2), 79–91.

Dong, M., Giles, W. H., Felitti, V. J., Dube, S. R., Williams, J. E., Chapman, D. P., et al. (2004). Insights into causal pathways for ischemic heart disease: adverse childhood experiences study. *Circulation*, *110*(13), 1761–1766. https://doi.org/10.1161/01.CIR.0000143074.54995.7F. [pii].

Dube, S. R., Anda, R. F., Felitti, V. J., Chapman, D. P., Williamson, D. F., & Giles, W. H. (2001). Childhood abuse, household dysfunction, and the risk of attempted suicide throughout the life span: findings from the Adverse Childhood Experiences Study. *JAMA*, *286*(24), 3089–3096. joc11276 [pii].

Dube, S. R., Anda, R. F., Felitti, V. J., Edwards, V. J., & Croft, J. B. (2002). Adverse childhood experiences and personal alcohol abuse as an adult. *Addictive Behaviors*, *27*(5), 713–725.

Dube, S. R., Felitti, V. J., Dong, M., Chapman, D. P., Giles, W. H., & Anda, R. F. (2003). Childhood abuse, neglect, and household dysfunction and the risk of illicit drug use: the adverse childhood experiences study. *Pediatrics*, *111*(3), 564–572.

Dube, S. R., Felitti, V. J., Dong, M., Giles, W. H., & Anda, R. F. (2003). The impact of adverse childhood experiences on health problems: evidence from four birth cohorts dating back to 1900. *Preventive Medicine*, *37*(3), 268–277.

Dunlop, B. W., & Nemeroff, C. B. (2007). The role of dopamine in the pathophysiology of depression. *Archives of General Psychiatry*, *64*(3), 327–337. 64/3/327 [pii] https://doi.org/10.1001/archpsyc.64.3.327.

Edwards, V. J., Anda, R. F., Gu, D., Dube, S. R., & Felitti, V. J. (2007). Adverse childhood experiences and smoking persistence in adults with smoking-related symptoms and illness. *The Permanente Journal*, *11*(2), 5–13.

Enoch, M. A. (2011). The role of early life stress as a predictor for alcohol and drug dependence. *Psychopharmacology*, *214*(1), 17–31. https://doi.org/10.1007/s00213-010-1916-6.

Felitti, V. J., Anda, R. F., Nordenberg, D., Williamson, D. F., Spitz, A. M., Edwards, V., et al. (1998). Relationship of childhood abuse and household dysfunction to many of the leading causes of death in adults. The Adverse Childhood Experiences (ACE) Study. *American Journal of Preventive Medicine*, *14*(4), 245–258. S0749379798000178 [pii].

Flaherty, E. G., Thompson, R., Litrownik, A. J., Theodore, A., English, D. J., Black, M. M., et al. (2006). Effect of early childhood adversity on child health. *Archives of Pediatrics & Adolescent Medicine*, *160*(12), 1232–1238. 160/12/1232 [pii] https://doi.org/10.1001/archpedi.160.12.1232.

Fonagy, P., Luyten, P., & Strathearn, L. (2011). Borderline personality disorder, mentalization, and the neurobiology of attachment. *Infant Mental Health Journal*, *32*(1), 47–69.

Forbes, C. E., Cox, C. L., Schmader, T., & Ryan, L. (2011). Negative stereotype activation alters interaction between neural correlates of arousal, inhibition and cognitive control. *Social Cognitive and Affective Neuroscience*, https://doi.org/10.1093/scan/nsr052. nsr052 [pii].

Frayn, D. H., Paris, J., & Zweig-Frank, H. (1991). Childhood experience and borderline personality disorder [12]. *American Journal of Psychiatry*, *148*(7), 952–953.

Frias, A., Palma, C., Farriols, N., Gonzalez, L., & Horta, A. (2016). Anxious adult attachment may mediate the relationship between childhood emotional abuse and borderline personality disorder. *Personality and Mental Health*, *10*(4), 274–284.

Frodl, T., Carballedo, A., Fagan, A. J., Lisiecka, D., Ferguson, Y., & Meaney, J. F. (2012). Effects of early-life adversity on white matter diffusivity changes in patients at risk for major depression. *Journal of Psychiatry and Neuroscience*, *37*(1), 37–45.

Frodl, T., Reinhold, E., Koutsouleris, N., Donohoe, G., Bondy, B., Reiser, M., et al. (2010). Childhood stress, serotonin transporter gene and brain structures in major depression. *Neuropsychopharmacology*, *35*(6), 1383–1390. npp20108 [pii] https://doi.org/10.1038/npp.2010.8.

Frodl, T., Reinhold, E., Koutsouleris, N., Reiser, M., & Meisenzahl, E. M. (2010). Interaction of childhood stress with hippocampus and prefrontal cortex volume reduction in major depression. *Journal of Psychiatric Research*, *44*(13), 799–807.

Furay, A. R., McDevitt, R. A., Miczek, K. A., & Neumaier, J. F. (2011). 5-HT1B mRNA expression after chronic social stress. *Behavioural Brain Research*, *224*(2), 350–357. S0166-4328(11)00478-5 [pii] https://doi.org/10.1016/j.bbr.2011.06.016.

Glaser, D. (2000). Child abuse and neglect and the brain—a review. *Journal of Child Psychology and Psychiatry, and Allied Disciplines*, *41*(1), 97–116.

Glaser, J. P., van Os, J., Portegijs, P. J., & Myin-Germeys, I. (2006). Childhood trauma and emotional reactivity to daily life stress in adult frequent attenders of general practitioners. *Journal of Psychosomatic Research*, *61*(2), 229–236. S0022-3999(06)00223-6 [pii] https://doi.org/10.1016/j.jpsychores.2006.04.014.

Gogtay, N., Giedd, J. N., Lusk, L., Hayashi, K. M., Greenstein, D., Vaituzis, A. C., et al. (2004). Dynamic mapping of human cortical development during childhood through early adulthood. *Proceedings of the National Academy of Sciences of the United States of America*, *101*(21), 8174–8179. https://doi.org/10.1073/pnas.0402680101. 0402680101 [pii].

Gogtay, N., & Thompson, P. M. (2010). Mapping gray matter development: implications for typical development and vulnerability to psychopathology. *Brain and Cognition*, *72*(1), 6–15. S0278-2626(09)00162-6 [pii] https://doi.org/10.1016/j.bandc.2009.08.009.

Goldman, J., Salus, M. K., Wolcott, D., & Kennedy, K. Y. (2003). What factors contribute to child abuse and neglect? In Office on Child Abuse and Neglect (Eds.), *A coordinated response to child abuse and neglect: The foundation for practice*. Washington, DC: Office on Child Abuse and Neglect. Available online at http://www.childwelfare.gov/pubs/usermanuals/foundation/foundatione.cfm. (Chapter 5).

Gould, F., Clarke, J., Heim, C., Harvey, P. D., Majer, M., & Nemeroff, C. B. (2012). The effects of child abuse and neglect on cognitive functioning in adulthood. *Journal of Psychiatric Research*, *46*(4), 500–506.

Graham-Bermann, S. A., & Seng, J. (2005). Violence exposure and traumatic stress symptoms as additional predictors of health problems in high-risk children. *The Journal of Pediatrics*, *146*(3), 349–354. S0022347604010522 [pii] https://doi.org/10.1016/j.jpeds.2004.10.065.

Grant, M. M., Cannistraci, C., Hollon, S. D., Gore, J., & Shelton, R. (2011). Childhood trauma history differentiates amygdala response to sad faces within MDD. *Journal of Psychiatric Research*, *45*(7), 886–895.

Green, J. G., McLaughlin, K. A., Berglund, P. A., Gruber, M. J., Sampson, N. A., Zaslavsky, A. M., et al. (2010). Childhood adversities and adult psychiatric disorders in the national comorbidity survey replication I: associations with first onset of DSM-IV disorders. *Archives of General Psychiatry*, *67*(2), 113–123. 67/2/113 [pii] https://doi.org/10.1001/archgenpsychiatry.2009.186.

Gump, B. B., Mackenzie, J. A., Bendinskas, K., Morgan, R., Dumas, A. K., Palmer, C. D., et al. (2011). Low-level Pb and cardiovascular responses to acute stress in children: the role of cardiac autonomic regulation. *Neurotoxicology and Teratology*, *33*(2), 212–219. S0892-0362(10)00170-4 [pii] https://doi.org/10.1016/j.ntt.2010.10.001.

Gunnar, M., & Quevedo, K. (2007). The neurobiology of stress and development. *Annual Review of Psychology*, *58*, 145–173. https://doi.org/10.1146/annurev.psych.58.110405.085605.

Gunter, T. D., Chibnall, J. T., Antoniak, S. K., Philibert, R. A., & Black, D. W. (2013). Childhood trauma, traumatic brain injury, and mental health disorders associated with suicidal ideation and suicide-related behavior in a community corrections sample. *The Journal of the American Academy of Psychiatry and the Law*, *41*(2), 245–255.

Hart, H., & Rubia, K. (2012). Neuroimaging of child abuse: a critical review. *Frontiers in Human Neuroscience*, *6*, 52.

Hasler, G., Fromm, S., Carlson, P. J., Luckenbaugh, D. A., Waldeck, T., Geraci, M., et al. (2008). Neural response to catecholamine depletion in unmedicated subjects with major depressive disorder in remission and healthy subjects. *Archives of General Psychiatry*, *65*(5), 521–531. 65/5/521 [pii] https://doi.org/10.1001/archpsyc.65.5.521.

Hedges, D. W., & Woon, F. L. (2011). Early-life stress and cognitive outcome. *Psychopharmacology*, *214*(1), 121–130. https://doi.org/10.1007/s00213-010-2090-6.

Heim, C., & Nemeroff, C. B. (2001). The role of childhood trauma in the neurobiology of mood and anxiety disorders: preclinical and clinical studies. *Biological Psychiatry*, *49*(12), 1023–1039. S000632230101157X [pii].

Heim, C., Newport, D. J., Bonsall, R., Miller, A. H., & Nemeroff, C. B. (2001). Altered pituitary-adrenal axis responses to provocative challenge tests in adult survivors of childhood abuse. *The American Journal of Psychiatry*, *158*(4), 575–581.

Heim, C., Newport, D. J., Mletzko, T., Miller, A. H., & Nemeroff, C. B. (2008). The link between childhood trauma and depression: insights from HPA axis studies in humans. *Psychoneuroendocrinology*, *33*(6), 693–710. S0306-4530(08)00069-3 [pii] https://doi.org/10.1016/j.psyneuen.2008.03.008.

Heim, C., Shugart, M., Craighead, W. E., & Nemeroff, C. B. (2010). Neurobiological and psychiatric consequences of child abuse and neglect. *Developmental Psychobiology*, *52*(7), 671–690.

Herman, J. P., Ostrander, M. M., Mueller, N. K., & Figueiredo, H. (2005). Limbic system mechanisms of stress regulation: hypothalamo-pituitary-adrenocortical axis. *Progress in Neuro-Psychopharmacology & Biological Psychiatry*, *29*(8), 1201–1213. S0278-5846(05)00269-1 [pii] https://doi.org/10.1016/j.pnpbp.2005.08.006.

Hines, M. (2011). Gender development and the human brain. *Annual Review of Neuroscience*, *34*, 69–88. https://doi.org/10.1146/annurev-neuro-061010-113654.

Howell, B. R., & Sanchez, M. M. (2011). Understanding behavioral effects of early life stress using the reactive scope and allostatic load models. *Development and Psychopathology*, *23*(4), 1001–1016. S0954579411000460 [pii] https://doi.org/10.1017/S0954579411000460.

Huether, G. (1998). Stress and the adaptive self-organization of neuronal connectivity during early childhood. *International Journal of Developmental Neuroscience*, *16*(3–4), 297–306. S0736-5748(98)00023-9 [pii].

Hunter, A. L., Minnis, H., & Wilson, P. (2011). Altered stress responses in children exposed to early adversity: a systematic review of salivary cortisol studies. *Stress*, *14*(6), 614–626.

Jackowski, A., Perera, T. D., Abdallah, C. G., Garrido, G., Tang, C. Y., Martinez, J., et al. (2011). Early-life stress, corpus callosum development, hippocampal volumetrics, and anxious behavior in male nonhuman primates. *Psychiatry Research*, *192*(1), 37–44. S0925-4927(10)00392-6 [pii] https://doi.org/10.1016/j.pscychresns.2010.11.006.

Johnson, D. E., Guthrie, D., Smyke, A. T., Koga, S. F., Fox, N. A., Zeanah, C. H., et al. (2010). Growth and associations between auxology, caregiving environment, and cognition in socially deprived Romanian children randomized to foster vs ongoing institutional care. *Archives of Pediatrics and Adolescent Medicine*, *164*(6), 507–516.

Johnston, J. A. Y., Wang, F., Liu, J., Blond, B. N., Wallace, A., Liu, J., et al. (2017). Multimodal neuroimaging of frontolimbic structure and function associated with suicide attempts in adolescents and young adults with bipolar disorder. *The American Journal of Psychiatry*, *174*(7), 667–675. https://doi.org/10.1176/appi.ajp.2016.15050652.

Jonson-Reid, M., Kohl, P. L., & Drake, B. (2012). Child and adult outcomes of chronic child maltreatment. *Pediatrics*, *129*(5), 839–845. https://doi.org/10.1542/peds.2011-2529.

Judge, S. (2003). Developmental recovery and deficit in children adopted from Eastern European orphanages. *Child Psychiatry and Human Development*, *34*(1), 49–62.

Karl, A., Schaefer, M., Malta, L. S., Dorfel, D., Rohleder, N., & Werner, A. (2006). A meta-analysis of structural brain abnormalities in PTSD. *Neuroscience and Biobehavioral Reviews*, *30*(7), 1004–1031. S0149-7634(06)00028-5 [pii] https://doi.org/10.1016/j.neubiorev.2006.03.004.

Karten, Y. J., Olariu, A., & Cameron, H. A. (2005). Stress in early life inhibits neurogenesis in adulthood. *Trends in Neurosciences*, *28*(4), 171–172. S0166-2236(05)00029-9 [pii] https://doi.org/10.1016/j.tins.2005.01.009.

Kendler, K. S., Bulik, C. M., Silberg, J., Hettema, J. M., Myers, J., & Prescott, C. A. (2000). Childhood sexual abuse and adult psychiatric and substance use disorders in women: an epidemiological and cotwin control analysis. *Archives of General Psychiatry*, *57*(10), 953–959. yoa9487 [pii].

Komatsu, H., Ohara, A., Sasaki, K., Abe, H., Hattori, H., Hall, F. S., et al. (2011). Decreased response to social defeat stress in mu-opioid-receptor knockout mice. *Pharmacology, Biochemistry, and Behavior*, *99*(4), 676–682. S0091-3057(11)00200-0 [pii] https://doi.org/10.1016/j.pbb.2011.06.008.

Koob, G., & Kreek, M. J. (2007). Stress, dysregulation of drug reward pathways, and the transition to drug dependence. *The American Journal of Psychiatry*, *164*(8), 1149–1159. 164/8/1149 [pii] https://doi.org/10.1176/appi.ajp.2007.05030503.

Koob, G. F., & Le Moal, M. (2001). Drug addiction, dysregulation of reward, and allostasis. *Neuropsychopharmacology*, *24*(2), 97–129. S0893-133X(00)00195-0 [pii] https://doi.org/10.1016/S0893-133X(00)00195-0.

Kreek, M. J., & Koob, G. F. (1998). Drug dependence: stress and dysregulation of brain reward pathways. *Drug and Alcohol Dependence*, *51*(1–2), 23–47. S0376-8716(98)00064-7 [pii].

Kuo, J. R., Khoury, J. E., Metcalfe, R., Fitzpatrick, S., & Goodwill, A. (2015). An examination of the relationship between childhood emotional abuse and borderline personality disorder features: the role of difficulties with emotion regulation. *Child Abuse & Neglect*, *39*, 147–155.

Ladd, C. O., Huot, R. L., Thrivikraman, K. V., Nemeroff, C. B., Meaney, M. J., & Plotsky, P. M. (2000). Long-term behavioral and neuroendocrine adaptations to adverse early experience. *Progress in Brain Research*, *122*, 81–103.

Lamont, A. (2012). *Child abuse and neglect statistics*. Canberra: Australian Government, Australian Institute of Family Studies, National Child Protection Clearinghouse. Available from http://www.aifs.gov.au/nch/pubs/sheets/rs1/rs1.html.

Lenroot, R. K., & Giedd, J. N. (2010). Sex differences in the adolescent brain. *Brain and Cognition*, *72*(1), 46–55. S0278-2626(09)00200-0 [pii] https://doi.org/10.1016/j.bandc.2009.10.008.

Lenroot, R. K., Schmitt, J. E., Ordaz, S. J., Wallace, G. L., Neale, M. C., Lerch, J. P., et al. (2009). Differences in genetic and environmental influences on the human cerebral cortex associated with development during childhood and adolescence. *Human Brain Mapping*, *30*(1), 163–174. https://doi.org/10.1002/hbm.20494.

Loman, M. M., Wiik, K. L., Frenn, K. A., Pollak, S. D., & Gunnar, M. R. (2009). Postinstitutionalized children's development: growth, cognitive, and language outcomes. *Journal of Developmental and Behavioral Pediatrics*, *30*(5), 426–434. https://doi.org/10.1097/DBP.0b013e3181b1fd08.

Lu, W., Mueser, K. T., Rosenberg, S. D., & Jankowski, M. K. (2008). Correlates of adverse childhood experiences among adults with severe mood disorders. *Psychiatric Services*, *59*(9), 1018–1026. 59/9/1018 [pii] https://doi.org/10.1176/appi.ps.59.9.1018.

Luo, F. F., Han, F., & Shi, Y. X. (2011). Changes in 5-HT1A receptor in the dorsal raphe nucleus in a rat model of post-traumatic stress disorder. *Molecular Medicine Reports*, *4*(5), 843–847. https://doi.org/10.3892/mmr.2011.516.

Malykhin, N. V., Carter, R., Hegadoren, K. M., Seres, P., & Coupland, N. J. (2012). Fronto-limbic volumetric changes in major depressive disorder. *Journal of Affective Disorders*, *136*(3), 1104–1113. S0165-0327(11)00687-2 [pii] https://doi.org/10.1016/j.jad.2011.10.038.

McGowan, P. O., Sasaki, A., D'Alessio, A. C., Dymov, S., Labonte, B., Szyf, M., et al. (2009). Epigenetic regulation of the glucocorticoid receptor in human brain associates with childhood abuse. *Nature Neuroscience*, *12*(3), 342–348. https://doi.org/10.1038/nn.2270.

Meiser-Stedman, R., Dalgleish, T., Smith, P., Yule, W., & Glucksman, E. (2007). Diagnostic, demographic, memory quality, and cognitive variables associated with acute stress disorder in children and adolescents. *Journal of Abnormal Psychology*, *116*(1), 65–79. 2007-01891-006 [pii] https://doi.org/10.1037/0021-843X.116.1.65.

Melcher, T., Born, C., & Gruber, O. (2011). How negative affect influences neural control processes underlying the resolution of cognitive interference: an event-related fMRI study. *Neuroscience Research*, *70*(4), 415–427. S0168-0102(11)00131-3 [pii] https://doi.org/10.1016/j.neures.2011.05.007.

Miskovic, V., Schmidt, L. A., Georgiades, K., Boyle, M., & MacMillan, H. L. (2009). Stability of resting frontal electroencephalogram (EEG) asymmetry and cardiac vagal tone in adolescent females exposed to child maltreatment. *Developmental Psychobiology*, *51*(6), 474–487. https://doi.org/10.1002/dev.20387.

Mithoefer, M. C., Wagner, M. T., Mithoefer, A. T., Jerome, L., & Doblin, R. (2011). The safety and efficacy of {+/-}3,4-methylenedioxymethamphetamine-assisted psychotherapy in subjects with chronic, treatment-resistant posttraumatic stress disorder: the first randomized controlled pilot study. *Journal of Psychopharmacology*, *25*(4), 439–452. 0269881110378371 [pii] https://doi.org/10.1177/0269881110378371.

Mueller, S. C., Maheu, F. S., Dozier, M., Peloso, E., Mandell, D., Leibenluft, E., et al. (2010). Early-life stress is associated with impairment in cognitive control in adolescence: an fMRI study. *Neuropsychologia*, *48*(10), 3037–3044.

NAPCAN. (2007). *Child abuse and neglect fact sheet (online)*. Canberra: National Association for Prevention of Child Abuse and Neglect. Available http://www.napcan.org.au/what.htm.

Navailles, S., Hof, P. R., & Schmauss, C. (2008). Antidepressant drug-induced stimulation of mouse hippocampal neurogenesis is age-dependent and altered by early life stress. *The Journal of Comparative Neurology*, *509*(4), 372–381. https://doi.org/10.1002/cne.21775.

Navalta, C. P., Polcari, A., Webster, D. M., Boghossian, A., & Teicher, M. H. (2006). Effects of childhood sexual abuse on neuropsychological and cognitive function in college women. *The Journal of Neuropsychiatry and Clinical Neurosciences*, *18*(1), 45–53. 18/1/45 [pii] https://doi.org/10.1176/appi.neuropsych.18.1.45.

Nemeroff, C. B. (2004). Neurobiological consequences of childhood trauma. *The Journal of Clinical Psychiatry*, *65*(Suppl 1), 18–28.

Noble, K. G., Tottenham, N., & Casey, B. J. (2005). Neuroscience perspectives on disparities in school readiness and cognitive achievement. *The Future of Children*, *15*, 71–89.

O'Halloran, C. J., Kinsella, G. J., & Storey, E. (2012). The cerebellum and neuropsychological functioning: a critical review. *Journal of Clinical and Experimental Neuropsychology*, *34*(1), 35–56. https://doi.org/10.1080/13803395.2011.614599.

O'Rand, A. M., & Hamil-Luker, J. (2005). Processes of cumulative adversity: childhood disadvantage and increased risk of heart attack across the life course. *The Journals of Gerontology Series B, Psychological Sciences and Social Sciences*, *60*, 117–124. Spec No. 2, 60/suppl_Special_Issue_2/S117 [pii].

Ochsner, K. N., & Gross, J. J. (2005). The cognitive control of emotion. *Trends in Cognitive Sciences*, *9*(5), 242–249. S1364-6613(05)00090-2 [pii] https://doi.org/10.1016/j.tics.2005.03.010.

Ochsner, K. N., Ray, R. D., Cooper, J. C., Robertson, E. R., Chopra, S., Gabrieli, J. D., et al. (2004). For better or for worse: neural systems supporting the cognitive down- and up-regulation of negative emotion. *NeuroImage*, *23*(2), 483–499. S1053-8119(04)00340-4 [pii] https://doi.org/10.1016/j.neuroimage.2004.06.030.

Oladeji, B. D., Makanjuola, V. A., & Gureje, O. (2010). Family-related adverse childhood experiences as risk factors for psychiatric disorders in Nigeria. *The British Journal of Psychiatry*, *196*(3), 186–191. 196/3/186 [pii] https://doi.org/10.1192/bjp.bp.109.063677.

Onozawa, K., Yagasaki, Y., Izawa, Y., Abe, H., & Kawakami, Y. (2011). Amygdala-prefrontal pathways and the dopamine system affect nociceptive responses in the prefrontal cortex. *BMC Neuroscience*, *12*, 115. 1471-2202-12-115 [pii] https://doi.org/10.1186/1471-2202-12-115.

Oomen, C. A., Soeters, H., Audureau, N., Vermunt, L., van Hasselt, F. N., Manders, E. M., et al. (2011). Early maternal deprivation affects dentate gyrus structure and emotional learning in adult female rats. *Psychopharmacology*, *214*(1), 249–260. https://doi.org/10.1007/s00213-010-1922-8.

Otte, C., Neylan, T. C., Pole, N., Metzler, T., Best, S., Henn-Haase, C., et al. (2005). Association between childhood trauma and catecholamine response to psychological stress in police academy recruits. *Biological Psychiatry*, *57*(1), 27–32. S0006-3223(04)01072-8 [pii] https://doi.org/10.1016/j.biopsych.2004.10.009.

Park, E., Cockrem, J. F., Han, K. H., Kim, D. H., Jung, M. H., & Chu, J. P. (2012). Stress-induced activation of ovarian heat shock protein 90 in a rat model of polycystic ovary syndrome. *The Journal of Obstetrics and Gynaecology Research*, *38*(2), 396–407. https://doi.org/10.1111/j.1447-0756.2011.01705.x.

Pastor, R., McKinnon, C. S., Scibelli, A. C., Burkhart-Kasch, S., Reed, C., Ryabinin, A. E., et al. (2008). Corticotropin-releasing factor-1 receptor involvement in behavioral neuroadaptation to ethanol: a urocortin1-independent mechanism. *Proceedings of the National Academy of Sciences of the United States of America*, *105*(26), 9070–9075. https://doi.org/10.1073/pnas.0710181105. 0710181105 [pii].

Pechtel, P., & Pizzagalli, D. A. (2011). Effects of early life stress on cognitive and affective function: an integrated review of human literature. *Psychopharmacology*, *214*(1), 55–70. https://doi.org/10.1007/s00213-010-2009-2.

Peper, J. S., Schnack, H. G., Brouwer, R. M., Van Baal, G. C., Pjetri, E., Szekely, E., et al. (2009). Heritability of regional and global brain structure at the onset of puberty: a magnetic resonance imaging study in 9-year-old twin pairs. *Human Brain Mapping*, *30*(7), 2184–2196. https://doi.org/10.1002/hbm.20660.

Pereda, N., & Gallardo-Pujol, D. (2011). Neurobiological consequences of child sexual abuse: a systematic review. *Revisión sistemática de las consecuencias neurobiológicas del abuso sexual infantil*, *25*(3), 233–239.

Pereda, N., Guilera, G., Forns, M., & Gomez-Benito, J. (2009). The international epidemiology of child sexual abuse: a continuation of Finkelhor (1994). *Child Abuse & Neglect*, *33*(6), 331–342. S0145-2134(09)00097-0 [pii] https://doi.org/10.1016/j.chiabu.2008.07.007.

Perry, B. D. (2009). Examining child maltreatment through a neurodevelopmental lens: clinical applications of the neurosequential model of therapeutics. *Journal of Loss and Trauma*, *14*, 240–255.

Perry, B. D., Pollard, R. A., Blakley, T. L., & Vigilante, D. (1995). Childhood trauma, the neurobiology of adaptation, and "use-dependent" development of the brain: how "states" become "traits". *Infant Mental Health Journal*, *16*(4), 271–291.

Pizzagalli, D. A., Holmes, A. J., Dillon, D. G., Goetz, E. L., Birk, J. L., Bogdan, R., et al. (2009). Reduced caudate and nucleus accumbens response to rewards in unmedicated individuals with major depressive disorder. *The American Journal of Psychiatry*, *166*(6), 702–710. appi.ajp.2008.08081201 [pii] https://doi.org/10.1176/appi.ajp.2008.08081201.

Polak, A. R., Witteveen, A. B., Reitsma, J. B., & Olff, M. (2012). The role of executive function in posttraumatic stress disorder: a systematic review. *Journal of Affective Disorders*, https://doi.org/10.1016/j.jad.2012.01.001. S0165-0327(12)00007-9 [pii].

Quesada, A. A., Wiemers, U. S., Schoofs, D., & Wolf, O. T. (2012). Psychosocial stress exposure impairs memory retrieval in children. *Psychoneuroendocrinology*, *37*(1), 125–136. S0306-4530(11)00166-1 [pii] https://doi.org/10.1016/j.psyneuen.2011.05.013.

Reed, P. L., Anthony, J. C., & Breslau, N. (2007). Incidence of drug problems in young adults exposed to trauma and posttraumatic stress disorder: do early life experiences and predispositions matter? *Archives of General Psychiatry*, *64*(12), 1435–1442. 64/12/1435 [pii] https://doi.org/10.1001/archpsyc.64.12.1435.

Rigby, K. (2003). *Bullying among young children: A guide for teachers and carers*. Canberra: Australian Government Attorney-General's Department. Available online at www.crimeprevention.gov.au.

Rudolph, K. D., Troop-Gordon, W., & Granger, D. A. (2011). Individual differences in biological stress responses moderate the contribution of early peer victimization to subsequent depressive symptoms. *Psychopharmacology*, *214*(1), 209–219. https://doi.org/10.1007/s00213-010-1879-7.

Rutter, M., Andersen-Wood, L., Beckett, C., Bredenkamp, D., Castle, J., Dunn, J., et al. (1998). Developmental catch-up, and deficit, following adoption after severe global early privation. *Journal of Child Psychology and Psychiatry, and Allied Disciplines*, *39*(4), 465–476.

Sapolsky, R. M. (1996). Stress, glucocorticoids, and damage to the nervous system: the current state of confusion. *Stress*, *1*(1), 1–19. I405N970008 [pii].

Sarnyai, Z., Shaham, Y., & Heinrichs, S. C. (2001). The role of corticotropin-releasing factor in drug addiction. *Pharmacological Reviews*, *53*(2), 209–243.

Scheeringa, M. S., Zeanah, C. H., Myers, L., & Putnam, F. (2004). Heart period and variability findings in preschool children with posttraumatic stress symptoms. *Biological Psychiatry*, *55*(7), 685–691.

Schilling, E. A., Aseltine, R. H., Jr., & Gore, S. (2007). Adverse childhood experiences and mental health in young adults: a longitudinal survey. *BMC Public Health*, *7*, 30. 1471-2458-7-30 [pii] https://doi.org/10.1186/1471-2458-7-30.

Schmahmann, J. D., & Caplan, D. (2006). Cognition, emotion and the cerebellum. *Brain*, *129*(Pt 2), 290–292. 129/2/290 [pii] https://doi.org/10.1093/brain/awh729.

Schmitt, J. E., Lenroot, R. K., Wallace, G. L., Ordaz, S., Taylor, K. N., Kabani, N., et al. (2008). Identification of genetically mediated cortical networks: a multivariate study of pediatric twins and siblings. *Cerebral Cortex*, *18*(8), 1737–1747. bhm211 [pii] https://doi.org/10.1093/cercor/bhm211.

Sepa, A., Frodi, A., & Ludvigsson, J. (2005). Mothers' experiences of serious life events increase the risk of diabetes-related autoimmunity in their children. *Diabetes Care*, *28*(10), 2394–2399. 28/10/2394 [pii].

Sepa, A., Wahlberg, J., Vaarala, O., Frodi, A., & Ludvigsson, J. (2005). Psychological stress may induce diabetes-related autoimmunity in infancy. *Diabetes Care*, *28*(2), 290–295. 28/2/290 [pii].

Shalev, U., Erb, S., & Shaham, Y. (2010). Role of CRF and other neuropeptides in stress-induced reinstatement of drug seeking. *Brain Research*, *1314*, 15–28. S0006-8993(09)01432-2 [pii] https://doi.org/10.1016/j.brainres.2009.07.028.

Shaw, P., Kabani, N. J., Lerch, J. P., Eckstrand, K., Lenroot, R., Gogtay, N., et al. (2008). Neurodevelopmental trajectories of the human cerebral cortex. *The Journal of Neuroscience*, *28*(14), 3586–3594. 28/14/3586 [pii] https://doi.org/10.1523/JNEUROSCI.5309-07.2008.

Shea, A., Walsh, C., MacMillan, H., & Steiner, M. (2005). Child maltreatment and HPA axis dysregulation: relationship to major depressive disorder and post traumatic stress disorder in females. *Psychoneuroendocrinology*, *30*(2), 162–178.

Sheu, Y. S., Polcari, A., Anderson, C. M., & Teicher, M. H. (2010). Harsh corporal punishment is associated with increased T2 relaxation time in dopamine-rich regions. *NeuroImage*, *53*(2), 412–419. https://doi.org/10.1016/j.neuroimage.2010.06.043.

Shonkoff, J. P., & Garner, A. S. (2012). The lifelong effects of early childhood adversity and toxic stress. *Pediatrics*, *129*(1), e232–e246. peds.2011-2663 [pii] https://doi.org/10.1542/peds.2011-2663.

Soloff, P. H., Feske, U., & Fabio, A. (2008). Mediators of the relationship between childhood sexual abuse and suicidal behavior in borderline personality disorder. *Journal of Personality Disorders*, *22*(3), 221–232. https://doi.org/10.1521/pedi.2008.22.3.221.

Soloff, P. H., White, R., Omari, A., Ramaseshan, K., & Diwadkar, V. A. (2015). Affective context interferes with brain responses during cognitive processing in borderline personality disorder: fMRI evidence. *Psychiatry Research*, *233*(1), 23–35. https://doi.org/10.1016/j.pscychresns.2015.04.006.

Stevens, S. E., Sonuga-Barke, E. J., Kreppner, J. M., Beckett, C., Castle, J., Colvert, E., et al. (2008). Inattention/overactivity following early severe institutional deprivation: presentation and associations in early adolescence. *Journal of Abnormal Child Psychology*, *36*(3), 385–398. https://doi.org/10.1007/s10802-007-9185-5.

Strine, T. W., Dube, S. R., Edwards, V. J., Prehn, A. W., Rasmussen, S., Wagenfeld, M., et al. (2012). Associations between adverse childhood experiences, psychological distress, and adult alcohol problems. *American Journal of Health Behavior*, *36*(3), 408–423. https://doi.org/10.5993/AJHB.36.3.11.

Surtees, P. G., Wainwright, N. W., Pooley, K. A., Luben, R. N., Khaw, K. T., Easton, D. F., et al. (2011). Life stress, emotional health, and mean telomere length in the European Prospective Investigation into Cancer (EPIC)-Norfolk population study. *The Journals of Gerontology Series A, Biological Sciences and Medical Sciences*, *66*(11), 1152–1162. glr112 [pii] https://doi.org/10.1093/gerona/glr112.

Takahashi, K., Sakamoto, K., & Kimura, J. (2012). Hypoxic stress induces transient receptor potential melastatin 2 (TRPM2) channel expression in adult rat cardiac fibroblasts. *Journal of Pharmacological Sciences*, *118*(2), 186–197. JST.JSTAGE/jphs/11128FP [pii].

Tanti, A., Kim, J. J., Wakid, M., Davoli, M. A., Turecki, G., & Mechawar, N. (2017). Child abuse associates with an imbalance of oligodendrocyte-lineage cells in ventromedial prefrontal white matter. *Molecular Psychiatry*, https://doi.org/10.1038/mp.2017.231.

Teicher, M. H., Andersen, S. L., Polcari, A., Anderson, C. M., Navalta, C. P., & Kim, D. M. (2003). The neurobiological consequences of early stress and childhood maltreatment. *Neuroscience and Biobehavioral Reviews*, *27*(1–2), 33–44. S0149763403000071 [pii].

Teicher, M. H., Anderson, C. M., & Polcari, A. (2012). Childhood maltreatment is associated with reduced volume in the hippocampal subfields CA3, dentate gyrus, and subiculum. *Proceedings of the National Academy of Sciences of the United States of America*, *109*(9), E563–E572. 1115396109 [pii] https://doi.org/10.1073/pnas.1115396109.

Teicher, M. H., Samson, J. A., Polcari, A., & McGreenery, C. E. (2006). Sticks, stones, and hurtful words: relative effects of various forms of childhood maltreatment. *The American Journal of Psychiatry*, *163*(6), 993–1000. 163/6/993 [pii] https://doi.org/10.1176/appi.ajp.163.6.993.

Teicher, M. H., Tomoda, A., & Andersen, S. L. (2006). Neurobiological consequences of early stress and childhood maltreatment: are results from human and animal studies comparable? *Annals of the New York Academy of Sciences*, *1071*, 313–323. 1071/1/313 [pii] https://doi.org/10.1196/annals.1364.024.

Thabrew, H., de Sylva, S., & Romans, S. E. (2012). Evaluating childhood adversity. *Advances in Psychosomatic Medicine*, *32*, 35–57. 000330002 [pii] https://doi.org/10.1159/000330002.

Thomas, C., Hypponen, E., & Power, C. (2008). Obesity and type 2 diabetes risk in midadult life: the role of childhood adversity. *Pediatrics*, *121*(5), e1240–e1249. 121/5/e1240 [pii] https://doi.org/10.1542/peds.2007-2403.

Tiemeier, H., Lenroot, R. K., Greenstein, D. K., Tran, L., Pierson, R., & Giedd, J. N. (2010). Cerebellum development during childhood and adolescence: a longitudinal morphometric MRI study. *NeuroImage*, *49*(1), 63–70. S1053-8119(09)00893-3 [pii] https://doi.org/10.1016/j.neuroimage.2009.08.016.

Tofoli, S. M. C., Baes, C. W., Martins, C. M. S., & Juruena, M. (2011). Early life stress, HPA axis, and depression. *Psychology & Neuroscience*, *4*(2), 229–234.

Tomoda, A., Suzuki, H., Rabi, K., Sheu, Y. S., Polcari, A., & Teicher, M. H. (2009). Reduced prefrontal cortical gray matter volume in young adults exposed to harsh corporal punishment. *NeuroImage*, *47*(Suppl 2), T66–T71. https://doi.org/10.1016/j.neuroimage.2009.03.005.

Tonmyr, L., Jamieson, E., Mery, L. S., & MacMillan, H. L. (2005). The relation between childhood adverse experiences and disability due to mental health problems in a community sample of women. *Canadian Journal of Psychiatry*, *50*(12), 778–783.

Treadway, M. T., Grant, M. M., Ding, Z., Hollon, S. D., Gore, J. C., & Shelton, R. C. (2009). Early adverse events, HPA activity and rostral anterior cingulate volume in MDD. *PLoS ONE*, *4*(3), e4887.

Twardosz, S., & Lutzker, J. R. (2010). Child maltreatment and the developing brain: a review of neuroscience perspectives. *Aggression and Violent Behavior*, *15*(1), 59–68.

UKDH. (2010). *Final reports from the Taskforce on the health aspects of violence against women and children*. London: United Kingdom Department of Health. Available online at http://www.dh.gov.uk/en/Publichealth/ViolenceagainstWomenandChildren/DH_113753.

Vaynman, S., Ying, Z., & Gomez-Pinilla, F. (2004). Hippocampal BDNF mediates the efficacy of exercise on synaptic plasticity and cognition. *The European Journal of Neuroscience*, *20*(10), 2580–2590. EJN3720 [pii] https://doi.org/10.1111/j.1460-9568.2004.03720.x.

Waldinger, R. J., Schulz, M. S., Barsky, A. J., & Ahern, D. K. (2006). Mapping the road from childhood trauma to adult somatization: the role of attachment. *Psychosomatic Medicine*, *68*(1), 129–135. 68/1/129 [pii] https://doi.org/10.1097/01.psy.0000195834.37094.a4.

West, R., Choi, P., & Travers, S. (2010). The influence of negative affect on the neural correlates of cognitive control. *International Journal of Psychophysiology*, *76*(2), 107–117. S0167-8760(10)00054-1 [pii] https://doi.org/10.1016/j.ijpsycho.2010.03.002.

Westbrook, J., & Berenbaum, H. (2017). Emotional awareness moderates the relationship between childhood abuse and borderline personality disorder symptom factors. *Journal of Clinical Psychology*, *73*(7), 910–921.

Witt, K., Milner, A., Spittal, M. J., Hetrick, S., Robinson, J., Pirkis, J., et al. (2018). Population attributable risk of factors associated with the repetition of self-harm behaviour in young people presenting to clinical services: a systematic review and meta-analysis. *European Child & Adolescent Psychiatry*, https://doi.org/10.1007/s00787-018-1111-6.

Witt, S. H., Streit, F., Jungkunz, M., Frank, J., Awasthi, S., Reinbold, C. S., et al. (2017). Genome-wide association study of borderline personality disorder reveals genetic overlap with bipolar disorder, major depression and schizophrenia. *Translational Psychiatry*, *7*(6), e1155https://doi.org/10.1038/tp.2017.115.

Woodward, S. H., Kaloupek, D. G., Streeter, C. C., Kimble, M. O., Reiss, A. L., Eliez, S., et al. (2007). Brain, skull, and cerebrospinal fluid volumes in adult posttraumatic stress disorder. *Journal of Traumatic Stress*, *20*(5), 763–774.

Woon, F. L., & Hedges, D. W. (2008). Hippocampal and amygdala volumes in children and adults with childhood maltreatment-related posttraumatic stress disorder: a meta-analysis. *Hippocampus*, *18*(8), 729–736. https://doi.org/10.1002/hipo.20437.

Woon, F. L., Sood, S., & Hedges, D. W. (2010). Hippocampal volume deficits associated with exposure to psychological trauma and posttraumatic stress disorder in adults: a meta-analysis. *Progress in Neuro-Psychopharmacology & Biological Psychiatry*, *34*(7), 1181–1188. S0278-5846(10)00233-2 [pii] https://doi.org/10.1016/j.pnpbp.2010.06.016.

Wray, N. R., Ripke, S., Mattheisen, M., Trzaskowski, M., Byrne, E. M., Abdellaoui, A., et al. (2018). Genome-wide association analyses identify 44 risk variants and refine the genetic architecture of major depression. *Nature Genetics*, *50*(5), 668–681. https://doi.org/10.1038/s41588-018-0090-3.

Wright, R. J. (2010). Perinatal stress and early life programming of lung structure and function. *Biological Psychology*, *84*(1), 46–56. S0301-0511(10)00012-8 [pii] https://doi.org/10.1016/j.biopsycho.2010.01.007.

Yasik, A. E., Saigh, P. A., Oberfield, R. A., & Halamandaris, P. V. (2007). Posttraumatic stress disorder: memory and learning performance in children and adolescents. *Biological Psychiatry*, *61*(3), 382–388. S0006-3223(06)00797-9 [pii] https://doi.org/10.1016/j.biopsych.2006.06.005.

Yehuda, R., Flory, J. D., Pratchett, L. C., Buxbaum, J., Ising, M., & Holsboer, F. (2010). Putative biological mechanisms for the association between early life adversity and the subsequent development of PTSD. *Psychopharmacology*, *212*(3), 405–417. https://doi.org/10.1007/s00213-010-1969-6.

CHAPTER 11

Physical Punishment and Offending in Two Successive Generations of Males

David P. Farrington*, **Catia G. Malvaso**†

*Institute of Criminology, Cambridge University, Cambridge, United Kingdom †School of Psychology, University of Adelaide, Adelaide, SA, Australia

1 Introduction

Longitudinal studies have provided clear evidence that childhood maltreatment is associated with an increased risk of delinquent or criminal behaviour in later life (for reviews, see Braga, Gonçalves, Basto-Pereira, & Maia, 2017; Maas, Herrenkohl, & Sousa, 2008; Malvaso, Delfabbro, & Day, 2016; Wilson, Stover, & Berkowitz, 2009). Physical punishment or abuse in particular has been shown to be a consistent predictor of youth offending and violence. Table 1 shows some key longitudinal studies that have examined the association between physical punishment or abuse and offending.

It has also been found that a number of risk factors other than and in combination with maltreatment can increase the risk of offending. These risk factors include characteristics of the child (e.g. difficult temperament and low intelligence), characteristics of parents (e.g. histories of incarceration, substance abuse, and mental illness), characteristics of peers (e.g. engaging in antisocial behaviour), and characteristics of the broader contextual environment (e.g. neighbourhood poverty). More longitudinal research is needed to gain a deeper insight into the complex interplay of these influences and the underlying mechanisms responsible for the increased risk of offending found among victims of childhood physical punishment and abuse.

Little is known about the similarities or differences in risk factors from one generation to the next. Although evidence is mixed (see Thornberry, Knight, & Lovegrove, 2012), a history of abuse is often cited as the most important risk factor for the later perpetration of abuse. Relationships between risk factors and offending have been found to be similar across generations (Farrington, Ttofi, Crago, & Coid, 2015). However, to the best of our knowledge, the extent to which the abuse-offending association is perpetuated across generations is unknown.

Child Abuse and Neglect. https://doi.org/10.1016/B978-0-12-815344-4.00011-8

Table 1: Key longitudinal studies relating child physical punishment or abuse to offending

Author (Date)	Sample Size	Offending Detail	Comparison Group	Controls (*N*)	Main Findings
Baskin and Sommers (2010)	2429	OR, J	Yes	3	Type of maltreatment showed mixed results; e.g. CPA was positively associated with violent and nonviolent arrests, but not total arrests; CSA was negatively associated with total and violent arrests and neglect with violent arrests only
Grogan-Kaylor, Ruffolo, Ortega, and Clarke (2008)	1180	SR, J	No	14	CPA, but not CSA or neglect, was associated with delinquency. A number of other risk factors predicted delinquency, including older age, male gender, receipt of child welfare services, decreased parental monitoring, poorer parent-youth and peer relationships, and youth trauma and psychopathology
Malvaso, Delfabbro, and Day (2017)	$N = 71{,}739$ ($n = 17{,}390$ for reduced sample)	OR, J	No	3	Young people who had records of substantiated maltreatment were just under 10 times more likely to be convicted of a youth offence compared with a general population estimate. Strongest predictors of convictions among maltreated youth were male gender, Aboriginal and Torres Strait Islander background, CPA, a greater number of substantiations for any type of maltreatment, maltreatment that started in childhood and persisted through adolescence, and placement in OHC
Mersky and Reynolds (2007)	1539	OR, J, A	Yes	11	Both CPA and neglect were associated with increases in violent and nonviolent offences. Maltreatment was a more consistent predictor of both violent and nonviolent offences among males but was only associated with an increased risk of violent petitions and adult convictions among females. Moderation effects were also found between maltreatment and public assistant receipt; maltreated children from families receiving assistance were more likely to have violent petitions than maltreated children from less disadvantaged families

Salzinger, Rosario, and Feldman (2007)	200	SR, J	Yes	7	The relationship between CPA and violent delinquency was mediated by adolescent attachment to parents and verbal and physical abuse in relationships with parents. Interactions between CPA, delinquency of friends and abusive relationships with best friends moderated the CPA-delinquency relationship. Male gender was also found to be a risk factor for later delinquency
Smith, Ireland, and Thornberry (2005)		OR, SR, J, A	Yes	8	Maltreatment in adolescence increased the odds for official arrest and self-reported general and violent offending in both late adolescence and early adulthood. Various other risk factors including race, gender, and community poverty contributed to offending outcomes. The strongest predictor, however, was previous offending. CPA was associated with violent offending in both late adolescence and early adulthood, CSA was associated with general offending in early adulthood only, and neglect was associated with arrest in both adolescence and adulthood and general and violent offending in adolescence
Stouthamer-Loeber, Wei, Homish, and Loeber (2002)	503	OR, J	Yes	20	Followed boys with substantiated maltreatment over 7 years and found almost half were involved in serious persistent delinquency by age 12, in contrast with only a fifth of controls. Maltreatment has unique effects on persistent serious delinquency; however, not living with biological parents and caretaker unemployment also increased delinquency risk. When interactions were considered, maltreatment no longer had a unique effect on delinquency, but a significant interaction was found between maltreatment and not living with biological parents

(Continued)

Table 1: Key longitudinal studies relating child physical punishment or abuse to offending—cont'd

Author (Date)	Sample Size	Offending Detail	Comparison Group	Controls (*N*)	Main Findings
Taussig (2002)	214	SR, J	No	17	CPA, but not CSA or neglect, was associated with increased delinquency. Low perceived classmate support and poorer behavioural conduct were associated with increased in delinquency, and social acceptance was associated with decreased delinquency
Widom and Maxfield (1996)	1575	OR, J, A	Yes	4	Being male, older, and African American and experiencing CPA and neglect (but not CSA) were associated with increased arrests for violent crime (juvenile or adult). Maltreated children began their criminal careers on average a year younger than their peers and were more likely to become chronic offenders
Zingraff, Leiter, Myers, and Johnsen (1993)	2886	OR, J	Yes	4	Maltreated children (including physically abused), compared with a sample of school children, were at increased risk for general and status offences but not property of violent offences. When compared with a sample of poor children, maltreatment predicted status offences only. Controls for age, gender, race, and family structure had varying effects in the different models but overall accounted for the direct influence of maltreatment on offending for most types of crime

Note: *OR*, official record; *SR*, self-report; *J*, juvenile outcomes; *A*, adult outcomes; *CPA*, child physical abuse; *CSA*, child sexual abuse; *OHC*, out-of-home care.

1.1 Child Physical Abuse and Offending

Despite evidence that suggests that the link between child physical abuse (and maltreatment more broadly) and offending holds after controlling for potential confounders, risk factors, and different study methodologies (see Braga et al., 2017), it is important to understand how the design and characteristics of different studies might influence findings. For example, in a meta-analytic review of reports examining the relationship between childhood exposure to violence and juvenile offending, Wilson et al. (2009) found large effect sizes for cross-sectional studies and small effect sizes for prospective longitudinal studies.

Cross-sectional studies of the abuse-offending link typically involve selecting a sample of incarcerated young offenders and examining their prior, often self-reported, experiences of abuse. These studies tend to have small samples and do not include appropriate comparison groups of nonoffending individuals, and their results can be influenced by biases associated with self-report measures of abuse. For example, young offenders might be motivated to try to minimise their responsibility for offending by attributing it at least partly to their earlier victimisation. Despite deepening our understanding of the accumulation of risk factors for young people involved in the criminal justice system, these studies provide limited insight into the possible causal relationship between abuse and offending.

Over the last decade, there has been a rapid increase in the publication of more methodologically rigorous studies using prospective longitudinal data. These studies have provided detailed examinations of the interactions between risk and protective factors that can influence the complex pathways from abuse to offending. However, there are still substantial inconsistencies in the way in which longitudinal studies are designed, how aspects of abuse and offending are operationalised, and which variables are included or controlled for in multivariate analyses (Malvaso, Delfabbro, & Day, 2018).

As an example, in the aforementioned meta-analytic review by Wilson et al. (2009), moderate (rather than small) effect sizes were found for longitudinal studies that examined the effects of direct victimisation (i.e. physical or sexual abuse) compared with those that measured the witnessing of domestic violence. This suggests that the way victimisation, violence, and abuse are operationalised can influence the results, and it might be that physical victimisation, rather than other forms of abuse and neglect, plays a more direct role in the broader maltreatment-offending association. The key advantage of longitudinal studies is that the date of onset of abuse is typically known. This information can be used to avoid retrospective bias and establish the correct temporal order between abuse and offending. In turn, longitudinal data can make researchers more confident that abuse is a predictor or possible cause of later offending behaviour.

Another issue concerns confounding factors. A range of risk factors (e.g. low socioeconomic status) have been found to predict both childhood physical abuse and offending behaviour.

Although longitudinal studies often include variables such as gender, race, and socioeconomic indicators in multivariate models testing the association between abuse and offending, fewer projects have measured other individual, familial, and contextual characteristics that likely play a role in mitigating or exacerbating risk.

A recent meta-analysis of studies examining the association between child maltreatment more broadly and later antisocial behaviour found that, although the total number of covariates included in analyses did not influence the association, a number of specific covariates did (Braga et al., 2017). For example, it was found that controlling for family stress, child-rearing practices, and the quality of parent–child relationships reduced the effect of maltreatment on antisocial behaviour. In other studies that have compared outcomes for maltreated with nonmaltreated groups of individuals over time, lower levels of parental education and parental criminality have also been found to increase the risk of offending (e.g. Smith et al., 2005; Stouthamer-Loeber, Loeber, Homish, & Wei, 2001; Widom & White, 1997). In research that specifically examined the consequences of physical abuse, low positive attachment to parents was found to mediate the association between abuse and delinquency (Salzinger et al., 2007).

The importance of school and educational factors in buffering the effects of abuse on offending has also been demonstrated (e.g. Smith, Park, Ireland, Elwyn, & Thornberry, 2013; Tyler, Johnson, & Brownridge, 2008). On the other hand, negative school experiences can exacerbate the risk. For example, Egeland, Yates, Appleyard, and van Dulmen (2002) showed that physical abuse was associated with alienation in preschool and this increased the risk of antisocial behaviour in adolescence through externalising problems. More examples have been found in studies examining the effects of maltreatment more broadly. For example, Brezina (1998) discovered that low school commitment, deviant attitudes, and anger all influenced delinquency. Associations can also extend into adulthood, with Topitzes, Mersky, and Reynolds (2011) finding that, among males in the Chicago Longitudinal Study, childhood externalising behaviour and adolescent socioemotional skills, school commitment and educational attainment, and prior delinquency fully explained the association between childhood maltreatment and adult arrests.

Another issue is the use of retrospective versus prospective measures of abuse, with each approach subject to both advantages and disadvantages. Retrospective measures likely introduce bias into studies, because of issues of recall, for example, those resulting from memory problems a long time after the event in question. Infantile amnesia and social desirability bias might also influence whether an individual is able or willing to report past experiences of abuse. As mentioned previously, the advantage of prospective measures of abuse is that the temporal order can be established and causality can be inferred. If we are able to determine that abuse preceded offending in time, then we can be more confident in testing the role of abuse in the causal pathway to offending.

Official records or administrative data that are collected by child protection agencies are commonly used as measures of child abuse and neglect. However, the use of administrative records can also be problematic because they can lead to an underestimate of the magnitude of the effect of abuse on offending, because not all children who experience abuse come to the attention of official child protection agencies. On the other hand, studies that limit their analyses to cases of abuse that have been verified or substantiated by child protection services may exaggerate the size of the association, by focusing only on those who have been most severely maltreated (Lansford et al., 2007). Finally, official records are also likely to introduce bias into the study because disadvantaged families and minority groups might be more likely to come to the attention of child protection services, potentially because of surveillance bias.

A number of studies have attempted to quantify the concordance between measures of abuse by comparing official records of maltreatment (collected both prospectively and retrospectively) and retrospective self-report measures of maltreatment. Smith, Ireland, Thornberry, and Elwyn (2008) found moderate concordance between official records and self-reported maltreatment but discovered a higher prevalence in self-reports. Brown, Cohen, Johnson, and Salzinger (1998) showed that only 17% of self-reported maltreatment was confirmed in official records, while 60% of official records were not self-reported in adulthood. Widom and Morris (1997) discovered that concordance varied according to the type of abuse, with sexual abuse being especially underreported by adults.

It has been suggested that the inclusion of multiple measures is ideal, so that any differences in outcomes depending on the way abuse is measured can be identified. To the best of our knowledge, no study has compared the concordance between maltreatment according to different reporters in successive generations. That is, we are not aware of any studies that have examined the extent to which prospectively measured reports of abuse by parents are concordant with retrospectively reported experiences of abuse by their children later in adulthood.

Relatedly, we have not found any studies that have examined the concordance between retrospectively and prospectively measured experiences of physical abuse collected over three generations. This type of analysis not only provides an assessment of the intergenerational transmission of abuse but also enables risk factors in successive generations to be compared. A history of maltreatment is often cited as the most important risk factor for later perpetration of maltreatment; however, evidence for the intergenerational transmission of abuse is mixed (Ben-David, Jonson-Reid, Drake, & Kohl, 2015; Leve, Khurana, & Reich, 2015; Thornberry et al., 2012; Widom, Czaja, & DuMont, 2015).

Theories of social selection suggest that the same types of parents who are likely to be engaged in criminal behaviour may also be more likely to physically punish or abuse their children. It might be that these individuals are more likely to be suffering from mental health problems, substance abuse, and economic insecurity, and these same risk factors have been shown to independently predict child maltreatment. Parental involvement in crime is also viewed as a risk factor for abuse because it is associated more generally with poorer-quality parenting and child-rearing environments. Another explanation is that of oversurveillance, that is, differential levels of monitoring or exposure to authorities based on socioeconomic status or race. Parents who are already known to one government system, such as the criminal justice system, might also be flagged in another, such as the child protection system. From an intergenerational perspective, understanding the reciprocal influences in the parent–child relationship is important in determining whether the cycle of physical punishment persists both within generations and across generations.

1.2 Aims of This Chapter

This chapter aims to investigate the relationship between physical punishment (or harsh discipline) and offending in the Cambridge Study in Delinquent Development (CSDD), which is a prospective longitudinal study of 411 London males from age 8 to 56. These males are now called generation 2 (G2) to distinguish them from their parents (generation 1 or G1) and their children (generation 3 or G3). The key questions addressed are the following:

1. To what extent are prospective and retrospective reports of physical punishment in these successive generations concordant?
2. To what extent does physical punishment by the G1 parents predict convictions of the G2 males?
3. To what extent does physical punishment by the G2 males predict convictions of the G3 males?
4. To what extent does physical punishment predict convictions after controlling for other childhood parental, child-rearing, and socioeconomic risk factors?

2 Method

2.1 The CSDD

The CSDD began in 1961, and for the first 20 years, it was directed by Donald West. David Farrington started working on it in 1969 and began directing the CSDD in 1982. The most recent data collections have been jointly directed by David Farrington and Jeremy Coid. The CSDD has been funded primarily by the Home Office and secondly by the Department of Health. The results of the study have been described in six books (Farrington, Piquero, & Jennings, 2013; Piquero, Farrington, & Blumstein, 2007; West, 1969, 1982; West & Farrington, 1973, 1977) and in five summary articles (Farrington, 1995, 2003; Farrington, Coid, & West, 2009; Farrington & West, 1981, 1990).

At the time they were first contacted in 1961–62, the G2 boys were all living in a working-class area of South London. The vast majority of the sample was chosen by taking all the boys who were then aged 8–9 and on the registers of six state primary schools within a 1 mile (1.6 km) radius of a research office that had been established. In addition to 399 boys from these 6 schools, 12 boys from a local school for educationally subnormal children were included in the sample, in an attempt to make it more representative of the population of boys living in the area. Therefore, the boys were not a probability sample drawn from a population, but rather a complete population of boys of that age in that area at that time.

Most of the G2 boys (357, or 87%) were White in appearance and of British origin, in the sense that they were being brought up by parents who had themselves been brought up in England, Scotland, or Wales. Of the remaining 54 boys, 12 were Afro-Caribbean, having at least one parent of West Indian (usually) or African origin. Of the remaining 42 boys of nonBritish origin, 14 had at least one parent from the North or South of Ireland, 12 had parents from Cyprus, and the other 16 boys were Caucasian and had at least one parent from another Western industrialised country.

On the basis of their fathers' occupations when they were aged 8, 94% of the G2 boys could be described as working class (categories III, IV, or V on the Registrar General's scale, describing skilled, semiskilled, or unskilled manual workers), in comparison with the national figure of 78% at that time. The majority of the boys were living in conventional two-parent families with both a father and a mother figure; at age 8, only 6% of the boys had no operative father, and only 1% had no operative mother. This was, therefore, overwhelmingly a traditional White, urban, working-class sample of British origin.

2.2 Interviews

The G2 males have been assessed or interviewed nine times, at ages 8, 10, 14, 16, 18, 21, 25, 32, and 48. At all ages except 21 and 25, the aim was to interview all the males who were still alive, and it was always possible to interview a high proportion: 405 (99%) at age 14, 399 (97%) at age 16, 389 (95%) at age 18, 378 (94%) at age 32, and 365 (93%) at age 48. At age 21, the aim was to interview all the convicted males and an equal number of randomly chosen unconvicted males, and 218 of the 241 target males (90%) were interviewed. At age 25, only 85 males were interviewed.

Between 2004 and 2013, efforts were made to interview the biological G3 children of the G2 males. There were 691 G3 children whose name and date of birth were known. Only children aged at least 18 (born up to 1995) were targeted. The ethical requirements of the South-East Region Medical Ethics Committee required that we contact the G2 male and/or his female partner in trying to interview the G3 children. Therefore, 20 children whose fathers refused at age 48 and 7 children whose fathers were dead at age 48 (and where no female partner was available) were not eligible to be interviewed. An additional six G3 children who had died and three who were disabled (one with Down's syndrome, one with mental health problems, and one with severe attention deficit-hyperactivity disorder), together with two who did not know that the G2 male was their father, were considered to be not eligible. Of the 653 eligible G3 children, 551 were interviewed (84.4%) at an average age of 25, 291 of the 343 G3 males (84.8%) and 260 of the 310 G3 females (83.9%). Of the remainder, 39 children refused, 33 parents refused, 13 children could not be traced, 14 were elusive (agreeing or not refusing but never being available to interview), and three were aggressive or problematic. This chapter focuses on the G3 males.

2.3 Criminal Record Searches of the G2 Males

These searches have been described in previous publications (e.g. Farrington, Ttofi, Crago, & Coid, 2014). The minimum age of criminal responsibility in England is 10. Recent searches of criminal records of the G2 males took place in July 2002 and December 2004 in the PNC, at which time most of the males were aged 51. A Home Office report (Farrington et al., 2006) and many previous analyses were based on the criminal records up to age 50 derived from these searches. A further search of the PNC was completed in March 2011, when most males were aged 57. The criminal records of the G2 males are therefore now known up to age 56 (Farrington et al., 2013).

For comparability with the G3 children, it was decided to count officially recorded cautions and convictions in the PNC, since cautions were routinely recorded on a national basis from 1995. In total, 177 G2 males were convicted up to age 56 (43.8% of 404 at risk) for a total of 909 offences, including 51 cautions. In this chapter, 'convictions' include cautions. Convictions were only counted if they were for 'standard list' (more serious) offences, thereby excluding minor crimes such as minor traffic infractions and simple drunkenness. The most common offences included were thefts, burglaries, and unauthorised takings of vehicles, although there were also quite a few offences of violence, vandalism, fraud, and drug abuse. The definition of what is a 'standard list' offence changed over time. In particular, common assault became a standard list offence in July 1995, drunk driving was added to the standard list from January 1996, and being drunk and disorderly was added in April 1997. All of these types of offences were counted.

2.4 Criminal Record Searches of the G3 Children

As mentioned, there were 691 G3 children whose name and date of birth were known. Their median year of birth was 1981, and more than half were born between 1977 and 1985. They were first searched in the microfiche records in 1994, and they were then searched in the PNC in 2003, 2006, and 2011–12. The median age at which they were last searched was 30, and more than half were last searched between ages 25 and 33. The 31 G3 children who were abroad could not be searched, but 656 of the remaining 660 were searched. These included 343 G3 males and 313 G3 females. Almost all were searched at least up to age 21.

2.5 Measures of Physical Punishment

Unless otherwise stated, the G1 family measures were based on psychiatric social worker interviews with the G1 parents when the G2 males were age 8–10. Harsh discipline at age 8 was a combination of three variables: cruel attitude, very strict discipline, and harsh quality of discipline. While this variable did not explicitly measure physical punishment, it is likely that almost all of those coded as receiving harsh discipline would have been receiving physical punishment. Also, at age 48, the G2 males were asked about the discipline they received from their G1 parents during their childhood, and those who said that they had been beaten or smacked were coded as receiving physical punishment. A 'smack' was defined as being struck with an open hand. 'Beating' was defined as being struck with an implement such as a cane, slipper, or strap or being thumped or kicked. This was a retrospective report.

At age 32, the G2 males who had children were asked what they did when their children were very naughty, and those who beat or smacked their children were coded as using physical punishment. At age 48, the G2 males were asked the same question, with the same coding, except that the answers could refer to the past and the present. The G3 males were also asked about the discipline that they had received from their G2 parents during their childhood, and again, those who said that they had been beaten or smacked were coded as receiving physical punishment. This was a retrospective report.

2.6 G1 Risk Factors at Age 8–10

For comparability, all risk factors were dichotomised, as far as possible, into the 'worst' quarter versus the remainder (see Farrington & Loeber, 2000).

Parental: Convictions of the G1 father and G1 mother up to age 32 were obtained from criminal record searches. (Age 32 was chosen for comparability between different generations.) Young G1 mothers were those who had their first child before age 21, and young G1 fathers were those who had their first child before age 23. These ages were also chosen for comparability across generations. Nervousness of the G1 father was based on social worker ratings and psychiatric treatment, while nervousness of the G1 mother was based on both of these measures plus a health questionnaire. Low interest in his children by the G1 father and low interest in the boy's education by the G1 parents were rated by the social workers.

Family: Uninvolved G1 fathers were identified by a questionnaire on the extent to which the G1 father joined in the G2 boy's leisure activities (see Farrington, 1989, Smith & Farrington, 2004, and West & Farrington, 1973, for more information about all G1 and G2 measures). The uninvolved G1 fathers rarely or never joined the G2 boy's leisure activities. Poor parental supervision referred to the extent to which the G1 parents knew what the G2 boy was doing when he was out. Parental conflict was also rated by the social workers based on their interviews with the G1 parents, and it referred to chronic tension or disagreement in many fields, raging conflicts, or estrangement. A disrupted family referred to the G2 boy's temporary or permanent separation from a G1 parent before his 10th birthday for reasons other than death or hospitalisation. Physical neglect of the G2 boy referred to noticeable neglect of his clothing, hygiene, or food, and 'boy not praised' meant that no special recognition was given to the G2 boy when he behaved well.

Socio-economic: Low G1 family income at age 8 was rated by the social workers. Large G1 family size referred to five or more children born to the G2 boy's mother up to his 10th birthday. Poor G1 housing was rated by the social workers and referred to living in dilapidated slum premises. Low socioeconomic status referred to G1 fathers who had an unskilled manual job when the G2 boy was age 8–10.

2.7 G2 Risk Factors

Most of the G2 risk factors were derived from the age 32 interview with the G2 male, when only 9% of the G3 children were age 10 or over.

Parental: Convictions of the G2 father and G2 mother up to age 32 were obtained from criminal record searches. As for G1, young fathers referred to G2 males who were under age 23 at the time of the birth of the G3 male, and young mothers referred to G2 mothers who were under age 21 at the birth of their first known child. (We only have records of children that the G2 female had with the G2 male.)

Family: Uninvolved G2 fathers were those who spent the least time in activities with their children each week (according to their reports at age 32). Poor parental supervision referred to the G2 father not knowing where his children were when they were out. Like physical punishment, this was also retrospectively reported by the G3 child. Parental conflict was based on the G2 father's report of frequent rows, and the G2 father also answered about whether he had a child living elsewhere at age 32. The G3 male, in his interview, reported on whether he had lived with his G2 father for the whole time period up to his 16th birthday or whether he had been separated at some stage.

Socioeconomic: Low take-home pay was reported by the G2 male at age 32. Large family size referred to the number of people living in the G2 male's household when he was age 32. Poor housing of the G2 male at age 32 was rated by the interviewer, based on whether the home was dirty, smelly, damp, neglected, overcrowded, or inadequately furnished; had vermin; or had structural problems. Low socioeconomic status at age 32 indicated that the G2 male had a semiskilled or unskilled manual job.

3 Results

3.1 Physical Punishment and Convictions

Table 2 shows the prevalence of the physical punishment variables. The cut-off point for G1 harsh discipline was arbitrary, since (as mentioned) the aim at age 8–10 was to

Table 2: Prevalence of physical punishment and convictions

	No	Yes	% Yes
G1 harsh discipline at 8 (P)	272	112	29.2
G1 physical punishment from G2 at 48 (R)	253	91	26.5
G2 physical punishment at 32 (P)	134	84	38.5
G2 physical punishment at 48 (P)	154	114	42.5
G2 physical punishment from G3 at 25 (R)	183	92	33.5
G2 convicted 10–21	272	137	33.5
G2 convicted 22–56	284	112	28.3
G3 convicted 10–21	274	69	20.1
G2 violent 10–21	365	44	10.8
G2 violent 22–56	347	49	12.4
G3 violent 10–21	306	37	10.8

Note: *P*, prospective; *R*, retrospective.

identify the 'worst' quarter on each risk factor. The other cut-off points are meaningful. Remarkably, 75% of the G2 males at age 48 said that they had been beaten or smacked during their childhood. It is known that the use of physical punishment by parents in England has decreased since the 1960s, and nowadays, it is widely disapproved. Because of the high prevalence of physical punishment overall, only the 26% who said that they had been beaten were counted as physically punished. About 40% of G2 males said that they physically punished their own children at ages 32 and 48. Reports of beating children were rare; for example, at age 48, only 4 G2 males said that they had beaten their children, while 110 said that they had smacked their children. The numbers are relatively small at age 32 because not that many G2 males had children at that age. Retrospectively, about one-third of the G3 children (at the average age of 25) said that they had been beaten or smacked during their childhood.

Table 2 also shows the prevalence of convictions. About one-third of the G2 males were convicted between ages 10 and 21, compared with only one-fifth of the G3 males. It is known that conviction rates have decreased over time in England. Over a quarter of the G2 males were convicted between ages 22 and 56. Fewer males were at risk of conviction between these ages because of deaths and emigration.

Because of interest in the cycle of violence, we have focused especially on convictions for violent offences (assault, wounding, robbery, threatening behaviour, and possessing an offensive weapon). Table 2 shows that 11% of G2 males and 11% of G3 males were convicted for violence between ages 10 and 21. It is known that the decrease in conviction rates in England is driven by a decrease in property crimes rather than in violence. Between ages 22 and 56, 12% of G2 males were convicted for violence. (For more information about violence in the CSDD, see Farrington, 2018.)

Table 3: Interrelations of physical punishment variables

Variable 1	Variable 2	Odds Ratio	Confidence Interval
G1 harsh discipline at 8 (P)	G1 physical punishment from G2 at 48 (R)	2.11	1.36–3.27
G1 harsh discipline at 8 (P)	G2 physical punishment at 32 (P)	1.09	0.64–1.86
G1 harsh discipline at 8 (P)	G2 physical punishment at 48 (P)	1.02	0.64–1.63
G1 physical punishment from G2 at 48 (R)	G2 physical punishment at 32 (P)	0.98	0.59–1.66
G1 physical punishment from G2 at 48 (R)	G2 physical punishment at 48 (P)	1.59	1.00–2.52
G2 physical punishment at 32 (P)	G2 physical punishment at 48 (P)	1.20	0.74–1.95
G2 physical punishment at 32 (P)	G2 physical punishment from G3 at 25 (R)	1.23	0.72–2.09

Note: *P*, prospective; *R*, retrospective.

Table 3 shows how the physical punishment variables were interrelated. Because of directional predictions, one-tailed statistical tests are used in this chapter, so that the 90% confidence interval is shown. Also, to take account of the clustering of children in families, the standard error of the logarithm of the odds ratio was increased by 10% for comparisons involving G3 children (see Farrington et al., 2015).

Remarkably, the retrospective report of his childhood physical punishment by the G2 male at age 48 was significantly related to the prospective measure of G1 harsh discipline by the psychiatric social workers when the G2 male was age 8 (odds ratio or OR=2.11). This is surprising, as the retrospective variable referred to the whole of childhood but the prospective variable was measured at age 8. There was no significant relationship between G1 harsh discipline at age 8 and the G2 male's use of physical punishment on his own children at ages 32 or 48. However, the G2 male's retrospective report at age 48 of his childhood physical punishment was (just) significantly related to his reported use of physical punishment on his own children at age 48. Since both reports were given in the same interview, they could perhaps be affected by reporting bias.

Surprisingly, the G2 male's use of physical punishment at age 32 was not significantly related to his use of physical punishment at age 48. However, it must be remembered that the average G3 child was under age 10 when the G2 male was age 32 but of course 16 years older when the G2 male was age 48, so that many of the age 48 reports were retrospective. Finally, the G2 male's use of physical punishment at age 32 was not significantly related to the G3 male's retrospective report of the physical punishment that he had received in childhood. However, the G2 male's report referred to all of his children, not specifically to the G3 male, and the G3 male's report referred to the physical punishment he had received from his parents, not specifically from the G2 male. Also, 26% of G3 males were separated from their G2 father at some stage (see Farrington et al., 2015).

3.2 Physical Punishment Versus Convictions

Table 4 shows that the G1 harsh discipline measure at age 8 significantly predicted later convictions and was a very strong predictor of convictions for violence (OR=4.09 for violence at 10–21). Similarly, the retrospective report of G1 physical punishment from the G2 male at age 48 was significantly related to later convictions and was strongly related to convictions for violence (OR=2.99 for violence at 10–21).

Surprisingly, the G2 male's report of his own use of physical punishment at age 32 was not significantly related to the convictions of the G3 male, although the trend was in the expected direction (25 vs 17% convicted). Disappointingly, the trend was in the opposite direction for violence. However, as mentioned, the G2 male's report referred to all of his children, and it is

Table 4: Physical punishment by parents versus convictions of sons

Physical Punishment	Conviction	% Convicted		Odds Ratio	Confidence Interval
		Not Punished	Punished		
G1 harsh discipline at 8 (P)	G2 convicted 10–21	29.0	42.9	1.83	1.25–2.68
G1 harsh discipline at 8 (P)	G2 convicted 22–56	23.1	37.6	2.00	1.34–2.99
G1 harsh discipline at 8 (P)	G2 violent 10–21	6.3	21.4	4.09	2.34–7.16
G1 harsh discipline at 8 (P)	G2 violent 22–56	9.0	20.2	2.57	1.52–4.36
G1 physical punishment from G2 at 48 (R)	G2 convicted 10–21	30.6	42.9	1.70	1.12–2.57
G1 physical punishment from G2 at 48 (R)	G2 convicted 22–56	25.6	35.6	1.60	1.04–2.47
G1 physical punishment from G2 at 48 (R)	G2 violent 10–21	7.1	18.7	2.99	1.64–5.44
G1 physical punishment from G2 at 48 (R)	G2 violent 22–56	10.0	17.8	1.95	1.10–3.44
G2 physical punishment at 32 (P)	G3 convicted 10–21	17.0	25.3	1.65	0.89–3.06
G2 physical punishment at 32 (P)	G3 violent 10–21	11.1	9.6	0.85	0.37–1.94
G2 physical punishment from G3 at 25 (R)	G3 convicted 10–21	15.0	32.2	2.69	1.55–4.68
G2 physical punishment from G3 at 25 (R)	G3 violent 10–21	6.7	18.9	3.26	1.57–6.75

Note: *P*, prospective; *R*, retrospective.

possible that his female partner was more important in rearing the G3 male. Interestingly, the G3 male's retrospective report of the physical punishment that he had received in childhood was significantly related to his convictions and especially to his violence (OR=3.26).

3.3 Family Risk Factors Versus Physical Punishment and Violence

In investigating the relationship between childhood physical punishment, other family factors, and violence, we focus on G1 harsh discipline and G2 physical punishment (retrospectively reported by the G3 male), because they were most strongly related to violence. For ease of exposition, we will refer to both of these measures as predictors of violence, although the second measure is not strictly predictive.

Table 5 shows the relationship between G1 harsh discipline at age 8 and 18 other G1 family risk factors measured at age 8–10. Harsh discipline was especially related to low

Table 5: G1 family risk factors versus harsh discipline and G2 violence

G1 Family Risk Factors	% Harsh Discipline			% Violent		
	Nonrisk	Risk	Odds Ratio	Nonrisk	Risk	Odds Ratio
Parental						
Convicted G1 father at 32	24.9	45.6	2.52[a]	7.7	23.5	3.65[a]
Convicted G1 mother at 32	26.6	60.0	4.15[a]	9.4	30.0	4.15[a]
Young G1 father	28.0	34.2	1.34	10.8	11.8	1.11
Young G1 mother	28.8	30.3	1.07	10.1	12.8	1.31
Nervous G1 father	25.8	46.2	2.47[a]	9.5	15.4	1.73
Nervous G1 mother	23.3	41.8	2.36[a]	8.6	14.6	1.83[a]
Low father interest in children	23.6	76.2	10.38[a]	9.8	11.6	1.21
Low parent interest in education	24.5	55.6	3.85[a]	8.0	23.8	3.59[a]
Child-rearing						
Uninvolved G1 father	24.3	41.5	2.21[a]	8.5	12.2	1.49
Poor supervision	23.1	55.6	4.16[a]	7.6	22.2	3.49[a]
Parental conflict	21.0	61.6	6.04[a]	7.6	20.5	3.15[a]
Disrupted family	25.9	40.0	1.91[a]	8.3	20.0	2.77[a]
Physical neglect of boy	25.3	57.8	4.04[a]	9.0	25.0	3.35[a]
Boy not praised	26.6	53.7	3.19[a]	9.3	22.0	2.75[a]
Socio-economic						
Low family income	25.1	42.7	2.23[a]	7.7	21.5	3.28[a]
Large family size	26.5	37.1	1.64[a]	8.2	19.4	2.70[a]
Poor housing	25.9	34.5	1.50[a]	8.7	14.7	1.81[a]
Low social class	26.6	39.5	1.80[a]	9.5	16.5	1.87[a]

[a] $P<.05$, one-tailed.

interest of the G1 father in his children (OR = 10.38), parental conflict (OR = 6.04), poor parental supervision (OR = 4.16), a convicted G1 mother (OR = 4.15), and physical neglect of the boy (OR = 4.04). Table 5 also shows the extent to which G1 family risk factors predicted G2 violence at age 10–21 (see also Farrington, 2018). The strongest predictors were a convicted G1 mother (OR = 4.15), a convicted G1 father (OR = 3.65), low parental interest in education (OR = 3.59), poor parental supervision (OR = 3.49), physical neglect of the boy (OR = 3.35), low family income (OR = 3.28), and parental conflict (OR = 3.15).

Table 6 shows the relationship between G2 physical punishment (retrospectively reported by the G3 male) and 14 other G2 family risk factors, mostly measured when the G2 male was age 32 (and the G3 male was under age 10). Physical punishment was significantly related to a convicted G2 mother (OR = 3.37), a convicted G2 father (OR = 2.61), a young G2

Table 6: G2 family risk factors versus physical punishment and G3 violence

G2 Family Risk Factors	% Physical Punishment			% Violent		
	Nonrisk	Risk	Odds Ratio	Nonrisk	Risk	Odds Ratio
Parental						
Convicted G2 father at 32	25.4	47.1	2.61[a]	5.7	18.6	3.75[a]
Convicted G2 mother at 32	31.8	61.1	3.37[a]	10.0	22.2	2.58
Young G2 father	30.8	42.6	1.67	10.4	10.9	1.06
Young G2 mother	30.5	50.0	2.28[a]	11.4	6.1	0.51
Child-rearing						
Uninvolved G2 father at 32	33.3	44.7	1.62	10.6	10.5	0.99
Poor supervision at 32	32.0	47.4	1.91[a]	7.2	19.3	3.07[a]
Poor supervision from G3	30.2	36.8	1.34	5.6	15.7	3.11[a]
Parental conflict at 32	30.1	43.5	1.79[a]	8.4	13.3	1.67
Separated from child at 32	35.5	34.0	0.94	9.5	14.9	1.66
Separation from G3	34.2	32.4	0.92	9.5	14.5	1.62
Socio-economic						
Low take-home pay at 32	31.3	41.3	1.54	8.0	15.9	2.19
Large family size at 32	30.3	44.3	1.82[a]	8.5	16.7	2.16[a]
Poor housing at 32	31.1	35.0	1.19	8.5	17.7	2.31[a]
Low social class at 32	35.0	29.8	0.79	9.1	16.7	1.99

[a] $P < .05$, one-tailed.

mother (OR = 2.28), poor parental supervision (OR = 1.91), large family size (OR = 1.82), and parental conflict (OR = 1.79). Table 6 also shows the extent to which G2 family risk factors predicted G3 violence at age 10–21 (see also Farrington, 2018). The strongest predictors were a convicted G2 father (OR = 3.75), poor supervision according to G3 (OR = 3.11), poor supervision according to G2 (OR = 3.07), a convicted G2 mother (OR = 2.58 but not significant because of small numbers), and poor housing (OR = 2.31).

Since G1 harsh discipline was significantly related to other family risk factors that also predicted violence, it is important to investigate whether G1 harsh discipline predicts violence independently of the other family risk factors. Therefore, G1 harsh discipline and all other strong (OR > 2.0) predictors of violence were entered into a forward stepwise logistic regression analysis. The other strong predictors of violence were a convicted G1 father, a convicted G1 mother, low parental interest in education, poor parental supervision, parental conflict, a disrupted family, physical neglect of the boy, boy not praised, low family income, and large family size.

Table 7 shows the results of the logistic regression analysis. Only three G1 risk factors significantly and independently predicted G2 violence: harsh discipline (which was the most important predictor and entered the equation first), a convicted G1 father, and low family income. The next most important predictor was a disrupted family, but its *P* value to enter the equation was only .078. In the final model, the partial OR values were 3.03 for harsh discipline, 2.71 for a convicted G1 father, and 2.60 for low family income.

A similar analysis was carried out for the predictors of G3 violence. In addition to physical punishment, a convicted G2 father, a convicted G2 mother, poor supervision at age 32, poor supervision according to the G3 male, low take-home pay, large family size, and poor housing were included in the analysis. Table 7 shows that only three G2 risk factors significantly and independently predicted G3 violence: a convicted G2 father, physical punishment, and poor housing. The similarity between the G2 and G3 results is remarkable. Poor parental

Table 7: Results of logistic regression analyses

Risk Factor	LRCS Change	*P*	Partial OR	*P*
G2 violence				
Harsh discipline	17.33	0.001	3.03	0.001
Convicted G1 father at 32	10.62	0.001	2.71	0.003
Low family income	6.63	0.005	2.60	0.004
G3 violence				
Convicted G2 father at 32	14.63	0.001	4.34	0.001
Physical punishment	4.49	0.017	2.54	0.024
Poor housing at 32	3.49	0.031	2.20	0.047
Poor supervision from G3	2.60	0.053	2.17	0.058

Notes: G2 violence, *N* = 384; G3 violence, *N* = 221; LRCS, likelihood ratio chi-squared; OR, odds ratio; *P* values one-tailed.

supervision according to the G3 male was on the borderline of statistical significance, and so, it is also shown in Table 7. In the final model, the partial OR values were 4.34 for a convicted G2 father, 2.54 for physical punishment, 2.20 for poor housing, and 2.17 for poor supervision.

4 Conclusions

No other longitudinal study has investigated the relationship between physical punishment and offending in two successive generations of males. Our conclusions are as follows: First, the retrospective reports of their childhood physical punishment by G2 males at age 48 were significantly related to the prospective measure of the harsh discipline that they had received 40 years before at age 8 (based on psychiatric social worker interviews with their G1 parents). However, the G2 male's prospective report of his use of physical punishment at age 32 was not related to the G3 male's retrospective report of the physical punishment that he had received in childhood. More research is needed on the concordance between prospective and retrospective reports of physical punishment and on the circumstances in which they are most likely to be concordant.

Second, G1 harsh discipline was a significant predictor of G2 convictions and an especially strong predictor of G2 convictions for violence between ages 10 and 21. Similarly, the retrospective report of G1 physical punishment from the G2 male at age 48 was significantly related to G2 convictions and especially strongly related to G2 convictions for violence between ages 10 and 21.

Third, the G3 male's retrospective report of the physical punishment that he had received in childhood was significantly related to his convictions between ages 10 and 21 and especially to his convictions for violence. However, the G2 male's report of his use of physical punishment at age 32 did not significantly predict convictions of the G3 male. More research is needed on the circumstances in which prospective and retrospective reports of physical punishment are likely to be most valid.

Last, while many childhood family risk factors predicted convictions for violence, physical punishment was one of the three most important independent predictors for both G2 and G3 males. The other two important predictors were convictions of the father and poverty (as measured by low income or poor housing). The similarity between the G2 and G3 results is remarkable.

5 Chapter Revision Questions

1. To what extent are prospective and retrospective reports of physical punishment concordant?
2. To what extent does physical punishment predict later convictions?
3. Does childhood physical punishment predict convictions for violence more strongly than convictions for other types of crimes?

4. What other family risk factors are most closely associated with physical punishment?
5. What are the strongest childhood predictors of later convictions for violence?
6. To what extent does physical punishment predict later convictions for violence after controlling for other family risk factors?

References

Baskin, D. R., & Sommers, I. (2010). Child maltreatment, placement strategies, and delinquency. *American Journal of Criminal Justice*, *36*(2), 106–119. https://doi.org/10.1007/s12103-010-9088-9.

Ben-David, V., Jonson-Reid, M., Drake, B., & Kohl, P. L. (2015). The association between childhood maltreatment experiences and the onset of maltreatment perpetration in young adulthood controlling for proximal and distal risk factors. *Child Abuse and Neglect*, *46*, 132–141.

Braga, T., Gonçalves, L. C., Basto-Pereira, M., & Maia, Â. (2017). Unraveling the link between maltreatment and juvenile antisocial behavior: a meta-analysis of prospective longitudinal studies. *Aggression and Violent Behavior*, *33*, 37–50. https://doi.org/10.1016/j.avb.2017.01.006.

Brezina, T. (1998). Adolescent maltreatment and delinquency: the question of intervening processes. *Journal of Research in Crime and Delinquency*, *35*(1), 71–88.

Brown, J., Cohen, P., Johnson, J. G., & Salzinger, S. (1998). A longitudinal analysis of risk factors for child maltreatment: findings of a 17-year prospective study of officially recorded and self-reported child abuse and neglect. *Child Abuse and Neglect*, *22*, 1065–1078.

Egeland, B., Yates, T., Appleyard, K., & van Dulmen, M. (2002). The long-term consequences of maltreatment in the early years: a developmental pathway model to antisocial behavior. *Children's Services: Social Policy, Research, and Practice*, *5*(4), 249–260.

Farrington, D. P. (1989). Later adult life outcomes of offenders and non-offenders. In M. Brambring, F. Losel, & H. Skowronek (Eds.), *Children at risk: Assessment, longitudinal research, and intervention* (pp. 220–244). Berlin, Germany: De Gruyter.

Farrington, D. P. (1995). The development of offending and antisocial behaviour from childhood: key findings from the Cambridge study in delinquent development. *Journal of Child Psychology and Psychiatry*, *36*, 929–964.

Farrington, D. P. (2003). Key results from the first 40 years of the Cambridge study in delinquent development. In T. P. Thornberry & M. D. Krohn (Eds.), *Taking stock of delinquency: An overview of findings from contemporary longitudinal studies* (pp. 137–183). New York: Kluwer/Plenum.

Farrington, D. P. (2018). Origins of violent behavior over the life span. In A. T. Vazsonyi, D. J. Flannery, & M. DeLisi (Eds.), *The Cambridge handbook of violent behavior and aggression.* (2nd ed.)(pp. 3–30). Cambridge, UK: Cambridge University Press.

Farrington, D. P., Coid, J. W., Harnett, L. M., Jolliffe, D., Soteriou, N., Turner, R. E., et al. (2006). *Criminal careers up to age 50 and life success up to age 48: New findings from the Cambridge study in delinquent development*. London: Home Office. [Research Study No. 299].

Farrington, D. P., Coid, J. W., & West, D. J. (2009). The development of offending from age 8 to age 50: recent results from the Cambridge study in delinquent development. *Monatsschrift fur Kriminologie und Strafrechtsreform (Journal of Criminology and Penal Reform)*, *92*, 160–173.

Farrington, D. P., & Loeber, R. (2000). Some benefits of dichotomization in psychiatric and criminological research. *Criminal Behaviour and Mental Health*, *10*, 100–122.

Farrington, D. P., Piquero, A. R., & Jennings, W. G. (2013). *Offending from childhood to late middle age: Recent results from the Cambridge study in delinquent development*. New York: Springer.

Farrington, D. P., Ttofi, M. M., Crago, R. V., & Coid, J. W. (2014). Prevalence, frequency, onset, desistance and criminal career duration in self-reports compared with official records. *Criminal Behaviour and Mental Health*, *24*, 241–253.

Farrington, D. P., Ttofi, M. M., Crago, R. V., & Coid, J. W. (2015). Intergenerational similarities in risk factors for offending. *Journal of Developmental and Life-Course Criminology*, *1*, 48–62.

Farrington, D. P., & West, D. J. (1981). The Cambridge study in delinquent development (United Kingdom). In S. A. Mednick & A. E. Baert (Eds.), *Prospective longitudinal research: An empirical basis for the primary prevention of psychosocial disorders* (pp. 137–145). Oxford, UK: Oxford University Press.

Farrington, D. P., & West, D. J. (1990). The Cambridge study in delinquent development: A long-term follow-up of 411 London males. In H.-J. Kerner & G. Kaiser (Eds.), *Kriminalitat:Personlichkeit, lebensgeschichte und verhalten.* [Criminality: Personality, behaviour and life history](pp. 115–138). Berlin, Germany: Springer-Verlag.

Grogan-Kaylor, A., Ruffolo, M. C., Ortega, R. M., & Clarke, J. (2008). Behaviors of youth involved in the child welfare system. *Child Abuse and Neglect*, *32*(1), 35–49. https://doi.org/10.1016/j.chiabu.2007.09.004.

Lansford, J. E., Miller-Johnson, S., Berlin, L. J., Dodge, K. A., Bates, J. E., & Pettit, G. S. (2007). Early physical abuse and later violent delinquency: a prospective longitudinal study. *Child Maltreatment*, *12*(3), 233–245. https://doi.org/10.1177/1077559507301841.

Leve, L. D., Khurana, A., & Reich, E. B. (2015). Intergenerational transmission of maltreatment: a multilevel examination. *Development and Psychopathology*, *27*(4), 1429–1442.

Maas, C., Herrenkohl, T. I., & Sousa, C. (2008). Review of research on child maltreatment and violence in youth. *Trauma, Violence & Abuse*, *9*(1), 56–67. https://doi.org/10.1177/1524838007311105.

Malvaso, C. G., Delfabbro, P., & Day, A. (2016). Risk factors that influence the maltreatment-offending association: a systematic review of prospective and longitudinal studies. *Aggression and Violent Behavior*, *31*, 1–15. https://doi.org/10.1016/j.avb.2016.06.006.

Malvaso, C. G., Delfabbro, P., & Day, A. (2017). The child protection and juvenile justice nexus in Australia: a longitudinal examination of the relationship between maltreatment and offending. *Child Abuse and Neglect*, *64*, 32–46. https://doi.org/10.1016/j.chiabu.2016.11.028.

Malvaso, C. G., Delfabbro, P., & Day, A. (2018). The maltreatment-offending association: a systematic review of the methodological features of prospective and longitudinal studies. *Trauma, Violence & Abuse*, *19*(1), 20–34. https://doi.org/10.1177/1524838015620820.

Mersky, J. P., & Reynolds, A. J. (2007). Child maltreatment and violent delinquency: disentangling main effects and subgroup effects. *Child Maltreatment*, *12*(3), 246–258. https://doi.org/10.1177/1077559507301842.

Piquero, A. R., Farrington, D. P., & Blumstein, A. (2007). *Key issues in criminal career research: New analyses of the Cambridge study in delinquent development*. Cambridge, UK: Cambridge University Press.

Salzinger, S., Rosario, M., & Feldman, R. S. (2007). Physical child abuse and adolescent violent delinquency: the mediating and moderating roles of personal relationships. *Child Maltreatment*, *12*(3), 208–219. https://doi.org/10.1177/1077559507301839.

Smith, C. A., & Farrington, D. P. (2004). Continuities in antisocial behaviour and parenting across three generations. *Journal of Child Psychology and Psychiatry*, *45*, 230–247.

Smith, C. A., Ireland, T. O., & Thornberry, T. P. (2005). Adolescent maltreatment and its impact on young adult antisocial behavior. *Child Abuse and Neglect*, *29*(10), 1099–1119. https://doi.org/10.1016/j.chiabu.2005.02.011.

Smith, C. A., Ireland, T. O., Thornberry, T. P., & Elwyn, L. (2008). Childhood maltreatment and antisocial behavior: comparison of self-reported and substantiated maltreatment. *American Journal of Orthopsychiatry*, *78*(2), 173–186. https://doi.org/10.1037/0002-9432.78.2.173.

Smith, C. A., Park, A., Ireland, T. O., Elwyn, L., & Thornberry, T. P. (2013). Long-term outcomes of young adults exposed to maltreatment: the role of educational experiences in promoting resilience to crime and violence in early adulthood. *Journal of Interpersonal Violence*, *28*(1), 121–156. https://doi.org/10.1177/0886260512448845.

Stouthamer-Loeber, M., Loeber, R., Homish, D. L., & Wei, E. (2001). Maltreatment of boys and the development of disruptive and delinquent behavior. *Development and Psychopathology*, *13*, 941–955.

Stouthamer-Loeber, M., Wei, E., Homish, D. L., & Loeber, R. (2002). Which family and demographic factors are related to both maltreatment and persistent serious juvenile delinquency? *Children's Services: Social Policy, Research, and Practice*, *5*(4), 261–272.

Taussig, H. N. (2002). Risk behaviors in maltreated youth placed in foster care: a longitudinal study of protective and vulnerability factors. *Child Abuse and Neglect*, *26*, 1179–1199.
Thornberry, T. P., Knight, K. E., & Lovegrove, P. J. (2012). Does maltreatment beget maltreatment? A systematic review of the intergenerational literature. *Trauma, Violence & Abuse*, *13*(3), 135–152. https://doi.org/10.1177/1524838012447697.
Topitzes, J., Mersky, J. P., & Reynolds, A. J. (2011). Child maltreatment and offending behavior: gender-specific effects and pathways. *Criminal Justice and Behavior*, *38*(5), 492–510. https://doi.org/10.1177/0093854811398578.
Tyler, K. A., Johnson, K., & Brownridge, D. A. (2008). A longitudinal study of the effects of child maltreatment on later outcomes among high-risk adolescents. *Journal of Youth and Adolescence*, *37*, 506–521.
West, D. J. (1969). *Present conduct and future delinquency*. London: Heinemann.
West, D. J. (1982). *Delinquency: Its roots, careers and prospects*. London: Heinemann.
West, D. J., & Farrington, D. P. (1973). *Who becomes delinquent?* London: Heinemann.
West, D. J., & Farrington, D. P. (1977). *The delinquent way of life*. London: Heinemann.
Widom, C. S., Czaja, S. J., & DuMont, K. A. (2015). Intergenerational transmission of child abuse and neglect: real or detection bias? *Science*, *347*(6229), 1480–1485.
Widom, C. S., & Maxfield, M. G. (1996). A prospective examination of risk for violence among abused and neglected children. *Annals of the New York Academy of Sciences*, *794*, 224–237.
Widom, C. S., & Morris, S. (1997). Accuracy of adult recollections of childhood victimization: part 2. childhood sexual abuse. *Psychological Assessment*, *9*(1), 34–46.
Widom, C. S., & White, H. R. (1997). Problem behaviours in abused and neglected children grown up: prevalence and co-occurrance of substance abuse, crime and violence. *Criminal Behaviour and Mental Health*, *7*, 287–310.
Wilson, H. W., Stover, C. S., & Berkowitz, S. J. (2009). The relationship between childhood violence exposure and juvenile antisocial behavior: a meta-analytic review. *Journal of Child Psychology and Psychiatry*, *50*(7), 769–779. https://doi.org/10.1111/j.1469-7610.2008.01974.x.
Zingraff, M. T., Leiter, J., Myers, K. A., & Johnsen, M. C. (1993). Child maltreatment and youthful problem behavior. *Criminology*, *31*, 173–202.

CHAPTER 12

Physical 'Discipline', Child Abuse, and Children's Rights

Bernadette J. Saunders
Monash University, Caulfield East, VIC, Australia

1 Introduction

Postman (1982) poignantly observed that "children are the living messages we send to a time we will not see". Parents and other adults acting in loco parentis are entrusted with the task of nurturing children; protecting them from harm; and, as far as possible, ensuring their optimal development. The United Nations Convention on the Rights of the Child (CRC) recognises that "the child, for the full and harmonious development of his or her personality, should grow up in a family environment, in an atmosphere of happiness, love and understanding" (United Nations Convention on the Rights of the Child, 1989). Ideally, each child will experience a happy and healthy childhood, and this will positively shape societies that will exist in the future.

It is perhaps unsurprising that this significant responsibility is sometimes perceived as more of a burden than a privilege. Indeed, adults characteristically hold ambivalent attitudes towards children (Lancy, 2015). Particularly in Western societies, children may be positively regarded as precious 'little angels' whom parents cherish and tend to overprotect (Lancy, 2017), especially from unfamiliar people and places external to the home, and as a source of stress and negative emotion. Children are commonly considered to be their parents' property, and parents are expected to discipline and control them. The idea that children should be seen but not heard is perhaps less strongly espoused than in the past, but children's presence is still decidedly unwelcome in many places that adults perceive to be their space (see Freeman, 2010; Saunders, 2013). An apt label for this discriminatory attitude towards children is 'childism', which Young-Breuhl defines as "a prejudice against children on the ground of a belief that [children] are property and can (or even should) be controlled, enslaved, or removed to serve adult needs" (Young-Bruehl, 2012). As a means of discipline and control, the types and extent of physical force that have lawfully and commonly been inflicted upon children have differed through time and across cultures, as has the extent to which such 'disciplinary' violence has been socially condoned as normative or, indeed, considered not to be violent at all.

Child Abuse and Neglect. https://doi.org/10.1016/B978-0-12-815344-4.00012-X

Historically, children have been regarded and treated as subordinates: lesser beings than adults. Indeed, Jenks (Jenks, 1996) and others (Hengst, 2003; Lee, 2001; Uprichard, 2008) have drawn attention to the persistent idea of children as 'becomings', cocooned in a socially constructed cage that can be protective but also limiting and, for many children, physically and emotionally frustrating and painful. Indeed, Waksler (1991) has explored the idea that descriptors that sit comfortably with notions of children as 'childlike', by which is meant incompetent, naïve, and dependent, strategically position them as inferior to adults and in need of adults' firm guidance and control, arguably to a greater extent than is either appropriate or necessary. In contrast, respectful recognition of children's competence and abilities exposes the negative impact of excessive adult-imposed constraints and reveals, as Alderson has observed, that "[t]reating children with respect can markedly increase their competence" (Alderson, 1992). Indeed, according children respect might, rather than or in addition to increasing children's competence, promote environments in which children's inherent competence is acknowledged rather than blindly denied. As Menkel-Meadow (1987) remarks, "each time we let in a new excluded group… each time we listen to a new way of knowing, we learn more about the limits of our current way of seeing".

Like adults, children ought to be recognised as both becomings, people in the future, and beings, people in the present (Lee, 2001; Uprichard, 2008) who actively and competently contribute to, and participate in, their families and society. Instead, even in the twenty-first century, many children's capabilities, inquisitiveness, and zest for life (often sadly lacking in adults' lives) are constrained, and their human rights to dignity and to physical and emotional integrity are not fully recognised. These children's positive sense of self, confidence in their abilities, and optimal development, both as a child and a future adult, are consequently stunted.

In this context, this chapter focuses on physical discipline, child abuse, and children's rights, all of which are interrelated. Drawing on the United Nations Committee on the Right of the Child (UNCRC) General Comment No. 8, corporal punishment is defined as follows:

> *Any punishment in which physical force is used and intended to cause some degree of pain or discomfort, however light. Most involves hitting ('smacking', 'slapping', 'spanking') children, with the hand or with an implement - a whip, stick, belt, shoe, wooden spoon, etc. But it can also involve, for example, kicking, shaking or throwing children, scratching, pinching, biting, pulling hair or boxing ears, forcing children to stay in uncomfortable positions, burning, scalding or forced ingestion (for example, washing children's mouths out with soap or forcing them to swallow hot spices). In the view of the Committee, corporal punishment is invariably degrading. (Committee on the Rights of the Child, 2006)*

World progress towards recognition of children's rights to physical integrity and to protection from humiliating and degrading treatment is detailed, and some of the reasons for the continuing tolerance of corporal punishment of children in family, school, and other institutional settings around the world are discussed. Attention is drawn to international law and the human rights context within which children's physical discipline continues to be tolerated in many countries, including Australia. Further, recognition is given to a growing awareness that the corporal punishment of children is not only an infringement of their human rights but also a disquieting public health concern. A selection of recent research studies on corporal punishment is reviewed, with a focus upon existing research and the need for further research that consults children and young people about child abuse and corporal punishment. Obstacles and pathways to legislative reform are considered, including the influence of language and tradition, perceptions of the child, children's status vis-à-vis adults, and questionable distinctions between corporal punishment of children and child abuse. Also discussed is recent research on parenting programs and approaches designed to challenge parents' use of corporal punishment to correct and control children's behaviour, and to promote nonviolent alternatives.

2 Background

Societies and their governments continue to allow the corporal punishment of children in family, school, and other institutional settings in too many countries around the world. A 2014 UNICEF report revealed that 80% of the world's children are corporally punished by their parents (Cappa et al., 2014). In 2019, it will be 40 years since Sweden progressively legislated, through its civil code, to prohibit corporal punishment of children in any setting. The primary aim of the ban was to be educative not punitive. It reflected an unprecedented legislative confirmation of the humanity of children; each child's uniqueness; and every child's human rights to dignity, physical and emotional integrity, and protection from harm. Children in Sweden 'have the right to care, security, and a good upbringing'. Children are to be treated with respect for their person and individuality and may not be subjected to physical discipline or other abusive behaviour (Sweden: Children and Parents Code, 1949).

Just over 10 years ago, New Zealand (NZ), amidst much contention, became the first English-speaking country to introduce a total ban on corporal punishment. In NZ's Crimes Act (2007), the use of force to correct a child's behaviour can no longer be justified or used as a defence to assault. Significantly, this has not led, as many New Zealanders feared, to the unjust criminalisation of large numbers of parents. Section 59(4) of the Act acknowledges police discretion to not prosecute behaviours "considered to be so inconsequential that there is no public interest in proceeding with a prosecution" (The Crimes (Substituted Section 59) Amendment Act, 2007). A final police review of policing activities (New Zealand Police, 2013), five years after the ban, identified growing numbers of child assault reports, suggesting enhanced community confidence in reporting incidents of concern, "and a slight increase in smacking and 'minor acts of physical discipline' incidents". However, the review noted that "due to the low prosecution rate (eight prosecutions for a 'smacking' event since the June 2007 law change), initial fears that 'good parents' would be criminalised continues to be proven wrong". The review acknowledged that some parents, following reports of 'minor acts of discipline', were referred to child welfare agencies for support and guidance. In 2015, Ireland became the only other English-speaking country to follow NZ's lead. Ireland's Children First Act (2015) states in s24A (1) "the common law defence of reasonable chastisement is abolished".

At the time of writing, 53 states have legally banned corporal punishment in all settings, including the home (Global Initiative to End All Corporal Punishment of Children & Save the Children Sweden, 2017). Countries have more readily prohibited corporal punishment in schools, 131 states; in penal institutions, 139 states; and in childcare settings, 60 states, and judges cannot sentence children to corporal punishment for engaging in criminal activities—in 165 states (Global Initiative, 2018). It seems, as Brehm and Boyle (2018) contend, that disapproval of school corporal punishment is emerging as 'a global norm' and a precursor to the much slower adoption of policies regulating the more private sphere of the home and family. The Global Initiative to End All Corporal Punishment of Children has, nevertheless, recognised that "there is a long way to go. Still, only 10% of the world's children are fully protected in law from all corporal punishment. And still, so long since the adoption of the Convention on the Rights of the Child, the statute books in far too many countries at best fail to prohibit corporal punishment of children, at worst specifically authorise corporal punishment of children and set out the details of how it should be inflicted" (Global Initiative, 2018).

Indeed, limiting rather than prohibiting violent responses to children has characterised legislative responses, particularly in English-speaking countries. This results in strengthening, rather than questioning, parents' perceived rights to punish children through physical means. Boundaries in 'secular law' specify means of and justifications for legitimately resorting to physical force: these boundaries include 'instruments' and 'sites of punishment', 'reasons for punishment', 'who can administer punishment', 'degree of force', 'risk of harm', and 'susceptibility to punishment' (McGillivray, 1997). McGillivray sharply discerns that corporal punishment law can be "a shifting geojurispudence of licit and illicit body contacts" (McGillivray, 1997). Specified limitations serve to reinforce children's low status and thwart rather than progress children's rights to the same, if not greater, protection from assault as adults are provided. These boundaries define, albeit fuzzily and objectionably, permissible violence towards children, increasing their vulnerability to both short and long-term adverse consequences (discussed in more detail below).

3 International Law and the Human Rights Context Within Which Children's Physical Discipline Continues to Be Tolerated

Preceded by two previous declarations, the Geneva Declaration on the Rights of the Child (1924) and the Declaration on the Rights of the Child (1959), the United Nations Convention on the Rights of the Child (1989) was adopted and opened for signature, ratification, and accession in November 1989. With the exception of the United States, all of the world's states have ratified it. However, many have not codified all of its principles in law. The Preamble to the CRC points out that:

> *In the Universal Declaration of Human Rights [1948], the United Nations has proclaimed that childhood is entitled to special care and assistance... [T]he child should be fully prepared to live an individual life in society... brought up... in the spirit of peace, dignity, tolerance, freedom, equality and solidarity... [Further], the need to extend particular care to the child has been stated in... the International Covenant on Civil and Political Rights [1966] (in particular in articles 23 and 24) [and] in the International Covenant on Economic, Social and Cultural Rights [1966] (in particular in article 10).*

As human beings, children's human rights to dignity and a violence-free childhood were thus documented well before the CRC, but the historical denial of children's rights, notwithstanding their documentation in previous human rights instruments, appears to have been the impetus for the CRC. Children, despite their humanity, have been denied their rights as people, "in much the same way as the term 'he' was supposed to incorporate 'she' but in fact served... to exclude and marginalise women" (Lansdown, 1995).

Four articles in the CRC particularly challenge the continuing legal and social tolerance of corporal punishment in children's childhoods. Article 19(1) of the CRC asserts that "States Parties shall take all appropriate legislative, administrative, social and educational measures to protect the child from all forms of physical or mental violence, injury or abuse, neglect or negligent treatment, maltreatment...while in the care of parent(s), legal guardian(s) or any other person who has the care of the child". Article 28(2) refers to 'school discipline' that should be 'administered in a manner consistent with the child's human dignity and in conformity with the present Convention'. In Article 37(a), State Parties are required to ensure that "no child shall be subjected to torture or other cruel, inhuman or degrading treatment or punishment," and Article 24(3) insists that "States Parties shall take all effective and appropriate measures with a view to abolishing traditional practices prejudicial to the health of children".

It is disquieting that the CRC does not explicitly mention corporal punishment. However, the above articles, together with UNCRC's interpretation of the CRC in their General Comments No. 8 (2006), "The right of the child to protection from corporal punishment and other cruel or degrading forms of punishment (arts. 19; 28, para. 2; and 37, inter alia)", and No. 13 (2011), "The right of the child to freedom from all forms of violence" (Committee on the Rights of the Child, 2011), condemn corporal punishment in any setting. These documents explicitly require countries that have ratified the CRC to remove defences to assault in existing legislation—variously described in English-speaking countries as 'lawful correction', 'reasonable chastisement', and 'justifiable assault'—and to instigate new legislation that explicitly prohibits the corporal punishment of children. As evidenced in NZ and other countries that have removed such defences in their criminal legislation, the criminalisation of parents ought not to be an overriding concern. Indeed, the UNCRC advise, in General Comment No. 8, that

> *40. The principle of equal protection of children and adults from assault, including within the family, does not mean that all cases of corporal punishment of children by their parents that come to light should lead to prosecution of parents. The de minimis principle - that the law does not concern itself with trivial matters - ensures that minor assaults between adults only come to court in very exceptional circumstances; the same will be true of minor assaults on children...*
>
> *41. Children's dependent status and the unique intimacy of family relations demand that decisions to prosecute parents, or to formally intervene in the family in other ways, should be taken with very great care. Prosecuting parents is in most cases unlikely to be in their children's best interests. It is the Committee's view that prosecution and other formal interventions (for example, to remove the child or remove the perpetrator) should only proceed when they are regarded both as necessary to protect the child from significant harm and as being in the best interests of the affected child. The affected child's views should be given due weight, according to his or her age and maturity.*

The following articles in international law further support moves to ban corporal punishment in childhood: Article 7 of the Universal Declaration of Human Rights 1948; Article 16 of the Convention Against Torture 1984; Article 7 of the International Covenant on Economic, Social, and Cultural Rights 1966; Article 7 of the International Covenant on Civil and Political Rights 1966; Article 11(5) of the African Charter on the Rights and Welfare of the Child 1999; Article 5 of the American Convention on Human Rights 1969; and Article 17 of the European Social Charter 1961, revised in 1996 (see Bitensky (2006) for a more detailed discussion).

4 Physical 'Discipline'—A Human Rights Violation and a Disquieting Public Health Concern

Children continue to be the only people who may be lawfully assaulted in the context of 'discipline', violating their human rights. It is now 30 years since the CRC came into force and over 12 years since the CRC Committee, composed of independent experts who monitor its implementation, were unequivocal in their affirmation of the child's right to protection from any degree of corporal or other cruel or degrading punishment. More recently in 2015, the United Nations General Assembly adopted the Sustainable Development Goals, setting priorities for the next 15 years (United Nations, 2015). Target 16.2 includes ending "all forms of violence against and torture of children," and indicator 16.2.1 measures the "proportion of children aged 1–17 years who experienced any physical punishment and/or psychological aggression by caregivers in the past month". The 2017 Report of the UN Secretary General on Goal 16 states that "[v]arious forms of violence against children persist, including discipline that relies on physical punishment and psychological aggression. In 76 countries (most are developing countries) with available data from 2005 to 2016, about 8 in 10 children from 1 to 14 years of age were subjected to some form of psychological aggression and/or physical punishment on a regular basis" (UN Secretary General, 2017). Clearly, human rights arguments alone have not persuaded many country's governments to responsibly fulfil their obligations under the CRC.

However, some progress, especially in the last 12 years, deserves recognition. Prior to 2006, only 16 countries had banned all corporal punishment. Three Scandinavian countries led the way, Sweden (1979), Finland (1983), and Norway (1987). Then followed mainly European countries—Austria (1989); Cyprus (1994); Denmark (1997); Latvia (1998); Croatia (1999); Germany, Bulgaria, and Israel (2000); Turkmenistan (2002); Iceland (2003); Romania and Ukraine (2004); and Hungary (2005). Post 2006, progress hastened with 37 countries taking this progressive step. Many countries are in Africa and Central/South America as well as Europe. As previously mentioned, there are only two English-speaking countries in this group. The most recent country to ban corporal punishment in 2017 is Lithuania preceded by Mongolia, Montenegro, Paraguay, and Slovenia in 2016; Benin, Ireland, and Peru in 2015; Andorra, Argentina, Bolivia, Brazil, Estonia, Malta, Nicaragua, and San Marino in 2014; Cabo Verde, Honduras, and TFYR Macedonia in 2013; South Sudan followed by Albania, the Republic of Congo, Kenya, Poland, and Tunisia in 2011; Costa Rica, Liechtenstein, Luxembourg, and the Republic of Moldova in 2008; the Netherlands, Portugal, Spain, Togo, Uruguay, and Venezuela in 2007; and Greece in 2006. Fortunately, for many children living in these countries, corporal punishment is no longer 'simply a fact of childhood' (McGillivray, 1997).

In 1981, a couple of years after Sweden codified children's right "to be treated with respect for their person and individuality and…not be subjected to physical discipline or other abusive behaviour" (Sweden: Children and Parents Code, 1949), Bean and Roberts, 1981 in a psychology lab at Idaho State University in the United States conducted a disciplinary time-out experiment. Twenty-four 'noncompliant preschool children' aged between 2 and 6 years old were subjected to "three experimental conditions: Parent Release, Child Release, or Control [and a] spanking procedure was used to inhibit premature escape from time-out for children in the Parent Release group". Through a one-way mirror, the 'experimenters' observed the children and their mothers. Mothers in the parent release group 'spanked' their child twice on the bottom when the child did not comply with her commands. Every child was spanked "at least once for premature escape from time out. The group mean number of spankings was 8.3…[s]panking [they stated] has been demonstrated to suppress noncompliance" (Bean & Roberts, 1981). In a similar experiment in 1983, children's compliance was forced after an average of eight spankings, yet the researchers concluded that there was "no support for the necessity of the physical punishment" (Day & Roberts, 1983). The contrast in attitudes to children in Sweden and the United States at that time is stark. Approaching 40 years later, it is hard to imagine such an abhorrent human experiment, and one can quite confidently assert that, today, university ethics committees in the English-speaking world at least would not allow such research to take place. The irony, however, is that the mothers' willingness to cause their children pain in these experiments as a means to force compliance is still considered by many in the English-speaking world as acceptable and even sometimes necessary. In many countries including Australia, assaults, colloquially described and minimised as 'smacking' and 'spanking', are normalised responses, especially to small, impressionable children. It is unlikely that the bodies of the children in the 'experiment' would have been bruised, and any red marks would have been transitory, so parental discipline of this nature would also most likely be of minimal if any concern to child protection services. Moreover, it would probably fall under the 'di minimis' principle in law. In countries that condone and normalise corporal punishment, the likelihood that parents who resort to this type of 'discipline' will receive nonstigmatising constructive support and guidance in their parenting strategies is also minimal, unless there is a determined effort to put an end to this breach of human rights.

It has long been recognised that, in some families, mild corporal punishment can quickly and unintentionally escalate, resulting in severe and even fatal abuse. As Gil observed over 40 years ago,

> *Whenever corporal punishment in child rearing is sanctioned, and even subtly encouraged by a society, incidents of serious physical abuse and injury are bound to happen, either as a result of deliberate, systematic, and conscious action on the part of perpetrators, or under conditions of loss of self-control. In either case, but especially in the latter, physical attacks on children tend to relieve [perpetrator's] tensions and frustrations. Clearly, then, these attacks are carried out to meet emotional needs...rather than educational needs of the victims, as is often claimed by advocates of corporal punishment. (Gil, 1975)*

Recent research confirms Gil's observations (Gershoff, 2002; Lee, Grogan-Kaylor, & Berger, 2014; Zolotar et al., 2014). In a study of child homicide between 1991 and 2005 in the state of New South Wales Australia, (Nielssen et al., 2009) concluded that the prohibition of corporal punishment, as a way of reducing child abuse, would save children's lives. Similarly, Crandall, Chiu and Sheehan (2006), in their US research into injury in the first year of a child's life, conclude that "with focused education and prevention efforts, including... attitudes towards physical discipline, we may decrease the burden of infant injury in this vulnerable population".

Of perhaps greater concern, given the large numbers of children who are regularly subjected to corporal punishment, is the increasing research findings about the short- and long-term effects of even mild corporal punishment on children and the future adults that they will become (Gershoff & Grogan-Kaylor, 2016). In 2016, Gershoff and Grokan-

Kaylor published a meta-analysis of 75 studies focusing on the effects of corporal punishment (Gershoff & Grogan-Kaylor, 2016). Significantly, they note that they did not find a major difference in outcomes whether children experienced common 'spanking' (defined as "hitting a child on their buttocks or extremities with an open hand") or 'physical abuse'. They found that 13 detrimental child outcomes, including aggression and antisocial behaviour, increase in internalising behaviours (e.g. fearfulness and social withdrawal) and externalising behaviours (e.g. bullying and negative disruption), low moral internalisation, mental health problems, alcohol and substance abuse, low self-esteem, impaired cognitive ability, decreased self-regulation, poor parent–child relationships, and enhanced risk of physical injury and severe abuse. Beyond childhood, particularly after a history of regular spankings, they found that corporal punishment was associated with mental health issues in adulthood, antisocial behaviours, and the intergenerational transmission of support for parents' use of corporal punishment as discipline. Moreover, they confirmed previous findings that 'milder and more severe physical punishment is linked and that the former may increase the risk that children will be physically abused'. Gershoff has also proposed that "parents' physical punishment of children [could] be considered a source of toxic stress that affects brain development"—"it is painful and distressing to the child; and the parent is not available as a source of comfort, in large part because the parent is the source of stress itself" (Gershoff, 2016). She highlights the need for prospective research to strengthen existing evidence that supports her claim.

Adding further weight to concerns about its undesirable impact, Durrant and Ensom (2017) reflected on what has been learnt form 25 years of corporal punishment research. They concluded that corporal punishment is not useful in child rearing, and it only jeopardises children's optimal development. They recommended 'alternative and positive approaches to discipline' (discussed further below).

5 Corporal Punishment From the Child's Perspective

Article 12(1) of the CRC states that "States Parties shall assure to the child who is capable of forming his or her own views the right to express those views freely in all matters affecting the child, the views of the child being given due weight in accordance with the [child's] age and maturity". As Freeman (1996) contends, Article 12 "recognises the child as a full human being with integrity and personality and the ability to participate freely in society". In countries where parents essentially maintain both ownership of children and an entitlement to use physical force as a parenting strategy, it follows that children's perspectives do not often form the basis of arguments for or against corporal punishment in childhood.

Increasingly, however, when given the opportunity, children as young as four have shared their experiences of corporal punishment and insightfully reflected on its nature, effects, and acceptability. Their recent lived experience provides the missing dimension, given much retrospective research, and research that seeks only adults' perspectives on this issue. When asked why children do not smack adults, a 6-year-old child in Willow and Hyder's (1998) research conducted 20 years ago in the United Kingdom asserted that "no one should smack anyone", and when asked why adults do not smack each other, a 5-year-old child insightfully answered, "because they must respect each other cos if they smacked each other they won't like each other". Seven-year-olds, in this UK research, said a smack is "painful, and it sets a wrong example," and "you feel like you don't like your parents any more".

Children around the world have described 'normal' punishment in varying ways. It could mean being hit with a hand on the leg, beaten with implements, pinched, having your head pushed against a wall, or forced to kneel on sharp objects. Yet despite differences, recurrent themes appear in children's accounts of their thoughts, feelings, and experiences. Many children have "described angry, uncontrolled [parents' and teachers'] responses that spiral and become more painful…[children have talked about feeling] heartbroken, resentful, emotionally torn, humiliated and worthless…[They have] explained how being hit diminishes their confidence, enhances their insecurity and reduces their potential…[They have] talked about learning that violence is a means to settle disputes but they know that there are better ways and that adults must decide to adopt them if hitting children is to stop…[They have] described feeling unloved, sad, betrayed and bewildered when deliberately hurt by parents who have loved and cared for them…[and they have] observed that disempowering rather than constructive outcomes result from physical chastisement" (Saunders, 2015).

In my 2005 research (Saunders, 2005; Saunders & Goddard, 2010) in Victoria, Australia, children between the ages of 8 and 17 years old shared their perceptions of their rights, their position in society vis-à-vis adults, and their diminished sense of self in contexts in which children were physically punished. The following quotes provide some insight into these children's responses:

> *[There's] the control…over you…There is…helplessness…with being a child…I don't think it's appropriate for [my parents] to physically punish me any more…'cause I think I am becoming a bit of a person, not a child anymore. (13yrs)*
>
> *…if adults [have] physical contact with someone, like punching 'em, it's against the law… they could go to jail, they could be charged with assault. And that's exact same for smacking. But…if you're a kid, and it's in the house, it's okay because they're your kids. If you are a kid, it doesn't really matter…You barely have any say. (9yrs)*
>
> *I'd like to say to…the government, to the parents, this is not the way to discipline, by hitting a child. Why? Think about it for a minute, any hitting, you can see a bruise but you can't see how it mentally affects someone and they'll carry that right through their childhood, right through their adulthood (12yrs)*

There needs to be more opportunities for the voices of both very young and older children to be heard. Their insights and views deserve greater respect, recognition, and 'due weight' in any informed discussion about physical 'discipline', child abuse, and children's rights.

6 Some Obstacles and Pathways to Recognition of Children's Rights and to Legislative Reform

Changes in people's attitudes and behaviours may be reflected in, or prompted by, law reform. Children's voices may be powerful in persuading adults to see corporal punishment from the child's perspective, if only they are willing to listen. Language also plays a significant role in both perpetuating and questioning the legitimacy of corporal punishment. A multifaceted approach is necessary to "create a new culture of childhood, one in which children are identified as persons and right holders" (Freeman, 1999). Indeed, Freeman declared 30 years ago that "[i]f we are to assert the dignity of all persons, to affirm equal respect for all persons, we must as a necessary precondition protect the bodily integrity of all. If we are concerned to eliminate the evil of child abuse, we must ultimately come to accept that corporal punishment of children is child abuse" (Freeman, 1988).

6.1 Distinguishing Corporal Punishment of Children From Child Abuse

Attempts to distinguish corporal punishment of children from child abuse are fraught with difficulties. Such distinctions must, of necessity, deny the child's rights to dignity and to protection from physical and emotional harm, as increasing research evidence suggests. Gershoff, Lee, and Durrant (2017) similarly contend that "the dichotomy between physical punishment and physical abuse is a false one that legitimises violence against children". It is notable that 11–17-year-olds in Mason and Falloon's (1999) research poignantly "described abusive behaviour as that perpetuated by persons who use power to control those they consider as lesser". They perceived abuse as "feeling let down by those with whom they are in an emotional relationship [and] discounted because of their age". Adults, they said, are "not allowed to smack anyone else but children," and a child "can't do anything back". They saw this context as integral to child abuse.

6.2 Language and Tradition

In the English-speaking world, words such as 'spanking' and 'smacking' effectively mask and minimise the habitual, and often ill-considered, use of various means of physically punishing children. The commonly expressed 'loving smack' is an oxymoron (Freeman, 1999; Freeman & Saunders, 2014). These two words serve to confuse an unnecessary, negative, hurtful act with a positive, caring motivation. Even the word 'discipline', literally meaning to constructively teach, has arguably become distorted in contexts that condone corporal punishment as discipline, and in which children are commonly hit to teach them, for example, not to hit others (for further discussion, see Durrant & Stewart-Tufescu, 2017; Saunders, 2017). Many parents corporally punish their children because that is what happened to them as a child. They believe that it did not do them any harm. They do not stop using it, even when they see its immediate physical and emotional impact on their children, prompting them to regret their actions. Of particular concern, tiredness, stress, anger, and loss of control often override consideration of better alternatives (Saunders, 2005; Saunders & Goddard, 2010).

Ngugi wa Thiong'o (1984) well recognises the power of words, observing that: "language is a carrier of a people's culture. Culture is a carrier of a people's values. Values are a carrier of a people's outlook or consciousness and sense of identity...languages [impose] the culture, values and consciousness carried by them". Changes in language have been powerful in uplifting the status of other disempowered groups in society, including women, people whose skin is not white, and people with a disability. Many disparaging or demeaning words have appropriately disappeared from customary communication. In contrast, children may be objectified through language – referred to as 'it'. They may be belittled in adultist insults, such as 'behaving like a child', 'being childish', and 'needing to grow up', and at adults' whims, they may ambiguously be characterised as 'painful little devils' or 'sweet little angels' (see Saunders, 2017; Saunders & Goddard, 2001). Children are often referred to as 'kids'. While this can be a term of endearment, it is also often preceded with words such as 'just' or used in a condescending manner. Critical, ageist attitudes are apparent in language used to refer to both the very young and the very old. 'Living a second childhood', for example is not seen to be a positive component of ageing. If children are to be respected, then the language used to refer to them must also be respectful. It should acknowledge their importance, their competence, and their humanity. At the same time, words used to describe violent and hurtful actions directed at them should not serve to deceive or to minimise children's experiences.

6.3 Recognition of Parents and Their Important Role in Society

As noted at the beginning of this chapter, parents and other people acting in loco parentis are vested with an enormous responsibility to respond to children's needs so that they can develop to their full physical, emotional, and intellectual potential. To fulfil this challenging role, parents from all socio-economic and cultural backgrounds should be recognised for the important role that they play, and be provided with education and support that will enable them to better respond to their children and to meet their children's needs to the greatest possible extent. Most parents want to be the best parents that they possibly can be.

6.4 The Importance of Parenting Programs and Supports, and Universal Education

Gershoff et al. (2017) have proposed strategies targeted at three levels of intervention to promote positive discipline and to dissuade parents from using corporal punishment. They discuss 'indicated intervention programs' that are targeted at parents who have maltreated their children or are considered likely to do so; 'selective prevention programs' that seek to educate all parents, including parents-to-be, and also professionals whose work brings them into contact with parents and their children; and 'universal prevention programs' that target all adults and children. They consider 20 existing programs and approaches in relation to their effectiveness in reducing corporal punishment and, importantly, changing 'the attitudes that maintain its legitimacy'. The approaches, including home visitation programs, group-based programs, media-based interventions, the engagement of medical professionals who work with families, and public education campaigns, all achieve some degree of success. Notably, these authors emphasise the significant role of law in articulating a society's morals and standards of behaviour. They note that, based on longitudinal pre- and post-ban studies of the effect of a corporal punishment ban on changing attitudes that support its use, there is increasing confidence in the positive impact of law reform.

A widely implemented strategy called 'Positive Discipline in Everyday Parenting' (PDEP) is a universal violence prevention program that was recently evaluated in 13 countries, divided according to their level of development—high, medium, or low (Durrant et al., 2017). This program aims to motivate parents to think about their long-term goals for their children rather than children's immediate obedience; enhancing parents' appreciation of the need to both warmly nurture their children while also providing a structure for learning; increasing parents' knowledge of normal childhood behaviours and development; and, finally, the integration of this learning as a means to approach parenting with constructive problem-solving in mind, rather than a punitive approach. Encouragingly, only one in five parents in each category were not convinced that PDEP would assist them to less often use corporal punishment.

7 Conclusion

Hitting and hurting children is wrong, "it is wrong to hit children as it is wrong to hit adults" (Freeman, 1999). Children are entitled to live in environments that nurture and promote their optimal development, whenever this is possible. Gershoff (2013) has contended that "we now know enough to stop hitting our children". The research evidence conclusively demonstrates that even a 'loving smack' does not contribute to children's well-being nor is it associated with improved child behaviour (Gershoff & Grogan-Kaylor, 2016). If we cherish our children and care about the society in which they will live in the future, why would we resort to corporal punishment knowing the risks to children's health and happiness both now and in the future? From a public health perspective, and on moral and human rights grounds, children's childhoods should be free from violence. As the 'primordial violence' (Straus, Douglas, & Medeiros, 2014) so embedded in the lives of too many children around the world, all manner of corporal punishment should become a regretted remnant of an unenlightened past.

8 Chapter Review Questions

1. What is the term for discrimination against children?
2. According to a 2014 UNICEF report, what percentage of the world's children are corporally punished by their parents?
3. In what year did New Zealand ban corporal punishment, and why is this particularly significant?
4. In 2018, how many countries had banned corporal punishment in all settings?
5. Which was the first country to ban corporal punishment in all settings, and in what year?
6. Which international convention came into being to safeguard the human rights of children, and in what year?
7. Which principle in law guards against the unnecessary criminalisation of parents?
8. Gershoff and Grokan-Kaylor's meta-analysis of 75 studies that focused upon the effects of corporal punishment found many detrimental outcomes—how many did they record in their article?
9. Which article in the UNCRC (1989) supports children's right to comment on issues that affect them?
10. What role do euphemisms, such as 'smacking' and 'spanking', play in perpetuating the legitimacy of corporal punishment as discipline?
11. Drawing on both increasing research evidence and international laws, the corporal punishment of children is concerning from at least two perspectives—what are these perspectives?

References

Alderson, P. (1992). The rights of children and young people. In A. Coote (Ed.), *The welfare of citizens: Developing new social rights* (pp. 153–180). London: Rivers Oram Press.

Bean, A. W., & Roberts, A. R. (1981). The effect of time-out release contingencies on changes in child non-compliance. *Journal of Abnormal Child Psychology*, *9*(1), 95–105.

Bitensky, S. (2006). *Corporal punishment of children: A human rights violation*. Ardsley: Transnational Publishers, Inc.

Brehm, H. N., & Boyle, E. H. (2018). The global adoption of National Policies Protecting Children from violent discipline in schools and homes, 1950-2011. *Law and Society Review*, *52*(1), 206–233.

Cappa, C., et al. (2014). *Hidden in plain sight: A statistical analysis of violence against children*. New York: UNICEF.

Children First Act. (2015). https://www.dcya.gov.ie/viewdoc.asp?fn=%2Fdocuments%2FChildren_First%2FChildrenFirstLegislation.htm.

Committee on the Rights of the Child. (2006). *General Comment No. 8 (2006): The right of the child to protection from corporal punishment and other cruel or degrading forms of punishment (articles 19, 28(2) and 37, inter alia)*.

Committee on the Rights of the Child. (2011). *General Comment No. 13 Article 19: The right of the child to freedom from all forms of violence, 56th Session 17 February 2011*. Available at:http://www.crin.org/docs/CRC.C.GC.13_en_AUV-1.pdf.

Crandall, M., Chiu, M., & Sheehan, M. D. (2006). Injury in the first year of life: Risk factors and solutions for high-risk families. *Journal of Surgical Research*, *133*, 7–10.

Day, D. E., & Roberts, M. W. (1983). An analysis of the physical punishment component of a parent training program. *Journal of Abnormal Child Psychology*, *11*(1), 141–152.

Declaration on the Rights of the Child. (1959). Available from: https://www.unicef.org/malaysia/1959-Declaration-of-the-Rights-of-the-Child.pdf.

Durrant, J., & Ensom, R. (2017). Twenty-five years of physical punishment research: What have we learned? *Journal of the Korean Academy of Child & Adolescent Psychiatry*, *28*(1), 20–24.

Durrant, J. E., & Stewart-Tufescu, A. (2017). What is "discipline" in the age of children's rights? *The International Journal of Children's Rights*, *25*(2), 359–379.

Durrant, J. E., et al. (2017). Parents' views of the relevance of a violence prevention program in high, medium, and low human development contexts. *International Journal of Behavioral Development*, *41*(4), 523–531.

Freeman, M. (1988). Time to stop hitting our children. *Childright*, *51*, 5–8.

Freeman, M. (1996). Children's education: A test case for best interests and autonomy. In R. Davie & D. Galloway (Eds.), *Listening to children in education*. London: David Fulton.

Freeman, M. (1999). Children are unbeatable. *Children & Society*, *13*, 130–141.

Freeman, M. (2010). The human rights of children. *Current Legal Problems*, *63*, 1–44.

Freeman, M., & Saunders, B. J. (2014). Can we conquer child abuse if we don't outlaw physical chastisement of children? *International Journal of Children's Rights*, *22*, 681–709.

Geneva Declaration on the Rights of the Child. (1924). Available from: http://www.un-documents.net/gdrc1924.htm.

Gershoff, E. (2002). Corporal punishment by parents and associated child behaviors and experience: A meta-analytic and theoretical review. *Psychological Bulletin*, *128*(4), 539–579.

Gershoff, E. (2013). Spanking and child development: We know enough now to stop hitting our children. *Child Development Perspectives*, *7*(3), 133–137.

Gershoff, E. (2016). Should parents' physical punishment of children be considered a source of toxic stress that affects brain development? *Family Relations*, *65*, 151–162.

Gershoff, E. T., & Grogan-Kaylor, A. (2016). Spanking and child outcomes: Old controversies and new meta-analyses. *Journal of Family Psychology*, *30*(4), 453–469.

Gershoff, E. T., Lee, S. L., & Durrant, J. E. (2017). Promising intervention strategies to reduce parents' use of physical punishment. *Child Abuse & Neglect*, *71*, 9–23.

Gil, D. (1975). Unraveling child abuse. *American Journal of Orthopsychiatry*, *45*(3), 346–356.

Global Initiative. (2018). *End corporal punishment of children*. Available from:http://endcorporalpunishment.org/.

Global Initiative to End All Corporal Punishment of Children & Save the Children Sweden. (2017). *Ending legalised violence against children: Global progress to December 2017*. London: Global Initiative to End All Corporal Punishment of Children.

Hengst, H. (2003). The role of the media and commercial culture in children's experiencing of collective identities. In B. Mayall & H. Zeiher (Eds.), *Children in generational perspective* (pp. 111–132). London: Institute of London.

Jenks, C. (1996). *Childhood*. London: Routledge.

Lancy, D. (2015). *The anthropology of childhood: Cherubs, chattel, changelings* (2nd ed.). Cambridge, United Kingdom: Cambridge University Press.

Lancy, D. F. (2017). *Raising children: Surprising insights from other cultures*. Cambridge: Cambridge University Press.

Lansdown, G. (1995). In C. Cloke & M. Davies (Eds.), *Children's rights to participation and protection: A critique, in participation and empowerment in child protection* (pp. 19–38). London: Pitman Publishing.

Lee, N. (2001). *Childhood and society: Growing up in an age of uncertainty*. Buckingham: Open University Press.

Lee, S. J., Grogan-Kaylor, A., & Berger, L. M. (2014). Parental spanking of 1-year-old children and subsequent child protection services involvement. *Child Abuse & Neglect*, *38*, 875–883.

Mason, J., & Falloon, M. (1999). A children's perspective on child abuse. *Children Australia*, *24*(3), 9–13.

McGillivray, A. (1997). He'll learn it on his body': disciplining childhood in Canadian law. *International Journal of Children's Rights*, *5*, 193–242.

Menkel-Meadow, C. (1987). Excluded voices: New voices in the legal profession making new voices in the law. *University of Miami Law Review*, *42*(29), 29–53.

New Zealand Police. (2013). *11th review of the Crimes (Substituted Section 59) Amendment Act 2007*.

Ngugi wa Thiong'o. (1984). The tension between national and imperialist china. *World Literature Written in English, 24*, 3–9.

Nielssen, O. B., et al. (2009). Child homicide in New South Wales from 1991 to 2005. *Medical Journal of Australia, 190*(1), 7–11.

Postman, N. (1982). *The disappearance of childhood.* New York: Delacorte Press.

Saunders, B. J. (2005). *Because there's a better way than hurting someone: An exploratory study of the nature, effects and persistence of 'physical punishment' in childhood, in Faculty of Arts.* Melbourne, Victoria, Australia: Monash University.

Saunders, B. J. (2013). Ending the physical punishment of children in the English-speaking world: The impact of language, tradition and law. *The International Journal of Children's Rights, 21*, 278–304.

Saunders, B. J. (2015). Ending corporal punishment in childhood: Advancing children's rights to dignity and respectful treatment. In A. Diduck, N. Peleg, & H. Reece (Eds.), *Law in society: Reflections on children, family, culture and philosophy: Essays in honour of Michael Freeman* (pp. 243–271). Leiden, the Netherlands: Brill|Nijoff.

Saunders, B. J. (2017). Words matter: Textual abuse of childhood in the English-speaking world, and the role of language in the continuing denial of children's rights. *International Journal of Children's Rights, 25*(2), 519–536.

Saunders, B. J., & Goddard, C. (2001). The textual abuse of childhood in the English-speaking world: The contribution of language to the denial of children's rights. *Childhood, 8*(4), 443–462.

Saunders, B. J., & Goddard, C. (2010). *Physical punishment in childhood: The rights of the child.* Chichester: John Wiley & Sons.

Straus, M. A., Douglas, E. M., & Medeiros, R. A. (2014). *The primordial violence: Spanking children, psychological development, violence, and crime.* New York: Routledge/Taylor & Francis Group.

Sweden: Children and Parents Code, 1949, Chapter 6, Section 1

The Crimes (Substituted Section 59) Amendment Act. (2007). http://www.legislation.govt.nz/act/public/2007/0018/latest/DLM407664.html.

UN Secretary General. (2017). *Progress towards the sustainable development goals.* Geneva: United Nations.Available from: http://www.un.org/ga/search/view_doc.asp?symbol=E/2017/66&Lang=E.

United Nations. (2015). *Sustainable development goals* Available from:https://sustainabledevelopment.un.org/?menu=1300.

United Nations Convention on the Rights of the Child. (1989). Available from: http://www.ohchr.org/EN/ProfessionalInterest/Pages/CRC.aspx.

Uprichard, E. (2008). Children as 'being and becomings': Children, childhood and temporality. *Children & Society, 22*, 303–313.

Waksler, F. (Ed.), (1991). *Studying the social worlds of children: Sociological readings.* London: Falmer Press.

Willow, C., & Hyder, T. (1998). *It hurts you inside: Children talking about smacking.* London: National Children's Bureau Enterprises.

Young-Bruehl, E. (2012). *Childism: Confronting prejudice against children.* New Haven and London: Yale University Press.

Zolotar, A., et al. (2014). Speak softly—and forget the stick: Corporal punishment and child physical abuse. *American Journal of Preventive Medicine, 35*, 364–369.

CHAPTER 13

Understanding the Nature and Dimensions of Child Sexual Abuse to Inform Its Prevention

Nadine McKillop
USC Law School, Faculty of Arts, Business and Law, USC Australia, Sippy Downs, QLD, Australia

Child sexual abuse (CSA) is a complex, multifaceted social phenomenon. The causes, nature, and dimensions of CSA are heterogeneous—they vary across individuals, circumstances, and over time. For example, the motivations, behaviours, and processes associated with CSA may look very different for someone who is contemplating (or "at risk of") abusing, than for someone who has just begun abusing, and for someone who has become persistent in their offending. Additionally, the dynamics of CSA vary across the different social spheres in which it occurs: domestic, organisational, public, and 'virtual' environments. This heterogeneity makes the task of preventing CSA difficult and, at times, overwhelming. The best way forward, now advocated by many in the field, is to create a comprehensive suite of prevention strategies that match these complexities. However, this can only be achieved when there is an accurate understanding of the nature and dimensions (e.g. the who, what, where, when, and how) of CSA, underpinned by a strong theoretical and empirical base, that helps to explain 'why' it occurs. Knowing these dimensions helps to delineate key targets for prevention to create a comprehensive, coordinated response to CSA.

In this chapter, I synthesise current developments in CSA prevention, framed within the public health approach to the problem. I begin by introducing the public health prevention model and demonstrating how it can be applied to inform and enhance CSA prevention efforts. Drawing on Bronfenbrenner's (1979) socio-ecological model and person-situation perspectives (Mischel, 1968; Wortley, 2008), key individual, ecological, and situational targets for prevention are then identified. Finally, I introduce Smallbone and Rayment-McHugh's (2017) prevention matrix designed specifically for sexual violence prevention and showcase some of the promising strategies proposed in this matrix. Smallbone, Marshall, and Wortley (2008, see also Smallbone & Rayment-McHugh, 2017) prevention frameworks have gained international attention because they conceptualise CSA as an interaction between individual-level vulnerabilities for offending and victimisation and the social and

Child Abuse and Neglect. https://doi.org/10.1016/B978-0-12-815344-4.00013-1

environmental conditions in which it occurs. In this way, prevention efforts extend beyond traditional 'individual-focused' approaches to the contexts and situations in which CSA incidents manifest.

Like them, I advocate for evidence-informed, tailored prevention approaches that address the unique dimensions of CSA, across the different settings in which it occurs. Aligned with the public health approach, the strategies discussed in this chapter are aimed at preventing these abuses from occurring in the first place and creating conditions conducive to early disclosure and that promote timely and appropriate responses and redress when CSA does occur. Before considering these strategies, however, it is necessary to demonstrate how the public health prevention model applies to CSA prevention.

1 The Public Health Prevention Model

The public health prevention model originated from the field of medicine (Dahlberg & Krug, 2002). Defining the nature and dimensions (e.g. who, what, where, when, and how) of a problem is at the core of this approach. From these foundations, prevention strategies are designed to address identified target areas; their effectiveness is then evaluated; and where positive effects are shown, these strategies are adopted more widely to help combat the problem (Dahlberg & Krug, 2002). A key strength of this model is its multifaceted approach to understanding and preventing the problem at an individual level and across the multiple (i.e. relationship, community, and societal) systems in which it occurs. It is only in the last two decades however that the utility of this multifaceted approach for preventing interpersonal (including sexual) violence has been formally recognised (Krug, Dahlberg, Mercy, Zwi, & Lozano, 2002).

1.1 Levels of Prevention

As shown in Fig. 1, under the public health prevention model, there are three levels of prevention. At the *primary* level, initiatives are 'universal'; they are directed indiscriminately at the general population with the aim of preventing illness or disease occurring in the first place (Dahlberg & Krug, 2002). Whole-of-community initiatives are intended to improve awareness and knowledge of the issue at hand and encourage proactive strategies to prevent its occurrence. They aim to change widespread beliefs and culture that filter down to other important systems (e.g. schools, families, and individuals) to promote well-being and resilience. It is through these awareness and education campaigns that we begin to see a reduction in new cases of the problem occurring in the community. For example, over the past two or so decades, there has been a dedicated approach to reducing cigarette smoking. Many of these campaigns have been implemented at the primary level with the aim of changing the prevailing social culture and acceptance of cigarette smoking (e.g. mass-media antismoking advertising and health risk education, school-based curricula, and increased consumer tax;

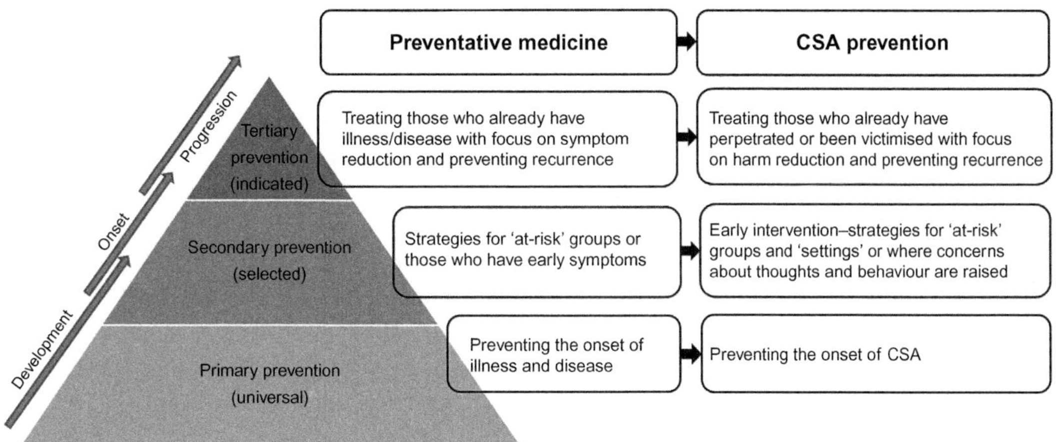

Fig. 1
Public health prevention approach to CSA.

Pierce, White, & Emery, 2012). At the same time, a decline in the prevalence of cigarette smoking has been observed in Australia and other Western countries (Greenhalgh, Bayly, & Winstanley, 2017; Pierce et al., 2012). In Australia, the prevalence of cigarette smoking has reduced to 14.3%. This effect is particularly evident among younger adults (18–44 years), 60% of whom have never smoked (Australian Bureau of Statistics, 2017).

At the *secondary* prevention level, the focus of initiatives is more 'selected'. Prevention approaches are directed at specific groups—those most at risk of becoming ill or those with early symptoms of disease—rather than universally applied. One example of this is Type 2 diabetes. Up to 58% of Type 2 diabetes can be prevented through healthy diet and weight and moderate physical activity (Diabetes Australia, 2018). There are also well-established risk factors associated with Type 2 diabetes such as family history of the disease (Molyneaux, Constantino, & Yue, 2004). Thus, identifying those with a family history of diabetes, monitoring blood sugar levels and diet, telephone support, and dedicated lifestyle programs are key ways to help reduce the occurrence of Type 2 diabetes among these 'at risk' individuals.

At the *tertiary* prevention level, the focus is on working with 'indicated' cases; those already suffering from illness or disease, with a focus on symptom reduction and preventing recurrence (Dahlberg & Krug, 2002). Using the two previous health issues discussed, treating symptoms of emphysema and throat or lung cancer are examples for cigarette smoking; for Type 2 diabetes, insulin and other medications are used to treat and control its progression.

We can approach CSA prevention in much the same way as cigarette smoking or diabetes. As shown in Fig. 1, locating CSA prevention within the public health prevention model also allows us to contemplate prevention strategies both before and after CSA occurs. This is important because motivations, behaviours, and processes of CSA are likely to change across the criminal career. In the same way that other experiences and consequences shape behaviour, so too does offending shape future offending. As such, what might be required to prevent a potential (has not yet begun abusing) or novice (has just begun abusing) offender from abusing may be very different to what is required to prevent reoffending by a persistent offender (Smallbone & McKillop, 2015).

From a public health perspective then, prevention strategies at the *primary* level are focused on universal promotion of 'safe, healthy environments and behaviours' to prevent CSA from occurring in the first place (Lyles, Cohen & Brown, 2009, p. 1). At a *secondary* level, prevention strategies are more selected; they address risk factors, known to increase vulnerability for perpetration or victimisation, to build a layer of resilience for those 'individuals' or 'contexts' most at risk, either before or in the very early stages of CSA. In those instances when CSA does occur, *tertiary*-level initiatives aim to reduce harms associated with CSA and prevent sexual reoffending or revictimisation. Whilst these levels of prevention specify time points for intervention, knowing the nature and dimensions of CSA provides direction on what prevention initiatives should target.

1.2 Targets for Prevention

A key feature of the public health approach is that it locates targets for prevention within the individual and the multiple systems in which they live and interact (Krug et al., 2002). This socioecological approach acknowledges the dynamic and reciprocal influences that these systems have on shaping behaviour, as illustrated in Fig. 2 (Bronfenbrenner, 1979; Dahlberg & Krug, 2002). At its most simple, the model has four systems, *individual*, *relationship*, *community*, and *society*, that link an individual's growth and behaviour to the ecological and situational influences in which their development occurs (Bronfenbrenner, 1979). Approaching CSA prevention from this perspective then allows us to identify and implement interventions across multiple systems whilst at the same time forestalling its development, onset, or progression. Over time, this multipronged approach should produce comprehensive and sustained prevention effects, compared with any single intervention alone (Dahlberg & Krug, 2002). For the purposes of this chapter, these systems are grouped into individual and ecological (relationship, community, and societal) factors. Additionally, situational factors are included within the examination of these systems.

1.2.1 Individual factors

At the *individual* level, targets for prevention include biological and personal factors—those identified in one's history that increase vulnerability to perpetration and/or victimisation. For instance, official statistics overwhelmingly implicate males as the main perpetrators of CSA (e.g. McCloskey & Raphael, 2005). The onset of CSA follows a bimodal pattern, peaking once in adolescence and again in middle adulthood (Hanson, 2002). In fact, youth

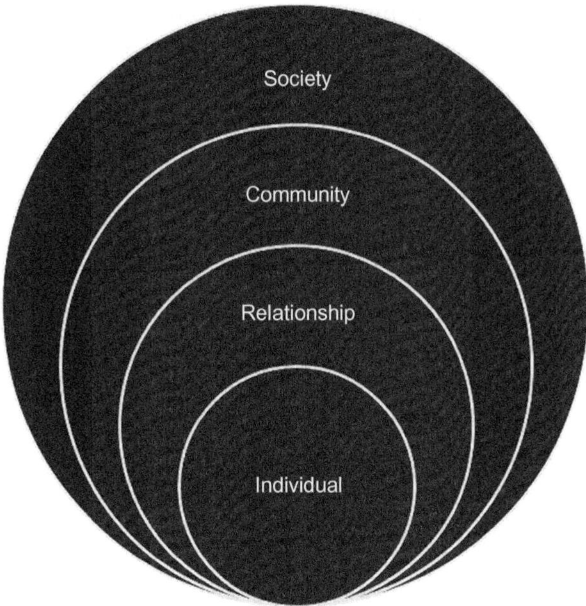

Fig. 2
The socio-ecological model (Bronfenbrenner, 1979).

are responsible for around 35%–50% CSA offences (Bourke & Donohue, 1996; Finkelhor, Ormrod, & Chaffin, 2009). Adolescents and adults tend to have very low sexual recidivism rates, typically engaging in nonsexual offending both before and after perpetrating CSA (Hanson & Bussière, 1998; Nisbet, Wilson, & Smallbone, 2004). However, among the few most persistent offenders, their sexual offending tends to originate in adolescence (see McKillop, Brown, Smallbone, & Pritchard, 2015).

In terms of vulnerability, both male and female children are victimised. However, the rate of female victimisation is at least double than that of boys (Finkelhor & Dziuba-Letherman, 1994). Middle-childhood (average age 11 years old) is the most vulnerable period for CSA, although children as young as infants can be victimised and girls tend to be younger than boys when abused (Finkelhor & Dziuba-Leatherman, 1994; McKillop, Brown, Wortley, & Smallbone, 2015). For victims, short- and long-term effects of CSA are well documented (Paolucci, Genuis, & Violato, 2001) and can vary, with worse outcomes (e.g. PTSD, depression, alcoholism, and suicide) linked to the relationship to the abuser, duration of abuse, level of intrusive behaviour, and negative responses to disclosure (Hebert, Parent, Daignault, & Tourigny, 2006). Many CSA victims are also at higher risk of revictimisation across the life course (Classen, Gronskaya Palesh, & Aggarwal, 2006).

Other than gender, there are no defining biological or psychological features common to all CSA perpetrators; some may offend in the absence of any prescribed psychological disturbance, and others can exhibit dangerous psychopathic traits (Smallbone & Rayment-McHugh, 2017). The presence of sexual deviance including paedophilia as an explanation has been a key focus of research (Seto & Lalumiere, 2010). Those who meet criteria for paedophilia are likely to be more persistent in their offending (Seto, 2008), and sexual deviance is the single major risk factor for reoffending (Hanson & Bussière, 1998). However, this does not help to explain the manifestation of the CSA in the absence of these traits; although some adults report preoccupation about sexual thoughts of children in the lead up to abusing, many adult abusers report that these incidents arise often in the absence of prolonged or compulsive thoughts or fantasies (McKillop, Smallbone, Wortley, & Andjic, 2012). Attachment-related difficulties and associated social and intimacy deficits appear more commonly among those who perpetrate CSA, rather than inherently sexually deviant motivations, at least at onset (Marsa et al., 2004; McKillop et al., 2012). Other individual-level psychosocial vulnerabilities identified as potential precursors to perpetrating CSA include emotion regulation problems, feelings of loneliness, emotional neediness, and low self-confidence (Quadara, Nagy, Higgins, & Siegel, 2015).

When identifying these individual-level vulnerabilities, it becomes evident that they cannot be considered in isolation from the other socio-ecological systems in which they are formed. Even for victims, vulnerabilities lie more in their environment than in themselves. These systems include relationships, community, and society.

1.2.2 Ecological factors

At the *relationship* level targets for prevention are those within one's close social circle (immediate or extended family and peers). In terms of developmental precursors to CSA, self-reported histories of known CSA offenders highlight adverse childhood histories and difficulties with social relationships. Polyvictimisation (i.e. exposure to multiple types of maltreatment), for example, has been linked to later onset of CSA (Leach, Stewart, & Smallbone, 2015). Similarly, risks for CSA victimisation arise from environmental vulnerabilities such as abuse and neglect, unstable home environments, disrupted attachment, family discord, and parental mental health problems (including alcoholism; Alexander, 1992).

In terms of the onset of CSA, consideration should be given to relationships in the settings in which CSA occurs. The domestic setting is the most common place for contact CSA to occur (see Smallbone & McKillop, 2016; also, Colombino, Mercado, Levenson, & Jeglic, 2011). Typically, these CSA incidents arise out of already long-standing relationships between the child and perpetrator, including familial (e.g. biological or stepchild and sibling or grandchild) and nonfamilial (e.g. neighbour, family friend, and babysitter) relationships (McKillop, Rayment-McHugh, Smallbone, & Bromham, 2018), where familiarity, trust, and authority become key facilitators of CSA. This is similar for both youth- and adult-perpetrated CSA (McKillop et al., 2018); few CSA incidents are perpetrated by strangers.

Boys tend to be more at risk of CSA by a nonfamily member, outside the home; girls by a family member, within the home and over a longer duration (McKillop, 2012). CSA incidents tend to arise during the daily routines for the perpetrator and child and often perpetrated when others are present nearby (McKillop, Brown, Wortley, & Smallbone, 2015). Subtle grooming (attention giving and nonsexual touching) that progresses to more explicit sexual discussions and behaviour might, in part, explain length to abuse, although many perpetrators report abusing in the absence of any long-term sexual motivations or thoughts and only become aware of these feelings in the moments before CSA (McKillop et al., 2018). This likely becomes more conscious and deliberate as offending progresses. In terms of development and onset then, these findings point to the importance of involving families as key targets for CSA prevention.

Social settings outside the home (e.g. schools, workplaces, and neighbourhoods) are key targets at the *community* level. For our purposes, I focus on youth-serving organisations; 'virtual' settings; and, to a lesser extent, public settings that are vulnerable to CSA incidents. Youth-serving community organisations (e.g. schools, churches, residential institutions, out-of-home care, and sporting clubs) tend to be 'at risk' places for CSA, accounting for around 5%–10% of CSA (Shattuck, Finkelhor, Turner, & Hamby, 2016). They are particularly conducive to youth-perpetrated CSA (Finkelhor et al., 2009), but adults who have legitimate access to children through paid or volunteer employment also abuse. Some adult perpetrators may have deliberately sought employment specifically for this purpose, most abuse however tends to arise out of their day-to-day interactions and routines with children (Smallbone & McKillop, 2016).

The 'virtual' setting is now an integral part of social interaction and communication particularly for youth and, by its very nature, creates copious opportunities for online and offline grooming, sexual exploitation, and blackmail, by individuals known and unknown to the victim (Quadara et al., 2015). The relatively depersonalised nature of this setting makes it difficult to formally regulate both content and interactions. Its boundless nature makes it difficult to limit the extent of revictimisation, once exploitation occurs. Finally, the public setting tends to be associated more with less frequent, stranger-perpetrated offences. Within these settings, those children left 'unguarded' for long periods of time and who appear emotionally vulnerable may be at a somewhat increased risk of CSA in this setting (Gallagher, Bradford, & Pease, 2008).

At the *societal* level, the focus is on fostering a social climate that does not tolerate CSA and has a widespread structural influence that permeates down to community-level perceptions, influencing behaviour and responses at the relationship and individual system levels. This can have a profound influence on encouraging victims to disclose abuse, without fear of judgement, blame, or stigma. Thus, it is key target for universal prevention initiatives.

1.2.3 Situational factors

Finally, *situational* factors (those 'in the moment' influences) within abuse settings are regarded as having the most direct and powerful influence on immediate behaviour (Smallbone et al., 2008; see also Smallbone & Cale, 2015). Smallbone and colleagues suggest that situations not only provide opportunities for motivated offenders to perpetrate CSA but also can dynamically influence one's behaviour. In terms of providing opportunities to offend, CSA occurs when there is a convergence of a vulnerable child, in the presence of a motivated offender and in the absence of a capable guardian (or bystanders) who could prevent its occurrence (Cohen & Felson, 1979). In terms of the dynamic nature of situations, Wortley (2008) suggests that behaviour is highly situation-dependent, and situations can be powerful enough to lead some individuals to depart from their usual behaviour and in the absence of conscious motivations, by prompting, pressuring, permitting, or provoking a response. These are what Wortley (2008) terms situational precipitators and help explain the onset of CSA in the absence of any long-standing preconceived sexual motivations.

The bimodal pattern of CSA onset reinforces the likelihood that contextual or situational conditions influence CSA perpetration. Adult-onset offending, for example, often occurs at a time when offenders have assumed a caretaking role (e.g. father or stepfather) or are entrusted with quasi-parental responsibilities (e.g. as an uncle, teacher, or sporting coach). For adolescence-onset offending, often, the offender is also given some caretaking responsibilities (e.g. offender is an older cousin or sibling). These caretaking roles increase opportunities for enacting abusive behaviour and potentially expose individuals to specific situations that might trigger offending motivations (e.g. during close physical (nonsexual) contact with a child; Smallbone et al., 2008). Addressing these situational risks should therefore form part of any prevention plan.

By applying the public health prevention model, this section identified the three levels of prevention and personal (individual), socio-ecological (relationship, community, and society), and situational (contextual and immediate precipitating) factors that form targets for CSA prevention. With this knowledge, the focus now turns to preventing and responding to the problem. A sample of promising prevention activities and resources aimed at making places safer, alongside more traditional individual-level-focused activities, is discussed to demonstrate how they can work together to form part of a comprehensive approach to CSA prevention.

2 Preventing and Responding to the Problem

In this section, I introduce a sample of innovative CSA prevention approaches, drawn from Smallbone and Rayment-McHugh's (2017) prevention matrix. The aim of these approaches is to provide the best protection against the occurrence of CSA in the first place and to guide effective responses when it does occur.

Prevention matrices are not new to crime prevention. Drawing on routine activities theory (Cohen & Felson, 1979), van Dijk and de Waard (1991) proposed a two-dimensional typology for crime prevention. This focused on three key target groups (offender, victims, and situations), linked across the three levels of prevention, with the aims of:

(1) reducing the propensities to offend,
(2) diminishing vulnerability of the potential victim,
(3) strengthening the level of guardianship in the environment (p. 485).

This conceptualisation shifted the focus of prevention to the situation in which crime occurs, in addition to the individuals involved, forming a matrix of activities aimed at potential and actual offenders, potential and actual victims, and settings (i.e. situational crime prevention; van Dijk & de Waard, 1991). This prevention matrix was predominantly applied to street crimes and crime in public and organisational settings, such as pubs and clubs.

Drawing on Tonry and Farrington's (1995) work, Smallbone et al. (2008) first proposed a 12-point prevention model along the same lines as van Dijk and de Waard but focused for the first time on the perpetration of sexual crimes. Key targets for this model were the offender, victim, situation, and community across the three prevention levels. More recently, this was refined to 9-point matrix that combines the situation and community into *abuse settings*, mapped to the primary, secondary, and tertiary levels of prevention (Smallbone & Rayment-McHugh, 2017; see Table 1). As discussed in Smallbone and McKillop (2015), focusing on abuse settings shifts the focus from the complexities of individuals to risky places or contexts.

Table 1: CSA prevention matrix

Prevention Levels / Prevention Targets	Primary Prevention (Universal)	Secondary Prevention (Selected)	Tertiary Prevention (Indicated)
(Potential) offenders	· General deterrence (e.g. public awareness campaigns)	· Helplines · Sexual ethics programs	· Therapeutic and risk management responses
(Potential) victims	· Protective behaviour programs · Improving guardianship (e.g. responsible bystander training)	· Developmental prevention (e.g. home nursing visits)	· Ameliorating harms · Preventing revictimisation
(Potential) settings	· Designing 'child safe' settings · Community/parent education	· Situational interventions (and safety planning) in at-risk settings	· Situational risk management with known sexual offenders

Adapted with permission from Smallbone, S., & Rayment-McHugh, S. (2017). Sexual crimes. In. Sidebottom, A., & Tilley, N. (Eds.), *Handbook of crime prevention and community safety* (2nd ed.), UK: Routledge (Chapter 20).

In this regard, prevention activities and resources are aimed at making places safer, alongside more traditional individual-level-focused activities (e.g. reducing propensities to offend or vulnerabilities towards victimisation).

2.1 Primary Prevention

There is a lot scope for universal, societal-level prevention strategies to target *potential* victims, offenders, bystanders (families, peers, and communities), and settings. These strategies, which utilise organised communication strategies (e.g. social (and other) media campaigns and messaging), can have a profound and wide-reaching influence on public perception, knowledge, and awareness, at the community and societal level, as well as achieving widespread shifts in attitudes and beliefs (Kemshall & Moulden, 2017). These campaigns move the responsibility of prevention onto the shoulders of the community by promoting awareness and debunking myths, regarding the contexts and dynamics (the who, when, what, where, and how) of CSA.

These campaigns are particularly important for breaking the silence and secrecy surrounding CSA, which is the most fundamental enabler of CSA. Other public campaigns have effectively mobilised public attitudes and action towards a public agenda (e.g. White Ribbon and domestic violence) and show profound impacts on reporting, disclosures, and responses for victims. Similarly, recent campaigns stemming from the *Royal Commission into Institutional Responses to Child Sexual Abuse* have increased the profile of CSA within the community, giving recognition and voice to those who have been harmed and for changes to be made at the community-level to stop these abuses from occurring and reoccurring.

As highlighted by Levine and Dandamudi (2016), resources and efforts directed towards potential CSA perpetrators have been largely overlooked. However, these same public awareness and education campaigns can serve more generally as a deterrence strategy for potential offenders (especially those who have just begun contemplating such thoughts or novice offenders) by sending messages about the wrongful nature of such acts, community intolerance of such acts, and the significant penalties for engaging in CSA. It may also increase their perceptions of risk, in terms of children identifying and speaking up or others noticing grooming or inappropriate behaviours.

Another prevention target has been to educate children on how to protect themselves. Many universal, group protective behaviour programs are implemented in schools and aim to improve children's knowledge and recognition of potentially abusive situations, teach resistance behaviours, and encourage abuse disclosure (i.e. recognise, resist, and report; Wurtele & Kenny, 2010). Although evaluations of these school campaigns indicate success in terms of children's ability to acquire and retain relevant concepts and implementation of these strategies in simulated conditions, evidence is limited regarding impact on reducing actual victimisation (Finkelhor, 2009; Walsh, Zwi, Woolfenden, & Shlionsky, 2015; Wurtele & Kenny, 2010). The emphasis on children to bear the responsibility of protecting themselves, often in the context of complex, dependent relationships with the perpetrator, has been met with criticism. As such, there has been a push for a more critical focus on involving parents and other potential bystanders in these programs as 'partners in prevention' (Wurtele & Kenny, 2010, p.111). This potentially strengthens the effect of these programs by extending the layer of protection through enhanced guardianship (monitoring), improving family communication and a shared responsibility for keeping children safe (Mendelson & Letourneau, 2015).

Beyond the family, responsible bystander programs are also an essential target for combatting both youth- and adult-perpetrated CSA. Like other education programs, bystander intervention programs aim to increase recognition of risky situations; enhance perceived responsibility; overcome barriers to intervening with peers; and build skills to intervene safely, before (e.g. noticing something concerning at school), during (e.g. by interrupting an offence), or after CSA (e.g. by providing timely and effective support) has occurred. Emerging evidence supports the effectiveness of bystander interventions in producing attitudinal and behavioural change among young adult participants (Banyard, Moynihan, & Plante, 2007), but follow-up studies are needed to determine their long-term impacts, including whether they result in actual reductions in sexual violence. Media-based bystander campaigns have proven useful for mobilising guardianship action. One impressive example is 'Who Are You?' (http://www.whoareyou.co.nz/) campaign, which could be adapted specifically for CSA prevention.

Yet another prevention target is abuse settings. There are many ways to increase safety within physical settings to make these environments safer for children. Prevention of CSA in domestic setting is facilitated best through making residents (usually parents) the agents of change, through universal awareness and parent education campaigns that equip them with knowledge and skills to enhance guardianship (Forehand et al., 2007). Chasan-Taber and Tabachnick (1999) found that many parents are receptive to engaging in education programs, with their concerns lying in the lack of knowledge on how CSA occurs and strategies to better protect children. The challenge here lies in engaging parents of dysfunctional families whose children may be more at risk of victimisation and whose parents may be less equipped to recognise CSA and intervene (Wurtele & Kenny, 2010). Some practical measures that may reduce opportunities to offend include 'open door' policies and designing communal play areas with direct line of sight; for those entering the home (e.g. babysitters and tutors), careful reference checks may be considered (Kaufman, Mosher, Carter, & Estes, 2006) as prevention measures.

For organisations, comprehensive induction processes, well-designed child-safe policies and codes of conduct, and effective staff supervision and training all contribute to building awareness and maintaining a strong child-safe, child-friendly culture that arms against abuse occurring and promotes disclosure and accountability when it does occur (Smallbone & McKillop, 2016). Open environments that allow easy line of sight to all activities involving children are effective situational prevention measures that facilitate natural surveillance and extended guardianship, minimising opportunities for CSA (Smallbone & McKillop, 2016). Similarly, improving children's safety in public settings (e.g. parks, pools, and beaches) can be achieved through environmental design to improve natural surveillance (increased lighting and visibility), electronic CCTV monitoring, and ensuring public amenities are in line of sight. The presence of place managers (e.g. park maintenance or security guards) to guard these spaces also reduces opportunities to offend (Smallbone & McKillop, 2016).

In terms of 'virtual' settings, despite the known concerns regarding Internet safety (e.g. sharing photos and divulging personal information; Wolak, Finkelhor, Mitchell, & Ybarra, 2008), the ever-evolving nature of technology makes the prevention of online and offline child sexual exploitation difficult. Practical strategies for those most at risk of victimisation (i.e. youth) include parental controls and house rules to regulate Internet use and filters to block content; this is best combined with parent education (Pellai & Caranzano-Maitre, 2015). For 'potential' offenders' pop-up warnings and messages that educate on the harms associated with viewing child exploitation material and potential prosecution have been suggested as deterrence strategies (Wortley & Smallbone, 2012).

Despite the Internet's potential for enabling CSA victimisation, it is perhaps also the most efficient tool for the prevention of CSA. The Internet (via social media particularly) can promote education and awareness of the risks pertaining to both CSA perpetration and victimisation, in both online and offline settings. Once prevention materials are developed, they can be widely disseminated, across all levels of the social ecology (individual, parents, and community members) as a cost-effective tool for improving knowledge about risks, how to detect at risk situations and safely intervene, and extend guardianship (Wolak et al., 2008).

The best line of defence, however, across all systems is ensuring open lines of communication between adults and young people about the healthy and unhealthy sexual behaviours and encouraging discussion and responses (where necessary) when questions or concerns arise—no matter how small they may seem.

2.2 Secondary Prevention

Much of the literature on those who have perpetrated CSA identify missed opportunities to work with individuals prior to the onset of their offending and in the very early stages of CSA. One initiative that seeks to intercept at this stage is the Stop It Now! campaign. Founded in 1992 by Fran Henry (the United States), Stop It Now! operates across the United States, the United Kingdom, Ireland, and the Netherlands. Advocating a public health approach to CSA, services offered by Stop It Now! reach across the primary and secondary prevention levels, targeting community through social media campaigns to educate and build awareness of this issue and its prevention, and early-intervention (e.g. confidential helplines) services for individuals concerned for others and individuals concerned about their own thoughts and behaviour (Denis & Whitehead, 2012). The German equivalent Prevention Project Dunkelfeld (PPD) targets potential (perpetrators) using social marketing to encourage them to seek early intervention (Schaefer et al., 2010). These campaigns all serve to encourage collective responsibility towards CSA prevention. Evaluations of the Stop It Now! services in Europe show continued increases in demand on the service (including a significant proportion concerned about their own feelings and behaviour towards children) and some positive outcomes resulting from intervention such as recognising and responding to risky behaviour (NatCen Social Research, 2014) and reframing CSA prevention as a collective responsibility. Of all the programs evaluated by Stop It Now! Wales, those targeting parents (Internet Safety and Parents Protect!) showed greatest improvements, reinforcing that parents are a receptive and significant resource for prevention (Hudson, 2018).

Another area of secondary prevention has been to engage with middle and early high-school children to prevent risky sexual attitudes and behaviours as part of a broader recognition of youth-perpetrated CSA. The rationale behind sexual ethics programs is to educate children about appropriate relationship behaviours at a time where they are also navigating puberty and when sexual interests, attitudes, and beliefs about intimate relationships and activity are salient (Schewe, 2007). Targeted towards peer-aged partners, these programs provide opportunities to build knowledge and skills regarding healthy, respectful, and consenting partnerships. The most rigorously evaluated program to date, Safe Dates, has demonstrated reductions in sexual dating violence across several outcome studies (Foshee et al., 2005). Social media campaigns such as 'Tea and Consent' (http://www.consentiseverything.com/) are also cost-effective measures that send powerful messages to youth about accountability and responsibility for their actions, with potential for widespread dissemination.

For 'at risk' children, family-based programs (e.g. parent education, home visiting, and nursing programs) that target vulnerable families to build resilience, strengthen attachment bonds, improve parenting, and create safer environments have shown promise in reducing child maltreatment (Olds, 2002). These programs tend to be more effective when implemented with 'at risk' families than when implemented universally (Holzer, Higgins, Bromfield, Richardson, & Higgins, 2006), indicating it is most effective as a secondary prevention measure.

2.3 Tertiary Prevention

Tertiary-level responses to CSA include offender custodial and community-based risk management and rehabilitation programs to prevent reoffending. Most rehabilitation programs for CSA offenders include cognitive-behavioural therapy (CBT) and relapse prevention components. The most recent meta-analytic review (Schmucker & Lösel, 2015) indicated that pharmacological and CBT approaches are most effective for adult CSA offenders. However, for youth who sexually harm, multisystemic therapy and CBT approaches appear most effective in reducing recidivism. Importantly though, context plays a role in treatment effectiveness, with community-based programs showing better outcomes than prison-based programs (MacKenzie, 2002). Furthermore, better outcomes are achieved when aftercare services have adequate release planning that engage community-based partners in the transition from prison, rather than sole reliance on surveillance and monitoring (Schaefer, Cullen, & Eck, 2016). These findings highlight the importance of postrelease supervision as an essential component of prevention, by supporting offenders through the challenging process of release and reintegration (Cullen & Gendreau, 2000), especially for those convicted of CSA.

One promising approach designed to address these reintegration risks and augment existing interventions, in the adult CSA population, is Circles of Support and Accountability (CoSA). Established in Canada in 1994, CoSA is underpinned by 'restorative justice' principles and helps offenders gain accommodation, employment, and financial assistance and engages with formal and social support networks as part of their reintegration from prison (Wilson & McWhinnie, 2013). With the initial success of these programs in reducing sexual and violent recidivism (Wilson, Cortoni, & McWhinnie, 2009; Wilson, Picheca, & Prinzo, 2007), CoSA has continued to expand, with success, across the United States (Minnesota; Duwe, 2018), the United Kingdom (Bates, Saunders, & Wilson, 2007), and more recently Australia. The most recent randomised control trial of CoSA (Duwe, 2018) showed significant reductions in rearrest rates for new sexual and general offences, over an average 6-year follow-up period, producing a state-fiscal benefit of $40,923 per participant. The findings also highlighted potential transferability to other violent offenders without a CSA history (Duwe, 2018). However, it remains a resource-intensive and low-volume program, making a broader-scale rollout of programs and sustainability challenging (Duwe, 2018).

Given the short and long-term impacts of CSA, timely and effective therapeutic interventions have been the focus of tertiary-level prevention for victims. Such interventions are aimed at reducing trauma-related symptoms as an immediate response to victims. However, efforts to reduce the occurrence of revictimisation across the lifespan have increased in recognition of the significant links between CSA and later victimisation (Classen et al., 2006). For children, individual- or group-based trauma-focused cognitive behavioural therapy (TF-CBT), integrated with parallel parent sessions (Trask, Walsh, & DiLilo, 2011), appears to be effective. Adults with a CSA history also seem to benefit from TF-CBT and present-focused CBT (PF-CBT; Classen, Cavanaugh, Kaupp, et al., 2011). There is some evidence that PF-CBT may help to reduce sexual revictimisation, but follow-up evaluation is required to determine outcomes (Classen et al., 2006).

In terms of abuse settings, interest is emerging around the utility of place-based approaches to augment existing offender and victim-focused prevention activities. For organisational settings, employment screening has been widely used to identify and prevent those convicted of CSA gaining employment within youth-serving organisations. However, these measures fall short of identifying the 'successful' perpetrator or those who begin abusing during their employment; they are also not helpful for screening youth who perpetuate these crimes (Smallbone & McKillop, 2016), so they should be regarded as a small, albeit necessary, component of prevention. For both organisations and homes, environmental safety audits can be used at a secondary or tertiary level to identify areas of vulnerability (closed or out-of-the-way places) to augment safety planning and risk management and reduce opportunities for CSA. For familial abuse, supported reunification strategies are also important. For the Internet, eSafety software to monitor search terms on known offenders' computers is a promising initiative (Elliott, Findlater, & Hughes, 2010).

3 Conclusion

CSA remains a global public health concern due to the physical and psychological health risks associated with victimisation and revictimisation over the life course. For some time, the prevention focus was reactive, responding to known incidents through law enforcement, criminal justice interventions, and rehabilitative efforts. As our understanding about the nature and dimensions of CSA has improved, there has been acknowledgement that these reactive measures are not sufficient to reduce the extent and impacts of CSA. Approaching CSA from a public health perspective facilitates a more comprehensive and proactive prevention approach that attends to the multidimensional nature of this social phenomena, providing multiple opportunities for targeted prevention despite its heterogeneity.

It is clear that we need to tackle CSA in three key ways: (1) precluding incidents occurring in the first place (through primary prevention and some aspects of secondary prevention); (2) working with individuals 'at risk' of perpetrating or being abused and 'at risk' settings (through secondary prevention); and (3) encouraging early disclosure, timely and appropriate intervention when CSA does occur to reduce recurrence and ultimately promote desistance (tertiary prevention). As argued elsewhere (Smallbone & McKillop, 2015)—and illustrated through the examples discussed—a comprehensive prevention framework that targets (potential) offenders, (potential) victims, specific situations, and relevant ecological (peer, family, organisational, and neighbourhood) systems, across all three prevention levels, provides the best armoury against CSA. Ultimately, the goal is to prevent CSA from occurring in the first place; in times when this fails, at the very least, there needs to be appropriate mechanisms in place to ensure children are given a voice and are provided with appropriate responses, and that perpetrators receive the help and interventions that lead to desistance.

4 Chapter Review Questions

1. What are some of the known characteristics of child sexual abuse?
2. Why is it important to understand the nature and dimensions of child sexual abuse when developing prevention programs?
3. Describe the three levels of prevention proposed by the Public Health Prevention Model. What is the aim of each prevention level? Use a health example to explain your answer.
4. There are four settings in which child sexual abuse occurs. What are some of the risks associated with each of these settings?
5. What is the socioecological model, and why is it be important for understanding and preventing child sexual abuse?
6. Three targets for prevention are set out in this chapter. What are they, and why should they be targets for prevention?
7. Describe the person–situation interaction model. How might ordinary situations influence sexually abusive behaviour?
8. Name three ways to prevent sexual abuse at the primary, secondary, and tertiary levels.

References

Alexander, P. C. (1992). Application of attachment theory to the study of sexual abuse. *Journal of Consulting and Clinical Psychology*, *60*, 185–195.

Australian Bureau of Statistics. (2017). *Australian smoking rates falling*. Available at:http://www.abs.gov.au/ausstats/abs@.nsf/mediareleasesbyCatalogue/E6DE72422D16BBB4CA258130001536C2?OpenDocument.

Banyard, V. L., Moynihan, M. M., & Plante, E. G. (2007). Sexual violence prevention through bystander education: an experimental evaluation. *Journal of Community Psychology*, *35*(46), 3–81.

Bates, A., Saunders, R., & Wilson, C. (2007). Doing something about it: a follow-up study of sex offenders participating in Thames Valley circles of support and accountability. *British Journal of Community Justice*, *5*(1), 19–42.

Bourke, M. L., & Donohue, B. (1996). Assessment and treatment of juvenile sex offenders: an empirical review. *Journal of Child Sexual Abuse*, *5*, 47–70.

Bronfenbrenner, U. (1979). *The ecology of human development: experiments by nature and design*. Cambridge: Harvard University Press.

Chasan-Taber, L., & Tabachnick, J. (1999). Evaluation of a child sexual abuse prevention program. *Sexual Abuse: A Journal of Research and Treatment*, *11*, 279–292.

Classen, C. C., Cavanaugh, C. E., Kaupp, J. W., et al. (2011). A comparison of trauma-focused and present-focused group therapy for survivors of childhood sexual abuse: a randomized control trial. *Psychological Trauma: Theory, Research, Practice and Policy*, *3*, 84–93.

Classen, C. C., Gronskaya Palesh, O., & Aggarwal, R. (2006). Sexual revictimization: a review of the empirical literature. *Trauma, Violence & Abuse*, *6*, 103–129.

Cohen, L. E., & Felson, M. (1979). Social change and crime rate trends: a routine activity approach. *American Sociological Review*, *44*, 588–608.

Colombino, N., Mercado, C. C., Levenson, J. J., & Jeglic, E. (2011). Preventing sexual violence: can examination of offense location inform sex crime policy?. *International Journal of Law and Psychiatry*, *34*, 160–167.

Cullen, F. T., & Gendreau, P. (2000). Assessing correctional rehabilitation: policy, practice, and prospects. In J. Horney (Ed.), *Criminal justice 2000: Volume 3—Policies, processes, and decisions of the criminal justice system* (pp. 109–175). National Institute of Justice: Washington, DC.

Dahlberg, L. L., & Krug, E. G. (2002). Violence: a global public health problem. In E. G. Krug, L. L. Dahlberg, J. A. Mercy, A. B. Zwi, & R. Lozano (Eds.), *World report on violence and health* (pp. 1–56). Geneva: World Health Organization.

Denis, D., & Whitehead, H. (2012). *Stop it now! UK & Ireland: helpline and campaign report 2002-2012*. Stop it Now! UK & Ireland: Birmingham.

Diabetes Australia. (2018). *Prevention*. Available at:https://www.diabetesaustralia.com.au/prevention.

Duwe, G. (2018). Can circles of support and accountability (CoSA) significantly reduce sexual recidivism? Results from a randomized controlled trial in Minnesota. *Journal of Experimental Criminology*, https://doi.org/10.1007/s11292-018-9325-7. published online 13 March 2018.

Elliott, I. A., Findlater, D., & Hughes, T. (2010). Practice report: a review of e-Safety remote computer monitoring for UK sex offenders. *Journal of Sexual Aggression*, *16*(2), 237–248.

Finkelhor, D. (2009). The prevention of childhood sexual abuse. *The Future of Children*, *19*, 169–194.

Finkelhor, D., & Dziuba-Leatherman, J. (1994). Victimization of children. *American Psychologist*, *49*, 173–183.

Finkelhor, D., Ormrod, R., & Chaffin, M. (2009). *Juveniles who commit sex offenses against minors*. Retrieved from Juvenile Justice Bulletin, U.S. Department of Justice, May 7, 2013, fromhttps://www.ncjrs.gov/pdffiles1/ojjdp/227763.pdf.

Forehand, R., Armistead, L., Long, N., Wyckoff, S. C., Kotchick, B. A., Whitaker, D., et al. (2007). Efficacy of a parent-based sexual-risk prevention program for African American preadolescents: a randomized controlled trial. *Archives of Pediatrics and Adolescent Medicine*, *161*, 1123–1129.

Foshee, V. A., Bauman, K. E., Ennett, S. E., Suchindran, C., Benefield, T., & Linder, G. F. (2005). Assessing the effects of the dating violence prevention program 'safe dates' using random coefficient regression modelling. *Prevention Science*, *6*, 245–258.

Gallagher, B., Bradford, M., & Pease, K. (2008). Attempted and completed incidents of stranger-perpetrated child sexual abuse and abduction. *Child Abuse and Neglect*, *32*, 517–528.

Greenhalgh, E. M., Bayly, M., & Winstanley, M. H. (2017). 1.3 Prevalence of smoking—adults. In M. M. Scollo & M. H. Winstanley (Eds.), *Tobacco in Australia: Facts and issues*. Melbourne: Cancer Council Victoria. Available at from http://www.tobaccoinaustralia.org.au/chapter-1-prevalence/1-3-prevalence-of-smoking-adults.

Hanson, R. K. (2002). Recidivism and age: follow-up data from 4,672 sexual offenders. *Journal of Interpersonal Violence*, *17*, 1046–1062.

Hanson, R. K., & Bussière, M. T. (1998). Predicting relapse: a meta-analysis of sexual offender recidivism studies. *Journal of Consulting and Clinical Psychology*, *66*, 348–362. https://doi.org/10.1037//0022-006x.66.2.348.

Hebert, M., Parent, N., Daignault, I. V., & Tourigny, M. (2006). A typological analysis of behavioral profiles of sexually abused children. *Child Maltreatment*, *11*, 203–216.

Holzer, P. J., Higgins, J. R., Bromfield, L. M., Richardson, N., & Higgins, D. J. (2006). The effectiveness of parent education and home visiting child maltreatment prevention programs. In *Child abuse prevention issues no. 24*: Australian Institute of Family Studies.

Hudson, K. (2018). Preventing child sexual abuse through education: the work of Stop It Now! Wales. *Journal of Sexual Aggression*, *24*(1), 99–113. https://doi.org/10.1080/13552600.2017.1383088.

Kaufman, K. L., Mosher, H., Carter, M., & Estes, L. (2006). An empirically based situational prevention model for child sexual abuse. *Crime Prevention Studies*, *19*, 101–144.

Kemshall, H., & Moulden, H. (2017). Communicating about child sexual abuse with the public: learning the lessons from public awareness campaigns. *Journal of Sexual Aggression*, *23*(2), 124–138. https://doi.org/10.1080/13552600.2016.1222004.

Krug, E. G., Dahlberg, L. L., Mercy, J. A., Zwi, A. B., & Lozano, R. (2002). *World report on violence and health*. Geneva: World Health Organization.

Leach, C., Stewart, A., & Smallbone, S. (2015). Testing the sexually abused-sexual abuser hypothesis: a prospective longitudinal birth cohort study. *Child Abuse and Neglect*, *51*, 144–153.

Levine, J. A., & Dandamudi, K. (2016). Prevention of child sexual abuse by targeting pre-offenders before first offense. *Journal of Child Sexual Abuse*, *25*(7), 719–737. https://doi.org/10.1080/10538712.2016.1208703.

Lyles, A., Cohen, L., & Brown, M. (2009). *Transforming communities to prevent child sexual abuse and exploitation: a primary prevention approach*. Oakland, CA: Prevention Institute.

MacKenzie, D. L. (2002). Reducing the criminal activities of known offenders and delinquents: crime prevention in the courts and corrections. In L. W. Sherman, D. P. Farrington, B. C. Welsh, & D. L. Mackenzie (Eds.), *Evidence-based crime prevention* (pp. 330–404). New York: Routledge.

Marsa, F., O'Reilly, G., Carr, A., Murphy, P., O'Sullivan, M., Cotter, A., et al. (2004). Attachment styles and psychological profiles of child sex offenders in Ireland. *Journal of Interpersonal Violence, 19*, 228–251.

McCloskey, K. A., & Raphael, D. N. (2005). Adult perpetrator gender asymmetries on child sexual assault victim selection: results from the 2000 national incident-based reporting system. *Journal of Child Sexual Abuse, 14*(4), 1–24.

McKillop, N. (2012). *The origins of child sexual abuse: An analysis of developmental and situational factors* [Unpublished dissertation]Griffith University.

McKillop, N., Brown, S., Smallbone, S., & Pritchard, K. (2015). Similarities and differences in adolescence-onset versus adulthood-onset sexual abuse incidents. *Child Abuse and Neglect, 46*, 37–46. https://doi.org/10.1016/j.chiabu.2015.02.014.

McKillop, N., Brown, S., Wortley, R., & Smallbone, S. (2015). How victim age affects the context and timing of child sexual abuse: applying routine activities approach to the first sexual abuse incident. *Crime Science, 4*(17), 1–10. https://doi.org/10.1186/s40163-015-0031-8.

McKillop, N., Rayment-McHugh, S., Smallbone, S., & Bromham, Z., 2018. *Understanding and preventing the onset of child sexual abuse in adolescence and adulthood*. Trends & issues in crime and criminal justice No. 554. Canberra: Australian Institute of Criminology. https://aic.gov.au/publications/tandi/tandi554.

McKillop, N., Smallbone, S., Wortley, R., & Andjic, I. (2012). Offenders' attachment and sexual abuse onset: a test of theoretical propositions. *Sexual Abuse: A Journal of Research and Treatment, 24*(6), 591–610.

Mendelson, T., & Letourneau, E. J. (2015). Parent-focused prevention of child sexual abuse. *Prevention Science, 16*, 844–852. https://doi.org/10.1007/s11121-015-0553-z.

Mischel, W. (1968). *Personality and assessment*. New York: Wiley.

Molyneaux, L., Constantino, M., & Yue, D. (2004). Strong family history predicts a younger age of onset for subjects diagnosed with type 2 diabetes. *Diabetes, Obesity and Metabolism: A Journal of Pharmacology and Therapeutics, 6*(3), 187–194. https://doi.org/10.1111/j.1462-8902.2004.00330.x.

NatCen Social Research. (2014). *A public health approach to tackling child sexual abuse: Research on Stop It Now! UK and Ireland and Stop It Now! Netherlands*. http://www.stopitnow-evaluation.co.uk. Retrieved 28/5/2016.

Nisbet, I. A., Wilson, P. H., & Smallbone, S. (2004). A prospective longitudinal study of sexual recidivism among adolescent sex offenders. *Sexual Abuse: A Journal of Research and Treatment, 3*, 223–234.

Olds, D. (2002). Prenatal and infancy home visiting by nurses: from randomized trials to community replication. *Prevention Science, 3*, 153–172.

Paolucci, E. O., Genuis, M. L., & Violato, C. (2001). A meta-analysis of the published research on the effects of child sexual abuse. *The Journal of Psychology, 135*, 17–36.

Pellai, A., & Caranzano-Maitre, M. (2015). Primary prevention of child sexual abuse: child focused interventions. *Irish Journal of Applied Social Studies, 15*(2). Article 4. Available at: https://arrow.dit.ie/ijass/vol15/iss2/4.

Pierce, J. P., White, V. M., & Emery, S. L. (2012). What public health strategies are needed to reduce smoking initiation? *Tobacco Control, 21*, 258–264. Available at: http://tobaccocontrol.bmj.com/content/tobaccocontrol/21/2/258.full.pdf.

Quadara, A., Nagy, V., Higgins, D., & Siegel, N. (2015). *Conceptualising the prevention of child sexual abuse: Final report*. Australian Institute of Family Studies. Research Report No. 33. Available at: https://www.childabuseroyalcommission.gov.au/sites/default/files/WEB.0061.001.0001.pdf.

Schaefer, G. A., Mundt, I. A., Feelgood, S., Hupp, E., Neutze, J., Ahlers, C. J., et al. (2010). Potential and Dunkelfeld offenders: two neglected target groups for prevention of child sexual abuse. *International Journal of Law and Psychiatry, 33*(3), 154–163. https://doi.org/10.1016/j.ijlp.2010.03.005.

Schaefer, L., Cullen, F., & Eck, J. (2016). *Environmental corrections: A New paradigm for supervising offenders in the community*. Thousand Oaks, CA: SAGE.

Schewe, P. A. (2007). Interventions to prevent sexual violence. In L. S. Doll, S. E. Bonzo, J. A. Mercy, D. A. Sleet, & E. N. Haas (Eds.), *Handbook of injury and violence prevention* (pp. 223–240). New York: Springer.

Schmucker, M., & Lösel, F. (2015). The effects of sexual offender treatment on recidivism. An international meta-analysis of sound quality evaluations. *Journal of Experimental Criminology*, *11*, 597–630.

Seto, M. (2008). *Pedophilia and sexual offending against children: Theory assessment, and intervention.* Washington, DC: American Psyclogical Association.

Seto, M. C., & Lalumiere, M. L. (2010). What is so special about male adolescent sexual offending? A review and test of explanations through meta-analysis. *Psychological Bulletin*, *136*, 526–575.

Shattuck, A., Finkelhor, D., Turner, H., & Hamby, S. (2016). Children exposed to abuse in youth-serving organizations: results from national sample surveys. *JAMA Pediatrics*, *170*, 1–4.

Smallbone, S., & Cale, J. (2015). An integrated life course developmental theory of sexual offending. In A. Blockland & P. Lussier (Eds.), *Sex offenders: A criminal careers approach* (pp. 1–44). New York: Wiley.

Smallbone, S., Marshall, W. L., & Wortley, R. (2008). *Preventing child sexual abuse: Evidence, policy and practice*. Cullompton, UK: Willan.

Smallbone, S., & McKillop, N. (2015). Evidence-informed approaches to preventing sexual violence and abuse. In P. D. Donnelly & C. L. Ward (Eds.), *Oxford textbook in violence prevention: Epidemiology, evidence, and policy*. Oxford: Oxford University Press.

Smallbone, S., & McKillop, N. (2016). Preventing child sexual abuse: a place based approach. In M. Finnane & Y. Smaal (Eds.), *The sexual abuse of children: Recognition and redress*. Monash University Press.

Smallbone, S., & Rayment-McHugh, S. (2017). Sexual crimes. In A. Sidebottom & N. Tilley (Eds.), *Handbook of crime prevention and community safety* (2nd ed.). UK: Routledge. [Chapter 20].

Tonry, M., & Farrington, D. P. (1995). Strategic approaches to crime prevention. In M. Tonry & D. Farrington (Eds.), *Building a safer society: Strategic approaches to crime prevention* (pp. 1–20). Chicago: University of Chicago Press.

Trask, E. V., Walsh, K., & DiLilo, D. (2011). Treatment effects for common outcomes of child sexual abuse: a current meta-analysis. *Aggression and Violent Behaviour*, *16*, 6–19.

van Dijk, J., & de Waard, J. (1991). A two-dimensional typology of crime prevention projects: with bibliography. *Criminal Justice Abstracts*, *23*, 483–503.

Walsh, K., Zwi, K., Woolfenden, S., & Shlionsky, A. (2015). *School-based education programmes, for the prevention of child sexual abuse. The Cochrane review*. John Wiley & Sons Ltd.

Wilson, R., Cortoni, F., & McWhinnie, A. (2009). Circles of support and accountability: a Canadian national replication of outcome findings. *Sexual Abuse: A Journal of Research and Treatment*, *21*, 412–430.

Wilson, R., & McWhinnie, A. (2013). Putting the 'community' back in community risk management of persons who have sexually abused. *International Journal of Behavioral Consultation and Therapy*, *8*(3–4), 72–79.

Wilson, R., Picheca, J., & Prinzo, M. (2007). Evaluating the effectiveness of professionally facilitated volunteerism in the community-based management of high-risk sexual offenders: Part Two—a comparison of recidivism rates. *The Howard Journal*, *46*(4), 327–337.

Wolak, J., Finkelhor, D., Mitchell, K. J., & Ybarra, M. L. (2008). Online "predators" and their victims: myths, realities, and implications for prevention and treatment. *American Psychologist*, *63*(2), 111–128. https://doi.org/10.1037/0003-066X.63.2.111.

Wortley, R. K. (2008). Situational precipitators of crime. In R. Wortley & L. Mazzerole (Eds.), *Environmental criminology and crime analysis* (pp. 48–66). Cullompton: Willan.

Wortley, R., & Smallbone, S. (2012). *Internet child pornography: Causes, investigation and prevention*. New York: Praeger.

Wurtele, S. K., & Kenny, M. (2010). Primary prevention of child sexual abuse: child- and parent-focussed approaches. In K. L. Kaufman (Ed.), *The prevention of sexual violence: A practitioner's handbook* (pp. 107–119). Holyoke, MA: NEARI Press. Suggested website https://ecsa.lucyfaithfull.org/.

PART 3

Management: Responding to Child Abuse

CHAPTER 14

False Reports in Child Abuse and Neglect Cases

Wayne Petherick
Faculty of Society and Design, Bond University, Gold Coast, QLD, Australia

1 Introduction

False reports are the proverbial third rail of the justice system. For those unfamiliar with the term, the third rail is that that carries the power in an electric rail system and the one that will kill you if touched. In political discourse, this is a term used to describe an issue too sensitive to discuss, and such issues not only are a product of modern times but also are likely as old as human interaction. Nor are they a product of modern literature on the subject. False reports were discussed in the professional literature at least as early as 1924, when Austrian jurist Hans Gross wrote *Criminal Investigation*. On the false report, Gross (1924, p. 98) notes "the importance of a minute interrogatory is clearly shown in the case where a complicated plot has been laid to deceive the Investigating Officer and the falsity of the depositions must be exposed."

The very suggestion that a falsehood could be conveyed by someone claiming victim status may enrage the listener and bring scorn upon the speaker. That someone would fabricate a harm or loss against them or specifically that they would falsely accuse another of a crime strikes at the heart of a social and moral imperative to tell the truth. The idea that a child would do this is even more distasteful. However repugnant the idea or practice may be, simply ignoring it or trying to silence those who speak of it does nothing to further understand the problem and even less to combat it or deal with its many effects. Some feel that to question a claim with the goal of establishing the truth is impolite or politically incorrect or that it discourages legitimate victims from coming forward (Petherick & Ferguson, 2015). As succinctly and logically stated by Rumney & McCartan (2017, p. 502), "to argue that discussions around false allegations are dangerous fails to distinguish careful, evidence-based approaches to the topic from ill-informed discussions, influenced by myths and mischaracterisation."

This chapter examines false reports as they apply to child abuse and neglect allegations. First, false reports will be defined, and the different types will be outlined. The incidence of false

Child Abuse and Neglect. https://doi.org/10.1016/B978-0-12-815344-4.00014-3

reports will follow before moving onto the motivations involved. The penultimate discussion is of the various effects of false reporting for all parties concerned, before closing with a discussion on assessing false reports.

This is an important discussion to have. Despite concerns that prosecuting false reporters undermines legitimate victims or discourages real victims from coming forward, the reality is that no such compunction exists in prosecuting those whom claims are made against. Admittedly, vetting at the investigative level may mean that no further action is warranted or taken, but even one case where the falsely accused is arrested, charged, or worse is too many. That is to say nothing of the stink that can follow the falsely accused. As stated by Hoyle, Speechley, and Burnett (2016, pp. 4–5)),

> *It is apparent that for those wrongly accused the effects are likely to be devastating, even when allegations do not lead to criminal sanctions. Indeed, an unknown number of abuse allegations do not lead to police inquiries or criminal proceedings at all, and are not recorded as crimes. Nevertheless, they may have a substantial impact. Some allegations do not go beyond informal complaints, but they may still affect their subject's employment or standing in the community. Others may be aired in employment tribunals or family courts, and even when they are not substantiated, their consequences may be severe. Finally, there are complaints which, though dealt with by the criminal process, end in acquittals or decisions by the Crown Prosecution Service to discontinue proceedings or to take 'no further action'. Here too, significant damage may be done to alleged 'perpetrators' in circumstances where there has been no finding of guilt.*

So, even with a null finding, the consequences can be severe and perhaps worse when the finding goes against the falsely accused. Consider the following brief account of a well-known case from relatively recent times (Kleven, 2012):

> *A Longview father, wrongly accused of raping his own child tearfully spoke out on national television with his daughter at his side.*
>
> *Cassandra Kennedy was 11 years old in 2001 when she accused her father of rape. Now, as a 23-year-old, she apologized to her now-free dad on "Katie."*
>
> *"Thank you for being a good dad and I'm sorry for my wrong perspective as a child about you," she told her dad, Thomas Edward Kennedy, on the show. "I'm glad you're here for me now."*
>
> *Last January, Cassandra told police she made up the rape allegations when she was a child.*
>
> *"I was just angry and upset because I felt like he wasn't around enough and you know, broken promises and stuff like that," Cassandra said. Host Katie Couric asked her if she had just wanted more of her dad, "I did. I wanted more of my dad."*
>
> *Thomas denied the rape allegations at the time but was convicted and sentenced to more than 15 years in prison. After serving nearly a decade, he was released and all charges against him were dismissed.*

When he was released, "I felt joy, I felt security. Knowing that my prayer had finally been answered. I had hope and faith all along," Thomas said.

As an innocent man in prison, Thomas said it was scary and horrible: not knowing from one second to the next what was going to come at him.

When he was released, and Cassandra, now an adult, was reunited with her dad, she feared his response.

"I didn't really know for sure what he was thinking or what he was going to say or anything like that. Then I saw he took his hand out from behind his back and had a bouquet of flowers for me. So I melted right there. It was awesome."

In April when Cassandra recanted her story, prosecutors said they were unsure whether she lied in 2001 or is lying now. Cowlitz County Prosecutor Sue Baur said there was sufficient evidence for a jury to convict Thomas Kennedy at the time.

"It's impossible for anyone to know what the truth is, isn't it?" Baur had said. "There is basically no way that a jury now would be able to convict [...] when she's recanting now. But, technically that doesn't mean that anybody has made a finding that she lied back then."

Baur said her office would not seek to have the case tried again, and that the statute of limitations prevents her office from charging the daughter with false reporting.

Based on the reported 'crime', Thomas Kennedy was arrested, prosecuted, and found guilty. He was sentenced to 15 years in prison and served 9 years before his daughter confessed to her malfeasance. Prosecutors decided not to charge Cassandra with her false report, claiming it will stop other false reporters from coming forward with their confessions, potentially causing the falsely accused to languish in jail.

So then, how did an 11-year-old make a claim that was so convincing? Kennedy initially got the idea from a friend and was able to adapt parts of her story to make her own version of events more believable (Ross, 2012). The reader familiar with investigative processes may ask the question "but surely the results of the sexual assault examination would have come back negative?" Ordinarily, they may have, but Kennedy's confession that she had sex with a boy about her own age in the second grade lead to a finding of a perforated hymen at examination, supporting the claim of her father's guilt (Ross, 2012).

Whilst most allegations of abuse will be true, there exist a number that are, for whatever reason, wholly or partially fabricated. These false reports are a problem for the criminal justice system, the individual accused, and the society to varying degrees. The reputation of the accused may be ruined, and police have to invest vast resources into needless investigations (Rassin & van der Sleen, 2005) diverting those resources from investigations to crimes involving legitimate victims. Society, through the taxation and welfare system, bears the financial burden of these claims, and there are an undetermined number of false victims getting help, support, and resources from victims of crime and other nonprofit or not-for-profit groups. Speaking specifically about stalking, but no less relevant to other victim's groups, Pathé (2002) believes these individuals should be identified and removed from the group as soon as possible because of the resource drain they represent. That is to say nothing of the cost to the falsely accused who has to fund a legal defence, which they will likely be unable to recuperate outside of civil litigation, which itself can be an expensive and emotional remedy with uncertain outcomes.

At this juncture and before moving onto the rest of this chapter, a note of caution is offered. Having been exposed to the ire of those who think discussions of this type are antivictim or that the author is personally antivictim, I would simply say that nothing could be further from the truth. Personally and professionally, I am provictim and believe in victim's rights. I believe that victims should be afforded every accommodation and service to help restore them to physical and emotional homeostasis following the horrible events they encounter. But I believe that this should be limited to actual victims of crime and further believe that we do a disservice to these actual victims by not treating the false claim as we should: as a crime and antisocial behaviour. For those who falsely report owing to mental disorder or defect, a recognition of the root cause of the disorder and associated treatment for it is warranted, with the final disposition of the case dictated by regional laws and mental health legislation. Many jurisdictions have laws against false reports, and many will prosecute these vigorously but usually only in those cases involving malice (as discussed later in this chapter). Prosecution will not usually be sought for those filing a report made with the best intentions that is later discovered to be false and rightly so. It should be noted though that whilst this is acceptable from a legal standpoint, even a report made under the veil of mistaken belief may still have ruinous consequences for the falsely accused, and therefore, false reports considered in this chapter include these as a type.

It is with this consideration in mind that this chapter is written and presented, such that we may educate ourselves on the presentation and fallout of false reports, so they may be better and earlier identified and their consequences buffered or eliminated. Not only do we owe this to real victims such that their plight is not diminished, but also we owe it to actual and potential false victims against whom these complaints are levelled.

2 What Is a False Report?

A false report is a mendacious claim made about an event or person that either is entirely untrue or contains some element of untruth. There are four basic elements in a claim, and any or all of these can be fabricated. These are the victim, the offender, the alleged act, and the circumstances. If a complete fabrication, then no aspects of it are true. If partial, then it may have some elements of truth such as the person involved, the location, or the actual behaviours engaged in or directed towards the 'victim'. For example, a change of heart following sex could lead the consensual sexual partner to be accused of rape, or evidence of consensual sex could be used to bolster a claim of sexual assault.

As this is a general term encompassing a variety of different contexts of claims, there are different types of false reports.

A false allegation is where one person wrongfully accuses another of victimisation, where the falsely accused becomes a victim. A false confession is a claim that someone was responsible for a crime they did not commit, and these may be particularly problematic as throughout criminal justice a confession is seen as common, potent, and persuasive (Kassin, 2017). False victimisation occurs when someone claims to have been victimised when in fact they have not been. A false denial is when someone denies doing something they are accused of, which they have in fact done. Another type not discussed in great frequency in the literature is the false retraction, though there is some research on the subject (Rieser, 1991; Tully, 2002). A false retraction occurs when a previous allegation of abuse was formally made and maintained over a period of time but is subsequently withdrawn (Sorensen & Snow, 1991), and these occur for any number of reasons including embarrassment or shame, love for the abuser, not wanting to be placed into foster or state care, and where the claimant has been coached or threatened. In the study by Sorensen and colleagues, false retractions occurred in 22% of the cases. According to Rieser (1991), a false allegation is one reason why a child would recant, so a false recantation would only follow any type of allegation (true or false); otherwise, there would be nothing to retract.

These could be considered the general types, but of course, there are other variants within these that may or may not be related to child abuse and neglect. For example, someone may make a false call to emergency services, someone may falsely make an insurance claim, or someone may falsely claim a welfare payment reserved for victims of crime. In the context of this work, the discussion is limited to those in child abuse and neglect.

For the purpose of this chapter, the four broad distinctions (false allegations, false confessions, false victimisation, and false denials) will suffice. It is necessary to point out that a false report may include only one of the above or more than one. If someone falsely claims to be a victim without naming their victimiser, then this is simply a false victimisation claim. Should they go on to name a suspect, then a false allegation would also be involved against the pseudoperpetrator. If that person is arrested, is interviewed, and subsequently confesses to something they did not do, then it would also include a false confession. Despite the seeming paradox—a confession for a crime one did not commit—these do happen. In the United States, there were 139 exonerations in 2017 (National Registry of Exonerations, 2018), and of these, 29 were false confessions (a record number), with the majority being for homicide ($n=22$, manslaughter $n=1$), then child sexual abuse ($n=16$), sexual assault ($n=3$), and child abuse ($n=1$). Interestingly, there were 14 cases of child sexual abuse (approximately 10%) that were perjured or false accusations also. Claims that no one would confess to a crime they did not commit are simply not supported by the literature and evidence, with coercive interview and interrogation strategies being a factor in these (Kassin, 2014).

Within child abuse and neglect, the false report may originate entirely with the child, or it may come from the parent or guardian, either as a genuine concern that the allegation is true and happening or in full knowledge that it is false. The child may also be recruited by the adult or caregiver and coached in what to say, such that their statement buttresses the overall allegation. Ironically, when a very young child provides an erudite explanation using vivid detail with language beyond their years, this may indicate coaching or subtle influence (O'Donohue, Benuto, & Cirlugea, 2013), signalling an elevated risk of false report.

3 How Common Are False Reports?

There is a widely held belief that false reports of sexual violence are commonplace, and there is much publicly accessible debate refuting this (see Lazard, 2017 as one example). There is also much discussion in the professional literature that they are not that common, with a 2% statistic being widely cited and discussed briefly below. But these discussions relate to all reports of sexual violence and are not limited solely to those that occur within the context of child abuse and neglect. Establishing this subpopulation within the general population of false reports may be difficult though there are studies available. One thing we do know from the literature is that false reports are not widely studied, and many of the studies that have been done are considerably dated. In one of these early studies, Wakefield and Underwager (1991) doubt the veracity of all abuse allegations, specifically identifying those in divorce allegations, as a serious concern. They claim that about three-quarters of their cases are deemed to be false, though these findings are not replicated in any other research. Their overall doubts are likely misplaced though their general caution is not: we must remain alert to the possibility of a false report.

Any findings about the incidence of false reports will be influenced by several variables, many relating to the inclusion and exclusion criteria of the research. If the researchers limit their cases only to those in which the false reports have been unequivocally proven, the result will be smaller sample sizes than studies where the inclusion criteria capture proven cases, whilst those with strong suspicion but not definitive proof will result in a larger sample. Given that proving a false report is difficult, studies using the first criteria may result in smaller sample sizes, limiting the degree to which they can be generalised to the larger population of false reporting. The waters are further muddied when a defendant accepts a plea bargain knowing they are innocent but decide to accept this fate instead of rolling the dice in a jury trial (Greer, 2000). Some studies include a number of unfounded claims in their data, and these should not necessarily be taken as false reports, rather cases in which there was insufficient evidence to arrest or convict or simply to support the allegation that the offence occurred. Such cases may be evidentiary and legally weak but could be entirely legitimate.

Further, because false allegations of sexual abuse and neglect in children are a subpopulation of the overall body of false reports, this will result in an inherently smaller sample yet again.

This appears to be the case, with some studies relying only on a handful of cases (or, in research parlance, a small *n*). It may also be true that this phenomenon is low in frequency and that there simply is not a large sample to draw from.

As stated, there is a widely held belief that the general rate of false reporting is only 2%. This, however, appears to have propagated throughout the literature from a common source that itself was based on faulty assumptions. As it is outside of the purview of this work to dissect the lineage of this argument, the author recommends reading *The Truth Behind Legal Dominance Feminism's Two Percent False Rape Claim* (Greer, 2000).

Even though not related to child abuse, it may be worth looking first at some of the research that has been done on false reports in sexual assault.

Her Majesty's Crown Prosecution Service Inspectorate in the United Kingdom published a report indicating a false-report rate for rapes of 11.8% or 164 out of 13,779 cases (Her Majesty's Crown Prosecution Service Inspectorate, 2002). Jordan (2004) investigated 164 rape and sexual assault allegations from police files and found that 33% ($n=62$) were classified by the police as false and in another 8% ($n=13$) the complainant said the claim was false. This is somewhat higher than that found by other studies.

In one of the earliest and most widely reported studies, Kanin (1994) studied 109 reported rapes over a 9-year period in the Midwestern United States. Kanin's study found that 41% of these rapes were false. The reasons for reporting ranged from revenge to attention seeking, and there were fluctuations of reports over the years studied (from 27% to 70%). Later, Kennedy and Witkowski (2000) replicated Kanin's study by examining forcible rape complaints between 1988 and 1997. Kennedy found that 32.3% ($n=22$) of the 68 reports were false.

Thoennes and Tjaden (1990) used information from mail and telephone surveys and interviews with legal and mental health professionals dealing with abuse cases. In the 6 months of the data collection for their study, over 9000 families with custody visitation disputes were served in the eight courts where records were kept for the study. They note that slightly less than 2% of those cases involved allegations of sexual abuse. The range across sites was between 1% and 8% though removing the site with the lowest incidence the average became 3%. It should be noted that this study was only interested in custody/visitation disputes and did not feature other situations such as divorce proceedings and inclusion of which would tend to increase the base rates. The authors suggest that half the cases were believed to involve abuse, whereas in 33%, no abuse was deemed to have happened and in the remaining 17% the investigators could not conclude one way or the other.

Lanning (2010) discusses situations that could be classified as regressed and situational child sexual abuse. In the regressed type, the abuse is the result of the stress and strain of a marital breakdown, and the offender 'regresses' to an earlier stage of development. In the situational type, the offender does not have a sexual preference for children but exploits a situation that arises for complex reasons. The final type is the false report, wherein the abuse is not actually happening. It is noted that proportionately, more false reports of sexual abuse are made in the context of divorce compared with other situations with Faller (1991, p. 88) providing some context as to why the false allegation may be more common in divorce than at other times:

> *The higher proportion of false allegations can be understood by contrasting the divorce situation with others. In intrafamilial sexual abuse, it is usually a major issue to convince nonabusive family members that the abuse occurred. Mothers may find it very difficult to believe that the man to whom they are married could sexually victimise their child. Quite the opposite may arise when parents are divorcing.*

In Faller's study of 136 cases, 19 were identified as false reports, with another 12 categorised as inconclusive and 'therefore possibly false' (p. 88). Taking 19 as the base rate for false reports that means that about 14% of the sample was false and including the 12 questionable cases, if all were false, would raise the base rate to approximately 23%. As noted elsewhere in this chapter though, questionable does not necessarily mean false.

Whilst the proportion of false reports would appear to be high in this study, only 'three cases in the sample appeared to be calculated untruths, evidently motivated by the desire to exclude the accused parent from the life of the child and of the accusing parent' (Faller, 1991, p. 89).

In a later study, Faller teamed up with Ellen deVoe (Faller & DeVoe, 1995) to further test the different contexts under which allegations may be made. Their sample consisted of 215 allegations of sexual abuse in the context of divorce, which involved 174 children. Of the sample, 41 children were subject to allegations of sexual abuse by more than one person. One hundred and thirty-two (a fraction over 75%) were alleged to have been abused by one person; 36 (a fraction over one-fifth) were said to have been abused by two people, four by three or more people, and two by four people. Most allegations (63.2%) involved females, the rest males.

For the relationship of divorce to allegations, 31 cases (14.4%) involved the discovery of sexual abuse following divorce. This discovery was the catalyst for the decision to divorce. The second largest group (54 cases, 25.1%) was where divorce preceded the discovery of previous sexual abuse that was reported as ongoing during the divorce. Of these, 18 cases were identified by the parent, whilst 36 cases were reported by the child after the marriage was over. The largest group (58 cases, 27%) involved those cases where the sexual abuse was reported to have started during or after the marriage breakup. Fifty of these were made by noncustodial parents and the remaining eight by custodial parents. For false and possibly false allegations, 31 (14.4%) had the appearance of falsity with an additional 14 (6.5%) possibly false. Of the total of 45 cases in this category, the majority ($n=34$) were based on misinterpretation by the adult, whilst 10 (4.7%) were 'knowingly false allegations' (Faller & DeVoe, 1995, p. 9), with another being unknown. In 27 of the cases, the allegation appeared unrelated to the divorce. The last category included those that were apparently false allegations by the child, happening in nine cases (4.2%) with nearly all cases being based on a misinterpretation by the parent, with one case appearing to be a deliberate false allegation. It should be noted that, regarding false reports of all colours, the motive or reason for the report is not important insofar as it being false or regarding the potential for negative effects to the falsely accused. That is, a well-meaning parent thinking they are acting in the best interest of the child will potentially have the same impact as a child or parent filing a deliberately false complaint.

One study examined 18 cases revolving around divorce and custody disputes from the Boulder County (Colorado) Sexual Abuse Team (McGraw & Smith, 1992). These authors note that "determining whether such allegations are reliable or fictitious presents a challenge to caseworkers who are apt to find themselves caught up in the highly charged atmosphere of divorce and custody proceedings" (p. 49). There were 290 cases overall, but only these 18 met the inclusion criteria: (1) The families were investigated by the sexual abuse team, and (2) the sexual abuse team assessed that the case involved a contested custody dispute. Within these 18 cases, 7 (39%) were deemed to be substantiated or likely valid, there was one (5.5%) recantation, another two (11%) were deemed to have insufficient information, and five (28%) involved unsubstantiated suspicion. The three remaining cases were deemed to be false reports, with two (11%) initiated by the adult and one (5.5%) initiated by the child. From this overall picture, one in six of these cases was therefore a false report.

The Department of Children and Families (2007) in Florida, the United States, has established procedures for determining whether a false report of child abuse has been made. They define a false report as a "report of abuse, neglect, or abandonment of a child to the central abuse hotline, which is maliciously made for the purpose of (a) harassing, embarrassing, or harming another person; (b) personal financial gain for the reporting person; (c) acquiring custody of a child; or (d) personal benefit for the reporting person in any private disputes involving the child" (p. 1). Because the tally is restricted to those cases resulting in calls to an abuse hotline, their number of false reports may be lower than the actual number of false reports because of the 'dark figure' of reports, which is the difference between the number reported to the hotline and the actual incidence of false reports. Also, as they only include those cases of malice, their numbers will exclude those resulting from the best intentions of the reporter or other reasons still culminating in mistaken beliefs, so the actual numbers will be smaller again still. This report identified 143 potential false-report cases, with 58 of these being referred to law enforcement. As the report does not provide the total number of reports made, we cannot calculate what proportion of the overall reports are false or potentially false.

Whilst not providing actual data or the results of empirical analysis, Martell (1988) discusses both their occurrence and the sensitive nature of their discussion, stating that "while many and perhaps most reports appear to be based on real events, some reports are wrong, either in whole or in part" (p. 618). Then (p. 618),

> *I have encountered many cases in which child asexual abuse allegations have been shown to be erroneous. Curiously, while relief is frequent when other social and psychological complaints have proved unfounded, in this area it has sometimes been difficult to even raise the possibility that an accusation is false.*

Martell identifies a number of categories of erroneous allegations, which will be briefly discussed in the coming section.

4 Motivations for False Reports

Motivation applies to any internal force that activates and directs behaviour (Roeckelein, 2006). Motive is not well understood even by those who seek to establish it; though, to be fair, it is difficult to establish even in the best of cases with the most abundant evidence. Speaking specifically to the motive for crime but equally applicable to false reports, only the offender may truly know or understand the motive (Leonard, 2001), and third parties may only be able to reconstruct the most likely motive from being and the evidence.

The motivations for false reports in child sexual abuse are not dissimilar to motivations for other types of false reporting. This is perhaps because the motives for antisocial and criminal behaviour are relatively uniform and occur across the spectra (see Brotto, Sinnamon, & Petherick, 2017; Petherick, 2015; Petherick & Sinnamon, 2014). From the available research on false reports in child abuse and neglect, it is known that such reports will come from one of three sources: the child themselves, a parent, or a third party. As such, there may be overall consistency between the motives in these cases and motives in general or other crimes, though with some variation based on who is doing the reporting. A child may be less likely to have profit or materialism motives for reporting and therefore have a more limited motivational range than an adult. It could also be that children have their own peculiar set of motives, though this hasn't yet been the subject of empirical investigation.

4.1 Child Custody

The overall goal of this false report is to secure an advantage in a child custody matter. When the false report is made formally as part of proceedings, I would refer to this as a *moral advantage* motive. This is designed specifically to undermine the integrity of another or their ability to provide a safe and nurturing environment, thus winning a moral advantage. If proven to be false, this may form the basis of a defamation claim.

4.2 Mental Disorder

There is a significance over representation of mental health issues in the population of false reporters (MacKay, 2014), and the issue of mental disorder in the context of motivation is a difficult one. The first reason is that mental disorders run the full gamut of psychological conditions from stress and anxiety to disorders involving paranoid or psychotic thinking and behaviour. Even the mildest of disorders could be claimed as the precipitant of the abuse, whilst someone suffering a florid delusional state may still refrain from hurting a child. There are some disorders that are inherently linked to false allegations, such as Munchausen syndrome and Munchausen syndrome by proxy, and any number of disorders with delusional elements. Some of these are reported in the literature on child abuse (Gehlawat, Gehlawat, Singh, & Gupta, 2015; Savvidou, Bozikas, & Karavatos, 2002) and on false allegations specifically (Karanfil, Akçan, & Orhan, 2011).

Another issue in disaggregating mental disorder from motivation is that we cannot 'turn back the clock' and take the mental disorder out of the equation to see if the behaviour still manifests. We are thus left to the skill of the mental health evaluator in determining the degree to which the disorder drove or guided the behaviour. Because causation is difficult to establish, under the law, an individual suffering from a mental disorder can only be held legally liable for the behaviour if it can be shown that the behaviour was outside of their control and that they knew what they were doing was wrong (see McGrath & Torres, 2010, for a thorough review of these and related issues).

4.3 Revenge

Revenge is perhaps one of the best and most widely understood motives because it is linked to an emotional state we have all experienced at one time or another. In motivational parlance, revenge is known as anger retaliatory (see Petherick, 2015; Petherick & Sinnamon, 2014). Revenge results from an actual event the person is responding to, or it can be the result of a faulty perception, that is, someone incorrectly perceives a grievance they feel needs to be corrected.

Revenge behaviour is linked to emotional states relating to restoration and justice and is generally frowned upon in Western societies where it may be viewed as childish and unethical (Grobbink, Derksen, & van Marle, 2015). Those who seek revenge may be perceived as morally weak or immature and lacking the ability to move beyond challenges that are a normal part of life. The tendency towards rumination over actual or perceived transgressions plays a role in the germination of revenge-based actions.

Certain motives are largely driven by activation in different parts of the brain. Revenge is considered a subtype of the anger-driven motives and as such will be moderated by the midbrain, specifically the amygdala, which is responsible for fear, anxiety, and aggression (Kalat, 2011). Family aggressive behaviour, closely linked to anger responses, is predicted in lab studies of higher right amygdala volumes (Saxbe et al., 2018). When an individual embarks on a revenge plan and the punishment is effective rather than symbolic, the dorsal striatum, part of the brain linked to rewards from goal-directed actions, is activated (de Quervain et al., 2004). Where there is a direct effect on the punisher, the ventral striatum is involved, with the dorsal striatum being involved where the punishment has a strong effect (Kirsch et al., 2009).

If a claim is made during divorce, this could be to give the claimant a moral advantage as discussed above. If anger or hatred of the accused is the cause, this may be to deprive them of custody or visitation rights, to get even for real or perceived infidelities, or to damage someone's occupational prospects (such as when they are required to have a clean criminal record for security clearances). These would all be examples of revenge-based motives.

4.4 Mistaken Belief

The research discussed elsewhere in this chapter would tend to indicate that most false claims are made with the best intentions, without any desire to mislead or specifically harm the other party. It is not unreasonable to expect that a concerned parent would allege abuse if they feel they have sufficient information to do so, even though no actual abuse is happening. As such, the mistaken belief is a claim that is made with the utmost confidence in authenticity that is not made with malice or any purpose other than a desire to protect the child. This may happen when, for example, a parent observes injuries innocently sustained that are interpreted as abuse.

4.5 Material Gain

Elsewise referred to as *profit-oriented* (Petherick & Sinnamon, 2014; Petherick, 2015), this may be the lesser applicable motivation in false reports of child abuse and neglect. To be sure, there may be cases where one parent files a false complaint against the other to win custody with the indirect benefit being child support or welfare payments. If this was done to punish the other parent through financial sanction, then this would be more suited to the classification of revenge above. If both purposes were served, then both motives could be said to be in operation.

4.6 Malingering

Malingering is when one pretends to be ill in order to secure benefit. According to MacKay (2014), malingering claims are not uncommon among young people, but they are not at all common in cases of child abuse. It is noted that whilst "malingered symptoms of dysfunction are not uncommon among young people in personal injury claims, they are not at all common in cases of alleged abuse" (MacKay, 2014, p. 86).

4.7 Concealment of Activities

A false report may be made to try and conceal any given range of activities. Upon finding out that their teenage daughter engaged in consensual sexual activity with an older partner, a story may be provided alleging that the sex was actually forced. The concerned parent is the one who is likely to make the allegation. Another analogous situation would be where one partner reports being forced into sex outside of an existing relationship (Heenan & Murray, 2006; Jordan, 2004). To cover up drug or alcohol use or a relapse during addiction, a claimant may allege sexual abuse as the catalyst to try and ameliorate the substance use.

Martell (1988) discusses a variety of categories of false reports "derived from review of several hundred cases seen during the past 12 years" (Martell, 1988, p. 619). These include simple misunderstandings, perhaps based on language or a misinterpretation of innocent contact; simple misreporting based on inherent suspicion where actions are invented or distorted so as to appear inappropriate; distortion through illness arising from emotional and mental illness; distortion by design, resulting from child custody and other judicial hearings; professional errors resulting from rescue fantasies, gender biases, therapeutic alliance with the client, or personal feelings of disgust; misrepresentation with the ultimate goal to curry favour or advantage from social and government services; and miscellaneous errors, such as partial false reports (wrong person is named) or to gain sympathy or attention.

5 Effects of False Reports

The effects of false reports are many and varied and will differ according to who makes the report, who the report is made against, the specific act(s) alleged in the report, and the circumstances of the allegation. Like many things related to criminal or antisocial behaviour, if there are contextual elements that explain the behaviour, these may be considered both socially and legally by adjudicators. The author is not suggesting for a moment that there are excuses for child abuse and neglect, just that these impact on perception and expectation, and have an impact on the actual or perceived effect of the false report.

5.1 Who Makes the Report

When the report is made by a parent or guardian with direct knowledge of the individuals and acts alleged, this may be seen to carry more weight than allegations made by those who claim second- or third-hand knowledge of the stated abuses. As a result, any accusations are likely to carry more weight and perhaps heighten or elevate response to the accusations. This means that, whether true or false, the claims may carry greater weight and thus the effects may be amplified.

It is likely that reported sexual abuse made by a mother of a daughter against a father may carry greater weight than that made by a father of a son or daughter against a mother. This is perhaps because of societal beliefs with some unlikely to think of women as sex offenders (Gakhal & Brown, 2011). This belief about perpetrators of sex offences may mean that allegations against a man by a woman are taken more seriously than allegations against a woman made by a man, this setting in motion a cascading sequence of events that will follow the accused through the criminal justice and/or child protection system.

Studies into investigative bias tend to show that there is a tendency to seek out inculpating evidence (that tends to indicate guilt) whilst ignoring that that is exculpatory (that tends to indicate innocence) as a rule. There are subtle differences in bias, the type of evidence that is needed or sought out, or in how that plays a role in guilt determination (see Ask & Granhag, 2005; Rassin, Eerland, & Kuijpers, 2010 as but two examples, admittedly with differing findings regarding the strength and nature of the bias).

5.2 Who the Report Is Made Against

False allegations made against parents may be particularly problematic because one of the primary and most critical roles of a parent is to protect the child. When allegations of abuse are levelled against a parent, outrage over the violation of this basic social tenet may blind investigators and others to the possibility that the claims are false, therefore leading to vigorous pursuit of the 'offending' parent. A false allegation made against a parent may be viewed as representing a more serious offence and involve either a more rigorous investigation into them, or the stacking up of charges against them, or perhaps even both.

A biological parent may be viewed as less predatory, and if the abuse allegations are made against a step-parent, this may reinforce the presumed legitimacy of the claim or lead to the belief that the step-parent has placed themselves within the family for access to potential victims. Over and above this, there is a tendency for stepchildren to be abused at higher rates than biological children, known as 'the Cinderella effect', based on the plight of Cinderella from the child's tale (Daly & Wilson, 1997). This effect has been widely discussed and cited, with Raine (2013) providing a useful summary of various studies on the subject.

Supporting this Cinderella effect, Lightcap, Kurland, and Burgess (1982) examined data from 24 two-parent households where there was at least one known victim of child abuse. Results show that stepchildren are abused at a higher rate by step-parents, accounting for more than 50% of the deviation from a normal distribution. Moreover, when both biological children and stepchildren lived in the same home, all the abuse relationships occurred between steprelations. The abusers are more commonly males than females (two-thirds to three-quarters of the time when considered across houses where there are steprelations and those where they are not). With regard to the crime of murder, step-parents kill at much higher rates than biological parents (Friedman, Cavney, & Resnick, 2012). According to evolutionary theory, this selective bias in victimisation increases the chance of passing along your own genes whilst simultaneously eliminating competing genes from the population.

Put simply, there is research showing that step-parents abuse at higher rates than biological parents, and this may be viewed as by-proxy validation of claims made where the accused is a step-parent. As a result, when a false claim is made against a step-parent, they may be viewed as inherently more liable and therefore more likely to be guilty. More rigorous prosecution may be undertaken leading to a greater chance of a miscarriage of justice.

When the report is made by one parent or child against the other parent, this can have a negative impact on the nonaccused parent. Ironically, though they are the parent who has carried the report to law enforcement or child protection agencies, they may be judged negatively owing to their perceived failure to protect the child(ren). Even when nothing has actually happened, an allegation has the potential to impact upon the parent–child relationship (Plummer & Eastin, 2007; Theimer & Hansen, 2017), and one or both parents may still be viewed pejoratively. This could take the form of "how could you let this happen under your roof?" or in questions about whether abuse may actually be happening, just not necessarily according to the reported instance. This may come about when the alleger is seen to be making a 'cry for help' by bringing other abuses to light by claiming false abuses.

5.3 Specific Acts Alleged in the Report

Whilst the author is not excusing one act over the next, it should go without saying that the different varieties of abuse and neglect will be judged differently according to their weight and impact. Abuse claimed to be the result of discipline that got out of hand may be viewed as less severe than sexual abuse with no organic origin or mitigation. Those who perceive errant disciplinary abuse may be more likely to attribute lesser long-term negative effects of this than other crimes like sexual abuse. A conviction may be more likely to follow if the accuser claims that they were a witness to the falsely claimed event (Myers, 1980). Studies have been conducted confirming this effect of varying natures and to varying degrees (Grubb & Harrower, 2009; Herzog, 2008; Myers, 1980).

Because of this, there may be bias in thinking that whilst not excusable, it is understandable that parents occasionally get carried away in the heat of the moment. This tendency towards less negative attribution of the act may mean that the accused is less likely to suffer lasting disdain. However, in the case of alleged sexual abuse, the accused and their family carry the stigma and revulsion along with suspicion that may follow them such as "they got away with it" (Hoyle et al., 2016) or the belief that "where there is smoke there is fire": that they may not have done this but surely they have done something else that has not been discovered. Where a guilty verdict is secured and the defendant continues to claim their innocence, it may have a negative influence on parole decisions, appeals, or any other consideration such as conditional work release (Hoyle et al., 2016).

5.4 Circumstances of the Allegation

The circumstances of the allegation are another important point to consider. A parent who is mentally ill who is claimed to have physically or sexually abused a child may be judged as less culpable than one who has no such affliction. Whilst drug and alcohol abuse is not generally considered an excuse under the law, there are examples of such defences being used successfully in cases of abuse (see Schenck & Mahowald, 1998, for an interesting discussion on alcohol abuse and sleepwalking as a legal defence, albeit it in a true not false allegation). Looking at the same argument from the other direction, a claim of abuse involving drug or alcohol intoxication where the parent is not known to consume alcohol or drugs may be seen as more likely to be false, even though the parent has simply been adept at hiding their history of use or abuse.

Beyond mental illness and intoxication, other circumstances that may influence the degree to which the false allegation of abuse is believed include the contextual circumstances of the claim, for either the accuser (whether child or adult) or the family in general. Instances involving family law matters may be fertile ground for abuse allegations (MacKay, 2014), as this may be a way to get leverage over the other parent in court. Any other evidence of conflict may similarly taint the view of those judging the accusation as true or false, such as general family discord or specific conflict between a parent and child. As with other points of contention discussed, if a specific issue can be identified, this may render the claim more believable than, say, one made in the absence of any contextual elements or where there is no conflict.

There are numerous potential factors involved in the effects of false allegations, and the above should be considered a good start, with the author being aware of the size and scope of this chapter as but one chapter in an edited volume. There is more research needed in this area in terms of the possible effects on the falsely accused and the myriad factors that play a role in this.

6 Assessing False Reports

There are a variety of ways to assess the validity of reports, ranging from investigative approaches revolving around collecting evidence to support or refute the allegations, to social science approaches that work to disprove aspects of the claim, to actuarial methods relying on empirical studies to develop what could most simply be classified as checklists, where each item has been found to account for a certain amount of the variance between true and false statements or claims.

In *Applied Crime Analysis* (Petherick, 2015), it is suggested that any report initially be treated as a hypothesis awaiting testing and verification. In accordance with the scientific method, this hypothesis is initially viewed as potentially false (i.e. it is a null hypothesis, that is, that nothing has happened), and when enough information is gathered to falsify this, there exists sufficient information to proceed with an actual inquiry on the grounds that there is actually something to investigate. Treating the allegation in this way will prevent a costly and time-consuming inquiry when no actual crime has been committed. This approach is also supported elsewhere and is cited as a common errors made in the assessment of allegations of child abuse (Mart, 2010). Specifically (pp. 333–334),

> *A second general problem seen in many child abuse related interviews is the failure of the investigator to understand his or her role. The investigator's role is, or should be, to develop information to assist the court through the use of a hypothesis testing model. This requires some explanation. In any case of alleged abuse there are a number of logical possibilities about the actual state of affairs. The matter has come to the authorities because the child is alleged to have said something to somebody that raised concerned that they have been abused.*
>
> ...
>
> *There are other possible hypotheses, but these are possibilities in nearly every CSA case. In a good forensic interview, the evaluator should come into the situation with no preconceptions and should not be favouring any of these possibilities.*

Petherick and Ferguson (2015) propose an initial examination of the evidence, followed by a thorough victimology and an analysis of the involvement of others, before looking to other behavioural considerations.

6.1 Examination of the Evidence

The available evidence will be dictated by the type of act being claimed and by the diligence of the reporter in documenting or keeping evidence, among other things. It is important to remember that the supporting evidence in any given case will range from nothing or virtually nothing to cases with a wealth of information. Every attempt must be made to reconstruct the physical evidence where possible, and it may be necessary to recruit other professionals if the analyst is not qualified to do so. Discrepancies between the claim and the evidence must be accounted for and explained. An examination of the parts of the claim that are substantiated and that are not should be undertaken, and then, an accounting of the disparities should be performed. Whilst this would represent a perfect world scenario, the reality may be that allegations and denials will be the word of one person against the other, as there is a lack of physical evidence in most cases of abuse (Bussey, 1995).

6.2 Victimology

Victimology involves a thorough study of the victim and all information relevant to their background. This includes information from a number of domains including demographic information; medical and psychological history; financial, residential, and work history; and criminal justice system history. As a warning sign for a false report, every attempt should be made to determine whether the claimant has made any false reports in the past, how many, and the circumstances under which they were made (see this author's other chapter in this volume for a detailed overview of the process for compiling a victimology).

6.3 Involvement of Others

In this author's experience, examining the involvement of others has been found to be a prudent and fruitful step in examining a false report. False reporters will often use others deliberately, or these others may be dragged into the situation unwittingly or without a desire to be involved. Determining how these others are used is perhaps more important than simply whether they are used in the first place (Petherick & Ferguson, 2015). These others may be employed to bolster claims, and they can also be used to refute them. For example, if the allegation names a number of witnesses, these could be used to support the aspects of the claims; though, if the reporter claims someone was a witness but refuses to name or identify them, this should raise suspicion. It should be obvious that this won't indicate a false report in every situation or scenario, as some will have a legitimate reason for not involving third parties. Every attempt should be made to examine the relationship to the reporter and how this person came to be involved.

In some cases, owing to shame, embarrassment, or guilt, there may be a reluctance to involve others, especially in cases involving sexual abuse that is likely to be viewed as a private matter. Where the claimant, either a parent or a child, seeks to involve others, it must be determined whether these others serve a purpose not directly related to furthering or resolving the allegation. In one false-report case from the author's files, numerous individuals were alleged to have witnessed the various behaviours described, though none were produced on request with various florid accounts of their absences provided in lieu of being interviewed (on an overseas cruise, had since moved to another country, and was too shy to be interviewed, among others).

6.4 Behavioural Considerations

Other behavioural considerations should also be considered. If someone claims to be traumatised by the event they are reporting but is laughing whilst recounting gruesome details, this could indicate duplicity (or perhaps discomfort, with the laughter being a sign of nervousness). No one sign should be taken as proof positive of mendacity as a result, and one is looking more for an overall impression. Any paradoxical behaviour on the part of the offender that is claimed should be further investigated, such as a claim that an attack or assault happened on a busy street at rush hour without producing any witnesses. In this examination, the analyst will already have a healthy understanding of what is supported by evidence and what is not because they have spent some time with the material.

After this process has been undertaken, the analyst would use their experience and knowledge of the research and literature to make a professional judgement about the truth or falsity of the claim. In one of the original articles on the subject, Wakefield and Underwager (1991) provide a number of considerations useful in differentiating real from false allegations. These are presented briefly below (pp. 461–464):

6.5 The Origin of the Original Disclosure

Important in this regard, "young children almost never initiate false allegations without influence from an adult. The child is influenced by an adult who already believes the suspected abuse is true" (Wakefield & Underwager, 1991, p. 461). It is suggested that the young child is unable to concoct elaborate lies and is susceptible to parental influence and that spontaneous admissions are more likely to be true. This is perhaps supported by other data in this chapter.

6.6 The Timing of the Allegation

Accusations may arise at any time, but those materialising after divorce or during visitation disputes may be more common. There may be substantive differences in reports occurring during a marriage without dissolution of the relationship than occurring during a custody battle. The chronology of events is important, especially as it relates to keystone events during divorce or custody.

6.7 The Age of the Child

Very young children may be particularly susceptible to the influences of the parent, and these influences must be evaluated as younger children are more dependent on the parent.

6.8 Behaviour of the Accusing Parent

There are a variety of potential responses to claims of abuse, from the child being mistaken to knowing the abuse was happening. It is noted that in false allegation cases, the parent quickly attempts to get sympathy by telling everyone without concern for shame or privacy. Should the parent seek out the help of professionals and not hear what they want, they may seek out the assurances of professionals who are willing to verify their claims.

6.9 Nature of the Allegations

A false allegation is perhaps more likely to involve a vague assertion rather than a specific accusation that is rich in detail or perhaps relies on the claimant's intuition rather than evidence, such as "something is just not right, I know it" (p. 463). It is important to consider the nature of the allegations in terms of whether they are consistent with known abuse behaviours or whether they are not probable. Bizarre behaviours involving multiple adults or satanic rituals are less likely to be true.

6.10 Characteristics of the Child's Statement

This involves an assessment of the statement to determine whether it has characteristics of true accounts of abuse. The details provided therein should be appropriate and expected for the child's age and emotional maturity. The statement to be assessed for validity must be obtained as soon as possible from the child, and it must be spontaneous and not influenced by leading questions.

6.11 Personality Characteristics of the Parties Involved

Parents making claims of abuse may be more likely to have personality disorders and other psychiatric issues; "therefore, in the absence of corroborating evidence, when the parent making the accusation is disturbed and the accused is psychologically normal, a false accusation should be considered" (p. 464).

6.12 Behaviour of the Professionals Involved

Professionals must remain open and objective and not make judgements about guilt or innocence. Put simply, this criterion involves the professional making judgements about the veracity of the claim before an investigation has been undertaken. "In cases that turn out to be false, a professional often very quickly reaches a decision that abuse has occurred, the decision is made on the basis of limited data, disconfirming data are ignored, and no alternative options are examined" (p. 464). Wakefield and Unterwager also note that a conclusion can be reached without talking to the person accused, even if that option is open to them.

O'Donohue et al., 2013 propose 10 dimensions to analyse when an allegation of child sexual abuse is made. They claim that "although it is reasonable to hypothesise that most allegations of childhood sexual abuse (CSA) are true, children would need to be infallible for every allegation made to be true" (O'Donohue et al., 2013, p. 296). These 10 criteria are reproduced verbatim from the original (p. 300). Since the original publication of these items, the authors have integrated critiques from other authors into the checklist (see O'Donohue, Benuto, & Cirlugea, 2014):

1. Outcry analysis: The general circumstances of the child's initial accusations should be determined and analysed for possible bias.
2. Stake analysis: Whether anyone who had significant contact with the child has a hidden agenda relevant to a guilty or not guilty verdict towards the accused should be established.

3. Parental/significant other suggestion: Whether a caregiver or parent has made leading statements or engaged in leading questioning with the child resulting in the child developing a false memory should be evaluated.
4. Forensic interview analysis: Whether biased interviewing techniques were practised should be evaluated.
5. Memory analysis: Whether memory errors (e.g. errors of omission or commission) may have occurred should be determined.
6. Sufficiency of details provided by the child: Whether the child can describe in an age-appropriate manner events that occurred before, during, and after in a way that makes a coherent, understandable narrative should be assessed.
7. Inconsistency analysis: A contradictory statement by logic contains falsehoods; thus, whether the child has provided inconsistent core details between or within statements should be assessed.
8. Logistical detail analysis: Whether the allegation contains logistical implausibilities should be assessed. For example, claims that the child was anally raped but did not experience pain would make the report logistically problematic.
9. Fantastical detail analysis: The presence or absence of fantastical details in the allegations should be examined.
10. Personological analysis: Whether the child suffers from any mental health problems or history that may indicate an increased probability of either truth-telling or problematic reports should be assessed.

O'Donohue and colleagues note that the model is intended to be used by forensic examiners such as psychologists, other mental health-care professionals, and forensic interviewers who may be called upon to analyse the result of forensic interviews.

Whilst not a checklist per se, the study of 18 child sexual abuse allegations by McGraw and Smith (1992) provides factors that were "particularly helpful in attempting to discriminate substantiated from fictitious allegations." These are (p. 56):

a. The lack of accompanying emotional abuse…However, such constricted emotional accounts are also seen in some substantiated cases where the child has posttraumatic stress disorder or in cases where the child has been subjected to serial interviews.
b. Fictitious reports may lack details. However, some children with untreated Post Traumatic Stress Disorder (PTSD) may provide an allegation that has significant detail but is derived from a past and not present episode of abuse.
c. The providing of unique detail within the allegation of the abuse was often helpful in sorting out whether an allegation was reliable. Substantiated cases typically had such detail. Again, a child with untreated PTSD may have provided such detail, but the detail was not consistent with the alleged, recent allegations but rather with a past episode of actual abuse.

d. ...A psychodynamic formulation was sought before defining a case as fictitious. An example of this would be a person with traits suggestive of a histrionic personality disorder who distorts or misperceives events. Again, more than one factor appearing fictitious was necessary before a case was deemed fictitious.

7 Conclusion

Whilst most abuse allegations are legitimate, the research shows that false reports do happen. As such, investigators, mental health professionals, advocates, child safety workers, and others need to remain aware that there is a possibility of falsity and thus approach any allegation with scepticism whilst maintaining an open mind. Not only will this guard against accepting any complaint uncritically, but also it may guard against what Hans Gross (1924) calls a *preconceived theory*, which is a hypothesis about what happened that takes hold before the full facts of the case are known. The motivations for false reports in child abuse and neglect cases are likely similar to those for other types of offending with some subtle differences by virtue of who makes the complaint. There are tools and methods available to help with the determination of false reports: Some are intuitive such as reports where the claims do not match the facts, whilst others are based on the empirical study of false-report cases. Whatever the approach, all of those involved in the case must work diligently to maximise service provision to legitimate victims whilst simultaneously reducing the error for miscarriages of justice such as the arrest and possible prosecution of the falsely accused.

8 Chapter Review Questions

1. False reports only happen in about 2% of sexual abuse claims, so they are not a cause of concern.
2. Identify three different motives for false reports.
3. A false retraction is often based on what other types of false report?
4. How might the circumstances of a false report impact on the effects of a false report?
5. Identify some of the mechanisms thought that a false report can be assessed.

References

Ask, K., & Granhag, P. A. (2005). Motivational sources of confirmation bias in criminal investigations: the need for cognitive closure. *Journal of Investigative Psychology and Offender Profiling*, 2(1), 43–63. https://doi.org/10.1002/jip.19.

Brotto, G., Sinnamon, G. C. B., & Petherick, W. A. (2017). Victimology and predicting victims of violence. In W. A. Petherick & G. C. B. Sinnamon (Eds.), *The psychology of criminal and antisocial behavior: Victim and offender perspectives*. San Diego: Academic Press.

Bussey, K. (1995). Allegations of child sexual abuse—accurate and truthful disclosures, false allegations and false denials. *Current Issues in Criminal Justice*, *7*, 176–192.

Daly, M., & Wilson, M. (1997). Crime and conflict: Homicide in evolutionary psychological perspective. *Crime and Justice*, *22*, 51–100.

de Quervain, D. J. F., Fischbacher, U., Treyer, V., Schellhammer, M., Schnyder, U., Buck, A., et al. (2004). The neural basis of altruistic punishment. *Science; Washington*, *305*(5688), 1254–1258.

Department of Children and Families. (2007). *False reports of child abuse, neglect or abandonment referred to law enforcement (Annual report no. 2005–2006)*. (pp. 1–6) Florida: Department of Children and Families. Retrieved from https://www.dcf.state.fl.us/programs/childwelfare/docs/2006LMRs/2006FalseReportsChildAbuseAbandonmentNeglectReport.pdf.

Faller, K. C. (1991). Possible explanations for child sexual abuse allegations in divorce. *Journal of Orthopsychiatry*, *61*(1), 86–91. https://doi.org/10.1037/h0079227.

Faller, K. C., & DeVoe, E. (1995). Allegations of sexual abuse in divorce. *Journal of Child Sexual Abuse; Binghamton*, *4*(4), 1–25.

Friedman, S. H., Cavney, J., & Resnick, P. J. (2012). Child murder by parents and evolutionary psychology. *Psychiatric Clinics of North America*, *35*(4), 781–795. https://doi.org/10.1016/j.psc.2012.08.002.

Gakhal, B. K., & Brown, S. J. (2011). A comparison of the general public's, forensic professionals' and students' attitudes towards female sex offenders. *Journal of Sexual Aggression*, *17*(1), 105–116. https://doi.org/10.1080/13552600.2010.540678.

Gehlawat, P., Gehlawat, V., Singh, P., & Gupta, R. (2015). Munchausen syndrome by proxy: an alarming face of child abuse. *Indian Journal of Psychological Medicine; Kottayam*, *37*(1), 90–92. https://doi.org/10.4103/0253-7176.150850.

Greer, E. (2000). The truth behind legal dominance feminism's two percent false rape claim figure. *Loyola of Los Angeles Law Review*, *33*(3), 947–972.

Grobbink, L. H., Derksen, J. J. L., & van Marle, H. J. C. (2015). Revenge: an analysis of its psychological underpinnings. *International Journal of Offender Therapy and Comparative Criminology*, *59*(8), 892–907. https://doi.org/10.1177/0306624X13519963.

Gross, H. (1924). *Criminal investigation: A practical handbook for magistrates, police officers and lawyers* (34rd ed.). New York: Sweet and Maxwell.

Grubb, A. R., & Harrower, J. (2009). Understanding attribution of blame in cases of rape: an analysis of participant gender, type of rape and perceived similarity to the victim. *Journal of Sexual Aggression*, *15*(1), 63–81. https://doi.org/10.1080/13552600802641649.

Heenan, M., & Murray, S. (2006). *Study of reported rapes in Victoria, 2000–2003* [Summary research report]. Melbourne, Victoria: Office of Women's Policy.

Her Majesty's Crown Prosecution Service Inspectorate. (2002). *A report on the joint inspection into the investigation and prosecution of cases involving allegations of rape (government report)* (pp. 1–83). Her Majesty's Inspectorate of Costabulary. Retrieved from https://www.justiceinspectorates.gov.uk/cjji/wp-content/uploads/sites/2/2014/04/ARC_20020401.pdf.

Herzog, S. (2008). An attitudinal explanation of biases in the criminal justice system: an empirical testing of defensive attribution theory. *Crime & Delinquency*, *54*(3), 457–481. https://doi.org/10.1177/0011128707308158.

Hoyle, C., Speechley, N. E., & Burnett, R. (2016). *The impact of being wrongly accused of abused in occupations of trust: Victim's voices*. Oxford: Oxford University Centre for Criminology. Retrieved from https://www.law.ox.ac.uk/sites/files/oxlaw/the_impact_of_being_wrongly_accused_of_abuse_hoyle_speechley_burnett_final_26_may.pdf.

Jordan, J. (2004). Beyond belief?: police, rape and women's credibility. *Criminal Justice*, *4*(1), 29–59. https://doi.org/10.1177/1466802504042222.

Kalat, J. W. (2011). *Biological psychology* (10th ed.). Belmont: Wadsworth Cengage.

Kanin, E. (1994). False rape allegations. *Archives of Sexual Behavior*, *23*(1), 81–92.

Karanfil, R., Akçan, R., & Orhan, F. O. (2011). False allegations of child sexual abuse and paranoid disorder: a report of 2 cases. *Turkish Journal of Psychiatry*, *22*(1), 53–57.

Kassin, S. M. (2014). False confessions. *Policy Insights from the Behavioral and Brain Sciences*, *1*(1), 112–121. https://doi.org/10.1177/2372732214548678.

Kassin, S. M. (2017). False confessions. *WIREs Cognitive Science*, *8*, 1–11. https://doi.org/10.1002/wcs.1439.

Kennedy, D. B., & Witkowski, M. (2000). False allegations of rape revisited: A replication of the Kanin study. *Journal of Security Administration*, *23*, 41–46.

Kirsch, P., Zimmermann, J., Schmitz, A., Lis, S., Gallhofer, B., Reuter, M., et al. (2009). What you did to others you did to me? Brain activation during altruistic punishment in a first person versus a third party dictator game. *NeuroImage*, *47*, S95. https://doi.org/10.1016/S1053-8119(09)70769-4.

Kleven, A. (2012). Tears and forgiveness as Longview dad, daughter speak on false allegations. *MYNorthwest*, December 11. Retrieved from http://mynorthwest.com/31502/tears-and-forgiveness-as-longview-dad-daughter-speak-on-false-rape-allegations/? Accessed 10 September 2018.

Lanning, K. (2010). *Child molesters: A behavioural analysis for professionals investigating the sexual exploitation of children* ((5th ed.). Washington, DC: National Centre for Missing and Exploited Children.1–195. Retrieved from http://www.missingkids.com/content/dam/ncmec/en_us/desktop/publications/nc70.pdf.

Lazard, L. (2017). *Here's the truth about false accusations of sexual violence*. NCMEC. Retrieved May 1, 2018, from http://theconversation.com/heres-the-truth-about-false-accusations-of-sexual-violence-88049(2017).

Leonard, D. P. (2001). Character and motive in evidence law. *Loyola of Los Angeles Law Review*, *34*(2), 439–536.

Lightcap, J. L., Kurland, J. A., & Burgess, R. L. (1982). Child abuse: A test of some predictions from evolutionary theory. *Ethology & Sociobiology*, *3*(2), 61–67.

MacKay, T. (2014). False allegations of child abuse in contested family law cases: the implications for psychological practice. *Educational and Child Psychology*, *31*(3), 85–96.

Mart, E. G. (2010). Common errors in the assessment of allegations of child sexual abuse. *Journal of Psychiatry and Law; London*, *38*(3), 325–343,263.

Martell, D. M. (1988). Clarifying erroneous child sexual abuse allegations. *American Journal of Orthopsychiatry*, *58*(4), 618–621.

McGrath, M., & Torres, A. N. (2010). Forensic mental health assessments. In W. A. Petherick, B. E. Turvey, & C. E. Ferguson (Eds.), *Forensic criminology*. San Diego: Academic Press.

McGraw, J. M., & Smith, H. A. (1992). Child sexual abuse allegations amidst divorce and custody proceedings: refining the validation process. *Journal of Child Sexual Abuse*, *1*(1), 49–57.

Myers, M. A. (1980). Social contexts and attributions of criminal responsibility. *Social Psychology Quarterly*, *43*(4), 405. https://doi.org/10.2307/3033960.

National Registry of Exonerations. (2018). Exonerations in 2017. In *The national register of exonerations* (pp. 1–22). Irvine: University of California. Retrieved from https://www.law.umich.edu/special/exoneration/Documents/ExonerationsIn2017.pdf?utm_source=National+Registry+of+Exonerations+Newsletter&utm_campaign=7008e6a520-EMAIL_CAMPAIGN_2018_03_07&utm_medium=email&utm_term=0_47e13608bc-7008e6a520-66652693.

O'Donohue, W., Benuto, L. T., & Cirlugea, O. (2013). Analyzing child sexual abuse allegations. *Journal of Forensic Psychology Practice*, *13*(4), 296–314. https://doi.org/10.1080/15228932.2013.822245.

O'Donohue, W., Benuto, L. T., & Cirlugea, O. (2014). Analyzing child sexual abuse allegations: further considerations. *Journal of Forensic Psychology Practice*, *14*(3), 237–246. https://doi.org/10.1080/15228932.2014.918476.

Pathé, M. (2002). *Surviving stalking*. Oxford: Oxford University Press.

Petherick, W. A. (2015). Motivations. In W. A. Petherick (Ed.), *Applied crime analysis: A social science approach to understanding crime, criminals, and victims*. ((1st ed.,)(pp. 148–171). Waltham: Academic Press.

Petherick, W. A., & Ferguson, C. E. (2015). False reports. In W. A. Petherick (Ed.), *Applied crime analysis: A social science approach to understanding crime, criminals, and victims*. Boston: Anderson Publishing.

Petherick, W. A., & Sinnamon, G. C. B. (2014). Motivations: Offender and victim perspectives. In W. A. Petherick (Ed.), *Profiling and serial crime: Theoretical and practical issues* (3rd ed.). Boston: Anderson Publishing.

Plummer, C. A., & Eastin, J. (2007). The effect of child sexual abuse allegations/investigations on the mother/child relationship. *Violence Against Women*, *13*(10), 1053–1071. https://doi.org/10.1177/1077801207305931.

Raine, A. (2013). *The anatomy of violence*. New York: Pantheon.

Rassin, E., Eerland, A., & Kuijpers, I. (2010). Let's find the evidence: an analogue study of confirmation bias in criminal investigations. *Journal of Investigative Psychology and Offender Profiling*, *7*(3), 231–246. https://doi.org/10.1002/jip.126.

Rassin, E., & van der Sleen, J. (2005). Characteristics of true versus false allegations of sexual offences. *Psychological Reports*, *97*, 589–598.

Rieser, M. (1991). Recantation in child sexual abuse cases. *Child Welfare*, *70*(6), 611–621.

Roeckelein, J. E. (Ed.), (2006). *Elsevier's dictionary of psychological theories* (1st ed.). Boston: Elsevier.

Ross, W. (2012). Casandra Kennedy recants rape charge against her father, freed after 9 years. *The Daily Beast*. Retrieved from https://www.thedailybeast.com/articles/2012/04/10/casandra-kennedy-recants-rape-charge-against-her-father-freed-after-9-years.

Rumney, P. N. S., & McCartan, K. F. (2017). Purported false allegations of rape, child abuse and non-sexual violence: nature, characteristics and implications. *The Journal of Criminal Law*, *81*(6), 497–520. https://doi.org/10.1177/0022018317746789.

Savvidou, I., Bozikas, V. P., & Karavatos, A. (2002). False allegations of child physical abuse: a case of Münchausen by proxy-like syndrome? *The International Journal of Psychiatry in Medicine*, *32*(2), 201–208. https://doi.org/10.2190/5AUK-YGF7-0Q58-A7EH.

Saxbe, D., Lyden, H., Gimbel, S. I., Sachs, M., Piero, L. B. D., Margolin, G., et al. (2018). Longitudinal associations between family aggression, externalizing behavior, and the structure and function of the amygdala. *Journal of Research on Adolescence*, *28*(1), 134–149. https://doi.org/10.1111/jora.12349.

Schenck, C. H., & Mahowald, M. W. (1998). An analysis of a recent criminal trial involving sexual misconduct with a child, alcohol abuse and a successful sleepwalking defence: arguments supporting two proposed new forensic categories. *Medicine, Science and the Law*, *38*(2), 147–152. https://doi.org/10.1177/002580249803800211.

Sorensen, T., & Snow, B. (1991). How children tell: the process of disclosure in child sexual abuse. *Child Welfare*, *70*(1), 3–15.

Theimer, K., & Hansen, D. J. (2017). Attributions of blame in a hypothetical child sexual abuse case: roles of behaviour problems and frequency of abuse. *Journal of Interpersonal Violence*, 1–22. https://doi.org/10.1177/0886260517716943.

Thoennes, N., & Tjaden, P. G. (1990). The extent, nature, and validity of sexual abuse allegations in custody/visitation disputes. *Child Abuse and Neglect*, *14*, 151–163.

Tully, B. (2002). The evaluation of retractions in sexual abuse cases. *Child Abuse Review*, *11*(2), 94–102. https://doi.org/10.1002/car.728.

Wakefield, H., & Underwager, R. (1991). Sexual abuse allegations in divorce and custody disputes. *Behavioural Sciences and the Law*, *9*, 451–468.

CHAPTER 15

Mandatory Reporting: Managing Disclosure and Information Gathering

Andrew Lowe
Queensland Police Service, Toowoomba, QLD, Australia

Mandatory reporting legislation—laws that place an onus on certain professionals to report suspected child abuse—forms part of a government response to detecting and preventing child abuse. It is the purpose of this chapter to discuss key components that are consistent across the various pieces of mandatory legislation. Specifically, attention will be given to legal terms such as *harm*, *reasonable suspicion*, and *reasonable belief*. This is done to inform professionals of various legal thresholds so that informed decisions can be made about their reporting obligations. Decision-making models will also be considered, providing professionals with a framework to help articulate their own decision-making processes when making a report to authorities of child abuse. The second part of this chapter provides advice to professionals around how to have conversations with children who self-disclose abuse. It acknowledges that these professionals are often one of the earliest persons a child discloses abuse to and addresses the need for professionals to be able to respond to these disclosures. Strategies are proposed to assist professionals in obtaining further information from the child in an appropriate manner that considers the evidentiary importance of these disclosures and helps to satisfy the professionals' suspicion or belief, informing their decision to report or not.

1 Mandatory Reporting

In 1962, Dr C. Henry Kempe and Dr Brandt F. Steele published the paper, 'The Battered Child Syndrome', introducing the concept of child abuse to medical practitioners. In subsequent editions of the paper, Kempe, Silverman, Steele, Droefemueller, and Silver (1985) described battered child syndrome as a "clinical condition in young children who have received serious physical abuse, generally from a parent or foster parent" (p. 143). Further, they identified that the clinical presentation can vary widely from those cases in which the trauma is very mild and is often unsuspected and unrecognised to those who exhibit the most florid evidence of injury to the soft tissues and skeleton (Kempe et al., 1985, p. 144).

Child Abuse and Neglect. https://doi.org/10.1016/B978-0-12-815344-4.00015-5

Regardless of the symptoms, Kempe et al. (1985) suggested that battered child syndrome should be considered for any case where a child exhibits possible trauma and neglect, and there are marked discrepancies with the information provided by the parents or caregivers. The greatest contribution of this publication, however, was not the identification of physical abuse indicators, rather it was the acknowledgement of the extent of the child maltreatment problem (Melton, 2005) and proposed responses by professionals when encountering this issue. Kempe et al. (1985) recommended that, in response to this problem, the physician should.

> *... report possible wilful trauma to the police department or any special children's protective service that operates in his community. The report that he makes should be restricted to the objective findings which can be verified and, where possible, should be supported by photographs and roentgenograms (p. 153).*

Kempe's conclusion that the best response was for health practitioners to report suspect abuse to appropriate authorities has subsequently had a significant impact on public policy regarding child abuse matters (Melton, 2005).

Since this was proposed in 1962, many jurisdictions across the world have enacted *mandatory reporting legislation* in a variety of forms. Mandatory reporting refers to statutory obligations placed on certain professional groups to report known or suspected cases of child abuse or neglect to relevant agencies charged with the investigation and response to child protection matters (Mathews, 2014; Mathews & Walsh, 2004; Walsh, Schweitzer, & Bridgstock, 2005). These professionals include, but are not limited to, teachers, medical professionals, mental health professionals, and police and are done with the goal of ceasing victimisation, providing health care and support interventions, and taking enforcement action against the perpetrator (Mathews, 2014; Mathews, Bromfield, Walsh, & Vimpani, 2015). Mandatory reporting legislation is based on three assumptions: (1) that children are not able to protect themselves and need others to act on their behalf, (2) that abusive parents will not voluntarily request assistance, and (3) that persons who deal children are ideally placed to detect abuse (Takis, 2008). This legislation forms part of government compliance with the *United Nations Convention on the Rights of the Child*, specifically Article 19, which states that.

> *States Parties shall take all appropriate legislative, administrative, social, and educational measures to protect the child from all forms of physical or mental violence, injury or abuse, neglect or negligent treatment, and maltreatment or exploitation, including sexual abuse, whilst in the care of parent(s), legal guardian(s), or any other person who has the care of the child (UN General Assembly, 1989).*

Ultimately, the intent of mandatory reporting laws is to protect children from serious harm and to assist parents and caregivers in decreasing the likelihood that harm will reoccur (Mathews & Walsh, 2014).

1.1 Defining Harm or Abuse

Each jurisdiction's guiding child protection legislation should have a working definition of *harm* or *abuse* contained within. Whilst there will be nuances between different jurisdictions or organisations, there will, however, be broader similarities, as most of these pieces of legislation or policy are guided by overarching international guidelines, namely, the World Health Organisation (2017), which proposes that

> *Child maltreatment, sometimes referred to as child abuse and neglect, includes all forms of physical and emotional ill-treatment, sexual abuse, neglect, and exploitation that results in actual or potential harm to the child's health, development or dignity. Within this broad definition, five subtypes can be distinguished—physical abuse, sexual abuse, neglect and negligent treatment, emotional abuse, and exploitation*

Definitions of abuse or harm, as seen above, often break these terms into subcategories—physical, sexual, emotional, and neglect—however, it is important to articulate the fundamental concepts of what 'harm' or 'abuse' is, so that when reporting this behaviour, the full circumstances and impacts can be identified. For this, core definitions of these terms should be considered.

'Abuse', within the context of child abuse and neglect, is defined as (1) the improper use of something and (2) cruel or violent treatment of a person or animal (Oxford Dictionaries, 2018). 'Harm' is defined as (1) physical injury, especially that is deliberately inflicted (Oxford Dictionaries, 2018). Both definitions imply that these are behaviours that are intentionally inflicted, not accidental; have an element of violence or impropriety when considering broader social norms; and result in an injury or detriment—whether it be physical or emotional. Both harm and abuse, therefore, contain two elements for consideration of professionals: (1) an intentional act and (2) a consequence. These differ from 'neglect'—"(1.1) the action of not taking proper care of someone or something; (1.2) failure to do something" (Oxford Dictionaries, 2018)—in that, it is not an intentional act, rather a failure to do something they are lawfully and morally obliged to do.

1.2 Reasonable Suspicion or Reasonable Belief

Mandatory reporting legislation inevitably will include a reporting threshold based on the professional having a *suspicion* or *belief* that child abuse has occurred (Mathews et al., 2015). These terms, within the legislative context, exist on a certainty continuum of increasing confidence from lowest to highest of (1) suspicion, (2) belief, and (3) knowledge. Defining these and articulating their differences can be challenging and have been identified as being problematic for professionals in deciding whether to report or not (Mathews & Walsh, 2004). Given that these terms are legal constructs, consideration must be given to precedent set in case law as to the meaning of each of the terms.

To demonstrate this continuum, the following fictional case study and discussion are used:

Case Study (Part 1): A classroom teacher is alerted to a change in a student's behaviour.

There are a number of reasons that could explain a child's change in behaviour, of which abuse is one of many. Based on this information alone, there is no evidence presented that can lead one to suspect abuse. It may, however, activate the teacher to pay closer attention to the child.

The least certain state of mind is *suspicion*. Consideration is given to Chief Justice Griffith's comments in the matter of *Caroll v Hasz* (1903):

> *The words 'suspected on reasonable grounds' are capable of being construed in two ways; they may mean that facts exist which would justify suspicion in the mind of anyone, or they may mean the existence of facts which, in the mind of some individual give rise to a suspicion which is reasonable – that is the words may be used in an objective or subjective sense. I think that they are used in the objective sense and have an absolutely impersonal meaning*

Suspicion is a state of mind, based on facts, which give rise to an apprehension of the existence of a matter (*R v Chan*, 1992). It is more than a possibility (*R v Rondo*, 2001) and is an inclination towards assenting to a proposition, rather than rejecting it (*George v Rockett*, 1990).

Case Study (Part 2): Later that day, the classroom teacher sees the child's shirt to be pushed up. The classroom teacher observes what appears to be a bruise running horizontally across the child's back. The mark is dark purple in colour and is observed to be a long straight line about 3 cm wide. A circular shape can be seen in the mark, which has broken the skin.

Whilst exact wound identification for evidentiary purposes can only be done by a medical professional, the classroom teacher uses their own experiences about what a bruise looks like to inform their interpretations. Similarly, the shape of the bruise looks, in the teacher's experience, or appears similar to how a belt and buckle are shaped. Whilst no explanation has yet been provided as to how the marks occurred, or (a) if they are bruises, (b) whether they were intentionally inflicted, or (c) if there was another explanation as to how this occurred, the teacher now has information that has raised an apprehension that the child has been physically abused. The teacher, therefore, *reasonably suspects* that the child has been abused.

Belief is more than suspicion (*R v Chan*, 1992) but is less than knowledge, as a person can hold a belief that a state exists whilst still having a degree of doubt about the matter (*R v Raad*, 1983).

Case Study (Part 3): Later that day, the classroom teacher speaks privately with the child, asking what happened to their back. The child replies that one of their parents, 'hit me with their belt'.

The disclosure by the child confirms the suspicion held by the classroom teacher and assists in formulating a *reasonable belief* that the child has been abused. It has now been identified that the act was caused by a caregiver and that the child has been struck with an implement. There is still some element of doubt, around the context of the strike, and whether it is intentional or accidental. However, there is a strong belief that physical abuse has occurred.

The highest end of certainty on the continuum is to have *knowledge* and to accept the truth of what is believed (*R v Fallon*, 1981; *R v Raad*, 1983). Given the high threshold that knowledge implies—that there is some direct evidence that leads the professional to, unequivocally, recognise that child abuse has occurred—knowledge of child abuse is not the typical threshold for reporting (Mathews & Kenny, 2008), as this may only come after an investigation is completed.

Scenario (Part 4): Having received a report of suspected abuse, investigative agencies speak with the child who discloses being struck multiple times by their parent with a belt after they became angry because the child would not clean their teeth. Further examination located multiple similar injuries across the child's body in various locations, which, on medical examination, were confirmed to be bruising and consistent with a belt. A belt was located at the home address that, when overlayed with the injuries, was an identical shape. When interviewed, the parent confirmed the version of the child and that the actions were not proportionate in their response to the child's behaviour.

There is no further doubt about the events, and knowledge of the full event is now held.

It should be noted that this example is designed to demonstrate the principles of suspicion, belief, and knowledge. There will be a multitude of factors that may activate a professional's suspicion. The absence of any of the evidence discussed above, such as injuries or disclosures by the child, should not preclude against reporting harm if the professional achieves a level of suspicion, regardless of what brings them to that state.

1.3 Decision Making and Reporting Harm

Despite the existence of legislation requiring professionals to report suspicions of child abuse and neglect to authorities, there are still a number who do not report suspected abuse. In their review of barriers to mandatory reporting in the United Kingdom and Ireland, Bunting, Lazenbatt, and Wallace (2010) cite research that 20% of Australian teachers had decided not to report suspected child abuse and neglect, whereas physicians were even higher with 43% deciding against reporting. Other international studies have shown that between 10% (Walsh et al., 2005) and 49% (Goebbels, Nicholson, Walsh, & Vries, 2008) of teachers failed to report suspect child abuse in their careers. In other professions, a study by Blaskett and Taylor (2003) suggested the nonreporting rate was 10% overall, with psychiatrists having the highest rate of nonreporting at 23%, and nurses the lowest at 4%. Whilst the rates of failing to report suspect child abuse and neglect vary across locations and professions, the reasons for nonreporting are more consistent. These reasons include, but are not limited to, a lack of knowledge around the process of reporting abuse (Alvarez, Donohue, Kenny, Cavanagh, & Romero, 2005; Blaskett & Taylor, 2003; Finlayson & Koocher, 1991); professional characteristics, attitudes, and beliefs such as a belief that the professional themselves is the best person to resolve the issue (Blaskett & Taylor, 2003; Bunting et al., 2010); subjective judgements about the child's best interests (Francis et al., 2012); a fear of litigation or retaliation or at least a breakdown of the professional working relationship with the family (Alvarez et al., 2005; Beck, Oglaff, & Corbishley, 1994; Kenny, 2004); a belief that child protection agencies don't respond properly (Blaskett & Taylor, 2003); a lack of any physical evidence (Beck et al., 1994; Bunting et al., 2010); and the professionals' interpretation regarding reporting thresholds (Finlayson & Koocher, 1991).

Rather than focussing on why professionals fail to report suspected abuse, consideration should be given to the processes that occur when deciding to report suspected abuse. Earlier works by Dalgleish (1988) suggest that this decision-making process involves a *judgement* (is this abuse?) and an *action* (will I report it?). First, meeting the *judgement threshold* involves the professional judging, the severity of the abuse based on the case characteristics, the professionals' previous experience, and personal values to decide whether a child has been harmed. Following this is the *action threshold*, where the professional decides whether to make a report to authorities (Dalgleish, 1988). In making this second decision, professionals must consider the consequences of the reporting on all parties involved, the quality of the suspicion, and where this lies within the professional's own threshold of risk in deciding whether to take action or not (Walsh, Farrell, Bridgstock, & Schweitzer, 2006).

A second systematic decision-making process has been proposed by Francis et al. (2012) and consists of four stages: (1) being alerted to the possibility of abuse or neglect, (2) gathering evidence, (3) deciding whether to report, and (4) processing the outcome of their action. In the first phase, *being alerted*, the professional is triggered to the possibility that a child has been abused or neglected, either from physical, behavioural, or social cues exhibited by the child (Francis et al., 2012). From this, a professional *gathers evidence* that involves either actively seeking information or 'watchful waiting' to see if the situation is a one-off event or an ongoing event (Francis et al., 2012). When *deciding to report*, the third phase, the professional must balance their reporting obligation against the information they have gathered (Francis et al., 2012). If the gathered evidence is the stronger of the two, then a report will be made. Alternatively, if the legal obligations placed on the professional are greater than the level of suspicion, it is likely that the report will not be made or at least deferred. Finally, the fourth phase, *processing the decision*, involves self-reflection on behalf of the professional on their decision (Francis et al., 2012).

Both of these models promote the need for information to support the presence of abuse, develop a suspicion, and inform the reporting decision (Walsh et al., 2006). This is supported by research conducted with education professionals, which has shown 'a strong relationship between teachers' detection (how likely is it that this child has been abused or neglected?) and reporting (how likely is it that you will report this case to the authorities?)' (Walsh, Bridgestock, Farrell, Rassafiani, & Schweitzer, 2008, p. 990). In other words, when the information held by professionals leads them to be reasonably convinced that child abuse occurred, they would be likely to report the abuse. Further to this, supporting research, analysing what information is most likely to convince a professional as to the existence of abuse, has indicated that there "can be no substitute for a child's own witness in deciding to report child abuse" (Crenshaw, Crenshaw, & Lichtenberg, 1995, p. 1106), meaning that how a professional handles a child's disclosure of abuse is directly related to informing their decision to report the abuse.

2 Information Gathering and Managing Disclosures

Perhaps, the most significant argument against mandatory reporting legislation is that by requiring professionals to report *suspected* abuse, it will produce an increased number of unfounded notifications to investigative agencies, thereby increasing the burden on already encumbered agencies and diverting resources (Mathews & Walsh, 2004; Queensland Law Reform Commission, 2015). In 2003, a study of the 2222 reports of harm lodged by Queensland teachers showed that 72% ($n=1597$) of these reports were subsequently substantiated by child protection agencies (Mathews & Walsh, 2004). A more detailed comparison of Australian substantiation rates across various jurisdictions was completed by Mathews et al. (2015), which produced the following results:

		Mandatory Reporters		Nonmandatory Reporters	
	Reports	Reports	Substantiated Reports	Reports	Substantiated Reports
ACT	75,382	37,272 (*49.5%*)	4074 (10.9%)	38,110 (50.5%)	4264 (11.2%)
NSW	1,022,486	–	–	–	–
NT	46,431	21,847 (*47.1%*)	5227 (23.9%)	24,847 (52.9%)	5279 (21.2%)
QLD	250,752	130,608 (*52.1%*)	63,731 (48.8%)	120,144 (47.9%)	56,076 (46.7%)
SA	269,315	142,153 (*52.8%*)	12,718 (8.9%)	127,162 (47.2%)	9277 (7.2%)
TAS	98,987	65,912 (*66.6%*)	8245 (12.5%)	33,075 (33.4%)	3028 (9.2%)
VIC	454,120	190,428 (*41.9%*)	36,888 (19.3%)	263,692 (58.1%)	41,180 (15.6%)
WA	79,136	39,315 (*49.7%*)	8637 (21%)	39,821 (50.3%)	9409 (23.6%)

Two issues of note are observed in these results. First is the degree of attrition when comparing the numbers of reports, and the numbers of which are ultimately substantiated. Second, there is little difference in the substantiation rates between mandatory reporters and those who don't have legal obligations to report. Arguments against mandatory reporting legislation use these results to suggest that this legislation is not effective and unnecessarily overburdens the child protection system. Alternatively, Mathews and Walsh (2004) suggest that the argument that is raised by these results should not be against mandatory reporting legislation, but "more precisely is against (a) insufficient resources, and (b) inaccurate reporting" (p. 34). This therefore highlights the need for increasing accuracy achieved through information gathering.

2.1 Why Do We Need to Speak to Children Disclosing Child Abuse?

Speaking to children who disclose child abuse is one of the main means to gather information as to what has happened, and from the professional's perspective, these conversations can help solidify their decision to report child abuse. In a study conducted by Finlayson and Koocher (1991), it was identified that psychologists were

> *significantly more likely to suspect sexual abuse if symptoms reported were highly specific than if they received ambiguous signs that might or might not be associated with sexual abuse. Virtually all respondents had a substantial degree of suspicion when the child made a direct statement regarding abuse. The respondents' degree of suspicion decreased as the clinical presentation of sexual abuse became more ambiguous (p. 469)*

This uncertainty was nearly eliminated when a direct communication of abuse was made (Finlayson & Koocher, 1991), meaning that how professionals handle these disclosures is vital to the overall child protection response. Further, there is a strong restorative purpose of having these conversations. By this, it is meant that adults who work with children may be the most trusted adults in a child's life, particularly if they have come from an abusive background (Mathews & Walsh, 2004). This trust is what facilitates "the making of disclosures by children about their experience" (p. 33), and people who work with children are often the first people to whom the child has disclosed the abuse. Therefore, if the disclosure of abuse is not handled appropriately, not only will this impact on the relationship between the child and the professional, but also it may create a barrier to the child in obtaining assistance to rectify the harm done to them.

In saying this, even before the conversation commences, some general principles must be discussed when being alerted to abuse against a child. These relate to nonverbal behaviours and attitudes when encountering these situations. First and foremost, the disclosures need to be dealt with sensitively, and the professional should avoid appearing shocked or other strong reactions, as this may impact how the child feels having finally made the disclosure (Crosson-Tower, 2003). Consideration should be given to the fact that "children often feel or are told that they are to blame for their own maltreatment and for bringing 'trouble' to the family" (p. 25), and as such, any negative response may reinforce this belief. Even though a disclosure of abuse may not be expected when interacting with children, when they do occur, the receiver must respond in a sensitive, comforting, and calm manner so as to prevent any reinforcement of negative beliefs. Most importantly, the child's statement must not be dismissed or delayed because the professional is unprepared for the conversation or believes that they should speak to someone more appropriate before continuing. The most serious consequence of these nonverbal behaviours is that the child stops engaging with the investigation and intervention, therefore not receiving the assistance required to prevent ongoing abuse. With the right conversation management strategies available to the professionals, such a situation can be avoided.

2.2 Having Conversations With Children Who Disclose Abuse

Having conversations with young persons who disclose abuse is *not* about investigating the child's allegations. There is never an expectation on individuals who work with children to investigate a child's disclosure (Best, 2001; Mathews, 2011). Rather than an investigative function, these initial conversations assist in the collection of information that allows the professional to establish their suspicions of harm and assist in making a decision around their legal obligations under mandatory reporting legislation and other professional obligations (Mathews, 2011). It also facilitates the provision of accurate advice to designated child protection investigators to help them in making decisions regarding the investigation and intervention strategy. The collection of additional information may also benefit the professional themselves in the ongoing therapeutic or pedagogical relationship with the child (Best, 2001; Mathews, 2011).

There is no template that can be applied to the sequence of questions one must ask a child who has disclosed abuse. Such a rigid approach may be detrimental to the disclosure process, rather than being responsive to what the child is saying in a specific situation. There are certainly many generic positive behaviours that can be followed when dealing with disclosures of abuse; however, these differ from having a prepared conversation script, which should be avoided. Shepherd and Griffiths (2013) identify several child-centred conversational behaviours, which include, but are not limited to, being courteous, speaking clearly, using simple vocabulary and short uncomplex sentences, remaining positive and nonjudgemental, and ensuring each other's meaning and understandings are the same. More specific behaviours are suggested by Crosson-Tower (2003), including (1) refraining from asking leading questions, (2) letting the child tell his story without probing for information, (3) explaining to the child the obligation to report the abuse, and (4) reassuring the child that the information will be handled in confidence.

The author proposes three specific strategies that can be adopted by professionals when speaking with children who have self-disclosed abuse, for the purpose of gathering accurate and reliable information and assisting in making an informed decision to meet their mandatory reporting obligations. These relate to both the actual conversation and postconversation behaviours that are important investigative considerations that may impact the professional. These include (1) listening, (2) asking open questions, and (3) maintaining the 'chain of disclosure'. It should also be noted that the term *interview* or *interviewer* will appear in the following sections. This should not be confused with *investigator*. The term interview or any derivative of this is used to denote a conversation with a purpose (Burgess, 1984).

2.2.1 Listening

It is widely acknowledged that the "best interviewers are those who listen a great deal more than they talk" (Wilson & Powell, 2001, p. 41). One of the greatest causes of consternation when speaking with children who disclose abuse or any other interview situation is the worry that the interviewer will be able to come up with the right question to ask at the right time (Wilson & Powell, 2001). This can be alleviated by focussing and listening on what the child is saying, rather than concentrating on what future questions will be. Listening to the verbal cues used by the child may identify further questions to be asked or even remove the need for further questions, depending on the level of information provided by the child. Active listening may also prompt further disclosures, simply because the child knows they are being heard, and "this is what matters most to a child in an interview" (p. 41). There are two strategies that can be used to demonstrate to the child that they are being heard. First is the use of minimal prompts (Wilson & Powell, 2001), such as head-nodding and other signs of understanding (e.g. 'uh-huh', 'ok', and 'mmm'). Second is the use of pauses after the child has finished speaking and before a further question is asked. An appropriate length pause presents a number of beneficial things to the conversation, as it "gives you time to observe the child, to think what you want to say, and to think how to say it" (Shepherd & Griffiths, 2013, p. 329); it is also the "best cue for the child to carry on talking" (p. 326).

2.2.2 Ask open questions

It is widely acknowledged that the type of questions asked by a person can influence their ability to accurately recall an incident (Bowles & Sharman, 2014; Lipton, 1977; Milne & Bull, 1999). It is therefore "imperative to understand the nature of questioning in order to conduct the most effective and nonbiased interview" (Milne & Bull, 1999, p. 26). To understand how to ask an open question, it is important to know not only what constitutes such a question but also what types of questions are *not* open questions. This section will discuss *open questions*, *specific or direct questions*, *closed questions*, and *leading and other inappropriate questions*, before exploring why open questions are so effective as an interview strategy.

Open questions are questions that "do not make assumptions or assume a particular answer" (Wilson & Powell, 2001, p. 53). Open questions are "framed in such a way that the *interviewee* is able to give an open, unrestricted answer, which, in turn, enables the interviewee to control the flow of the information in the interview [emphasis added]" (Milne & Bull, 1999, p. 22). These questions are often framed as an instruction or request for more detail (Shepherd & Griffiths, 2013; Wilson & Powell, 2001). An example of an open question is

Open Question:
"You said that someone touched your privates, tell me everything about that."

No restrictions or parameters are placed on the child's version, allowing them to speak inhibited by nothing other than the extent to which the child wishes to speak. Similar questions may be structured around instructions such as '*tell*', '*explain*', or '*describe*' to initiate free disclosure from the child or expand on what they have previously said (Shepherd & Griffiths, 2013).

Compared with open questions, *specific or direct questions* are, as the name suggests, more focussed on details within the child's version. Specific questions ask for precise information and require few words in response (Milne & Bull, 1999). These questions "focus the child's attention on a narrow or specific aspect of the event that may need to be clarified but would not otherwise be provided during the child's account of the event" (p. 23). Such questions may commence with the following words—*who*, *what*, *when*, *where*, *why*, and *how*. An example of a specific or direct question is

---

Specific or Direct Question:
"What colour was his shirt?"

Specific questions can be useful to obtain further detail but should be used cautiously (Wilson & Powell, 2001). This level of detail would certainly be in the parameters of an interview by investigators and child protection agencies; however, the level of detail sought may exceed what is needed to develop a professional's reasonable suspicion of abuse. Considering that error rates in accounts may increase with the use of these questions (Wilson & Powell, 2001), their use should be minimised in these contexts.

Closed questions further direct the child towards specific information and provide even further restrictions on the range of answers, usually either a 'yes' or 'no' (Wilson & Powell, 2001). An example of a closed question is

---

Closed Question:
"Did this happen in your bedroom?"

Whilst these questions are less taxing on the child's verbal ability (Wilson & Powell, 2001), they can restrict the flow of conversation and should only be used if other questioning approaches have been unsuccessful (Milne & Bull, 1999). Again, this level of detail would most likely be outside the scope of what is required by the professional to establish a reasonable suspicion of abuse.

Of all the question types, *leading and other inappropriate questions* are questions that, unanimously agreed, should be avoided because of the adverse effect they have on the child's evidence (Bowles & Sharman, 2014; Lipton, 1977; Milne & Bull, 1999; Wilson

& Powell, 2001). Leading questions are "so worded that it is not neutral; i.e. it suggests to the witness, by its form or content, what the answer should be, lead him to the desired answer, or indicates the questioners point of view" (Hibberd & Worring, 1981 cited in Milne & Bull, 1999, p. 25). Leading questions "assume the existence of facts that have not yet been proved or have not already been mentioned" (Milne & Bull, 1999, p. 25). Given that the purpose of a leading question is to prompt the desired response, the chance of incorrect information being provided in response to these questions is high and therefore should be avoided (Lipton, 1977; Shepherd & Griffiths, 2013; Wilson & Powell, 2001). Other inappropriate questions include *forced-choice questions*, where a small number of alternatives are provided for the witnesses to select, with the risk being that the correct answer is not among those answers, and *multiple questions*, where multiple questions asked are answered in one meaning that misunderstandings can occur as which question is to be answered or to which question the answer relates (Milne & Bull, 1999).

From the perspective of professionals seeking to gather more information so as to support a reasonable suspicion or belief that child abuse has occurred, there would be little cause to obtain the 'fine grain' detail through the use of probing and closed-style questions. In fact, it has been acknowledged that probing for answers in these situations can do more harm to the overall investigation (Crosson-Tower, 2003). To avoid this, it is recommended that open-ended questions be used as much as possible to obtain information from a child who has self-disclosed abuse. By focussing on open-ended questions when gathering information, a number of positive outcomes occur. These include, but are not limited to, (1) providing the most accurate information, (2) providing the most accurate information from vulnerable persons, (3) minimising the risk of evidence contamination, and (4) allowing the interviewee to speak longer about the topics under examination.

First and foremost, open-ended questions provide more accurate information (Hershkowitz, Lamb, Stenberg, & Esplin, 1997; Milne & Bull, 1999). Research in controlled environments, where participants watch a staged event, has shown that interviewee responses to open questions are generally accurate (Lipton, 1977). Results from these tests vary between 83% (Lipton, 1977) and 91% (Milne & Bull, 1999) of accurate responses. It should be noted, however, that in these simulated tests, participants "only freely recalled 21% of the facts simulated" (p. 21). Other question types provided a greater volume of information; however, the accuracy decreased with their use (Lipton, 1977). What this demonstrates is that open questions do not necessarily get all or even the majority of information but what information is provided is largely accurate and reliable. Whilst this may be an issue for investigators and child protection agencies who require significantly more detail to satisfy legal requirements in either the criminal or child protection systems, this is not necessary for professionals dealing with initial disclosures of abuse. By utilising open-ended questions, the professional will likely produce sufficient and reliable information about the abuse to satisfy whether a reasonable suspicion exists.

Similar results are seen regarding accuracy rates of information provided by vulnerable persons with the use of open-ended questions. Whilst vulnerable persons, particularly persons with an intellectual disability, may not perform as well in an interview situation, they can still produce accurate and reliable information when questioned with mainly open-ended questions and other positive interviewer behaviour (Bowles & Sharman, 2014). Results have demonstrated that persons with an intellectual disability, both adults and children, produce fewer details when questioned, but their information was *no less accurate* than those without an intellectual disability (Bowles & Sharman, 2014). Given that children with some form of disability are overrepresented with respect to child abuse victimisation, with reported incidence ranging from 4% to 70% (Australian Institute of Family Studies, 1996), the potential to encounter a victim of child abuse with a vulnerability is, therefore, a possibility. Professionals who adopt open-ended questions to explore disclosures will use the same approach regardless of the existence of a vulnerability.

Open-ended questions also minimise "the risk that the interviewer will impose his or her view of what happened on the interviewee" (Milne & Bull, 1999, p. 22). This is largely due to the fact that the interviewee is doing the most of the talking, as open-ended questions elicit longer responses than other question types (Hershkowitz et al., 1997; Shepherd & Griffiths, 2013). It also means that the child is "less likelihood of being confronted with a question about which no response can be made, and it is unlikely *for witnesses to volunteer information* about which they are unsure" (Lipton, 1977, p. 91). By providing the child with greater opportunity to speak openly, the interviewer gains information that is untainted by their own perspective and also gives him/her time to think about how to respond to this disclosure. More importantly, the interviewer can refocus on simply *listening* to what the child has to say about what has occurred to him/her, rather than worrying about what to say or do next.

3 Maintaining the 'Chain of Disclosure'

The *chain of disclosure* is discussed by Shepherd and Griffiths (2013) and proposes that a verbal disclosure of an offence should be treated like other forms of evidence:

> *The witness's account is akin to an item of evidence and raises the issue of the chain of continuity. Every time he or she has spoken to someone, or been spoken to, about it this is akin to more than one hand holding the item. On each occasion, the material is liable to be contaminated (Shepherd & Griffiths, 2013, p. 313).*

This places an obligation on professionals to maintain accurate records of the conversation around the disclosures of abuse. Doing so serves two purposes: (1) contemporaneous notes for use in criminal proceedings and (2) allowing investigators to assess the evidentiary reliability of the child's statements and consider any contamination issues. The first aspect is particularly important in allegations of sexual abuse as, in some jurisdictions, evidence may be called from the person or persons to whom the child has disclosed the abuse, prior to making the complaint to authorities (Australian Law Reform Commission, 2010). This is referred to as a *fresh complaint* or *preliminary complaint*. By virtue of being one of the first persons the child discloses to, the professional may be considered a witness in any future criminal proceedings. The documentation of the disclosure will be of benefit to both the professional and authorities in the preparation of this testimony.

Second is the issue of credibility assessment. This is not about the credibility of the child, rather credibility of how the disclosure was made. Take, for instance, the following statement:

Report of Harm:
Isabelle (11 years of age) has disclosed to the notifier that her brother had raped her. They were in his bedroom when this occurred.

Ideally, a report made to investigative agencies should report the verbatim disclosure; however, this example appears to be an unequivocal report of abuse. When considering the questions that were asked that resulted in this disclosure, more interpretations can be made. If it was obtained by using a series of inappropriate questions, for example,

Inappropriate:
"My brother did something bad to me"
Q: What do you mean something bad? (Direct Question)
A: Something with his rude part.
Q: With his penis? (Closed/Leading Question)
A: Yes.
Q: Did he rape you? (Closed/Leading Question)
A: I don't know.
Q: Did he have sex with you? Did you say no? (Closed/Multiple Question)
A: Yes.
Q: What were you doing when it happened? (Direction Question)
A: Playing his PlayStation.
Q: You were in his room. (Leading/Closed Question)
A: Yes.

Three things should be noted about this example: (1) the number of questions that the interviewer is having to ask to gain information, meaning that there is a greater cognitive load on the interviewer to generate questions; (2) that the interviewer is the one controlling the interview, not the person in possession of the information; and (3) that interviewer contamination is occurring, in that their beliefs around the event are being discussed, rather than exploring the child's recollection. Its weight as evidence is far less than it would be, had it been obtained using open-ended questions:

Appropriate:

"My brother did something bad to me"

Q: Tell me everything about what your brother did to you. (Open Question)

A: I was sitting on the floor in his room playing with his PlayStation. He came in and sat down next to me and asked me if I wanted to see something cool, and I said yes. He pulled his pants down and showed me his rude part, but it looked different. I said that it was gross. He told me to touch it, and I said no; then, he put it near my face and told me to kiss it, but I said no. He grabbed my head and put it in my mouth. I didn't like it, but he was holding my head, and I couldn't move.

In short, the strength of the disclosure would change depending on the questioning strategies used in the interview or conversation (Hershkowitz et al., 1997). Documenting not only the disclosures but also the questions asked when gathering information is an important consideration for professionals to whom a child self-discloses abuse. Not only does it provide the ability to assess the strength of the evidence, but also it allows the professional to reflect on their conversation with the child and ideally improves their practise in future instances of a similar nature.

4 Conclusion

Given the potential for professionals in occupations that interact with children to encounter a disclosure of abuse, it is important that they are equipped to handle these disclosures and satisfy mandatory reporting obligations imposed upon them by virtue of their position. Understanding the thresholds required to make a report, namely, the conditions of having a 'reasonable suspicion' or 'reasonable belief', and articulating the decision-making process that notifies progress through remove uncertainty around whether to make a report or not. This will add to the efficacy of the mandatory reporting system, ensuring that at-risk children receive support and so that nonabuse matters do not overburden the child protection system. Considering that one of the strongest factors around whether to report suspected abuse or not is whether a disclosure has been made by a child, having conversations with, and gathering further information from children who self-disclose abuse is an important aspect. This, however, can be a challenging experience for professionals unaccustomed with managing reports of abuse. Questions are often raised about what and how to ask a child about these events, so as to gather additional information in an evidentially sound manner, to help support the professional's decision to report or not, and also to demonstrate to the child that their concerns are being taken seriously. To achieve these objectives, a number of strategies can be adopted by professionals. These include, but are not limited to, actively listening to what the child is saying, asking open-ended questions based on what the child has already disclosed, and maintaining documentation of the conversation ensuring the *chain of disclosure* is articulated appropriately. As professionals who work with children are often one of the first people whom the child may disclose the abuse to, it is vital that they manage the conversation and gather information appropriately, so as to achieve the best outcome for the child.

5 Chapter Review Questions

1. What is mandatory reporting, and what is its intent?
2. Who is considered a mandatory reporter?
3. Define harm, abuse, and neglect.
4. Define and articulate the difference between suspicion, belief, and knowledge, providing examples from your professional context.
5. What are the common barriers to professionals meeting their mandatory reporting obligations?
6. Drawing on the models of Dalgleish (1988) and Francis et al. (2012), what are the key principles in decision-making with regard to reporting suspected harm?
7. What necessitates speaking to children about disclosures of abuse?
8. Construct your own 'checklist' for managing disclosures of abuse by children, include the key elements outlined in this chapter.

References

Abuse. (2018). *In Oxforddictionaries.com*. Retrieved from https://en.oxforddictionaries.com/definition/abuse.

Alvarez, K. M., Donohue, B., Kenny, M. C., Cavanagh, N., & Romero, V. (2005). The process and consequences of reporting child maltreatment: a brief overview for professionals in the mental health field. *Aggression and Violent Behaviour*, *10*, 311–331.

Australian Institute of Family Studies. (1996). *Child maltreatment and disabilities*. Retrieved from https://aifs.gov.au/cfca/publications/child-maltreatment-and-disability#ref.

Australian Law Reform Commission. (2010). *Family violence—A national legal response*. ALRC Report 114 Sydney: Australian Law Reform Commission.

Beck, K. A., Oglaff, J. R. P., & Corbishley, A. (1994). Knowledge, compliance, and attitudes of teachers toward mandatory child abuse reporting in British Columbia. *Canadian Journal of Education*, *19*(1), 15–29.

Best, R. (2001). Where child protection systems and schools meet. *Australian and New Zealand Journal of Law and Education*, *6*(1), 3–13.

Blaskett, B., & Taylor, S. C. (2003). *Facilitators and inhibitors of mandatory reporting of suspected child abuse*. Canberra: Australian Institute of Criminology.

Bowles, P. V., & Sharman, S. J. (2014). A review of the impact of different types of leading interview questions on child and adult witnesses with intellectual disabilities. *Psychiatry, Psychology and Law*, *21*(2), 205–217.

Bunting, L., Lazenbatt, A., & Wallace, I. (2010). Information sharing and reporting systems in UK and Ireland: professional barriers to reporting child maltreatment concerns. *Child Abuse Review*, *19*, 187–202.

Burgess, R. G. (1984). Autobiographical accounts and research experience. In R. G. Burgess (Ed.), *The research process in educational settings: Ten case studies* (pp. 251–270). Lewes: The Falmer Press.

Carroll v Hasz. (1903). *St R Qd 250*.

Crenshaw, W. B., Crensaw, L. M., & Lichtenberg, J. W. (1995). When educators confront child abuse: an analysis of the decision to report. *Child Abuse & Neglect*, *19*(9), 1095–1113.

Crosson-Tower, C. (2003). *The role of educators in preventing and responding to child abuse and neglect*. Washington, DC: U.S. Department of Health and Human Services.

Dalgleish, L. I. (1988). Decision making in child abuse cases: applications of social judgement theory and signal detection theory. In B. Brehmer & C. R. B. Joyce (Eds.), *Human judgement: The SJT view* (pp. 317–360). North Holland: Elsevier Science Publishers.

Finlayson, L. M., & Koocher, G. P. (1991). Professional judgement and child abuse reporting in sexual abuse cases. *Professional Psychology: Research and Practice*, *22*(6), 464–472.

Francis, K., Chapman, Y., Sellick, K., James, A., Miles, M., Jones, J., et al. (2012). The decision-making processes adopted by rurally located mandated professionals when child abuse or neglect is suspected. *Contemporary Nurse*, *41*(1), 58–69.

George v Rockett. (1990). *170 CLR 104; 93 ALR 483; [1990] HCA 26.*

Goebbels, A. F. G., Nicholson, J. M., Walsh, K., & Vries, D. (2008). Teachers' reporting of suspected child abuse and neglect: behaviour and determinants. *Health Education Research*, *23*(6), 941–951.

Harm. (2018). *In Oxforddictionaries.com*. Retrieved from https://en.oxforddictionaries.com/definition/harm.

Hershkowitz, I., Lamb, M. E., Stenberg, K. J., & Esplin, P. W. (1997). The relationships among interviewer utterance type, CBCA stores and the richness of children's responses. *Legal and Criminological Psychology*, *2*, 169–176.

Kempe, C. H., Silverman, F. N., Steele, B. F., Droefemueller, W., & Silver, H. K. (1985). The battered child syndrome. *Child Abuse & Neglect*, *9*, 143–154.

Kenny, M. C. (2004). Teachers attitude toward and knowledge of child maltreatment. *Child Abuse & Neglect*, *28*, 1311–1319.

Lipton, J. P. (1977). On the psychology of eyewitness testimony. *Journal of Applied Psychology*, *62*(1), 90–95.

Mathews, B. (2011). Teacher education to meet the challenges posed by child sexual abuse. *Australian Journal of Teacher Education*, *36*(11), 13–32.

Mathews, B. (2014). Mandatory reporting laws and identification of child abuse and neglect: consideration of differential maltreatment types, and a cross-jurisdictional analysis of child sexual abuse reports. *Social Sciences*, *3*, 460–482.

Mathews, B., Bromfield, L., Walsh, K., & Vimpani, G. (2015). *Child abuse and neglect: a socio-legal study of mandatory reporting in Australia—Report for the Australian government*. Brisbane: Queensland University of Technology.

Mathews, B., & Kenny, M. C. (2008). Mandatory reporting legislation in the United States, Canada and Australia: a cross-jurisdictional review of key features, differences, and issues. *Child Maltreatment*, *13*(1), 50–63.

Mathews, B., & Walsh, K. (2004). Issues in mandatory reporting of child sexual abuse by Australian teachers. *Australia & New Zealand Journal of Law and Education*, *9*(2), 3–17.

Mathews, B., & Walsh, K. (2014). Mandatory reporting laws. In A. Hayes & D. Higgins (Eds.), *Families, policy and the law: Selected essays on contemporary issues for Australia* (pp. 131–142). Melbourne: Australian Institute of Family Studies.

Melton, G. B. (2005). Mandated reporting: a policy without reason. *Child Abuse & Neglect*, *29*, 9–18.

Milne, R., & Bull, R. (1999). *Investigative interviewing: Psychology and practice*. Chichester: John Wiley & Sons.

Neglect. (2018). *In Oxforddictionaries.com*. Retrieved from https://en.oxforddictionaries.com/definition/neglect.

Queensland Law Reform Commission. (2015). *Review of child protection mandatory reporting laws for the early childhood education and care sector*. Brisbane: Queensland Government.

R v Chan. (1992). *28 NSWLR 421, 437; 63 A Crim R 242.*

R v Fallon. (1981). *28 SASR 394; 4 A Crim R 411.*

R v Raad. (1983). *3 NSWLR 344.*

R v Rondo. (2001). *126 A Crime R 562; [2001] NSWCCA 540.*

Shepherd, E., & Griffiths, A. (2013). *Investigative interviewing: The conversation management approach* (2nd ed.). Oxford: Oxford University Press.

Takis, A. (2008). The mandatory reporting debate. *Macquarie Law Journal*, *8*, 125–152.

UN General Assembly. (1989). Convention on the rights of the child. *Treaty Series*: Vol. 1577. United Nations. Retrieved from http://www.ohchr.org/EN/ProfessionalInterest/Pages/CRC.aspx.

Walsh, K., Bridgestock, R., Farrell, A., Rassafiani, M., & Schweitzer, R. (2008). Case, teacher and school characteristics influencing teachers' detection and reporting of child physical abuse and neglect: Results from an Australian survey. *Child Abuse and Neglect*, *32*(10), 983–993.

Walsh, K., Farrell, A., Bridgstock, R., & Schweitzer, R. (2006). The contested terrain of teachers detecting and reporting child abuse and neglect. *Journal of Early Childhood Research*, *4*(1), 65–76.

Walsh, K., Schweitzer, R., & Bridgstock, R. (2005). *Critical factors in teachers' detecting a reporting child abuse and neglect: Implications for practice*. Albion: Abused Child Trust.

Wilson, C., & Powell, M. (2001). *A guide to interviewing children: Essential skills for counsellors, police, lawyers and social workers*. Crows Nest: Allen & Unwin.

World Health Organisation. (2017). *Child maltreatment*. Retrieved from http://www.who.int/topics/child_abuse/en/.

CHAPTER 16

Virtue Ethics and Good Professional Judgement in Child Protection

Karen Broadley
RMIT University, Melbourne, VIC, Australia

1 Introduction

During my 20+ years as a youth worker and child protection practitioner, I often thought about, talked about, and reflected on my daily work with children, young people, and families. Rarely, however did I write about it, except in my official capacity when writing case notes and court reports.

A reoccurring theme in many conversations I had with colleagues over my years of practice and in my own reflections is related to the expectations placed on practitioners and managers to think and act by referring explicitly to rules, manuals, practice standards, procedures, checklists, risk factors, and key performance indicators and so on. The requirement to comply with prescribed rules and checklists was a source of constant discomfort to me and many of my colleagues. Not only did I find it annoying that such tasks took up time that could have been better spent more productively, but also it was a way of practice that failed to appreciate the nature of child protection practice and the importance of good professional judgments that went beyond rule following. There were times when children, young people, and families were caused harm because they were not treated as people with their own unique capacities, experiences, and situations. Their voices and perspectives were devalued and given insufficient weight within assessments and decision-making processes. Professional judgement was not exercised, and the experience and intuition of practitioners were disregarded.

The typically unthinking and unquestioning compliance with these prescribed modes of practice was maintained in part by collective fear and habit; it was a fear of being blamed and held responsible should tragedy occur. Indeed, in child protection systems and many other public systems, ticking boxes and following rules are seen by many workers as offering some form of protection to the individual and organisation. For the worker and the organisation, relying on professional judgement and working beyond specified procedures are deemed to

Child Abuse and Neglect. https://doi.org/10.1016/B978-0-12-815344-4.00016-7

be high risk. A practitioner who thinks and acts beyond 'the rules' will be required to take responsibility for the consequences of her actions should tragedy occur. She risks being labelled careless or fool. "Why didn't she just follow the guidelines?"

After leaving child protection, I continued thinking about this culture of fear and compliance that caused harms and was antithetical to the exercise of good professional judgement. I was concerned about the consequences of that for children, young people, and families. Over time, I did further reading, thinking, and writing. Munro (2002, p. 2) affirmed my sense that something was wrong when she said.

> *... there is a problem in how many child protection services are trying to improve practice; the dominant view has been that progress can be achieved by a more formalised and prescriptive approach. The increase in empirical research and the development of guidelines, checklists, procedures and risk assessment instruments exemplify this approach. The problem is that many of the people who are on the receiving end of these developments – the front-line workers – are very sceptical about them and use them half-heartedly. There is a widespread feeling that they fail to capture key elements of working effectively with families. These formal aids are often seen as a device for protecting management from outside criticism rather than for protecting children from abuse.*

Through my reading, I also came to realise that modern institutions generally have a tendency to rely on 'technical rational' methods to solve 'wicked problems'. This became particularly apparent to me after reading Rittel and Webber (1973) and their discussion about 'wicked problems' that are social and, by their nature, difficult to define, ambiguous, and often hard (if not impossible) to achieve agreement on. I saw then how the problem of working out how to best protect and prevent children from being abused and neglected is indeed a classic 'wicked problem'. As such, it cannot be understood and responded to as if it is a technical problem, with prescribed rules, manuals, and checklists. Seeing my work as a practitioner through the work of Rittel and Webber (1973) further affirmed my sense that something was wrong and that the dominant mode of operating in child protection in the way I just explained is inappropriate.

Part of my reflection also involved reading and thinking more about ethics. With time, I came to understand that these technical rational methods of practice are also informed by utilitarian and deontological ethical traditions. I came to see how both utilitarian theories (which focus on consequences, outcomes, and the greatest good for the greatest number) and deontological theories (which focus on duties and rule following) encourage an overly prescriptive approach (Lovat & Gray, 2007; MacIntyre, 2003; McBeath & Webb, 2002). These ethical traditions discourage us to consider the uniqueness of individuals and the particularities of the context, the children and young people themselves, and their experiences and perspectives.

I also began to realise how neoliberal policy in conjunction with utilitarian thinking had come to permeate every aspect of the child and family welfare field. I realised that attempts to use technical means to solve 'wicked problems' attracted people because it seemed to provide easy, efficient, objective, and 'value for money' solutions. At the same time, it has hindered the ability of practitioners to exercise professional discretion and judgement and to engage with children and young people in meaningful ways.

My reading also led me to Aristotle and Virtue Ethics as offering a possible way forward (Bessant, 2009; Lawler & Salzman, 2013; MacIntyre, 2003; McBeath & Webb, 2002; Oakley & Cocking, 2001; Schwartz & Sharpe, 2010). I felt a connection with this ethical tradition and believed it fitted well with my own experiences and viewpoints, because it requires clarity about human thought and action, and it values thinking and good judgments. All this I considered critical for good decision making in child protection.

This chapter is an exercise in reflective practice that draws in my experiences, conversations, deliberations, and insights gained from my long involvement in youth work and child protection work. It also draws from Aristotle's virtue ethics that I use as an organising framework to describe professional judgement. By borrowing some fundamental insights from Aristotle and drawing from my own experiences, I explain what good professional judgement 'looks like', how it is learned, and how modern child protection systems hinder its development. I also recommend ways forward.

2 Aristotle and Virtue Ethics

Virtue ethics was an ancient ethical theory largely forgotten in favour of other ethical theories (mainly utilitarianism and deontology) until quite recently. However, in 1958, Elizabeth Anscombe published 'Modern Moral Philosophy' and criticised utilitarianism and deontology and recommended a return to Aristotelian moral theory (Slote, 2010). Since then, there has been a resurgence of virtue ethics (Bessant, 2009) (see, e.g. Oakley & Cocking, 2001; Schwartz & Sharpe, 2010), and it is now considered to be one of the major forms of ethical theory (Slote, 2010).

According to Aristotle, one of the most important questions in life relates to "what happiness is, what activities it consists in, and how to become happy" (MacIntyre, 2003, p. 57). Aristotle says that the first step towards answering this question is to recognise that every rational activity aims to realise a goal that is seen as good. There is a goal that relates to human life as a whole that Aristotle calls *eudaemonia* (i.e. flourishing) (Bessant, 2009; MacIntyre, 2003). This is both subjective (e.g. some people may aim for political achievement, whilst others aim for enjoyment) and universal (e.g. all people desire good physical health for themselves and their children) (Bessant, 2009). There are also goals that relate to various professions. For example, the goal of teaching is to educate students, the goal of doctoring is to promote health and to relieve suffering, and the goal of child protection is to advance the safety and wellbeing of children (Schwartz & Sharpe, 2010). All of these goals help individuals, families, and communities to attain 'goods' (such as safety, health, and education) that play a crucial role in their flourishing (Bessant, 2017; Oakley & Cocking, 2001; Schwartz & Sharpe, 2010).

Although many ethical theorists disagree about how *eudaemonia* is to be described, it is generally agreed that virtuous living is its main component and precondition (Lawler & Salzman, 2013; Oakley & Cocking, 2001; Slote, 2010). Virtue ethicists agree that having a virtuous character, with virtuous character traits, and living a habitually virtuous life is good for individuals, families, and communities (Oakley & Cocking, 2001). They agree that virtue ethics is all about character, but this does not mean that virtue ethics ignores doing because action follows being (Lawler & Salzman, 2013; Oakley & Cocking, 2001).

2.1 Virtue Ethics and Child Protection Work

For the child protection practitioner, virtue ethics provides a useful ethical framework to draw from because it offers clarity about what is good—that is, it offers a foundation for child protection practice that can be used to achieve goods such as physical, emotional, and social safety and wellbeing, which are all important if children are to flourish (Bessant, 2009).

Virtue ethics also emphasises the importance of good character (Bessant, 2009; Oakley & Cocking, 2001; Schwartz & Sharpe, 2010). This means it is important for child protection practitioners to display virtues such as courage, endurance, honesty, kindness, generosity, and determination. It is not sufficient for child protection practitioners to display the virtues just because they lead to good consequences or because it is their duty, i.e. listed in the organisational code of ethics, practice manual, or procedures. It is necessary that virtuous actions arise out of good character, which means having an appropriate disposition and motivation, i.e. the desire to protect children and help families. Lovat and Gray (2007) argue that those who practise social work must have compassion and a desire to support, to help, and to be generally in service to others. They suggest that those who do not have this other-centred approach will struggle in the profession. McBeath and Webb (2002, p. 1023) similarly state.

> *... if a social worker does not recognise his or her moral identity and calling, then one may wonder whether such a person ought to do social work at all.*

2.2 Practical Wisdom

Aristotle highlighted three types of knowledge. The first is *episteme*, which is scientific, universal, invariable, and context-independent. It is achieved with the aid of analytical rationality (Flyvbjerg, 2001). We use it when we draw from theories and empirical evidence. The second is *techne*, which is craft and art, and as an activity, it is concrete, variable, and context-independent (Flyvbjerg, 2001). The third is *phronesis*, which involves values and ethics. *Phronesis* can be translated as 'practical common sense' (Flyvbjerg, 2001, p. 56) or 'practical wisdom' (Schwartz & Sharpe, 2010, p. 5). *Phronesis* has been described as the 'governing virtue' (Oakley & Cocking, 2001, p. 15) and the 'master excellence' (Schwartz & Sharpe, 2010, p. 6). It is the virtue that coordinates the other virtues. The child protection practitioner possessing practical wisdom does not exclusively rely on a rule book of general, context-independent truths (i.e. practice manuals and research-based evidence). He also considers the uniqueness of individuals, their experiences, and perspectives. By drawing from a repertoire of knowledge and from his experience, emotion, and intuition, he just knows how to behave and decide in the "right way to do the right thing in a particular circumstance, with a particular person, at a particular time" (Schwartz & Sharpe, 2010, p. 6).

The concept of *phronesis*, which essentially involves the ability to make good judgments in social practice, is at the heart of and can enhance our understanding of what good professional judgement might 'look like' (Kinsella & Pitman, 2012).

> *Phronesis... is an intellectual virtue that implies ethics. It involves deliberation that is based on values, concerned with practical judgment and informed by reflection. It is pragmatic, variable, context-dependent and oriented toward action (Kinsella & Pitman, 2012, p. 2).*

3 Good Professional Judgement

Drawing from Aristotle's concept of *phronesis*, I now outline seven elements of good professional judgement. These are (1) understanding and working to achieve the *telos* or the goal of practice, (2) analytical reasoning, (3) using intuition, (4) drawing from experience, (5) reflective practice, (6) the appropriate use of emotion, and (7) exercising Aristotle's 'golden mean'.

3.1 The Goal of Practice

Exercising good professional judgement requires that we are guided by the proper goal of an activity. Aristotle's word for the proper goal of practice was *telos*, e.g. the *telos* of teaching is to educate students. However, there is disagreement about whether practitioners should focus narrowly on protecting children from incidents of child abuse and neglect (viz. physical and sexual abuse and criminal neglect) or whether their focus should be broadened. Bryce (2018, p. 1) points to the "growing emphasis on children's wellbeing, development and universal right to quality of life and fair treatment." The former, narrow focus tends to aim at short-time safety, whilst the latter broader focus tends to include the child's longer-term development and quality of life.

Although traditionally, child protection systems have been inclined towards former, 'forensic focus', there is a current trend towards a more encompassing focus than is inclusive of cumulative harm (Bryce, 2018). Indeed, multiple studies show that cumulative harm can be more damaging to a child's behavioural, cognitive, and socio-emotional development in the long term than other types of abuse (Broadley, 2014; Bryce, 2018). Aiming for children's safety, wellbeing, and healthy development in the long and the short term is undoubtedly a good goal to have. It involves thinking about what it might take for a child to flourish and thrive.

Turning to controversies about the goal of healthcare can help us to think further about the goal of child protection practice. According to Oakley and Cocking (2001), some define health as an absence of disease, whilst others argue there are broader more positive elements of health as well, such as having a positive state of physical, mental, and social wellbeing. Oakley and Cocking suggest that regardless of these disputes, the idea that doctors should serve the goal of health is not really controversial. The more important task is for a doctor to articulate what the goal of a particular intervention with a particular patient is and then to show how this goal contributes to their flourishing. The question about whether the goal should be widened to enhance health rather than to only cure illness depends on a number of factors including the availability and allocation of resources.

Regardless of the disputes regarding the goal of child protection practice, the idea that child protection practitioners should service the goal of child safety and wellbeing is not controversial. Child protection practitioners must have clarity about the final purpose or *telos* of child protection practice, and this can be achieved by asking whether their actions and decisions are oriented towards the flourishing of a particular child in a particular situation. Knowing the proper things to aim at in a particular context with a particular child and families will also be informed by factors such as availability and allocation of resources.

3.2 Analytical Reasoning

> *... we first lay down the end, and then examine the ways and means to achieve it. If it appears that any of several [possible] means will reach it, we consider which of them will reach it most easily and most finely... (Arist. EN III.3, 1112b15–18, trans. Irwin, 1985).*

Good professional judgement is informed by analytical reasoning. The practitioner draws from theoretical and empirical knowledge that is particular to their field. Problems are identified; options are considered; and the pros, cons, and risks associated with each option are weighed. A choice is made about what seems best suited to solve the problem and achieve the goal. Describing, measuring, and solving problems may initially involve the practitioner turning to the use of checklists, procedures, risk assessment tools, and manuals. Munro (2010) agrees that many child protection systems in Australia and internationally have practice manuals containing detailed procedures setting out the correct way to practise in ways that can be readily performed and ticked off.

The use of manuals and checklist may be helpful and important, but not sufficient to good practice. In the 'real world', problems and solutions do not arrive labelled neatly on our desks. They must be constructed from the messiness of human lives and relationships (Schön Donald, 1983). In the real 'world', the future cannot be predicted by using a particular formula or risk assessment tool. Thinking, deciding, and acting well in an uncertain and risky world requires the virtues, analytical reasoning, and intuition.

3.3 Intuition

> *... some people when in a state of opinion do not hesitate, but think they know exactly... there need be no difference between knowledge and opinion in this respect; for some men are no less convinced of what they think than others of what they know ... (Arist. EN VII. 3 1146b27–9, trans. Ross, 2009).*

Aristotle placed emphasis on the use of intuition. Intuition is the ability to instantaneously and accurately form an opinion about what is best or true, without conscious reasoning or independent evidence. It is internalised and involves making decisions and taking actions spontaneously without forethought (Calder, 2015; Flyvbjerg, 2001; Schön Donald, 1983). It draws from our existing knowledge about people, relationships, and the incredibly complex world we inhabit and from our experiences with particulars, detecting patterns, and similarities and differences within patterns and is refined through trial and error (Schwartz & Sharpe, 2010). The complexity and speed at which these processes occur is what makes an intuitive 'opinion' that may lack evidence and reasoned forethought difficult to articulate and substantiate.

Intuition plays a crucial role in the exercise of good professional judgement in child protection (Coles, 2002; Munro, 2002). It is important because analytical decision making is often inappropriate in the midst of child protection work that is fast-paced, sometimes involving urgent responses. Even in the day-to-day activities of gathering and organising information about child safety, practitioners must draw on their intuition. Deciding what information to gather and selecting and organising the information to make an assessment require intuition. For example, when interviewing a child or young person about suspected abuse or witnessing violence, the wise practitioner will know that no two children will relate their experiences of abuse in the same way. In order to respond to each child's unique situation and needs, the practitioner must make quick intuitive decisions about what questions to ask, how to ask them, and how much silence to allow between questions, without making the child feel uncomfortable. Schwartz and Sharpe (2010) describe this ability as 'framing'. They explain that in framing a scene, we separate a picture from its surroundings. We exclude to the outside the information we consider irrelevant, whereas what is inside we choose as relevant and worthy of attention. We pull out and interpret the relevant particulars of a situation automatically, without conscious thought or deliberation, and we unconsciously recognise patterns, and we understand how the current situation is similar and different from other situations we have encountered. We are also mindful of the purpose of the assessment and the decision that is to be made. It is by framing that we know which children need more rapport building and time to develop trust so they feel able to talk about abuse. It is by framing that we know which parts of the practice manual to prioritise over others, which rules are relevant, and when rules should be bent (Schwartz & Sharpe, 2010). Although practice manuals are important, it is by exercising our intuitive skills and drawing from our experience that we know how to use them.

3.4 The Importance of Experience

> *... some people who lack knowledge but have experience are better in action than others who have knowledge (Arist. EN VI.8, 1141b17–19, trans. Irwin, 1985).*

Virtue ethics places emphasis upon experience (Bessant, 2009; Lovat & Gray, 2007; McBeath & Webb, 2002; Schwartz & Sharpe, 2010). Flyvbjerg (2001) goes as far as to say that "more than anything else, *phronesis* requires *experience*" (p. 57). The ability to detect complex patterns and recognise similarities and differences between the past and the present requires experience (Dreyfus, 2004; Flyvbjerg, 2001; Schwartz & Sharpe, 2010). Thinking and acting well in the face of risk and uncertainty requires experience. It is by trial and error and sometimes long hard experience that we grow and become wise.

Although practical wisdom is learned through experience, not just any experience will do. It is important to have social experiences that cultivate such learning. Good professional judgement is something we learn from the professional communities we practise within—from observing respected others, that is, our mentors, teachers, and leaders. It is in community that we learn how to evaluate our own conduct, we look to experienced others to guide us, and we receive feedback for our mistakes (Lawler & Salzman, 2013; Schwartz & Sharpe, 2010).

> *It is a central claim of virtue theory...that virtues are shaped in a community and culture by narratives and role models judged to be virtuous. Virtues are learned – and can only be learned – within particular communities; they can be sustained only in those communities; they get their content from communities; they get their worth and convey worth only from and in community; and they act back on communities to sustain them (Lawler & Salzman, 2013, p. 448).*

Not only it is experience that leads to learning, but also it is necessary to reflect on that experience.

3.5 Reflective Practice

Virtue ethics places emphasis on reflection (Kinsella & Pitman, 2012; Lovat & Gray, 2007; McBeath & Webb, 2002). "Whatever else phronesis might be, we can safely say that it involves reflection" (Kinsella, 2012, p. 37).

Reflection involves the ability to be self-aware, to assess one's motives, to be bravely self-critical, to acknowledge failures, and to figure out whether a particular action or intervention has or has not worked and why (Schwartz & Sharpe, 2010). In a nutshell, it is the practitioner evaluating her own performance—"am I doing a good job?"

Schön Donald (1983) argues that good professional judgement occurs through two types of reflection—'reflection in action' and 'reflection on action'. The former involves reflecting on actions and words, feelings, theories, and values, in the midst of the 'action'. Reflecting and evaluation, he says, occurs rapidly in order to assess whether a different course or approach to action should be taken—e.g. whilst in the process of interviewing a child about suspected child abuse. The latter—reflection on action—involves reflecting on actions already taken and what could have been done differently and considering what can be learnt. This involves the practitioner talking things over with a supervisor or colleague or in a reflective practice group session, questioning why he acted a certain way and what was happening for him and for others involved. Learning, Schön argues, occurs when the practitioner thinks critically, critiquing and questioning his own decisions and actions.

Reflection should be more than an individual process; it should also be a public social process. It should attend to collective thought and be concerned with practice as a whole (Coles, 2002; Kinsella, 2012). It should question taken-for-granted knowledge and practices. Kinsella (2012, p. 45) states

> *Reflexivity goes beyond reflection to interrogate the very conditions under which knowledge claims are accepted and constructed, and it recognises the sociality of that process.*

3.6 Use of Emotion

Our emotions play a central role in signalling what is valuable and important for a person's flourishing, and they interact with reasoning to guide our social decisions (Lawler & Salzman, 2013; Schwartz & Sharpe, 2010). For example, compassion which that is a feeling of sympathy and concern for the suffering of others can signal what matters and what must be attended to. But compassion (as with other emotions), as a first impression judgement, must be tested through cognitive reasoning before it can be judged as a genuine virtue, real and true for human flourishing (Lawler & Salzman, 2013).

Emotions play a central role in exercising good professional judgement in child protection (Calder, 2015; Hill, 2010). Calder suggests that a practitioner's sense of personal disturbance can signal potential risks and dangers for a particular child and that if such emotions are absent, then practitioners can lose contact with a vital source of information to inform their assessment. Hill (2010, p. 61) agrees that emotions "can be seen as giving clues about the experience of service users." However, emotion as a first impression judgement must be rigorously tested through reasoning and reflection (both individual and collective, i.e. in supervision). We must be aware of how our emotions can impact on and may even distort how we gather and select information and how we interpret information to form judgments. Many things, including practitioners' own personal past experiences and future expectations, can impact on this process (Calder, 2015; Hill, 2010). For example, compassion for a struggling parent may inhibit our ability to recognise child abuse in the home. We might see things in a way that will fit in with what we want to see, even if this involves omitting or distorting certain factual details.

It is important for practitioners to work in an organisation where they are encouraged and enabled to talk about and understand their emotions. Practitioners must be supported to ask themselves questions such as "what are my emotions telling me?" "Are my emotions telling me more about myself than the other person?" Detecting human cruelty and suffering in the form of child abuse is deeply disturbing and emotional work. It is important that practitioners not be cut off from their emotions, and it is equally important that they not be blindly driven by them.

3.7 The 'Golden Mean'

> *For both excessive and deficient exercises ruin strength; and likewise, too much or too little eating or drinking ruins health, while the proportionate amount produces, increases, and preserves it. The same is true, then, of temperance, bravery, and the other virtues. For if, e.g., someone avoids and is afraid of everything, standing firm against nothing, he becomes cowardly, but if he is afraid of nothing at all and goes to face everything, he becomes rash… bravery, then, (is) ruined by excess and deficiency but preserved by the mean (Arist. EN II.3, 1104a15–26, trans. Irwin, 1985).*

The idea of the 'golden mean' is essential to Aristotle's definition of virtue (Lawler & Salzman, 2013), and it is essential to good professional judgement in child protection. The golden mean is the desirable middle between two extremes, between excess and deficiency, both of which are vices (Bessant, 2009). Practitioners who exercise the golden mean understand that virtuous actions often lie in the mean between two extremes (e.g. the mean between providing support to parents and the exercise of authority and control over parents). They know when a virtue needs to be moderated so as not to become a failing and the cause of harm (Bessant, 2009). They also know that the golden mean is not necessarily the midpoint between two extremes; it is the right balance in a particular circumstance and with a particular child and family. Some situations may require the extreme—for example, exercising authority, investigating and controlling an abusive parent who is unwilling to engage with support and treatment.

Wise practitioners also know how to find the right balance between conflicting virtues, goals, needs, rights, and interests, in the right situation, with the right person. They know for example, how to balance the virtues of truth and kindness and caring too much and detachment. They know how to balance the child's need for autonomy and the child's need for beneficence (Beauchamp & Childress, 2001) and how to balance parental rights and child rights—"child protection workers have to walk a tightrope, balancing the conflicting rights of the family members" (Munro, 2002, p. 1). They know how to balance the goal of ensuring a child's safety and the goal of maximising a child's welfare—for although removal from birth family may increase a child's safety, it may harm them emotionally, socially, and developmentally (Munro, 2002). They are not preoccupied with 'risk', and they are not passive towards 'risk'. Their virtues and wisdom help them to identify risk, and as they act to reduce risk, they are aware that they may create new and other unintended risks to children, families, and even entire communities—and this is where the balancing acts come into play.[1] They know that doing the right thing involves attention to context, experience, and intuition *and* attention to risk assessment tools, rules, and rationality. Embracing one of these extremes may make it easier to conceptualise and 'solve' problems, but it inhibits real understanding and can seriously compromise good outcomes for children and families. By utilising Aristotle's golden mean, practitioners value the universal and the particular. They are wary of rules and rationality dominating practice (Flyvbjerg, 2001).

Aristotle believed that by self-awareness, we can come to know our own natural tendencies and avoid (what is to us) the easier extreme. Do I have a tendency towards support and empowering of vulnerable parents? Or do I have a tendency towards investigating and gathering evidence about their alleged crimes against children? Aristotle said.

> *We must also examine what we ourselves drift into easily. For different people have different natural tendencies toward different goals, and we shall come to know our own tendencies form the pleasure or pain that arises in us. We must drag ourselves off in the contrary direction; for if we pull far away from error, as they do in straightening bent wood, we shall reach the intermediate condition (Arist. EN II.9, 1109b3-6, trans. Irwin, 1985).*

4 Hindering and Encouraging the Development of Good Professional Judgement

It is important to recognise the role of institutions in either encouraging or discouraging the development of professional judgement. Schwartz and Sharpe suggest that some institutions encourage the development of practical wisdom whilst others discourage it by design. Kinsella and Pitman (2012, p. 8) agree that structurally and systemically, some organisations actively mitigate the development of practical wisdom. Holding practitioners accountable for not exercising good professional judgement in these contexts not only is unfair but also avoids recognising and dealing with the broader problems at play.

[1] See Broadley (2014) under section heading 'Assessments must be informed by the statutory requirement to cause no further harm' regarding harms that are caused by the very systems and interventions designed to protect children from harm.

4.1 Ignoring the Central Role of Emotion Can Erode the Development of Professional Judgement

Child protection work is typically highly emotional, sometimes deeply disturbing work. Practitioners need to be well supported to 'manage' their emotions, and not be cut off from them or unconsciously or consciously driven by them. Such capacities can only be developed in a system where leaders and supervisors understand the significance of such intense emotions, are willing and able to validate them, contain them, and cope with them (Hill, 2010, p. 26).

Ample literature reports on the failure of child protection leaders and managers to acknowledge and appropriately respond to the practitioner's emotional life (Goddard & Hunt, 2011; Hill, 2010). Heavy workloads and time pressures, managerial requirements to complete forms, and tick boxes can squeeze out time to provide practitioners with the support they need (Goddard & Hunt, 2011; Schwartz & Sharpe, 2010). Moreover, there is a common view that to be 'professional' is to be detached and unemotional (Goddard & Hunt, 2011) and that to express emotion is a sign of weakness (Hill, 2010).

When leaders in organisations fail to acknowledge and respond to the child protection practitioner's emotional life, other less helpful methods of managing emotions are often put in place, and these methods can be detrimental to the exercise of good professional judgement. For example, practitioners themselves can become preoccupied with rules and checklists. They can do this in order to remove emotion from their practice and to avoid making their own professional judgments. They can rely on the rules to protect them from blame if tragedy occurs, because a poor outcome can be blamed on poorly designed rules (Dreyfus, 2004). They need not feel anxious about pleasing supervisors, because their performance will be evaluated by how well they follow the rules. Ultimately, the over-reliance on manuals and procedures do not address the complex realities and uncertainties of practice and deprive practitioners of learning opportunities.

Another ultimately unhelpful way of protecting practitioners, teams, and workforces from the difficult business of appropriately expressing, understanding, and coping with emotion is by the use of bureaucratic structures (Hill, 2010). For example, a common structure of child protection systems is for practitioners to be separated into programs. Those in the intake program decide whether or not a child protection investigation is required, investigation and assessment teams decide whether a (children's court) legal framework is required, and those in case management program do the longer-term work with children and families who are on long-term court orders. This structure separates practitioners from the ongoing emotional impact of the work (i.e. needing to have an ongoing working relationship with a family whose child they have removed from parental care). However, important questions must be asked about whether these structures may compromise good outcomes for children and families by denying practitioners the opportunity to build therapeutic relationships with their clients (Hill, 2010). A therapeutic relationship fundamentally involves empathy and the use of rather than the avoidance of emotion. Of course, some situations (e.g. threats and violence towards practitioners) may legitimately require a change of practitioner.

4.2 Key Performance Indicators Can Reshape the Goal of Practice by Encouraging Practitioners to Prioritise Elements That Are Measured Over Those That Are Not

Since 1995, the Australian Productivity Commission has been reporting on the performance of child protection services in each jurisdiction (Tilbury, 2002). The introduction of key performance indicators to measure the 'success' or not of particular activities was motivated by neoliberal concerns about efficiency and effectiveness (Tilbury, 2002). According to the Productivity Commission Report, one measure of child protection effectiveness is ensuring notifications are responded to and investigations are completed in a 'timely and appropriate manner' (Productivity Commission, 2017, p. 10)

Although timeliness of the first visit to families is undoubtedly important, the danger here is that the activities that are measured can take priority over activities that are not measured. A key performance indicator such as this can come to dominate and reshape the goal of practice, making it difficult for practically wise practitioners to exercise good professional judgement (Schwartz & Sharpe, 2010). "Reporting on indicators ... (makes) some areas of work important and others invisible" (Tilbury, 2003, p. 9) such as the follow-up work that is done with families after the first visit is complete.

Findings in the Victorian Ombudsman's (2009) report confirm this to be the case:

> *There is evidence that departmental staff conduct the initial visit to families well. However, there is also evidence that further investigation following the initial visit is sometimes poorly planned and executed. This is reported to arise from the department's constant shuffling of resources in order to respond to new matters and meet performance measures (p. 34).*

and

> *At interview, senior departmental staff said cases were regularly allocated for the sole purpose of attempting a first visit to the family. Once a visit has been attempted, the department has met its performance target, and the case may then be de-allocated and staff redeployed to other matters where similar action is required to comply with the performance measure (p. 35).*

Focusing on the timeliness of the first visit to the detriment of follow-up work may actually cause families more harm than good by 'stirring up problems' and providing no solutions and by making families more suspicious of 'the welfare' and more sceptical of child protection workers, regarding them as unhelpful. A wise practitioner may, for good reasons, in a particular situation, prefer to delay the first visit, disregard the key performance indicator, and conduct the first visit only when there is the capacity for quality follow-up work to be done. In some cases, it may even be preferable to not visit at all if it is known that there is insufficient time for quality follow-up work to occur. However, a system of measurement that concentrates on the first visit and measures a practitioner's performance (and offers promotion) by how well they adhere to these rules can discourage the exercise of good professional judgement.

5 The Way Forward

We must find better ways to evaluate the performance of child protection practitioners and the systems they work within. We all need to do our jobs better and learn from our mistakes. But adherence to rules, standards, and key performance indicators is not the only or best way to evaluate performance. Key performance indicators may provide fast and efficient, quantifiable, and easily measureable methods of evaluating practice, but they are not wise enough or nuanced enough to provide the information we need. Moreover, they can reshape the goal (changing the *telos*) of practice by encouraging practitioners to focus on the elements that are measured. If adherence to key performance indicators becomes a dominant mode of practice, it can become more difficult for the handful of wise practitioners to do their work as they know it should be done (Schwartz & Sharpe, 2010). Careful and systematic evaluation can provide the information we need. Reflective practice sessions, case presentations, child death inquiries, and serious case reviews—all these can assist to improve practice.

Accountability is also important. Child protection practitioners are delegated the power to make life-and-death decisions in relation to children and families. Such decisions should only be made under the condition that they are accountable. Their professional judgments must be justified judgments. By explaining and justifying their decisions, practitioners make their decisions, themselves, and their organisation more trustworthy (Molander, Grimen, & Eriksen, 2012). But accountability must go beyond the public reporting of performance measures—which tell us little about the quality of decision making and whether practitioners are exercising good professional judgement—and of course, performance measures can be manipulated (Ombudsman, 2009). Accountability to the children's court is an important accountability mechanism. Other forms of accountability include encouraging independent research into child protection and particularly child protection decision making. Unfortunately, such research is scarce (Goddard & Tucci, 2008). Darlington and Scott (2002, p. 24) suggest that this may be because.

> *... government departments, may be concerned with the potential political ramifications of the research and at times research proposals may be thwarted, ostensibly on ethical grounds.*

Finally, practitioners must to be well supported to manage their emotions. On a positive note, the Victorian child protection 'Leading Practice' guide (Gibbs, Dwyer, & Vivekananda, 2014) for leaders and managers emphasises leadership, supervision and management, and working with emotions as pivotal for good outcomes for children and families. Translating these values and ideas into practice requires significant organisational culture change and time.

6 Conclusion

In this chapter, I have drawn from Aristotle's virtue ethics to describe good professional judgement and consider how it is learned. Good professional judgement involves values and ethics, and it goes beyond strict adherence to rules and manuals. It is context-specific and concerned with particulars, and it is constantly in flux. Practitioners face multiple goals and value conflicts, requiring delicate balancing acts. They must be mindful of rules, procedures, and manuals *and* draw on their intuition, emotions, and experience. Practitioners must understand that the future cannot be objectively known—no matter how sophisticated the risk assessment tool. Practitioners can only infer the future from the present, and their knowledge about both is incomplete (Yuengert, 2012). In most situations, there is no 'right' answer, but only 'an all things considered' best answer, for that particular situation, people, and time. Practitioners must also be able to use reasoning to defend and justify their decisions and actions as being appropriate to the situations and the people involved. They need to be well supported by the organisations they work within.

After 20+ years as a youth worker and child protection worker, this 'must list' of requirements still seems daunting. "This work is not for the faint hearted, and while it can be challenging, it can also be immensely rewarding" (Victorian Government, 2011, p. 10). But the work can only be rewarding if those doing the work feel like they are doing *good* work. When practitioners do good work, this is not only good for children and families but also good for practitioners themselves. Practitioners are more likely to find their work satisfying, stay in the work, and gain experience. Through practice, they are able to develop their capacity to make even better professional judgments, and this in turn becomes even more satisfying, it makes them happy, and this creates a virtuous circle (Schwartz & Sharpe, 2010). Doing good work contributes to their flourishing and also the flourishing of children and families.

Virtue ethics and good professional judgement in child protection by Karen Broadley.

7 Chapter Review Questions

1. Why is the problem of child abuse and neglect described as a 'wicked problem'?
2. Drawing from Aristotle's virtue ethics, what are the main elements of good professional judgement in child protection work?
3. Virtue ethics emphasises the importance of character. What virtues are important for child protection practitioners to display? Why are these virtues important?
4. What does it mean for a child protection practitioner 'to use emotion appropriately'? Give examples.

5. What is the different between 'reflection in action' and 'reflection on action'? Why are both important? How can reflective practice be developed?
6. Drawing from Aristotle's 'golden mean', brainstorm some 'balancing acts' intrinsic to child protection work.
7. What are key performance indicators? How can they reshape the goal of practice? Why is this a problem?
8. What organisational factors in child protection hinder/promote the development of good professional judgement?

References

Beauchamp, T. L., & Childress, J. F. (2001). *Principles of biomedical ethics*. USA: Oxford University Press.

Bessant, J. (2009). Aristotle meets youth work: a case for virtue ethics. *Journal of Youth Studies*, *12*(4), 423–438.

Bessant, J. (2017). Self-care in public and community sector workplaces. *International Journal of Public Administration*, *40*(2), 126–137.

Broadley, K. (2014). Equipping child protection practitioners to intervene to protect children from cumulative harm. *Australian Journal of Social Issues*, *49*(3), 284–365.

Bryce, I. (2018). A review of cumulative harm: a comparison of international child protection practices. *Children Australia*, *43*(1), 23–31. https://doi.org/10.1017/cha.2018.3.

Calder, M. C. (2015). *Risk in child protection: Assessment challenges and frameworks for practice*. Jessica Kingsley Publishers.

Coles, C. (2002). Developing professional judgment. *Journal of Continuing Education in the Health Professions*, *22*(1), 3–10.

Darlington, Y., & Scott, D. (2002). *Qualitative research in practice: Stories from the field*. St Leonards, NSW: Allen & Unwin.

Dreyfus, S. E. (2004). The five-stage model of adult skill acquisition. *Bulletin of Science, Technology & Society*, *24*(3), 177–181.

Flyvbjerg, B. (2001). *Making social science matter: Why social inquiry fails and how it can succeed again*. Cambridge University Press.

Gibbs, J., Dwyer, J., & Vivekananda, K. (2014). *Leading practice: A resource guide for child protection leaders*. Melbourne: Department of Human Services.

Goddard, C., & Hunt, S. (2011). The complexities of caring for child protection workers: the contexts of practice and supervision. *Journal of Social Work Practice*, *25*(4), 413–432.

Goddard, C., & Tucci, J. (2008). *Policy analysis: Responding to child abuse and neglect in Australia*. Melbourne: Australian Childhood Foundation Protecting Children, Child Abuse Prevention Research Australia.

Hill, A. (2010). *Working in statutory contexts*. Cambridge: Polity Press.

Irwin, T. (1985). *Aristotle Nicomachean ethics. Translated with introduction and notes*. Hackett Publishing.

Kinsella, E. A. (2012). Practitioner reflection and judgement as phronesis: a continuum of reflection and considerations for phronetic judgement. In E. A. Kinsella & A. Pitman (Eds.), *Phronesis as professional knowledge*: Springer.

Kinsella, E. A., & Pitman, A. (2012). *Phronesis as professional knowledge*. Springer.

Lawler, M. G., & Salzman, T. A. (2013). Virtue ethics: natural and Christian. *Theological Studies*, *74*(2), 442–473.

Lovat, T., & Gray, M. (2007). Towards a proportionist social work ethics: a Habermasian perspective. *British Journal of Social Work*, *38*(6), 1100–1114.

MacIntyre, A. (2003). *A short history of ethics: A history of moral philosophy from the Homeric age to the 20th century*. Routledge.

McBeath, G., & Webb, S. A. (2002). Virtue ethics and social work: being lucky, realistic, and not doing ones duty. *British Journal of Social Work*, *32*(8), 1015–1036.

Molander, A., Grimen, H., & Eriksen, E. O. (2012). Professional discretion and accountability in the welfare state. *Journal of Applied Philosophy*, *29*(3), 214–230.
Munro, E. (2002). *Effective child protection*. London, Thousand Oaks, CA: SAGE.
Munro, E. (2010). Learning to reduce risk in child protection. *British Journal of Social Work*, *40*(4), 1135–1151.
Oakley, J., & Cocking, D. (2001). *Virtue ethics and professional roles*. Cambridge University Press.
Ombudsman Victoria. (2009). *Own motion investigation into the Department of Human Services Child Protection Program*. . Retrieved from Melbourne.
Productivity Commission. (2017). *Report on government services 2015–2016*. . [Retrieved from Canberra].
Rittel, H. W. J., & Webber, M. M. (1973). Dilemmas in a general theory of planning. *Policy Sciences*, *4*(2), 155–169.
Ross, W. D. (2009). *Nicomachean ethics (Oxford world's classics)*. Oxford University Press.
Schön Donald, A. (1983). *The reflective practitioner: How professionals think in action*. New York: Basic Books.
Schwartz, B., & Sharpe, K. (2010). *Practical wisdom: The right way to do the right thing*. New York: Riverhead Books.
Slote, M. (2010). Virtue ethics. In J. Skorupski (Ed.), *The Routledge companion to ethics*: Routledge.
Tilbury, C. (2002). Performance measurement in child protection. *Australian Social Work*, *55*(2), 136–146.
Tilbury, C. (2003). Repeated reports to child protection: interpreting the data. *Children Australia*, *28*(3), 4.
Victorian Government. (2011). *Child protection workforce: The case for change*. . Retrieved from Melbourne.
Yuengert, A. (2012). *Approximating prudence: Aristotelian practical wisdom and economic models of choice*. Springer.

CHAPTER 17

Decision-Making Guidelines for the Child Protection Intake Phase

Karen Broadley
RMIT University, Melbourne, VIC, Australia

1 Introduction

Most advanced industrialised countries have seen significant increases in notifications[1] about child abuse and neglect (Broadley, Goddard, & Tucci, 2014). Whether this is primarily due to the increase in public awareness, including the introduction of mandatory reporting, a widening of the definition of child abuse and neglect to include emotional abuse and witnessing of domestic violence, or an actual increase in the numbers of children being abused and neglected, is unclear (Munro, 2002). What is clear is that this increase in notifications has resulted in increased workloads for statutory child protection practitioners. Furthermore, the requirement placed on practitioners to 'screen out' increasing numbers of cases based on minimal, primarily second-hand information via telephone conversations makes good decision-making particularly difficult. In many Australian states and territories, only a small proportion of notifications are transferred to a child protection investigation. The majority are 'screened out', by being referred to the voluntary service system (Australian Institute of Health and Welfare, 2014), or closed with no further action taken. The situation is similar in other countries, for example the United States (López, Fluke, Benbenishty, & Knorth, 2015). Making decisions about which cases require an investigation and the urgency "becomes akin to searching for the proverbial needle in the haystack" (Scott, 2006, p. 9). However, exercising good professional judgement is important. Poor decision-making can result in abused children continuing to be abused or wasting scarce resources on unnecessarily investigating innocent families.

Although there is a plethora of literature in relation to child protection practice generally, research on decision-making is minimal (Stokes & Schmidt, 2012). Admittedly, there are descriptive studies that describe child protection decision-making as it actually occurs. These

[1] Some jurisdictions use the term child protection 'notification', whilst others refer to a 'report'. In this chapter, I have chosen to use the term 'notification' so as not to confuse the term with a written 'report'.

Child Abuse and Neglect. https://doi.org/10.1016/B978-0-12-815344-4.00017-9

capitalise on the use of vignettes (e.g. see Arad-Davidzon & Benbenishty, 2008; Britner & Mossler, 2002; Osmo & Benbenishty, 2004; Stokes & Schmidt, 2012), interviewing of child protection practitioners (e.g. see Platt, 2006a, 2006b), and analysis of case files (e.g. see English, Wingard, Marshall, Orme, & Orme, 2000). However, normative studies are sorely lacking. With this lack of clear guidelines, it is not surprising that decisions are prone to bias, factual error, and peculiar and unexplained inconsistencies (Arad-Davidzon & Benbenishty, 2008; Osmo & Benbenishty, 2004; White, Hindley, & Jones, 2015). Arad-Davidzon and Benbenishty (2008, p. 108) suggest "the idiosyncratic nature of decision-making is a major problem in child welfare."

In this chapter, I provide decision-making guidelines for the intake phase.[2] In doing so, I draw from more than 20 years working within Victoria's child and family welfare system and the statutory child protection system. In some sense therefore, this chapter is an exercise in reflective practice (Schön Donald, 1983). The guidelines I provide are also informed by empirical studies—i.e. risk factors associated with child abuse and neglect, relevant theories, and descriptive studies that describe child protection decision-making as it actually occurs. However, the guidelines should *not* be used as a checklist. I argue that good decisions rely on the exercise of professional judgement, which includes using intuition and emotion, drawing from the practitioner's own experience and reflection, and exercising Aristotle's golden mean (see previous chapter).

The guidelines I present focus initially on the *information-gathering* process. I then consider how to organise and evaluate the information provided to the practitioner by considering the (1) *risk* to the child, the (2) *truthfulness* of the allegations, and whether there is sufficient (3) *safety* for the child.

Whilst I rely primarily on Australian and English material with a particular focus on the state of Victoria (given this is where my experiences lie), I suggest that the problem of exercising good professional judgement is not unique to Australia, but common to child protection systems internationally. In this way, I suggest that the guidelines presented in this chapter have international relevance.

Before I present the guidelines, I briefly describe child protection programs in the Australian context.

2 The Australian Context

As a federation of states and territories, Australia does not have one unified child protection system, but eight different systems with laws and policies to guide decision-making (Bromfield & Higgins, 2005). This diversity means there is a lack of high-quality surveillance

---

[2] In different places, 'intake' is named differently, for example 'front end' (Hughes, Rycus, Saunders-Adams, Hughes, & Hughes, 2013, p. 508).

data (Broadley et al., 2014). This makes it impossible to know the magnitude of the child abuse and neglect problem (because there are no clear and uniform definitions of child abuse and neglect across jurisdictions) and to know whether incidence of child abuse and neglect is increasing or decreasing (because there is no consistent use of definitions over time) (Broadley et al., 2014). However, there are a range of similarities between systems. For example, over the past decade, there has been strong nationwide shift towards a public health approach to child protection (see Broadley et al., 2014) by providing support to all children and families, especially those who are affected by risk factors such as mental illness, disabilities, social isolation, or other types of disadvantage. In this way, we have shifted away from the older, more forensic style of child protection intervention.

2.1 Child Protection Intake Programs

Child protection intake programs are broadly similar in all Australian states and territories. Intake is a central office, with notifications about child abuse and neglect being primarily received by telephone. A few individuals may attend the office personally to make a notification, send a letter, or send an e-mail.[3] Intake practitioners take a record about the child's details. A check is then made for any child protection history. If there is information in the notification to suggest a criminal offence has occurred, a report will be made to the police. Follow-up telephone calls may be made to education, health, and welfare services to obtain information relevant to the child's safety (Bromfield & Higgins, 2005). Ultimately, the intake practitioner, in conjunction with their supervisor, must determine whether the reported concerns (in conjunction with the information gathered from other education, health, and welfare services) meet the threshold for statutory intervention and the priority. Cases that are not referred for a child protection investigation are referred to either a voluntary family support service or other specialist service or closed with no further action taken (Bromfield & Higgins, 2005).

3 The Child Protection Intake Phase: Guidelines to Inform Practice

Upon receiving a notification about child abuse and neglect, the practitioner must

- Gather information about the child and family details and about the nature and severity of the concerns for the child.

There are three important questions the practitioner must ask herself:

- What is the *risk* of harm to the child?
- Might the allegations be *true*?
- Is there sufficient *safety* for the child?

[3] In all states and territories, legislation exists to protect the identity of persons making a notification.

Although it is important for the practitioner to gather and analyse information about *risk*, *truth*, and *safety* simultaneously, the initial focus must be on *risk* to the child (as I will soon explain). By drawing from her intuition and experience, the practitioner will decide how to organise the information-gathering process, which telephone calls to prioritise, which pieces of information are irrelevant, which are worthy of attention, and when enough information has been gathered for a decision to be made (Schwartz & Sharpe, 2010). Inexperienced practitioners should be mentored by experienced practitioners who have a reputation for being practically wise and who themselves make good professional judgments (Broadley, see previous chapter).

3.1 Information Gathering

The information gathering will centre on concerns relating to one or more of five different abuse types—physical abuse, sexual abuse, emotional abuse, neglect, and exposure to family violence. It is important that practitioners have a good understanding of the different abuse types and indicators of abuse. It is important for them to know that according to theories of multitype maltreatment, many children who are abused or neglected are subjected to multiple forms of abuse and neglect (Price-Robertson, Rush, Wall, & Higgins, 2013). White et al. (2015), for example found that neglect (as opposed to other abuse types) is a particularly strong predictor of all other abuse types. Goddard and Bedi (2010, p. 7) found there were 'high rates of overlap' between intimate partner violence and child physical and sexual abuse. Vachon et al. (2015, p. 1140) found that child sexual abuse is 'almost always accompanied' by other types of child abuse and neglect.

3.1.1 The five "W" questions

When I worked as a child protection practitioner, I used the five 'W' questions (what, who, when, where, and why) as useful guide to the initial stages of the information-gathering process (Broadley et al., 2014). This guide, however, should *not* be used as a type of prescriptive checklist. By exercising good professional judgement (i.e. drawing from their intuition and experience and critically reflecting on their own practice), practitioners will know when *not* to ask some of these questions:

- *What happened?* This involves questions about the incident or concerns. For example, in relation to physical abuse, it might be important to obtain a description of the incident and what was said and done. Was it a punch, a slap, or kick? How many times? Are there or were there injuries, where on the body, what do they look like? Has the child been medically examined? Has a report been made to the police? The same type of questions in relation to previous incidents may also be asked. It is also important to distinguish between facts, assumptions, and opinions.
- *Who was involved?* This involves questions about the age, sex, and ethnicity of the child and family members and whether there were witnesses to the incidents or concerns. This

also may involve questions about the child's and family's support network, both informal and formal.

- *When did it happen?* This may involve questions in relation to the date and time of the incident, whether anything similar has previously occurred and, if so, how many times and when?
- *Where did it happen?* This may involve questions about the location—for example, the home, the street, and the shops.
- Finally, the question about *why* it happened will be informed by well-considered 'who', 'what', 'when', and 'where' questions (Broadley et al., 2014).

If there is an alleged criminal offence (physical or sexual assault, significant neglect, or family violence), it is important that this be immediately reported to the police.

3.1.2 Follow up telephone calls

After taking the notification and checking for previous child protection notifications, the practitioner may make follow-up telephone calls to education, health, and welfare services (e.g. the police, a hospital, a family support service, a drug and alcohol service, or the child's school) to verify and/or obtain further information relevant to the child's safety (Bromfield & Higgins, 2005). Although many professionals are bound by rules of client confidentiality, these rules do not apply if the professional believes that providing the information is necessary to protect a child from current or future harm. Parents and children rarely have input into decision-making in the intake phase. Informing parents by telephone about a notification that has been made about the safety of their children is usually inappropriate. It can increase the stress and anxiety already experienced by many vulnerable parents (especially those with disabilities, substance use problems, conflictual relationships, facing socio-economic hardship, and isolation). It can increase the risk of harm to the child (e.g. if the parent believes the child has been revealing 'family secrets'). Furthermore, information gathered from a parent by telephone is likely to present a far more optimistic picture than what is really happening for the child.

3.1.3 Incorporating the views of other professionals and appropriate experts

It is important to place value and weight on the views and recommendations of professionals who have regular contact with the child. In the case of indigenous children and children from culturally and linguistically diverse backgrounds, it is important to seek specialist cultural advice. It also important to ask the notifier what he or she expects as a result from making the notification. In situations where the family is to be referred out to a family support service or other specialist services, it may be appropriate to request that the notifier makes this referral for the family. It may be more beneficial for someone the family knows (such as a school teacher or school counsellor) to make the referral than for this task to be undertaken by the statutory service that will then necessitate informing the family that a child protection notification has been received.

3.2 Focusing on Risk

A judgement of *risk* in the child protection context involves a combination of the *severity* and *likelihood* of abuse or further abuse to the child (Munro, 2002). A judgement of risk will also be informed by the particularities of the *context* (Schwartz & Sharpe, 2010).

3.2.1 Severity of harm to the child

According to many child protection experts and descriptive studies, the initial focus must be on the severity of the harm (e.g. Child Welfare Information Gateway, 2008; English et al., 2000; Morton & Salovitz, 2006; Platt, 2006a, 2006b; Platt & Turney, 2014). Drake (2013, p. 243) goes as far as to say that consideration of severity should be the starting point of any assessment and that there is little point in proceeding through the assessment if the severity is not high:

> *If the precipitating event is not severe, then it is hard to see the value in such formalised evidence gathering or documentation, because juvenile or criminal court action will almost certainly not occur in any event.*

The practically wise practitioner will understand the difficulties associated with making a judgement about severity. He will understand that it is not possible to arrange different types of abuse and neglect on a continuum from least to most severe. Although there are some who argue that the more severe cases are those involving sexual and physical abuse and that the less severe cases are those involving emotional abuse and chronic neglect (see, e.g. English et al., 2000; Child Welfare Gateway, 2008 who point to this argument), other researchers argue differently (Bryce, 2018; English et al., 2000; Vachon et al., 2015). Flaherty and Goddard (2008, p. 5) believe neglect is "arguably the most damaging type of child maltreatment with regard to the long term consequences for the child's cognitive, socio-emotional and behavioural development, and is particularly detrimental if it occurs early in life." Platt and Turney (2014, p. 1477) agree that to reduce children's experiences of abuse and neglect onto a "point on a measuring stick demonstrates a failure to understand the meaning and impact of the experience for that particular child." When making a judgement about the severity of an abusive incident, the practically wise practitioner will consider the range of other factors including the particularities of the context, the age, the functioning and voice of the child, and the child's experiences and history.

Although cases involving sexual abuse, physical abuse (where there is visible injury), domestic violence, and criminal neglect may not necessarily be the most severe cases, they should, if they constitute a possible criminal offence (which in Victoria they do), be immediately reported to the police.

3.2.2 The likelihood of harm to the child

Risk assessment also involves a consideration about the *likelihood* of future harm to a child. In Aristotle's time, there was not a well-developed theory of probability,[4] and therefore,

[4] See Munro (2002), for an explanation about probability theory.

the Aristotelian approach emphasises the important role of experience for making such a judgement (Yuengert, 2012; see previous chapter). When individuals rely on their experience of situations in the past to inform actions in the present, it is because they believe that the best predictor of the future is the past. They are assuming that it is likely 'for the most part' (Yuengert, 2012, p. 78) that present situations will turn out similarly to previous situations. "Probability theory replaces statements such as 'for the most part' and 'in the majority of cases' with more exact relationships between action and consequence" (Yuengert, 2012, p 78), i.e. a more exact relationship between variables describing individual or family characteristics and the occurrence of child abuse and neglect. However, in reality, neither experience nor empirically derived risk factors can provide a sure guide for action because "no two decision contexts are exactly alike and the differences between them may be crucial" (Yuengert, 2012, p. 69). There are many families experiencing many risk factors who do not abuse their children and some families experiencing no risk factors who do abuse their children.

In the child protection context (as in the criminal justice and other contexts), the process of risk assessment generally falls into one of two categories—the 'actuarial approach' and the 'professional judgment approach' (Broadley, 2016). The actuarial approach to risk assessment is a technical prescriptive approach often involving tick-box tools that draw from probability theory. Shortcomings of the actuarial tools are well documented and include the following:

- They are unable to accommodate the unique characteristics of each individual child and family (Goddard, Saunders, Stanley, & Tucci, 1999; Price-Robertson & Bromfield, 2011).
- They tend to exclude children's voices and other important perspectives from the assessment (Goddard et al., 1999; Price-Robertson & Bromfield, 2011).
- They are usually not suited for use with indigenous communities and other ethnic groups (Price-Robertson & Bromfield, 2011).
- They tend to focus on future harm and not on what is currently happening to the child (Goddard et al., 1999; Munro, 2002).
- For the most part, they have been developed without any specific regard to the severity of the abuse (Morton & Salovitz, 2006).
- They undermine the importance of professional experience and intuition (Goddard et al., 1999; Price-Robertson & Bromfield, 2011).

The professional judgement approach to risk assessment has been described as decision-making that is drawn from the practitioner's personal, practice, and cultural knowledge, where relevant information, patterns of meaning, and individual's own stories are filtered into a decision that is consistent with the organisational and social context (Stokes & Schmidt, 2012). Decision-making is also informed by empirically derived risk factors associated with child abuse and neglect (Stokes & Schmidt, 2012).

3.2.3 The particularities of the context

The professional judgement approach to risk assessment must also be informed by the particularities of the context—because every context is different. In drawing from the literature and from my own experience, I group these particularities under eight headings: (1) the pattern and history of harm to the child, (2) parental functioning, (3) parental history, (4) parental intent, (5) ecological factors, (6) child's age, (7) child's functioning, and (8) child's voice. I will go through these one at a time.

- The pattern and history of harm

Many researchers agree that it is important for the intake practitioner to check whether previous notifications have been made about the safety of the child (Child Welfare Information Gateway, 2008; Hughes et al., 2013; Platt, 2006b). (Fluke, Merkel-Holguin, & Schene, 2013, p. 546) suggest

> *... it is a common practice for child welfare professionals to review prior reports of child maltreatment when determining pathway assignment ...*

A history of multiple notifications indicates two things. Firstly, it indicates that the child has experienced multiple episodes of abuse and neglect, and although the episodes may not seem severe when considered in isolation, the resulting cumulative harm may be severe (Bryce, 2018). Secondly, a history of multiple notifications indicates a likelihood of future child abuse and/or neglect. In their systematic review of the research, White et al. (2015) found previous episodes of maltreatment to be one of the most consistently identified factors as predicting future maltreatment.

A high likelihood of future harm can be reduced by well-matched interventions. Some programs, for example may target parents to improve their parenting (e.g. parenting education programs) or address a particular problem (e.g. substance abuse problem). However, if information contained in previous notifications indicates that parents have not been able to achieve and sustain change despite receiving previous treatment and support services, then important questions must be asked about why change might occur this time. Maybe the parents are unwilling or unable to change? Maybe something different should be tried? It is important not to assume an inability or refusal to change. The origins of youth work, social work, and other helping professions lie in the understanding that individuals can and do change, particularly when they receive the support and assistance they need. Nevertheless, child safety must be prioritised.

- The functioning of the parents

It is important to gather information about the functioning of the parents (Turney, Platt, Selwyn, & Farmer, 2012).

Most children notified to statutory child protection services live within families with multiple and complex problems including parental substance abuse, mental illness, and family violence (Bromfield, Lamont, Parker, & Horsfall, 2010; Munro, 2002). These three problems have been referred to as the toxic trio. They often cooccur and are interrelated. They are also related to other problems such as poverty, unemployment, and social isolation (Bromfield et al., 2010).

It is important to note that substance abuse can be both the cause and the consequence of cooccurring problems. For example, substances can be used to self-medicate or to escape distressing mental health symptoms related to child abuse and neglect whilst at the same time exacerbating or even precipitating mental health conditions (Laslett, Dietze, & Room, 2013; Meredith & Price-Robertson, 2011). Children and young people who have grown up in disadvantaged neighbourhoods, where there are increased social problems, are at greater risk of developing substance use problems, and such problems can keep them trapped within a cycle of poverty and disadvantage. Potts (2005, p. 190) says that "poor living conditions are seen as both a cause and effect of parental drug misuse."

Gathering information about the functioning of the parents is important for two reasons. Firstly, this information informs a judgement about *severity* of harm. Problems such as parental substance abuse and family violence *in and of themselves* cause harm to children (Goddard & Bedi, 2010). Furthermore, according to theories of cumulative risk, children who are forced to live with multiple risk factors fare worse than those who live with fewer risk factors and certainly more than those who live with no risk factors. Multiple risk factors *in and of themselves* can raise the severity of the harm to the child (MacKenzie, Kotch, & Lee, 2011). Secondly, this information is important because the problems of parental substance abuse, mental illness, and family violence have consistently been shown to increase the *likelihood* of child abuse and neglect (White et al., 2015).

As previously stated, the likelihood of future harm can be reduced by suitable interventions. However, it is important to recognise that some parental problems can actually interfere with parental capacity to change. In relation to parental substance abuse, Holland et al. (2014, p. 13) suggest that it can become 'a major barrier' and often *the* major barrier to achieving change. They suggest it is not only the result of other problems (such as mental illness, family violence, or social isolation) but also a 'powerful reinforcer and creator of further problems for families'.

It is important to consider the particularities of each unique situation. For example, if the child has a relationship with a trusted adult who can provide support and use influence on the child's behalf, the child may experience some emotional healing from previous abuse (reducing severity) and may be less likely to be targeted as a victim in the future (reducing likelihood).

- Whether the perpetrator has been responsible for incidents of child abuse, neglect and/or intimate partner violence in the past

Researchers agree that it is important for the intake practitioner to inquire whether the parent has a history of sexual assault or violence against another child or previous partner (Britner & Mossler, 2002). Obtaining a criminal record check on an alleged perpetrator will reveal if the parent has a prior criminal conviction in relation to violence, sexual assault, or crimes against children. A telephone call to the police can be a source of additional information about the parents, whether, for example there have been police call-outs in response to domestic violence. If the checks reveal that the parent or primary carer has perpetrated abuse or violence against other children or other partners, this may make it more likely that acts of violence will be perpetrated against the notified child. In their systematic review of the research, White et al. (2015) found parental history of assaultive behaviour to be commonly associated with child abuse and neglect.

However, it is also important to consider the following factors: (i) the severity of the previous incident, (ii) the time that has passed since the previous incident, (iii) the programs and treatment undertaken by the perpetrator since the previous incident, (iv) the feedback from the treatment provider about progress since the previous incident, and (v) the character, functioning, and life situation of the parent at the time of the previous incident compared with currently.

- The intent to cause harm

Although there is no consensus amongst experts about whether the intent to cause harm is a necessary component of child abuse and neglect, some suggest that notions of culpability, responsibility, motive, and intent are important to many practitioners when making decisions about which cases warrant child protection investigation and which cases do not (Platt, 2006a, 2006b; Platt & Turney, 2014).

There are cases where the relevance of intent will be quite straightforward. For example, a parent who accidently injures his child by running over him as he backs the car from the driveway should be viewed differently from the parent who intentionally drives the car over his child with a desire to harm his child. Although the harm to the child may be severe, an accidental injury may reduce the likelihood of future harm to the child. However, if the accident occurred whilst the parent was substance affected, the parent will be viewed as being more responsible, and future harm may be considered more likely.

Other cases are more complex. Consider a mother with substance abuse problems whose partner has been sexually abusing her 12-year-old daughter. Although it is important not to blame the mother (assuming she had no knowledge of the abuse) and deflect attention away from the perpetrator, it is also important for the mother to act protectively, prioritise the safety and needs of her daughter, and engage with support and services as necessary, to reduce the likelihood of future harm. Intent must be considered in conjunction with a range of other factors.

- Ecological factors

Various risk and protective factors within the child's ecology also impact on the child's safety and wellbeing. White et al. (2015), for example found that children who live in families where there are low levels of social support, low family income, poor home conditions, and housing instability are more likely to suffer child abuse and neglect. It is important to remember that some wealthy parents also abuse their children. However, wealth can buffer children from experiencing abuse and neglect, and it can buffer the effects of child abuse and neglect. For example, wealthy parents who abuse substances and who neglect their children will have greater access to resources that can act as protective factors (e.g. babysitters, holiday camps, tutors, and legal resources). They are not restricted by the lack of resources to living in violent neighbourhoods.

- The age of the child

Research on child protection decision-making suggests that practitioners in the field consider the age of the child when making a decision about whether a child protection investigation is warranted (Child Welfare Information Gateway, 2008; Hughes et al., 2013). There is good reason for this. It is statistically shown that younger children are at greater risk of child abuse and neglect than older children (White et al., 2015).

The most obvious reason is that the more fragile physique of younger children means that injury is easier to inflict and the damage is more severe. A range of other factors make it more likely for them to be targets. For example, infants and very young children are unable to provide, fend, or speak up for themselves should their needs not be provided for or their safety threatened. Additionally, the task of caring for an infant is generally more exhausting and consuming than caring for an older child. It can be difficult for parents without adequate resources and support to manage these demands.

- The functioning of the child

It is important to consider the child's physical and mental capacities when determining the severity and likelihood of harm to the child (Arad-Davidzon & Benbenishty, 2008; Morton & Salovitz, 2006; Turney et al., 2012).

It is important to know whether a child has a disability and, if so, the nature and severity of the disability. Children with disabilities and physical health problems are more likely to suffer child abuse and neglect, particularly if they are socially isolated, have low visibility within the community, or unable to communicate what has happened to them (White et al., 2015).

It is also important for practitioners to consider whether childhood problems may be an indicator of child abuse and neglect. Knowledge of trauma theory, for example will alert practitioners to the possibility that problems such as delay in meeting developmental milestones and disturbed behaviours may be indicative of child abuse and neglect (Price-Robertson et al., 2013). The experience of repeated or ongoing early psychological trauma has been shown to impede children's physical, cognitive, emotional, psychological, and social development (Price-Robertson et al., 2013). However, it is also important for practitioners to remember that some 'disturbed' behaviours may not be connected to abuse and neglect and some abused children show no signs of trauma.

- The voice of the child

In most instances, the voiced experiences and expressed wishes of the child will not be relevant to decision-making in the intake phase. Of course, it will be relevant if the child himself or herself makes the notification to child protection or if say a teacher is the notifier and has information about the child's expressed wishes (if say a child tells her teacher she is scared when she is at home). In cases such as these, the child's voice should be given weight and impact on decision-making.

It is important to point out that wherever possible, children's voices should be listened to and given weight. This should occur in every other phase of child protection involvement (e.g. during investigation, case planning, and decisions about placement in out-of-home care).

3.3 Might the Allegations Be True?

If the severity of the alleged harm is *low*, then, regardless of likelihood, there is little value in gathering further information (Drake, 2013) because the case will not warrant a child protection investigation. However, if the severity of the alleged harm is *sufficiently high* to warrant child protection investigation, then, regardless of likelihood, the practitioner must determine whether the allegations *might* be true, If one or two telephone calls can determine that an allegation is clearly not true, then not only this will protect innocent parents from being investigated, but also it will save child protection practitioner's valuable time. However, if the severity of the alleged harm is *very high*, then it may be important not to waste valuable time making telephone calls in order to find out whether the allegations are clearly not true. The case may need to be regarded as urgent and promptly transferred to a child protection investigation. Practitioners must draw from relevant empirical and theoretical knowledge and their experience and intuition to exercise good professional judgement.

Consider, for example a notification made by a noncustodial parent stating that his 3-year-old daughter is being chronically neglected by her mother (who is the notifier's expartner) who allegedly uses drugs on a daily basis. The notifier says that his child is nonverbal and has not commenced toilet training. As a result of some targeted questioning, the intake practitioner believes the allegations have arisen more out of assumption than fact that the relationship between the parents is acrimonious. The child regularly attends childcare. The practitioner checks the file and finds no notifications in the past. Although the practitioner suspects the allegations to be vexatious, the alleged drug use and the young age of the child caution the practitioner that the severity of the harm *could* be high. Therefore, a follow-up phone call to the childcare centre is warranted. If the outcome is that the childcare centre supervisor has no concerns about the child's attendance, functioning or presentation, or the mother's presentation, then the case may be closed. If the childcare centre supervisor does relay concerns, but not sufficiently high in severity to warrant a child protection investigation, then a conversation with the supervisor about what the centre may be able to do to support and recommend services to the mother may be appropriate. If the child is older, then the severity may be lower (given older age of the child), likelihood may be lower (no history of notified concerns over a greater number of years may mean a lower likelihood of there being concerns in the future), and no follow-up telephone calls may be necessary. Of course, the practitioner may lean on the side of caution and time permitting and may make a telephone call to the principal or vice-principal of the child's school. However, a wise practitioner will also remember that making telephone calls to children's schools can be stigmatising to children and families and that this should not occur carelessly or without just reason.

Researchers have found that professional notifiers are more likely to be viewed as more trustworthy than community and family members (Child Welfare Information Gateway, 2008; Hughes et al., 2013). Allegations of child abuse arising out of matrimonial-type disputes have a reputation for being vexatious (Platt, 2006b). Corroboration from other sources might be particularly important in these situations (Platt, 2006a, 2006b). However, a practitioner may have a 'gut feeling' about the trustworthiness of a notifier that goes beyond a rational explanation based on whether the notifier is or is not a professional, and this should inform the decision-making.

3.4 Is There Safety?

Finally, the practitioner must turn to the question of safety. The word *safety* implies greater certainty than the word *likelihood*. In cases where the severity of the alleged harm is high and meets the threshold for child protection intervention and where the allegations might be true, the question of safety is paramount. There are two things for the practitioner to consider.

3.4.1 The access the perpetrator has to the child

White et al. (2015) in their research found that 'high perpetrator access' increased the risk to the child.

Consider the previous case example of a 12-year-old child, who has disclosed sexual abuse perpetrated by her mother's partner. The child made a statement to the police. The police officer informs the child protection intake practitioner that although the child's statement seems credible, there is no certainty about whether there will be enough evidence to take the case to criminal court. The alleged offender is still living free and unchecked in the community. The intake practitioner considers the severity of the alleged abuse to be high and believes the allegations to be probably (or at the very least 'might be') true. Ensuring the alleged perpetrator has no access to the child is crucial. If information gathered from police reveals that the mother supported her daughter to make the statement and has consequently separated from the alleged perpetrator, there *may* be sufficient safety for the child. The case *may* be closed with a referral to a specialist sexual assault service to provide counselling, advice, and support to the mother and daughter, with the counselling service agreeing to make a notification should they suspect the mother has reunited with the alleged perpetrator or if they suspect the alleged perpetrator is having contact with the child or if the mother disengages with their service. However, if it appears the mother will continue to live with or have contact with the alleged perpetrator, then the case will certainly require a child protection investigation.

3.4.2 Whether there is parental cooperation with support services and intention and capacity to change

Many researchers consider the willingness and ability of the parents to change as a crucial part of the assessment (Hughes et al., 2013; Morton & Salovitz, 2006; Platt & Turney, 2014). Child safety can be increased by the introduction of appropriate, well-matched interventions.

In the case study just mentioned, the mother may have told the police of her intention to separate from her partner. However, if a child protection history check reveals the mother has a history of linking up with and reuniting with dangerous partners and an unwillingness or inability to link in with support services, then this may cast doubt on the mother's willingness or ability to follow through with protective action this time. A recommendation for a child protection investigation will almost certainly be required.

Regardless of intent, it is crucial for parents facing problems related to sexual assault, violence, disability, substance misuse, and others to link in with appropriate support services and begin to demonstrate an increased capacity to provide for their children and keep their children safe. Nonoffending parents (of child sexual abuse and of family violence) are not responsible for the harm that is inflicted on themselves or their children. The perpetrators are responsible for this. However, nonoffending parents do have a responsibility to accept the necessary supports, so they can ensure the future safety of their children.

4 Conclusion

In this chapter, I have provided guidelines for decision-making in the child protection intake phase. Knowledge of decision-making guidelines such as these is integral but not sufficient to exercising good professional judgement. It is crucial for practitioners to use intuition and emotion, to draw from experience, and to reflect on that experience. It is also crucial for practitioners to exercise virtues such as empathy, sensitivity, warmth, honesty, resiliency, resourcefulness, and cooperativeness. In order for practitioners to negotiate the uncertainty of decision-making in the child protection intake phase, they must be calm and alert—having the capacity to adjust quickly to changing circumstances and new information.

Furthermore, good professional judgement exists and develops within particular organisational contexts. It is learnt from observation and support within a learning environment, not simply by adhering to guidelines and rules (Stokes & Schmidt, 2012). Referring to guidelines such as these is nevertheless important. Such guidelines can help practitioners to be clear and explicit about how they reached a conclusion, and they can make decision-making more transparent and open to review (Munro, 2002). Such guidelines may also reduce some of the uncertainty and stress associated with making such quick and difficult decisions in resource- and time-poor environments.

5 Chapter Review Questions

1. What steps might a child protection practitioner take as she gathers information about child safety in the intake phase?
2. What information might be important to seek from what professionals? Give examples.
3. How might the practitioner go about organising the information?
4. Why must the initial focus of the assessment be on the severity of harm?
5. Define 'risk'.
6. How might the concept of risk and the activities of risk assessment be both a help and a hindrance to good judgement in the intake phase? In child protection work generally?
7. Consider the 12-year-old (the 12-year-old previously mentioned, who has been sexually abused) who has been sexually abused by her mother's partner. How might other factors (i.e. the eight listed factors in Section 3.2 commencing with pattern and history of harm) impact on decision-making? Give examples.
8. Consider how Aristotle's virtue ethics might be applied to decision-making in the intake phase as distinct from other phases (i.e. investigation phase and long-term phase).

Acknowledgement

The author wishes to acknowledge support through an Australian Government Research Training Program and thank Professor Judith Bessant at RMIT University for her very helpful comments.

References

Arad-Davidzon, B., & Benbenishty, R. (2008). The role of workers' attitudes and parent and child wishes in child protection workers' assessments and recommendation regarding removal and reunification. *Children and Youth Services Review*, *30*(1), 107–121.

Australian Institute of Health and Welfare. (2014). *Child Protection Australia 2012–2013 (Vol. Cat. no. CWS. 49)*. Canberra: AIHW.

Britner, P. A., & Mossler, D. G. (2002). Professionals' decision-making about out-of-home placements following instances of child abuse. *Child Abuse & Neglect*, *26*(4), 317–332.

Broadley, K. (2016). Making the decision to remove a child from parental care: twelve decision making criteria. *Children Australia*, *41*(2), 90–97.

Broadley, K., Goddard, C., & Tucci, J. (2014). *They count for nothing: Poor child protection statistics are a barrier to a child-centred national framework*. Melbourne: Australian Childhood Foundation and Child Abuse and Prevention Australia, Monash University.

Bromfield, L., & Higgins, D. (2005). National comparison of child protection systems. *Child Abuse Prevention Issues*, *22*, 1–31.

Bromfield, L., Lamont, A., Parker, R., & Horsfall, B. (2010). Issues for the safety and wellbeing of children in families with multiple and complex problems. (Clearinghouse publications). *Family Matters*, *88*, 76.

Bryce, I. (2018). A review of cumulative harm: a comparison of international child protection practices. *Children Australia*, *43*(1), 23–31. https://doi.org/10.1017/cha.2018.3.

Child Welfare Information Gateway. (2008). *Differential response to reports of child abuse and neglect*. March 2016, fromhttp://centerforchildwelfare.fmhi.usf.edu/kb/trdiver/differential_response.pdf.

Drake, B. (2013). Differential response: what to make of the existing research? A response to Hughes et al. *Research on Social Work Practice*. 1049731512474492.

English, D. J., Wingard, T., Marshall, D., Orme, M., & Orme, A. (2000). Alternative responses to child protective services: emerging issues and concerns. *Child Abuse & Neglect*, *24*(3), 375–388.

Flaherty, N., & Goddard, C. (2008). Child neglect and the little children are sacred report. *Children Australia*, *33*(1), 5–11.

Fluke, J. D., Merkel-Holguin, L., & Schene, P. (2013). Thinking differentially: a response to issues in differential response. *Research on Social Work Practice*, *23*(5), 545–549.

Goddard, C., & Bedi, G. (2010). Intimate partner violence and child abuse: a child centred perspective. *Child Abuse Review*, *19*, 5–20.

Goddard, C., Saunders, B. J., Stanley, J. R., & Tucci, J. (1999). Structured risk assessment procedures: instruments of abuse? *Child Abuse Review*, *8*, 251–263.

Holland, S., Forrester, D., Williams, A., & Copello, A. (2014). Parenting and substance misuse: understanding accounts and realities in child protection contexts. *British Journal of Social Work*, *44*(6), 1491–1507.

Hughes, R. C., Rycus, J. S., Saunders-Adams, S. M., Hughes, L. K., & Hughes, K. N. (2013). Issues in differential response. *Research on Social Work Practice*, *23*(5), 493–520. 1049731512466312.

Laslett, A., Dietze, P., & Room, R. (2013). Carer drinking and more serious child protection case outcomes. *British Journal of Social Work*, *43*(7), 1384–1402.

López, M., Fluke, J. D., Benbenishty, R., & Knorth, E. J. (2015). Commentary on decision-making and judgments in child maltreatment prevention and response: an overview. *Child Abuse and Neglect*, *49*, 1–11.

MacKenzie, M. J., Kotch, J. B., & Lee, L.-C. (2011). Toward a cumulative ecological risk model for the etiology of child maltreatment. *Children and Youth Services Review*, *33*(9), 1638–1647.

Meredith, V., & Price-Robertson, R. (2011). *Alcohol misuse and child maltreatment*. In *National child protection clearinghouse resource sheet*. Melbourne: Australian Institute of Family Studies.(pp. 1–7).

Morton, T. D., & Salovitz, B. (2006). Evolving a theoretical model of child safety in maltreating families. *Child Abuse & Neglect*, *30*(12), 1317–1327.

Munro, E. (2002). *Effective child protection*. London, Thousand Oaks, CA: SAGE.

Osmo, R., & Benbenishty, R. (2004). Children at risk: rationales for risk assessments and interventions. *Children and Youth Services Review*, *26*(12), 1155–1173.

Platt, D. (2006a). Investigation or initial assessment of child concerns? The impact of the refocusing initiative on social work practice. *British Journal of Social Work*, *36*(2), 267–281.

Platt, D. (2006b). Threshold decisions: how social workers prioritize referrals of child concern. *Child Abuse Review*, *15*(1), 4–18.

Platt, D., & Turney, D. (2014). Making threshold decisions in child protection: a conceptual analysis. *British Journal of Social Work*, *44*(6), 1472–1490.

Potts, N. C. (2005). Problem drug use and child protection: interagency working and policies in Scotland. *Infant*, *1*(6), 189–193.

Price-Robertson, R., & Bromfield, L. (2011). *Risk assessment in child protection*. Australian Institute of Family Studies.

Price-Robertson, R., Rush, P., Wall, L., & Higgins, D. (2013). Rarely an isolated incident. *Child Family Community Australia*, *15*, 1–11.

Schön Donald, A. (1983). *The reflective practitioner: How professionals think in action*. New York: Basic Books.

Schwartz, B., & Sharpe, K. (2010). *Practical wisdom: The right way to do the right thing*. New York: Riverhead Books.

Scott, D. (2006). *Sowing the seeds of innovation in child protection*. Centre for Excellence in Child and Family Welfare.

Stokes, J., & Schmidt, G. (2012). Child protection decision making: a factorial analysis using case vignettes. *Social Work*, *57*(1), 83–90.

Turney, D., Platt, D., Selwyn, J., & Farmer, E. (2012). *Improving child and family assessments turning research into practice*. London: Jessica Kingsley Publishers.

Vachon, D. D., Krueger, R. F., Rogosch, F. A., & Cicchetti, D. (2015). Assessment of the harmful psychiatric and behavioral effects of different forms of child maltreatment. *JAMA Psychiatry*, *72*(11), 1135–1142.

White, O. G., Hindley, N., & Jones, D. P. H. (2015). Risk factors for child maltreatment recurrence: an updated systematic review. *Medicine, Science and the Law*, *55*(4), 259–277.

Yuengert, A. (2012). *Approximating prudence: Aristotelian practical wisdom and economic models of choice*. Springer.

CHAPTER 18

Eight Core Principles of Neurobiologically Informed Interventions for Trauma From Childhood Maltreatment

Grant C.B. Sinnamon

Bela Menso Brain and Behaviour Centre, Gold Coast, QLD, Australia

1 Introduction

Until relatively recently, the literature presented the view that treatments for psychological trauma in children and adolescents showed little efficacy. For example, in reference to treatment efficacy for posttraumatic stress disorder (PTSD) in children and adolescents, the Australian Psychological Society commissioned a literature review on evidence-based treatments for mental illness and psychological disorder that stated that (as of January 2010) "… no recent studies were found to indicate the effectiveness of any interventions for this disorder" (Australian Psychological Society, 2010, p. 144). However, there is a growing body of literature that is providing evidence that many of the identified psychosocial impairments manifest by trauma in young people including child maltreatment can be overcome. Child maltreatment and in particular maltreatment resulting from experiences of domestic and family violence (DFV) are known to be particularly insidious, pervasive, and resistant to treatment. The complexity of the affront caused by this form of traumatic experience crosses boundaries and includes the potential for a host of biopsychosocial insults including the physical alteration of neurobiological developmental trajectory, physiological wellbeing, and genetics, through to psychosocial offence around a child's sense of betrayal and abandonment (Dvir, Ford, Hill, & Frazier, 2014; Perry & Sullivan, 2014; Sullivan, 2012; Teicher, Andersen, Polcari, Anderson, & Navalta, 2002; van der Kolk, 2003). Within these effects, there are a host of potential comorbidities around physical development and health; psychological and emotional development and wellbeing; personality formation; intellectual and cognitive function; and the development and consolidation of the cognitive, behavioural, and emotional factors involved in a child's capacity for successful social engagement.

The evidence base for successful intervention in childhood trauma continues to develop, and duplicable intervention methods are becoming more widely recognised and included in

Child Abuse and Neglect. https://doi.org/10.1016/B978-0-12-815344-4.00018-0

a broad array of professional development and training programs globally. In addition, the area of developmental trauma is being increasingly viewed through the lens of developmental and functional neuropsychiatric mechanics. In this way, symptoms are being reduced to their neurofunctional correlates in recognition of the neurophysiological mediation of almost all human biopsychosocial operations.

In simple terms, as we develop, the interplay between genetics, the environment, and the influences of our own unique experiences on these factors contribute to the way in which we develop our physical mechanics and our psychological competencies, traits, and schemas. Certain experiences will interact with our unique physiological factors and will drive adaptation of our brains and bodies. Some elements of ourselves, both physical and psychological, will be stimulated regularly and will therefore develop as an adaptation to this stimulation. These become stronger and more sensitive and so take on a role as dominant neurofunctional processes. Conversely, if there are areas that are not regularly stimulated, encouraged, and nurtured, they will not develop and will remain underdeveloped and, comparatively speaking at least, be deficit in functionality to those that have been regularly 'exercised'.

For example, children exposed to threatening, chaotic, or inconsistent environmental stimuli will have threat physiology activated on a regular basis. This will become stronger and more sensitive to activation. This is an appropriate adaptation in our fight-or-flight physiology to make engaging in survival-guaranteeing (or at least survival-enhancing) behaviours more likely and more rapid. However, when this is the regular and consistent pattern of our neurological activation, our neural pathways that provide us with our ability to perceive enriching experiences such as happiness, joy, peace, and love are not being activated and will not develop to the same extent.

This is where we could spend substantial time discussing the fundamentals of neuron theory and developmental physiology and anatomy. For the purposes of this chapter, I will not venture down that particular 'rabbit hole' and will instead try to keep this at a more practical level. So, to summarise, our development, growth, and continued rejuvenation and recovery throughout life is a product of the interplay between our unique nature, nurture, and adventure. What gets stimulated regularly will develop and remain strong and dominant; what does not will not develop and will remain weak and subverted. This is the very basis of all learning, physical development, and the health and wellbeing of our biological structures, systems, and functions.

What is very important to note here is that (1) our thoughts, emotions, motivations, behaviours, sense of reality, and ultimately very capacity for sentience are all manifestations of the physical elements of ourselves; (2) our early-life experiences, both good and bad, hold an exponentially greater influence on our physical development than our experiences in later periods of our life; and (3) our central nervous system is a part of our physical selves and therefore influenced in the same way.

So, when a child is exposed to trauma, abuse, and/or neglect, such as that experienced through DFV, the patterns of stimulation they experience will drive neurological and physiological development accordingly. If we use this knowledge to help us plan treatment when working with trauma in children, then the emerging evidence suggests that we can have vastly improved outcomes. There are a number of foundational principles that underpin using this model for successful trauma treatment in people exposed to DFV. When these principles are put into action, they can be summarised as involving the following:

1. Downregulation of the neurological and peripheral physiology involved in and that are reactionary to threat response activation. This is done by dampening and ultimately weakening the dominant unresourceful neural pathways that have been sensitised to threat and protective reactivity (e.g. fear responses, hypervigilance, and reflexive aggression). In addition, the process includes the following:
   a. The initial external control of the triggers that mediate the activation and character of the emotional and behavioural responses to these physiological processes
   b. The teaching of competency to self-regulate these processes
2. The stimulation and strengthening of the more resourceful but presently deficit pathways that have remained underdeveloped due to a lack of activation
3. The integration of functionally disconnected neural circuitry in an appropriately sequenced and contextualised manner (Coates & Gaensbauer, 2009; Perry, 2006, 2009; Perry, Pollard, Blakley, & Vigilante, 1995)

The author has forwarded eight fundamental principles of effective neurodevelopmental practice that have been garnered from the research and clinical literature. These are not new or unique to this chapter but are rather based upon the empirically supported principles of neurodevelopment and neurorehabilitation. Together, these form an integrated foundation for working with trauma, and in particular, trauma experienced through maltreatment at the hands of primary carer or close-relational perpetrators. These principles are presented in Table 1:

The literature supports these principles, and I would argue that effective prevention programs and clinical interventions aimed at repairing maltreatment-induced neurological deficits should be considerate of these principles.

2 Eight Core Principles of Neurodevelopment and Neurorehabilitation

2.1 Principle 1: Social Affiliation, Attachment, and Empathy Are Essential for Healthy Neurodevelopment

In studies of resilience in children who experience maltreatment, one of the primary reoccurring themes is that healthy attachment and social affiliation, more than any other factor, predict positive outcomes and appropriate resolution of adverse experience (Ozbay et al., 2007; Perry, 2009; Stalker, Gebotys, & Harper, 2005). Generally, social affiliation

Table 1: Eight core principles of neurodevelopment and neurorehabilitation

	Principles
1.	Attachment (bonding, connectedness, empathy, and social affiliation)
2.	Sequential brain development
3.	Use-dependent neural development
4.	Neuroplasticity
5.	Neuroarchitecture mirrors neuroarchaeology
6.	Intervention sequencing must mirror developmental sequence (address lowest-order function first)
7.	Formal intervention in the early stages of post-extreme trauma is not always the best policy. Attend to immediate needs first
8.	Prevention is always better than cure—builds resilience and competency. Healthy development (relationships, enriching environment, etc.) builds resilience naturally

appears to moderate both the genetic and environmental risks of maltreatment, offering strong resilience to stress. Biologically, this appears to be conferred through three primary physiological systems—the HPA axis, the monoamine system, and the central oxytocin pathways (Aslund et al., 2011; Bartz & Hollander, 2006; Charney, 2003; Enoch, Steer, Newman, Gibson, & Goldman, 2010; Heinrichs, Baumgartner, Kirschbaum, & Ehlert, 2003; Ozbay et al., 2007; Southwick, Vythilingam, & Charney, 2005). While more research is needed to fully elucidate the mechanisms by which social affiliation inoculates against stress and trauma, it is clear that positive social supports mitigate the risk of trauma-induced or precipitated psychopathology, the neurological dysfunction associated with these psychopathologies (e.g. PTSD), the onset of medical comorbidities, and ultimately early mortality (Southwick et al., 2005). In children, the primary social affiliation mechanism is parental attachment (or that of the primary caregiver).

Social support is considered to have two dimensions. The first is its structural dimensions. That is the physical size of the social network and the frequency of social interaction within the network. The second is the functional dimension. The functional dimension includes the quality elements such as the emotional (e.g. feeling loved, being emotionally connected, and receiving and giving of empathic support and emotional safety) and instrumental characteristics (e.g. practical support, physical assistance, and protection) (Charney, 2003; Ozbay et al., 2007). Though both may be important, in the context of exposure to maltreatment and other trauma, particularly in children, it is the functional elements that research has illustrated to be of greatest importance (Perry, 2009; Southwick et al., 2005). These functional characteristics are those most associated with positive attachment that is associated with improved resilience (Bartley, Head, & Stansfeld, 2007; Heinzer, 1995).

In essence, poor attachment and being socially isolated elevate stress reactivity in the immature brain through upregulating autonomic and HPA axis function (Charmandari, Kino, Souvatzoglou, & Chrousos, 2003; Charmandari, Tsigos, & Chrousos, 2005; Charney, 2003;

Southwick et al., 2005). This then impinges on brain development by interfering with critical period neuronal hyperplasticity and the cellular mechanics involved in basic cell function as well as signalling and genetic expression. Many of the processes around social connection and attachment are dependent upon the expression of oxytocin and vasopressin (Bartz & Hollander, 2006). Oxytocin appears to mediate HPA axis reactivity to stressors (Heinrichs et al., 2003). Therefore, positive attachment appears to mediate stress reactivity in children helping to mitigate the potential for any deleterious effects on neurodevelopmental processes.

In a psychosocial context, children are heavily dependent upon their caregivers in early-life. During this period, a child will come to associate all of its physiological and emotional states with those with whom it is most consistently socially engaged. Further, because of this high level of dependence, these states will generally be a product of the interactions with primary caregivers. In a positive relational environment, the infant will associate comfort, satiation, curiosity, safety, learning and knowledge, and other positive and endearing characteristics with its caregiver(s). In a less positive relationship, where caregivers are inattentive, inconsistent with care, emotionally volatile, poor at meeting the physical and emotional needs of the child, or openly abusive or neglectful, then the young person will come to associate fear, threat, confusion and other negative characteristics with the caregiver(s). Over time, these associations can become generalised as the representative perception of all adults and authority figures. In this way, core schemas around notions of trust versus mistrust and self-worth and self-identity are maladaptively established.

Positive and endearing characteristics are associated with internal biochemistry that enhances learning, growth, and resilient psychosocial development. Negative experiences result in upregulated stress reactivity as an adaptive feature of surviving within a volatile physical environment. This internal biochemistry is neurotoxic and highly deleterious to the requirements of healthy neurodevelopment—resulting in neural deficits that correspond to physical, emotional, psychological, and cognitive impairments.

Memory of these experiences will also serve to create various 'templates' (emotional and behavioural) for social interaction. Volatile, stress reactive experiences will create templates that stimulate negative and maladaptive responses, while positive emotionally secure and rewarding experiences will create templates that motivate responses of an empathic, trusting, and mutually supportive nature.

The importance of secure attachment and the protection against early-life stressors that it brings is further emphasised by the highly disproportional emotional valence of early-childhood experiences. The rapid growth and organisation of the human brain in early life means, by necessity, it is also highly malleable and reactive to stimulation. This is a positive feature when it comes to learning languages, learning to walk, and other desirable developmental goals; however, adverse experiences also provide organisational frameworks for neurodevelopment. Repetition of adverse experience—whether through physical repetition of the experience or through reliving memories of the event—means that the highly plastic neural pathways will be influenced by the pattern of stimulation and develop accordingly (see use-dependent development, principle 3, and plasticity, principle 4).

This is an important feature of learning and adaptation. If a child receives cues indicating a high-threat environment, then it makes sense that brain processes will adapt to reflect a need for hyperreactive stress responses (e.g. reflexive physiological preparedness for action or escape) and stronger activation of emotional states that will motivate self-preservation behaviours. For example, increased fear response will motivate removal from a threat (including dissociation), or increased anger may motivate more aggressive self-defence behaviours and produce higher pain thresholds. A child developing in a low-attachment, high-threat environment is in little need of adaptive responses that promote social affiliation, connectedness, happiness, or skills in advanced mathematics.

Children developing within environments with strong positive attachments will adapt according to the presented stimuli and the needs of the environment. This reflects the value of empathy in the context of social interaction. In a more positive social environment, the neurodevelopmental needs are significantly different. Attachment and social affiliation help provide safety and security from predation and physical threat, therefore resulting in the need for more advanced methods of advancing within the group. The demand on neural responses is therefore less about physical threat management and more about intellectual differentiation and empathic participation in the group. This provides some evolutionary impetus for the way in which attachment, social affiliation, and environmental security impact neurodevelopmental processes and sequence (Heckhausen, 2000; Nevo, 2011; Sheridan, 2005).

Recent studies have started to show the pervasive impact that the absence of healthy relationships with primary carers can have on the physical mechanics of young children. The research shows that humans are genetically programmed for attachment bonds in childhood and their absence results in physiological adaptation to our genetics in order to compensate (Barr et al., 2008; Blum et al., 2015; Brodsky, 2016; Cicchetti, Rogosch, & Toth, 2011; Csala et al., 2015; Liu, Lou, Lavebratt, & Forsell, 2015; Olsson et al., 2013). Adaptation to poor attachment also includes changes in the integrity of ribonucleic acid (RNA). The effect of which is to alter our DNA and therefore our genotype and to impact physiological function at its most fundamental level (Blum et al., 2015; Cicchetti et al., 2011; Olsson et al., 2013; Scofield et al., 2015). RNA is one of the four foundational molecules that are essential for the existence of life. It plays a crucial role in the core mechanics of biological function including the regulation, expression, coding, and decoding of our genes. RNA is also essential for cellular function, including our neurons, as it is involved in several vital roles within our cells. One of these is to synthesise proteins by linking various amino acids together to form proteins essential for cellular function and messaging (Chen et al., 2006). Therefore, the absence of positive attachment relationships in early life can have a substantial impact on our genetics, genetic expression, and foundational capacity for our physiology to maintain life.

Ultimately, attachment is a core principle of neurological development and function, and the absence of strong and positive attachment relationships with primary carers in early life represents a serious risk to our health, wellbeing, and long-term morbidity. Therefore, interventions that seek to treat the impacts of trauma and neglect associated with DFV must address any issues of attachment and social affiliation as a priority.

2.2 Principle 2: Sequential Brain Development

The brain develops in sequence from the lower-order, least complex structures of the brainstem and progresses through to the higher-order and more complex structures of the cortex (Pechtel & Pizzagalli, 2011). Development proceeds through four distinct vertically integrated regions—the brainstem, diencephalon and cerebellum, limbic system, and cortex (Pechtel & Pizzagalli, 2011; Perry, 2006, 2008). These regions are significantly interconnected; however, they each undertake distinct functions with lower regions performing primary regulatory and sensorimotor tasks and the higher structures of the limbic and cortical regions performing complex tasks relating to social and cognitive function.

While the majority of neurons are already present at birth, it is the micro neurodevelopmental processes (e.g. synaptogenesis) taking place during the first several years of life that dictate, to a significant degree, the developmental progress of the brain's structures and functions. The brainstem, responsible for primary survival regulation such as cardiovascular and respiratory function, develops largely in utero and throughout the first months of life. Conversely, the higher cortical regions do not develop until the structures and functions of the lower-order regions have. Therefore, higher cognitive function such as language, abstract reasoning, behaviour inhibition, and sentience develop later in life. With each region having a different schedule of development, each region also has differing periods during which they will be at a heightened sensitivity for disruption. The earlier the disruption, the lower the region of the brain that is primarily impacted. The challenge for higher cortical functioning is that, without appropriate subcortical brain development in the lower regions of the brain, the cortical regions will lack the scaffolding and structural integrity to fully develop their own functional capacities. Therefore, the younger a person is when they are exposed to the neurodevelopmentally disruptive impacts of experiences such as DFV, the more potentially pervasive the impact will be.

The process is mediated by a number of chemical and electrical processes that stimulate pathway development. Many of the key mediators such as the monoamine system (noradrenergic, serotonergic, and dopaminergic systems) are also among the most sensitive to disruptions from trauma such as that experienced through DFV. The monoamine system is particularly sensitive and is involved in mediating myriad functions across a wide distribution network in the brain. Therefore, disruption to the development and functioning of these three monoamine networks can result in wholesale dysfunction. If disruption occurs in early development from influences such as in utero exposure to teratogens or from exposure to DFV in early life, then the resulting dysfunction will be pervasive across lower- and higher-order brain functions.

Brain-derived neurotrophin factor (BDNF) is integral to critical period hyperplasticity in the brain through its role in stimulating acetylcholine (ACh) release (Garcia et al., 2010; Knipper et al., 1994). During early life, BDNF continually stimulates the release of ACh, which in turn creates a perpetual state of hyperplasticity in the developing brain. This means a child's brain is hypersensitive to experience. Each experience will generate synaptogenesis resulting in increased synaptic connections between the neurons that are involved in sensing, storing (learning and remembering), interpreting, signalling, and responding to that experience (Hall, Vetreno, & Savage, 2014). When a child experiences a traumatic event, BDNF stimulation of ACh can be affected. When this happens, the hyperplasticity essential for optimal brain development that characterises the critical period is interrupted or prematurely terminated. The result of this ACh release interruption on developmental period hyperplasticity can be substantial and pervasive (Kuczewski, Aztiria, Leanza, & Domenici, 2005).

A further implication of sequential development is the nature of the sequence of hemisphere-specific development. As the brain develops in a vertically sequenced manner, the brain also progresses in a switching pattern from right brain to left. Similar to the heightened risks associated with region-specific developmental trajectories, hemispheric development faces heightened periods of developmental risk. A failure to successfully switch developmental focus from hemisphere to hemisphere at the appropriate time can result in hemispheric dominance and corresponding hemispheric weaknesses. A host of impaired functions reflect hemisphere-specific deficits (Bellis, Billiet, & Ross, 2008; Dobel, Putsche, Zwitserlood, & Junghofer, 2008; Landau, Auerbach, Gross-Tsur, & Shalev, 2003; Pitchford, Funnell, De Haan, & Morgan, 2007; Plante, Boliek, Mahendra, Story, & Glaspey, 2001; Spitzer et al., 2004). Therefore, interventions must account for both vertical and horizontally sequenced development trajectories (see intervention sequencing must mirror developmental sequencing: principle 6).

2.3 Principle 3: Use-Dependent Neurodevelopment

Ultimately, brain function is a confluence of the learning and adaptation that occurs through experience. Brains are developmentally and functionally use-dependent, which means they will adapt based upon the way in which the structures and systems are stimulated—much in the same way that an individual builds muscle through exercise. This has been evidenced at a cellular level with the activation of Purkinje cells stimulating development, protein expression, and dendritic proliferation (Wanner, Baader, Oberdick, & Schilling, 2000). Ultimately, the brain regions that are most active will develop dominant activation mechanisms, while those less active pathways and structures will be underdeveloped and deficit (Perry, 2008; Perry et al., 1995; Wanner et al., 2000).

In this way, brain development is dependent upon the sensory experiences of early life. Activation of various systems, in particular the noradrenergic system and the HPA axis, in response to threatening, aversive, or inconsistent and confusing sensory experience, results in activation-dependent development. This process results in the differentiation of the as yet undifferentiated neural systems into a threat-dominant response network. This is clearly evidenced clinically in the behavioural, affective, and physiological response patterns observed in child and adult survivors of childhood maltreatment (Carpenter, Shattuck, Tyrka, Geracioti, & Price, 2011; Eisen, Qin, Goodman, & Davis, 2002; Heim & Nemeroff, 2001; Nemeroff, 2004; Pervanidou & Chrousos, 2010; Pine et al., 2005; van der Kolk, 2003).

Alterations to brain structures, signalling pathways, chemical and electrical distribution networks, and communication systems have a direct relationship to the nervous system's operational viability (performance). Given the impact of chronic stressors during childhood on the structures and systems of the brain, it is not surprising that functionality in the brains of children and adults with a history of exposure to DFV in childhood is compromised. This adaptive response to adversity in early life ultimately becomes a self-reinforcing network with heightened reactivity of threat pathways further strengthening the activation-dependent neural networks. Therefore, successful interventions aimed at treating the functional, affective, and behavioural consequences must necessarily involve the breakdown of the maladaptive dominant pathways prior to any attempts to improve the deficit networks.

2.4 Principle 4: Neuroplasticity

The underlying principle of neurobiologically based intervention is that neural pathways and neural functions can be intentionally manipulated to prune maladaptive pathways and functionality and produce new or altered networks and function. This is the basis of neuroplasticity. The process of neuroplasticity has been clearly demonstrated in numerous studies and is a core factor of both healthy neurodevelopment and adaptive neurobiology in the face of brain insult (Dimyan & Cohen, 2011; Karunanayaka et al., 2010; Lillard & Erisir, 2011; Voytek et al., 2010; Whitall et al., 2011). In neuromodulated intervention for maltreatment-induced impairment, the processes of neuroplasticity are engaged to reduce the maladaptive threat-sensitive neurology, to stimulate the development of more resourceful neural pathways, and to integrate brain function both vertically (brainstem to cortex) and horizontally (hemispheric integration).

Neuroplasticity underpins all learning and development, as well as decremental functional processing associated with neurodegenerative disorders. The idea that the brain is malleable is the essential principle of all growth, change, adaptation, and learning. It is central to everything we do that involves some form of alteration to our thoughts, feelings, motivations, and behaviours, from falling in and out of love; acquiring a taste for particular foods and drinks; and learning to do mathematics, to read, to kick a football, to ride a bike, or to do a somersault. Equally, it is the process by which we learn to feel afraid of a particular scenario or person, by which we come to automatically think of ourselves or others in a particular way (I am stupid, unworthy, ugly, etc., or 'they' are dangerous, nice, etc.), and by which we learn to behave in response to a threatening situation (run away, cower, attack, etc.).

An essential factor of plasticity is purpose. As an organism, we humans are programmed for survival. The plasticity of our brains is programmed to support this prime objective. Therefore, plasticity processes will always prioritise surviving before thriving (Gericke, 2008; Korn & Faber, 1996). Therefore, if we want to take advantage of the principle of plasticity therapeutically, then we must remove threats and provide a safe, stable, nurturing, and highly predictable environment. In this way, we can help those we work with to engage change processes around their feelings, thoughts, motivations, and behaviours that will help them thrive. If we do not provide this sense of safety and stability, then the fundamental neurological processes underpinning functional outputs in the areas of feelings, thoughts, motivations, and behaviours will continue in survival mode, despite our best intentions and the client's/patient's desires to the contrary. This is a factor of fundamental biological function and cannot be circumvented and is the reason that unconditional positive regard and trust between the therapist and the client/patient is the single most accurate predictor of achieving beneficial outcomes from therapeutic intervention (Ivey, Ivey, & Zalaquett, 2009; Jennings, Sovereign, Bottorff, Pederson-Mussell, & Vye, 2005). Therefore, it doesn't matter whether you are involved in assisting trauma survivors through traditional counselling or general psychological support, as a case manager, residential support worker, lawyer or law enforcement officer, or in a more clinical or medically oriented position such as clinical psychologist, general practitioner, or psychiatrist; ensuring you engage in an environment and in a manner that offers a sense of safety, security, and predictability, is essential in order to promote successful change in line with the fundamental objectives of neuroplastic priority. If not, then you may inadvertently contribute to maintaining a neurological state of survival that may not only sustain any trauma-related presentation but also prime the individual for further trauma.

2.5 Principle 5: Neuroarchitecture Mirrors Neuroarchaeology

The structure and function of the brain mirrors the developmental influences of early life. All of our behaviours, emotions, and cognitions are adaptations to experience. This experience influences the use-dependent structural and functional development of the brain. Therefore, our history of neurological stimulation (neuroarchaeology) is reflected in our neurological structure and function (neuroarchitecture).

This underpins the clinical importance of obtaining as detailed a patient history as possible. A particular characteristic of many patients presenting with a history of DFV or some other form of adverse familial history is that a detailed history may prove elusive. They may not know the details of much of their early-life history; parents of abused or neglected children will not necessarily disclose these details accurately (if at all); children may end up in out-of-home care, and carers (including government agencies) may not be aware of full details; adopted children and their adoptive parents may have no way of obtaining details of early-life history (particularly if an overseas adoption); and many adolescent or adult survivors of childhood maltreatment may present with psychopathologies that inhibit capacity to either remember or disclose truthful recollections of early-life experience (e.g. personality disorder and dissociative disorder) (Alaggia, 2010; Bernard-Bonnin, Hebert, Daignault, & Allard-Dansereau, 2008; Diseth, 2005; Dube, Williamson, Thompson, Felitti, & Anda, 2004; Foynes, Freyd, & Deprince, 2009; Leichsenring, Leibing, Kruse, New, & Leweke, 2011; Sciolla et al., 2011). Moreover, both the neurophysiological sequelae from trauma and the neuropsychiatric sequelae from some of the treatments associated with trauma such as some of those for depression or psychosis can have a remarkable adverse impact on cognitive function including memory (Ang et al., 2017; Baune, Czira, Smith, Mitchell, & Sinnamon, 2012; Kozicky, Torres, Bond, Lam, & Yatham, 2012; Pechtel & Pizzagalli, 2011; Sheu, Polcari, Anderson, & Teicher, 2010).

However, there is a growing body of literature showing a strong functional correlation between psychological and physiological function and that this correlation can be further correlated to specific neurological function. That is to say that observations of physical and psychological function can provide insights into neuroarchitecture. One example is the relationship between psychological disorder and vestibular function (Lee et al., 2018; MacDowell et al., 2018; Naranjo et al., 2017; Smith, Wilkinson, Bodani, Bicknell, & Surenthiran, 2018; Walker, Kantaris, & Chambers, 2018; Yu, Xue, Zhang, & Zhou, 2018). Research into these relationships is showing strong correlations between the physical functions of the vestibular system that are managed by the brain, such as balance, coordination, visual-ocular reflex (VOR), and spatial orientation, and psychological and cognitive function in areas such as anxiety; depression; threat perception and fear response; risk–reward prediction; and executive performance such as decision-making, planning, working memory, and set maintenance or shift (Blini, Tilikete, Farne, & Hadj-Bouziane, 2018; Fuchs, 2018; Lee et al., 2018; Lopez, Nakul, Preuss, Elziere, & Mast, 2018; Schindler & Bartels, 2018; Smith, 2017).

In turn, deficits in both of these functional dimensions—psychological-cognitive and physiological—have been correlated to early-life trauma across types including teratogenic (such as exposure to alcohol in utero), sexual, psychological, and corporal (Hill, Steinhauer, Locke-Wellman, & Ulrich, 2009; Jirikowic et al., 2013; Kooistra et al., 2009; Lamela & Figueiredo, 2018; Purewal Boparai et al., 2018; Radziej, Schmid, Dinkel, Zwergal, & Lahmann, 2015).

Therefore, the literature provides strong evidence that our neuroarchitecture mirrors our neuroarchaeology. Moreover, even with only a relatively poor historical picture, the impact of childhood maltreatment can be predictably evidenced in the structure and function of both the central and peripheral nervous systems.

Given that experience is mirrored in the development and structures of the brain, diagnostic processes of neurological deficits can often be readily undertaken through assessment of function. For example, brainstem deficits may be indicated by the presence of deficits to functions known to be controlled by brainstem structures such as dysregulation in autonomic function and arousal, cardiovascular regulation or respiration, or heightened and aversive responses to external stimulation (e.g. touch and sound). Functional deficits in physical and behavioural characteristics will then be largely correlated with activation or functional patterns in specific brain regions (Gump et al., 2011; Napadow et al., 2008; Perry, 2009; Sharma, Sagar, Deepak, Mehta, & Balhara, 2011). Clinically, this provides a new avenue for diagnostic accuracy and therapeutic intervention. For example, a child with a history of child maltreatment may be experiencing challenges with learning to read. Reading behaviours may be put down to challenges associated with environmental challenges associated in being able to engage in learning or may be identified as being characteristic of dyslexia. Understanding the relationship between neuroarchaeology and neuroarchitecture and functional basis for ocular performance, an alternative hypothesis may be that the early-life factors have inhibited the development of extraocular eye motion control and that this is impacting the ability to control essential visual requirements for reading such as saccadic eye control (Agarwal et al., 2016; Gimse, Tjell, Bjorgen, & Saunte, 1996; James et al., 2018; Liversedge, Rayner, White, Findlay, & McSorley, 2006; Paolozza, Titman, Brien, Munoz, & Reynolds, 2013; Reynolds, Nicolson, & Hambly, 2003).

Understanding the relationship between life experience and neural structures and function allows for more accurate intervention when faced with performance, emotional, cognitive, or behavioural challenges. Therefore, understanding that neuroarchitecture mirrors neuroarchaeology is an essential principle of developing effective intervention strategies for those who have experienced childhood maltreatment such as DFV.

2.6 Principle 6: Intervention Sequence Must Mirror Neurodevelopmental Sequence

This principle has its origins in the now discredited early evolutionary biological theory that 'ontogeny recapitulates phylogeny' (Gilbert & Barresi, 2017). Recapitulation theory hypothesised that the development of an embryo from fertilisation to gestation or hatching (a period called ontogeny) goes through stages that resemble the successive stages in the evolution of the animal's ancestry (known as phylogeny) (Ehrlich, Holm, & Parnell, 1963). Forwarded by Ernst Haeckel in the 1870s, the theory was a restatement or clarification of the biogenetic law or embryological parallelism (Gilbert & Barresi, 2017). This was originally known as the Meckel-Serres law after the original proponents Etienne Serres and Johann Meckel.

As an articulate evolutionary biology theory, according to Ehrlich et al. (1963, p. 66),

> *Its shortcomings have been almost universally pointed out by modern authors, but the idea still has a prominent place in biological mythology. The resemblance of early vertebrate embryos is readily explained without resort to mysterious forces compelling each individual to reclimb its phylogenetic tree.*

However, the theory is echoed in widely accepted cognitive-developmental theory that in essence argues "… both biological evolution and the stages in the child's cognitive development follow much the same progression of evolutionary stages as that suggested in the archaeological record" (LeCron-Foster, 2005, p. 387).

As a principle for neurodevelopment and therapeutic interventions, it is argued that, just as higher-order association cortices develop off the back of lower-order sensorimotor structures (Gogtay & Thompson, 2010; Pechtel & Pizzagalli, 2011; Shaw et al., 2008), intervention that is aimed at repairing maltreatment-induced neurodevelopmental impairments should also follow a similar sequence. Therefore, intervention needs to follow developmental sequencing in order to allow the brain to develop according the natural structural and functional patterning. Once assessment has identified the location of the lowest-order functional deficits, then intervention processes should address these lower-order deficits first. As lower-order function is improved, then the intervention can progress in a hierarchical manner, much the same way as the normal trajectory of childhood neurodevelopment would follow.

The sequencing makes practical sense as much as it is argued to be a neurological imperative. If a child has dysregulated autonomic responses, they will present with behavioural characteristics such as hypervigilance, hypermotility, rapid and irregular eye movement, and inability to maintain a singular focus of attention (de Young, Kenardy, & Cobham, 2011; Diseth, 2005; Howell, 2011; Lee & Hoaken, 2007; Passarotti & Pavuluri, 2011). This symptom presentation is consistent with brainstem dysregulation (Aisa et al., 2009; Bergman, Sarkar, Glover, & O'Connor, 2010; Geva & Feldman, 2008; Talge, Neal, & Glover, 2007). Any attempt to work at a cognitive or affective level with a child with this pattern of presentation will be unsuccessful as they lack the functional capacity to engage prefrontal or limbic regulation processes. Therefore, regulation of the presentation of autonomic hyperarousal needs to be addressed before intentional cognitive therapeutic processes are engaged. As dysautonomia of this nature is a result of hyperreactivity of the brainstem, lower regions of the brain must necessarily be the focus of initial therapeutic attention.

Intervention must also consider the hemispherically unique functional patterns. If developmental insult inhibits appropriate right–left brain switching and development, then a range of impairments may ensue. For example, hemispheric functional imbalance is associated with, among many other things, language delays (Kurup & Kurup, 2003; Loman, Wiik, Frenn, Pollak, & Gunnar, 2009; Plante et al., 2001), poor auditory processing (Bellis et al., 2008), emotional dysregulation and stronger negative emotional responses (Carmona,

Holland, & Harrison, 2009; Kujala, Lepisto, Nieminen-von Wendt, Naatanen, & Naatanen, 2005; Thomas, Johnstone, & Gonsalvez, 2007), and attachment dysfunction (Schore, 2002).

2.7 Principle 7: Formal Intervention Not Always the Best Policy

Early formal therapeutic intervention for DFV-related trauma is NOT always the most appropriate course of action. After experiencing traumatic events such as DFV, people need time to process their experience, settle in to new living arrangements, and attend to the myriad of immediate needs that require attending to. Those who have gone through such experiences need to be treated both uniquely and holistically. Therefore, before engaging in any type of formal intervention, 'other' immediate needs should be considered and addressed as necessary. As a part of this process, a person's nonclinical needs are seen as equally important to the ultimate success of any intervention and support program. In this way, people can be treated in the context of their whole life story rather than only being seen in the context of their trauma. In this initial stage of intervention and support, attending to immediate needs is done without any expectations of therapeutic engagement or long-term behavioural change but rather is a part of preparing the space for the individual or family unit, to have the greatest opportunity to be helped in all areas of need.

This is supported by the fact that for long-term positive change to occur, there must be a sense of safety, stability, and predictability. These will not be present in the immediate aftermath of trauma or in the immediate wake of removal from an acute or chronic high-stress and traumatic environment. Providing assistance with immediate needs will allow the establishment of a safe, regulated, stable, and predictable environment. Over time therapeutic engagement, to the extent it may be deemed necessary, can be introduced.

Often, the extended family members, friends, and professional helpers of those who have been through DFV undergo a form of parallel processing. Originally, the concept of parallel processing had its foundations in the psychoanalytic theory of transference and countertransference (Calvert, Crowe, & Grenyer, 2016). Parallel process was argued to occur when the therapist recreated the emotional experiences and/or relationship they had with the client, within their supervisory relationship (Hyland, 2016). In the context of mental health and trauma-related situations, parallel processing involves those close to the 'victim' or 'patient' (including professional helpers and support workers from any number of disciplines), becoming caught in the same emotional upheaval and dysregulation as they are going through. In this way, the therapist, carer, friend, or family member parallels the contextual elements of the client/patient, such as anxiety, depression, fear, or other emotional or behavioural factor. This experience is usually directed towards the victim/patient and can therefore direct a victim's key supporters to want to prematurely engage or overengage in care, support, or therapeutic activities due to their own fears, anxieties, and insecurities they have for them. Those supporting someone who is dealing with a traumatic experience must be reflective and self-aware to ensure they are able to identify moments when they may start to parallel process what is happening for the person they are supporting.

Attending to immediate needs without any expectation of 'fixing', the individual may include any number of actions including the following:

- Immediate safety needs.
- Physical shelter/living arrangements.
- Food, clothing, etc.
- Ensuring environment is regulated, stabilised, reassuring, and predictable.
- Medical treatment and medication/physical health needs.
- Educational, employment, and social needs.
- Emotional needs.
- Advocacy to appropriate support services: successful intervention and support will likely require a multidisciplined 'team-oriented' approach.

Before any formal 'therapeutic' intervention, attending to the immediate needs will help provide the platform for natural or self-healing to occur. There is evidence that engaging in formal therapeutic processes too early may increase trauma outcomes rather than reduce them. This is known as trauma priming (Gist, 2015; Robinson, 2008). Individuals may be further sensitised or primed for trauma if they are forced to actively engage with their experiences in the immediate aftermath of the events. Instead, providing for the immediate physical and social needs of the individual and ensuring they are emotionally safe and psychologically protected from further traumatising experiences allow for the opportunity for the individual to integrate the experience and potentially deal with it without formal intervention processes.

Over time, if there is evidence that acute traumatic responses are becoming chronic trauma (PTSD), then formal therapeutic intervention will become warranted. However, as stated, there is good research from a number of sources suggesting that many individuals will naturally heal from traumatic stressors without formal intervention if these immediate needs are attended to appropriately in the immediate aftermath of a traumatic event or immediately after being removed from a traumatic environment (Gist, 2015; Kavan, Elsasser, & Barone, 2012; Robinson, 2008).

2.8 Principle 8: Prevention Is Better Than a Cure

In all matters of health and wellbeing, prevention is always better than a cure. Prevention involves two elements: (1) reducing the risk of DFV and other traumas occurring that involves recognising potential high-risk environmental factors and providing the external supports and resources to help reduce the risk and (2) ensuring adequate access to education, training, and developmental environments that provide opportunities to develop competency in dealing with challenging experiences and the resilience to overcome trauma and adversity when it arises. If people are taught resilience and have a strong social support network, then they are generally pretty good at resolving trauma from adverse experiences. Other factors do influence the ability to cope; however, the argument that prevention is always better than a cure still stands.

2.8.1 Reducing the risk of DFV occurring

To say prevention is better than a cure seems like an obvious statement to make; however, it is a fact of our social structures and political priority that we often avoid engaging with preventative strategy, and instead, we attend to issues as after-the-fact remedial endeavours. The issue of DFV is no exception to this. Familial supports, mentorship, healthy families, and social wellbeing programs, engaging vulnerable individuals and families with both formal and informal support and protection networks, are just some ways that DFV can be prevented before life challenges, home and financial stressors, relationship breakdowns, predatory perpetrators, and the maladaptive abusive outcomes they manifest can insidiously embed themselves into a relational or family environment. In locations where such programs have been instigated, the issues of DFV have been seen more in terms of it being a human rights issue than purely a legal one, and reports of a reduction in DFV has followed (Foshee et al., 2015; Frohmader, Dowse, & Didi, 2015; Goodman, Banyard, Woulfe, Ash, & Mattern, 2016).

Preventing DFV has also been identified as an area where intergenerational vulnerability is extremely high. Children who are exposed to DFV are at significantly higher risk of being involved in DFV when they are older as either a victim or a perpetrator (Bottoms et al., 2016; Foshee et al., 2015, 2016; Howarth et al., 2015; Storer, Casey, Carlson, Edleson, & Tolman, 2016). As a result, many programs aimed at preventing DFV are taking an intergenerational approach and engaging young people exposed to DFV with the aim of preventing them from perpetuating the cycle of perpetrators and victims (Foshee et al., 2016; Foshee, Dixon, et al., 2015; Howarth et al., 2015).

2.8.2 Prevention through teaching competency and resilience

This early-intervention model is mirrored in the argument to prevent children of all backgrounds from becoming either perpetrators or victims of DFV in the first instance. Advocates for early engagement with all children argue that we can largely prevent DFV through teaching children respect, emotional and relational competency, and resilience before they are exposed to the stressors of life that contribute to DFV via maladaptive coping strategies and poor self-schemas and related self-defeating belief systems (Stoever, 2014).

Like programs that could prevent DFV from occurring in the first place, the issue of competency and resilience training is also largely ignored. The evidence from competency and resilience programs both of a generic nature (e.g. general life skill programs) and with a specific orientation (e.g. academic, relationship, parenting, work, stress management, military, or competency and resilience skill programs) has demonstrated that these skills can have immense benefit and should be given a primary focus during childhood or at other key times identified as opportune for engaging in competency and resilience skill training (e.g. relationship and parenting programs or as a part of a high school positive education program) (Bursch et al., 2017; Herrenkohl & Favia, 2016; Kemper & Khirallah, 2015; Magen & DeLisser, 2017).

The research shows that there are some specific elements in developing resilience. These are the following:

2.8.2.1 Predictability and flexibility

Competency and resilience comes, in part, from having the ability to predict the actions and reactions of those around you, being able to understand the cause-and-effect relationships within your environment, being able to differentiate between subtle nuances and variations of behaviour and communications, and being able to predict and evaluate risk and reward that may be inherent in any course of action. Along with this skill comes the ability to be flexible in one's own behaviour choices so that plans, behaviours, and choices can be altered to most resourcefully meet the needs of the environment from moment to moment.

Animal models have shown that when a rat is given random electric shocks, the stress that results will impact the immune system and result in stomach ulcers. However, if the rat is given a warning (a light comes on or a bell is rung), then the rat can predict that the shock is coming and predict that it will not continue for very long. Rats given this preshock warning do not get ulcers.

Our ability to predict our environment and act appropriately provides us with the foundations for control and competency. Having control and the competency to successfully manage that control is essential to being resilient.

2.8.2.2 Outlet for managing and resolving stressors

An essential element of developing resilience is to have outlets to help manage stress. By far, the greatest outlet is aerobic exercise. There are a number of potential outlets to help manage stress. Exercise, hobbies, mental activities, meditation and yoga, social activities, watching movies or television, video games, and numerous other activities, as long as they are enjoyable and diversionary (i.e. take your mind and body away from any stressors for a period of time), then they can act as an outlet to reduce stress.

Once again, animal models show that giving rats random electric shocks will ultimately result in stomach ulcers via immune-mediated processes. However, if, after the shock is administered, the rat is able to engage in a diversionary activity to alleviate stress, then they do not get ulcers. Activities for the rat include things such as a running wheel to provide aerobic exercise or a piece of wood for the rat to gnaw on. Human equivalents might be to go to gym or for a run or to get a massage.

A second part of having an outlet and managing stressors is to have the ability to resolve our stressors. Problem-solving, planning, and decision-making skills, as well as having access to assistance, are all integral to this process. Developing competency in these areas and developing an appropriate support and resource network will once again provide the mechanics and the competency to maintain control and deal with stressors as they arise.

2.8.2.3 Social affiliation

The final cornerstone to resilience is being socially affiliated. Protective and life enhancing social affiliation has two components and along with exercise make up the three most significant predictors of mental and physical health, wellbeing, and longevity.

The first element of social affiliation is having a select group of close intimate connections. These are the few close people who are there for you no matter what. They are the people to whom you can tell your greatest hopes, dreams, fears, and mistakes. These are the 'warts and all' friends and family.

The second element of social affiliation is the extent to which you connect with others on a daily basis. These are the everyday interactions a person has with others, not the intimate connections, but the everyday connections encountered throughout the day. If there are a number of these connections and they are for the most part positive, then this helps create resilience and is protective against the negative impacts of stress.

Encouraging, supporting, and teaching people the skills necessary to develop a small number of close intimate relationships and to have the confidence and presence to look up and acknowledge those around them as they go about their daily activities will provide a level of social affiliation that has a profound effect on their resilience and ability to deal with adversity.

These elements of resilience are also pivotal to having the skills, confidence, and self-worth to make decisive choices when faced with a situation in which you or people you love and/or have responsibility for are placed under threat. In this way, developing these three elements of resilience is essential to preventing exposure to situations in which DFV might occur or dealing with such a situation more decisively when faced with it.

Ultimately, developing resilience is vital to preventing DFV and other intimate environment human-to-human forms of maltreatment. Developing resilience can be undertaken through a variety of processes. Resilience-promoting neurodevelopment and function can be encouraged through the following:

- Active and intentional engagement to promote attachment, empathy, connection, and investment in the welfare of others. For adults, parents, carers, and mentors, this means being present when interacting with others. Being present, being aware and engaged, and being congruent with an attitude of care and concern, all provide a valuable role model and send an important message that the other person is valued and respected. This, in turn, helps build trust and investment.

- Teach resilience skills. Provide deliberate programs and opportunities to learn competency skills and develop the core elements of resilience.
- Be what you want others to become. Modelling the competency skills and the resilience behaviours you want to develop in others is essential to develop trust and connection. Model the elements of resilience detailed above so that others can observe them in action. Incongruent behaviours quickly lead to mistrust, confusion, resentment, and insecurity.
- Open, clear, and honest communications. Providing and encouraging open communication help establish a template for interacting that others can observe, learn, and emulate.

The above factors all provide the active and intentional application of the principle of use-dependent development and neuroplasticity.

3 Summary and Conclusion

In perhaps a timely counter to the pessimistic outlook presented by the statistics that detail the prevalence of DFV in our communities and the devastating biopsychosocial consequences to individuals and the damage to our social institutions, clinical research is providing an increasing body of evidence in support of the positive potential for successful intervention in both child and adult survivors of childhood maltreatment such as that experienced through DFV. While significantly more research is needed to provide a consensus of evidence-based interventions, neurobiologically sound principles for intervention based on current understanding are required in the present in order to help inform and guide current practice models. In this chapter, a set of eight core principles have been presented that I contend are important considerations when implementing interventions and preventative programs in support of child and adult survivors of DFV and other trauma. However, as with any intervention protocol engaged in response to what are largely preventable pathologies, I leave my final statement to be a reiteration of the eighth and perhaps most important principle. That is an acknowledgment that prevention is always preferable to a cure.

4 Chapter Summary

- Until relatively recently, the literature presented the view that treatments for psychological trauma in children and adolescents showed little efficacy. However, there is a growing body of literature that is providing evidence that many of the identified psychosocial impairments manifest by trauma in young people including child maltreatment can be overcome.
- Child maltreatment and in particular maltreatment resulting from experiences of DFV are known to be particularly insidious, pervasive, and resistant to treatment.

The complexity of the affront caused by this form of traumatic experience crosses boundaries and includes the potential for a host of biopsychosocial insults including the physical alteration of neurobiological developmental trajectory, physiological wellbeing, and genetics, through to psychosocial offence around a child's sense of betrayal and abandonment.

- The area of developmental trauma is being increasingly viewed through the lens of developmental and functional neuropsychiatric mechanics. In this way, symptoms are being reduced to their neurofunctional correlates in recognition of the neurophysiological mediation of almost all human biopsychosocial operations.
- As we develop the interplay between genetics, the environment, and the influences of our own unique experiences, these factors contribute to the way in which we develop our physical mechanics and our psychological competencies, traits, and schemas.
- Some elements of ourselves, both physical and psychological, will be stimulated regularly and will therefore develop as an adaptation to this stimulation. These become stronger and more sensitive and take on a role as dominant neurofunctional processes. Conversely, if there are areas that are not regularly stimulated, encouraged, and nurtured, they will not develop and will remain underdeveloped.
- When a child is exposed to trauma, abuse, and/or neglect, such as that experienced through DFV, the patterns of stimulation they experience will drive neurological and physiological development accordingly.
- If we use this knowledge to help us plan treatment when working with trauma in children, then the emerging evidence suggests that we can have vastly improved outcomes.
- A number of foundational principles underpin this approach including the following: (1) downregulation of the neurological and peripheral physiology involved in and that are reactionary to threat response activation; (2) the stimulation and strengthening of the more resourceful, but presently deficit, pathways that have remained underdeveloped due to a lack of activation; and (3) the integration of functionally disconnected neural circuitry in an appropriately sequenced and contextualised manner.
- Successful intervention is based on eight core principles:
  1. Attachment (bonding, connectedness, empathy, and social affiliation).
  2. Sequential brain development.
  3. Use-dependent neural development.
  4. Neuroplasticity.
  5. Neuroarchitecture mirrors neuroarchaeology.
  6. Intervention sequencing must mirror developmental sequence.
  7. Attend to immediate needs first. Formal intervention in the early stages of postextreme trauma is not always the best policy.
  8. Prevention is always better than cure—build resilience and competency.

5 Chapter Review Questions

1. According to the literature, what is the most effective intervention for childhood trauma?
2. What are the three steps posited in the chapter to neurofunctionally address the impact of childhood maltreatment?
3. Downregulation involves two broad processes. Describe them.
4. Describe the principle of social affiliation.
5. Describe the principle of sequential brain development.
6. Describe the principle of use-dependent brain development.
7. Describe the principle of neuroplasticity and the impact of survival prioritisation.
8. How does brain structure relate to experience?
9. During the planning of an intervention, what principle must be considered when structuring the treatment?
10. What is the risk if formal treatment is undertaken too early, and what principle does this relate to?
11. When considering prevention, what are the two elements to be considered? Describe them.
12. Name and describe the elements that research argues are important for resilience.

References

Agarwal, M., Ulmer, J. L., Chandra, T., Klein, A. P., Mark, L. P., & Mohan, S. (2016). Imaging correlates of neural control of ocular movements. *European Radiology*, *26*(7), 2193–2205. https://doi.org/10.1007/s00330-015-4004-9.

Aisa, B., Elizalde, N., Tordera, R., Lasheras, B., Del Río, J., & Ramírez, M. J. (2009). Effects of neonatal stress on markers of synaptic plasticity in the hippocampus: implications for spatial memory. *Hippocampus*, *19*(12), 1222–1231.

Alaggia, R. (2010). An ecological analysis of child sexual abuse disclosure: considerations for child and adolescent mental health. *Journal of the Canadian Academy of Child and Adolescent Psychiatry*, *19*(1), 32–39.

Ang, M. S., Abdul Rashid, N. A., Lam, M., Rapisarda, A., Kraus, M., Keefe, R. S. E., et al. (2017). The impact of medication anticholinergic burden on cognitive performance in people with schizophrenia. *Journal of Clinical Psychopharmacology*, *37*(6), 651–656. https://doi.org/10.1097/JCP.0000000000000790.

Aslund, C., Nordquist, N., Comasco, E., Leppert, J., Oreland, L., & Nilsson, K. W. (2011). Maltreatment, MAOA, and delinquency: sex differences in gene-environment interaction in a large population-based cohort of adolescents. *Behavior Genetics*, *41*(2), 262–272. https://doi.org/10.1007/s10519-010-9356-y.

Australian Psychological Society. (2010). *Evidence-based psychological interventions in the treatment of mental disorders: A literature review* (3rd ed.). Melbourne: Australian Psychological Society.

Barr, C. S., Schwandt, M. L., Lindell, S. G., Higley, J. D., Maestripieri, D., Goldman, D., et al. (2008). Variation at the mu-opioid receptor gene (OPRM1) influences attachment behavior in infant primates. *Proceedings of the National Academy of Sciences of the United States of America*, *105*(13), 5277–5281. https://doi.org/10.1073/pnas.0710225105.

Bartley, M., Head, J., & Stansfeld, S. (2007). Is attachment style a source of resilience against health inequalities at work? *Social Science and Medicine*, *64*(4), 765–775. S0277-9536(06)00507-7, [pii] https://doi.org/10.1016/j.socscimed.2006.09.033.

Bartz, J. A., & Hollander, E. (2006). The neuroscience of affiliation: forging links between basic and clinical research on neuropeptides and social behavior. *Hormones and Behavior*, *50*(4), 518–528. S0018-506X(06)00169-3, [pii] https://doi.org/10.1016/j.yhbeh.2006.06.018.

Baune, B. T., Czira, M. E., Smith, A. L., Mitchell, D., & Sinnamon, G. (2012). Neuropsychological performance in a sample of 13-25 year olds with a history of non-psychotic major depressive disorder. *Journal of Affective Disorders*, *141*(2–3), 441–448. https://doi.org/10.1016/j.jad.2012.02.041.

Bellis, T. J., Billiet, C., & Ross, J. (2008). Hemispheric lateralization of bilaterally presented homologous visual and auditory stimuli in normal adults, normal children, and children with central auditory dysfunction. *Brain and Cognition*, *66*(3), 280–289. S0278-2626(07)00147-9, [pii] https://doi.org/10.1016/j.bandc.2007.09.006.

Bergman, K., Sarkar, P., Glover, V., & O'Connor, T. G. (2010). Maternal prenatal cortisol and infant cognitive development: moderation by infant-mother attachment. *Biological Psychiatry*, *67*(11), 1026–1032.

Bernard-Bonnin, A. C., Hebert, M., Daignault, I. V., & Allard-Dansereau, C. (2008). Disclosure of sexual abuse, and personal and familial factors as predictors of post-traumatic stress disorder symptoms in school-aged girls. *Paediatrics & Child Health*, *13*(6), 479–486.

Blini, E., Tilikete, C., Farne, A., & Hadj-Bouziane, F. (2018). Probing the role of the vestibular system in motivation and reward-based attention. *Cortex*, *103*, 82–99. https://doi.org/10.1016/j.cortex.2018.02.009.

Blum, K., Febo, M., Smith, D. E., Roy, A. K., 3rd, Demetrovics, Z., Cronje, F. J., et al. (2015). Neurogenetic and epigenetic correlates of adolescent predisposition to and risk for addictive behaviors as a function of prefrontal cortex dysregulation. *Journal of Child and Adolescent Psychopharmacology*, *25*(4), 286–292. https://doi.org/10.1089/cap.2014.0146.

Bottoms, B. L., Peter-Hagene, L. C., Epstein, M. A., Wiley, T. R., Reynolds, C. E., & Rudnicki, A. G. (2016). Abuse characteristics and individual differences related to disclosing childhood sexual, physical, and emotional abuse and witnessed domestic violence. *Journal of Interpersonal Violence*, *31*(7), 1308–1339.

Brodsky, B. S. (2016). Early childhood environment and genetic interactions: the diathesis for suicidal behavior. *Current Psychiatry Reports*, *18*(9), 86. https://doi.org/10.1007/s11920-016-0716-z.

Bursch, B., Lloyd, J., Mogil, C., Wijesekera, K., Miotto, K., Wu, M., et al. (2017). Adaptation and evaluation of military resilience skills training for pediatric residents. *Journal of Medical Education and Curricular Development*, *4*. 2382120517741298.

Calvert, F. L., Crowe, T. P., & Grenyer, B. F. (2016). Dialogical reflexivity in supervision: an experiential learning process for enhancing reflective and relational competencies. *The Clinical Supervisor*, *35*(1), 1–21.

Carmona, J. E., Holland, A. K., & Harrison, D. W. (2009). Extending the functional cerebral systems theory of emotion to the vestibular modality: a systematic and integrative approach. *Psychological Bulletin*, *135*(2), 286–302. 2009-02580-009, [pii] https://doi.org/10.1037/a0014825.

Carpenter, L. L., Shattuck, T. T., Tyrka, A. R., Geracioti, T. D., & Price, L. H. (2011). Effect of childhood physical abuse on cortisol stress response. *Psychopharmacology*, *214*(1), 367–375. https://doi.org/10.1007/s00213-010-2007-4.

Charmandari, E., Kino, T., Souvatzoglou, E., & Chrousos, G. P. (2003). Pediatric stress: hormonal mediators and human development. *Hormone Research*, *59*(4), 161–179. https://doi.org/10.1159/000069325. [69325 [pii].

Charmandari, E., Tsigos, C., & Chrousos, G. (2005). Endocrinology of the stress response. *Annual Review of Physiology*, *67*, 259–284. https://doi.org/10.1146/annurev.physiol.67.040403.120816.

Charney, D. S. (2003). The psychobiology of resilience and vulnerability to anxiety disorders: implications for prevention and treatment. *Dialogues in Clinical Neuroscience*, *5*(3), 207–221.

Chen, C., Li, J. G., Chen, Y., Huang, P., Wang, Y., & Liu-Chen, L. Y. (2006). GEC1 interacts with the kappa opioid receptor and enhances expression of the receptor. *The Journal of Biological Chemistry*, *281*(12), 7983–7993. https://doi.org/10.1074/jbc.M509805200.

Cicchetti, D., Rogosch, F. A., & Toth, S. L. (2011). The effects of child maltreatment and polymorphisms of the serotonin transporter and dopamine D4 receptor genes on infant attachment and intervention efficacy. *Development and Psychopathology*, *23*(2), 357–372. https://doi.org/10.1017/S0954579411000113.

Coates, S., & Gaensbauer, T. J. (2009). Event trauma in early childhood: symptoms, assessment, intervention. *Child and Adolescent Psychiatric Clinics of North America*, *18*(3), 611–626. S1056-4993(09)00028-5, [pii] https://doi.org/10.1016/j.chc.2009.03.005.

Csala, I., Egervari, L., Dome, P., Faludi, G., Dome, B., & Lazary, J. (2015). The possible role of maternal bonding style and CHRNB2 gene polymorphisms in nicotine dependence and related depressive phenotype. *Progress in Neuro-Psychopharmacology & Biological Psychiatry*, *59*, 84–90. https://doi.org/10.1016/j.pnpbp.2015.01.012.

de Young, A. C., Kenardy, J. A., & Cobham, V. E. (2011). Trauma in early childhood: a neglected population. *Clinical Child and Family Psychology Review*, *14*(3), 231–250.

Dimyan, M. A., & Cohen, L. G. (2011). Neuroplasticity in the context of motor rehabilitation after stroke. *Nature Reviews Neurology*, *7*(2), 76–85.

Diseth, T. H. (2005). Dissociation in children and adolescents as reaction to trauma—an overview of conceptual issues and neurobiological factors. *Nordic Journal of Psychiatry*, *59*(2), 79–91.

Dobel, C., Putsche, C., Zwitserlood, P., & Junghofer, M. (2008). Early left-hemispheric dysfunction of face processing in congenital prosopagnosia: an MEG study. *PLoS One*, *3*(6), e2326. https://doi.org/10.1371/journal.pone.0002326.

Dube, S. R., Williamson, D. F., Thompson, T., Felitti, V. J., & Anda, R. F. (2004). Assessing the reliability of retrospective reports of adverse childhood experiences among adult HMO members attending a primary care clinic. *Child Abuse & Neglect*, *28*(7), 729–737. https://doi.org/10.1016/j.chiabu.2003.08.009. [S0145213404001516 [pii].

Dvir, Y., Ford, J. D., Hill, M., & Frazier, J. A. (2014). Childhood maltreatment, emotional dysregulation, and psychiatric comorbidities. *Harvard Review of Psychiatry*, *22*(3), 149–161. https://doi.org/10.1097/HRP.0000000000000014.

Ehrlich, P., Holm, R., & Parnell, D. (1963). *The process of evolution*. New York: McGraw-Hill.

Eisen, M. L., Qin, J., Goodman, G. S., & Davis, S. L. (2002). Memory and suggestibility in maltreated children: age, stress arousal, dissociation, and psychopathology. *Journal of Experimental Child Psychology*, *83*(3), 167–212. [https://doi.org/S0022096502001261 [pii].

Enoch, M. A., Steer, C. D., Newman, T. K., Gibson, N., & Goldman, D. (2010). Early life stress, MAOA, and gene-environment interactions predict behavioral disinhibition in children. *Genes, Brain, and Behavior*, *9*(1), 65–74. GBB535, [pii] https://doi.org/10.1111/j.1601-183X.2009.00535.x.

Foshee, V. A., Benefield, T., Dixon, K. S., Chang, L.-Y., Senkomago, V., Ennett, S. T., et al. (2015). The effects of moms and teens for safe dates: a dating abuse prevention program for adolescents exposed to domestic violence. *Journal of Youth and Adolescence*, *44*(5), 995–1010.

Foshee, V. A., Dixon, K. S., Ennett, S. T., Moracco, K. E., Bowling, J. M., Chang, L.-Y., et al. (2015). The process of adapting a universal dating abuse prevention program to adolescents exposed to domestic violence. *Journal of Interpersonal Violence*, *30*(12), 2151–2173.

Foshee, V. A., Reyes, H. L. M., Chen, M. S., Ennett, S. T., Basile, K. C., DeGue, S., et al. (2016). Shared risk factors for the perpetration of physical dating violence, bullying, and sexual harassment among adolescents exposed to domestic violence. *Journal of Youth and Adolescence*, *45*(4), 672–686.

Foynes, M. M., Freyd, J. J., & Deprince, A. P. (2009). Child abuse: betrayal and disclosure. *Child Abuse and Neglect*, *33*(4), 209–217. S0145-2134(09)00033-7, [pii] https://doi.org/10.1016/j.chiabu.2008.11.001.

Frohmader, C., Dowse, L., & Didi, A. (2015). Preventing violence against women and girls with disabilities: integrating a human rights perspective. *Human Rights Defender*, *24*, 11.

Fuchs, D. (2018). Dancing with gravity-why the sense of balance is (the) fundamental. *Behavioral Sciences (Basel)*, *8*(1). https://doi.org/10.3390/bs8010007.

Garcia, N., Santafe, M. M., Tomas, M., Lanuza, M. A., Besalduch, N., & Tomas, J. (2010). Involvement of brain-derived neurotrophic factor (BDNF) in the functional elimination of synaptic contacts at polyinnervated neuromuscular synapses during development. *Journal of Neuroscience Research*, *88*(7), 1406–1419. https://doi.org/10.1002/jnr.22320.

Gericke, G. S. (2008). An integrative view of dynamic genomic elements influencing human brain evolution and individual neurodevelopment. *Medical Hypotheses*, *71*(3), 360–373. https://doi.org/10.1016/j.mehy.2008.03.048.

Geva, R., & Feldman, R. (2008). A neurobiological model for the effects of early brainstem functioning on the development of behavior and emotion regulation in infants: implications for prenatal and perinatal risk. *Journal of Child Psychology and Psychiatry, and Allied Disciplines*, *49*(10), 1031–1041.

Gilbert, S. F., & Barresi, M. J. F. (2017). Development and evolution: developmental mechanisms of evolutionary change. In *Developmental Biology* (11th ed.). Sunderland, MA: Sinauer Associates.

Gimse, R., Tjell, C., Bjorgen, I. A., & Saunte, C. (1996). Disturbed eye movements after whiplash due to injuries to the posture control system. *Journal of Clinical and Experimental Neuropsychology*, *18*(2), 178–186. https://doi.org/10.1080/01688639608408273.

Gist, R. (2015). *Psychological debriefing*. Hoboken, NJ: Wiley.

Gogtay, N., & Thompson, P. M. (2010). Mapping gray matter development: implications for typical development and vulnerability to psychopathology. *Brain and Cognition*, *72*(1), 6–15. S0278-2626(09)00162-6, [pii] https://doi.org/10.1016/j.bandc.2009.08.009.

Goodman, L. A., Banyard, V., Woulfe, J., Ash, S., & Mattern, G. (2016). Bringing a network-oriented approach to domestic violence services: a focus group exploration of promising practices. *Violence Against Women*, *22*(1), 64–89.

Gump, B. B., Mackenzie, J. A., Bendinskas, K., Morgan, R., Dumas, A. K., Palmer, C. D., et al. (2011). Low-level Pb and cardiovascular responses to acute stress in children: the role of cardiac autonomic regulation. *Neurotoxicology and Teratology*, *33*(2), 212–219. https://doi.org/S0892-0362(10)00170-4 [pii] https://doi.org/10.1016/j.ntt.2010.10.001.

Hall, J. M., Vetreno, R. P., & Savage, L. M. (2014). Differential cortical neurotrophin and cytogenetic adaptation after voluntary exercise in normal and amnestic rats. *Neuroscience*, *258*, 131–146. https://doi.org/10.1016/j.neuroscience.2013.10.075.

Heckhausen, J. (2000). Evolutionary perspectives on human motivation. *American Behavioral Scientist*, *43*(6), 1015–1029. https://doi.org/10.1177/00027640021955739.

Heim, C., & Nemeroff, C. B. (2001). The role of childhood trauma in the neurobiology of mood and anxiety disorders: preclinical and clinical studies. *Biological Psychiatry*, *49*(12), 1023–1039.

Heinrichs, M., Baumgartner, T., Kirschbaum, C., & Ehlert, U. (2003). Social support and oxytocin interact to suppress cortisol and subjective responses to psychosocial stress. *Biological Psychiatry*, *54*(12), 1389–1398. [https://doi.org/S0006322303004657 pii].

Heinzer, M. M. (1995). Loss of a parent in childhood: attachment and coping in a model of adolescent resilience. *Holistic Nursing Practice*, *9*(3), 27–37.

Herrenkohl, T. I., & Favia, L. A. (2016). Building resilience by teaching and supporting the development of social emotional skills and wellness in vulnerable children. In U. Kumar (Ed.), *The Routledge international handbook of psychosocial resilience* (pp. 346–354). London: Routledge.

Hill, S. Y., Steinhauer, S. R., Locke-Wellman, J., & Ulrich, R. (2009). Childhood risk factors for young adult substance dependence outcome in offspring from multiplex alcohol dependence families: a prospective study. *Biological Psychiatry*, *66*(8), 750–757. https://doi.org/10.1016/j.biopsych.2009.05.030.

Howarth, E., Moore, T. H., Shaw, A. R., Welton, N. J., Feder, G. S., Hester, M., et al. (2015). The effectiveness of targeted interventions for children exposed to domestic violence: measuring success in ways that matter to children, parents and professionals. *Child Abuse Review*, *24*(4), 297–310.

Howell, K. H. (2011). Resilience and psychopathology in children exposed to family violence. *Aggression and Violent Behavior*, *16*(6), 562–569.

Hyland, M. E. (2016). The story of motivational concordance. In S. Trusz & P. Bąbel (Eds.), *Interpersonal and intrapersonal expectancies* (pp. 35–40). New York: Routlege.

Ivey, A. E., Ivey, M. B., & Zalaquett, C. P. (2009). *Intentional interviewing and counselling: Facilitating client development in a multicultural society* (7th ed.). Belmont, CA: Brooks/Cole Cengage Learning.

James, S. S., Papapavlou, C., Blenkinsop, A., Cope, A. J., Anderson, S. R., Moustakas, K., et al. (2018). Integrating brain and biomechanical models—a new paradigm for understanding neuro-muscular control. *Frontiers in Neuroscience*, *12*, 39. https://doi.org/10.3389/fnins.2018.00039.

Jennings, L., Sovereign, A., Bottorff, N., Pederson-Mussell, M., & Vye, C. (2005). Nine ethical values of master therapists. *Journal of Mental Health Counseling*, *27*(1), 32–47.

Jirikowic, T. L., McCoy, S. W., Lubetzky-Vilnai, A., Price, R., Ciol, M. A., Kartin, D., et al. (2013). Sensory control of balance: a comparison of children with fetal alcohol spectrum disorders to children with typical development. *Journal of Population Therapeutics and Clinical Pharmacology*, *20*(3), e212–e228.

Karunanayaka, P., Schmithorst, V. J., Vannest, J., Szaflarski, J. P., Plante, E., & Holland, S. K. (2010). A group independent component analysis of covert verb generation in children: a functional magnetic resonance imaging study. *NeuroImage*, *51*(1), 472–487.

Kavan, M. G., Elsasser, G. N., & Barone, E. J. (2012). The physician's role in managing acute stress disorder. *American Family Physician*, *86*(7), 643–649.

Kemper, K. J., & Khirallah, M. (2015). Acute effects of online mind–body skills training on resilience, mindfulness, and empathy. *Journal of Evidence-Based Complementary and Alternative Medicine*, *20*(4), 247–253.

Knipper, M., da Penha Berzaghi, M., Blochl, A., Breer, H., Thoenen, H., & Lindholm, D. (1994). Positive feedback between acetylcholine and the neurotrophins nerve growth factor and brain-derived neurotrophic factor in the rat hippocampus. *The European Journal of Neuroscience*, *6*(4), 668–671.

Kooistra, L., Ramage, B., Crawford, S., Cantell, M., Wormsbecker, S., Gibbard, B., et al. (2009). Can attention deficit hyperactivity disorder and fetal alcohol spectrum disorder be differentiated by motor and balance deficits? *Human Movement Science*, *28*(4), 529–542. https://doi.org/10.1016/j.humov.2009.01.007.

Korn, H., & Faber, D. S. (1996). Escape behavior—brainstem and spinal cord circuitry and function. *Current Opinion in Neurobiology*, *6*(6), 826–832.

Kozicky, J. M., Torres, I. J., Bond, D. J., Lam, R. W., & Yatham, L. N. (2012). Comparison of neuropsychological effects of adjunctive risperidone or quetiapine in euthymic patients with bipolar I disorder. *International Clinical Psychopharmacology*, *27*(2), 91–99. https://doi.org/10.1097/YIC.0b013e32834e3bea.

Kuczewski, N., Aztiria, E., Leanza, G., & Domenici, L. (2005). Selective cholinergic immunolesioning affects synaptic plasticity in developing visual cortex. *The European Journal of Neuroscience*, *21*(7), 1807–1814. https://doi.org/10.1111/j.1460-9568.2005.04014.x.

Kujala, T., Lepisto, T., Nieminen-von Wendt, T., Naatanen, P., & Naatanen, R. (2005). Neurophysiological evidence for cortical discrimination impairment of prosody in Asperger syndrome. *Neuroscience Letters*, *383*(3), 260–265. S0304-3940(05)00421-0, [pii] https://doi.org/10.1016/j.neulet.2005.04.048.

Kurup, R. K., & Kurup, P. A. (2003). Hypothalamic digoxin and hemispheric chemical dominance: relation to speech and language dysfunction. *The International Journal of Neuroscience*, *113*(6), 797–814. https://doi.org/10.1080/00207450390200936. F9879Q8KWFX3262F [pii].

Lamela, D., & Figueiredo, B. (2018). Childhood physical maltreatment with physical injuries is associated with higher adult psychopathology symptoms. *European Psychiatry*, *53*, 1–6. https://doi.org/10.1016/j.eurpsy.2018.04.008.

Landau, Y. E., Auerbach, J. G., Gross-Tsur, V., & Shalev, R. S. (2003). Speed of performance of children with developmental right hemisphere syndrome and with attention-deficit hyperactivity disorder. *Journal of Child Neurology*, *18*(4), 264–268.

LeCron-Foster, M. (2005). Symbolism: the foundation of culture. In T. Ingold (Ed.), *Companion encyclopedia of anthropology* (pp. 366–395). New York: Routlege.

Lee, V., & Hoaken, P. N. S. (2007). Cognition, emotion, and neurobiological development: mediating the relation between maltreatment and aggression. *Child Maltreatment*, *12*(3), 281–298.

Lee, J. O., Lee, E. S., Kim, J. S., Lee, Y. B., Jeong, Y., Choi, B. S., et al. (2018). Altered brain function in persistent postural perceptual dizziness: a study on resting state functional connectivity. *Human Brain Mapping*, https://doi.org/10.1002/hbm.24080.

Leichsenring, F., Leibing, E., Kruse, J., New, A. S., & Leweke, F. (2011). Borderline personality disorder. *The Lancet*, *377*(9759), 74–84.

Lillard, A. S., & Erisir, A. (2011). Old dogs learning new tricks: neuroplasticity beyond the juvenile period. *Developmental Review*, *31*(4), 207–239.

Liu, J. J., Lou, F., Lavebratt, C., & Forsell, Y. (2015). Impact of childhood adversity and vasopressin receptor 1a variation on social interaction in adulthood: a cross-sectional study. *PLoS One*, *10*(8), e0136436. https://doi.org/10.1371/journal.pone.0136436.

Liversedge, S. P., Rayner, K., White, S. J., Findlay, J. M., & McSorley, E. (2006). Binocular coordination of the eyes during reading. *Current Biology*, *16*(17), 1726–1729. https://doi.org/10.1016/j.cub.2006.07.051.

Loman, M. M., Wiik, K. L., Frenn, K. A., Pollak, S. D., & Gunnar, M. R. (2009). Postinstitutionalized children's development: growth, cognitive, and language outcomes. *Journal of Developmental and Behavioral Pediatrics*, *30*(5), 426–434. https://doi.org/10.1097/DBP.0b013e3181b1fd08.

Lopez, C., Nakul, E., Preuss, N., Elziere, M., & Mast, F. W. (2018). Distorted own-body representations in patients with dizziness and during caloric vestibular stimulation. *Journal of Neurology*, https://doi.org/10.1007/s00415-018-8906-8.

MacDowell, S. G., Wellons, R., Bissell, A., Knecht, L., Naquin, C., & Karpinski, A. (2018). The impact of symptoms of anxiety and depression on subjective and objective outcome measures in individuals with vestibular disorders. *Journal of Vestibular Research*, *27*(5–6), 295–303. https://doi.org/10.3233/VES-170627.

Magen, E., & DeLisser, H. M. (2017). Best practices in relational skills training for medical trainees and providers: an essential element of addressing adverse childhood experiences and promoting resilience. *Academic Pediatrics*, *17*(7), S102–S107.

Napadow, V., Dhond, R., Conti, G., Makris, N., Brown, E. N., & Barbieri, R. (2008). Brain correlates of autonomic modulation: combining heart rate variability with fMRI. *NeuroImage*, *42*(1), 169–177.

Naranjo, E. N., Cleworth, T. W., Allum, J. H. J., Inglis, J. T., Lea, J., Westerberg, B. D., et al. (2017). Threat effects on human oculo-motor function. *Neuroscience*, *359*, 289–298. https://doi.org/10.1016/j.neuroscience.2017.07.024.

Nemeroff, C. B. (2004). Neurobiological consequences of childhood trauma. *The Journal of Clinical Psychiatry*, *65*(Suppl 1), 18–28.

Nevo, E. (2011). Evolution under environmental stress at macro- and microscales. *Genome Biology and Evolution*, *3*, 1039–1052. evr052, [pii] https://doi.org/10.1093/gbe/evr052.

Olsson, C. A., Moyzis, R. K., Williamson, E., Ellis, J. A., Parkinson-Bates, M., Patton, G. C., et al. (2013). Gene-environment interaction in problematic substance use: interaction between DRD4 and insecure attachments. *Addiction Biology*, *18*(4), 717–726. https://doi.org/10.1111/j.1369-1600.2011.00413.x.

Ozbay, F., Johnson, D. C., Dimoulas, E., Morgan, C. A., Charney, D., & Southwick, S. (2007). Social support and resilience to stress: from neurobiology to clinical practice. *Psychiatry (Edgmont)*, *4*(5), 35–40.

Paolozza, A., Titman, R., Brien, D., Munoz, D. P., & Reynolds, J. N. (2013). Altered accuracy of saccadic eye movements in children with fetal alcohol spectrum disorder. *Alcoholism, Clinical and Experimental Research*, *37*(9), 1491–1498. https://doi.org/10.1111/acer.12119.

Passarotti, A. M., & Pavuluri, M. N. (2011). Brain functional domains inform therapeutic interventions in attention-deficit/hyperactivity disorder and pediatric bipolar disorder. *Expert Review of Neurotherapeutics*, *11*(6), 897–914.

Pechtel, P., & Pizzagalli, D. A. (2011). Effects of early life stress on cognitive and affective function: an integrated review of human literature. *Psychopharmacology*, *214*(1), 55–70.

Perry, B. D. (2006). The neurosequential model of therapeutics: applying principles of neuroscience to clinical work with traumatized and maltreated children. In N. Boyd Webb (Ed.), *Working with traumatized youth in child welfare* (pp. 27–52). New York: Guilford Press.

Perry, B. D. (2008). Child maltreatment: the role of abuse and neglect in developmental psychopathology. In T. P. Beauchaine & S. P. Hinshaw (Eds.), *Textbook of child and adolescent psychopathology* (pp. 93–128). New York: Wiley.

Perry, B. D. (2009). Examining child maltreatment through a neurodevelopmental lens: clinical applications of the neurosequential model of therapeutics. *Journal of Loss and Trauma*, *14*, 240–255.

Perry, B. D., Pollard, R. A., Blakley, T. L., & Vigilante, D. (1995). Childhood trauma, the neurobiology of adaptation, and "use-dependent" development of the brain: how "states" become "traits". *Infant Mental Health Journal*, *16*(4), 271–291.

Perry, R., & Sullivan, R. M. (2014). Neurobiology of attachment to an abusive caregiver: short-term benefits and long-term costs. *Developmental Psychobiology*, *56*(8), 1626–1634. https://doi.org/10.1002/dev.21219.

Pervanidou, P., & Chrousos, G. P. (2010). Neuroendocrinology of post-traumatic stress disorder. *Progress in Brain Research*, *182*, 149–160. S0079-6123(10)82005-9, [pii] https://doi.org/10.1016/S0079-6123(10)82005-9.

Pine, D. S., Mogg, K., Bradley, B. P., Montgomery, L., Monk, C. S., McClure, E., et al. (2005). Attention bias to threat in maltreated children: implications for vulnerability to stress-related psychopathology. *The American Journal of Psychiatry*, *162*(2), 291–296. 162/2/291, [pii] https://doi.org/10.1176/appi.ajp.162.2.291.

Pitchford, N. J., Funnell, E., De Haan, B., & Morgan, P. S. (2007). Right-hemisphere reading in a case of developmental deep dyslexia. *Quarterly Journal of Experimental Psychology (Hove)*, *60*(9), 1187–1196. 780414111, [pii] https://doi.org/10.1080/17470210701425845.

Plante, E., Boliek, C., Mahendra, N., Story, J., & Glaspey, K. (2001). Right hemisphere contribution to developmental language disorder: neuroanatomical and behavioral evidence. *Journal of Communication Disorders*, *34*(5), 415–436. https://doi.org/S0021-9924(01)00059-4 [pii].

Purewal Boparai, S. K., Au, V., Koita, K., Oh, D. L., Briner, S., Burke Harris, N., et al. (2018). Ameliorating the biological impacts of childhood adversity: a review of intervention programs. *Child Abuse & Neglect*, *81*, 82–105. https://doi.org/10.1016/j.chiabu.2018.04.014.

Radziej, K., Schmid, G., Dinkel, A., Zwergal, A., & Lahmann, C. (2015). Psychological traumatization and adverse life events in patients with organic and functional vestibular symptoms. *Journal of Psychosomatic Research*, *79*(2), 123–129. https://doi.org/10.1016/j.jpsychores.2015.05.005.

Reynolds, D., Nicolson, R. I., & Hambly, H. (2003). Evaluation of an exercise-based treatment for children with reading difficulties. *Dyslexia*, *9*(1), 48–71. discussion 46-47 https://doi.org/10.1002/dys.235.

Robinson, R. (2008). Reflections on the debriefing debate. *International Journal of Emergency Mental Health*, *10*(4), 253–259.

Schindler, A., & Bartels, A. (2018). Integration of visual and non-visual self-motion cues during voluntary head movements in the human brain. *NeuroImage*, *172*, 597–607. https://doi.org/10.1016/j.neuroimage.2018.02.006.

Schore, A. N. (2002). Dysregulation of the right brain: a fundamental mechanism of traumatic attachment and the psychopathogenesis of posttraumatic stress disorder. *The Australian and New Zealand Journal of Psychiatry*, *36*(1), 9–30. [https://doi.org/996 [pii].

Sciolla, A., Glover, D. A., Loeb, T. B., Zhang, M., Myers, H. F., & Wyatt, G. E. (2011). Childhood sexual abuse severity and disclosure as predictors of depression among adult African-American and Latina women. *The Journal of Nervous and Mental Disease*, *199*(7), 471–477. https://doi.org/10.1097/NMD.0b013e31822142ac. 00005053-201107000-00009 [pii].

Scofield, M. D., Boger, H. A., Smith, R. J., Li, H., Haydon, P. G., & Kalivas, P. W. (2015). Gq-DREADD selectively initiates glial glutamate release and inhibits cue-induced cocaine seeking. *Biological Psychiatry*, *78*(7), 441–451. https://doi.org/10.1016/j.biopsych.2015.02.016.

Sharma, R. K., Sagar, R., Deepak, K. K., Mehta, M., & Balhara, Y. P. (2011). Clinical and autonomic functions: a study of childhood anxiety disorders. *Annals of Saudi Medicine*, *31*(3), 250–257. AnnSaudiMed_2011_31_3_250_81533, [pii] https://doi.org/10.4103/0256-4947.81533.

Shaw, P., Kabani, N. J., Lerch, J. P., Eckstrand, K., Lenroot, R., Gogtay, N., et al. (2008). Neurodevelopmental trajectories of the human cerebral cortex. *The Journal of Neuroscience*, *28*(14), 3586–3594. 28/14/3586, [pii] https://doi.org/10.1523/JNEUROSCI.5309-07.2008.

Sheridan, S. R. (2005). A theory of marks and mind: the effect of notational systems on hominid brain evolution and child development with an emphasis on exchanges between mothers and children. *Medical Hypotheses*, *64*(2), 417–427. S0306-9877(04)00483-9, [pii] https://doi.org/10.1016/j.mehy.2004.09.002.

Sheu, Y. S., Polcari, A., Anderson, C. M., & Teicher, M. H. (2010). Harsh corporal punishment is associated with increased T2 relaxation time in dopamine-rich regions. *NeuroImage*, *53*(2), 412–419. https://doi.org/10.1016/j.neuroimage.2010.06.043.

Smith, P. F. (2017). The vestibular system and cognition. *Current Opinion in Neurology*, *30*(1), 84–89. https://doi.org/10.1097/WCO.0000000000000403.

Smith, L., Wilkinson, D., Bodani, M., Bicknell, R., & Surenthiran, S. S. (2018). Short-term memory impairment in vestibular patients can arise independently of psychiatric impairment, fatigue, and sleeplessness. *Journal of Neuropsychology*, https://doi.org/10.1111/jnp.12157.

Southwick, S. M., Vythilingam, M., & Charney, D. S. (2005). The psychobiology of depression and resilience to stress: implications for prevention and treatment. *Annual Review of Clinical Psychology*, *1*, 255–291. https://doi.org/10.1146/annurev.clinpsy.1.102803.143948.

Spitzer, C., Willert, C., Grabe, H. J., Rizos, T., Moller, B., & Freyberger, H. J. (2004). Dissociation, hemispheric asymmetry, and dysfunction of hemispheric interaction: a transcranial magnetic stimulation approach. *The Journal of Neuropsychiatry and Clinical Neurosciences*, *16*(2), 163–169. https://doi.org/10.1176/appi.neuropsych.16.2.163. 16/2/163 [pii].

Stalker, C. A., Gebotys, R., & Harper, K. (2005). Insecure attachment as a predictor of outcome following inpatient trauma treatment for women survivors of childhood abuse. *Bulletin of the Menninger Clinic*, *69*(2), 137–156. https://doi.org/10.1521/bumc.69.2.137.66508.

Stoever, J. K. (2014). Teach your children well: preventing domestic violence. *Seattle Journal for Social Justice*, *13*, 515.

Storer, H. L., Casey, E. A., Carlson, J., Edleson, J. L., & Tolman, R. M. (2016). Primary prevention is? A global perspective on how organizations engaging men in preventing gender-based violence conceptualize and operationalize their work. *Violence Against Women*, *22*(2), 249–268.

Sullivan, R. M. (2012). The neurobiology of attachment to nurturing and abusive caregivers. *Hastings Law Journal*, *63*(6), 1553–1570.

Talge, N. M., Neal, C., & Glover, V. (2007). Antenatal maternal stress and long-term effects on child neurodevelopment: how and why? *Journal of Child Psychology and Psychiatry, and Allied Disciplines*, *48*(3–4), 245–261.

Teicher, M. H., Andersen, S. L., Polcari, A., Anderson, C. M., & Navalta, C. P. (2002). Developmental neurobiology of childhood stress and trauma. *The Psychiatric Clinics of North America*, *25*(2), 397–426 [vii–viii].

Thomas, S. J., Johnstone, S. J., & Gonsalvez, C. J. (2007). Event-related potentials during an emotional Stroop task. *International Journal of Psychophysiology*, *63*(3), 221–231. S0167-8760(06)00288-1, [pii] https://doi.org/10.1016/j.ijpsycho.2006.10.002.

van der Kolk, B. A. (2003). The neurobiology of childhood trauma and abuse. *Child and Adolescent Psychiatric Clinics of North America*, *12*(2), 293–317 [ix].

Voytek, B., Davis, M., Yago, E., Barceló, F., Vogel, E. K., & Knight, R. T. (2010). Dynamic neuroplasticity after human prefrontal cortex damage. *Neuron*, *68*(3), 401–408.

Walker, A., Kantaris, X., & Chambers, M. (2018). Understanding therapeutic approaches to anxiety in vestibular rehabilitation: a qualitative study of specialist physiotherapists in the UK. *Disability and Rehabilitation*, *40*(7), 829–835. https://doi.org/10.1080/09638288.2016.1277393.

Wanner, I., Baader, S. L., Oberdick, J., & Schilling, K. (2000). Changing subcellular distribution and activity-dependent utilization of a dendritically localized mRNA in developing Purkinje cells. *Molecular and Cellular Neurosciences*, *15*(3), 275–287. https://doi.org/10.1006/mcne.1999.0824. S1044-7431(99)90824-2 [pii].

Whitall, J., McCombe Waller, S., Sorkin, J. D., Forrester, L. W., Macko, R. F., Hanley, D. F., et al. (2011). Bilateral and unilateral arm training improve motor function through differing neuroplastic mechanisms: a single-blinded randomized controlled trial. *Neurorehabilitation and Neural Repair*, *25*(2), 118–129.

Yu, Y. C., Xue, H., Zhang, Y. X., & Zhou, J. (2018). Cognitive behavior therapy as augmentation for sertraline in treating patients with persistent postural-perceptual dizziness. *BioMed Research International*, *2018*, 8518631. https://doi.org/10.1155/2018/8518631.

CHAPTER 19

Understanding Childhood Maltreatment and Subsequent Revictimisation: A Singapore Perspective

Dongdong Li, Chi Meng Chu, Grace S. Chng, Ming Hwa Ting
Centre for Research on Rehabilitation and Protection, Ministry of Social and Family Development, Singapore, Singapore

1 Introduction

Child maltreatment is a global problem. According to the World Health Organisation (WHO, 2016), approximately a quarter of the adult population reported being physically abused as children, whereas one in five women and one in 13 men reported being sexually abused as children. These statistics highlight the need to address the issue of child maltreatment and subsequent revictimisation, particularly with WHO reporting an estimated fatality rate of >40,000 deaths each year due to child maltreatment (WHO, 2016).

In this chapter, we explore the phenomenon of childhood maltreatment from a Singapore perspective. Specifically, we focus on the prevalence of different types of maltreatment, possible predictors and effects of childhood maltreatment, and some of the possible interventions that attempt to address the negative consequences caused by maltreatment.

2 Managing Childhood Maltreatment in Singapore

Singapore is an independent island state in Southeast Asia with a total population of 5.6 million according to Singapore Department of Statistics (DOS, 2017b). The management of child protection cases in Singapore is guided by interministry child abuse protocols first developed in 1999 and the National Standards for Protection of Children that was introduced in 2002 by the then Ministry of Community Development, Youth and Sports (known today as Ministry of Social and Family Development, MSF). Similar to how WHO has conceptualised maltreatment (Butchart et al., 2006), childhood maltreatment in Singapore is broadly defined as any act of omission or commission by a caregiver that results in actual or potential harm to children and young persons (CYP) under 16 years (MSF, 2016). The standards set a

Child Abuse and Neglect. https://doi.org/10.1016/B978-0-12-815344-4.00019-2

framework for different systems, such as the judicial system, police, healthcare services, schools, and child protection agencies, to handle child protection cases.

The Child Protective Service (CPS) of the Ministry of Social and Family Development (MSF) oversees the investigation of child abuse allegations and the subsequent protection of children. When a case is referred to CPS, the intake unit would assess, using a tool, if the case meets the threshold for statutory intervention. If it does, the case is then referred to the investigation unit, which conducts a social investigation on the case and assesses the immediate safety of the child. The investigation officer also assesses the level of intervention that should be accorded to the family and if there is a necessity for the application of a Care and Protection Order to ensure the necessary safeguards to keep the CYP safe. Following the social investigation and assessment of the likelihood of future harm to the CYP, the family is then referred for services. This is to either suitable community services or CPS' intervention unit, for ongoing intervention to address needs to ensure the safety of the child.

The legal protection for children in Singapore is guided mainly by the Children and Young Persons Act, which is largely based on child protection legislations in the United Kingdom. However, cross-cultural studies have shown that the meaning of child maltreatment varies across Western and Asian cultures (Deater-Deckard & Dodge, 1997). For example, strict discipline (such as caning) is viewed as a sign of parental concern and involvement rather than child abuse in Asian societies (Elliott, Tong, & Tan, 1997; Lau, Liu, Yu, & Wong, 1999). Such differences in the sociocultural context will not only change the antecedents but also moderate the effects of childhood maltreatment (Gershoff, 2002). For example, it was found that the Singapore public strongly disapproved of sexual abuse (Elliott et al., 1997), and accordingly, Singaporean women with childhood sexual abuse history reported worse psychological adjustment compared with women from the United States with a sexual abuse history (Back et al., 2003). Additionally, societal perceptions are subjected to change over time. Following on the above example of strict discipline in Asian societies, the perspective of physical discipline in Singapore is also changing. In 2004, a study by the Singapore Institute of Mental Health demonstrated that fewer Singaporean parents are resorting to physical discipline, with 68% out of the 230 parents revealing that they used reasoning alone as a form of parental discipline (Lee, 2004). These results suggest the importance of cultural sensitivity in CPS studies.

3 Prevalence of Maltreatment in Singapore

Guided by the National Standards, childhood maltreatment in Singapore is operationalised as four main types, specifically physical abuse, sexual abuse, neglect, and emotional/psychological abuse (MSF, 2016). For example, child neglect is defined as when "a parent or caregiver fails to provide adequate food, shelter, clothing, medical care and supervision or forces a child to do things inappropriate for his/her age" (p. 8).

Prevalence of childhood maltreatment is low in Singapore, though there are a rising number of cases over the past few years (MSF, 2016). For year 2016, a total of 3035 enquiries were received by CPS, out of which 873 were investigated (MSF, 2017a). In the same year, there are 836,000 resident children and youth aged 19 years and below (DOS, 2017a), which translates to a national prevalence of maltreatment of around 1/1000. This figure is lower than the overall estimated worldwide prevalence rates based on informant report (4/1000 for sexual abuse and 3/1000 for physical and emotional abuse) and self-report (>10% for all abuse types) (Stoltenborgh, Bakermans-Kranenburg, Alink, & IJzendoorn, 2015).

Table 1 presents a summary of studies conducted in Singapore with the prevalence rate of different types of maltreatment among children who entered the national child protection system. All these studies were conducted by the Ministry and used full cohorts of cases to ensure representativeness (with the only exception of Liu et al., 2016). The samples of these studies included children placed under out-of-home care who had relatively low risk in terms of maltreatment and revictimisation (37.3% of the cases did not report any abuse experience at all) and high risk cases who experienced severe trauma and were referred to psychological services.

Among all maltreatment types, physical abuse is consistently reported as the dominant abuse type despite the different sample characteristics, ranging from 31.4% for children under out-of-home care (Liu et al., 2016) to 60% among those substantiated cases and 72% for those referred to psychological services (Chen, 2016). The prevalence rate for sexual abuse

Table 1: Prevalence of abuse among children in the national child protection system

Study	Sample	Prevalence of Abuse			
		Physical (%)	Sexual (%)	Emotional (%)	Neglect (%)
Liu et al. (2016)	721 children who were residing under out-of-home care between 2011 and 2013	31.4	11.1	17.5	38.4
Li, Chu, Ng, and Leong (2014)	1750 child protection closed cases between 2002 and 2009[a]	43.5	15.9	<20	20.5
Keong (2017)	580 child protection cases under investigation between 2014 and 2015	50	18	26	46
MSF (2016)	1316 substantiated cases between 2005 and 2014[a]	60	30	5	6
Chen (2016)	292 child protection cases (63% of all abuse cases between 2011 and 2013) who were referred for further psychological assessment and intervention	72	45	56	36
Chng, Li, Chu, Ong, and Lim (2018)	440 families under investigation between 2014 and 2015	49	21	25	42

[a] Percentage from these two studies was based on primary abuse type only.

followed the same trend, in that the rate is lowest among children in care at slightly over 10%, whereas 30% of the substantiated cases and 45% of the cases referred to psychological services had sexual abuse experiences. The prevalence of emotional abuse and neglect tended to be lower in studies where only the primary type of abuse was reported (Li et al., 2014), especially so with samples that consisted of only substantiated cases (MSF, 2016). A possible reason could be that emotional abuse and neglect were less visible to detect, and yet, they were often present for cases that were substantiated as physical or sexual abuse cases.

4 Predictors of Maltreatment and Revictimisation

Despite the efforts to prevent maltreatment and recurrence, there are children who are involved with CPS on multiple occasions. According to Thompson and Wiley (2009), the rate of reentry ranged from 16% to 62% depending on the length of follow-up. In an 8-year follow-up study, the reentry rate was as high as 67% for children aged 4–12 years (Proctor et al., 2012). In comparison, the reentry rate for Singapore was significantly lower. Using the administrative records of 1750 child protection cases closed between 2002 and 2009 in Singapore, Li et al. (2014) found that the overall reentry rate was 10.5%, ranging from 3.9% (within 1 year) to 16.5% (within 8 years after case closure). A more recent study with 580 cases that entered CPS between March 2014 and December 2015 showed a similar 1-year reentry rate of 3% (Keong, 2017).

Many studies in this area have been guided by the ecological-transactional framework of human development and child maltreatment (Belsky, 1993; Bronfenbrenner, 1977; Cicchetti & Lynch, 1993; Sameroff, 1975). This framework posits that risk factors occur at different levels, from specific child characteristics to broad sociocultural contexts (Sidebotham & Heron, 2006). Past studies have shown that risk factors on the following three proximal levels are of the most interest to CPS: (1) child case characteristics, (2) household environment, and (3) parental background. According to the ecological-transactional model, the most proximal factors occur at the child level, including children's characteristics such as gender and race. The second proximal level is the family environment, such as family structure and household income, which interacts directly with children's characteristics. The third proximal level is parental background, such as parental age and parental education.

4.1 Child Case Characteristics

Past studies have examined the reentry risk based on children's demographic and case characteristics. For demographic background, majority of the studies found that the risk of CPS reentry decreases with age (Connell, Bergeron, Katz, Saunders, & Tebes, 2007; Fluke, Shusterman, Hollinshead, & Yuan, 2008; Fuller & Nieto, 2009; Kahn & Schwalbe, 2010; Lipien & Forthofer, 2004). Moreover, the risk of CPS reentry is higher for Caucasian children as compared with minority groups such as African American (Connell et al., 2007; Fuller & Nieto, 2009; Kahn & Schwalbe, 2010; Lipien & Forthofer, 2004) and does not differ across gender (Fuller & Nieto, 2009; Hélie, Laurier, Pineau-Villeneuve, & Royer, 2013; Kahn & Schwalbe, 2010; Lipien & Forthofer, 2004; Thompson & Wiley, 2009). In contrast, there are studies reporting inconsistent age, gender, and race differences. For example, one study reported that the risk of reentry was lower for infants and young children who receive more services (Palusci, 2011). Another study reported that girls had a slightly higher risk of reentry than boys (Fluke et al., 2008). Similarly, there are also studies reporting that some minority groups, such as the African Indian and Alaskan (Fluke et al., 2008) and aboriginal descent (Hélie et al., 2013), had higher risk of CPS reentry. These inconsistent findings might be due to methodological differences and the lack of consideration for cultural contexts, thus highlighting the importance of culturally relevant studies with good methodological rigour.

As for case characteristics, past studies have consistently shown that prior involvement in CPS predicts a higher risk of reentry (English, Marshall, Brummel, & Orme, 1999; Fluke et al., 2008; Hélie et al., 2013). As for service duration in CPS, the results were mixed. Some studies found that a shorter service period was indicative of higher risk of reentry (Jonson-Reid, 2003; Yampolskaya, Mowery, & Dollard, 2013), whereas others found no significant effect of length of service (Hélie et al., 2013). With regard to case types, there are inconsistent findings as well; some studies reported that sexual abuse cases were the least likely to experience reentry as compared with physical abuse and neglect cases, possibly because sexual abuse cases were more likely to receive extensive services that reduce the likelihood of CPS reentry (Connell et al., 2007; Fuller & Nieto, 2009; Lipien & Forthofer, 2004). However, other researchers found that physical or sexual abuse cases have higher risk of CPS reentry (Thompson & Wiley, 2009). In another study, physical abuse cases had no significant difference with sexual abuse or neglect cases (Kahn & Schwalbe, 2010). These discrepancies in findings could be due to the level and effectiveness of services provided to clients in different studies and again imply the necessity of context-based research (Kahn & Schwalbe, 2010).

In Singapore, child case characteristics, such as child's age at entry, case type, case closure result, and duration of case, have been associated with a higher risk of CPS reentry (Li et al., 2014). Additionally, in a sample of emotionally abused cases, children with mental health conditions or academic difficulties were found to be 8.01 times and 3.65 times, respectively, as likely as children without such characteristics to experience a recurrence of harm while the case was still open in CPS (Keong, 2017). These findings highlight that child-level factors influence possible CPS outcomes in Singapore and provide preliminary evidence to inform practitioners on certain issues to look out for when assessing cases that enter CPS.

4.2 Household Environment and Parental Background

Household environment also ranked among the most important proximal factors that were associated with CPS engagement and reentry (Li et al., 2014). Past studies have shown that household poverty is one of the strongest predictors of child maltreatment and CPS reentry

(Connell et al., 2007; Kahn & Schwalbe, 2010; MacKenzie, Kotch, & Lee, 2011; Sidebotham & Heron, 2006). In addition, studies have documented that nonintact families (such as single-parent or reconstituted families), large families, and families with violence exposure tended to have higher risk (Fowler et al., 2013; Palusci & Ondersma, 2012; Proctor et al., 2012). As for parental background, it is now widely recognised that parental problems are strongly related to CPS reentry of a child (Sidebotham & Heron, 2006). The extant literature suggests that young parents, lower parental educational achievement, and unemployment status were found to be consistently strong indicators of CPS engagement and reentry (Begle, Dumas, & Hanson, 2010; MacKenzie, Kotch, & Lee, 2011; Sidebotham & Heron, 2006). All these factors might affect the risk of CPS reentry through influencing the household environment and parent–child interactions. For example, a single teenage mother with low educational achievement was less likely to provide a safe, stable, and nurturing home environment for her child to thrive in adverse events (Schofield, Lee, & Merrick, 2013). Therefore, repeated and chronic child abuse was more likely to occur in such households (Belsky, 1993).

In Singapore, mother's unemployment status, family size, and household income have been associated with the increased likelihood of CPS reentry (Li et al., 2014). Child protection cases with unemployed mothers were 1.91 times as likely to reenter CPS as compared with those employed. Families with household income of less than $1500 were 1.96 times as likely as those with household income of more than $1500 to reenter CPS, and a family size of seven or more individuals was found to be 2.10 times as likely as family size of 4–6 individuals to reenter CPS. Additionally, a separate study found that caregivers who justified abuse were 5.94 times as likely as children whose caregivers did not justify abuse to experience a recurrence of harm (Keong, 2017). Chng et al. (2018) also identified four family typologies in a sample of 440 families who had CPS contact: (a) The large household group was intergenerational, and majority lived with extended family members, (b) the harsh parenting group showed high levels of parenting problems and the caregiver justifying his abuse/neglect, (c) the high criminality group had high levels of caregiver substance abuse and caregiver arrest and incarceration history, and (d) the low disadvantage group that had low probability of the eight familial risk factors measured. As compared with the family group that had low levels of family risk factors, the harsh parenting group was found to be twice as likely to have recurrence of harm. Differences were also seen across the family typologies with regard to the child's age at entry into CPS and abuse types. These findings point to the importance of looking beyond direct interventions with the child. There is a critical need to support and strengthen the family as a means of enabling a safe, stable, and supportive environment for the child to return to.

4.3 Cumulative Risk

The ecological-transactional framework provides guidelines on identifying a set of risk factors for each level and emphasises the importance of the interplay of a variety of factors at multiple levels. Factors at different levels influence each other reciprocally and dynamically throughout human development (MacKenzie, Kotch, Lee, Augsberger, & Hutto, 2011). Past studies have tested mediation effects and interaction effects among different factors (Connell et al., 2007; Sidebotham & Heron, 2006), but these are usually limited to two- or three-way interaction, which may not sufficiently describe the complex interplay of multiple factors.

This limitation warrants the integration of the ecological-transactional model with a cumulative risk model (MacKenzie, Kotch, & Lee, 2011). A cumulative risk model assumes that the accumulation of risk factors, rather than any single particular risk factor, has higher predictive power for negative outcomes (Begle et al., 2010). In fact, the cumulative risk model has been empirically supported in many areas of social, medical, and psychological domains (Appleyard, Egeland, Dulmen, & Alan Sroufe, 2005; Begle et al., 2010; MacKenzie, Kotch, & Lee, 2011; Tarren-Sweeney, 2008). In child maltreatment studies, it was found that a cumulative model of ecological-transactional risk provides enhanced predictive capacity of repeated child maltreatment (MacKenzie, Kotch, & Lee, 2011).

Li et al. (2014) tested the cumulative model in a sample of Singaporean child protection cases as pertaining to seven risk factors identified to be associated with CPS reentry: child's age at entry, case type, case closure result, duration of the case, household income, family size, and mother's unemployment status. The cumulative score for each case ranged from zero to more than five. The results showed that as compared with cases with no risk factors, those that had five or more risk factors were 36 times more likely to reenter CPS. With a reduction in the number of risks, the hazard ratios also decreased in magnitude. These results validated the utility of a cumulative risk score and could provide a basis to determining which cases to concentrate on for better resource allocation.

5 Impact of Childhood Maltreatment

The negative effects of child maltreatment are well documented in research literature (Trocmé, Tourigny, MacLaurin, & Fallon, 2003). According to a recent meta-analysis, child maltreatment may lead to a range of long-term mental health problems, chronic diseases, and risky lifestyles (Norman et al., 2012). Therefore, protecting children from maltreatment and the associated adverse outcomes remains the primary goal of state child welfare agencies (Connell et al., 2007). In this section, the impact of childhood maltreatment on internalising and externalising behaviours is discussed in relation to a few characteristics of maltreatment, including maltreatment history, the cumulative effect of multiple maltreatment, the differential effects of maltreatment subtypes, and the age of onset.

5.1 Maltreatment History

Research in Western contexts has demonstrated that children with a history of childhood maltreatment have a much higher risk of being arrested and/or referred for delinquent offences or a higher rate of recidivism for youth offenders with such history (Fagan, 2005; Jonson-Reid, 2002; Kelley, Thornberry, & Smith, 1997; Ryan, 2006; Swanston et al., 2003; Widom & Maxfield, 2001). In a large-scale study of 18,676 children and youth, Ryan and Testa (2005) found that the delinquency rates for substantiated victims of childhood maltreatment were on average 47% higher than those who were not maltreated. Similarly, a longitudinal study of 1575 individuals showed that maltreated children were significantly more likely to be arrested as a juvenile (27.4% vs 17.2%) and adult (41.6% vs 13.9%) when compared with their nonmaltreated counterparts (Widom & Maxfield, 2001). In addition, a study on Arizona administrative data revealed that those cases that were dually involved with both the child protection and youth justice systems were twice as likely to recidivate (62% vs 30%) as compared with delinquency only cases (Halemba, Siegel, Lord, & Zawacki, 2004). In a more recent study on youth who simultaneously received services from the child welfare and juvenile justice agencies ($N=1148$), 56% of the maltreated offenders reoffended during a 5-year period as compared with 41% of their nonmaltreated counterparts (Huang, Ryan, & Herz, 2012). Research in Singapore also provided supporting evidence for this relationship. In a study of Singapore youth offenders (that used propensity score matching), it was found that maltreated youth offenders were 1.38 times as likely as their nonmaltreated counterparts (57% vs 38%) to reoffend with a follow-up period of up to 7.4 years (Li, Chu, Goh, Ng, & Zeng, 2015). The study replicated the findings from Western jurisdictions and thus further established the robust relationship between maltreatment and delinquent outcomes regardless of culture differences.

From a retrospective angle, the extant literature also suggests that a substantial proportion of youth offenders are likely to have a history of child maltreatment. In a study of childhood maltreatment prevalence across public service sectors, 77.6% of youth from the juvenile justice sample ($N=229$) had reported being maltreated, with 57.3% having experienced multiple forms of maltreatment (Miller, Green, Fettes, & Aarons, 2011). King and colleagues (2011) showed that 65%–75% of youth offenders ($N=1735$) reported having experienced physical abuse, whereas 10%–40% were reportedly sexually abused during their childhood. Furthermore, Moore, Gaskin, and Indig (2013) found that 60% of young offenders have a history of childhood abuse or neglect, with females being almost 10 times as likely to report three or more types of serious child maltreatment compared with males. Similar results were found in Singapore as well, which documented that 6% of a large cohort of youth offenders had childhood maltreatment (Li et al., 2015). It is highly likely that this rate is due to under-reporting. Nevertheless, this 6% is still substantially greater than that (<1%) of the general population. In a smaller study with 79 female residents admitted to an adolescent female residential facility for both delinquency and protection reasons, it was also shown that more than two-thirds had past victimisation experiences (Chu, Thomas, & Ng, 2009).

5.2 Multiple Maltreatment

Multiple maltreatment refers to exposure to multiple types of abuse in child maltreatment studies. This concept has been expanded to broader notions such as 'polyvictimisation' and 'adverse childhood events', which include other types of victimisation from crime, violence, and traumatic experiences (Felitti et al., 1998; Finkelhor, Ormrod, & Turner, 2007). A strong cumulative effect was consistently found in the literature in both Western and Asian countries on internalising and externalising behaviours (Appleyard et al., 2005; Hahm, Lee, Ozonoff, & Van Wert, 2010; Kim & Cicchetti, 2010; Suliman et al., 2009). For example, in a large-scale study with 18,341 Chinese adolescents from Hong Kong and Mainland China, Chan (2013) reported that almost one in seven (14%) respondents emerged as polyvictims. Polyvictims were more likely to report PTSD and depressive symptoms, self-harm ideation, and poor physical and mental health.

In a Singapore study with 132 child protection cases receiving psychological services, Goh (2015) found that 81% of the children had multiple maltreatment, which is related to higher levels of PTSD and depression. In another Singapore study with children in care, Liu et al. (2016) reported that more than one-third of the children had multiple maltreatment, and these children demonstrated poorer life functioning and more behavioural and emotional needs. Similar results on the cumulative effect of multiple maltreatment were found in a study with Singapore youth offenders, in that more adverse childhood events are related to higher levels of aggressive behaviours (Lim, 2017).

5.3 Subtypes of Maltreatment

Research suggests that different forms of maltreatment may affect child functioning differently, though the results usually differ among studies, especially when the subtype comparisons were made within groups of maltreated children (Manly, Cicchetti, & Barnett, 1994; Manly, Kim, Rogosch, & Cicchetti, 2001; Tanaka, Wekerle, Schmuck, & Paglia-Boak, 2011; Torchalla, Strehlau, Li, Schuetz, & Krausz, 2012). The inconsistent findings are largely due to different operational definitions used to define subtypes of maltreatment, the cooccurring nature of maltreatment subtypes, and different analytic approaches used to examine the associations. Similar to many other studies, Manly et al. (2001) examined the effects of different subtypes of maltreatment on child functioning by comparing maltreated groups with a nonmaltreated control group. The majority of significant differences were actually found between the maltreated groups and the nonmaltreated control group, but not between the different maltreated groups. This might explain the inconclusive findings in a study conducted with a sample of Singapore child protection cases, as >70% had more than one type of maltreatment (Chen, 2016). Nevertheless, it is important to investigate the differential effects of maltreatment subtypes within groups of maltreated children, who usually experienced multiple types of maltreatment, as these findings will be particularly relevant for local child welfare service planning and resource allocation decisions. For example, knowing that maltreatment subtype or combination of subtypes is associated with which outcomes may help policymakers and individual caseworkers better tailor intervention services to meet the needs of maltreated children.

5.4 Age of Onset

Age of onset of maltreatment is one of the maltreatment dimensions that has received much attention in the literature. From the perspective of developmental psychopathology, the manifestations of maltreatment may vary depending on whether stage-specific tasks at different developmental levels are successfully negotiated (Cicchetti & Toth, 1995). Therefore, the earlier the maltreatment occurs in a child's life that interrupts the child's successful negotiation of stage-specific tasks, the more likely the child will fail to achieve important developmental milestones (e.g. development of self-regulations skills), which, in turn, compromises the successful negotiation of future developmental tasks and leads to greater likelihood of future psychopathology (Cicchetti, 1987).

Research in the area of developmental traumatology suggests that maltreatment experiences in early childhood may cause alterations in biological stress systems and adverse brain development in maltreated children, which are likely to contribute to delays in, or failures of, multisystem developmental achievements (e.g. in behavioural and emotional regulation) (De Bellis et al., 2002; De Bellis & Kuchibhatla, 2006). It is believed that failure to self-regulate behaviours and emotions may lead to externalising and internalising symptomatology in maltreated children that continues into adulthood and results in psychopathology (Cicchetti, Rogosch, & Thibodeau, 2012; De Bellis et al., 1999). Therefore, from a developmental point of view, an earlier age of onset of maltreatment could be predicted to have a more detrimental effect on child outcomes. This is supported by a Singapore study where age of onset of first maltreatment predicted maltreated children's parent-reported externalising symptomatology (Chen, 2016).

6 Responding to Child Maltreatment in Singapore

The negative effects of child maltreatment, as discussed above, are clear. Unfortunately, it is not possible to eradicate this problem entirely. However, to maximise the potential of such individuals to experience optimal outcomes despite being exposed to early adversities, MSF has been working on various initiatives for the early detection, better management, interventions, and prevention of child maltreatment.

6.1 Decision-Making Tools

Moving towards evidence- and research-based practice, MSF has put in place a suite of initiatives ranging from the use of structured case management and decision-making tools such as the Child and Adolescent Needs and Strengths (CANS) and the Structured Decision Making (SDM) tool. The use of structured case management and decision-making tools not only plays a crucial role in ensuring that clients receive a good standard of care but also helps in creating a common language and vocabulary among case workers from various agencies, which then ensures that clients receive consistent care in a transparent manner.

In 2011, MSF collaborated with John S. Lyons, the author of CANS, to develop a localised Singaporean version of the tool. The objective of introducing this new tool was to facilitate case management through cultivating a common framework for communicating the needs and strengths of the individuals in out-of-home care due to care and protection grounds. Having a common communication framework is essential because not only are there multiple children's homes in Singapore but also some children in out-of-home care transit between various children's homes or foster care. Research using local data has demonstrated both the reliability and validity of this tool (Heng & Liu, 2014; Liu et al., 2014).

In 2013, MSF began a customisation of a suite of decision support tools, known as the SDM system adapted from the Children's Research Centre from the United States (CRC, 2017). This system seeks to structure critical decision points, to increase consistency and accuracy in decision-making, and to make use of collected data to inform policy and practice. The tools developed under SDM encompass both community and CPS tools. Community tools are developed to strengthen general and sector expertise in timely identification of incidents of child abuse, such as the Sector-Specific Screening Guide and the Child Abuse Reporting Guide. Assessment tools for CPS were also developed to support clarity, transparency, and articulation of the various decision-making points, such as screening and response priority assessment, safety assessment, family strengths and needs assessment, and likelihood of future harm assessment and reassessment. The SDM system aims to increase safety, reduce risks, and promote permanency planning for the child. Through the use of these evidence-based tools, especially the actuarial likelihood of future harm assessment, CPS is better able to focus its attention and resources to intervene in families that require them, thereby minimising the potential negative effects of maltreatment and enabling better outcomes.

6.2 Interventions

As discussed in an earlier section, the impact of child maltreatment is highly detrimental; multitype maltreatment and an earlier age at onset can exacerbate problems, with possible escalation to the juvenile justice system. For maltreated children who demonstrate complex emotional and behavioural issues, MSF set up the therapeutic group homes and pilot small group care homes in 2013 and 2017, respectively, to provide targeted and more intensive care and supervision for children with complex needs and challenging behaviours (MCYC, 2017). By providing intensive and specialised services to these children, the objective is to mitigate the negative effects of maltreatment they may have experienced.

As familial issues are often the reason children enter into child protection and welfare, MSF has also invested in programs to strengthen and preserve families. The Positive Parenting Program (Triple P) equips families with positive parenting skills in place of physical punishment. The trauma-focused cognitive behavioural therapy is given to families who have experienced abuse. The Safe and Strong Families (SSF) program, an intensive home-based program to work with families with child protection concerns, is also being piloted. SSF works to equip these families with skills and support resources to enable them to keep their children safe in their families.

6.3 Engaging the Community

Three specialist community resources in the form of Child Protection Specialist Centres (CPSCs) were set up in 2012 and 2017. They bring child protection expertise into the community to increase awareness and to provide support and consultation to community professionals on child protection issues. They manage moderate risk cases and are an alternative for some families to receive help in their community, instead of directly entering into CPS. Currently, MSF is monitoring the evaluation of the CPSCs to determine effectiveness and ascertaining the necessity for more centres.

As part of the SDM tools, the Child Abuse Reporting Guide (CARG) has also been developed in collaboration with community stakeholders, such as schools, preschools, family service centres, hospitals, and social services. Professionals working in the community have been trained in the CARG for timely identification of child protection concerns and to efficiently decide whether to report these concerns to CPS or to take an alternative course of action.

6.4 Prevention Efforts

As part of public education, MSF launched a 3-year 'Break the Silence—Against Family Violence' campaign in November 2016 (MSF, 2017b). The campaign included videos, roadshows, and social media (#breakthesilenceSG), to educate the public on family violence, sources of help, and the importance of public response. As child abuse is part of family violence, these public education efforts have been helpful in educating the public on reporting abuse when they witness one. There was an increase in enquiries received by MSF, from 2022 enquiries in 2015 to 3035 enquiries in 2016. From the enquiries received, more serious cases of abuse are being rightly flagged up for statutory intervention.

7 Conclusion

Child maltreatment is a highly complex issue; there is a need to better define child maltreatment with contextual sensitivity, to more clearly identify and understand the antecedents and impact of child maltreatment and revictimisation, and to work towards improving the timeliness and effectiveness of our response to this problem. There is no working back to undo the crushing effects of child maltreatment; thus perhaps, the better solution is in prevention and early detection. In Singapore, upstream work is becoming more pertinent as we witness downstream outcomes of child maltreatment. Hence, equipping the community to detect child maltreatment has to be simultaneously emphasised as we continue to improve our child protection system with better decision-making tools and more targeted interventions. Lastly, practice changes have to be aligned with an evidence-based approach; continual research and evaluation should underpin the efforts we make in child protection work in order to increase the quality of decisions and allow for better resource allocation.

8 Chapter Review Questions

1. What is the definition of child maltreatment in Singapore?
2. What is the national prevalence rate of child maltreatment?
3. Out of the four main abuse types, which is the most dominant in Singapore? How does this compare with other countries?
4. Describe three child case characteristics that predict maltreatment and revictimisation.
5. Describe three household environment and parental background factors that predict maltreatment and revictimisation.
6. What is cumulative risk, and why is this important to understand in the context of child maltreatment?
7. What is multiple maltreatment, and what are some outcomes linked to this?
8. Name two responses to child maltreatment as outlined in the chapter.

Acknowledgements

We would like to express our sincere thanks to the staffs and management of Child Protective Service, Ministry of Social and Family Development for their support and assistance for this chapter. We would like to also thank Chen Jiaoyu, Melissa Keong, and Amanda Goh for their valuable contribution.

References

Appleyard, K., Egeland, B., Dulmen, M. H., & Alan Sroufe, L. (2005). When more is not better: the role of cumulative risk in child behavior outcomes. *Journal of Child Psychology and Psychiatry*, *46*(3), 235–245.

Back, S. E., Jackson, J. L., Fitzgerald, M., Shaffer, A., Salstrom, S., & Osman, M. M. (2003). Child sexual and physical abuse among college students in Singapore and the United States. *Child Abuse & Neglect*, *27*(11), 1259–1275.

Begle, A. M., Dumas, J. E., & Hanson, R. F. (2010). Predicting child abuse potential: an empirical investigation of two theoretical frameworks. *Journal of Clinical Child and Adolescent Psychology*, *39*(2), 208–219.

Belsky, J. (1993). Etiology of child maltreatment: a developmental ecological analysis. *Psychological Bulletin*, *114*(3), 413–434.

Bronfenbrenner, U. (1977). Toward an experimental ecology of human development. *American Psychologist*, *32*(7), 513–531.

Butchart, A., Phinney Harvey, A., Mian, M., Furniss, T., Kahane, T., & Organization, W. H. (2006). *Preventing child maltreatment: A guide to taking action and generating evidence*. World Health Organization and International Society for Prevention of Child Abuse and Neglect.

Chan, K. L. (2013). Victimization and poly-victimization among school-aged Chinese adolescents: prevalence and associations with health. *Preventive Medicine*, *56*(3–4), 207–210.

Chen, J. (2016). *Maltreatment onset and subtypes predict internalising and externalising symptomatology in maltreated children* [Master of Psychology (Clinical)]. James Cook University.

Chng, G. S., Li, D., Chu, C. M., Ong, T., & Lim, F. (2018). Family profiles of maltreated children in Singapore: a latent class analysis. *Child Abuse & Neglect, 79*, 465–475.

Chu, C. M., Thomas, S. D., & Ng, V. P. (2009). Childhood abuse and delinquency: a descriptive study of institutionalized female youth in Singapore. *Psychiatry, Psychology and Law, 16*(Suppl. 1), S64–S73.

Cicchetti, D. (1987). Developmental psychopathology in infancy: illustration from the study of maltreated youngsters. *Journal of Consulting and Clinical Psychology, 55*(6), 837–845. https://doi.org/10.1037/0022-006x.55.6.837.

Cicchetti, D., & Lynch, M. (1993). Toward an ecological/transactional model of community violence and child maltreatment: consequences for children's development. *Psychiatry, 56*(1), 96–118.

Cicchetti, D., Rogosch, F. A., & Thibodeau, E. L. (2012). The effects of child maltreatment on early signs of antisocial behavior: genetic moderation by tryptophan hydroxylase, serotonin transporter, and monoamine oxidase a genes. *Development and Psychopathology, 24*(3), 907–928. https://doi.org/10.1017/s0954579412000442.

Cicchetti, D., & Toth, S. L. (1995). A developmental psychopathology perspective on child abuse and neglect. *Journal of the American Academy of Child & Adolescent Psychiatry, 34*(5), 541–565.

Connell, C. M., Bergeron, N., Katz, K. H., Saunders, L., & Tebes, J. K. (2007). Re-referral to child protective services: the influence of child, family, and case characteristics on risk status. *Child Abuse & Neglect, 31*(5), 573–588. https://doi.org/10.1016/j.chiabu.2006.12.004.

CRC. (2017). *Development of the SDM® likelihood of future harm, assessment for Singapore*. NCCD Children's Research Center.

De Bellis, M. D., Keshavan, M. S., Clark, D. B., Casey, B. J., Giedd, J. N., Boring, A. M., et al. (1999). Developmental traumatology: II. Brain development. *Biological Psychiatry, 45*(10), 1271–1284. https://doi.org/10.1016/s0006-3223(99)00045-1.

De Bellis, M. D., Keshavan, M. S., Shifflett, H., Iyengar, S., Beers, S. R., Hall, J., et al. (2002). Brain structures in pediatric maltreatment-related posttraumatic stress disorder: a sociodemographically matched study. *Biological Psychiatry, 52*(11), 1066–1078.

De Bellis, M. D., & Kuchibhatla, M. (2006). Cerebellar volumes in pediatric maltreatment-related posttraumatic stress disorder. *Biological Psychiatry, 60*(7), 697–703. https://doi.org/10.1016/j.biopsych.2006.04.035.

Deater-Deckard, K., & Dodge, K. A. (1997). Externalizing behavior problems and discipline revisited: nonlinear effects and variation by culture, context, and gender. *Psychological Inquiry, 8*(3), 161–175.

DOS. (2017a). *Age pyramid of resident population*. Retrieved from http://www.singstat.gov.sg/statistics/visualising-data/charts/age-pyramid-of-resident-population.

DOS. (2017b). *Population trends, 2017*. Retrieved from Singapore: Department of Statistics. http://www.singstat.gov.sg/docs/default-source/default-document-library/publications/publications_and_papers/population_and_population_structure/population2017.pdf.

Elliott, J. M., Tong, C. K., & Tan, P. M. (1997). Attitudes of the Singapore public to actions suggesting child abuse. *Child Abuse & Neglect, 21*(5), 445–464.

English, D. J., Marshall, D. B., Brummel, S., & Orme, M. (1999). Characteristics of repeated referrals to child protective services in Washington state. *Child Maltreatment, 4*(4), 297–307.

Fagan, A. A. (2005). The relationship between adolescent physical abuse and criminal offending: support for an enduring and generalized cycle of violence. *Journal of Family Violence, 20*(5), 279–290.

Felitti, V. J., Anda, R. F., Nordenberg, D., Williamson, D. F., Spitz, A. M., Edwards, V., et al. (1998). Relationship of childhood abuse and household dysfunction to many of the leading causes of death in adults: the adverse childhood experiences (ACE) study. *American Journal of Preventive Medicine, 14*(4), 245–258.

Finkelhor, D., Ormrod, R. K., & Turner, H. A. (2007). Polyvictimization and trauma in a national longitudinal cohort. *Development and Psychopathology, 19*(1), 149–166.

Fluke, J. D., Shusterman, G. R., Hollinshead, D. M., & Yuan, Y.-Y.T. (2008). Longitudinal analysis of repeated child abuse reporting and victimization: multistate analysis of associated factors. *Child Maltreatment, 13*(1), 76–88. https://doi.org/10.1177/1077559507311517.

Fowler, P., Henry, D., Schoeny, M., Landsverk, J., Chavira, D., & Taylor, J. (2013). Inadequate housing among families under investigation for child abuse and neglect: prevalence from a national probability sample. *American Journal of Community Psychology*, *52*(1/2), 106–114. https://doi.org/10.1007/s10464-013-9580-8.

Fuller, T., & Nieto, M. (2009). Substantiation and maltreatment rereporting a propensity score analysis. *Child Maltreatment*, *14*(1), 27–37.

Gershoff, E. T. (2002). Corporal punishment by parents and associated child behaviors and experiences: a meta-analytic and theoretical review. *Psychological Bulletin*, *128*(4), 539–579.

Goh, A. (2015). *Effects of multiple victimisation on children and adolescents in the child protection system* [Master of Psychology (Clinical)]. James Cook University.

Hahm, H. C., Lee, Y., Ozonoff, A., & Van Wert, M. J. (2010). The impact of multiple types of child maltreatment on subsequent risk behaviors among women during the transition from adolescence to young adulthood. *Journal of Youth and Adolescence*, *39*(5), 528–540.

Halemba, G. J., Siegel, G. C., Lord, R. D., & Zawacki, S. (2004). *Arizona dual jurisdiction study final report*. National Center for Juvenile Justice. Retrieved May 5, 2014 from http://www.cwla.org/programs/juvenilejustice/AZDualJurStudy.pdf.

Hélie, S., Laurier, C., Pineau-Villeneuve, C., & Royer, M.-N. (2013). A developmental approach to the risk of a first recurrence in child protective services. *Child Abuse & Neglect*, *37*(12), 1132–1141. https://doi.org/10.1016/j.chiabu.2013.05.001.

Heng, M. M., & Liu, D. (2014). In *Reliability and validity of the child and adolescent needs and strengths (CANS) in Singapore Paper presented at the 9th international conference for child and adolescent psychopathology (ICCAP)*.London, UK: University of Roehampton.

Huang, H., Ryan, J. P., & Herz, D. (2012). The journey of dually-involved youth: the description and prediction of rereporting and recidivism. *Children and Youth Services Review*, *34*(1), 254–260.

Jonson-Reid, M. (2002). Exploring the relationship between child welfare intervention and juvenile corrections involvement. *American Journal of Orthopsychiatry*, *72*(4), 559–576.

Jonson-Reid, M. (2003). Foster care and future risk of maltreatment. *Children and Youth Services Review*, *25*(4), 271–294.

Kahn, J. M., & Schwalbe, C. (2010). The timing to and risk factors associated with child welfare system recidivism at two decision-making points. *Children and Youth Services Review*, *32*(7), 1035–1044. https://doi.org/10.1016/j.childyouth.2010.04.011.

Kelley, B. T., Thornberry, T. P., & Smith, C. A. (1997). *In the wake of childhood maltreatment*. Washington, DC: National Institute of Justice. Retrieved June 12, 2014, from https://www.ncjrs.gov/pdffiles1/165257.pdf.

Keong, M. (2017). *Child maltreatment in Singapore: An analysis of familial factors* [Honours]. National University of Singapore.

Kim, J., & Cicchetti, D. (2010). Longitudinal pathways linking child maltreatment, emotion regulation, peer relations, and psychopathology. *Journal of Child Psychology and Psychiatry*, *51*(6), 706–716.

King, D. C., Abram, K. M., Romero, E. G., Washburn, J. J., Welty, L. J., & Teplin, L. A. (2011). Childhood maltreatment and psychiatric disorders among detained youths. *Psychiatric Services*, *62*(12), 1430–1438.

Lau, J. T. F., Liu, J. L. Y., Yu, A., & Wong, C.-K. (1999). Conceptualization, reporting and underreporting of child abuse in Hong Kong. *Child Abuse & Neglect*, *23*(11), 1159–1174.

Lee, H. C. (2004, September 17). *Most parents here don't cane kids, shows study*. Singapore: The Straits Times. Retrieved from Http://www.corpun.com/sgd00409.htm.

Li, D., Chu, C. M., Goh, J. T. L., Ng, I. Y., & Zeng, G. (2015). Impact of childhood maltreatment on recidivism in youth offenders: a matched-control study. *Criminal Justice and Behavior*, *42*(10), 990–1007.

Li, D., Chu, C. M., Ng, W. C., & Leong, W. (2014). Predictors of re-entry into the child protection system in Singapore: a cumulative ecological–transactional risk model. *Child Abuse & Neglect*, *38*(11), 1801–1812.

Lim, R. W. (2017). *Adverse childhood experiences and aggression in juvenile offenders in Singapore: Exploring the moderating influence of prosocial peers and social support* [Honours]. National University of Singapore.

Lipien, L., & Forthofer, M. S. (2004). An event history analysis of recurrent child maltreatment reports in Florida. *Child Abuse & Neglect*, *28*(9), 947–966.

Liu, D., Chu, C. M., Neo, L. H., Ang, R. P., Tan, M. Y. L., & Chu, J. (2016). Multiple trauma exposure and psychosocial functioning in Singaporean children in out-of-home care. *Psychological Trauma: Theory, Research, Practice, and Policy*, *8*(4), 431.

Liu, D., Tan, M. Y. L., Lim, A.Y.-Y., Chu, C. M., Tan, L. J., & Quah, S. H. (2014). Profiles of needs of children in out-of-home care in Singapore: school performance, behavioral and emotional needs as well as risk behaviors. *Children and Youth Services Review*, *44*, 225–232.

MacKenzie, M. J., Kotch, J. B., & Lee, L.-C. (2011). Toward a cumulative ecological risk model for the etiology of child maltreatment. *Children and Youth Services Review*, *33*(9), 1638–1647. https://doi.org/10.1016/j.childyouth.2011.04.018.

MacKenzie, M. J., Kotch, J. B., Lee, L.-C., Augsberger, A., & Hutto, N. (2011). A cumulative ecological–transactional risk model of child maltreatment and behavioral outcomes: reconceptualizing early maltreatment report as risk factor. *Children and Youth Services Review*, *33*(11), 2392–2398. https://doi.org/10.1016/j.childyouth.2011.08.030.

Manly, J. T., Cicchetti, D., & Barnett, D. (1994). The impact of subtype, frequency, chronicity, and severity of child maltreatment on social competence and behavior problems. *Development and Psychopathology*, *6*(1), 121–143.

Manly, J. T., Kim, J. E., Rogosch, F. A., & Cicchetti, D. (2001). Dimensions of child maltreatment and children's adjustment: contributions of developmental timing and subtype. *Development and Psychopathology*, *13*(4), 759–782.

MCYC. (2017). *HomeSweetHome@Admiralty, 4 more group homes to be set up for vulnerable children*. Retrieved from www.mcyc.sg/services/homesweethomeadmiralty, 13 July 2017 Straits Times.

Miller, E. A., Green, A. E., Fettes, D. L., & Aarons, G. A. (2011). Prevalence of maltreatment among youths in public sectors of care. *Child Maltreatment*, *16*(3), 196–204.

Moore, E., Gaskin, C., & Indig, D. (2013). Childhood maltreatment and post-traumatic stress disorder among incarcerated young offenders. *Child Abuse & Neglect*, *37*(10), 861–870.

MSF. (2016). *Protecting children in Singapore*. Retrived from Ministry of Social and Family Development. https://www.msf.gov.sg/publications/Documents/Hi%20res_Child%20Protection%202016_2.pdf.

MSF. (2017a). *Child abuse investigations* Retrived from https://www.msf.gov.sg/research-and-data/Research-and-Statistics/Pages/Child-Abuse-Investigations.aspx.

MSF. (2017b). *More singaporeans stepping forward to break the cycle of violence*. Retrieved from https://www.msf.gov.sg/media-room/Pages/More-Singaporeans-stepping-forward-to-break-the-cycle-of-violence.aspx.

Norman, R. E., Byambaa, M., De, R., Butchart, A., Scott, J., & Vos, T. (2012). The long-term health consequences of child physical abuse, emotional abuse, and neglect: A systematic review and meta-analysis. *PLoS Medicine*, *9*(11). https://doi.org/10.1371/journal.pmed.1001349.

Palusci, V. J. (2011). Risk factors and services for child maltreatment among infants and young children. *Children and Youth Services Review*, *33*(8), 1374–1382. https://doi.org/10.1016/j.childyouth.2011.04.025.

Palusci, V. J., & Ondersma, S. J. (2012). Services and recurrence after psychological maltreatment confirmed by child protective services. *Child Maltreatment*, *17*(2), 153–163. https://doi.org/10.1177/1077559511433817.

Proctor, L. J., Aarons, G. A., Dubowitz, H., English, D. J., Lewis, T., Thompson, R., et al. (2012). Trajectories of maltreatment re-reports from ages 4 to 12: evidence for persistent risk after early exposure. *Child Maltreatment*, *17*(3), 207–217. https://doi.org/10.1177/1077559512448472.

Ryan, J. P. (2006). Dependent youth in juvenile justice: do positive peer culture programs work for victims of child maltreatment? *Research on Social Work Practice*, *16*(5), 511–519.

Ryan, J. P., & Testa, M. F. (2005). Child maltreatment and juvenile delinquency: investigating the role of placement and placement instability. *Children and Youth Services Review*, *27*(3), 227–249.

Sameroff, A. (1975). Transactional models in early social relations. *Human Development*, *18*(1–2), 65–79.

Schofield, T. J., Lee, R. D., & Merrick, M. T. (2013). Safe, stable, nurturing relationships as a moderator of intergenerational continuity of child maltreatment: a meta-analysis. *Journal of Adolescent Health*, *53*(4 Suppl), S32–S38. https://doi.org/10.1016/j.jadohealth.2013.05.004.

Sidebotham, P., & Heron, J. (2006). Child maltreatment in the children of the nineties: a cohort study of risk factors. *Child Abuse & Neglect*, *30*(5), 497–522. https://doi.org/10.1016/j.chiabu.2005.11.005.

Stoltenborgh, M., Bakermans-Kranenburg, M. J., Alink, L. R., & IJzendoorn, M. H. (2015). The prevalence of child maltreatment across the globe: review of a series of meta-analyses. *Child Abuse Review*, *24*(1), 37–50.

Suliman, S., Mkabile, S. G., Fincham, D. S., Ahmed, R., Stein, D. J., & Seedat, S. (2009). Cumulative effect of multiple trauma on symptoms of posttraumatic stress disorder, anxiety, and depression in adolescents. *Comprehensive Psychiatry*, *50*(2), 121–127.

Swanston, H. Y., Parkinson, P. N., O'Toole, B. I., Plunkett, A. M., Shrimpton, S., & Oates, R. K. (2003). Juvenile crime, aggression and delinquency after sexual abuse: a longitudinal study. *British Journal of Criminology*, *43*(4), 729–749.

Tanaka, M., Wekerle, C., Schmuck, M. L., & Paglia-Boak, A. (2011). The linkages among childhood maltreatment, adolescent mental health, and self-compassion in child welfare adolescents. *Child Abuse & Neglect: The International Journal*, *35*(10), 887–898.

Tarren-Sweeney, M. (2008). Predictors of problematic sexual behavior among children with complex maltreatment histories. *Child Maltreatment*, *13*(2), 182–198.

Thompson, R., & Wiley, T. R. (2009). Predictors of re-referral to child protective services: a longitudinal follow-up of an urban cohort maltreated as infants. *Child Maltreatment*, *14*(1), 89–99.

Torchalla, I., Strehlau, V., Li, K., Schuetz, C., & Krausz, M. (2012). The association between childhood maltreatment subtypes and current suicide risk among homeless men and women. *Child Maltreatment*, *17*(2), 132–143. https://doi.org/10.1177/1077559512439350.

Trocmé, N. M., Tourigny, M., MacLaurin, B., & Fallon, B. (2003). Major findings from the Canadian incidence study of reported child abuse and neglect. *Child Abuse & Neglect*, *27*(12), 1427–1439.

Widom, C. S., & Maxfield, M. G. (2001). *An update on the cycle of violence*. Washington, DC: National Institute of Justice. Retrieved on June 14, 2014, from www.ncjrs.gov/pdffiles1/nij/184894.pdf.

World Health Organization (WHO). (2016). *Media centre: Child maltreatment. Fact sheets*. Retrieved from http://www.who.int/mediacentre/factsheets/fs150/en/.

Yampolskaya, S., Mowery, D., & Dollard, N. (2013). Predictors for readmission into children's inpatient mental health treatment. *Community Mental Health Journal*, *49*(6), 781–786. https://doi.org/10.1007/s10597-013-9592-8.

CHAPTER 20

Understanding Child Maltreatment Across Ethnic Minority Communities in Australia: Physical Abuse, Neglect, Witnessing Domestic and Family Violence, and Child Sexual Abuse

Jatinder Kaur
JK Diversity Consultants, Accredited Mental Health Social Worker, M.SocWk, M.Soc.Admin, B.A. (Psy), Cleveland, QLD, Australia

1 Introduction

Globalisation has significantly shifted the population demographics of Australia to a multicultural society, with a rich diversity of cultures, languages, religions, and ethnicities. The 2016 ABS Census data reflects that Australia is experiencing its fastest growth in overseas migration from South Asia, specifically from China and India. Of Australia's population of 24 million, 75% of Australians identified with an ancestry other than Australian as their first response, and 45% reported having at least one parent who was born overseas. Over 200 languages are spoken in Australia, with 21% of the population reported speaking a language other than English (ABS, 2017). Further, as a resettlement country, Australia accepts 13,756 refugee humanitarian entrants on annual permanent basis. Governments at both federal and state levels have developed multicultural policy frameworks, which aim to address the needs of migrants and refugees who settle in Australia.

Social workers are required to demonstrate "culturally competent, safe, and sensitive practice" when working with migrant and refugee communities in Australia (AASW Code of Ethics 2010, p. 17) including those working within the child protection system (CPS). This chapter will examine child maltreatment within various ethnic minority communities and outline the complex interactions of race, ethnicity, social class, patriarchy, religion, immigration status, and linguistic diversity and how these impact on ethnic minority families who come to the attention of CPS. The term 'ethnic minority' is deemed a more culturally

Child Abuse and Neglect. https://doi.org/10.1016/B978-0-12-815344-4.00020-9

inclusive and appropriate term to describe those communities that have a migration history and are minorities in at least one of the four main dimensions of ethnicity outlined by O'Hagan (1999)—race, language, culture, and religion. In Australia, the term culturally and linguistically diverse (CALD) is also commonly used in the research and policy landscape to refer to migrant and refugee communities.

2 Child Protection and Cultural Diversity

In Australia, approximately 1 in 33 children are involved in the CPS, with 73% reentering the system. The total number of children and young people placed into out-of-home care (OOHC) stands at 46,448 (AIHW, 2017). It is well documented that there is an over-representation of Aboriginal and Torres Strait Islander children and young people in CPS and OOHC. However, what remains unknown are the "numbers of children and young people from migrant and refugee backgrounds who have been placed in OOHC" (Kaur, 2012, p. 17). Culture influences child protection practice in two key ways: Firstly, considerations of abusive and protective behaviour towards children are culturally bound, and secondly, culture informs the range of professional responses to abuse (Connolly, Crichton-Hill, Ward, 2006, p. 23). According to Sawrikar (2009), "The national and state-based research on the needs of CALD families in the CPS is nascent but limited…similarly, the international literature is relatively scant" (p. 27).

In 2006, the author was employed as a frontline child protection officer in Queensland (Australia) and witnessed firsthand the challenges and complexity within the CPS in dealing with cross-cultural differences and assessment of child maltreatment across ethnic minority families. Kaur (2007) conducted a small exploratory research study into cross-cultural competence for child protection workers and their engagement and assessment with families from CALD backgrounds in the statutory system. The study highlighted the need for child protection officers to have the opportunity to attend CALD specific training and a need for the development of cross-cultural competence training specific to child protection (Kaur, 2007, p. 6). It also "identified key concerns in the provision of child protection practice, policy and service delivery when working with migrant and refugee families" (Kaur, 2007, p. 7). In 2012, Kaur was commissioned to undertake a research literature review on the needs of CALD and refugee families within the Australian CPS. The *Cultural Diversity and Child Protection* report (Kaur, 2012) was one of the first publications of its kind to review the available Australian research. It also established a 'baseline knowledge' for policymakers, legal practitioners, and researchers and proposed a number of recommendations to governments. This report highlighted the critical gaps in identifying the needs of migrant and refugee communities who become involved with CPS, a lack of data and research, and the prevalence rates of child maltreatment across migrant and refugee communities groups (Kaur, 2012). These findings were further supported by Dr Pooja Sawrikar (2017) who reported that within the CPS, there had been "slow research and poor data collection with ethnic minorities." She argued that,

> *more aggressive accusation of why research on cultural issues has been slow to get proper attention is institutional racism: not acting quickly in ways that could promote equity perpetuates and maintains disadvantage for some groups (Sawrikar, 2017, p. 46).*

The current knowledge base of CPSs, assessment, and intervention has traditionally been established on research and clinical experience from First World countries, for example the United Kingdom, the United States, Canada, and Europe. There is a need for more 'culturally specific research and clinical understanding' (Connolly, Crichton-Hill, Ward, 2006, p. 25) of child maltreatment across ethnic minority groups.

Ethnic culture includes "language, worldview, dress, food, styles of communication, notions of wellness, healing techniques, child-rearing patterns, and self-identity" (Abney, 2002, p. 477). According to Fontes (2005), 'ethnic culture' is what sets groups apart from each other ('us' and 'them'); it affects behaviour we consider abusive and nonabusive, which is not static. 'Ethnic culture' is multifaceted, evolving, and rapidly changing (Fontes, 2005, p. 4). Fontes (2005) proposes using 'ethnic culture' as a third circle in the Bronfenbrenner (1979) ecological models of child development. She argues that including 'ethnic culture' allows the practitioners to consider different ways of working with the child (individually), the child's family (kinship), religious and cultural/community leaders, and child's school and other services (Fontes, 2005). This approach allowed the practitioner to understand where they fit in the child's ecosystem and how this will impact on their understanding of 'ethnic culture' (Fontes, 2005, p. 3).

Australia does not have a unified statutory CPS; instead, each state and territory has its own legislation, policy, and practice guidelines with regard to child protection and welfare issues (Bromfield & Higgins, 2005). In 2009, the Council of Australian Governments (COAG) endorsed the National Framework for Protecting Australia's Children 2009–20; however, there remain significant discrepancies between jurisdictions in relation to definition of child abuse and maltreatment, risk assessment and decision making tools, and statutory interventions including foster/kinship care placements. There is neither universality regarding child-rearing standards nor the definition of child abuse or maltreatment (Korbin, 1991). Korbin (1991) has identified three levels that need to be considered when formulating culturally appropriate definitions of child maltreatment:

1. Acknowledgement of cultural differences in child-rearing practices
2. Deviations from the culturally appropriate child-rearing practices of any specific cultural group are considered by that cultural group to be abusive
3. Circumstances exist where societal harm undermines children's wellbeing beyond the control of the parent (e.g. poverty)

The international literature has identified that CPS practitioners can use contradictory approaches when intervening with families from migrant or refugee backgrounds (Maitra, 2005). According to Fontes (2005), there are two approaches used in child protection assessment, the first being 'false positive' (where caseworkers incorrectly assume an act is abusive) or the second being a 'false negative', which occurs when caseworkers fails to recognise a given practice as maltreatment, using cultural practices as justification (Fontes, 2005). Williams and Soydan (2005) suggested a trap for new workers (possible from the white Anglo-dominant culture) is either an ethnocentric worldview (e.g. caseworkers' own bias, stereotype of different ethnic groups, and making assumptions) or extreme cultural relativism (e.g. where the use of culture is justified and supersedes the rights of every child to be safe from harm—e.g. female genital mutilation). Child protection work is one of the most challenging areas within the human services, with this challenge further exacerbated when practitioners are navigating the complex myriads of ethnic, racial, and linguistic diversity when working with multicultural families (Kaur, 2009).

3 Child Maltreatment Across Diverse Cultures

It is imperative that CPS seek to understand the many causal factors involved in child maltreatment and develop a cultural perspective that encompasses culture, ethnicity, religion, and language when working with migrant and refugee families involved with CPS (Kaur, 2012, p. 12). The common risk factors that bring families to the attention of CPS include domestic and family violence (DFV), substance abuse, and mental illness (Bromfield, Lamont, Parker, & Horsfall, 2010) along with poverty. The literature has identified five main subtypes of child abuse and neglect (maltreatment):

1. Physical abuse
2. Neglect
3. Child sexual abuse (CSA)
4. Emotional abuse
5. Witnessing of domestic and family violence (DFV)

In the majority of cases reported to CPS, there would likely be multiple presentations and comorbidity abuse types for the same child. There are a number of additional factors that impact on migrant and refugee families coming to the attention of CPS. Diagram A outlines the emerging framework and how the premigration journey and resettlement in Australia can lead to child maltreatment or DFV. Whilst migrant and refugee families are subject to the above risk factors, they also experience a number of unique challenges and stressors that may impact on them and lead to their involvement with CPS. For more detailed review on this area, see Sawrikar, 2017.

4 Cross-Cultural Child Protection Assessment Framework

Practitioners working in the CPS need to ensure all assessments allow for cultural, racial, linguistic, religious, social, political, and economic factors when determining whether or not child maltreatment has occurred across migrant and refugee communities. These factors are displayed in Diagram A: cross-cultural child protection assessment framework.

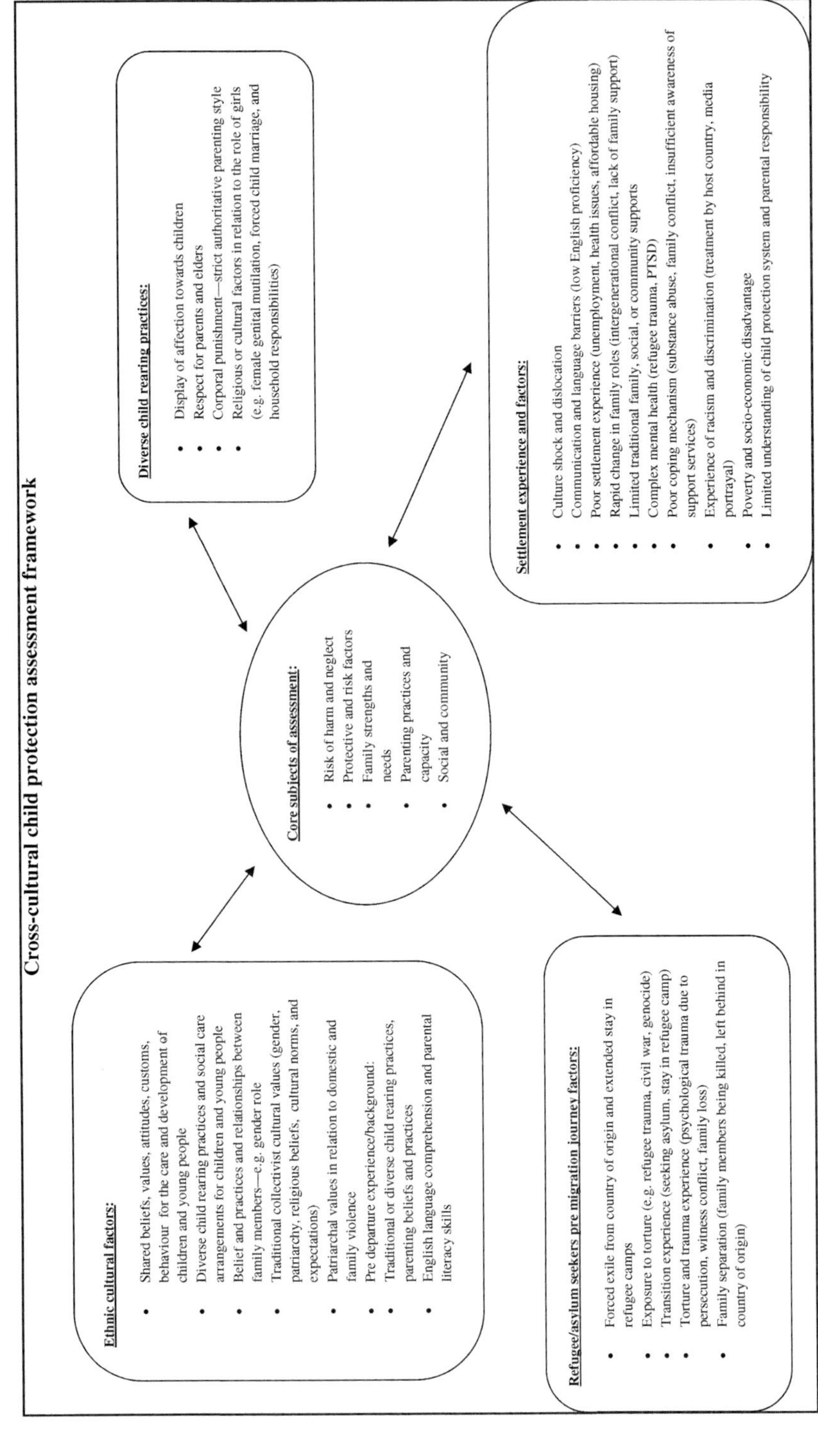
Cross-cultural child protection assessment framework
Diverse child rearing practices:
• Display of affection towards children
• Respect for parents and elders
• Corporal punishment—strict authoritative parenting style
• Religious or cultural factors in relation to the role of girls (e.g. female genital mutilation, forced child marriage, and household responsibilities)
Ethnic cultural factors:
• Shared beliefs, values, attitudes, customs, behaviour for the care and development of children and young people
• Diverse child rearing practices and social care arrangements for children and young people
• Belief and practices and relationships between family members—e.g. gender role
• Traditional collectivist cultural values (gender, patriarchy, religious beliefs, cultural norms, and expectations)
• Patriarchal values in relation to domestic and family violence
• Pre departure experience/background:
• Traditional or diverse child rearing practices, parenting beliefs and practices
• English language comprehension and parental literacy skills
Core subjects of assessment:
• Risk of harm and neglect
• Protective and risk factors
• Family strengths and needs
• Parenting practices and capacity
• Social and community
Settlement experience and factors:
• Culture shock and dislocation
• Communication and language barriers (low English proficiency)
• Poor settlement experience (unemployment, health issues, affordable housing)
• Rapid change in family roles (intergenerational conflict, lack of family support)
• Limited traditional family, social, or community supports
• Complex mental health (refugee trauma, PTSD)
• Poor coping mechanism (substance abuse, family conflict, insufficient awareness of support services)
• Experience of racism and discrimination (treatment by host country, media portrayal)
• Poverty and socio-economic disadvantage
• Limited understanding of child protection system and parental responsibility
Refugee/asylum seekers pre migration journey factors:
• Forced exile from country of origin and extended stay in refugee camps
• Exposure to torture (e.g. refugee trauma, civil war, genocide)
• Transition experience (seeking asylum, stay in refugee camp)
• Torture and trauma experience (psychological trauma due to persecution, witness conflict, family loss)
• Family separation (family members being killed, left behind in country of origin)

5 Culturally Sensitive Practice

A culturally sensitive approach in social work entails a recognition that all clients, regardless of their cultural background, will have much in common, yet they will have different 'worldviews' (Lee & Greene, 1999). Ideally, a culturally sensitive practitioner would have the skills and knowledge to recognise the different worldviews of migrant and refugee families (Kaur, 2009). Cultural sensitivity also implies an understanding by practitioners of the impact of racism and racial abuse and the ways of challenging this at an institutional and individual level (Thoburn, Chand, & Proctor, 2005). According to Dominelli and Campling (2002), "to successfully address issues of oppression, antioppressive interventions have to encompass social relations at the personal, organisational, and cultural levels" (p. 85). Social workers need to be conscious of power and authority and how 'othering processes' can serve to exclude based on a number of social categories including race, gender, age, disability, sexual orientation, mental health, and class and how this 'othering' can manifest within various government institutions (Dominelli & Campling, 2002).

The qualitative findings from the exploratory research study (Kaur, 2007) explored the concepts of 'culturally sensitive practice in child protection'; the caseworkers identified the following cross-cultural skills when working with migrant and refugee families involved with CPS:

- Caseworkers to engage, be respectful, and build responsive relationships when working with multicultural families
- Caseworkers to demonstrate an understanding of effective diverse child-rearing practices and norms
- Cross-cultural communication (using interpreter) and engagement
- Referral for culturally appropriate support services
- Placing the child with kin or extended family network (Kaur, 2009, p. 30).

Additionally, these findings are consistent with Pooja Sawrikar's (2017) research with child protection caseworkers in NSW CPS.

6 Child Protection Ethnic Case Studies

The emerging framework in understanding child maltreatment across migrant and refugee communities in Australia is illustrated in Diagram B. This diagram is to assist practitioners to better understand how child maltreatment occurs within ethnic minority groups. For the purpose of this chapter, case studies will be presented in relation to different ethnic culture and how child maltreatment occurs within that context (these ethnic case studies are based on the author's experience in working with multicultural families within CPS and mental health context in Australia and the names have been deidentified).

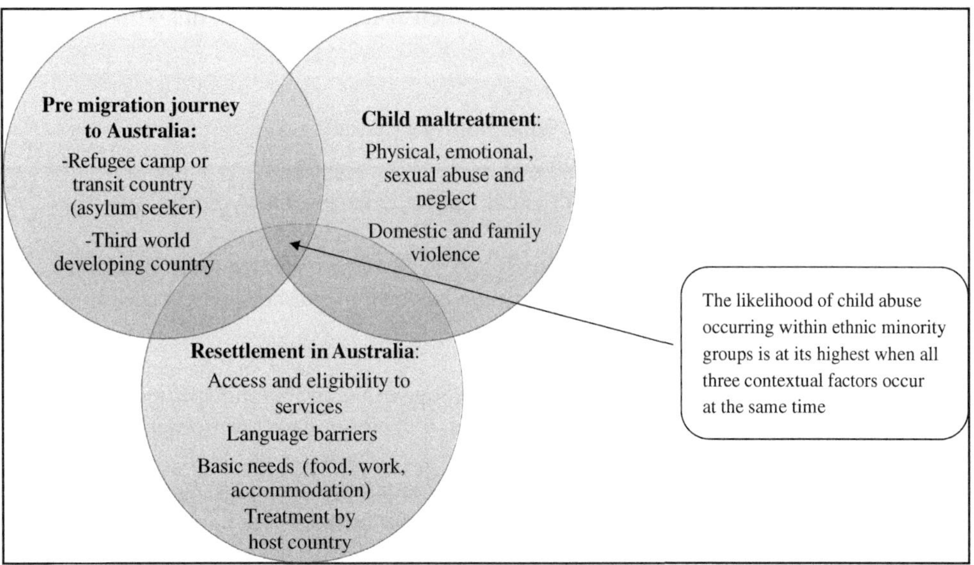

7 Physical Abuse

In Australia, there have been two major research studies examining child maltreatment across migrant and refugee communities. The 3-year research study by Sawrikar (2017) examined child maltreatment across the following groups: Chinese, Lebanese, Pacific Islander (Samoan and Tongan), and Vietnamese along with two reference groups of Anglo-Saxon and Indigenous participants in NSW. Physical abuse was the most common primary harm type among the CALD groups. The South Australian 3-year research study with refugee communities (Lewig et al., 2009) examined prevalence of child protection notifications involving refugee families across African (subSaharan), Middle Eastern, and Vietnamese groups. This study found that the most common harm types reported were neglect (leaving children without adult supervision), physical abuse, and exposure to domestic violence. Research has found the migration experience (forced and voluntary) and family separation for both migrant and refugee families is a significant factor with regard to individual families functioning and parenting capacity and their ability to successfully resettle in a new host country (Babacan, 2006, pp. 5–6). The South Australian study, which explored refugee experiences, identified the following risk factors that precipitated CPS involvement (Lewig et al., 2009):

- Communication and language barriers
- Premigration experience including trauma and separation of extended family
- Issues associated with domestic violence, such as alcohol abuse, mental illness, and in some families acceptance of physical violence towards women
- Cultural difference in parenting style

- The lack of family support, particular for women who are sole parents with a large number of children
- Traditional patriarchal family structures
- The lack of information about acceptable family practices

Case study 1: Somali young boy (physical abuse, witness DFV, and neglect)

Child protection notification concerns

The school observed bruises on Jumahl's arms and back of his neck. He often does not have food in his lunch box. Over the past term, he has become withdrawn in classroom and isolated.

Background history information

'Jumahl' is a 12-year-old Somali boy, who is struggling with learning and speaking English. He came to Australia under the refugee humanitarian program with his mother, stepfather, and four siblings (three sisters and one brother younger than him). His biological father was killed in the Somali civil war, and his mother had to flee from their village. She was raped by the militia, and her youngest daughter is the product of that rape. The family stayed in the UN refugee camp before being resettled in Australia. Since arriving in Australia, Jumahl's stepfather is unemployed and frequently goes out to meet his Somali friends where he drinks alcohol and gambles. His stepfather is very controlling, and all family members are fearful of him. Jumahl's mother works as a support worker in aged care, and she struggles to manage the child care responsibilities and household. Last month, police were also called to the house due to a domestic violence incident argument.

Assessment

The child protection practitioner would need to take into consideration the following cross-cultural factors and language barriers in conducting the assessment and investigation around the concerns for Jumahl's safety and wellbeing:

- English comprehension and understanding of Australian child protection legislation
- Child-rearing practices within African-Somali culture and cultural views on corporal punishment
- Risk assessment and harm in relation to children's wellbeing—e.g. Jumahl's physical bruises, emotional harm due to witnessing DFV in the home, possible grief and loss around biological father's death, and social isolation
- The prevalence of DFV within African-Somali culture and the stepfather's understanding of Australian laws around DFV and child protection
- Factors around poverty and poor settlement experience (unemployment and low English proficiency)
- Impact of ongoing refugee trauma for stepfather and poor coping skills (drinking alcohol and gambling behaviour)

Outcome of investigation

The child protection investigation outcome was substantiated for physical harm and emotional harm. The family was referred to a 12-month family intervention support service to address parenting issues, mental health and trauma, English language program, and men's behaviour support program.

For newly arrived African refugee families, Renzaho, Green, Mellor, and Swinburn (2011) found that African parents tended to remain authoritarian in their role and attempt to control their children, based on the traditional parenting styles that reinforce obedience and respect, through corporal punishment and strict compliance of rules and expectations in their children. Within the medical literature, there is growing interest in 'cultural practice' in the context of child maltreatment, such as coining, faith healing, female genital circumcision (mutilation), medical neglect, and bruising in ethnic minority children (Raman & Hodes, 2012).

8 Witnessing Domestic and Family Violence

There has been little Australian research examining the prevalence of DFV within migrant and refugee communities and their presentation to CPS (Kaur & Atkin, 2018). The two Australian research studies, Sawrikar (2017) and Lewig et al. (2009) found that witnessing DFV was one of the most common issues experienced by CALD and refugee families. Practitioners need to be aware of the multiple factors that impact on women from migrant and refugee backgrounds and prevalence of DFV. These factors include social isolation, limited English, unemployment, trauma, gender roles, and traditional values and patriarchal beliefs (Pittaway & Rees, 2005–2006; Rees & Pease, 2007). Refugee women are more vulnerable to DFV due to the premigration journey and contextual factors related to the experience of multiple and interrelated issues of custody and access issues, parental separation, family breakdown, racial discrimination, prearrival experiences of domestic violence, and community/cultural pressures to keep the family intact (Ghafournia, 2011; Rees & Pease, 2007; Vaughan et al., 2015). Social workers need to consider utilising antioppressive frameworks and to examine the multidimensional levels of oppression experienced by women from diverse backgrounds including race, culture, ethnicity, religion, sexual orientation, age, disability, class, patriarchy, and mental health (Kaur & Atkin, 2018).

Case study: Indian Sikh girls (witness DFV and emotional harm)

Child protection concerns

Eldest daughter (6 years old) told her teacher that 'Daddy was hitting mummy, and she was bleeding'. Police were called to the house, took out protection order, and called the ambulance.

Background history

'Sonia' is from an Indian (Punjabi-Sikh) family and had an arranged marriage with Mr. Singh. Within a few months of marriage, he started to complain about her parents 'interfering' in their personal affairs. He asked her to make choice between him and her parents. Sonia 'cut herself off' from her family despite living 10 min from her parents to appease her husband. The family violence first started with verbal arguments over money/finances. She was the main breadwinner and educated in Australia and was able to earn more money than Mr. Singh. He started to control the finances and, without her knowledge or consent, used her money to send back to his family in India. Mr. Singh's extended family started meddling in their marriage and 'encouraged Mr. Singh to control his wife'. The in-laws were also disappointed that Sonia gave birth to two daughters and did not produce a son. Mr. Singh would frequently be physically violent towards Sonia. During their marriage, he continued to be violent and was abusive to her in front of his two daughters and other relatives, yet no family member intervened. Police were called on several occasions (by the neighbours). She wanted to 'preserve her marriage' for the sake of her daughters and denied the allegations of family violence and lied about how she got her injuries (bruises on face and head wounds).

Assessment and outcome

Child protection and police took statements from Sonia and interviewed the girls. The outcome was substantiated for emotional harm. The girls were referred to counselling as they had bad dreams and were struggling at school. Sonia was diagnosed with depression and referred to a psychiatrist. She moved back with her parents after the DV court hearing to rebuild her life. Mr. Singh went back to India due to the shame and has no contact with his daughters.

Case study: Maori young girl (exposure to DFV and physical and emotional harm)

Aroha is a 15-year-old Maori Pacific Islander girl who is sleeping rough in the city. She became homeless due to family violence between her parents and being beaten by her father for not showing respect. She says that "many young Maori women accept violence in relationships' and that there is perception 'it's ok to hit a woman, if she is Maori and lippy (being smart mouth)." She talked about the movie (Once Were Warriors), "I see Beth and Jake all the time; many young Maori people beat their own girlfriends and then bash another male Maori young man who beats his partner." Aroha disclosed that many Pacific Islander young people feel ashamed when they become homeless and don't ask for people for support.

9 Child Sexual Abuse

There is very little research that has explored the topic of sexual abuse and sexual assault within migrant and refugee communities in the child protection context (Kaur, 2012). The exhaustive literature review by Sawrikar and Katz (2017) on CSA and ethnic minority communities highlighted that victims appeared to be at higher risk of suicidality. They posited that this was potentially due to the many barriers to engage with professional help-seeking in this group, with the most common associated with protecting the family's name (2017). Within the US context, Fontes (2005) highlighted that shame around CSA intersects with ethnic culture in many ways, such as feeling responsible for the abuse, failure to protect, fate, damaged goods, virginity, predictions of a shameful future, revictimisation, and the layers of shame produced by cultural oppression. Through the premigration journey, refugee women and girls may have experienced rape, sexual assault, war, civil unrest, refuge, and detention camps with the multiple experiences of trauma having a serious impact on the mental health of refugee women (Allimant & Ostapiej-Piatkowski, 2011). Refugee girls accompanying these women are at further risk of either experiencing similar experiences or have been exposed to sexual violence and may not have a 'protective parent' (if the mother was also a victim of physical and sexual violence) in their resettlement country.

10 Royal Commission Into Institutional Responses to Child Sexual Abuse

In 2017, the author was approached to provide expert evidence to the final hearing for the Royal Commission into Institutional Responses to CSA in relation to vulnerability for children and young people from migrant or refugee backgrounds. These factors include the lack of awareness around child sexual abuse and potential sexual grooming behaviours; English language skills and newly arrived families who would not have the capacity to disclose CSA due to cultural and religious barriers (in most diverse cultures, anything about sex is taboo, and there is lot of stigma); and newly arrived refugees who have complex trauma and mental health issues that may compromise or impair their capacity to be a 'protective parent' (mothers), particular potential for paedophiles (including stepfathers) who may target vulnerable women who have children. My recommendations to the Royal Commission were that Australian child protection authorities need to develop community education strategies that are culturally responsive, around the nature and definition of child abuse, especially sexual abuse, and recognising the signs of grooming. The following case studies (names that have been changed were provided to highlight these issues to the Royal Commission).

Case study: Online sexual grooming

A mother was Australian born from Palestine but was not practicing Muslim; she had five children, the eldest being a 15-year-old daughter. The mother went to Jordan to remarry. The new stepfather's motive was to marry the mother to access her 15-year-old daughter. The stepfather was a very traditional Muslim male and started grooming the 15-year-old via social media (Facebook). He pretended to be younger male and used a fake profile and started an online relationship with her. Eventually, the mother found out and her 15-year-old daughter was devastated that the person she was in love with 'was her stepfather'. Mother kicked out the stepfather; the daughter developed a serious mental illness (depression, and tried to commit suicide on few occasions). This case study was disclosed when young girl accessed hospital mental health service.

Case study: Sexual grooming within place of worship

Concerns were raised around a Hindu priest who was very friendly with Hindu Indian young women in the congregation. The community members trusted him with their issues. He was involved in many couple disputes, and eventually, it came to light that he would 'seek out' the divorced women for his own pleasure/relationship. The priest targeted many women, including an underage 17-year-old from the congregation. He would groom the women with gifts (gold jewellery and attention) and convince them to have sexual relations. Eventually, he was caught out by the community, and he absconded to Fiji before any victim was able to contact police and make a formal complaint against him. This priest stayed in Fiji for a few years. No criminal charges were laid. The same priest has returned back to Australia and has been accepted back into the Hindu community, 'as he has reformed himself' and currently has access to women and children. There were no working with children checks done as he was never charged for any child related offences.

11 Forced Child Marriage

In recent years, the media has raised concerns of the 'underground' practice of forced and servile child marriages occurring within some migrant and refugee communities in Australia. The Australian Attorney General Department released a discussion paper (AGD, 2012) that identified a number of factors that contributed to this practice those being to control unwanted behaviour and sexuality, prevent unsuitable relationships (outside ethnic, cultural, religious, or caste group), protect 'family honour', protect perceived cultural and religious ideals, settle debts, ensure property and wealth remain within family, and assist claims for residence and citizenship. Some of the harmful consequences associated with forced and servile marriage include interruption of education, emotional and physical abuse, rape, and unwanted pregnancy. This practice is not condoned by any religious faith or prescribed in any religious texts.

Case study 2: Muslim teenage girl (child sexual abuse and forced child marriage)

Child protection notification concerns

The school reports that Yasmin has been absent from high school for the past week, and the teacher holds concerns that she has been taken back to Jordan against her will to be married.

Background history information

Yasmin is a 16-year-old Jordanian Muslim girl; she is the eldest in her family and has two younger brothers. Her mother suffers from depression and chronic back pain. Her father is very controlling and a strict Muslim and community elder. Yasmin was working on school project over the past few months with fellow students that included two teenage boys. After school, the Imam saw Yasmin at the local library being 'friendly' with these boys and reported this back to her father. That night, her father beat Yasmin to teach her a lesson as they felt she brought shame onto their family. He also beat the mother as he blamed her for 'bad parenting' and 'spoiling her'. After that incident, Yasmin became withdrawn from her studies and started 'self-harming' on her wrists. She was afraid to tell her friends or teachers about what happened at home.

Forced child marriage and child sexual abuse

By the time child protection authorities informed the Federal police, Yasmin and her father had already departed Australia for Jordan. There is no extradition treaty with Jordan, and as a consequence, the Australian embassy could not intervene. Yasmin was forced to marry her first cousin who was 28 years old under Islamic law, despite her not consenting to the marriage. Her father told her he 'would kill her' if she did not comply with the marriage. She was raped multiple times by her husband and physically beaten whilst in Jordan. She had no one to seek help or support from.

Intervention

She arrived back in Australia after 3 months and was in the early stage of pregnancy. She was flagged by the Federal police at the airport, and they were able to assist her once she arrived. The child protection authorities intervened (Yasmin came into care and protection). Federal police also laid criminal charges against the father and husband. Few years later, Yasmin was able to get her marriage annulled. She was shunned by her mother, brothers, and extended family and was blamed for bringing 'dishonour' to her family.

12 Child Sexual Trafficking

The Asia-Pacific is known to be a region of origin, transit, and destination for human and child sexual trafficking. Reported cases of child trafficking include bonded and exploitative forms, including domestic service and factory work. Sexual exploitation involves child prostitution or production of child pornography and forced marriage (Larsen, 2011). The case study below that has been deidentified was the first Australian prosecution case for child sexual trafficking from Asia-Pacific region.

Case study: Child sex trafficking

A Thai mother was charged for sexual trafficking of her 9-year-old daughter for prostitution. The mother had set up massage business and taught her daughter Thai massage, masturbation of men, and oral sex. The mother told the court that she brought her daughter over from Thailand to pay the bills and that "if she wanted to be rich, she had to work hard." The judge rejected her claims, and she was sentenced to a 9-year jail sentence and was convicted of child trafficking offences.

13 Conclusion

There is a dire need for more research and data collection into understanding child maltreatment and prevalence rates across ethnic minority communities within Australia. This chapter has focused on using the 'ethnic-sensitive' framework to illustrate how child maltreatment can occur within migrant and refugee families and how the complex interactions of race, ethnicity, social class, patriarchy, religion, immigration status, premigration refugee trauma, and linguistic diversity can also contribute to child maltreatment. It is critical that CPS practitioners become culturally sensitive and utilise a cross-cultural child protection framework to assess and support ethnic minority families who become involved with the statutory system.

14 Chapter Review Questions

1. In your own words, explain what it means to be culturally competent.
2. Identify some of the gaps in cultural competency, in child protection.

3. What do we need to consider when formulating culturally appropriate definitions of child maltreatment?
4. What factors need to be considered when making assessments with regard to migrant and refugee families?
5. Identify and explain cross-cultural skills necessary when working with migrant and refugee families, as highlighted by Kaur (2009).
6. What risk factors might precipitate refugee involvement with CPS?
7. Identify cultural considerations, relevant to working with migrant and refugee families experiencing DFV.
8. Reflect on your own professional practice and identify ways in which you will adjust your practice and upskill in order to be more culturally competent.

References

AASW. (2010). *Australian association of social workers code of ethics*, Retrieved from https://www.aasw.asn.au/practitioner-resources/code-of-ethics.

Abney, V. (2002). Cultural competency in the field of child maltreatment. In J. E. B. Myers, L. Berliner, J. Briere, C. Terry Hendrix, C. Jenny, & T. A. Reid (Eds.), *The APSAC handbook on child maltreatment* (pp. 477–486). Thousand Oaks, CA: Sage.

ABS. (2017). *3412.0- Migration, Australia, 2015–16* Retrieved from http://www.abs.gov.au/AUSSTATS/abs@.nsf/mf/3412.0.

AIHW. (2017). *Child protection Australia 2015–16*, Retrieved from http://www.aihw.gov.au/publication-detail/?id=60129558626.

Allimant, A., & Ostapiej-Piatkowski, B. (2011). *Supporting women from CALD backgrounds who are victims/survivors of sexual violence: Challenges and opportunities for practitioners, Australian centre for the study of sexual assault (ACSSA) Wrap, No. 9*. (pp. 1–16). Melbourne: Australian Institute of Family Studies. https://aifs.gov.au/sites/default/files/publication-documents/w9.pdf.

Attorney General Department. (2012). *Discussion paper on forced and servile marriage*. https://www.ag.gov.au/Consultations/Documents/Consultationonforcedandservilemarriage/Discussion%20Paper%20for%20Public%20Release%20forced%20and%20servile%20marriage.pdf.

Babacan, H. (2006). *Literature review: Service/response models in child protection for culturally diverse communities*. Report commissioned and prepared for the Department of Child Safety Queensland.

Bromfield, L., & Higgins, D. (2005). *National comparison of child protection systems*. National Child Protection Clearinghouse, Issues 22. Australian Institute of Family Studies (AIFS). Accessed online: https://aifs.gov.au/cfca/sites/default/files/publication-documents/issues22.pdf.

Bromfield, L., Lamont, A., Parker, R., & Horsfall, B. (2010). *Issues for the safety and wellbeing of children in families with multiple and complex problems' (NCPC Issues No. 33)*. Melbourne: National Child Protection Clearinghouse. https://aifs.gov.au/cfca/publications/issues-safety-and-wellbeing-children-families.

Bronfenbrenner, U. (1979). *The ecology of human development: Experiments by nature and design*. Cambridge, MA: Harvard University Press.

Connolly, M., Crichton-Hill, Y., & Ward, T. (2006). *Culture and child protection: Reflexive responses*. Jessica Kingsley Publishers.

Dominelli, L., & Campling, J. (2002). *Anti-oppressive social work theory and practice*. New York: Palgrave Macmillan.

Fontes, L. (2005). *Child abuse and culture: Working with diverse families*. New York: Guilford Press.

Ghafournia, N. (2011). Battered at home, played down in policy: migrant women and domestic violence in Australia. *Aggression and Violent Behaviour*, *16*(3), 207–213.

Kaur, J. (2007). 'Working with families from culturally and linguistically diverse communities in Queensland': an Australian exploratory study. *Children Australia*, *32*(4), 17–24.

Kaur, J. (2009). Developing 'culturally sensitive' practice when working with CALD communities in child protection—an Australian exploratory study. *Developing Practice*, *23*(Autumn/Winter), 22–35.

Kaur, J. (2012). *Cultural diversity and child protection: A review of the Australian research on the needs of culturally and linguistically diverse (CALD) and refugee children and families*. Retrieved from http://www.jkdiversityconsultants.com.au/Cultural_Diversity_&_Child_Protection_Kaur2012_A4.pdf.

Kaur, J., & Atkin, N. (2018). Nexus between domestic violence and child protection—multidimensional forms of oppression impacting on migrant and refugee women in Australia. *Australian Social Work Journal*, *71*(2), 238–248.

Korbin, J. E. (1991). Cross-cultural perspectives and research directions for the 21st century. *Child Abuse and Neglect*, *15*, 67–77.

Larsen, J. (2011). *The trafficking of children in the Asia–Pacific. Trends & issues in crime and criminal justice no. 415*. Canberra: Australian Institute of Criminology. https://aic.gov.au/publications/tandi/tandi415.

Lee, M. Y., & Greene, G. J. (1999). A teaching framework for transformative multicultural social work education. *Journal of Ethnic and Cultural Diversity in Social Work*, *12*(3), 1–28.

Lewig, K., Arney, F., & Salveron, M. (2009). *The working with refugee families project*. Australian Centre for Child Protection.

Maitra, B. (2005). Culture and child protection. *Current Paediatrics*, *15*, 253–259.

O'Hagan. (1999). Culture, cultural identity and cultural sensitivity in child and family social worker. *Child & Family Social Work*, *4*(4), 269–281.

Pittaway, E., & Rees, S. (2005–2006). Multiple jeopardy: domestic violence and the notion of cumulative risk for women in refugee camps. *Women Against Violence: An Australian Feminist Journal*, *18*, 18–25.

Raman, S., & Hodes, D. (2012). Cultural issues in child maltreatment. *Journal of Paediatrics and Child Health*, *48*, 30–37.

Rees, S., & Pease, B. (2007). Domestic violence in refugee families in Australia. *Journal of Immigrant & Refugee Studies*, *5*(2), 1–19.

Renzaho, A. M. N., Green, J., Mellor, D., & Swinburn, D. (2011). Parenting, family functioning and lifestyle in a new culture: the case of African migrants in Melbourne, Victoria. *Child & Family Social Work*, *16*, 228–240.

Sawrikar, P. (2009). *Interim report 1—Culturally appropriate service provision for culturally and linguistically diverse (CALD) children and families in the New South Wales (NSW) child protection system: Literature review*. Sydney: NSW Department of Community Services. https://www.sprc.unsw.edu.au/media/SPRCFile/20_Report_Cald_Families_LitRvw.pdf.

Sawrikar, P. (2017). *Working effectively with ethnic minorities and across cultures in western child protection systems*. London and New York: Routledge, Taylor & Francis Group.

Sawrikar, P., & Katz, I. (2017). The treatment needs of victims/survivors of child sexual abuse (CSA) from ethnic minority communities: a literature review and suggestions for practice. *Children and Youth Services Review*, *79*, 166–179.

Thoburn, J., Chand, A., & Proctor, J. (2005). *Child welfare services for minority ethnic families. The research reviewed*. London: Jessica Kingsley Publishers.

Vaughan, C., Murdolo, A., Murray, L., Davis, E., Chen, J., Block, K., Quiazon, R., & Warr, D. (2015). ASPIRE: A multi-site community-based participatory research project to increase understanding of the dynamics of violence against immigrant and refugee women in Australia. *BMC Public Health*, *15*, 1283. https://doi.org/10.1186/s12889-015-2634-0. Open access article: https://bmcpublichealth.biomedcentral.com/track/pdf/10.1186/s12889-015-2634-0.

Williams, C., & Soydan, H. (2005). When and how does ethnicity matter? A cross-national study of social work responses to ethnicity in child protection cases. *British Journal of Social Work*, *35*(6), 901–920.

CHAPTER 21

Child Abuse and Neglect and the Judicial System: The Limits of Legal Enterprise

Rosemary Sheehan
Monash University, Melbourne, VIC, Australia

Effective child protection needs to be an integrated response where legal process is part of a collaborative response within the child welfare arena. However, the framing of child protection as a sociolegal enterprise limits this enterprise and distracts from a broader child welfare focus. The legal framework for child protection investigation and intervention clearly intends to provide for the protection of children where a child is at risk of harm or has been harmed but fits uneasily in this framework for responding to the often long-term and complex problems of individuals and families. The dominance of 'risk' as the benchmark for deciding harm or likelihood of harm has led to judicial and adversarial processes that seek out incidents of abuse or evidence of behaviours that cause harm or are likely to harm the child. The adversarial paradigm that operates in the court system creates considerable tension between the child protection and legal systems and distracts from concentrating on the child protection concerns and how a child's best interests are best determined.

This chapter argues that the emphasis on discrete episodes of maltreatment excludes the majority of child protection cases. The number of children on care and protection orders in Australia continues to rise despite significant attempts by many jurisdictions to divert children and families away from statutory intervention and increasing family supports to maintain children in their family's care. Child protection matters brought before the court increasingly involve long-term factors such as poverty, parental mental illness, substance abuse, and domestic violence, which impact on the lives of the children and their families. They are cases that are often more difficult to prove legally; there is little agreement between legal and welfare systems about definition and recognition of the impact of these factors on children, and the child protection service struggles to present the type of evidence of demonstrated behaviour and events that the Court seeks and fits readily into legislative parameters about proof of harm and the need for care and protection.

Contemporary thinking regarding child protection suggests shifting the focus from that of solely legal and right-based approaches to more holistic and multidisciplinary contributions,

Child Abuse and Neglect. https://doi.org/10.1016/B978-0-12-815344-4.00021-0

recognising that a child's best interests are better understood when all facets of concerns are assessed rather than just those that meet legal criteria. It is suggested that a legal process which recognises the unique role of the child welfare jurisdiction but that minimises disputation, is agreement-focussed, is more child-centred, and works collaboratively with key child welfare professionals is a better way to resolve the child's best interests. Whilst the court system is significant in its responsibility for children at risk of child maltreatment, this chapter argues that it needs to be part of a continuum or responses and engage with the broader community of child welfare concern, to bring a broader understanding to deciding what children's best interests are.

1 Child Protection and the Legal Process

The task of assessing whether or not a child is sufficiently at risk of child abuse to justify child protection intervention is one of the hardest tasks undertaken in the welfare field. This task is made more difficult because legal decisions about children brought to court often differ from child protection recommendations about the need for formal and statutory intervention to protect a child from harm. Legal and welfare professionals use different frames of references to deal with child abuse cases and can differ in how they view harm and risk to children. Whilst there will be factors common to their decision-making, the absence of a shared common decision-making model in child abuse matters across legal and welfare professionals leads to considerable variation in how child abuse is defined and in what behaviours constitute abuse and how seriously they are to be taken. How judicial officers decide whether or not a child is in need of protection, in legislative terms, and how they assess a parent's failure to protect are left to their discretion and their own individual criteria they use to explain child abuse.

The legal system exerts a powerful influence on the child protection system in Australia and specifically directs system and service responses. Court proceedings have become part of the core business of the child protection service, and great emphasis is given to using highly structured and standardised risk assessment measures to gather evidence that is acceptable to the Court (Allen Consulting Group, 2003). The Victorian Ombudsman (Office of the Victorian Ombudsman, 2009) reported that 'approximately 50% of child protection worker time is spent servicing Children's Court work and subsequent protection orders, even though only 7.3% of the total number of reports made to the department result in legal intervention being initiated in the Children's Court' (p. 12).

Child protection concerns sit uneasily within the Australian legislative framework. Each of Australia's eight state and territory child welfare jurisdictions has its own distinct child protection legislation (Australian Institute of Health and Welfare (AIHW), 2017; Bromfield & Higgins, 2005; Sheehan & Borowski, 2013). In Victoria, it is the *Children, Youth and Families Act,* 2005 that supplies the legal framework for child protection investigations and interventions. Child protection matters are thus identified and understood within this complexity of statutory responses and in a context that emphasises legal grounds as the criteria for considering statutory intervention and uses court proceedings to adjudicate child welfare matters. Judicial officers report that they first ensure their decisions are in accordance with legal principles but then refer to their views and intuition about cases before they form their decision (Sheehan & Borowski, 2013).

The National Framework for Protecting Australia's Children (Australian Government Department of Social Services, 2009–2020)—Australia's overarching child protection framework—advocates a 'whole of community' approach where child protection is 'everyone's responsibility' and uses a public health model to promote the health and wellbeing of children and the reduction in child abuse and neglect across Australia (The Council of Australian Governments, 2009). Yet the operationalisation of child protection in Australia is aligned with judicial and adversarial processes and separated from the broader child welfare and family support systems set up to respond to vulnerable families (Allen Consulting Group, 2003). This is strongly influenced by a generally held view that protection of the privacy of family life and parental autonomy is an Australian value, which is reflected not only in the framing of child welfare legislation but also in the choice of legal remedies to perceived problems in child-rearing. The Victorian Ombudsman, in his 2009 review of the child protection program, noted that "the current legal system perversely encourages disputation rather than cooperation in the protection of children" (Office of the Victorian Ombudsman, 2009, p. 57) when the remit of the child welfare jurisdiction is to respond "to concerns about child abuse and neglect often in circumstances of acute family disadvantage or marginalisation" (Victorian Law Reform Commission [VLRC], 2010, p. 312) and what is needed to decide these matters is expertise other than legal training (VLRC, 2010, p. 364). When the law is the predominant arbiter of how maltreatment is defined, this influences child protection practice to consider more what might or might not be accepted by the court as the threshold for intervention rather than solely relying on professional judgement about risk of harm to a child.

2 Child Protection Legislation

Child protection legislation in Victoria that directs that harm to a child 'may be constituted by a single act, omission or circumstance or accumulate through a series of continuing acts, omissions or circumstances' (CYFA s.162 (2)) and links this harm to the grounds for making a child protection order, which turn on physical, sexual, and emotional abuse of a child; a failure to provide for the child's health and development; and child abandonment. Yet child protection grounds set out in the Victorian legislation are not accompanied by a clear definition on what is considered 'harm to a child' (Bromfield & Miller, 2012; Sheehan, 2012).

The legal framework provides no clear guidance for judicial officers around how what is understood as significant physical, sexual, or emotional harm or failure to provide for a child's physical development. The application of the test of significant harm is highly variable and contested and shaped by who is applying the lens for its definition (Dickens, 2007; Masson, 2010). Whilst there is common acknowledgement that child protection legislation needs to move away from looking for episodes of abuse and singular events, to more effectively respond to the often long-term and complex problems of individuals and families, child protection workers must demonstrate to the court evidence of discrete episodes of maltreatment that have caused harm or are likely to harm the child.

The dominance of 'risk' as the benchmark for deciding harm or likelihood of harm to a child pervades these legal processes; considerable attention has been given to developing risk assessment instruments to gather the hard evidence favoured by the legal system to identify situations of child maltreatment and to justify decisions made by the child protection service (Braye & Preston-Shoot, 2006). Children's experiences of maltreatment are rarely clear-cut, and their complexity is underpinned by individual and social problems and family dysfunction (Price-Robertson, Rush, Wall, & Higgins, 2013; Sheehan, 2012). This emphasis on discrete episodes of maltreatment excludes the majority of child protection cases that are generally of a more chronic nature and about cumulative harm, rather than 'specific dangerous parental behaviour's (Allen Consulting Group, 2003, p. 29).

Whilst legislation promotes the 'best interests' of the child (see: *CYFA*: s.10) as the paramount concern of the court, how best interests are defined is not set out in the legislation, nor is there any guidance about how they might be understood. Conflicting aims in the protection of children from harm, maintaining children with their parents (see: *CYFA*: s.11), and ensuring adequate care of the child with the minimum child protection necessary to secure the child's welfare and safety (see: *CYFA* s.10 (2) (a)) all strike an uneasy balance that can lead to courts persevering with families who are unable to provide a child with the requisite care and safety they need for their wellbeing and development (Allen Consulting Group, 2003).

The *Children, Youth and Families Act,* 2005 considers that children's views and wishes are central to deciding their best interests (s. 11). In Victoria, children aged 11 and over instruct a solicitor appointed by Victorian Legal Aid, and the child's wishes are conveyed to the Court by adult legal practitioners. The legislation also provides in exceptional circumstances for best interests representation for children who are not mature enough to provide instruction. In these cases, the legal representative must act according to what he/she believes are the best interests of the child and communicate these to the Court. Yet how these processes are undertaken and whether or not it is the child's voice may be debateable. In Victoria, a legal representative appointed to act on a child's behalf is not required to have any particular training in working with children or knowledge of child welfare; it is left to the individual legal practitioner to develop (Sheehan, 2003). The predominant requirement is knowledge of the law and a capacity to engage in legal process.

Child welfare legislation is challenged by the difficult and uncertain nature of the social and individual problems that child protection workers respond to on a daily basis (Braye & Preston-Shoot, 2006). Moreover, child protection legislation in Victoria—and this is typical of Australian child protection legislation in general—sets out overlapping interests that are not easily reconciled: the family's interest to live as it chooses without external interference; the state's interest in the protection of vulnerable children; and the child's interest in exercising their own rights, which might differ from those of family and state especially when their wellbeing is being determined. How the child welfare, legal, and adult service systems (e.g. mental health, substance abuse, and family violence) define child abuse and neglect may overlap but will differ because they each serve a different purpose. In the absence of shared frameworks, legal and child protection systems find it almost impossible to develop agreed approaches about risks and consequences of maltreatment.

Certainly, court outcomes are often viewed by child protection as a compromise, legally driven and based on an accommodation of parent's and children's instructions to their legal representatives and on what they will agree to do rather than based on the child's developmental and welfare needs (Sheehan, 2006).

3 Child Protection in the Australian Context

The prevalence of child maltreatment within Australia is increasing at a concerning rate. The rate of children receiving child protection services in Australia increased from 26.0 per 1000 children in 2012–13 to 30.2 per 1000 children in 2015–16. In the 12 months between 2015 and 2016, 162,175 (30.2 per 1000) Australian children received child protection services (investigation, care and protection order, and/or out-of-home care), with 73% previously investigated or on orders (AIHW, 2017). Of children receiving child protection services in 2015–16, 115,024 were the subject of an investigation (21.4 per 1000), 61,723 were on a care and protection order (11.5 per 1000), and 55,614 were in out-of-home care (10.4 per 1000). Emotional abuse and neglect were the most common primary and cooccurring types of substantiated abuse and neglect, followed by physical abuse and sexual abuse. Younger children were more likely to be the subjects of substantiations of child maltreatment than those in older age groups, with infants (children aged under 1 year) the most likely (16.1 per 1000 children). This pattern was consistent across all jurisdictions.

In 2015–16, almost 48,000 care and protection orders were issued across jurisdictions, with almost 13,500 children admitted to an order during that time. Nationally, in 2015–16, more children were admitted to care and protection orders (13,500) than were discharged from orders (almost 11,000). At 30 June 2016, almost 52,000 children were on a care and protection order: rate of 9.6 per 1000 Australian children.

The increase in demand for Australian child protection services can be attributed to a range of complex factors (e.g. legislative changes, inquiries into child protection systems, and increased public awareness) (AIHW, 2017). Bromfield and Arney (2008) suggest one explanatory factor for the overall increase in child protection concerns is the complex family situations of these children: the strong connection between child abuse and neglect, domestic violence, parental substance abuse, and parental mental health. Certainly, there is a clear relationship between socio-economic disadvantage and contact with child protection services (VLRC, 2010, p. 35), characterised by housing instability, poverty, low education, social isolation, and neighbourhood disadvantage (Bromfield & Arney, 2008; Stanley, 2011), and parental factors such as mental illness and intellectual disability (McConnell & Llewellyn, 2002). They are cases that are more difficult to prove legally; there is little agreement between legal and welfare systems about definition and recognition of the impact of these factors on children, and the child protection service struggles to present the type of evidence of demonstrated behaviour and events that the Court seeks and fits readily into legislative parameters about proof of harm and the need for care and protection.

In addition, the demand for child protection services is confronted by a range of systemic issues such as a lack of suitable placements for children in care, access and resource limitations hindering early and timely family intervention, and fragmented interagency collaboration, all of which limit the capacity for effective service delivery. These systemic issues also include differing approaches by the legal and child welfare processes, high caseloads in child protection, high staff turnover, and the lowering of staff morale, all of which impact on child protection service delivery (Bromfield, Arney, & Higgins, 2014; Price-Robertson, Bromfield, & Lamont, 2014; Sheehan & Borowski, 2013).

4 Legal Responses to Child Protection Systems

Australia's 'child protection' orientation, which underpins Australia's child protection systems, is associated with this rising demand for child protection services (Price-Robertson et al., 2014). This orientation, shared with New Zealand, the United Kingdom, the United States, and Canada, is distinguished from the 'family service' approach that informs many Western European and Scandinavian countries (Price-Robertson et al., 2014). The 'family service' orientation frames child abuse within the context of social, economic, and psychological difficulties that result in family dysfunction, and the presence of child maltreatment is not necessary in order to receive assistance from government and other services who respond to these difficulties. In this orientation, there is a range of entry points and services that respond to families, and the presence of child maltreatment is not necessary in order to receive assistance. It is seen as working in partnership with the parent, with a legal response as the last resort (Price-Robertson et al., 2014).

The 'child protection' orientation frames child abuse and the protection of children from harm as the most significant concerns. Child protection focusses on receiving a report or notification about child protection concern, and statutory intervention is sought by presenting evidence to a court, subject to adversarial, standardised, and evidence-based procedures (Price-Robertson et al., 2014). This system is separated from wider family support services and focusses on families where there is a high or immediate need for intervention (Allen Consulting Group, 2003).

There are many different types of legal system and responses to the problem of child protection in different national political, legal, and cultural traditions. Child protection systems that, both in practice and legislatively, tend to focus on incidents, rather than the resulting harm to a child's welfare or development (Dickens, 2007), set up a threshold of significant harm in order to justify statutory intervention. But it is often difficult in child welfare matters to identify a 'decisive event' that can satisfy legal requirements and that a threshold of significance has been reached (Dickens, 2007). Definitions of neglect and 'thresholds' for protective intervention are a common area of contention in the adjudication of child welfare matters (Dickens, 2007; Scott, 2014) and take away from a focus on the impact on the child, rather than the severity or incidence of specific abusive acts or omissions (Scott, 2014, p. 9). Equally, the lack of clear definition on what constitutes 'adequate parenting' or a 'safe environment' for children (Hood, 2014; Scott, 2013) means many children who experience maltreatment are not captured by incident-focussed assessments (Spratt, 2012). The prescriptive policies and procedures associated with the 'incident-based' approach to child maltreatment, which is embedded in Australian law, not only try to reduce the complexity and uncertainty that underpins child protection but also fail to reflect the reality of practice with complex families (Buckley, Tonmyr, Lewig, & Jack, 2014; Munro, 2011).

As in Australia, Canada's child welfare systems similarly operate on a 'threshold approach', and families have to meet a minimum level of dysfunction in order to access services (Saskatchewan Ministry of Social Services, 2010). This notion of 'threshold' is, as just noted, in direct contrast to what characterises the majority of child welfare concerns, where harm is often cumulatively "the result of neglect stemming from poverty, substance abuse, mental health problems, and inadequate housing" (Saskatchewan Ministry of Social Services, 2010, p. 5). The rate of Canadian protection investigations driven by urgent child protection needs (generally severe physical or sexual abuse or neglect) has remained steady at approximately 6 investigations per 1000 children. But the rate of investigations involving other maltreatment types, most particularly around chronic needs, doubled over the same period, rising from 15 to 33 investigations per 1000 children (Trocmé, Kyte, Sinha, & Fallon, 2014). Such statutory demand has led to many Canadian jurisdictions adopting differential response models separating acute safety concerns from those related to longer-term development and wellbeing needs (Trocmé et al., 2014). It has suggested a more collaborative approach to child and family welfare, minimising court involvement (Saskatchewan Ministry of Social Services, 2010), and favouring greater emphasis on early intervention and family support.

5 A Problem-Solving Approach

In the United States, which also operates within an adversarial system, the 'juvenile and family courts' or dependency courts as they are known take a problem-solving approach to the adjudication of child protection matters and involve welfare and other professionals (Boles, Young, Moore, & DiPirro-Beard, 2007). The children's judge works with the main agencies involved in child protection (e.g. police, education, health and mental health, child and family support services, and child protection) to meet and debate the administrative issues that impact on decision-making and services for children. These integrated justice system responses bring together multidisciplinary contributions to understand harm and risk in child maltreatment matters (Wheeler, Carson, & Fox, 2006) and are best observed in family dependency treatment courts (FDTC) (Worcel, Furrer, Green, Burrus, & Finnigan, 2008), where there is intensive judicial monitoring of cases and interprofessional collaboration with representatives from child welfare and treatment systems, along with frequent appearances by parents to monitor progress, in order to produce more positive outcomes for children and their families.

This case management approach, embedded with therapeutic justice principles, involving a single judge devoted to this group of cases (Gatowski et al., 2002), also underpins the 'one family, one judge policy' as featuring in cases involving very young children brought before the Inner London District Court (in England). Cases involving children aged from birth to 2 years of age are assigned to a specific judge who hears the case each time it appears and coordinates the contributions of professionals about the child's developmental needs and parental competency and motivation. Considerable emphasis is placed on good initial risk assessment and multidisciplinary contributions. London's Family Drug and Alcohol Court is also a specialist problem-solving court (Harwin et al., 2011) working in partnership with a multidisciplinary team of practitioners who carry out assessments, develop an individual intervention plan, and provide regular reports on parental progress to the court and to all others involved in the case. The court monitors parent's progress, and judges speak directly to parents and social workers, to find ways of resolving problems that may have arisen (Harwin et al., 2011). It is an approach that is markedly different from ordinary proceedings in Australia's Children's Courts: There is little judicial continuity across hearings, there are no specialist teams attached to the court, child and family assessments are provided by a range of different experts that may take considerable time to appear, there are no hearings without lawyers, and there is little coordination of services for parents. It has to be acknowledged that Victoria has introduced its own FDTC, (Levine, 2012) modelled on the English approach, and a specialist list for hearing child sexual abuse matters (Sheehan, 2016) to provide more of a problem-solving approach to resolving these particular groups of cases.

Specialist problem-solving courts that are seen as more practical and interventionist in approach now feature in criminal justice systems in the United Kingdom, the United States,

Canada, Australia, and New Zealand, to deal with issues such as drug misuse, domestic violence, and mental health problems (Harwin et al., 2011, p. 16). Their focus on longer-term outcomes rather than simply deciding a sentence or order combines specially trained judges or magistrates, multidisciplinary collaboration in the court setting, who monitor an individual's progress in complying with designated services (Harwin et al., 2011). Where this has been extended to children's court matters, the focus is on parental behaviour and the extent to which they are demonstrating motivation and capacity to care for their children and comply with orders (Harwin et al., 2011, p. 16). The use of 'alternatives to conventional court proceedings' (*Family Justice Review* 3.171–3.186) is encouraged in England and Wales (Taylor-Gooby, 2011), as mediation-type approaches in child protection are seen as cheaper, more individualised, less traumatic, and more stabilising for children (Hayes & Houston, 2007; Patton, 2006; Thoennes, 2009); in the United States, child dependency proceedings increasingly rely on such approaches in deciding child protection matters (Jordan, 2009; Patton, 2006), albeit retaining judicial oversight of such mediation approaches.

The Family Court of Australia has also implemented problem-solving approaches to deciding postseparation parenting disputes involving serious allegations of child abuse. The Magellan case management system, introduced in 1998, is a judge-led, time-limited, interorganisational approach to the resolution of disputes about children. It can order expert investigations and assessments from the state child protection service and gather views from relevant professionals about children's needs and parenting issues. The aim is to resolve a case within 6 months, and judges play an active role in managing cases as they progress through the court (Higgins, 2007).

Child protection service systems across Australia are struggling to respond to the increasingly complex problems and multiple needs of vulnerable families (Sammut & O'Brien, 2009). Whilst children's courts have broadened their interest in the protection of children from a wider spectrum of events that damage child development, child protection workers believe that legislation and legal process fail to support this. The adversarial paradigm that operates across Australian Children's Courts creates considerable tension between the child protection and legal systems and distracts from concentrating on the nature and merit of child protection concerns and how a child's best interests are best determined. The Victorian Law Reform Commission in their report on the child protection system (2010, p. 204) described how magistrates acknowledged the adversarial nature of the court, noting it was their role to hear and determine the issues raised by parties and it was not for them to decide what must be discussed. The VLRC (2010) and the Office of the Victorian Ombudsman (2009) noted that a child's best interests are better understood when all facets of concerns are assessed rather than just those that meet legal criteria. Yet, child welfare legislation in Australia continues to maintain adversarial and highly legalised processes to deal with child abuse that diminish the significance and utility of welfare contributions. There is little accommodation of the kind of multidisciplinary contributions that are necessary to both make sense of and effectively respond to these increasingly complex problems.

Whilst Humphreys et al. (2009) observe that in Victoria, as in many other jurisdictions in Australia, there has been renewed investment in early intervention/prevention approaches, particularly those targeting the first 3 years of life and the development of initiatives to enhance child and family health and wellbeing, the 'forensic lens' is still evident in policy and practice, given the interrelationship between legislation and intervention in child protection matters. This is especially evident for Indigenous Australians, who very often live in communities of socio-economic disadvantage, where the burden of substance abuse and family violence is pervasive. There is a disconnect between legislation and child protection approaches to working with families, where risks are low but services needed, without court orders and all that the forensic approach brings with this. Humphreys et al. (2009) observe that whilst there is a need for tertiary statutory child protection, the more it is constructed as the principal conduit for welfare concerns about children, the more closely aligned it is with legal obligation, the more children's best interests are predominantly cast in terms of legislative parameters around risk and safety (Australian Government Department of Social Services, 2009–2020).

The Victorian Ombudsman's investigation into the child protection system found that "the forensic examination of activity…lead(s) more families (to) becoming ensnared in resource intensive and often counter-productive contested processes" (2009, p. 65). The overlap between mental health, disability, drug and alcohol, and domestic violence sectors indicates that the protection of children needs to reflect shared responsibility. The Victorian Law Reform Commission suggested child welfare jurisdiction needs to minimise disputation and work on agreement as a better way to resolve the child's best interests—especially "when parties will usually have important ongoing relationships" (2010, p. 209). They suggested the development of legislative principles that encourage early resolution of child protection matters and the legal process as problem solving in its approach, accommodating interprofessional contributions decision makers need to decide about a child's development and wellbeing (VLRC, 2010, p. 214). There needs to be formal child welfare guidance incorporated into court process, as is the case in England and Wales, so that there are shared frameworks to assess child protection concerns and develop an agreed child protection plan developed collaboratively with the court. What is also necessary is that legal decision makers have formal knowledge and education in child development, the effect of trauma on children, and the impact of parental mental illness and exposure to drugs and family violence on children (submission by the Director of Victorian Paediatric Forensic Medical Service to the VLRC, 2010, p. 365).

This need for service integration is a theme common to child protection commentators (Bromfield, Lamont, Parker, & Horsfall, 2010). The Council of Australian Governments

(2009) suggests that focussing solely on legal and right-based approaches to child protection fails to offer the broader understanding to deciding a child's best interests that is central to deciding child protection matters (Horsfall, Bromfield, & McDonald, 2010).

Despite the legislative changes that have generally been introduced into Australian child protection legislation, a legal process remains embedded in an adversarial legal system with a high threshold for statutory intervention—significant harm—and the belief that discrete incidents of abuse are generally necessary to satisfy a court that the grounds for child protection have merit. There is considerable emphasis on individual rights of parents and children and a requirement to demonstrate parental incapacity or misconduct that commits considerable child protection time to gathering evidence for formal legal proceedings. There remains a gap in providing legislative guidelines about what constitutes child maltreatment (apart from the child abuse grounds that initiate a protection application) or about how the court should decide significant harm and parental responsibility, leaving these to the discretion of the magistrate. Whilst there is general agreement about broad definitions of what constitutes serious physical and sexual abuse, it is difficult to achieve consensus on what constitutes abuse where a child is not seriously or gravely harmed. The unique role of the child welfare jurisdiction needs to be acknowledged by processes that promote decisions about a child's development and wellbeing and minimises disputation, recognising that "concerns about child abuse and neglect are often in circumstances of acute family disadvantage or marginalisation" (VLRC, 2010, p. 312) and need broader responses to family complexity than can be offered by an adversarial legal process.

6 Chapter Review Questions

1. What approach best recognises a child's best interests, which incorporates all facets of concern rather than just those that meet legal criteria?
2. How does an emphasis on legalism divert social work from its core aims with respect to child protection?
3. How might you develop a shared common decision-making model in child abuse matters across legal and welfare professionals?
4. Could Australia's child protection systems adapt to a 'family service' orientation? What principles would be developed to underpin this?
5. What might a problem-solving approach to managing child abuse matters in the children's courts look like?
6. What has driven Australia to adopt an adversarial legal system with a high threshold for statutory intervention in matters of child protection?
7. How might you develop definitions of what constitutes child maltreatment and introduce these into legislation?
8. What are the implications for child protection and the justice system of taking a social work practice framework to the interpretation of child protection matters?

References

Allen Consulting Group. (2003). *Protecting children: The child protection outcomes project.* Melbourne: Victorian Department of Human Services.

Australian Government Department of Social Services. (2009–2020). *National framework for protecting Australia's children.* Canberra https://www.dss.gov.au/our-responsibilities/families-and-children/publications-articles/protecting-children-is-everyones-business.

Australian Institute of Health and Welfare (AIHW). (2017). *Child protection Australia 2015–16.* Canberra https://www.aihw.gov.au/reports/child-protection/child-protection-australia-2015-16/notes.

Boles, S., Young, N., Moore, T., & DiPirro-Beard, S. (2007). Sacramento dependency drug court: development and outcomes. *Child Maltreatment, 12*(2), 161–171.

Braye, S., & Preston-Shoot, M. (2006). *Teaching, learning and assessment of law in social work education.* Bristol: The Policy Press.

Bromfield, L., & Arney, F. (2008). *Developing a road map for research: Identifying the priorities for a national child protection research agenda (child abuse prevention issues no. 28).* Melbourne: Australian Institute of Family Studies, National Child Protection Clearinghouse.

Bromfield, L., & Higgins, D. (2005). *National comparison of child protection systems (child abuse prevention issues no. 22).* Melbourne: Australian Institute of Family Studies, National Child Protection Clearinghouse.

Bromfield, L., & Miller, R. (2012). *Cumulative harm—best interests case practice model: Specialist practice resource.* Department of Human Services. viewed 13 August 2014 http://www.dhs.vic.gov.au/for-service-providers/children,-youth-and-families/child-protection/specialist-practice-resources-for-child-protection-workers/cumulative-harm-specialist-practice-resource.

Bromfield, L., Arney, F., & Higgins, D. J. (2014). Contemporary issues in child protection intake, referral and family support. In A. Hayes & D. J. Higgins (Eds.), *Families, policy and the law: Selected essays on contemporary issues for Australia* (pp. 121–129). Melbourne: Australian Institute of Family Studies.

Buckley, H., Tonmyr, L., Lewig, K., & Jack, S. (2014). Factors influencing the uptake of research evidence in child welfare: a synthesis of findings from Australia, Canada and Ireland. *Child Abuse Review, 23*(1), 5–16.

Children, Youth and Families Act (Victoria) (2005).

Dickens, J. (2007). When a child care case is taken to court in England and Wales, child neglect and the law: catapults, thresholds and delay. *Child Abuse Review, 16*, 77–92.

Gatowski, S., Dobbin, S., Litchfield, M., Halemba, G., Siegel, G., & Gunn, R. (2002). *Texas 65th Judicial District Children's Court: Evaluation of model court activities 1999–2001.* Texas: El Paso.

Harwin, J., Ryan, M., Tunnard, J., Pokhrel, S., Alrouh, B., Matias, C., et al. (2011). *The family drug & alcohol court (FDAC) evaluation project: Final report.* Conducted by Brunel University, funded by the Nuffield Foundation.

Hayes, D., & Houston, S. (2007). Lifeworld, system and family group conferences: Habermas's contribution to discourse in child protection (2007). *British Journal of Social Work, 37*(6), 987–1006.

Higgins, D. J. (2007). *Cooperation and coordination: An evaluation of the family court of Australia's Magellan case-management model.* Canberra: Family Court of Australia.

Horsfall, B., Bromfield, L., & McDonald, M. (2010). Are social marketing campaigns effectivein preventing child abuse and neglect? NCPC Issues No. 32—October 2010. Melbourne, Victoria: AIFS.

Hood, R. (2014). Complexity and integrated working in children's services. *British Journal of Social Work, 44*(1), 27–43.

Humphreys, C., Harries, M., Healy, K., Lonne, B., Mendes, P., McHugh, M., & Sheehan, R. (2009). Shifting the child protection juggernaut to earlier intervention. *Children Australia, 34*(3), 5–8.

Jordan, K. (2009). Need to be heard: Increasing child participation in protection mediation through the implementation of model standards (2009). *Family Court Review, 47*(4), 715–736.

Levine, G. (2012). *A study of family drug treatment courts in the United States and the United Kingdom: Giving parents children the best chance of reunification.* Report for the Winston Churchill Memorial Trust of Australia. https://www.churchilltrust.com.au/media/fellows/2011_Levine_Greg.pdf.

Masson, J. (2010). (Mis)understandings of significant harm. *Child Abuse Review, 19*, 291–298. Published online 21 June 2010 in Wiley InterScience (www.interscience.wiley.com)https://doi.org/10.1002/car.1129.

McConnell, D., & Llewellyn, G. (2002). Stereotypes, parents with intellectual disability and child protection. *Journal of Social Welfare and Family Law*, *24*(3), 297–317.

Munro, E. (2011). *The munro review of child protection—final report: A child-centred system*. United Kingdom: Department for Education. viewed 1 October 2017 https://www.gov.uk/government/publications/munro-review-of-child-protection-final-report-a-child-centred-system.

Office of the Victorian Ombudsman. (2009). *Own motion investigation into the department of human services child protection program*. Melbourne, Victoria: Office of the Victorian Ombudsman.

Patton, W. (2006). *Legal ethics in child custody and dependency proceedings: A guide for judges and lawyers*. England: Cambridge University Press.

Price-Robertson, R., Bromfield, L., & Lamont, A. (2014). *International approaches to child protection: What can Australia learn? CFCA Paper No. 23*. Melbourne: Australian Institute of Family Studies.

Price-Robertson, R., Rush, P., Wall, L., & Higgins, D. (2013). *Rarely an isolated incident: Acknowledging the interrelatedness of child maltreatment, victimisation and trauma*. Australia: Australian Institute of Family Studies. viewed 19 September 2014 https://www3.aifs.gov.au/cfca/publications/rarely-isolated-incident.

Sammut, J., & O'Brien, T. (2009). *Fatally flawed: The child protection crisis in Australia*. NSW: Centre for Independent Studies.

Saskatchewan Ministry of Social Services. (2010). *For the good of our children and our youth*. Saskatchewan, Canada: Saskatchewan Ministry of Social Services.

Scott, D. (2013). *Meeting children's needs when the family environment isn't always 'good enough': A systems approach*. Australia: Australian Institute of Family Studies. viewed 26 September 2014 https://www3.aifs.gov.au/cfca/publications/meeting-childrens-needs-when-family-environment-isnt.

Scott, D. (2014). *Understanding child neglect*. Australia: Australian Institute of Family Studies. viewed 26 September 2014 https://www3.aifs.gov.au/cfca/sites/default/files/publication-documents/cfca20.pdf.

Sheehan, R. (2003). The marginalisation of children by the legal process. *Australian Social Work*, *56*(1), 12–25.

Sheehan, R. (2006). Emotional abuse and neglect: The legal response. *Child Abuse Review*, *15*(1), 38–54.

Sheehan, R. (2012). Deciding the best interests of the child: legal responses to child protection concerns. In R. Sheehan, H. Rhoades, & N. Stanley (Eds.), *Vulnerable children and the law: International evidence for improving child welfare, child protection and children's rights* (pp. 333–346). London: Jessica Kingley Publishers.

Sheehan, R. (2016). Legal responses to child sexual abuse cases in the Children's Court of Victoria: Study findings on a case-management approach. *Journal of Social Welfare and Family Law*, *38*(3), 287–301.

Sheehan, R., & Borowski, A. (2013). *Australia's children's courts today and tomorrow*. New York: Springer.

Spratt, T. (2012). Why multiples matter: reconceptualising the population referred to child and family social workers. *British Journal of Social Work*, *42*, 1574–1591.

Stanley, N. (2011). *Children experiencing domestic violence: A research review research in practice series*. Dartington Hall, Totnes, England: Dartington and the University of Sheffield. www.rip.org.uk.

Taylor-Gooby, P. (2011). Taking advantage: informal social mechanisms and equal opportunities policies. *International Journal of Sociology and Social Policy*, *31*, 253–271. [Online]. Available at https://doi.org/10.1108/01443331111141255.

The Council of Australian Governments. (2009). *Protecting children is everyone's business: National framework for protecting Australia's children 2009–2020*. (The National Framework), Annual Report http://www.fahcsia.gov.au/sa/families/pubs/Pages/pac_report_to_COAG.aspx.

Thoennes, N. (2009). What we know now: findings from dependency mediation research. *Family Court Review. An Interdisciplinary Journal*, *47*, 21–37. https://doi.org/10.1111/j.1744-1617.2009.00237.x.

Trocmé, N., Kyte, A., Sinha, V., & Fallon, B. (2014). Urgent protection versus chronic need: clarifying the dual mandate of child welfare services across Canada. *Social Sciences*, *3*, 483–498.

Victorian Law Reform Commission. (2010). *Protection applications in the children's court: Final report*. Victoria: Melbourne.

Wheeler, M., Carson, L., & Fox, J. (2006). Family dependency treatment court: applying the drug court model in child maltreatment. *Drug Court Practitioner Fact Sheet*, *5*(1), 1–8.

Worcel, S., Furrer, C., Green, B., Burrus, S., & Finnigan, M. (2008). Effects of family treatment drug courts on substance abuse and child welfare outcomes. *Child Abuse Review*, *17*(6), 427–443.

CHAPTER 22

Public (Mis)perceptions of Individuals Who Sexually Abuse Children and the Implications Thereof

Amelie Pedneault
Department of Criminal Justice and Criminology, Washington State University, Pullman, WA, United States

1 Public Perceptions of Those Who Commit Child Sex Crimes

Child sexual abuse is a critical problem, with a yearly estimate of more than 2 million children subjected to sexual abuse or sexual exploitation (United Nations Children's Fund, 2014). In addition, some victims who are sexually abused as children incur severe and long-lasting consequences as a result of their victimisation, including negative physical and mental health outcomes, decreased educational achievement, and problematic behaviours (Beitchman et al., 1992; Browne & Finkelhor, 1986; Cashmore & Shackel, 2013; Green, 1993; Paolucci, Genuis, & Violato, 2001). It is therefore unsurprising that members of the public have very negative views of those who harm children sexually.

Individuals who commit sexual crimes are viewed more negatively by members of the public compared with offenders who commit crimes that are nonsexual in nature. For example, previous empirical results have demonstrated that sex offenders are considered worse than murderers (Quinn, Forsyth, & Mullen-Quinn, 2004) and are feared more than terrorists (Human Rights Watch, 2007). When specifically comparing sexual offenders with violent offenders, members of the public endorsed more severe punishment of individuals who commit the crime of fondling compared with those who hit their victims (Rogers & Ferguson, 2011). In addition, the public is least supportive of restoring the voting rights of sex offenders upon their reentry into society when compared with various other types of offenders (Chiricos, Padgett, Bratton, Pickett, & Gertz, 2012; Manza, Brooks, & Uggen, 2004). Overall, members of the public loathe and fear individuals who commit sexual crimes (Harper & Harris, 2017; Spencer, 2009), and these individuals are frequently described by terms such as *monster*, *predator*, and *animal* (Douard, 2008; Pickett, Mancini, & Mears, 2013; Simon, 1998; Spencer, 2009).

Child Abuse and Neglect. https://doi.org/10.1016/B978-0-12-815344-4.00022-2

The term 'sex offender' is applied to individuals who commit a range of crimes of a sexual nature of varying severities. However, not all sexual crimes have an equal negative perception among members of the public: Individuals who victimise children are perceived most negatively because their victims are particularly vulnerable and seen as deserving of protection against predation and abuse (Mears, Mancini, Gertz, & Bratton, 2007). Unsurprisingly, a study using vignettes has found that individuals victimising younger children were viewed more negatively than those targeting older victims (Rogers, Hirst, & Davies, 2011). In various investigations of public support for punishment in various types of sexual crimes, results consistently indicate agreement with more severe punishment of sexual crimes against children. For example, incarceration was almost universally agreed upon (with 97% support) as the appropriate punishment in cases of sexual contact of a child, and it was deemed appropriate by 80% of respondents for indecent exposure to children; by contrast, only 46% of respondents supported incarceration if the victim was an adult (Mears et al., 2007). Another study found that 97% of respondents supported registration and community notification for individuals who sexually abuse a neighbourhood child or their own child, compared with 71% for individuals who rape their spouse and 65% in cases involving statutory rape (Kernsmith, Craun, & Foster, 2009). Those results all indicate that offenders who victimise children are viewed extremely negatively. This is further reflected in public support for inflicting even the most severe form of punishment; a study found that a greater proportion of respondents (51%) agreed with imposing the death penalty for sexual crimes against children compared with crimes against adults (only 27%) (Mancini & Mears, 2010).

There are a series of myths that are commonly accepted by members of the public regarding sexual crimes and their perpetrators that might explain these negative perceptions. First is the idea that sexual crimes are on the rise, with studies demonstrating that 77% of Americans believe that the frequency of sexual crime has increased (Levenson, Brannon, Fortney, & Baker, 2007). This heightened level of public concern is also endorsed by legislators who regard sexual offending as a growing problem (Sample & Kadleck, 2008). These perceptions are contrary to a body of evidence indicating that the reality is quite the opposite (Finkelhor & Jones, 2004, 2006, 2012; Lonsway & Archambault, 2012). For instance, in the case of child sexual abuse, Finkelhor and Jones concluded that there is "fairly consistent and convergent evidence from a variety of sources pointing to large declines in sexual abuse from 1992 to 2010" (Finkelhor & Jones, 2012, p. 3).

A second inaccurate belief is that strangers perpetrate most child sexual abuse. This can be explained in part not only by a number of highly publicised cases of child abduction and murder by strangers (see Section 2) but also by a more general pattern of biased media coverage overemphasising the stories of sexual crimes against children committed by strangers (Kitzinger, 2004). This focus on the perpetration of child sexual abuse by strangers is contrary to a body of empirical findings documenting the high prevalence of incest and sexual abuse by acquaintances. As early as 1894, a medical textbook included cases of incest in a presentation of child sexual abuse in the United States (Gibb, 1894). Similarly, an author noted in 1913 that "a surprising number of little girls have first become involved in wrongdoing through the men in their own households" (Addams, 1913). It is now a well-established and important fact that a majority of individuals committing child sexual abuse are members of the child's family or social circle and utilise their relationships to access the child and cover the abuse. For example, a study found that 81% of victimisers of children were acquainted to, had previously seen, or were family members of their victims (Finkelhor, Hammer, & Sedlack, 2008), while another established that 87.2% of children were abused by a family member, acquaintance, or someone in a close relationship (Maguire & Singer, 2011). Notwithstanding this evidence, the public continues to believe that children are most at risk of sexual harm from strangers, with one recent study establishing that 54% of respondents believed that more than half of all sex offenders were strangers to their victims (Socia & Harris, 2016) and another one establishing that 30% of respondents were more worried about sexual abuse of a child by a stranger than a known perpetrator, compared with about 12% who endorsed the opposite (Craun & Theriot, 2008).

A final perception of the public relates to assumed high rates of sexual recidivism and the lack of treatment efficacy for individuals who commit sexual crimes. A number of studies demonstrate that members of the public are pessimistic when estimating the risk of sexual reoffence by convicted offenders. For example, a recent study determined that 83% of respondents believed that half or more of registered sex offenders were at high risk to commit a new sex offence (Socia & Harris, 2016), while 98% of respondents in another study said it was 'true' that sexual offenders recidivate sexually (Katz-Schiavone, Levenson, & Ackerman, 2008), yet another study found that 68% of the public believed that sexual offenders reoffend at a much higher rate than other criminals and respondents also estimated that 76% of child molesters will reoffend (Levenson et al., 2007). These estimates indicate a grossly incorrect belief in members of the public who overestimate the recidivism risk in light of meta-analytic results that found that only about 13.4% of individuals convicted of a sexual crime were reconvicted over a 5-year follow-up period (Hanson & Bussière, 1998). Specifically, for individuals who commit child sexual abuse, results indicated that 12.7% of them recidivate sexually. Additionally, a sizeable number of respondents in various studies believed that treatment of sexual offenders does not work to reduce their recidivism (Mancini, 2013; Payne, Tewksbury, & Mustaine, 2010; Rogers & Ferguson, 2011), discounting empirical results indicating that sexual offenders who receive treatment are less likely to commit additional sexual and nonsexual crimes (Duwe & Goldman, 2009; Hanson, Bourgon, Helmus, & Hodgson, 2009; Lösel & Schmucker, 2005). Further, it appears that this belief in the inevitability of recidivism is even more pronounced for individuals who commit sexual abuse of a child compared with those who sexually victimise adults. Another study found significantly higher agreement that individuals with a history of child sexual abuse would commit a new sexual crime (Fisher & Pedneault, 2016). Respondents in the same study also disagreed more strongly with statements that these offenders could be successfully rehabilitated and never offend again, compared with those who victimise adults.

To paraphrase the title of a recently published article, understanding public opinions of individuals who commit sexual crimes and specifically of those who victimise children necessitates an understanding of the vulnerability of victims abused by offenders who are constructed as monstrous and who present unmanageable risk of reoffence (Pickett et al., 2013), in spite of the stark contrast of these opinions to empirical results on these topics. An importunate disconnect exists between the empirical reality and what the public believes about individuals who commit child sexual abuse.

2 Moral Panic, Punitive Legislation, and Crime Control Theatre

In his book titled *Folk Devils and Moral Panic*, sociologist Stanley Cohen first utilised the term 'moral panic' to describe a widespread fear of a group of individuals who are perceived to threaten society's safety or core values (Cohen, 2014). In reacting to a moral panic, new laws are often enacted that target and control the group causing this fear in the community. Cohen's construction of moral panic is particularly applicable to understanding the ways in which the public now conceptualises child sexual abuse, as well as the resultant outcry and the punitive and reactive legislation that has been implemented in many Western countries.

Over the last century, moral panics regarding sexual crimes have occurred cyclically in the United States (Jenkins, 2004), and a number of notable cases, often involving the sexual murder of a child, have fuelled public fear during each panic wave. For example, Jesse Pomeroy of Massachusetts sadistically murdered two young children in 1874; he became the youngest person convicted of first-degree murder in Massachusetts at the time and initially received the death penalty (Jenkins, 2004). The crimes of Albert Fish in the early 20th century—including the murder, mutilation, and cannibalism of children (Schechter, 1990, 1994)—were instrumental to the second wave of panic that spread in the following decades, bolstered by cases such as a series of sexually motivated murders of children in 1937, and the 'Horror Week' of 1949 in which three young girls were murdered within the span of a few days (Jenkins, 2004). The third wave of moral panic unfolded first in the context of growing public concern over the ritualistic satanic abuse of children (Nathan, 1991; Victor, 1998) and false allegations made against day care centres following recovered memories of children submitted to questionable interrogation techniques by therapists (de Young, 2004a, 2004b). Also particularly salient to the third wave of moral panic were a number of horrific crimes against children, including the murder of 6-year-old Adam Walsh, whose decapitated head was found a week later; the kidnapping and murder of 11-year-old Jacob Wetterling, which went unsolved for 27 years; the rape and murder of 7-year-old Megan Kanka by a neighbour with a history of sexual assault against children; and the abduction, rape, and murder of 9-year-old Jessica Lunsford by a convicted sexual offender living nearby (Terry, 2015). In most of these cases, the victim was a vulnerable young child who was victimised, tortured, and killed by a stranger.

Each wave of moral panic has resulted in the adoption of a plethora of punitive statutes over time. During the first wave, a number of eugenic statutes were implemented, including some that imposed the castration and sterilisation of those identified as 'perverts', with the hopes that such measures would prevent the hereditary transmission of their deviant sexual inclinations (Jenkins, 2004). The second panic wave birthed a number of provisions targeting sexual psychopaths, allowing the indefinite confinement of individuals under civil commitment statutes, implemented not for punishment but for the prevention of crimes likely to be committed in the future (Freedman, 1987). Finally, the third and most recent wave, which has been described as an "unparalleled growth in sex crime laws" (Mancini, 2014, p. 152), was characterised by the implementation of memorial laws (Surette, 2007), in which legislation is named after a specific case (e.g. Adam Walsh Child Protection and Safety Act, 2006; Jacob Wetterling Crimes Against Children and Sexually Violent Offender Registration Act, n.d.; Megan's Law, n.d.). Over time, the cumulative effect of this legislation has imposed an increasingly heavier and more punitive legal regimen on individuals convicted of sexual crimes, including periodic registration with law enforcement and notification of the community (Levenson & Zgoba, 2015), restrictions on place of residence and work, and attempts to impose capital punishment for child sexual abuse (Rayburn Yung, 2015). Also notable was the resurgence of legislation imposing civil commitment (Harris, 2015) and castration (Scott & del Busto, 2015), which had been implemented in the previous two waves of moral panic. These pieces of legislation rarely involved rational choice considerations, such as costs and benefits, and were emotionally driven (Griffin & Miller, 2008; Surette, 2007; Tonry, 2004).

In each moral panic wave, there has been a proliferation of stories about the rarest forms of sexual offending against children (Brayford & Deering, 2012), often involving a stranger and the kidnapping and murder of the victim. These crime characteristics are very infrequent; an analysis indicated that there were only 105 'stereotypical' kidnappings of children by strangers reported to law enforcement in 2011, only half of which were sexually motivated and 92% of which did not involve the murder of the victim (Wolak, Finkelhor, & Sedlack, 2016). However, legislation is still created specifically to prevent crimes such as these from happening. There are important limitations in typifying such rare cases as representative of the child sexual abuse phenomenon and devising prevention strategies and implementing policies based on them. The reactionary and punitive legislation that has ensued as a result of these sensational but atypical cases has been mostly found ineffective in preventing child sexual abuse. For example, multiple studies conducted in the United States could not attribute a reduction in sexual crimes to registration and community notification laws (Ackerman, Sacks, & Greenberg, 2012; Sandler, Freeman, & Socia, 2008; Vásquez, Maddan, & Walker, 2008; Zgoba, Witt, Dalessandro, & Veysey, 2008). Similar findings have been noted for residence restrictions, mainly establishing that individuals who sexually recidivate do not live closer to locations where children congregate (Nobles, Levenson, & Youstin, 2012;

Socia, 2012; Zandbergen, Levenson, & Hart, 2010). On the other hand, the adoption of these policies entails a number of collateral consequences for offenders after their release, including housing instability, employment difficulties, financial hardship, threats, and harassment, all of which hinder successful reentry to society (Calkins Mercado, Alvarez, & Levenson, 2008; Lasher & McGrath, 2010; Levenson, 2008; Levenson & Tewksbury, 2009; Tewksbury, 2005; Zgoba, Levenson, & McKee, 2008).

This legislation can be seen as having symbolic value: it appears to control sexual crime but lacks effectiveness. This phenomenon has previously been termed *crime control theatre*, defined as "a public response or set of responses to crime which generate the appearance, but not the fact, of crime control" (Griffin & Miller, 2008, p. 160). Empirical investigations have demonstrated that the concept of crime control theatre is an applicable framework to understand public support for regulating individuals adjudicated for sexual crimes in the United States (Budd & Mancini, 2016; Socia & Harris, 2016). In addition, some authors have applied the proverbial children's tale *The Emperor's New Clothes* to sex offender laws, arguing that because this legislation has been passed in the name of protecting vulnerable victims against sexual harm, it is therefore above criticism and widely accepted as effective, without consideration for its lack of empirical support (Levenson & D'Amora, 2007).

Notwithstanding the demonstrated lack of effectiveness of this type of legislation, many countries have adopted similar special legislation against individuals convicted of sexual offences. For example, in its 2016 Global Survey, the Office of Sex Offender Sentencing, Monitoring, Apprehending, Registering, and Tracking counted 30 countries with laws governing the registration of sex offenders at the national and/or provincial level, including Australia, Canada, France, Germany, the Republic of Ireland, New Zealand, Portugal, South Africa, South Korea, Spain, Taiwan, the United Kingdom, and the United States, as well as 16 other countries that had considered or were considering such legislation, including Austria, Belgium, Finland, Israel, and Switzerland (SMART Office of Sex Offender Sentencing, Monitoring, Apprehending, Registering, and Tracking, 2016). This seems to indicate that public concern with sexual violence can be understood at a global level, with little consideration of the growing body of research establishing that specific legislation targeting sex offenders is not effective in preventing the perpetration of sexual abuse.

3 Terminology and Prevention

The terminology utilised might be critical when communicating to the public about sexual crimes against children and the individuals who commit such offences. Generally, the public uses terminology like 'paedophile' and 'child molester' indiscriminately to describe various types of contact and noncontact sexual behaviours between an adult and someone under 18 years old. In spite of its frequent usage in public discourse, it should be remembered that paedophilia has a much narrower medical definition: paedophilic disorder is included in the current (fifth) version of the Diagnostic and Statistical Manual of Mental Disorders (American Psychiatric Association, 2013) and applies to a fixed set of circumstances. The term should be used only in cases involving sexual attraction to prepubescent children (13 years old and younger) by an individual who is at least 16 years old and 5 years older than the child he or she is attracted to, with fantasies and urges lasting for at least 6 months and causing the individual to act upon these urges or to be in a distressed state because of them. Paedophilia should therefore be reserved to describe the condition of individuals with a predominant sexual interest in prepubescent children (Jahnke, Imhoff, & Hoyer, 2015) and does not imply child sexual abuse (McDonald, 2016).

As can be observed in Fig. 1, which presents worldwide relative interest for specific terms based on the volume of searches in Google, the terms 'paedophile' and 'child molester' have been frequently looked up since 2004. A higher level of interest is specifically noted for the term 'paedophile/paedophile' over time, especially compared with searches for 'child sexual abuse', for which the relative public interest has decreased. However, one should remember that this use of terminology has evolved over time, as depicted in Fig. 2, in which the frequency of the terms 'paedophile/paedophile' and 'child molester' in English books was plotted between 1940 and 2008. Inspection of this graph shows an 83.8-fold increase in uses of 'paedophile/paedophile' and a 57.7-fold increase for 'child molester' over the 1960–2008 time period; this suggests this terminology (especially the term 'paedophile') has become a much more common part of the public discourse when referring to individuals who commit child sexual abuse.

As the use of the term 'paedophile' has become more common recently, it is particularly interesting to examine its social construction over time. Jenkins notes the first uses of

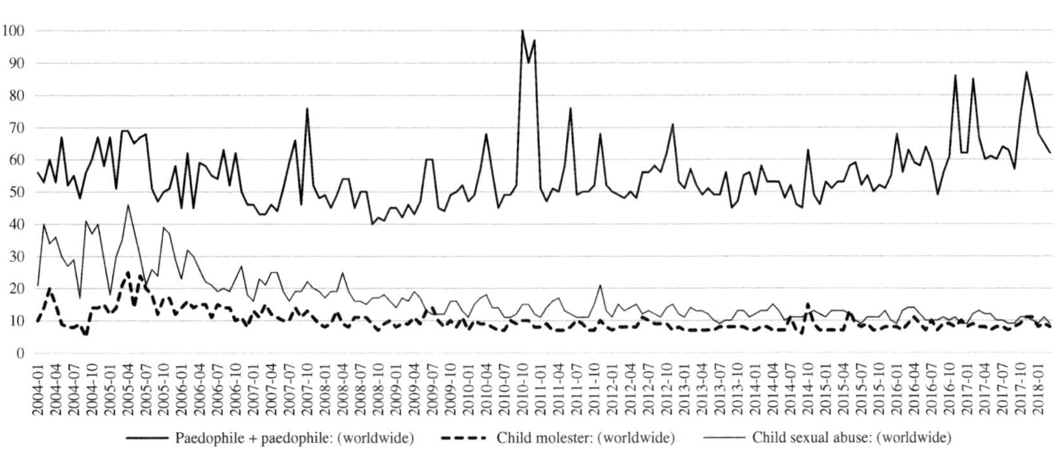

Fig. 1
Interest level in terms 'paedophile' and 'child molester' versus 'child sexual abuse' worldwide in Google searches, 2004–18.

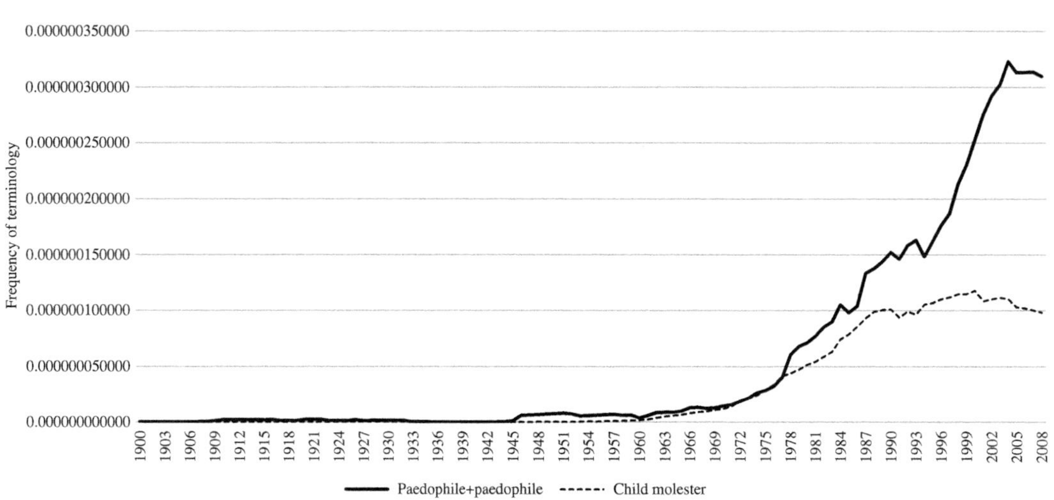

Fig. 2
Google NGram: Trends in historical use of terms 'paedophile', 'paedophile', and 'child molester' in all English books contained in Google Books, 1900–2008.

paedophilia in the English language in the 1880s in the work of von Krafft-Ebing on sexual perversions (Jenkins, 2004). Schofield remarks, however, that the term acquired new social meaning after the 1970s, specifically through its construction as a problem of increased importance (Schofield, 2004). By the 1990s, the paedophile "emerged as arguably the most feared and vilified of all 'predatory strangers'" (Schofield, 2004, p. 121) and was prominently featured in media content as an evil monster (Thomas, 2005). A notable pattern in this construction of the paedophile, one that is reminiscent of one of the myths presented in Section 1, is that of 'stranger danger'. Illustrating this point, Jewkes (2004, p. 94) wrote, "it is paedophiles who have come to be the recipients of moral outrage in the 21st century. And more specifically, it is paedophile strangers, not paedophiles within the family, who are the bogeymen of modern Britain." Interestingly, this association between paedophilia and stranger danger has led to the development of related ideas, such as the 'paedophile van'. This concept has received its own entry on Urban Dictionary Pedophile van, 2011) and describes the characteristics of a vehicle that is considered practical for the purpose of luring and abducting a child for sexual motivations. This constitutes another conceptual and terminological example linking the concepts of paedophilia and sexual abuse of children by strangers.

Similar changes in the meaning of 'paedophile' are noted in the representation of paedophiles in popular culture over time. An initial, marked historical pattern is a lack of representation of child sexual abuse in movies. Specifically, paedophiles and sex offenders were absent from Hollywood films until the 1950s, with a few rare instances in European movies (Kohm & Greenhill, 2011). Kohm noted a shift in this pattern, with representations of paedophiles as unidimensional villains emerging in the 1970s in movies that often conveyed violence by vigilantes as the appropriate way of dealing with individuals with paedophilia (Kohm, 2017). A more sinister version of paedophiles surfaced in the 1990s as they were increasingly represented in visual media as perverted neighbours hiding in plain sight within areas where children should be safe (Rafter, 2007). It was argued that many of these films served to better articulate the public's calls for retribution in cases of child sexual abuse (Kohm, 2017), in parallel to the exceptional media coverage of the rarest incidents of child sexual abuse in the midst of the third wave of moral panic, as described in the section of this chapter on moral panic, punitive legislation, and crime control theatre.

As with sexual offenders in general, an examination of public opinions about individuals with paedophilia indicates a number of misconceptions. First, the public believes that all paedophiles sexually abuse children. For example, 90% of a sample of respondents believed that paedophiles engaged in fondling children, and 76% believed that paedophiles engaged in sex with children (McCartan, 2004). A subsequent study found that 69% of respondents believed paedophiles to engage in sexual abuse of children, with only 12% acknowledging that it might not be the case (McCartan, 2010). Generally, paedophiles are seen as putting children and adolescents in danger, even more so than sexual sadists (Jahnke et al., 2015). It appears that the notions of paedophilia and child sexual abuse have become interchangeable for members of the public, ignoring research showing that many individuals with paedophilia—that is those who are sexually interested in prepubescent children—do not perpetrate child sexual abuse (Cantor & McPhail, 2016) and that at least half of all individuals who sexually abuse children do not have paedophilia (Seto, 2008).

This lack of distinction between the paedophilic condition (i.e. sexual interest in prepubescent children) and abusive behaviours (i.e. sexual abuse of children) is problematic in light of the second inaccurate belief, which is that paedophilia is uncontrollable. An analysis of US federal debates about sex offender legislation identified multiple instances in which legislators refer to the lack of control of paedophiles as a known fact (Lynch, 2006). A more recent study using survey data found that members of the public believed paedophilia was less controllable than alcohol abuse, antisocial tendencies, and sexual sadism (Jahnke et al., 2015). Interestingly, this belief is not false, considering the growing body of research pointing to neurodevelopmental differences in paedophiles that occur in utero and in early development (Knight & King, 2012; Seto, 2012). However, this perception of uncontrollability is quite problematic, considering the foregoing inaccurate belief in which the condition and sexually abusive behaviours are seen as one and the same. It follows that individuals with paedophilia are constructed as predisposed to sexually abusing children and very likely to recidivate upon release because they cannot control their sexual urges. Not surprisingly, large proportions of the public agree that individuals with paedophilia are better dead or imprisoned (Jahnke et al., 2015).

Overall, the use of language and terminology appears to have a significant influence on framing the issue of child sexual abuse with the public. It is unlikely that using terms such as 'paedophile' can be the starting point of an informed public discussion about child sexual abuse, considering the paedophile's mythical construction as a stranger and predator motivated by uncontrollable urges. Calder also urged caution in the use of such terminology: "the use of words like 'beast' and 'monster'...does give people the impression that ordinary men do not commit these crimes, therefore reinforcing inaccurate beliefs about offenders" (as cited in Greer, 2003, p. 128). In addition, this 'paedophile' myth also ultimately delegitimises any consideration of other causes of child sexual abuse by refusing to account for other possible explanations, such as opportunities and social or structural causes (Cowburn & Dominelli, 2001; Richards, 2017).

Therefore, it is likely that indistinctively referring to perpetrators of child sexual abuse as 'paedophiles' or 'child molesters' is counterproductive in building an accurate body of knowledge among members of the public about the issue of child sexual abuse. This assertion is further supported by recent findings demonstrating that the term 'sex offender' activates a set of stereotypes and inaccurate beliefs about these individuals in members of the public, compared with the utilisation of the more neutral label "people who have committed crimes of a sexual nature" (Harris & Socia, 2016). Instead, it is possible that the recent adoption by the US Department of Justice of a policy recommending the use of person-first language (e.g. 'person with a felony conviction') instead of crime-first language (e.g. 'criminal') might be a critical change to implement in the public discourse about child sexual abuse (Denver, Pickett, & Bushway, 2017). This will mean referring to 'child molesters' as "individuals who have committed a sexual crime against a child" and to 'paedophiles' as "individuals with paedophilia." The fundamental difference between these phrases is their focal point: the individual versus the crime they once committed or their mental disorder. Using this human-focused terminology might be a promising way of communicating about the issue with the public, as it refutes mythical constructions of these individuals as 'other' and 'nonordinary' and instead situates the discussion about prevention on those within children's circles of trust, where it is most likely to be impactful.

4 Chapter Review Questions

1. What are some inaccurate beliefs that members of the public hold about individuals who sexually abuse children?
2. According to Cohen, what are the core elements of a moral panic?
3. What are memorial laws?
4. Explain the concept of crime control theatre and discuss how it is manifested in the context of sex offender legislation.
5. Discuss the dangers of adopting sex offender legislation based on atypical cases.
6. How is the concept of 'paedophile' as understood by the public different from the DSM diagnostic for paedophilia?
7. What is the difference between person-first and crime-first language?
8. Discuss the possible role of terminology in preventing the sexual abuse of children.

References

Ackerman, A. R., Sacks, M., & Greenberg, D. F. (2012). Legislation targeting sex offenders: are recent policies effective in reducing rape? *Justice Quarterly*, *29*(6), 858–887. https://doi.org/10.1080/07418825.2011.566887.

Adam Walsh Child Protection and Safety Act. (2006). *Pub L. 109-248 § 501(1)(A)*.

Addams, J. (1913). *A new conscience and an ancient evil*. New York, NY: Macmillan.

American Psychiatric Association. (2013). *Diagnostic and statistical manual of mental disorders* (5th ed.). Washington, DC: American Psychiatric Association.

Beitchman, J. H., Zucker, K. J., Hood, J. E., DaCosta, G. A., Akman, D., & Cassavia, E. (1992). A review of the long-term effects of child sexual abuse. *Child Abuse & Neglect*, *16*(1), 101–118. https://doi.org/10.1016/0145-2134(92)90011-F.

Brayford, J., & Deering, J. (2012). Media influences on public perceptions of sex offenders: impact on policy and practice. In J. Brayford, F. Cowe, & J. Deering (Eds.), *Sex offenders: Punish, help, change or control? Theory, policy and practice explored* (pp. 52–68). New York, NY: Routledge.

Browne, A., & Finkelhor, D. (1986). Impact of child sexual abuse: a review of the research. *Psychological Bulletin*, *99*(1), 66–77. https://doi.org/10.1037/0033-2909.99.1.66.

Budd, K. M., & Mancini, C. (2016). Crime control theatre: public (mis)perceptions of the effectiveness of sex offender residence restrictions. *Psychology, Public Policy, and Law*, *22*(4), 362–374.

Calkins Mercado, C., Alvarez, S., & Levenson, J. (2008). The impact of specialized sex offender legislation on community reentry. *Sexual Abuse*, *20*(2), 188–205. https://doi.org/10.1177/1079063208317540.

Cantor, J. M., & McPhail, I. V. (2016). Non-offending pedophiles. *Current Sexual Health Reports*, *8*(3), 121–128. https://doi.org/10.1007/s11930-016-0076-z.

Cashmore, J., & Shackel, R. (2013). *The long-term effects of child sexual abuse*. Australian Institute of Family Studies.

Chiricos, T., Padgett, K., Bratton, J., Pickett, J. T., & Gertz, M. (2012). Racial threat and opposition to the re-enfranchisement of ex-felons. *International Journal of Criminology and Sociology*, *1*, 13–28.

Cohen, S. (2014). *Folk devils and moral panics: The creation of the mods and rockers* (3rd ed.). London: Routledge.

Cowburn, M., & Dominelli, L. (2001). Masking hegemonic masculinity: reconstructing the paedophile as the dangerous stranger. *The British Journal of Social Work*, *31*(3), 399–415. https://doi.org/10.1093/bjsw/31.3.399.

Craun, S. W., & Theriot, M. T. (2008). Misperceptions of sex offender perpetration: considering the impact of sex offender registration. *Journal of Interpersonal Violence*, *24*(12), 2057–2072. https://doi.org/10.1177/0886260508327706.

de Young, M. (2004a). *The day care ritual abuse moral panic*. Jefferson, NC: McFarland & Co.

de Young, M. (2004b). The devil goes to day care: McMartin and the making of a moral panic. *Journal of American Culture*, *20*(1), 19–25. https://doi.org/10.1111/j.1542-734X.1997.00019.x.

Denver, M., Pickett, J. T., & Bushway, S. D. (2017). The language of stigmatization and the mark of violence: experimental evidence on the social construction and use of criminal record stigma. *Criminology*, *55*(3), 664–690. https://doi.org/10.1111/1745-9125.12145.

Douard, J. (2008). Sex offender as scapegoat: the monstrous other within. *New York Law School Law Review*, *53*(1), 31–52.

Duwe, G., & Goldman, R. A. (2009). The impact of prison-based treatment on sex offender recidivism: evidence from Minnesota. *Sexual Abuse*, *21*(3), 279–307. https://doi.org/10.1177/1079063209338490.

Finkelhor, D., Hammer, H., & Sedlack, A. J. (2008, August). *Sexually assaulted children: National estimates and characteristics*. US Department of Justice. Retrieved from https://www.ncjrs.gov/pdffiles1/ojjdp/214383.pdf.

Finkelhor, D., & Jones, L. M. (2004). *Explanations of the decline in child sexual abuse cases*. Washington, DC: US Department of Justice.

Finkelhor, D., & Jones, L. M. (2006). Why have child maltreatment and child victimization declined? *Journal of Social Issues*, *62*(4), 685–716. https://doi.org/10.1111/j.1540-4560.2006.00483.x.

Finkelhor, D., & Jones, L. M. (2012). *Have sexual abuse and physical abuse declined since the 1990s?*. Durham, NH: Crimes Against Children Research Center.

Fisher, L. R., & Pedneault, A. (2016). *Washington residents' perceptions of sex offenders and sex offender policies*. Olympia, WA: Washington State Statistical Analysis Center.

Freedman, E. B. (1987). "Uncontrolled desires": the response to the sexual psychopath, 1920–1960. *The Journal of American History*, *74*(1), 83–106. https://doi.org/10.2307/1908506.

Gibb, W. T. (1894). Indecent assault upon children. In A. McLane Hamilton & L. Godkin (Eds.), *A system of legal medicine* (pp. 649–657). New York, NY: E. B. Treat.

Green, A. H. (1993). Child sexual abuse: immediate and long-term effects and intervention. *Journal of the American Academy of Child & Adolescent Psychiatry*, *32*(5), 890–902. https://doi.org/10.1097/00004583-199309000-00002.

Greer, C. (2003). *Sex crime and the media*. Cullompton, Devon, UK: Willan Publishing.

Griffin, T., & Miller, M. K. (2008). Child abduction, AMBER alert, and crime control theater. *Criminal Justice Review*, *33*(2), 159–176. https://doi.org/10.1177/0734016808316778.

Hanson, R. K., Bourgon, G., Helmus, L., & Hodgson, S. (2009). The principles of effective correctional treatment also apply to sexual offenders: a meta-analysis. *Criminal Justice and Behavior*, *36*(9), 865–891. https://doi.org/10.1177/0093854809338545.

Hanson, R. K., & Bussière, M. T. (1998). Predicting relapse: a meta-analysis of sexual offender recidivism studies. *Journal of Consulting and Clinical Psychology*, *66*(2), 348–362. https://doi.org/10.1037/0022-006X.66.2.348.

Harper, C. A., & Harris, A. J. (2017). Applying moral foundations theory to understanding public views of sexual offending. *Journal of Sexual Aggression*, *23*(2), 111–123.

Harris, A. J. (2015). The civil commitment of sexual predators: a policy review. In R. Wright (Ed.), *Sex offender laws: Failed policies, new directions* (2nd ed., pp. 219–239). New York, NY: Springer.

Harris, A. J., & Socia, K. M. (2016). What's in a name? Evaluating the effects of the "sex offender" label on public opinions and beliefs. *Sexual Abuse*, *28*(7), 660–678. https://doi.org/10.1177/1079063214564391.

Human Rights Watch. (2007). No easy answers. Sex offender laws in the US. *Human Rights Watch*, *19*(4G).

Jacob Wetterling Crimes Against Children and Sexually Violent Offender Registration Act, n.d. 42 U.S.C. § 14071.

Jahnke, S., Imhoff, R., & Hoyer, J. (2015). Stigmatization of people with pedophilia: two comparative surveys. *Archives of Sexual Behavior*, *44*(1), 21–34. https://doi.org/10.1007/s10508-014-0312-4.

Jenkins, P. (2004). *Moral panic: Changing concepts of the child molester in modern America*. New Haven, CT: Yale University Press.

Jewkes, Y. (2004). *Media and crime* (1st ed.). London: Sage.

Katz-Schiavone, S., Levenson, J. S., & Ackerman, A. R. (2008). Myths and facts about sexual violence: public perceptions and implications for prevention. *Journal of Criminal Justice and Popular Culture*, *15*(3), 291–311.

Kernsmith, P. D., Craun, S. W., & Foster, J. (2009). Public attitudes toward sexual offenders and sex offender registration. *Journal of Child Sexual Abuse*, *18*(3), 290–301. https://doi.org/10.1080/10538710902901663.

Kitzinger, J. (2004). Images of abusers: stranger-danger, the media, and the social currency of everyday knowledge. In K. Throsby & F. Alexander (Eds.), *Gender and interpersonal violence. Language, action and representation* (pp. 139–156). London, UK: Palgrave Macmillan.

Knight, R. A., & King, M. W. (2012). Typologies for child molesters: the generation of a new structural model. In B. K. Schwartz (Ed.), Vol. 7. *The sexual offender* (pp. 1–32). Kingston, NJ: Civic Research Institute.

Kohm, S. (2017). Representing the pedophile. In M. Brown & E. Carrabine (Eds.), *International handbook of visual criminology* (pp. 190–201). New York, NY: Routledge.

Kohm, S. A., & Greenhill, P. (2011). Pedophile crime films as popular criminology: a problem of justice? *Theoretical Criminology*, *15*(2), 195–215. https://doi.org/10.1177/1362480610388974.

Lasher, M. P., & McGrath, R. J. (2010). The impact of community notification on sex offender reintegration: a quantitative review of the research literature. *International Journal of Offender Therapy and Comparative Criminology*, *56*(1), 6–28. https://doi.org/10.1177/0306624X10387524.

Levenson, J. S. (2008). Collateral consequences of sex offender residence restrictions. *Criminal Justice Studies, 21*(2), 153–166. https://doi.org/10.1080/14786010802159822.

Levenson, J. S., Brannon, Y. N., Fortney, T., & Baker, J. (2007). Public perceptions about sex offenders and community protection policies. *Analyses of Social Issues and Public Policy, 7*(1), 137–161. https://doi.org/10.1111/j.1530-2415.2007.00119.x.

Levenson, J. S., & D'Amora, D. A. (2007). Social policies designed to prevent sexual violence: the emperor's new clothes? *Criminal Justice Policy Review, 18*(2), 168–199. https://doi.org/10.1177/0887403406295309.

Levenson, J., & Tewksbury, R. (2009). Collateral damage: family members of registered sex offenders. *American Journal of Criminal Justice, 34*(1), 54–68. https://doi.org/10.1007/s12103-008-9055-x.

Levenson, J. S., & Zgoba, K. M. (2015). Sex offender residence restrictions: the law of unintended consequences. In R. Wright (Ed.), *Sex offender laws: Failed policies, new directions* (pp. 180–189). New York, NY: Springer.

Lonsway, K. A., & Archambault, J. (2012). The "justice gap" for sexual assault cases: future directions for research and reform. *Violence Against Women, 18*(2), 145–168. https://doi.org/10.1177/1077801212440017.

Lösel, F., & Schmucker, M. (2005). The effectiveness of treatment for sexual offenders: a comprehensive meta-analysis. *Journal of Experimental Criminology, 1*(1), 117–146. https://doi.org/10.1007/s11292-004-6466-7.

Lynch, M. (2006). Pedophiles and cyber-predators as contaminating forces: the language of disgust, pollution, and boundary invasions in federal debates on sex offender legislation. *Law & Social Inquiry, 27*(3), 529–557. https://doi.org/10.1111/j.1747-4469.2002.tb00814.x.

Maguire, M., & Singer, J. K. (2011). A false sense of security: moral panic driven sex offender legislation. *Critical Criminology, 19*(4), 301–312. https://doi.org/10.1007/s10612-010-9127-3.

Mancini, C. (2013). Examining factors that predict public concern about the collateral consequences of sex crime policy. *Criminal Justice Policy Review, 25*(4), 450–475. https://doi.org/10.1177/0887403412473475.

Mancini, C. (2014). *Sex crime, offenders & society*. Durham, NC: Carolina Academic Press.

Mancini, C., & Mears, D. P. (2010). To execute or not to execute? Examining public support for capital punishment of sex offenders. *Journal of Criminal Justice, 38*(5), 959–968. https://doi.org/10.1016/j.jcrimjus.2010.06.013.

Manza, J., Brooks, C., & Uggen, C. (2004). Public attitudes toward felon disenfranchisement in the United States. *Public Opinion Quarterly, 68*(2), 275–286. https://doi.org/10.1093/poq/nfh015.

McCartan, K. (2004). 'Here There Be Monsters': the public's perception of paedophiles with particular reference to Belfast and Leicester. *Medicine, Science and the Law, 44*(4), 327–342. https://doi.org/10.1258/rsmmsl.44.4.327.

McCartan, K. F. (2010). Student/trainee-professional implicit theories of paedophilia. *Psychology, Crime & Law, 16*(4), 265–288. https://doi.org/10.1080/10683160802614144.

McDonald, D. (2016). Who is the subject of queer criminology? Unravelling the category of the paedophile. In M. Ball, A. Dwyer, & T. Crofts (Eds.), *Queering criminology* (pp. 102–120). Basingstoke: Palgrave Macmillan.

Mears, D. P., Mancini, C., Gertz, M., & Bratton, J. (2007). Sex crimes, children, and pornography: public views and public policy. *Crime & Delinquency, 54*(4), 532–559. https://doi.org/10.1177/0011128707308160.

Megan's Law, n.d. 42 USC 13701.

Nathan, D. (1991). Satanism and child molestation: constructing the ritual abuse scare. In J. T. Richardson, J. Best, & D. G. Bromley (Eds.), *The satanism scare* (pp. 75–94). New York, NY: Aldine de Gruyter.

Nobles, M. R., Levenson, J. S., & Youstin, T. J. (2012). Effectiveness of residence restrictions in preventing sex offense recidivism. *Crime & Delinquency, 58*(4), 491–513. https://doi.org/10.1177/0011128712449230.

Paolucci, E. O., Genuis, M. L., & Violato, C. (2001). A meta-analysis of the published research on the effects of child sexual abuse. *The Journal of Psychology, 135*(1), 17–36. https://doi.org/10.1080/00223980109603677.

Payne, B. K., Tewksbury, R., & Mustaine, E. E. (2010). Attitudes about rehabilitating sex offenders: demographic, victimization, and community-level influences. *Journal of Criminal Justice, 38*(4), 580–588. https://doi.org/10.1016/j.jcrimjus.2010.04.029.

Pedophile van. (2011). *Urban dictionary*. Retrieved from https://www.urbandictionary.com/define.php?term=pedophile%20van.

Pickett, J. T., Mancini, C., & Mears, D. P. (2013). Vulnerable victims, monstrous offenders, and unmanageable risk: explaining public opinion on the social control of sex crime. *Criminology*, *51*(3), 729–759. https://doi.org/10.1111/1745-9125.12018.

Quinn, J. F., Forsyth, C. J., & Mullen-Quinn, C. (2004). Societal reaction to sex offenders: a review of the origins and results of the myths surrounding their crimes and treatment amenability. *Deviant Behavior*, *25*(3), 215–232. https://doi.org/10.1080/01639620490431147.

Rafter, N. (2007). Crime, film and criminology: recent sex-crime movies. *Theoretical Criminology*, *11*(3), 403–420. https://doi.org/10.1177/1362480607079584.

Rayburn Yung, C. (2015). Child rapists and capital punishment. In R. Wright (Ed.), *Sex offenders laws: Failed policies, new directions* (2nd ed., pp. 240–255). New York, NY: Springer.

Richards, K. (2017). Born this way? A qualitative examination of public perceptions of the causes of pedophilia and sexual offending against children. *Deviant Behavior*, 1–17. https://doi.org/10.1080/01639625.2017.1335526.

Rogers, D. L., & Ferguson, C. J. (2011). Punishment and rehabilitation attitudes toward sex offenders versus nonsexual offenders. *Journal of Aggression, Maltreatment & Trauma*, *20*(4), 395–414. https://doi.org/10.1080/10926771.2011.570287.

Rogers, P., Hirst, L., & Davies, M. (2011). An investigation into the effect of respondent gender, victim age, and perpetrator treatment on public attitudes towards sex offenders, sex offender treatment, and sex offender rehabilitation. *Journal of Offender Rehabilitation*, *50*(8), 511–530. https://doi.org/10.1080/10509674.2011.602472.

Sample, L. L., & Kadleck, C. (2008). Sex offender laws: legislators' accounts of the need for policy. *Criminal Justice Policy Review*, *19*(1), 40–62. https://doi.org/10.1177/0887403407308292.

Sandler, J. C., Freeman, N. J., & Socia, K. M. (2008). Does a watched pot boil? A time-series analysis of New York State's sex offender registration and notification law. *Psychology, Public Policy, and Law*, *14*(4), 284–302.

Schechter, H. (1990). *Deranger: The shocking true story of America's most fiendish serial killer*. New York, NY: Pocket Books.

Schechter, H. (1994). *Depraved: The shoking true story of America's first serial killer*. New York, NY: Pocket Books.

Schofield, K. (2004). Collisions of culture and crime: media commodification of child sexual abuse. In J. Ferrell, K. Hayward, W. Morrison, & M. Presdee (Eds.), *Cultural criminology unleashed* (pp. 121–131). London, UK: Glasshouse Press.

Scott, C., & del Busto, E. (2015). Chemical and surgical castration. In R. Wright (Ed.), *Sex offender laws: Failed policies, new directions* (2nd ed., pp. 190–218). New York, NY: Springer.

Seto, M. C. (2008). *Pedophilia and sexual offending against children*. Washington, DC: American Psychological Association.

Seto, M. C. (2012). Is pedophilia a sexual orientation? *Archives of Sexual Behavior*, *41*(1), 231–236. https://doi.org/10.1007/s10508-011-9882-6.

Simon, J. (1998). Managing the monstrous: sex offenders and the new penology. *Psychology, Public Policy, and Law*, *4*(1/2), 452–467. https://doi.org/10.1037/1076-8971.4.1-2.452.

SMART Office of Sex Offender Sentencing, Monitoring, Apprehending, Registering, and Tracking. (2016). *Global survey of sex offender registration and notification systems*. Washington, DC: Department of Justice, Office of Justice Program.

Socia, K. M. (2012). The efficacy of county-level sex offender residence restrictions in New York. *Crime & Delinquency*, *58*(4), 612–642. https://doi.org/10.1177/0011128712441694.

Socia, K. M., & Harris, A. J. (2016). Evaluating public perceptions of the risk presented by registered sex offenders: evidence of crime control theater? *Psychology, Public Policy, and Law*, *22*(4), 375.

Spencer, D. (2009). Sex offender as homo sacer. *Punishment & Society*, *11*(2), 219–240. https://doi.org/10.1177/1462474508101493.

Surette, R. (2007). *Media, crime, and criminal justice: Images, realities and policies*. Belmont, CA: Wadsworth.

Terry, K. J. (2015). Sex offender laws in the United States: smart policy or disproportionate sanctions? *International Journal of Comparative and Applied Criminal Justice*, *39*(2), 113–127. https://doi.org/10.1080/01924036.2014.973048.

Tewksbury, R. (2005). Collateral consequences of sex offender registration. *Journal of Contemporary Criminal Justice*, *21*(1), 67–81. https://doi.org/10.1177/1043986204271704.

Thomas, T. (2005). *Sex crime: Sex offending and society*. Portland, OR: Willan.

Tonry, M. (2004). *Thinking about crime: Sense and sensibility in American penal culture*. Oxford, UK: Oxford University Press.

United Nations Children's Fund. (2014). *Hidden in plain sight. A statistical analysis of violence against children*. New York, NY: UNICEF.

Vásquez, B. E., Maddan, S., & Walker, J. T. (2008). The influence of sex offender registration and notification laws in the United States: a time-series analysis. *Crime & Delinquency*, *54*(2), 175–192.

Victor, J. S. (1998). Moral panics and the social construction of deviant behavior: a theory and application to the case of ritual child abuse. *Sociological Perspectives*, *41*(3), 541–565. https://doi.org/10.2307/1389563.

Wolak, J., Finkelhor, D., & Sedlack, A. J. (2016). *Child victims of stereotypical kidnapping known to law enforcement in 2011*. US Department of Justice, Office of Justice Program.

Zandbergen, P. A., Levenson, J. S., & Hart, T. C. (2010). Residential proximity to schools and daycares: an empirical analysis of sex offense recidivism. *Criminal Justice and Behavior*, *37*(5), 482–502. https://doi.org/10.1177/0093854810363549.

Zgoba, K. M., Levenson, J., & McKee, T. (2008). Examining the impact of sex offender residence restrictions on housing availability. *Criminal Justice Policy Review*, *20*(1), 91–110. https://doi.org/10.1177/0887403408322119.

Zgoba, K., Witt, P., Dalessandro, M., & Veysey, B. (2008). *Megan's law: Assessing the practical and monetary efficacy*. [No. 225370].

Biography

Amelie Pedneault is an Assistant Professor in the Department of Criminal Justice and Criminology at Washington State University. She earned her PhD in Criminology from Simon Fraser University in 2015, after completing her doctoral research at the Centre for Research on Sexual Violence. Her research examines various aspects of sexual offending, including, more recently, a large-scale study of public opinions about people who commit sexual crimes in Washington State.

Index

Note: Page numbers followed by *f* indicate figures, *t* indicate tables and *b* indicate boxes.

G

H

I

J

L

M

R

9780128153444